GREEK OARED SHIPS

900 – 322 B.C.

GREEK OARED SHIPS

900–322 B.C.

BY

J.S.MORRISON

President of University College, Cambridge

AND

R.T.WILLIAMS

Senior Lecturer in Classics in the University of Durham

CAMBRIDGE

AT THE UNIVERSITY PRESS

1968

Published by the Syndics of the Cambridge University Press
Bentley House, P.O. Box 92, 200 Euston Road, London, N.W. 1
American Branch: 32 East 57th Street, New York, N.Y. 10022

© Cambridge University Press 1968

Library of Congress Catalogue Card Number: 67-19504

Printed in Great Britain
at the University Printing House, Cambridge
(Brooke Crutchley, University Printer)

CONTENTS

CONTENTS

THE CLASSICAL PERIOD:
480–322 B.C.

Plates are to be found between page 336 and page 337

PREFACE

Chapters 1, 2, 4 and 7 are the work of R. T. Williams, except that some of chapter 7 was written by J. S. Morrison on the basis of his article 'The Greek Trireme' in the *Mariner's Mirror* 1941. The section on ship-sheds in chapter 8 was contributed by J. R. Blackman. The introduction, chapters 3, 5 and 6, the section on dockyards in chapter 8, chapters 9–12 and the general index are by J. S. Morrison. The model shown in Plate 23 was made by Sinclair Morrison. R. T. Williams made the collection of photographs from which the plates were selected.

We are greatly indebted to Captain Stephen Roskill, R.N., who read the manuscript, and made many valuable suggestions for the improvement of the text. We also wish to thank the authorities of all the institutions which were kind enough to give us permission to use their photographs in our plates. Further acknowledgements are made in the catalogues of chapters 1, 2, 4 and 7. We are also immeasurably indebted to the skill and patient care of the staff of the Cambridge University Press.

J.S.M.
R.T.W.

I wish to record my gratitude to the Leverhulme Foundation and to Churchill College, who between them made it possible for me to take sabbatical leave during the year 1965 and thus complete my part of this book.

J.S.M.

ABBREVIATIONS

For authors' names used as an abbreviation: see Bibliography

ABL	See Bibliography: C. H. E. Haspels
ABS	See Bibliography: Sir John Beazley
ABV	See Bibliography: Sir John Beazley
AD	Antike Denkmäler
AJA	American Journal of Archaeology
AM	Mitteilungen des Deutschen Archäologischen Instituts: Athenische Abteilung
Arch. Anz.	Archäologischer Anzeiger
ARV	See Bibliography: Sir John Beazley
AV	See Bibliography: E. Gerhard
AZ	Archäologische Zeitung
BM	British Museum
BPhW	Berliner Philologische Wochenschrift
BSA	Annual of the British School of Archaeology at Athens
BSR	Annual of the British School of Archaeology at Rome
CQ	Classical Quarterly
CR	Classical Review
CVA	Corpus Vasorum Antiquorum
Development	See Bibliography: Sir John Beazley
Diels–Kranz	Die Fragmente der Vorsokratiker, 5th ed.
Eph. Arch.	Ephemeris Archaiologike
F.Gr.Hist.	Die Fragmente der Griechischen Historiker von F. Jacoby
FR	See Bibliography: Furtwängler
GHI	See Bibliography: M. N. Tod
Gleichnisse	See Bibliography: R. Hampe
Histoire	See Bibliography: G. Perrot
IG	Corpus Inscriptionum Graecarum, editio minor
JdI	Jahrbuch des Deutschen Archäologischen Instituts
Jh	Jahreshefte des Österreichischen Archäologischen Instituts
JHS	Journal of Hellenic Studies

Mon. Ined.	Monumenti inedite publicato dall'Instituto di Corrispondenza Archeologica
NC	Numismatic Chronicle
NM	National Museum at Athens
O	See Bibliography: E. Kunze
Phylakopi	See Bibliography: T. D. Atkinson
PW*RE*	Paulys Encyclopädie der classischen Alterthumswissenschaft
RA	Revue Archéologique
RM	Mitteilungen des Deutschen Archäologischen Instituts: Römische Abteilung
S	See Bibliography: E. Kunze
Sagenbilder	See Bibliography: R. Hampe
SEG	Supplementum Epigraphicum Graecum
SIG	Sylloge Inscriptionum Graecarum, ed. W. Dittenberger, third edition
TAPA	Transactions and Proceedings of the American Philological Association

INTRODUCTION

The subject of this book is not one of the great literary, historical or philosophical problems with which the student of the Greek civilization of antiquity is faced. The book is written in the belief that those who have an interest in those problems may be ready to see that civilization illustrated, perhaps even illumined, by an examination of some part of its constant background of seafaring.

The constant and close reliance on the sea, and on the ships that sailed it, could not have failed to influence the language of the ancient Greeks, the metaphors and pictures in which their ideas were expressed. The result is that passages of Greek poetry and prose writing are often inscrutable without a knowledge of the nautical practice which lies behind them, and modern ignorance has led on occasion to corruption of the text. More frequently, historical events depend for their correct assessment on a knowledge of nautical matters. Unless we know what rowing in a *trieres* meant, we can hardly expect to understand the battles and voyages, the problems of training, transport and supply in the fleets of the fifth and fourth centuries. Finally, one of the joint authors was led to the subject in an attempt to find an explanation for a simile in Plato. In the myth of Er in the tenth book of the *Republic* Plato illustrates his picture of the universe saying that it is bound with a bond of light 'like the *hupozomata* of *triereis*'.

Torr's *Ancient Ships** is a fine book, but now rather out of date. It is also unscientific in its treatment of evidence. Koester's '*Das Antike Seewesen*'† is equally unscientific. It covers less ground than Torr and is equally out of date. Casson's recent *The Ancient Mariners*‡ takes a much wider canvas than we shall attempt, and is accordingly unable to treat the evidence of Greek antiquity in detail. Modern works of reference are most unsatisfactory. One example is perhaps sufficient. Liddell–Scott–Jones gives under *trieres* Tarn's explanation of the rowing system, apparently unaware that such a system is totally unsupported by any evidence, is based on the demonstrably untrue assumption that two-level ships did not exist before the *trieres*, and requires furthermore a length of hull and of oar which conflicts with the evidence,

---

* Cambridge, 1894.　　　　† Berlin, 1923.　　　　‡ London, 1959.

unmistakable in the case of the hull at least.* Under the names for the three classes of oarsmen, *thranites*, *zugios* and *thalamios*, Liddell–Scott–Jones gives a completely different, and more sensible, explanation of the oar system. If we look under *tetreres* and *penteres* we find no explanation at all.

The main object of this book will be to collect all the evidence for the Greek oared ship between 900 and 322 B.C. We shall draw the conclusions which seem to us necessary both about the oar systems and about the other features of these ships. But we hope that if the reader considers that we have drawn the wrong conclusion we shall at any rate have provided the material with which a better conclusion may be reached.

Representations of Greek oared ships are preserved from earlier centuries than the eighth. These early examples appear to be simple oared ships rowed at one level, and to have had the characteristic build of the later ships, an L-shaped keel with the lower limb of the L lengthened and terminating forward in a ram. We have no literary texts to enlarge our knowledge of these ships, unless the Linear B tablets with their references to rowers can be taken to be such. In the eighth century a flourishing Greek civilization around the eastern basin of the Mediterranean had close connections with the sea, over which passed virtually all its main lines of communication. This civilization produced epic poems, in particular the *Iliad* and *Odyssey* in which sea voyages play so large and intimate a part. It also produced, at Athens, the pottery of the Geometric style, on which contemporary oared ships frequently appear, more probably for their own sake than as illustrating a story, although some are certainly illustrations.

In the following centuries at Athens first black- and then red-figure pottery makes reference to oared ships, and the growing volume of literature of all kinds provides a commentary, particularly explicit in the historians. In the fifth and fourth centuries, when the *trieres* becomes the universal 'capital' ship, while the production of literature is in full flood, the supply of representations of ships shrinks to a mere handful. While the black-figure painter often decorated his vases with ships as objects interesting for their own sake, the red-figure painter is an illustrator; and ships, or more frequently the sterns of ships, appear only as stage properties in scenes of mythology. The painter will then only show a *trieres* by anachronism. It is fortunate however that we have a ship portrait in relief on stone from the end of the fifth century.

* For arguments against Tarn's theory see *Mariner's Mirror* 27 (1941), 14–44 and *CQ* XLI (1947), 122–35.

INTRODUCTION

Epigraphy supplies a limited amount of information in the fifth century. The decree of Themistocles before Salamis, preserved in a fourth-century version, is perhaps more valuable for its intrinsic interest than for the information it gives. But in the fourth century the 'naval lists', inventories of ships and their gear as they were handed on annually from one board of dockyard supervisors at Piraeus to another, supplement and enlarge in many important respects the knowledge of the contemporary oared ships which we can derive from literature and art.* The naval lists tell us that in the year 330–329 B.C. the *tetreres* had been introduced into the fleets of Athens. Five years later the *penteres* appears in an inventory. We shall consider the possible reasons for, and the nature of, the new developments, but we shall not pursue the history of the oared ship beyond this vital stage in its evolution. The subsequent history of the oared ship merges with the history of the fleets of Alexander's successors, of Carthage, Rome and Byzantium. We close our account with the year when Macedonian troops occupied the naval installations of Athens, and brought to an end once for all the era in which a city-state, with a few hundred *triereis*, had been able to dominate the civilized world.

NOTE ON TERMINOLOGY

For the benefit of Greekless readers no Greek appears in the text or footnotes. Arabic numerals in the text refer the reader to the Greek texts collected in separate sections of each chapter. A number of Greek words do nevertheless appear in the text in English letters, the names of things the nature of which is being discussed, e.g. *histion, hupozoma*. Quantities are marked in the Glossary of Greek words. Where there is a convenient anglicized form of a word or name, e.g. pentekontor, trierarch, *Persians* (for the title of Aeschylus' play), this has usually been used. In the case of the names for ship types, *trieres, tetreres, penteres*, we have thought best to retain the transliterated Greek forms rather than adopt the convenient anglicized forms of the Latin *triremis*, etc., familiar though they are to English readers. Our reason is the lack of certainty that the *trieres, tetreres* and *penteres* were in fact identical to the *triremis, quadriremis* and *quinqueremis*.

---

* The foundations of the study of these lists were laid by August Boeckh's great work *Urkunden über das Seewesen des Attischen Staates*: hergestellt und erläutet von A. Boeckh, Berlin, 1840 (vol. III of his *Staatshaushaltung der Athener*). All subsequent workers in this field must acknowledge a debt to him.

THE HOMERIC PERIOD: 900–700 B.C.

οὐ γὰρ Φαιήκεσσι μέλει βιὸς οὐδὲ φαρέτρη,
ἀλλ’ ἱστοὶ καὶ ἐρετμὰ νεῶν καὶ νῆες ἐΐσαι,
ᾗσιν ἀγαλλόμενοι πολιὴν περόωσι θάλασσαν.
Homer, *Odyssey* 6, 270–2

‘For the Phaeacians take no interest in the bow and
the quiver, only in masts and ships’ oars and balanced
ships, in which they take delight as they cross the
grey sea.’

I

SHIPS OF THE BRONZE AGE

SUMMARY

The earliest purely Greek representations of an oared ship come from Volos in Thessaly on the Middle Helladic (i.e. Bronze Age) vase found in 1956 (BA. 1, Pl. 1 *a*). Most authorities suppose that the Greeks began to arrive in Greece during this period and added their culture to that of the existing people, who had close affinities with Crete, the Islands and S.W. Asia Minor. There is disagreement as to the area from which the Greeks came: those who believe that they came by sea from N.W. Anatolia may point to these ships as some slight support for their theory, for they resemble the ships on the silver dagger blade from Dorak in Phrygia of the third millennium B.C.* That the place where the vase was found (Kastro tou Golou) has been identified with the site of the ancient Iolkos, with which the Argonaut myth is closely associated, led the excavator, Theochares, to call these ships 'a significant promise of Iolkos' developing maritime enterprise which eventually led to the launching of the good ship *Argo*'. It is interesting to note that even at this early date Greek ships were equipped with a ram, which determined naval tactics for centuries.

By the Mycenaean period (Late Bronze Age) it is clear from the Linear B tablets found at Pylos in Messenia that the oared warship was an important element in the defence strategy of the Homeric Nestor, for they record† tallies of crews drawn from various Pylian townships detailed for service at Pleuron in order to face the threat of some external danger. Perhaps only by coincidence the best preserved of Mycenaean ship representations comes from Messenia (BA. 2, Pl. 1 *b*): from this, and to some extent from the others, it is possible to get some idea of the ships in use during the Mycenaean era.

Mycenaean warships were certainly equipped with the ram (BA. 2 and 6, and probably 3, Pl. 1 *c*, and 5), propelled by both oar and sail (BA. 2–4) and

---

* Particularly as to the ram and the arrangement of the oars on four of the ships. Mellaart, *Illustrated London News*, 28 November 1959.

† Ventris and Chadwick, *Documents in Mycenaean Greek*, An. 1 and An. 610.

steered by steering oars from the stern (BA. 2 and 5). The balustrades at bow and stern above the level of the gunwale presuppose platforms fore and aft. Bow and stern are high, but there is no uniformity about the method of decorating them. The chief controversy arises over the interpretation of the horizontal and vertical lines between bow and stern. The interpretation which seems most likely will be mentioned first. The upper horizontal represents the line of the near-side gunwale, the lower line the line of the keel. This interpretation gives all the ships a seaworthy appearance, puts them in proportion, and in the case of BA. 3 is unimpeachable. The verticals between the horizontals in BA. 2 can be explained as decoration; for not only was this method of decoration used on later ships (e.g. Boeotian fibulae, Arch. 13–16, Pl. 8*d*; Corinthian plaque, Arch. 44; and the Etruscan amphora, Louvre E. 752), but on the terracotta model, BA. 7, on which there can be no doubt as to what is the hull, there are similar vertical markings on the outside. It would be a mistake to imagine that because the painter leaves an area reserved in the colour of the clay, he intended to represent void. On certain Geometric ships (Geom. 2–6) the rectangles formed by such vertical lines represent 'rooms' (i.e. rowing spaces) of the oarsmen, since tholepins appear one in each rectangle. Thus BA. 2 has space for 25 such 'rooms', and may therefore be of pentekontor size. But it must be noted that whereas on the Mycenaean ships the vertical lines appear to be only decorative, on the Geometric ships the lines may represent a structural feature. On BA. 3 and 4 there is a single vertical amidships between the two horizontals. This may represent a mast, but if so, why is it shown *outside* the hull? It may be a single vertical on a roughly drawn ship in place of the series which appears on the carefully drawn BA. 2. However, a parallel for the rendering of the mast outside the hull can be found on BA. 8: this latter is not a warship with ram, but a merchantman, and has a hold; the side of the ship is cut away so that we can see what is going on below.

The other interpretations of these verticals make a thoroughly unseaworthy ship. It has been suggested* that the upper horizontal represents a deck and the verticals its supports: on this interpretation the hull must consist only of the lower horizontal, and thus be several times shallower than its own superstructure. The same objection may be made against the interpretation which makes the upper line a rail and the verticals its supports. There

* Kirk, 118.

8

may well have been rails on Mycenaean ships, but not of the height shown in the painting.*

The sail on BA. 3 is made up of small squares, and thus conforms to Geometric practice (see Geom. 7–9 and p. 54).

CATALOGUE

BA. 1. Plate 1 *a* (after Theochares). Fragments of a matt-painted Middle Helladic vase from Volos (Iolkos). *c.* 1600 B.C. Theochares, *Archaeology* 1958, 15; Lord William Taylour, *The Mycenaeans*, 163, fig. 74; Orlandos, *Ergon* 1956, 46; E. Vermeule, *Greece in the Bronze Age*, fig. 43 *a*.

Two ships to right. The better-preserved group of fragments shows a prominent ram and part of the bow aft. The hull was decorated with a zigzag pattern within an ellipse.† There are five diagonal lines painted downwards from the keel just aft of the ram, but these diagonal lines did not continue along the hull: they have been interpreted as oars, but in this case it is surprising that they are set so near the ram and that they are not apparently continuous.‡ To judge from the other bow there were similar diagonal lines above the bow, and the top corner of the bow on Pl. 1 *a* has been restored on this evidence. Theochares also restored a second pair of oar groups further aft balancing those forward, but there is no apparent evidence for these nor for the shape of the stern. A short piece of a thick diagonal line in front of the bow on the second group of fragments has been ingeniously restored by Theochares as part of the steering oar of the other ship.

BA. 2. Plate 1 *b* (drawn by W. Dodds after Kourouniotes). Mycenaean pyxis from the Tragana Tholos Tomb, Messenia. Kourouniotes, *Eph. Arch.* 1914, 108, figs 13–15; Casson, *The Ancient Mariners*, pl. 3 *b*; Furumark, *Mycenaean Pottery*, 333, fig. 56, 40, ship 2 (dated to Late Helladic III c, 1; but wrongly drawn); E. Vermeule, *Greece in the Bronze Age*, fig. 43 *b*; Kirk 118, B. iv.

Ship to right. A continuous thick line runs from the top of the stern post to the end of the short ram: above it is a thinner horizontal line with verticals between the two (for a discussion of this hull see Summary). The stern post is high, inclines slightly aft, and has a bulbous end. The stern compartment has a balustrade and contains a large steering oar with a tiller attached by a pin. The bow compartment too has a balustrade, surmounted by a fish ensign. Several reproductions of this ship inadvertently omit the protrusion in front of the stem together with the decoration immediately behind it. The bow is high. A single rope (forestay) runs from the bow to the top of what must be the mast. The top of the mast has a ring on each side (cf. Arch. 94, Pl. 21 *e*).

---

* On Geometric ships it will be argued that the painter was trying to represent both the profile and the plan views, but Mycenaean painters do not seem to be addicted to such distortions (compare the correctly drawn Mycenaean with the distorted Geometric chariots).

† For a parallel for this decoration cf. the zigzag decoration on at least one ship from the Early Cycladic 'frying pan' (Tsountas, *Eph. Arch.* 1899, 90, fig. 22) or Hipponax' advice to Mimnes (see below, p. 120).

‡ But see the Dorak ships, p. 7 above, for a parallel.

Three ropes run upwards from the stern: Kourouniotes restored two of these as running to the mast-top (backstays) and the third, the lowest one, to the sailyard, as in Pl. 1 *b*; but in BA. 4 this lowest rope seems also to be attached to the mast. The sail is stylized into a small ellipse.

The restoration in Pl. 1 *b* is indicated by lighter ink.

BA. 3. Plate 1*c* (drawn by W. Dodds after Froedin and Persson). Stirrup vase from Asine, House G. Froedin and Persson, *Asine*, fig. 207, 2; Furumark, *Mycenaean Pottery*, 333, fig. 56, 40, ship 3 (he dates to Late Helladic III c); Kirk, fig. 5; Casson, *The Ancient Mariners*, pl. 3*c*; E. Vermeule, *Greece in the Bronze Age*, fig. 43*d* (but the ram has been refined in the drawing).

It is not clear at first sight whether the protrusion on the left is a steering oar or a ram. In shape it is more like a steering oar and the swelling at its extremity tells against a ram, but does not preclude it, for the second vertical from the right of the sail is just as irregular, and the whole ship is very roughly drawn. Against the steering oar theory it may be argued that the protrusion is clearly an extension of the keel line and not an oar set over the gunwale. It is more likely, on balance, to be the ram, with the line of the ram continuing along the bottom of the hull, as in BA. 2. The horizontal line above is the gunwale. Oars are painted roughly across the hull; the two nearest the stern alone reach the gunwale; although these are called oars, they may well correspond to the verticals painted on the hull of the more careful BA. 2. In the centre of the hull is a thicker vertical which seems to be the mast; that the mast is seen through the hull is a piece of distortion which may be paralleled on BA. 8, where figures are seen standing in the bottom of the hold. At the stern the keel does not curve upwards as in BA. 2, but has an elbow. The stern is high and has six protrusions on the inner side and two on the outer. The bow has a straight stem post, and bow screens. The sail is composed of small squares, but there are no ropes.

BA. 4. Fragments from Phylakopi. *JHS* Suppl. IV, pl. 32, figs 11 *a, b* (Late Helladic III); Kirk 116, B. 1.

(*a*) Ship to left. The stern ends in four divisions; the stem post is plain and curved. Three ropes from the stern to the mast repeat the arrangement of BA. 2. The horizontal line on either side of the fragment, just below the level of the tops of the bow and stern, seems too low for a yard, but the line does not continue to the bow, so that it cannot be part of the hull.

(*b*) Section of the hull of another ship facing right. Part of the lower hull line is crossed by oars as in BA. 3. On the left is part of the steering oar. On the right, cutting the lower horizontal almost at right-angles, is a thicker line in what must be the same position as the thick central line in BA. 3, which was there interpreted as a mast. Part of the upper horizontal (gunwale) remains at the top of the fragment.

BA. 5. Mycenaean fragment from Eleusis. Skias, *Eph. Arch.* 1898, 71, fig. 11.

Ship to right. The fragment breaks just before the ram. Below the narrow hull are seven rowing oars and two steering oars: the stern is curved.

BA. 6. Mycenaean fragment of a terracotta model from Phylakopi. *JHS* Suppl. IV, pl. 40, 37.

Bow of ship with a short ram. The stem is concave in outline.

Other Mycenaean ship representations are not warships; they include:

BA. 7. Terracotta model from Phylakopi. *JHS* Suppl. IV, fig. 180; *BSA* iii, 23.

A ship without a ram. Vertical bands are painted on the inside (to represent ribs or benches) *and* on the outside. This gives support to the theory (see Summary) that the verticals on the Pylos vase, BA. 2, are not supports of any kind, but decoration. There is an eye on each side of the bow.

BA. 8. Krater from Enkomi. *Swedish Cyprus Expedition*, I, pl. cxxi, 3–4; Furumark, *Mycenaean Pottery*, 333, fig. 56, 40 (dated to Late Helladic III B); Wace and Stubbings, *A Companion to Homer*, 542, fig. 65; E. Vermeule, *Greece in the Bronze Age*, pl. xxxii, A.

Two ships, probably merchantmen.

BA. 9. Miniature stool of terracotta from Phylakopi. *JHS* Suppl. IV, fig. 181.

Stern of ship.

BA. 10. Carving on stone stele, Dramesi (Hyria?). Blegen, *Hesperia* Suppl. 8 (1949), pl. 7 (Late Helladic I); E. Vermeule, *Greece in the Bronze Age*, fig. 43 c.

Rough carvings of what are probably merchantmen. There is a similar carving on a stele of Late Cypriot III date from Enkomi (Schaeffer, *Enkomi-Alasia*, pl. 10).

BA. 11. Stirrup jar from Skyros. E. Vermeule, *Greece in the Bronze Age*, fig. 43 f (Late Helladic III c).

This ship without a ram and having a high curving stern and bow with a figure-head resembles the ships of the Sea Peoples depicted on Egyptian relief sculptures (*Medinet Habu*, vol. I, Publications of the Oriental Institute, University of Chicago, no. 8, 1930, pl. 37).

2

SHIPS OF THE GEOMETRIC PERIOD

PROTOGEOMETRIC

Geom. 1. Plate 1*d* (after Kirk). Cretan bell-krater. Heraklion VI, 8. Desborough, *Protogeometric Pottery*, 241 (dated to *c.* 900 B.C.); Kirk, fig. 6.

Two ships in silhouette. It is difficult to be sure which is the stem and which the stern. The left-hand end is drawn thicker and squarer than the right-hand end, and high solid side screens of this sort are characteristic of bows rather than of sterns. If the left-hand end then is the bow, the protrusion at this point should be the ram. The shape of this protrusion may look a little like the blade of a steering oar, but if it is a steering oar it is surprising that the artist has omitted the loom, although he had no means in this pure silhouette technique of indicating the part between the blade and the loom. This may not be the Attic Geometric way of indicating the ram (this is a Cretan vase and the large majority of Geometric versions are Attic), yet it is clear from the Aristo-nothos krater (Arch. 5, Pl. 9) that the downward pointing ram of this sort did exist. Apart from the ram, six horizontal planks protrude in front. The keel curves upwards towards the stern, from which four planks protrude.

THE DIPYLON GROUP. LATE GEOMETRIC I.
c. 760–*c.* 735 B.C.

NOTES ON THE INTERPRETATION OF GEOMETRIC PICTURES OF THIS PERIOD

This Dipylon Group* consists of monumental grave vases often over five feet high and is called after the Dipylon cemetery at Athens, where they were found. They were decorated not only with Geometric ornament, but also

---

* Most of these vases are fragmentary and dispersed over Europe and America; and it has been a subject of study to attribute the fragments to their parent vases (Kunze and Villard) and the vases to their painters: in this last pursuit Chamoux, Coldstream, Davison, Kunze, Nottbohm, and Villard have done and are still doing much. The chief painter is called the Dipylon master or the Painter of Athens 804 after his outstanding work: an associate of his has been called by Miss Davison the Kunze painter after the scholar who first isolated him, while still other hands have been identified among the general products of this workshop and others. There is as yet no firm agreement about these painters and their works, and the problems are complicated by the fact that more than one painter sometimes worked on the same vase (Davison, 29 ff.). The Geometric period as a whole has problems of chronology, but the dates given to the Group are those of Davison, which have won a wide measure of agreement (see Coldstream's review of her work in *JHS* 1963, 212).

with funeral scenes, chariot processions, ships, and land and sea battles. In view of the perversity of perspective in this Group an essential preliminary to the examination of the ship representations would seem to be a glance at the other subjects which were represented.

The krater Louvre A. 517 (Pl. 3a), which is decorated not only with a ship, but also with horses, chariots, and a funeral scene, will provide a suitable illustration. First, the horses: immediately striking is the narrow body and long neck. This predilection for a form with a narrow waist may be seen in the wasplike waist of their human beings, and it will be seen in the narrow hulls of their ships, while the extenuated necks of their horses will correspond to the exaggeratedly high bows and sterns. Then, the way the hindlegs of the two horses and the twin tails and sheaths are neatly fitted into a common rump is reminiscent of the smoothness with which the two groups of lines (A, B, and C, D, E, see below) are fitted into the bow and stern. Secondly, the chariots: there is probably a serious distortion here, for while the rail in front of the charioteer is shown in more or less correct perspective, the rail which is seen behind the warrior is considered by authorities* to be the rail on the side of the car, because a rail, if in the rear position, would have seriously impeded mounting on the move. Sometimes† the whole floor of the chariot is shown in plan view as well as in profile. Again, the far-side wheel is placed alongside the near-side wheel and the chariot floor adjusted accordingly, as if the chariot were a four-wheeler: but even here the painter would not be consistent; if he has room in his frieze, both wheels are shown side by side; if he is pressed, simply one is shown.‡ Finally, the funeral scene, the ceremonial laying out of the corpse: the position of the blanket, in plan view above the corpse, and of the corpse, which presumably should be covered by the blanket, tilted on its side, shows the liberties which could be taken with perspective.

Distortion, then, both imposed by limitation of technique and for its own sake, combination of plan view with the profile, irregularity of per-

---

* Lorimer, *Homer and the Monuments*, 320.

† This can be observed in its most extreme form on such pieces as Louvre A. 547 (*CVA* pl. 14; Davison, fig. 22) or Athens 990 (Davison, fig. 23), and in a less marked form in Louvre A. 522 (*CVA* pl. 4, 3; Kunze *O* pl. II, 2).

‡ E.g. the Sydney krater 46. 41 (*Handbook*, 244–5, figs. 48–9), where the left-hand car is squeezed and only one wheel is shown, but in the same frieze on the right-hand car the greater space allows two to be shown. Cf. also Webster, *From Mycenae to Homer*, 206—it is one of the characteristics of Geometric art that 'a chariot must show both its wheels, its rails, front and floor'. In later phases of Geometric and certainly by Protoattic one wheel becomes the rule.

spective generally, and inconsistency in rendering the same subject are all factors which may be met with in interpreting the ships of this Dipylon Group.

These ships are of a single kind, a warship with ram, and certain conventional rules are observed by the painters; these are as follows:

I. A ship's side is painted with the design seen in fig. 1.

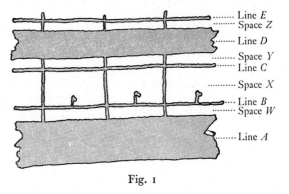

Fig. 1

A, B, C, D, and *E* are horizontal lines, of which *A* and *D* are considerably thicker than the others: *W, X, Y,* and *Z* are spaces, reserved in the colour of the clay, between these horizontal lines. Verticals cut through the horizontals and spaces at regular intervals. Sometimes small hooked uprights (tholepins) appear between the verticals on line *B* or starting from *A* and extending above *B*. Sometimes a mast and sail are included, in which case no tholepins are shown (Geom. 7–8, Pl. 2*c* and *d*): once (Geom. 9, Pl. 3*b*) oarsmen are set on line *D*, when tholepins are also omitted.

II A. When oarsmen are inserted in space *X* and sitting on line *B*, the verticals (and tholepins) are omitted as in fig. 2.

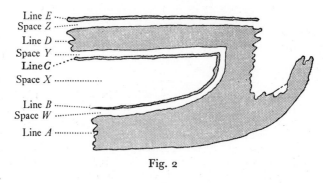

Fig. 2

The horizontal lines remain the same: fig. 2 shows *A* and *B* curving upwards towards the stern. On line *E* may be placed either another row of oarsmen (Geom. 10, Pl. 3*c*, and 14) or corpses (Geom. 11, Pl. 4*a*).

II B. The lines *C*, *D*, and *E* are omitted, once when a pile of corpses is placed above line *B* instead of oarsmen, so that there is no room for these horizontals (Geom. 16, Pl. 4*c*), and on another occasion when a krater handle comes down so low over the ship that there is no room for more than a single line of oarsmen (Geom. 17, Pl. 4*d*).

Interpretation of the Lines and Spaces

Line *A* is clearly the hull, but not necessarily the whole of the hull. Just above line *B* appear tholepins; hence *B* must be the gunwale, and thus the reserved space *W* is not a gap between two timbers, but decoration of a kind which appears frequently in this place on later representations of Greek ships.* This seems as far as one can go with certainty. For the rest (*C*, *D*, and *E*), three solutions have been put forward: (1) *C*, *D*, and *E* represent a rail. (2) *C*, *D*, and *E* represent a deck for which the verticals are the supports. (3) *C*, *D*, and *E* represent the far side of the ship.

1. It is very unlikely that the rail would be so high above the gunwale, or that the rail itself would be deeper than the whole of the hull.

2. The deck theory cannot be dismissed so summarily. There are three kinds of decks which could have been used—(*a*) a watertight deck covering the ship; (*b*) a deck, or rather gangway, along the centre line of the ship; (*c*) decks, or rather gangways (Greek: *parodoi*), only along the sides of the ship. The first seems to be ruled out both by Thucydides' statement (1, 14[3]) that it was only after Salamis that Athenian ships were completely decked (see below, pp. 160 ff.), and by certain objections levelled against (*c*). The second type, the central deck, has been turned down by Kirk,† because it would have interfered with the raising and the lowering of the mast. This seems sound, but it is at the same time likely that a central *gangway* at the level of the benches would have been employed. Thirdly, the side decks have the strongest claims for consideration and these have been clearly put forward by Kirk. If it were certain that the painter was thinking only of the

---

* Similarly, a reserved edge on a shield does not warrant the assumption that there were apertures at this point. There is nothing to suggest that the bottom of line *A* is the water-line and not the keel-line.

† *BSA* xliv, 127.

profile view of the ship, and if the difficulties in (i) and (ii) below could be explained away, then C, D, and E might well represent a deck. But this is not certain; in fact, in view of the perverse perspective noted above, some distortion involving a combination of the profile view with the plan view is to be expected. The main arguments against the deck theory are as follows:

(i) The height of the 'deck' above the gunwale is such that the ship would be top-heavy—i.e. the comparatively great depth of space X should preclude a deck theory: nor can it be argued that space X is made larger than fact in order to accommodate the rowers, because space X is at its deepest in some examples where there are no rowers (Geom. 2–3).

(ii) In some ships warriors stand with their feet in space X (Geom. 2, Pl. 1 e). If space X is a gap between gunwale and deck, their position would be impossible to explain, especially in view of the Geometric predilection for placing figures on the top of a line, even if they do not in fact belong there.*

(iii) When rowers are sitting above C, D, and E (Geom. 10, Pl. 3 c and d, and 14), it is usually assumed, because, among other reasons, their oars disappear over the far side of the ship, that these are the far-side oarsmen (incl. Kirk). If this is the case, it is more logical to assume that they are *sitting on the far side* of the ship as well, for their position above D and E corresponds exactly to that of the near-side oarsmen above line B.

(iv) After the Geometric style proper and its tradition had been superseded (under tradition may be included the representations of the first half of the seventh century) there is no sign of a 'deck' on Greek ship representations until the fifth century. If the deck theory is maintained, one must assume an advance in naval construction, in a period when shipping is known to have been restricted, which was paradoxically forgotten during a period of expansion.

3. Whereas A and B represent the hull, i.e. the profile view, we suggest that the spaces and lines above represent the plan view. Space X is the centre of the ship between the two sides; lines D and C balance A and B and represent the far side of the ship;† the verticals will be the benches, which are omitted when rowers are inserted above B. It is more than likely that the benches will be in line with the ribs of the ship, and that the supports of a rail

---

* Cf. the practice of putting the warrior or charioteer on top of the plan view of the chariot (Hirschfeld krater, Davison, fig. 25).

† Pernice, *AM* 1892, 285 ff., has already suggested that the artist was attempting to show the far side of the ship.

would be in line with these too: the verticals top line E in a manner suggesting that E is a rail, so that the verticals where they cross space X represent the benches, where they cross lines C and D represent side ribs, and above D are supports for the rail E. Even if this detailed explanation of the lines and spaces is a little in the air, it need not invalidate the general theory that there is a combination of the profile and the plan view. Nor is there any evidence to preclude it: there are two cases (Geom. 16–17, Pl. 4) where C, D, and E are omitted altogether; that the painter felt he could omit them without doing violence to the ship suggests the parallel of the chariot wheels; for where the painter had the room, the two wheels of the chariot were placed side by side; but when space was restricted, only one wheel was painted, which completely overlapped the second. Thus correct perspective was adopted only when room was restricted; usually the painter spread himself into the third dimension. This theory alone explains the position of the feet of the warriors standing not only on D and E but also in space X, for space X is the centre of the ship and where they should be standing, otherwise they are attracted to lines D and E in accordance with the Geometric style.

Some support for this theory that the lines C, D, and E and the spaces X, Y, and Z represent the plan view of the ship may be gained from the Geometric boat with the bizarre helmsman in the Heraklion Museum (Pl. 1f). If the horizontal lines which are joined by the uprights on the left of the helmsman are regarded as the thick line A on the Dipylon ships and the space above these lines below the port gunwale is regarded as space W and the gunwale itself, defined in black, as line B, then the space on the line of the helmsman's left leg equals space X, the line between his legs equals line C, the space along his right leg equals space Y, the two lines joined by the uprights equal the very thick line D, the space above, below the starboard gunwale, equals space Z and the gunwale itself with its black paint equals line E. It is true that the Heraklion boat, although Geometric in style, is not *Attic* Geometric, and the lines and spaces on a skiff of this sort should not be expected to correspond closely with those of a larger oared ship, yet the parallel is evident and might be said at least to counter the objection to this theory relating certain lines and spaces on the Dipylon ships to the plan view that we have no idea what the inside of a Geometric ship looked like.

CATALOGUE

Section 1

The ships in this section are of the type noted in fig. 1 above with verticals and tholepins. They are part of scenes of fighting, in which corpses are nearly always prominent. These scenes are set on one side of the shoulder zone of the krater, i.e. between, not under, the handles: on the other side of the vase, the main side, the funeral scene is depicted with mourners around the bier. It might be imagined that the ship scene represents the way in which the dead man met his death, but there was too little time between death and burial for a vase of this size to be made to order. The significance of these ship scenes will be discussed on p. 41.

Kunze has distinguished four such kraters and these correspond to Geom. 2–5: there is a strong possibility that Geom. 6 provides the ship scene for a fifth krater.

Geom. 2. Plate 1*e* (photo: Chuzeville). Attic krater (fragmentary). Louvre A. 527 (upper part of the vase as restored in the Louvre). *CVA* 11, pls 2, 2 and 3, 7 (where see bibliography: add R. T. Williams, *JHS* 1958, pl. 13*c* (right); Kunze *O* pl. IV, 1 below r. (his krater II); Davison, fig. 13*a* and *c* (by the Kunze painter); Chamoux, *La Civilisation grecque*, pl. 28); Kirk, no. 7*a–b*, pl. 38, 1.

On the shoulder zone of the krater one (?) ship in two fragments, A. 527 and 535, faces left in a battle scene. Line *A* (see fig. 1) is rather attenuated; on line *B*, midway between each pair of verticals, there are regular hooks which can only be tholepins. The verticals run from *A* right through *B*, *C*, *D*, and *E*. There are parts of five figures remaining on board; three or perhaps four stand on *B*, one stands in space *X* above the others, carrying a rectangular shield:* the figure on the ram is covered by the so-called Dipylon shield.† The ram tapers to a sharp point. The hatched stem post on the high bow curves forward before curving aft, and whether there is a final curve upwards is doubtful, for there is a break at this point: the stem post seems to begin at the inboard side of the bow screen; if this is so, either the lower part of the post must be in two sections, one for the port side of the screen, another for the starboard, or the bow must be planked over beneath the end of the post and the post must run down the centre of it; the latter seems the more likely. There are four planks protruding from the stem. An 'eye' in the form of a wheel with sixteen spokes decorates the bow, the after half of which has a balustrade.

Geom. 3. Attic krater fragment. Louvre A. 534. *CVA* pl. 3, 8 (where see bibliography: add R. T. Williams, *JHS* 1958, pl. 13*c* (left); Davison, fig. 13*c* (left); Kunze *O* pl. IV, 1 (below on left); Snodgrass, *Early Greek Armour*, pl. 3*c*); Kirk no. 8. Villard has mounted this fragment in the Louvre

---

* See Snodgrass, *Early Greek Armour and Weapons*, 61.
† See Snodgrass, 58; also p. 42 below.

as part of the other side of Geom. 2, but Kunze (*AJA* 1957, 306–7) argues that the other side to that should be a prothesis scene and gives this fragment to a companion piece, which he suggests is Louvre A. 522 (his krater I). But the ship under the handle on this latter krater (here Geom. 17) is not easily distinguishable as being by the same hand as this Louvre A. 534, which is certainly by the same hand as the ship on A. 527 (Geom. 2). See p. 26 for the painters.

Part of the bow (ram missing) and a great part of the hull of a ship identical in style to Geom. 2 remain. There were at least five figures (one again has a rectangular shield and on his left an archer) standing on line *B*.

Geom. 4. Plate 2*a* (photo: Chuzeville). Fragments of an Attic krater. Louvre A. 528. *CVA* pl. 7, 7–8 (where see bibliography); Kirk nos 9–10. Kunze (*S* 166 ff.) thinks that this frieze is the upper part of his krater III, of which the lower part is the base of Villard's A. 527, but he had, with qualifications, included also the following Geom. 5 (3), which must be excluded from this vase, because it has a different treatment to the interior (cf. Villard).

Fight on a ship. The larger fragment (A. 528) gives part of the bow and hull of a ship to left. The arrangement of the lines, spaces and verticals is the same as on the preceding except that space *X* is not so deep and the verticals and tholepins are painted more heavily. There are three planks projecting from the hatched stem post: three belaying pins (or the top of the balustrade) appear behind its base. The 'eye' consists of a wheel with eight spokes surrounded by dots. At least one plank protrudes from the stem. There are three figures aboard: the archer on the right stands on line *D*, the left-hand figure with an arrow through his neck, on the bow platform, and the central figure seems to be stepping up onto the platform. On the extreme left appear the arm and spear of another figure, who is placed too high to be standing on the ram.

The second fragment, A. 537, shows the stern probably of the same ship. Of the horizontal lines only *D* and *E* survive. The stern has a balustrade and a high stern post with projecting planks. One warrior seizes one of the spears stored in the stern compartment (see below, p. 48); two other warriors stand on line *D*, facing each other; aft of the ship lies a corpse.

Geom. 5. Plate 2*b* (no. 3; photo: Chuzeville). Attic krater fragments in the Louvre and Athens NM. (1) Louvre CA 3362 (1). *CVA* pl. 7, 15 (where see bibliography); Kirk, no. 13, pl. 39, 1. (2) Athens NM. Kunze *O* pl. V, 1; Kirk, no. 12. (3) Louvre CA 3362 (2). *CVA* pl. 7, 16; Kirk, no. 26. Kunze (*O* p. 167) places (1) and (2) in the shoulder zone of his krater IV (both fragments are unglazed on the inside). Villard (*CVA*) says that (1) and (3) (interior unglazed) belong almost certainly to the same zone of the same krater. If both are correct, (1) should be the bow of the left-hand ship of (3), and (2) the stern of the right-hand ship of (3) (but see below at (3)).

The fragments depict a battle at sea.

(1) This fragment shows the forepart of a ship to left similar in style to Geom. 4 with the conventional lines and spaces and tholepins: the bow tholepin rests on line *B*, the next one on *A*. There are the remains of a balustrade in the bow compartment, the outside of which is decorated with an 'eye' of eight spokes. Part of the leg of a warrior stands on line *D*, and beneath the bow there floats part of a corpse.

(2) Section of an identical ship towards the stern depicting two warriors opposing each other on line *D*. The stroke tholepin and three others rise from line *A*.

(3) The ram of one ship almost touches the stern of another. Two corpses lie beneath the ships and the leg of a third can be seen above the steering oars of the left-hand ship and the uppermost protruding plank of the right-hand ship. The right-hand ship has an 'eye' in the style of Geom. 4, and the left-hand ship shows planks protruding from the stern. If this fragment belongs to (1) and (2) there should be tholepins between the verticals, but it is not clear from the small section that remains of the verticals of the left-hand ship whether there were. The lines seem to be of too uniform a thickness for verticals alternating with tholepins and yet they are too close together for a succession of verticals. Kirk (loc. cit.) had doubts but seems to have thought that there were no tholepins. Until their presence can be established, the attribution of this fragment to the zone should be held in question. If it should be necessary to withdraw this fragment, (1) and (2) might well belong to the same ship.

Geom. 6. Attic krater fragments in the Louvre and Athens NM. (1) Athens. Pernice, *AM* 1892, 287, no. 23 and fig. 7; Kirk, no. 11. (2) Louvre CA 3364. *CVA* pl. 8, 1.

(1) The Athens fragment shows the bow (less ram) of a ship to left in a style close to Geom. 4, but here there is an 'eye' of sixteen spokes and there is a clear balustrade behind the hatched stem post, against which there rest three spears. There are four protruding planks on the stem and two on the after side of the bow compartment.

(2) The Louvre fragment shows the tip of a ram of one ship and the steering oar of a ship in front; beneath the ram is the head and chest of a corpse. The style is close to that of Geom. 5 (3), but this fragment cannot be part of that krater as this has internal glazing (see Villard); but it may be found to belong to the above Athens fragment when that can be checked.

The question arises whether these two fragments, if they go together, belong to one of the preceding four kraters. It is unlikely that Geom. 2 and 3 had room for a second ship in their respective panels, but even if they had, the style of this Athens fragment conforms rather to Geom. 4 and 5 with the shallower space *X*. It seems possible from a purely superficial examination that the tip of the ram on this CA 3364 (2) could belong to the bow of Geom. 4 and the chest of the corpse on this fragment belong to the legs of the corpse on Geom. 4, but neither the thickness of the two pieces nor their interior treatment really corresponds, and such a join would anyhow hardly have escaped Villard. Geom. 5, as has been stated, must be ruled out because that has its interior unglazed. There remains the strong possibility that Geom. 6 represents the ship painting for a fifth krater, and here Louvre A. 517 (*CVA* pl. 1) must be a strong candidate, which, as it stands, lacks a ship scene on the reverse side of the shoulder zone, and whose ship under the handle (Geom. 9) corresponds closely in style to this Athens fragment.*

Section 2

All the fragments except the last krater in this section represent ships with their sails raised. No men are shown on the ship except for the helmsman. Tholepins are omitted, but the arrangement of horizontal lines, spaces and verticals remains as in section 1. Kunze has shown (*O* 166 ff.) that the fragments come from two companion kraters, his kraters III and IV, and from the lowest zone in those kraters. Parts of the upper halves of these kraters can be seen in Geom. 4 and 5 respectively.

It may reflect the painter's feeling for form that he introduces the sail at the lowest zone and avoids there to some extent at least the human figure: in the shoulder zone a vertical accent is required to balance the horizontal handles, but towards the base of the vase the sail provides a satisfactory stable horizontal accent.

Geom. 7. Attic krater. Louvre A. 527 (lower part; it includes A. 526 and 538) and Louvre A. 539 and 540. *CVA* pls 2, 2; 3, 9–10; 7, 10–11 and 14 (where see bibliography); Kirk, no. 14, pl. 40, 1 (left); no. 17 *a–c*, pl. 39, 6, 9 and 5. Kunze gives this lower part of Louvre A. 527 to his krater III (*O* 166 ff.). Davison accepts Villard's restoration with some adjustments (31, n. 30). Kunze adds the Louvre fragments A. 539 and 540, which Villard keeps apart. Kirk added the Athens fragment (Geom. 8 (3)) but is refuted by Villard (*CVA* p. 5, n. 1).

On the fragment, old no. A. 526, the forepart of a ship is shown facing left. Lines and spaces are as in the preceding section, but the tholepins are omitted and a rectangular sail is added, decorated with squares six deep: a sheet is attached to the second vertical of the hull, and a sailyard brace to a belaying pin in the after part of the bow compartment. There are three more belaying pins in the forward part. The stem post is unhatched and the bow is decorated with an 'eye' of eight spokes. The style is less elaborate than in section 1.

The fragment A. 538 gives the stern of a similar ship in the same zone. As Kirk has pointed out (103, n. 18), this stern cannot come from the same ship as A. 526 (nor apparently did Villard intend it to be so regarded, see *CVA* p. 4), because the squares of the sail are here eight deep, not six, as on A. 526. A sailyard brace and a

---

* I have since observed that Kunze in a footnote (*S* 55, n. 26) has already attributed the Athens fragment to Louvre A. 517, but to the area under the left handle. I believe the presence of the tholepins on the ship tells against this position (the ship under the right handle, Geom. 9, has no tholepins). If the Louvre fragment CA 3364 does belong to the Athens fragment, they cannot belong to the handle area, because CA 3364 has part of a second ship—too large a composition for such a small space.

sheet are attached to the hull. The helmsman with a sword at his waist holds the sail; his legs do not appear below line *D*.

The fragment A. 540 provides the stern compartment behind the helmsman of A. 538. Kirk (no. 17*b*) thinks that this stern does not fit A. 538, but Kunze (*O* 167, n. 4) disagrees.

Two more fragments (A. 539) give more of perhaps the same sail (eight squares deep) and a part of the hull.

Geom. 8. Plate 2*c* (no. 1) and *d* (no. 3) (photos: German Archaeological Institute, Athens). Fragments of a similar krater. Athens NM. (1) Kunze *O* pl. VI, 1; Pernice, fig. 1; R. T. Williams, *Greece and Rome* 1949, pl. 85, 1*b*; Kirk, no. 15. (2) Kunze *O* pl. V, 3; Pernice, fig. 3; Kirk, no. 16. (3) Kunze *O* pl. VI, 2; Kirk, no. 14, pl. 40, 1 (right; Kirk mistakenly thought that this could be combined with Geom. 7); Pernice, fig. 2 and Snodgrass, *Early Greek Armour*, pl. 1, 1 omit the left-hand fragment. Kunze combines these fragments in his krater IV (see Geom. 5 for the upper part of the krater).

(1) The forepart of a ship sailing to left is in identical style to Geom. 7, except that four planks protrude from the stem and there are four spears in the bow compartment. This fragment also shows the mast with a bisected V top and halliards.

(2) This fragment gives the stern perhaps of the same ship, again in identical style to Geom. 7. Here the helmsman holds the sail with one hand and with the other the sailyard brace, which is tied to the balustrade in the bow compartment. Part of the steering oars can be observed on the edge of the fragment. The long neck of a flying bird appears just above the stern horn (cf. the bird on Geom. 7). It might be that the neck of this bird belongs to the body on (1), but then this will have to be the stern of another ship.

(3) Mid section and stern of another ship has the after half of the sail complete with the same details as in (2), but here there is an additional rope (probably a brailing rope) running from the centre of the after half of the sail to line *D*. Three spears are stored in the stern compartment.

Geom. 9. Plate 3*a* and *b* (photo: Chuzeville). Attic krater. Louvre A. 517. *CVA* pl. 1 (where see bibliography: add R. T. Williams, *JHS* 1958, pl. 13*a*); Kirk, no. 18, pl. 38, 2. This krater is considered by many to be by the Dipylon master (see below on the painters).

Under the handle there is painted a complete ship to left. The lines, spaces and verticals correspond to the composition in this section, but the four protrusions from the stem, the hatched stem post, the balustrade in the bow compartment, the 'eye' of sixteen spokes, correspond to those on Geom. 6 in section 1, though here there are no tholepins. This ship has no sail, but it might be argued that the centrepiece of the handle precluded its inclusion and the painter inserted four oarsmen to fill the sides.

Section 3

This section illustrates the practice, mentioned in category IIA and B above, of omitting the vertical lines (and tholepins) when space *X* is filled with oarsmen. On two occasions lines *C*, *D*, and *E* are omitted as well

(Geom. 16–17). Kunze has attributed Geom. 10–13, 16–17 to a single painter (but see notes on painters below, p. 26).

Geom. 10. Plate 3*c* and *d* (photo: Chuzeville). Attic krater fragments. Louvre A. 530. *CVA* pl. 6, 5, 7–9 (where see bibliography); Kirk, nos 28 and 22.

The lowest zone but one of the krater represents a ship being rowed to the left, a corpse beneath, and warriors standing in front of the bow and behind the stern. All that remains of the ship is part of the ram, which is long and thin, and the after section. The design of the hull is as represented in fig. 2 with the omission of the verticals. On line *B* are seated oarsmen straining at the oars, which have a spade-shaped blade: above line *E* is seated another set of oarsmen in similar attitudes with their oars set over the far-side gunwale. Kirk (loc. cit.) admits that they must be the far-side oarsmen (and not a higher bank), but being wedded to a deck theory for the explanation of lines *C*, *D*, and *E*, says that they are seated on a deck. If he believes that the ship is drawn in correct perspective and that *C*, *D*, and *E* represent a deck, any rowers shown rowing from that 'deck' must be there in fact. Therefore these fragments to us support the theory that the lines *C*, *D*, and *E* represent the far side of the ship, and just as the near-side rowers are seated on the near side (lines *A* and *B*), so the far-side oarsmen must be seated on the far side of the ship (lines *C*, *D*, and *E*). In the stern compartment the helmsman armed with a sword holds one of the steering oars with his left hand and raises a long-fingered right hand. The second steering oar can be seen behind.

Another fragment (old number A. 533, *CVA* pl. 6, 5: Kirk, no. 22) shows a section of the forepart of another ship to the left in the same zone (*sic* Villard, but Kunze rejects the attribution in *AJA* 1957, 307). There are two oarsmen on line *B*, but the place of oarsmen on lines *D* and *E* is taken by two figures, one standing, the other seated, both holding ropes, and beyond them a pile of corpses. There is no room in the frieze for a sail or a mast mounted, so that they are best interpreted as raising or lowering the mast by the forestays (cf. Geom. 16).

Geom. 11. Plate 4*a* (photo: German Archaeological Institute, Athens). Fragments of another krater now in Brussels (ex Louvre A. 531) augmented by fragments in Athens. Kunze *S* pl. 4; Davison, fig. 13; Giraudon 29663; Chamoux, *RA* 1945, 1, 86, fig. 8; Matz, pl. 13*b*; Brann, *Antike Kunst* 1959, pl. 18, 3; Kirk, no. 21. By the same painter as Geom. 10, whom Davison calls the Kunze painter.

A ship in identical style to that on Geom. 10 is rowed to the left in the lowest zone but one of a krater. Eight oarsmen have survived (there is room for about four more): the far-side oarsmen are here replaced by a pile of large corpses. There is no balustrade in the stern, where the helmsman sits under the horn holding the loom of one of the steering oars. The fragment on the extreme left gives part of the stem post curved back so that it is parallel to the hull. Beneath it are the bow screens edged with hatching and decorated with maeander in white paint. One figure transfixed by a spear collapses near the blade of the steering oar.

Kunze thinks it is possible that these fragments belong to the same frieze as Geom. 12–13.

23

Geom. 12. Plate 4*b* (photo: German Archaeological Institute, Athens). Attic krater fragment. Athens NM. Pernice, fig. 8; Kunze *S* pl. 9, 4; Kirk, no. 27.

This fragment shows part of a bow to left, from which advances a warrior, who might have been drawing a bow. Only the forward bottom edge of the stem post remains and this is hatched. A strip below it is decorated with a maeander in white paint. The stem has five planks protruding; the 'eye' is in the form of a wheel with eight spokes. The only other ship on which the stem post does not curve forward from its base, but immediately begins its upward and backward curve, is on the Warsaw (ex Königsberg) fragment, Geom. 16, where there is also similar figure painting (Kunze attributes the two to the same hand). It has been suggested that the warrior in front of the bows is Protesilaus, who was killed on landing at Troy (*Il.* II, 695).

Geom. 13. Attic fragment of a krater. Athens NM. Kunze *S* pl. 9, 5.

Only the lower part of the stern survives on this fragment and two or three oars with their spade-shaped blades and the usual striped blade of the steering oar. Beneath is a fallen warrior transfixed by a sword. Kunze rightly attributes this to the same painter and perhaps to the same frieze as Geom. 11 and 12.

Geom. 14. Fragments of another krater. Louvre A. 532. *CVA* pl. 7, 2–3 and 5 (where see bibliography: add R. T. Williams, *Greece and Rome* 1949, pl. 86, 2*a*); Kirk, nos 29, 30, and 25, pl. 39, 3–4.

CVA pl. 7, 2 shows the section of a ship being rowed to left. The upward curve of lines *A* and *B* indicates a point near the stern. Rowers are seated above both lines *B* and *E*, and the oars of the latter again go over the far side of the ship, so that the artist must be representing the far-side oarsmen. A section of a ship in the same zone appears in *CVA* pl. 7, 5, of which only the oarsmen above line *B* have survived.

Villard also attributes to the same zone *CVA* pl. 7, 3, but this ship has verticals without oarsmen and the combination of the two styles in the same zone seems unlikely, so Kunze seems right in keeping it apart (*AJA* 1957, 307, where he suggests that a fragment in Athens (Germ. Inst. Photo 4294) may belong to our Geom. 14).

Geom. 15. Krater fragment. Athens NM. Pernice, fig. 4; Kirk, no. 24.

A section of the bows has two oarsmen sitting on line B. Below their feet is a small vertical joining *A* and *B*: above their heads a single thick line; the fragment breaks at this point and it is impossible to tell whether there were other horizontals. The drawing is suspect both at this point and at the hull on the left of the fragment. It cannot be connected with any of the above, because it has a different dividing pattern below the picture.

Geom. 16. Plate 4*c* (i) and (ii) ((i) after *Mon. Ined.*; (ii) photo: Warsaw Museum*). Attic krater fragments. Warsaw 142172 (ex Königsberg A. 18). *Mon. Ined.* IX, pl. 40, 3; Lullies, *Antike Kleinkunst in Königsberg*, pl. 2; Kirk, fig. 2; *CVA* pl. 2, 4 and 6 (but only the bow of the ship is illustrated here). Kunze (*O* 168) attributes this fragment to the same hand as his kraters I and II.

* This lacks the fragment with the ram; the three fragments which make up the rest of the ship, Professor Michalowski informs us, are not in Warsaw.

A fight at sea. This ship belongs to the category of IIB on p. 15, in which lines *C*, *D*, and *E* are omitted, not because a different type of ship is being represented or because the vase is of a different date from the rest in the Group (Kunze and Nott-bohm make it contemporary), but because, in this case, a pile of corpses has been introduced above line *B* and into space *X*, so that there is simply no room for the other horizontals. Two figures in the bow are holding ropes in the same attitude as was depicted on Geom. 10, which was there interpreted as the raising or lowering of the mast: the mast can here be seen inclined slightly forwards. There are the remains of a figure seated in the stern corresponding to the figures in the bows who may also be taking part in the operation. There is one halliard just forward of the mast. The stern is similar to the others in this section; looms and blades of the steering oars can be discerned. The bow compartment lacks a balustrade aft of the bow screens, but is decorated with the usual 'eye', here of four spokes. Several planks protrude from the stem. On the long ram lies one corpse; there is another casualty behind the stern.

Geom. 17. Plate 4*d* (photo: Chuzeville). Attic krater. Louvre A. 522. *CVA* pl. 4 (where see biblio-graphy: add Kunze *O* pl. II; R. T. Williams, *Greece and Rome* 1949, pl. 86, 2*c*; *JHS* 1958, pl. 13*f*; Davison, fig. 15*a–b*); Kirk, no. 5.

A complete ship faces right under the handle. Line *B* is thicker than usual. Lines *C*, *D*, and *E* are here omitted because the centre-piece of the handle came down too low over the oarsmen's heads; the actual handle is missing, but its print in the clay can be clearly seen in the photograph. The attitude of the thirteen oarsmen is unique. They sit with their heads to the stern, chests to the front, and each with his right hand holds his own oar vertically over the gunwale and with his left hand holds the oar of the man behind him; the stroke oarsman seems to have no oar and to be grasping with his right either the stern balustrade or the oar of an invisible far-side oarsman. They are perhaps performing some starting drill: Kirk (loc. cit.) dismisses the theories of Cartault (a stopping or turning manœuvre—and rightly, for why should each man hold the oar of the man behind him, and where is the helmsman?), and of Assmann (ceremonial greeting), but is misled by his own incorrect early classification into saying that the strange position is a 'singularly naïve attempt simply to portray rowers in action'. For this krater belongs to the main output of the Dipylon Group and Kunze and Davison are both convinced that it is by the same hand as Geom. 2 (but see notes on painters, p. 26). Above the balustrade of the stern compartment the stern continues in unusual thickness before it tapers. The bow screens are high and have a balustrade aft.

Under the other handle of this krater there is the tip of the ram and the mid section of a ship with verticals and lines *A*, *B*, *C*, *D*, and *E* (see *CVA* pl. 4, 2). Kirk, no. 19, says that these parts do not belong to the krater, but Villard, p. 6, makes it clear that they are connected to its body.

Geom. 18. Krater fragment. Louvre A. 536. *CVA* pl. 7, 9 (where see bibliography); Kirk, no. 23.

The fragment shows the lower forward section of a ship to left on the lowest figured zone of a krater. Line *B* is thick, as on Geom. 16, but the fragment breaks at the shoulders of the two oarsmen, so that it is not certain whether lines *C*, *D*, and *E* were present or not: the verticals are absent. Five small fish swim below the hull. This is not in the style of the preceding fragments.

NOTES ON THE PAINTERS OF THE SHIPS IN THE DIPYLON GROUP

As has been mentioned in the Introduction to the Dipylon Group (see above, p. 12) the scattered fragments are being attributed to their respective kraters and attempts are being made to ascribe these kraters to their respective painters. It is not intended to make another list of ascriptions of whole vases but merely to tabulate the conclusions regarding the painters of the ships, for some of these conclusions seem to conflict with those of recent authorities on Geometric painting. Since it has already been seen that more than one hand was working on Louvre A. 527 (Geom. 2 and 7)*, it seems possible that this disagreement may be due to the fact that a subordinate, perhaps even a specialized painter, was assigned the task of painting a ship scene on a vase which was, in the main, the handiwork of another.

On the table below, the ships are allotted to individual painters, and the attribution of the larger pieces to which they belong, made by the most recent authorities, is noted in each case. It will be seen that the only serious discrepancy occurs in the case of the ships of our section 3, Geom. 10–18, Pl. 3*c*–4*d*. The bulk of these Kunze and, to a lesser extent, Davison ascribe to the so-called Kunze painter, but to the same painter they also give Louvre A. 527 (or rather Davison gives the whole krater A. 527, as restored in the Louvre, Geom. 2 (Pl. 1*e*) and 7, but Kunze allows only the upper part, Geom. 2), and it is here that the difficulty arises. The painter of the ships in this section 3, who may be called ship painter 3, has a quite different style from that of the ship painter of A. 527. His omission of the verticals and the insertion of oarsmen is not in itself the mark of a different painter, but it is accompanied by the omission of the stern balustrade and by the adoption of quite different detailing in the bow; the stem post does not curve forward at the base (Geom. 12, Pl. 4*b*, and 16, Pl. 4*c*); bow screens are hatched at the edges and areas picked out in a maeander of white paint (Geom. 11–12); more planks protrude at the stem than in the ships of other painters (Geom. 12 and 16). The

* See Davison.

Relation of the ship painters to the main painters

Cat. No.	Museum No.	Attributions of the composite pieces	Ship painter
Geom. 2	Louvre A. 527 (upper part)	Kunze (krater II) and Davison to Kunze painter	1 −
Geom. 3	Louvre A. 534	Kunze (krater I) and Davison to Kunze painter. Villard gives this to Geom. 2	1 −
Geom. 4	Louvre A. 528	Kunze (krater III) to Dipylon workshop	1
Geom. 7	Louvre A. 527 (lower part)	Kunze (krater III) to Dipylon workshop. Villard mounts this with Geom. 2	1
Geom. 5	Louvre CA. 3362 + Athens	Kunze (krater IV; same hand as III) to Dipylon workshop. Villard to same hand as A. 527	1
Geom. 8	Athens	Kunze to krater IV	1
Geom. 9	Louvre A. 517	Nottbohm and Davison to Dipylon master	1 +
Geom. 6	Athens	Kunze and Williams to Louvre A. 517	1 +
Geom. 10	Louvre A. 530	Kunze to Kunze painter	3
Geom. 11	Brussels + Athens	Kunze and Davison to Kunze painter	3
Geom. 12–13	Athens	Kunze to Kunze painter	3
Geom. 14–15	Louvre A. 532 + Athens		3
Geom. 16	Warsaw (ex Königsberg)	Kunze to Kunze painter; Nottbohm to Dipylon workshop	3
Geom. 17	Louvre A. 522	Kunze combines with Geom. 3. Kunze and Davison to Kunze painter. Villard to a separate workshop	2

ship on Louvre A. 522, Geom. 17 (Pl. 4*d*), included in this section by virtue of its build-up, has a style which has points of difference with painter 3; it has a form of stern which occurs nowhere else, a bow relieved of all detail, and a crew, lacking helmsman and his steering oars, of different stamp—differences which seem enough to warrant an ascription to another painter, our ship painter 2. It may be significant that Villard thought this vase (A. 522) belonged to a quite different context from Davison and Kunze, yet the ship under the other handle of this same vase was constructed like those in sections 1 and 2, though too little remains of it to risk an attribution.

Most of the ship fragments which make up sections 1 and 2 come from five kraters, according to Kunze's classification. Of the ships on these fragments, Geom. 4, 5, 7 and 8 (Pl. 2) are by one painter, ship painter 1, and, in fact, Kunze attributed the two kraters from which these fragments come to one painter (his kraters III and IV). Louvre A. 517 (Pl. 3*a*) is considered to be from the same hand as Athens 804, the Dipylon master; the ship under one handle (Geom. 9, Pl. 3*b*) and a possible candidate for a place elsewhere on the vase (Geom. 6) show greater confidence and precision than the ships of painter 1, but they are very close indeed, and it is hard to separate them; I have compromised by attributing them to ship painter 1 +. The ships on Louvre A. 527 (upper), Geom. 2, and Louvre A. 534, Geom. 3 (Pl. 1 *e*), are identical in style, and although this painter makes a shallower line *A* and a deeper space *X* than other painters and falls a little below the level of the central works of painter 1, again I find it impossible to distinguish him from painter 1 and would call him painter 1 −.

If, as I have suggested, ship painter 1 +, 1, and 1 − are one and the same, it means that he painted for the Dipylon master on Louvre A. 517 and for the Kunze painter on Louvre A. 527 and on Kunze's kraters III and IV, which Kunze simply attributes to the Dipylon workshop.

LATE GEOMETRIC II. *c.* 735–*c.* 710 B.C.

CATALOGUE

Section 4

The following ships, while having some common characteristics, are later than those in the Dipylon Group and show its influence. Only Geom. 19 seems to be of any importance or interest.

Geom. 19. Plate 4*e* (after Murray). Attic spouted bowl. London 1899, 2–19, 1. Murray, *JHS* 1899, pl. 8; Koester, pl. 19; Moll, B, VI *a*, 12; Hampe, *Sagenbilder*, pl. 22 *b*; Kirk, no. 40, fig. 4; Matz, pl. 14; Hampe, *Gleichnisse*, pl. 18 *b*. Nottbohm (*JdI* 58, 1 ff.) attributed this vase to the workshop of the painter of Athens 804 (i.e. the Dipylon master), but it is generally agreed to be later than this implies, and Davison attributes it to her Sub-Dipylon Workshop (p. 67).

Ship to right. The stern is high and the stern compartment has a screen, in which there seems to be a large port partly closed by a Dipylon-type shield: the helmsman can just be made out above the screen, and his steering oars, which are shown crossing the porthole, protrude behind the stern and are identical with those in the Dipylon Group. In the bow compartment the stem post is hatched and S-shaped: on the platform aft are set four pegs (cf. Geom. 7) and aft again there is a balustrade: a single plank protrudes at the stem. The tapering ram resembles those of the previous group. First, the horizontal lines of the ship: the lowest thick line, line *A* of the Dipylon Group, represents the hull; above is a thin horizontal on which the 'lower' oarsmen sit, placed much higher than line *B* (Dipylon) so that we see their legs; this line ought to be the gunwale because upon it can be made out the tholepins of these oarsmen: above are two thin horizontals connected with the 'upper' oarsmen, one for their feet and one on which they seem to sit (these lines may correspond to the Dipylon *C*, *D*, and *E*); the upper line has tholepins, so that this too was intended to be a gunwale.

Secondly, the verticals: in the Dipylon Group these were omitted when oarsmen were inserted, but here they are omitted only in the space where the bodies of the 'lower' oarsmen appear. In the Dipylon Group we regarded the 'upper' oarsmen as the far-side oarsmen, and the fact that it is only the blades of the near-side oarsmen that are represented below the hull should lead to the same decision here. There is, however, one feature at least which might point to a two-level ship: whereas there are twenty oarsmen 'below', there are nineteen 'above'; such a discrepancy would be out of the question in a single-level ship, but normal in a two-level one (cf. the ships of undoubted two levels, Arch. 85 ff.). Yet there appears to be no hull structure represented which could house two levels. It is difficult to choose between the two alternatives—a single-level ship in the Dipylon tradition showing the far-side oarsmen as well as the near-side or an incorrectly painted two-level ship.

Behind the stern are two figures, a male (presumably the captain about to go aboard) holding the wrist of a female. It has been suggested that the female is being abducted and that the scene represents the Rape of Helen by Paris or, less likely, of Ariadne by Dionysus. Kirk has replied to this suggestion by asserting that the grasping of the wrist indicates greeting or farewell, so that the scene might be a farewell—a departure for Troy, or more likely, in view of the Theban provenience of the vase, the departure of the *Argo*.* The wreath which the female holds may then be intended to crown the departing ship: Jason would be the captain, and the female perhaps Hera herself, who had supported Jason, or Hypsipyle, whom Jason left on Lemnos with all the other widows. If one has no faith, however, in the epic content of these scenes, it will simply be a scene of departure, but for the believers the presence of the Dipylon shield in the bow compartment, a shield which was obsolete at the time of painting,† will indicate that the painter had in mind some episode in saga.

Geom. 20. Attic fragment. Athens NM 287 from the Acropolis. Graef 299; probably Kirk, no. 20a.

Mid section of a hull (line A only appears) with three verticals. The looms of three oars cross the reserved rectangles between the verticals, but in an opposite direction from those on Geom. 19, and the blades protrude beneath the hull. This fragment and the next have been placed in this section following Kirk's remark (loc. cit.) that the drawing recalls Geom. 19.

Geom. 21. Attic fragment. Athens NM 288 from the Acropolis. Graef 300; Kirk, no. 20b.

A fish head and two oar blades similar to those on Geom. 20.

Geom. 22. Attic krater fragment. Louvre CA. 3361. *CVA* pl. 7, 13.

Section of hull (lines A and B only appear on the fragment). There are two oar blades beneath the hull. An oblique line above B suggests a leg, but there are also verticals: the combination of oars, legs, and verticals is more likely in this section than in the Dipylon Group.

* Other ship representations found in Thebes include Geom. 33 and 42; ship representations are also frequent on Boeotian fibulae. This Attic bowl may have been made specially for a Theban client.
† Webster, *BSA* 1955, 41, and see also Summary, p. 41.

Geom. 23. Fragment of Attic krater. Louvre CA. 3359. *CVA* pl. 7, 4.

Stern of ship to right. It has a high stern post and there are the remains of four oars-men and the helmsman. Part of the sail with diagonal hatching has survived. Villard (loc. cit.) includes this fragment with the Dipylon finds, and it is presumably con-temporary with them, but the style of the ship, as far as can be seen, is alien to that in the Dipylon Group.

Geom. 23 *bis*. Attic fragment. Athens, Agora P. 8885. Brann, *Athenian Agora VIII*, pl. 16 and 43, 277.

Bow of ship to left. The actual bow compartment is clearly influenced by the Dipylon Group, but the rendering of the hull with its careless painting of the horizontal and uprights is alien.

Geom. 24. Fragment of a plaque. Athens, from the N. slope of the Acropolis, Well *A*, *A–P* 1682. Boardman, *BSA* 1954, 195, fig. 2.

The plaque shows part of the ram and bow of a ship to left with a protrusion from the stem. The style is identical to that of the Dipylon fragments.

Section 5

The first four representations have certain common characteristics and have often been bracketed together, but they are of disputed date. Geom. 26 and 27, coming from the same grave, Kahane (loc. cit.) placed in his Strict Geometric period, *c.* 850–*c.* 800, and in his view they were just preceded by Geom. 28, the Eleusis skyphos: this last vase, however, Young* regarded as Late Geometric, and, as Davison has pointed out,† there is a close simi-larity between it and the Copenhagen jug, Geom. 29, which is clearly Late. The New York krater, Geom. 25, Richter (loc. cit.) places in the first half of the eighth century: Davison says (130) that it seems to precede the Di-pylon Group, but that it bears little resemblance to any krater or vase in that Group, and she points to features which seem to be Late: Marwitz (loc. cit.) has recently made a very strong case for a late date for this krater which it will be hard to refute.

The late date is accepted here because the ships show a more natural and developed perspective than those in the Dipylon Group itself. It is assumed that just as there was a development from the distorted perspective of chariots in the Dipylon Group to a more correct form in latest Geometric and Protoattic, so, in the last half century or so of Geometric, ships in more or less correct perspective should follow those rendered in a distorted perspective.

* 'Late Geometric Graves', *Hesperia* Suppl. 2, 79.
† 107; but on 130 she says it may yet come before the Dipylon Group.

Geom. 25. Plates 5 and 6*a* and *b* (photos: the Metropolitan Museum of Art, Fletcher Fund 1934). Attic krater. New York 34. 11. 2. Richter, *Bull. Metr. Mus.* (1934), 170, figs 1–3; Kirk, no. 6; Davison, fig. 138; Arias and Hirmer, *History of Greek Vase Painting*, pl. 7; Marwitz, *Antike Kunst* 1961, pls 17–18.

Scenes of fighting on and near two ships, which face right. One is complete apart from the ram and a section amidships; of the other there remain a large section of the stern, two sections amidships (one with a sail), another fragment showing the ram, and another the top of the stem post. The ram is thin. Above the solid black representing the lower part of the hull there are two thin horizontal lines intersected by verticals, of which only alternate ones reach the upper horizontal, at least as far as the step in the thick base line at the stern, from which point all the verticals reach the top horizontal. There are two projections from the stern post and three projections aft. The blade of one steering oar can be seen beneath the stern. The stern compartment is defined by a balustrade. In the bow the bow screens are decorated with an 'eye' in the form of a Union Jack in a reserved square: the stem post curves backward. In the bow of the ship (*a*) there are four spears, one of which is being seized by the warrior on the ram. In (*b*) there is a mast and part of a narrow rectangular cross-hatched sail with ropes attached: the arbitrary reduction of the sail's size to provide room for the figures is noticeable.

The interpretation of the horizontals is problematical. Kirk asserts that the upper horizontal is a deck, the one immediately below, a longitudinal beam, implying presumably that the top of the thick line below defines the gunwale; but in that case the superstructure is about twice as high as the hull—a quite unseaworthy ship. Admittedly there is distortion anyhow in that the warriors are standing on the topmost line, but that position is in accordance with the Geometric style. From a structural point of view it is more likely that the gunwale is defined by the line above the solid base. The stripes below this line will be decorative (cf. the diagonal lines in this position on the following ships, Geom. 28–30). These stripes are extended above the gunwale; the shorter ones may be the tholepins,* the longer ones supports for the upper horizontal, which will be a rail, although it is impossible to rule out the alternative that here, as in the preceding vases of the Dipylon Group, the plan view may in some way be incorporated with the profile.

The scenes of fighting are vividly portrayed. An invader has climbed onto the ram of (*a*), brandishes his own spear and seizes another from the store in the bows. He is faced by an archer, who bends his knee in the best style and aims an arrow at the invader. The archer is supported by a warrior behind who hurls his spear. In the stern two warriors grapple at close quarters armed with swords, one holding the other by his helmet (the arc over and behind the head set with short spurs is the conventional way of rendering the helmet at this time). On ship (*b*) a helmeted warrior†

---

* That these shorter lines are tholepins is supported by the fact that in the stern compartment, where tholepins would not be required, and indeed are never found, the lines are extended to reach the upper horizontal.   † Not the helmsman, who would hardly be wearing a helmet.

is in a firm position in the stern. In front of him a duel with swords takes place. Further forward a warrior with a shield stands over another, part of whose shield can be seen on the edge of the fragment, but the wounded warrior himself has fallen on the other side of the mast. However, the treatment of the hair of this reclining figure has led Marwitz (loc. cit. p. 43) to ask whether it may not be a woman. In Book 9 (ll. 39 ff.) of the *Odyssey* Odysseus and his men rape some Ciconian women and provoke an attack upon their ships, but this vase-painting rather invokes the memory of the battle by the ships in *Iliad* xv and in particular of Teucer, the archer, and his brother Ajax fighting side by side, of whom the painter might have been thinking when painting the two figures in the bow of (*a*). In the stern of the same ship the warrior holding another by his helmet crest recalls the action of Menelaus towards Paris in *Iliad* iii, 369. Here we see promise of the great narrative painting which is fulfilled in Athens in the next two centuries.

Geom. 26. Plate 6*c* (after Kirk). Attic cup. Athens, market. Kahane, *AJA* 1940, pl. 21, 6; Kirk, fig. 1.

Two metopes, each containing a ship. The ram is long and solid: the bow compartment has bow screens, at the level of which the stem is concave, but above, the high stem post curves forward, then aft, parallel to the hull. From the top of the stern post a line runs unbroken along the lower part of the hull and into the bow compartment. Above this line between the bow and the stern is a horizontal, which is probably the line of the gunwale. Thirteen vertical lines cross the hull and extend above the gunwale. The stern compartment shows a screen and two steering oars.

Geom. 27. Attic hydriskos. Whereabouts unknown. Kahane, *AJA* 1940, pl. 22, 1; Kirk, no. 2.

Two ships stern to stern. The line which forms the stern post runs right along the bottom of the ship and into the bow compartment to form the ram. Above this line, between the bow and the stern, runs a second horizontal. As on Geom. 26, verticals intersect these two horizontals, but the verticals are here more widely spaced. The bow and stern also resemble those on Geom. 26. The mast has a yard with fore and rear brace; there is also a rope from either end of the yard to a point where the mast cuts the gunwale (see p. 56 and cf. the later Assyrian relief of Sennacherib, Koester, fig. 7).

Geom. 28. Plate 6*d* (after Skias). Attic skyphos. Eleusis 741. Skias, *Eph. Arch.* 1898, pl. 5, 1; Koester, pl. 30*b*; Kourouniotes, *Eleusis*, fig. 48; see Webster, *BSA* 1955, 44, n. 43 for further references and add Davison, fig. 137*a–b*; Marwitz, *Antike Kunst* 1961, pl. 19, 7. Kirk, no. 3.

On this ship too the line of the stern continues along the lower part of the hull right to the tip of the ram. Another line above defines the gunwale; between the lower and the upper line there are diagonals, which because of their angle cannot be supports of any kind, but must be ornamental (cf. the similar diagonals on the shield of the right-hand warrior). Above the gunwale are five vertical posts, which are probably rather heavily painted tholepins. In the stern compartment there is a large steering oar, aft of which is a balustrade with two of its planks extending beyond the stern; the stern is high and curves well forward. The bow compartment has a screen and a balustrade: the stem post inclines slightly forward, then curves aft. The archer is again prominent in the defence of the ship: on either side are warriors with Dipylon shields (see p. 42).

Geom. 29. Attic jug. Copenhagen 1628. *CVA* 11, pl. 73, 4*a*; Furtwängler, *AZ* 1885, pl. 8, 1; Lorimer, *BSA* 1947, 78, fig. 1; Kirk, no. 3; Webster, *BSA* 1955, 45, fig. 2; Davison, fig. 133 (attributed to her Burly Workshop (post Dipylon Group)).

Fight on and around a ship. The essential parts of stem and stern are missing, so that it is impossible to be sure which way the ship is facing. One figure on the left seems to be standing on what ought to be the ram, and yet the curve of the post here suggests the stern. At this curve stand three spears, in front of which sits a figure who might be the helmsman holding the steering oar. Below the line on which he is sitting there is a strip decorated with diagonals, the angle of which precludes the possibility that the top line is a deck or even a rail. From the bottom of the hull there emerge six oars. There are two solid protruding planks from the curved line on the left.

On the left of the ship a warrior with a Dipylon shield collapses backwards. In front of him another, holding sword in one hand and a round shield* in front of him with the other, tries to get aboard. Facing the latter, over the helmsman, a defender brandishes his spear. An archer covers the right-hand end of the ship and wards off two enemy spearsmen.

Geom. 30. Attic fragment. Louvre. Torr, *RA* 1894, 17, fig. 3; Kirk, no. 35*a*.

A ship to right which resembles those in this section. Common features are the diagonals at the top of the hull (Geom. 28 and 29), mast, sail and rigging (Geom. 27) and the general shape of the bows (all except Geom. 29).

Geom. 31. Attic fragment. Louvre S. 529. Torr, fig. 4; Giraudon 33860; Kirk, no. 35*b*.

Right-hand corner of sail and rigging in the same arrangement as on Geom. 30. Kirk has suggested that it comes from the same hand as Geom. 30.

Section 6

This section consists of a group of representations partly from vases of non-Attic manufacture (Geom. 32–4) and partly from vases which, though Attic, have ships of a build closer to Corinthian than Athenian (Geom. 35–7). The ship on the Toronto bowl below, Geom. 42, which was thought to have been made in Corinth, but is now suspected to be Attic,† has a similar bow and stern (although it has a different hull structure). In this and in Geom. 35–7 the bow and stern compartments do not seem to be built up to the same extent as the Athenian; the stem post is much shorter and inclines forward;

---

* Snodgrass, *Early Greek Armour*, 49 ff.   † Tölle, *Arch. Anz.* 1963, 655–6.

the ram is thicker and curves upward. If late Geometric Attic artists paint ships of a style which approximates to what is later seen to be Corinthian, one must conclude that Corinthian ships were of some importance at this time (see below, p. 158).

Geom. 32. Plate 6*e* (photo: G. Buchner). Western Greek Geometric krater from Pithecusae. Buchner, *RM* 1953–4, 42, fig. 1, pls 14–16, 1; additional fragments included in *Expedition* 1966, vol. 8, no. 4, p. 8; Brunnsaker, *Opuscula Rom.* IV, 1962, 165 ff.

Around the body of the vase there runs a scene of shipwreck with an upturned ship (righted in Pl. 6*d*) and the crew in the water with the fish, the largest of which is swallowing a sailor. The ram is shorter than most Attic examples and curves upwards. One of the steering oars is still in position below the curving stern in spite of the ship's having capsized; the other may have been painted in the hatched area. The hull is deep with a reserved strip at gunwale level surmounted by a beam which projects beyond stem and stern. Eleven verticals divide this reserved area up into 'rooms' and extend well above the beam. The beam seems to be a rail and the verticals its supports. The style of the ship is closer to Corinthian than to Attic representations.

Geom. 33. Protocorinthian Geometric jug from Thebes. Berlin 3143. Furtwängler, *JdI* 1888, 248, figs *a–b*; Johansen, *Les Vases sicyoniens*, pl. 1, 3; Payne, *Protokorinthische Vasenmalerei*, pl. 2; *Necrocorinthia*, fig. 1*e*; Kirk, no. 37.

Ship to left. The ram is thin and curves upwards. The hull is cut by eight verticals which extend just above the gunwale. In the stern with its steering oar there is a screen decorated with an 'eye'. The bows are high and the screen here is also decorated with an 'eye' in the form of two concentric circles. There is a buffer-like protrusion from the stem on the line of the gunwale. The stem post curves backwards and has four extensions. The mast has one forestay and two backstays: for the fitting at the top of the mast cf. Arch. 94.

Geom. 34. Fragment of Argive Geometric from the Heraeum at Argos. Athens NM (on exhibition 1958).

Bow of ship with ram and thick stem post.

Geom. 35. Fragment of Attic krater. Athens, Agora P. 6094 and P. 2400. Burr, *Hesperia*, II, 1933, 623, fig. 90 (P. 2400), and Thompson, *Hesperia*, VI, 1937, 122, fig. 66*a* (P. 6094); Brann, *Athenian Agora VIII*, pl. 22, 379 (both fragments).

Bow and mid section of ship to left. The fabric of the vase is Attic, but the ship type seems to be Corinthian. The shape of the bow and the 'eye' closely resembles that on the Toronto bowl (Geom. 42). The stocky stem post inclines forward, while the projection inclining aft can be paralleled on later Corinthian ships (Arch. 41–2). The four verticals projecting above the gunwale are probably tholepins. Below the gunwale is a reserved strip intersected by verticals, which represents not void but solid hull, as is suggested by the Protoattic fragments, Arch. 3 ff., where the bodies of the marines or oarsmen are cut off below the level of the top horizontal, i.e. the gunwale.

Geom. 35 *bis*. Fragment of Attic krater. Athens, Agora P. 25329. Brann, *Athenian Agora VIII*, pl. 22, 380.

Stern of what is apparently a similar ship to the last, showing the stern post and part of the stern compartment below. Brann says that the four lines crossing the stern post are spears; this may be correct, but they may equally well represent the frame of a screen such as occurs behind the helmsman on the Protoattic fragment, Arch. 4.

Geom. 36. Attic krater fragment from the Kerameikos, Athens. R. Tölle, *Arch. Anz.* 1963, 655, fig. 11.

Bow of ship to left similar to the last. The ram is thick and curves upward: there is a short projection from the stem. The short stem post inclines forward: beneath it the 'eye' consists of a linear circle within a reserved circle. Along the hull is a reserved strip. Aft of the bow a fragment shows four of the oarsmen.

Geom. 37. Attic krater fragment from the Agora, P. 26817. R. Tölle, *Arch. Anz.* 1963, 656, fig. 12.

Centre section and stern of a similar ship to left. Above the lowest part of the hull, which is solid black, is a reserved area marked by verticals at regular intervals and two horizontals near the gunwale, which probably represent the two timber wales of the gunwale, while the verticals, since a rower is framed within a pair, may represent ribs or struts. There are nine of the crew's oarsmen seated at the level of the gunwale. Under the curving stern sits the helmsman with a steering oar.

Section 7

In the representations of this section the painter is depicting ships with oarports either square or rounded. The presence of ports does not mean that the artist must be representing a two-level ship, but simply that the gunwales were now being raised as a protection for the oarsmen. However, a strong case for a two-level ship may be made out for Geom. 42–4.

Geom. 38. Plate 7*a* (photo: Antikensammlungen, Munich). Attic jug. Munich 8696. Hampe, *Gleichnisse*, pl. 7, 11; Webster, *From Mycenae to Homer*, 28*a*–*b*; Davison, fig. 84; Brann, *Antike Kunst* 1959, pl. 19, 1.

A scene of shipwreck. The ship is capsized with one figure astride the keel and ten others in the sea. The hull has eight approximately circular portholes. The bow with the spoked 'eye' is similar to other Late Geometric representations, but the stem post begins to curve upward from the after end of the bow screens. In the stern compartment there is a balustrade; the stern horn is as thick and as high as the stem post. The gunwale planking projects from the stern and the steering oar crosses the aft porthole. This is a most vivid representation of a shipwreck and those who believe it is Odysseus riding the keel may well be right.

Geom. 39. Plate 7*b* (after Hood). Attic cup. University of Tasmania 31. Hood, *Greek Vases in the University of Tasmania*, pl. 3; *AJA* 1967, pls 31–2.

After half of ship to right. At an angle of 45 degrees to the stern is a solid plank-like appendage which might have been mistaken for a steering oar, if the steering oar had not appeared farther forward and been of a different shape with its loom probably behind the stern horn. Hood suggested that it was a gang-plank. The stern horn curves forward and upward. The hull is represented by rectangles, similar to the huge port-like apertures on Geom. 38 and 40. In two of these apertures there seem to be seated figures, while another figure sits above the gunwale. The remains of three oars cross the hull. Two figures climb aboard, each with two spears in his left hand, followed by four armed men and two mourning females—a scene of departure. The vase has been attributed (see Hood) to the same workshop as the last.

Geom. 40. Plate 7*c* (after Kirk). Attic fragment from the Acropolis. Athens NM 251. Graef 259; Pernice, fig. 9; Koester, fig. 22; Kirk, no. 33, pl. 40, 2.

Middle section of a ship to right. Four large oval ports set in the hull frame rowers who are partially covered by Dipylon-type shields. The oars have little indication of blades. This fragment and the next represent the Geometric artist's attempt to represent an oarsman rowing through a port; the port has to be grossly enlarged in order to show the oarsman.

Geom. 41. Attic fragment from the Acropolis. Athens NM 252. Graef 260; Pernice, fig. 10; Kirk, no. 34.

This smaller fragment is in identical style to Geom. 40, but shows only a single oarsman.

Geom. 42. Plate 7*d* (photo: Royal Ontario Museum, University of Toronto). Protocorinthian bowl from Thebes. Toronto C. 199. Robinson, Harcum and Iliffe, *Greek Vases in Toronto*, no. 113, vol. I, p. 27, vol. II, pl. 81; Payne, *Protokorinthische Vasenmalerei*, pl. 3; Koester, pl. 20; Hampe, *Sagenbilder*, pl. 22*a*; Matz, pl. 18; Lane, *Greek Pottery*, pl. 10B; R. T. Williams, *JHS* 1958, pl. XIV*a*; Kirk, no. 38.

Complete ship to left. Along the hull there are twenty semicircular ports, on the straight sides of which are set tholepins. The top of the gunwale is defined by a reserved line, where sit nineteen oarsmen with spade-shaped blades which cross the hull. Above the gunwale also there is a tholepin for each oar. In the stern compartment there is a balustrade, below which the hull is hatched; here sits a diminutive helmsman at the steering oars: the stern horn is low and plain except for a single projection, and one plank also projects from the stern. The ram is pointed, but, unlike the Attic, there is an almost immediate rise in the outline of the stem from the tip of the ram. A very short stem post inclines slightly forward. The bow screen is decorated with an 'eye' in the form of a circle in a reserved square, and below, a strip of Geometric pattern. Running along the stem and then curving aft along the hull of the bow compartment is a reserved line. In the bow compartment sits a diminutive bow officer (*prorates*). For arguments that this represents a two-level ship see the Summary, p. 38.

Geom. 43. Plate 7*e* (after Kirk). Attic fragment from the Acropolis. Athens NM 265. Graef 276; Pernice, fig. 5; Kirk, no. 31, pl. 40, 3; R. T. Williams, *JHS* 1958, pl. XIV *b*.

Middle section of a ship to left. Above the gunwale are reserved squares alternating with painted rectangles. The squares are clearly ports, for in each of them are the arms of rowers. Above the squares and rectangles are two horizontal lines joined by verticals. Above these are three more rowers: between the left and centre oarsmen is a section of the mast. For the position of the oars and the relative position of the rowers see the Summary, p. 39, where an attempt is made to relate this representation to two-level ships.

Geom. 44. Plate 7*f* (after Kirk). Attic fragment from the Acropolis. Athens NM 266. Graef 277; Pernice, fig. 6; Kirk, no. 32, pl. 40, 4; R. T. Williams, *JHS* 1958, pl. XIV *c*.

Middle section of a ship to left. A band just below the gunwale is decorated with diagonal hatching. The other horizontal feature above consists of two lines bounding a lozenge chain. Between these two horizontal features, probably representing wales, there are verticals which form rectangles; every other rectangle is divided into small squares; in the remainder are set the heads and chests of rowers. Three such rowers remain on the fragment, but above the lozenge chain there are parts of three more. For the position of the oars and the theory that this fragment like the last may represent a two-level ship see the Summary, p. 39. The detail of the eye of the top left oarsman is incised (see J. M. Cook, *BSA* 1934–5, 171, n. 3).

SUMMARY

Bow and Stern

The ram, appearing in Greece in the first half of the second millennium, is a constant feature in Geometric ship representations, although Geometric painters may have exaggerated its length and taper. The bow and stern compartments were noted in Mycenaean: in Geometric ships they seem more solid and extensive. Planks protrude from both stem and stern. The 'eye'* appears once in Mycenaean but is constant in the larger-scale Geometric representations. The term 'eye' is apt enough for post-Geometric ships, where a realistic eye is sometimes painted on the side of the bow, but in Geometric it nearly always takes the form of a wheel with a varying number of spokes. It is surprising that one of the many Homeric ship epithets has not been associated with this constant decorative feature. The epithet *amphielissa* may perhaps be translated quite literally: 'revolving on both sides', as these

---

* The 'eye' may not have been decorative or apotropaic but may have 'represented or disguised a hawse-pipe through which the anchor-cable ran'. (Kirk, 132.)

spoked wheels on either side of the bow might have seemed to do (but see p. 45). One decorative feature which did not occur on Mycenaean ships but is characteristic of Geometric is the high, curving stem or horn at both bow and stern. Here again the painters may have exaggerated the height and the curve, but it cannot be doubted that these horns were a feature of the ships of the time, which went out of fashion later, particularly at the bow, but which gave rise to the Homeric epithet noted on p. 45.

The absence of tholepins on Mycenaean ships may be attributed to the smallness of the scale of their representations, and they should not be regarded as a Geometric invention, but that they impressed Homer is clear from the epithet *polukleïs*, 'with many tholepins' (see p. 45).

As has been noted in the introduction to the Dipylon Group the significance of the lines *C*, *D*, and *E* on the side of its ships has been widely debated, and that interpretation has there been advocated which seems to conform most closely to the Geometric style generally—that the painter was incorporating the far side of the ship into the profile view. The main structural development of ships in the Geometric period does not appear until its close, when the gunwale was built up in order to protect the oarsmen, so that portholes were formed, which could be semicircular (Geom. 42) or square (Geom. 39, 43–4) or roughly circular (Geom. 38, 40–1). In later ships of undoubted two levels (e.g. Arch. 85) the lower level of oarsmen row through ports; it is therefore necessary to examine those Geometric examples which show oarsmen at apparently two levels and through ports for the possibility of two-level construction at this period.*

Two-level ships

First the Toronto bowl (Geom. 42, Pl. 7*d*), which shows nineteen oarsmen sitting on the top of the ship with tholepins in front of them: at a lower level are twenty ports with a tholepin in each port. It has been suggested that the oarsmen visible are the far-side men: but if this had been so, their oars should have dipped into the sea on the far side of the ship. It has been suggested too that they are the near-side rowers but placed above the gunwale instead of in their correct position behind the ports, so that they may be clearly seen: but it is very unlikely indeed that the painter would have done such violence to his ship as to invent another set of tholepins for the crew on the topmost

* Cf. *JHS* 1958, 121 ff.

line of the ship. There remains the probability that this is a two-level ship of which only the upper level is manned. The lower level is not manned perhaps because the artist could hardly insert the oarsmen at this scale and with the silhouette technique without completely filling the ports; in fact, this Corinthian artist has adopted the same solution as the Attic painter Exekias on the sixth-century vessel, Arch. 52. Another pointer to a two-level ship is the numerical difference between the nineteen rowers above and the twenty ports below, for a similar ratio occurs on undoubted two-level ships as a result of the echelon formation of the levels, a formation which can be seen here, for each oarsman sits not above a port, but above the intervening planked space. This ship certainly does not look as though the painter had taken liberties with perspective; in fact it is, in appearance, the most seaworthy vessel that has yet appeared. Weinberg* attributes the vase to his Linear Geometric, which extends from the third into the last quarter of the eighth century; Payne† says that it is a little later than the strictly Geometric period: it is clear from these authorities that the vase belongs to the last quarter of the eighth century and not before.

On the two Attic fragments, Geom. 43–4 (Pl. 7*e* and *f*), the ports are square, and there are rowers at two levels. On Geom. 43 the rowers are clearly arranged not one immediately above the other, but in echelon, the correct formation for two banks, if one judges from undoubted two-level ships of the sixth century. Now as to the question of the side on which the oars of the upper rowers extend into the water—they extend over the far side apparently, and not the near side, as they should do, if these are going to be two-level ships, but then the lower oarsmen as well, at least in two cases, have their oars on the far side, as it were. The oars of the bottom left and centre rowers on Geom. 44 do not run over the area that is decorated with diagonals, and the oar of the bottom left rower on Geom. 43 does not protrude in the right place below the keel. It is clear that the painter does not continue the oars of either bank over the gunwale and downwards across the hull, but picks them up, not too carefully, below the keel. The artist's reason for so doing is probably that he wishes to avoid over-complicating the design of his ship with the frequent diagonals of the oars. It seems, therefore, that the most natural and likely conclusion is that the painters of the Toronto bowl and these two Attic fragments were trying to render two-level ships.

* *AJA* 1941, 30 and *Corinth* vii, 89.   † *Protokorinthische Vasenmalerei.*

Nor do I think that the fact that Homer does not mention crews of the particular size which the Toronto bowl suggests, 39×2, should invalidate the two-level theory. By the time that these vases were painted (the use of incision on Geom. 44* suggests a date close to the end of Geometric and the beginning of Protoattic) Homeric formulae had become crystallized and it seems unlikely that bards would have a list of conversions to keep up with the latest naval developments. One place where a change might be expected would be in the Catalogue of Ships (*Il.* II, 494 ff.), which is recognized as being among the latest parts of Homer, and here a ship of the Boeotians is recorded as carrying 120 men (cf. p. 46 for Crews in Homer).

Size of ships

This conclusion leads on to the question of the size of Geometric ships generally. A clue may be gained from the number of rowers or of tholepins or, when both these are absent, from the number of 'rooms' formed by the verticals. Single examples, of course, cannot be reliable because a painter could extend or reduce the length of his ship according to the space available, but an examination of a number of complete or nearly complete ships does tend towards some conclusion.

The BM bowl, Geom. 19, has nineteen oarsmen on the far side, twenty on the near side; the Toronto bowl too has nineteen, but this, it has been argued, is a two-level ship. The Louvre fragment, Geom. 3, has nineteen, perhaps twenty, rooms with tholepins (the break in the fragment occurs just before the stern and there would be room for no more than one extra). Geom. 8 (3) in Athens would have about nine rooms aft of the mast; Geom. 8 (1) also in Athens has nine rooms before the mast. On the other hand, the Louvre krater, A. 517, Geom. 9, has fifteen 'rooms', and Geom. 17 has thirteen oarsmen, but both the latter are ships under a handle and it might well be that the painter was restricted to this particular size by reasons of space rather than because he had a ship of this definite size in mind. These statistics at least tend to the conclusion that there was a standard ship with about forty oarsmen and perhaps a smaller one with about thirty. This conclusion may be thought to be weakened by the New York krater, Geom. 25, for although one of its ships seems to have about twenty-five 'rooms', which is a suitable number, the other has about thirty-

* See catalogue, p. 37.

six, a number too large altogether for archaic naval engineering. A full discussion of the literary evidence concerning the size of the ships of the period will be found in chapter 3.

Sail and rigging, etc.

The archaeological evidence for mast, sail, rigging and steering oar is presented with the literary evidence in chapter 3.

Significance of ship scenes

The question* whether any of the scenes involving ships on these Geometric vases are meant to illustrate saga or epic is closely tied up with the larger problem, whether there exist any such illustrations at all anywhere in Geometric art. Those who deny that such illustrations exist† try to explain away centaur scenes‡ as belonging to folktale rather than to saga, and the scenes which involve an apparent pair of Siamese twins (which the other school contends represents Aktorione–Molione of *Iliad* XXIII, 638) as a technical device of an artist who finds he has not enough space for two separate figures but too much for one:§ the painting which shows a man wringing the necks of the last of a row of birds‖ (which the other school interprets as Herakles and the Stymphalian birds) would presumably be regarded as the portrait of a despairing Attic poultry farmer. The ship scenes are regarded by this school as illustrations of a not uncommon feature of the everyday life of a maritime people; but it is necessary for this school to present some supporting evidence for Athenian interest in naval affairs at this time other than the ship representations themselves.

The first duty of the school which believes that there are illustrations of saga and epic in Geometric art is to show that saga and epic were available to the Athenians in the second half of the eighth century. This has been done by Webster;¶ and now that the ships, Geom. 25–8, which had been thought to belong to the period 825–775, have been shown to be later, there is no ground for Kirk's statement (p. 146) that it would be necessary, if one wished

---

* The suggestion that the scenes on these funeral vases illustrated the achievements of the dead person fails because there was too little time between death and burial for one of these monumental vases to be 'ordered', thrown, painted and fired.

† Kirk, *BSA* 1949, 44 ff., makes a good case.

‡ Copenhagen amphora, *CVA* 11, pl. 73, 3; Webster, *BSA* 1955, 49, fig. 3. For further examples see list in Dunbabin, *The Greeks and their Eastern Neighbours*, 77 ff.   § Cook, *BSA* 1934–5, 206.

‖ Ny Carlsberg jug, Brommer, *Herakles*, 25, pl. 18; Davison, fig. 131.

¶ *BSA* 1955, 38 f., 'Homer and Geometric Vases'. Hampe in *Sagenbilder* may be regarded as the earliest advocate of this school.

to associate ship representations and epic, to postulate the wide propagation of saga on the mainland as early as the end of the ninth century in view of the above representations, which he thought belonged to this period. Next, turning to the Ny Carlsberg jug, one would have great difficulty in arguing seriously that the subject could be anything else than Herakles killing the Stymphalian birds. This same subject occurs on a seventh-century Boeotian fibula along with a man killing a lion; the latter can hardly be anything else than Herakles and the Nemean Lion, especially as another fibula shows Herakles and the Hydra.* Therefore, it seems very likely that Geometric paintings† of a man killing a lion will be Herakles and the Nemean Lion. Again, since the Aktorione–Molione twins also occur on Boeotian fibulae,‡ it is unreasonable to deny that the subject could have been treated by Geometric artists a generation before. Further, Brann seems to have discovered a representation of the death of Astyanax on a fragment from the Agora.§

Most of the members of this school would concur up to this point, but the next step, which is not taken by all, is to embrace the scenes of more general application—shipwrecks, fights around ships, funeral games and the like—within the scope of illustrations of saga and epic. This step Webster has made much easier to take by his suggestion that the presence of a figure of eight or Dipylon shield on a Geometric vase marked a scene as heroic.‖ By this criterion many of our scenes of fighting in and around ships may be identified as illustrations of epic, such as the Fight for the Ships (*Iliad* xv) or Achilles' raid on Lyrnessos (*Iliad* xx, 191) or Odysseus' raid on the Ciconians (*Od.* 9, 39); the scene on the London bowl from Thebes (Geom. 19) as an epic rape or departure.

There is one point on which both schools would agree—that the ship, with its contrast of straight lines and curves, was a subject which had a great appeal for the Geometric artist.¶

---

* Brommer, *Herakles*, pls 3 and 8; Hampe, *Sagenbilder*, pls 1 and 2. The arguments are Webster's.
† *Kerameikos* V, 1, pl. 69; Dunbabin, op. cit. pl. 1, 2.   ‡ Hampe, *Sagenbilder*, pls 9 and 14.
§ *Antike Kunst* 1959: Brann regards the fr. as Late Geometric, but Coldstream (*JHS* 1964, 217) as Early Protoattic, *c.* 690.
‖ *BSA* 1955, 41 f. The figure of eight shield was the large body shield used by the Minoans. It seems to have gone out of use in Crete and Greece by the end of the fourteenth century and was replaced by a small circular shield with a single central grip. The hoplite shield with its loop for the upper arm and the grip on the edge was introduced in the eighth century. There is no place in armour development for a return to the figure of eight shield in the eighth century and later. Webster extends an original suggestion of Lorimer (*Homer and the Monuments*, 156), that in the seventh century the introduction of such a shield into a painting was a deliberate archaism and marked the scene as heroic, to include the eighth century as well. Snodgrass, *Early Greek Armour*, 58 concurs.
¶ Cf. Kirk, 151 f.

3

LITERARY TEXTS

THE DATING OF THE LITERARY EVIDENCE

By Homer we shall mean the two great epic poems, the *Iliad* and the *Odyssey*.*
We shall also make reference to two of the older Homeric hymns, the *Hymn
to Apollo* and the *Hymn to Dionysus*, as well as to Hesiod's *Works and Days*. These
are all examples of oral poetry; that is to say, they were put together for
recitation by a professional poet who had a repertory of traditional material,
passed on from one poet to another, but not written down. Writing, in the
form of the Linear B syllabary, had been known and used in the administra-
tion of the centralized economy of a Mycenaean palace, but with the break-
up of the Mycenaean empire the use of writing had been discontinued, and it
was not until the middle of the seventh century that it was taken up again,
and then with an alphabet newly derived from Phoenicia. There is general
agreement that the great epics were composed in the head of one or, more
probably, two poets, the *Iliad* near the beginning of the eighth century and
the *Odyssey* towards its end. The two Homeric hymns with which we are
concerned are likely to have been composed at the beginning of the seventh
century. The second half of the seventh century marks the transition from
oral to literary poetry, and it is then that the poems of the oral tradition are
likely to have been written down. All the representations of ships listed in the
previous chapters come then within the period of oral poetry.†

A salient feature of oral poetry is the technique of using and reusing
formulae, from phrases and lines to passages of several lines, to describe
common objects, occurrences or actions.‡ The longer formulae are seldom
repeated exactly; the elements are combined in different ways to meet the
requirements of the poet's tale. Ships, and the common practices associated
with them, provide some of the best examples of formulaic composition. The

---

* Texts: books of the *Iliad* are indicated by Roman numerals, books of the *Odyssey* by Arabic
numerals throughout.

† For an account of Greek oral poetry see further T. B. L. Webster, *From Mycenae to Homer*, London,
1964, and G. S. Kirk, *The Songs of Homer*, Cambridge, 1962.

‡ See D. L. Page, *The Homeric Odyssey*, Oxford, 1955, 70.

43

detailed description of common objects and practices is another, and a most engaging, characteristic of heroic poetry. This characteristic, taken together with the formulaic technique, enables us to gain a more exact knowledge of Greek ships and seafaring at the period to which the descriptions refer than at almost any other time in antiquity.

The period to which they refer is not however very easily or narrowly determinable. Stubbings* says: 'There is no reason to doubt that the Homeric descriptions of nautical procedure, both sailing and rowing, are true to their period and stock lines such as "sitting in due order they smote the grey sea with their oars"[1] may well have been traditional in epic for centuries.' By 'their period' he may mean the period to which they refer, but it seems very unlikely that poets, putting together stock material in the eighth century, would have used descriptions which did not apply generally to contemporary ships. On the other hand we should not expect complete consistency. We shall find, in fact, that there are traces of one method of joining the planks of a carvel-built ship in the *Iliad* and of another in the *Odyssey* (see below, p. 50). The former may survive in a formular line from Mycenaean times, or it may be a practice which was becoming obsolete only at the end of the ninth century. Fortunately the problem of dating is not of very great consequence, since the representations of Mycenaean ships which we possess indicate that the main features of the ships of the Geometric period were already present in the ships of the Mycenaean age, i.e. high, curving stern, ram-shaped bow, balustraded platforms fore and aft, and steering oar. We can safely suppose that the Homeric descriptions would apply in general to the ships of the Geometric period although the descriptions may well contain material which derives from Mycenaean times.

TEXTS

1. IV, 580: ἑξῆς δ' ἑζόμενοι πολιὴν ἅλα τύπτον ἐρετμοῖς.

EPITHETS

The epithets which the Homeric poet gives to his ship, according to the normal practice of heroic poetry, may be taken as a useful indication of the impression which it made on those who saw and used it. Above all else the

---

* A. J. B. Wace and F. H. Stubbings, *A Companion to Homer*, London, 1962, 541. See also Kirk, op. cit. 327, who regards 'typical scenes like setting sail' as belonging to one category of pre-existing material.

Homeric ship seemed swift[1] and capacious[2], and its black colour is mentioned almost as often[3]. These three characteristics far outshine all others, and find equal emphasis in each of the great epic poems. Ships were in fact the quickest form of transport, their carrying capacity was a constant marvel, and their black colour, the result presumably of the pitch applied externally, which made them watertight, was always striking. It was a matter of wonder too that they could cross the sea[4].

A number of epithets emphasize particular aspects. They are bilaterally symmetrical[5]. They 'twist round at each end'[6], or 'have upright horns'[7], a reference to the horn-like ornament of bow and stern (*akrostolion*: see below, pp. 47 and 133) which is such a constant feature of all Geometric representations. The epithet *koronis*[8] may mean curved (from *koronos*) and thus refer to the upward curve of the stern visible in Mycenaean and Geometric pictures, or, if it is to be connected with *korone*, a crow, it may refer to the beak-like bow. A group of epithets is connected with the bow and stern platforms[9], the oarsmen's thwarts[10], the oars[11], and tholepins[12]; others with the painting of certain parts of the hull in special colours[13]. Finally there are the naïvely appreciative epithets[14] "well-built", "very beautiful".

TEXTS

1. θοή fifty times in the *Iliad*, fifty-two times in the *Odyssey*.
   ὠκεῖα once in the *Iliad*, twice in the *Odyssey*.
   ὠκύπορος nine times in the *Iliad*, twice in the *Odyssey*, ὠκύαλος twice in the *Odyssey*.

2. γλαφυρή forty times in the *Iliad*, twenty-two times in the *Odyssey*.
   κοίλη twenty-one times in the *Iliad*, nineteen times in the *Odyssey*.
   μεγακήτης twice in the *Iliad*.

3. μέλαινα thirty-nine times in the *Iliad*, forty-three times in the *Odyssey*.

4. ποντόπορος thirteen times in the *Iliad*, six times in the *Odyssey*.

5. ἐΐση nine times in the *Iliad*, ten times in the *Odyssey*.

6. ἀμφιέλισσα seven times in the *Iliad*, twelve times in the *Odyssey* (but see above, p. 37, for a possible alternative meaning).

7. ὀρθοκραιράων twice in the *Iliad*.

8. κορωνίς fifteen times in the *Iliad*, twice in the *Odyssey*.

9. ἐΰσσελμος fourteen times in the *Iliad*, fifteen times in the *Odyssey*.

10. ἐΰζυγος twice in the *Odyssey*. πολύζυγος once in the *Iliad*.

11. ἐπήρετμος five times in the *Odyssey*. ἐείκόσορος once in the *Odyssey*.
    δολιχήρετμος three times in the *Odyssey*.

12. πολυκλήϊς seven times in the *Iliad*, three times in the *Odyssey*. Also once in Hesiod.

13. κυανόπρωρος -ειος three times in the *Iliad*, ten times in the *Odyssey*.
    μιλτοπάρῃος once in the *Iliad*, once in the *Odyssey*.
    φοινικοπάρῃος twice in the *Odyssey*.

14. εὐεργής once in the *Iliad*, ten times in the *Odyssey*.
    περικαλλής once in the *Odyssey*.

THE SHIP'S COMPANY

When in the *Iliad* Odysseus is sent by Agamemnon to take Chryseis and a hecatomb (an unspecified number of bulls and goats for sacrifice) to Chryse, the ship's crew is twenty, and in the *Odyssey* crews of twenty are common[1]. On one occasion in the *Odyssey* a twenty-oared ship is described as 'a broad merchantman (*phortis*) which crosses the mighty deep'[2]. It is possible then that when the oarsmen are only twenty the ship may be either a small one accommodating only twenty oarsmen or a larger one in which there is plenty of room for cargo in addition to the oarsmen. The fifth-century *triereis* which were employed as horse-transports with a diminished crew may be compared (see below, p. 248).

The Catalogue of Ships in the *Iliad* includes a few instances where besides the number of ships the number of men is added. The Boeotians, who have pride of place, are said to have had fifty ships: 'in each went a hundred and twenty young men of the Boeotians'[3]. The poet does not say that they all rowed at once. A Late Geometric picture (see above, Geom. 19, Pl. 4*e*) shows thirty-nine oarsmen, and hence, unless the artist is showing the oarsmen of both port and starboard side, a ship of seventy-eight oarsmen. Thucydides, commenting on the Catalogue, shows that he regards the Boeotians as all oarsmen (see below, pp. 67–8). It is possible that Thucydides is right in his interpretation of Homer, more probable that some of the Boeotians were passengers.

Nothing is said in the Catalogue about the number of men who rowed Achilles' fifty ships, but later we are told that 'in each fifty comrades sat at the tholepins',[4] and that Achilles appointed five captains for his fleet. Similarly, the Boeotian fleet had five *archoi* and the fleet from Bouprasion and Elis had four for forty ships[5]. Each of Philoctetes' seven ships is said to have had a complement of fifty oarsmen[6].

In the *Odyssey* the poet is mostly concerned with single ships. When Odysseus is to be sent home from Phaeacia, Alcinous suggests the launching of a brand-new ship with a complement of fifty-two[7]. The ship would later have been called a pentekontor, with fifty oarsmen and two officers. On another occasion Odysseus divides his ship's company into two, and sends Eurylochus off to reconnoitre Circe's palace with twenty-two men. Since six of his men have just been eaten by the Cyclops, his original crew must have been fifty with two officers, himself and Eurylochus[8].

It may reasonably be concluded from this evidence that in the eighth century the normal 'capital ship' was the pentekontor, with fifty oarsmen and two officers, although larger ships were known. These ships were often assembled in fleets of fifty ships with commanders for each squadron of ten ships. Ships of twenty oarsmen were also used.

TEXTS

1. 1 309; 1 280, 2 212 (= 4 669), 4 778, 9 322 νηὸς ἐεικοσόροιο μελαίνης.
2. 9 323 φορτίδος εὐρείης, ἥ τ' ἐκπεράᾳ μέγα λαῖτμα.
3. II 509–10 ἐν δὲ ἑκάστῃ | κοῦροι Βοιωτῶν ἑκατὸν καὶ εἴκοσι βαῖνον.
4. XVI 169–70 ἐν δὲ ἑκάστῃ | πεντήκοντ' ἔσαν ἄνδρες ἐπὶ κληῖσιν ἑταῖροι.
5. II 494–5, 618–19.
6. II 719–20 ἐρέται δ' ἐν ἑκάστῃ πεντήκοντα | ἐμβέβασαν.
7. 8 34–6 ἀλλ' ἄγε νῆα μέλαιναν ἐρύσσομεν εἰς ἅλα δῖαν
   πρωτόπλοον, κούρω δὲ δύω καὶ πεντήκοντα
   κρινάσθων κατὰ δῆμον, ὅσοι πάρος εἰσὶν ἄριστοι.
8. 10 203 ff., 9 289 (two), 311 (two), 344 (two).

HULL AND GEAR

Except for the occasion of Odysseus' mission to Chryse the ships in the *Iliad* are beached, drawn high up on the Trojan shore[1]. In the battle by the ships the Greeks fight from the stern platforms, or poops, of their ships. Hector grasps the stern of Protesilaus' ship, 'holding the *aphlaston* in his hand'[2]. The *aphlaston* is the stern ornament, the forward curving 'horn' visible in all pictures of ships' sterns by Geometric painters (e.g. Geom. 7, 8, 9, 11, 14, 17, 25, 28). We may infer that the *aphlaston* of a beached ship stood about seven feet from the beach. When earlier Hector hits Lycophron with his spear, Lycophron falls from the stern to the ground[3]. Ajax 'with great strides traverses the *ikria* of the ships'[4]. *Ikria* is a plural noun used for the poop on which the helmsman has his seat. In Odysseus' shipwreck the mast falls on the helmsman's head, and he plunges from the *ikria* 'like a diver'[5]. Its

47

construction is described when Odysseus builds his improvised boat. Circe had bidden him 'build *ikria* on the boat, high so that it may carry you over the misty sea'. He uses for the purpose 'many uprights' and 'long *epenkenides*'[6]. Constructions of upright and longitudinal timbers are visible in the sterns of Geometric ships (e.g. Geom. 8 (3), Pl. 2 *d*; Geom. 9, Pl. 3 *a* and *b*), and appear to make the helmsman's seat. The derivation of the word *epenkenis* from *ankon* (an elbow) has been recognized, but not the further possibility that *epenkenis* may mean an elbow-rest. The longitudinal planks would perform just this function for the helmsman. The *ikria* is the place where Telemachus would have slept if Nestor had not given him shelter[7], and the place where Odysseus did sleep during his passage home in the Phaeacian ship[8]. Athena sits next to Telemachus there when they set out from Ithaca, and so does Theoclymenus on his return[9]. The *ikria* in the stern is mentioned most often, but a glance at the Geometric pictures shows a similar structure in the bows. The bow *ikria* is in fact mentioned once. When Odysseus stands armed on the look-out for Scylla, he stations himself in 'the *ikria* of the bow'[10]. On two occasions we find that spears are kept in the *ikria* without further specification. In four pictures spears are shown stacked in the bows (Geom. 6, 8 (1), 25, 29; Pls 2 *d*, 5, 6 *a* and *b*), and in one they are shown stacked in the stern (Geom. 4, 8 (3); Pl. 2 *a*, 2 *d*)[11].

The word *eüsselmos*, used as an epithet for ships frequently in the *Iliad* and *Odyssey*, implies the presence of a *selma* or of *selmata* in ships. But these latter words do not in fact occur in either poem. A clue to what is indicated by the epithet may be provided by a phrase in the *Hymn to Dionysus* (VII) which Allen regards as comparatively old[12].* *Selma* there means the bow platform. Later occurrences of the word (see below, pp. 196–7) seem to refer to the bow and stern platforms. It seems safe to conclude that *selma* takes the place of *ikria* in this context after Homer.

We may return to the battle by the ships. Ajax, hard pressed by the Trojan missiles, 'stepped back a little, in fear of his life, to the seven-foot *threnus* and left the *ikria* of the balanced ship'[13]. This seven-foot *threnus* is likely to have been the stout beam which we can observe in later ships (see below, p. 198) projecting on each side of the hull below and forward of the helmsman's seat. In the Homeric ship it would have stood about three feet from the beach and might have served as a convenient step for men leaving or

* T. W. Allen, *The Homeric Hymns*², Oxford, 1936, cvii and 379.

going on board the ship from the shore. Ajax would then have stepped back to this beam either inside, or more probably, outside the hull, when he was driven from the stern *ikria*. This beam, inside the ship, would have been in the right position to provide a footrest for the helmsman. Elsewhere in the Homeric poems the word does in fact mean a footrest[14]. The seven-foot *threnus* may have given its name to the *thranites*, the uppermost of the three classes of oarsmen in the *trieres* (see below, p. 284). Liddell–Scott–Jones say that the *threnus* was perhaps the helmsman's bench. Although there is visible in later ships, e.g. the fifth-century bronze model of a simple long ship (Clas. 20; Pl. 27 *b*), a beam projecting on each side of the ship and forming the fulcrum for the attachment of the steering oar (and also possibly the seat of the helmsman inside the hull), it seems unlikely that such a beam would have been as much as seven foot long at that point in the rapidly tapering stern. A more difficult consequence of this interpretation is that we should have to infer from the passage in the *Iliad* that the helmsman's seat was forward of the *ikria* and not part of it at all.

In Eumaeus' hut Odysseus in disguise tells a lot of tall stories about how he reached Ithaca. In the last he recounts his escape from the crew of a Thesprotian ship who were intending to sell him into slavery. As they took their meal on the beach, Odysseus, who had been left tied up in the ship, slipped the knots, put a ragged garment over his head, climbed down to 'the planed *epholkaion*', lowered his body into the water and swam off[15]. In later ships there were projections on each side of the bows, or rather a beam laid across the bows, the ends of which formed projections known as *epotides* and usually translated 'catheads'. It is possible then that the *epholkaion* was a similar beam to the seven-foot *threnus* but in the bows instead of the stern; and that it, like the *threnus*, afforded a step for anyone going over the side. Such projecting beams are visible in the bow of the clay model, Clas. 21. Odysseus does not say that the *epholkaion* was in the bows; but, if the stern was beached, the bow was the only part of the ship from which he could have made his escape by swimming. It was also the part furthest from his captors on the beach. A beam projecting on each side of the bow would have been useful for the attachment of a towing rope. It is from this practice presumably that it got its name *epholkaion*, i.e. towing bar.

The making of ships' timber is often in the mind of the poet of the *Iliad*[16]. Hector's heart is as hard as a shipwright's adze[17]. Heroes fall in battle like pine trees felled in the mountains for ship-timbers[18]. The nice balance of a hard-fought fight is compared to the accuracy with which a clever ship-wright makes his planks true and fitting snugly together[19]. Menelaus and Meriones, bringing the dead Patroclus from the battle, are compared to mules putting out all their strength to carry a huge ship's timber down from the mountain side[20].

Agamemnon tells the Greeks that after nine years at Troy the planks of their ships are rotten and the cords (*sparta*) have worked loose[21]. As Casson has pointed out,* Aulus Gellius and Pliny both assume that Homer is talking of the twine with which the planks were sewn together when he talks of the cords which have worked loose. Such a method of boat-building has been common east of Suez for many centuries.† Aeschylus later speaks of a ship 'sewn with flax'[22]; and the scholiast observes there: 'They used to drill ships and sew them together with cords, and the phrase in Homer "mending ships"[23] indicates the process of sewing them together.' It seems clear that at some period, at any rate in Mycenaean times and very probably later, a ship's sides[24] were built of long deal planks laid flush edge to edge carvel-fashion and accurately adzed to fit, and that these were then sewn together with cords of papyrus or hemp. In the *Odyssey*, however, when Odysseus makes the skin of planks for his improvised boat, he is described as using the more sophisticated method of joining the planks edge to edge by mortise and tenon (*harmonia*) fixed externally with dowel-pins (*gomphoi*)[25]. We may suppose that this method was in use in the eighth century, while the other still survived possibly in practice, certainly in the traditional language of the poet of the *Iliad*.

Odysseus' boat, being improvised, had no keel or frames. He had to rely on the joints to hold the planks together[26]. A proper ship had a keel (*tropis*). In the shipwreck the planking of the hull parts company with the keel, and Odysseus lashes keel and mast together and rides on them[27].

The name for the forefoot, or forward part of the keel, seems to be *steira*. The word is used in both *Iliad* and *Odyssey* in a formular passage describing the beginning of a sea voyage. The wind fills the sail; 'and about the *steira* the surging wave sang aloud as the ship went on her way'[28]. Liddell–Scott–Jones regard the word *steira* as a feminine form of *stereos*, an adjective mean-

---

* L. Casson, 'New Light on Ancient Rigging and Boatbuilding', *American Neptune* XXIV, 2 (1964), pp. 90 ff.

† James Hornell, *Water Transport*, Cambridge, 1946, pp. 192–3, 234–7, Pl. xxviiiB.

ing 'hard', and compare the definition by Hesychius of *steroma* as *tropis* (i.e. keel) and the use of *sterigma* by Nonnus and *stereoma* by Theophrastus to mean a ship's keel[29]. It is perhaps interesting to note further that in the picture of the world drawn by Parmenides at the end of the sixth century there is a *stereon* in the middle of the universe, and that Philolaus in the fourth century apparently took over this feature and called it 'the leading element which the creator god laid down as a keel for the sphere of the whole'[30]. The practice of hauling up and down beaches made it necessary for the keel to be made of the hardest wood available (see below, p. 279). The *steira* is not then the stem, a post stepped into the keel, but the forward end of the keel itself. We must think of a ship like those drawn in the Geometric pictures.

A ship is described once in the *Iliad* as *poluzugos* and twice in the *Odyssey* as *eüzugos*, i.e. with many or with good *zuga*. *Zuga* are not mentioned otherwise in the *Iliad*, but in the *Odyssey* reluctant passengers are bound under them and bronze gifts are stowed in the same place[31]. Alcinous, on the latter occasion, makes a special tour of inspection to see that the cargo will not get in the way of the oarsmen. There seems to have been nowhere else to put it. Later, in Herodotus, *zuga* mean the cross-planks laid on top of the sides of a vessel, and in Sophocles the *zugon* is expressly connected with rowing[32]. There seems little doubt that the *zuga* of the Homeric ship were the rowing thwarts.

The Geometric pictures have suggested to some scholars that the ships shown had an overall deck (e.g. Geom. 2–6, 7–9, 10, 11, 14, 15, 25). We have argued that the artist when he draws what appears to be a deck is presenting the far gunwale above the near gunwale by a kind of primitive perspective for which there are parallels in Geometric painting, e.g. in the representation of the wheels of chariots (see above, p. 13). The two levels of oarsmen which appear in the later Geometric representations do not of course involve a deck between each level, as is shown e.g. by the black-figure vase-paintings of such ships (Arch. 85 ff., Pls 20–1). A deck, when it occurs, covers all the oarsmen. That the Homeric ship did not have an overall deck seems clear from two considerations: first, that such a deck is never mentioned, and second, that in Odysseus' shipwreck when the mast falls 'all the tackle was thrown into the bottom of the ship'[33]. The period at which the *katastroma*, a light overall deck, was introduced will be discussed later (see below, pp. 161–2). There is no sign of it in Homer.

Three further minor fixtures are mentioned, two connected with the mast and one with the oars. The *histopede* appears to have been a raised footing for the mast, just as *histodoke* was the crutch which received the mast when it was struck[34]. The *mesodme* in which the mast was set when it had been stepped was probably, since in other contexts *mesodme* means a cross-beam, a thwart in the middle of the ship with a slot to take the mast. It is not to be identified with the *histopede*, although it is liable to be regarded as part of it[35]. When Odysseus passed the Sirens the poet says that he was tied *in* the *histopede*. The mast, we are told, had been lowered. Odysseus' body must have taken its place in the *histopede* and *mesodme*. The painters of the scene on the black- and red-figure vases, who depicted Odysseus tied to the mast, had not paid sufficient attention to the text.

The *kleïdes* at which the oarsmen sit in the *Iliad* and the *Odyssey* are undoubtedly tholepins[36]. The later word for tholepins, *skalmoi*, is not used in the older poems, and appears first in the *Hymn to Dionysus*[37]. Elsewhere in Homer the word *kleïs* means a key, or a collarbone, i.e. a hook-shaped object, and hook-shaped fittings are clearly visible on the gunwale of Geometric ships (e.g. Geom. 2–6). On one occasion a ship's crew are told to make fast their oars to the *kleïdes* and then go ashore, ready to sail after dinner. What they do is described as 'fitting the oars in leathern loops'[38]. A leathern loop passed round an oar and over a hook-shaped tholepin would keep the oar at the tholepin as the oarsman came forward for his stroke.

The movable gear of the Homeric ship may be conveniently divided here into the two categories employed later in the Athenian dockyards: 'wooden gear' and 'hanging gear' (*skeue xulina, skeue kremasta*: see below, p. 289). The most important of the wooden gear are the oars, the mast and the sailyard, while the hanging gear consists of the sail and the various kinds of ropes.

The rowing oars in Homer are usually called *eretma*[39]. *Kope*, the later word for an oar, means a sword-handle in the *Iliad* and *Odyssey* and a key-handle in the *Odyssey*. In the latter poem it is also used in its later sense of an oar[40].

In the *Iliad* the helmsmen are said to hold *oieïa* in their hands. A parallel word, *oiekes*, which later becomes the word for the tiller, is used in the same poem to mean the attachments to the yoke of a mule in a mulecart[41]. It seems likely then that *oieïon* means a tiller. The steering oar of the ship depicted on the Bronze Age Pylos vase (BA. 2) clearly has a tiller attached by a pin. A similar tiller also appears on a Geometric picture (Geom. 4).

Geometric ships are sometimes depicted with one steering oar. Some, like the later ships, have two (e.g. the Late Geometric ships in Geom. 19 and 42). Since *pedon* is used twice in the *Odyssey* to mean the blade of a rowing oar, it seems likely that *pedalion*, which is not found in the *Iliad*, may mean properly the steering oar blade as opposed to the tiller. Odysseus equips his makeshift boat with only a single *pedalion*, and the employment of one only might seem the result of its makeshift nature if it were not that elsewhere in the *Odyssey* a single steering oar appears to have been used[42]. It is possible that although two were normally fitted, as in later times, both were not always used. These confident conclusions as to the respective meanings of *oieïon* and *pedalion* appear to be confounded by the passage in the *Odyssey* where the Cyclops is throwing rocks at Odysseus' departing ship. His throw twice falls short of the ship 'and did not quite reach the tip of the *oieïon*'[43], clearly here not the tiller but the blade itself. We may explain the usage as the naming of a part for the whole and compare *kope*, which begins by meaning a handle and ends by meaning the whole oar. Alternatively, we may suppose that *oieïon* and *pedalion* both mean the whole steering oar.

There is no answer in Homer to the question whether the blade of the steering oar was moved laterally or was turned on its long axis. The former method would have been more effective with a small blade and a small ship. Nor do we know whether the two steering oars were joined together or moved independently.

The mast (*histos*) is mentioned four times in the *Iliad* and frequently in the *Odyssey*. In both poems the word also means a loom[44]. On the Geometric pictures the masts are shown (as in Geom. 8, 25, 27, 30, 33, 43) no taller than the bow and stern ornaments. It looks as if they have been reduced in size to fit into the space available, and the shape, and sometimes size, of the sail altered for the same purpose. In the shipwreck, as we saw, the mast falls and brains the helmsman (see p. 47 above). If the ship was a pentekontor rowing twenty-five men a side at one level, it could not have been less than eighty-five feet in length (i.e. 3×25 for the oarsmen $+ 10$ for bow and stern). If the mast was stepped at the middle point between bow and stern (as the word *mesodme* suggests: see above, p. 52), it must have been 42 feet high to have struck the helmsman as it fell. In the sixth-century black-figure picture of a heroic ship on the François vase (Arch. 33, Pl. 11 *a* and *b*), the mast is shown resting on the *histodoke* with its top six feet or so short of the helmsman. It seems likely then that the story in the *Odyssey* is a tall one and that the mast of a large heroic ship was about 35 feet long. It was apparently made of pine[45].

The only references to the sailyard in either poem come in connection with Odysseus' makeshift boat. 'In the boat he made a mast, and a sailyard (*epikrion*) to fit it[46].' The ladders and gang-planks we find in later ships are not mentioned in Homer. As has been suggested above, the Homeric ships, whose stern ornament could be grasped by an attacker, were not high enough in the stern to need a ladder, and the projecting *threnus* and *epholkaion*, at stern and bow, provided a step, which was all that was necessary. Finally, we learn in the *Iliad* of the long poles with which the Greeks 'fought high up from their black ships'. These appear to have been great pikes built up of many pieces of wood and tipped with bronze, which were carried on board for use in fighting at sea[47]. There are no sea-fights in the *Iliad* or *Odyssey*, but these pikes come in useful in the battles by the ships at Troy. When Ajax uses one in the *Iliad* it is described as twenty-two cubits in length and clamped together with hoops[48].

Ships of the Bronze Age and the Geometric period are shown with a single sail, usually rectangular, apparently composed of a large number of small rectangles (see Geom. 7, 8, 25, 30–1). In both *Iliad* and *Odyssey* crews set out, spreading or hoisting *histia*, and brail up *histia* on their return[49]. The word used for sail is a plural one. The singular number is used in one phrase: 'the wind filled the middle of the sail (*meson histion*)'. This phrase is repeated in the *Hymn to Dionysus*, where the singular is used twice for a sail[50] according to the later usage. The evidence of the pictures is decisive as to the number of sails. There certainly cannot have been more than one on each ship. An explanation for the use of the plural may be found in the many pieces of cloth out of which the sail must have been made. No ancient loom would have been large enough to make a sail of, say, 25 feet square, all in one piece. It is therefore possible that the hatching of the sails in the Geometric pictures represents these smaller pieces, though there seem to be far too many of them. If the sail is 25 feet square, thirty-nine pieces of 4 feet square would be sufficient. This conclusion is perhaps confirmed when we find Calypso bringing Odysseus *pharea*, pieces of cloth, to make the sails of his boat[51]. If it is accepted, the phrase 'the wind filled the middle of the sail' may be taken literally: 'the wind filled the middle piece of those of which the sail was made'. Homeric sails seem to have been white[52].

There is no mention in Homer of the side screens (*pararrumata*, or *pararruseis*) of which we hear later (see below, p. 302), but Odysseus 'protected his makeshift boat throughout with wicker mats to keep out the waves'[53]; and it is likely that some sort of light screen was normally used above the gunwale. The framework for such a screen is shown very clearly in the heroic ship on the François vase (Pl. 11*a–b*) and a similar screen seems to be shown together with the far gunwale in a sort of decorative amalgam on a number of Geometric pictures (Geom. 25 in particular).

The generic name for ropes in Homer seems to be *hopla*, although this word does not appear in the *Iliad*. Sometimes the word seems to be used more widely for all ships' gear[54], but in general ropes only are meant. When the wind blows fair, Telemachus gives his companions the order to lay hold of the *hopla*. They then hoist the mast, make it fast with the forestays (*protonoi*), and haul up the white sail with well-twisted ox-leathers. When the operation is finished they secure the *hopla* and take their ease. Elsewhere the operation is condensed into a single phrase, 'after toiling at the *hopla*'[55].

The forestays are mentioned in the *Iliad* in a formula of return. 'The crew lay the mast on the crutch, striking it with the forestays[56].' In the shipwreck the wind 'breaks both the forestays of the mast' with the result that it falls backwards[57]. It seems clear that the two *protonoi* are shrouds leading from the top of the mast to the gunwale on each side of the ship. They keep the mast in position, helped by the *epitonos*, a leather stay which is mentioned in the shipwreck passage in the *Odyssey* as remaining attached to the mast when the ship breaks up. This stay is usually taken to be a backstay in contrast to the *protonoi*, which are called forestays. If, as seems clear, the *protonoi* are shrouds, we have no clue from them as to the *epitonos*. It is attached to the mast but might as well be secured forward as aft. Two Geometric pictures (Geom. 10 and 16) suggest the lowering of the mast by means of the forestays. The Pylos ship (BA. 2) shows one rope clearly running from the top of the mast to the bow and three running from the stern *ikria* in the direction of the top of the mast or the ends of the sailyard. The fragmentary condition of the jug does not let us know where they end.

In the *Odyssey* Telemachus' crew hoist the sail with twisted ox-leathers. Leathers are also used as halliards in the *Hymn to Apollo*[58]. In a Spartan ivory relief of the end of the seventh century (see below, Arch. 31, Pl. 10*d*) two men are shown hoisting sailyard and sail, the halliards falling vertically from the top of the mast on each side. Two such ropes are to be seen on each side of the mast in a Geometric picture (Geom. 8) and can therefore be identified securely as halliards. On one occasion in the *Odyssey* ships' *hopla* are divided into *speira* and *peismata*. The latter, as we shall see, are mooring ropes. In the break-up of Odysseus' ship the sailyard (*epikrion*) and *speiron* fall far away in the sea[59]. The *speiron* must then be one, possibly any one, of the ropes associated with the sailyard and sail.

Odysseus employs three types of ropes in his makeshift boat: *huperai*, *kaloi*, and *podes*[60]. There is another reference to the last type in the *Odyssey*. Odysseus declares that he always kept the ship's *pous* in his hand, never handing it over to one of his comrades[61]. The *pous*, then, is the rope attached to one of the lower corners of the sail. It is shown in two Geometric pictures (Geom. 7 and 8). The other lower corner is presumably made fast. The helmsman holds one in his hand so that he can let it go in a squall. The nature of *kaloi* is made clear by a specific description in Herodotus (see below, pp. 299 f.). They are the brailing ropes which are made fast to the bottom edge of the sail and pass up the forward face of the sail through rings at certain intervals, then over the top of the sailyard and aft to the helmsman, who is thus able to brail up the sail without moving from his seat. These ropes are not identifiable in the Geometric pictures, but the vertical ropes depending from the sailyard in the ivory relief (Arch. 31, Pl. 10 *d*) are brailing ropes. Lastly, *huperai* are probably the ropes attached to each end of the sailyard and used to brace them round. These are visible in the Geometric pictures (Geom. 8 (3), Pl. 2 *d*). *Podes* and *huperai* seem to be lumped together under the phrase '*hopla* on each side of the sail' in the *Hymn to Dionysus*. When the wind began to fill the middle of the sail, 'the crew made the ropes taut on each side'[62].

Finally, there are the different ropes used for mooring. The formula is given in a passage of the *Iliad*: 'they threw out anchor-stones (*eunai*) and made stern-cables fast'[63]. The ship is moving towards the beach stern first. Out of the bows perforated stones are dropped with cables attached, known suitably as 'sleepers' and referred to elsewhere as 'hold-fasts of swift ships'[64]. Lines are then run out astern and made fast on the beach.* On another occasion in the *Iliad* it is proposed that a ship should ride at anchor off shore,

---

* Cf. Knight's *Modern Seamanship*, 13th ed. 1960, p. 227, where a method of mooring a ship using shore lines to secure the stern and two anchors to hold the bow in position is called 'the Mediterranean Moor'.

that is to say, with anchors out fore and aft; and similarly in the *Odyssey* a crew moor their ship well out from the shore and leave her there[65]. On a foreign shore men sleep beside the shore lines. When they leave they untie them[66]. The word *peisma* is used for mooring ropes generally. On the Cyclops' island the anchorage is excellent. There is no need of a *peisma*, nor is it necessary to drop anchor-stones or make fast shore lines[67]. In the Laestrygonian harbour, again, the shelter was excellent. Odysseus 'kept his ship outside, making fast *peismata* from a rock', presumably in deep water. In the emergency that ensues his caution enables him to make his escape quickly, merely cutting his mooring ropes[68]. The ship which Alcinous provided for Odysseus was prepared and moored ready for departure in a similar way, but not for the same reason. When he leaves, all the crew have to do is to let go the mooring rope from a pierced stone, a kind of bollard at the dockside[69]. It is from a ship's *peisma* that the serving girls are strung up across the hall by Odysseus in his vengeance[70]. The word can however be used in a general sense, e.g. of the makeshift rope which Odysseus makes of twisted osiers to tie up the stag he has killed[71].

Once in the *Odyssey* the material out of which a *hoplon* is made is said to be papyrus[72]. Like the *peisma* just mentioned, it was presumably laid. Leathers were, we have seen, used where a particularly reliable rope was required, e.g. for halliards. These may have been plaited.

TEXTS

1. I 485–6   νῆα μὲν οἵ γε μέλαιναν ἐπ' ἠπείροιο ἔρυσσαν
        ὑψοῦ ἐπὶ ψαμάθοις.

2. XV 716–17   Ἕκτωρ δὲ πρύμνηθεν ἐπεὶ λάβεν οὐχὶ μεθίει
        ἄφλαστον μετὰ χερσὶν ἔχων.

   IX 241   στεῦται γὰρ νηῶν ἀποκόψειν ἄκρα κόρυμβα.

3. XV 435   νηὸς ἀπὸ πρύμνης χαμάδις πέσε.

4. XV 676   ἀλλ' ὅ γε νηῶν ἴκρι' ἐπῴχετο μακρὰ βιβάσθων.

5. 12 413–14   ὁ δ' ἄρ' ἀρνευτῆρι ἐοικὼς | κάππεσ' ἀπ' ἰκριόφιν.

6. 5 163–4   ἀτὰρ ἴκρια πῆξαι ἐπ' αὐτῆς
        ὑψοῦ, ὥς σε φέρησιν ἐπ' ἠεροειδέα πόντον.

   252–3   ἴκρια δὲ στήσας, ἀραρὼν θαμέσι σταμίνεσσι,
        ποιεῖ· ἀτὰρ μακρῇσιν ἐπηγκενίδεσσι τελεύτα.

7. 3 352–3   οὔ θην δὴ τοῦδ' ἀνδρὸς Ὀδυσσῆος φίλος υἱὸς
        νηὸς ἐπ' ἰκριόφιν καταλέξεται.

8. 13 74–5   νηὸς ἐπ' ἰκριόφιν γλαφυρῆς, ἵνα νήγρετον εὕδοι, πρύμνης.

9. 2 416–18   ἂν δ' ἄρα Τηλέμαχος νηὸς βαῖν', ἄρχε δ' Ἀθήνη, νηΐ δ' ἐνὶ πρύμνῃ κατ' ἄρ' ἕζετο· ἄγχι δ' ἄρ' αὐτῆς ἕζετο Τηλέμαχος.

15 285–6   ἐν πρύμνῃ δ' ἄρ' ἔπειτα καθέζετο, πὰρ δὲ οἷ αὐτῷ εἷσε Θεοκλύμενον.

10. 12 229–30   εἰς ἴκρια νηὸς ἔβαινον | πρῴρης.

11. 15 282–3   ὣς ἄρα φωνήσας οἱ ἐδέξατο χάλκεον ἔγχος καὶ τό γ' ἐπ' ἰκριόφιν τάνυσεν νεὸς ἀμφιελίσσης.

55 1–2   εἵλετο δ' ἄλκιμον ἔγχος, ἀκαχμένον ὀξέϊ χαλκῷ νηὸς ἀπ' ἰκριόφιν.

12. *Hymns*, VII 47–8   λέων δ' ἐπὶ σέλματος ἄκρου δεινὸν ὑπόδρα ἰδών.

13. XV 728–9   ἀλλ' ἀνεχάζετο τυτθόν, ὀϊόμενος θανέεσθαι θρῆνυν ἐφ' ἑπταπόδην, λίπε δ' ἴκρια νηὸς ἐΐσης.

14. XIV 240   ὑπὸ δὲ θρῆνυν ποσὶν ἧσει.   Cf. 19 57.

15. 14 350–2   ξεστὸν ἐφόλκαιον καταβὰς ἐπέλασσα θαλάσσῃ στῆθος, ἔπειτα δὲ χερσὶ διήρεσσ' ἀμφοτέρῃσι νηχόμενος. See L-S-J s.v. ἐφέλκειν.

16. II 135   δοῦρα νεῶν.   9 498 νήϊα δοῦρα.   12 67 πίνακας νεῶν.

17. III 60–2   αἰεί τοι κραδίη πέλεκυς ὥς ἐστιν ἀτειρής, ὅς τ' εἶσιν διὰ δουρὸς ὑπ' ἀνέρος, ὅς ῥά τε τέχνῃ νήϊον ἐκτάμνῃσιν.

18. XIII 390–1 = XVI 483–4   ἠὲ πίτυς βλωθρή, τήν τ' οὔρεσι τέκτονες ἄνδρες ἐξέταμον πελέκεσσι νεήκεσι νήϊον εἶναι.

19. XV 410–12   ἀλλ' ὥς τε στάθμη δόρυ νήϊον ἐξιθύνει τέκτονος ἐν παλάμῃσι δαήμονος, ὅς ῥά τε πάσης εὖ εἰδῇ σοφίης ὑποθημοσύνῃσιν Ἀθήνης . . .

20. XVII 742–4   οἱ δ' ὥς θ' ἡμίονοι κρατερὸν μένος ἀμφιβαλόντες ἕλκωσ' ἐξ ὄρεος κατὰ παιπαλόεσσαν ἀταρπόν ἢ δοκὸν ἠὲ δόρυ μέγα νήϊον . . .

21. II 135   καὶ δὴ δοῦρα σέσηπε νεῶν καὶ σπάρτα λέλυνται.

22. Aeschylus, *Supplices*, 134–5 (Murray) πλάτα . . . λινορραφής τε | δόμος ἅλα στέγων δορός.

23. 14 383   νῆας ἀκειόμενον.

24. XV 381–2   οἱ δ' ὥς τε μέγα κῦμα θαλάσσης εὐρυπόροιο νηὸς ὑπὲρ τοίχων καταβήσεται . . .

Cf. 12 420–1   ὄφρ' ἀπὸ τοίχους | λῦσε κλύδων τρόπιος· τὴν δὲ ψιλὴν φέρε κῦμα.

25. 5 243–8   αὐτὰρ ὁ τάμνετο δοῦρα· θοῶς δέ οἱ ἤνυτο ἔργον.
      εἴκοσι δ' ἔκβαλε πάντα, πελέκκησεν δ' ἄρα χαλκῷ,
      ξέσσε δ' ἐπισταμένως, καὶ ἐπὶ στάθμην ἴθυνεν.
      τόφρα δ' ἔνεικε τέρετρα Καλυψώ, δῖα θεάων.
      τέτρηνεν δ' ἄρα πάντα καὶ ἥρμοσεν ἀλλήλοισι,
      γόμφοισιν δ' ἄρα τήν γε καὶ ἁρμονίῃσιν ἄρασσεν.

26. 5 361–2   ὄφρ' ἂν μέν κεν δούρατ' ἐν ἁρμονίῃσιν ἀρήρῃ
      τόφρ' αὐτοῦ μενέω καὶ τλήσομαι ἄλγεα πάσχων.

27. 12 424–5   τῷ ῥ' ἄμφω συνέεργον ὁμοῦ τρόπιν ἠδὲ καὶ ἱστόν,
      ἑζόμενος δ' ἐπὶ τοῖς φερόμην ὀλοοῖς ἀνέμοισιν.

28. 1 481–2 = 2 427–8 (with slight variation)
      ἐν δ' ἄνεμος πρῆσεν μέσον ἱστίον, ἀμφὶ δὲ κῦμα
      στείρῃ πορφύρεον μεγάλ' ἴαχε νηὸς ἰούσης.

29. Theophrastus, *Historia Plantarum*, v vii 3; Nonnus, *Dionysiaca*, 40 451.

30. Diels–Kranz, 44 A 17: see *Journal of Hellenic Studies*, LXXV (1955), p. 65.

31. 9 98–9   τοὺς μὲν ἐγὼν ἐπὶ νῆας ἄγον κλαίοντας ἀνάγκῃ,
      νηυσὶ δ' ἐνὶ γλαφυρῇσιν ὑπὸ ζυγὰ δῆσα ἐρύσσας.

  13 20–2   καὶ τὰ μὲν εὖ κατέθηχ' ἱερὸν μένος Ἀλκινόοιο,
      αὐτὸς ἰὼν διὰ νηὸς ὑπὸ ζυγά, μή τιν' ἑταίρων
      βλάπτοι ἐλαυνόντων, ὁπότε σπερχοίατ' ἐρετμοῖς.

32. Herodotus, 2 96 ζυγὰ ἐπιπολῆς τείνουσι αὐτῶν.
   Sophocles, *Ajax*, 249–50
      ἢ θοὸν εἰρεσίας ζυγὸν ἑζόμενον | ποντοπόρῳ ναΐ μεθεῖναι.

33. 12 410–11   ἱστὸς δ' ὀπίσω πέσεν, ὅπλα τε πάντα
      εἰς ἄντλον κατέχυνθ'.

34. 12 178–9   οἱ δ' ἐν νηΐ μ' ἔδησαν ὁμοῦ χεῖράς τε πόδας τε
      ὀρθὸν ἐν ἱστοπέδῃ.

  1 434   ἱστὸν δ' ἱστοδόκῃ πέλασαν προτόνοισιν ὑφέντες. Cf. Ap. Rh.

35. 2 424–5 = 15 289–90   [4 1632.
      ἱστὸν δ' εἰλάτινον κοίλης ἔντοσθε μεσόδμης
      στῆσαν ἀείραντες.

Cf. 19 37 and 20 354 for non-nautical use.

36. E.g. XVI 169–70   ἐν δὲ ἑκάστῃ
      πεντήκοντ' ἔσαν ἄνδρες ἐπὶ κληΐσιν ἑταῖροι.

  2 419   ἂν δὲ καὶ αὐτοὶ βάντες ἐπὶ κληΐσι καθῖζον.

37. *Hymns*, VII 42   πάντες δὲ σκαλμοὶ στεφάνους ἔχον.

38. 4 782 = 8 53   ἠρτύναντο δ' ἐρετμὰ τροποῖς ἐν δερματίνοισι.

39. See 38 and 1 435   τὴν δ' εἰς ὅρμον προέρεσσαν ἐρετμοῖς.

40. 9 489   ἐμβαλέειν κώπῃς.   12 214 κώπῃσιν ἁλὸς ῥηγμῖνα. . .τύπτετε.

41. XIX 43   οἵ τε κυβερνῆται καὶ ἔχον οἰήϊα νηῶν.
   XXIV 268–9   κὰδ δ' ἀπὸ πασσαλόφι ζυγὸν ἦρεον ἡμιόνειον
      πύξινον ὀμφαλόεν, εὖ οἰήκεσσιν ἀρηρός.

42. 7 328 = 13 78 (var.) ἀναρρίπτειν ἅλα πηδῷ.

    5 255 πρὸς δ' ἄρα πηδάλιον ποιήσατο, ὄφρ' ἰθύνοι.

Cf. *ib.* 270 and 315.

    3 281 πηδάλιον μετὰ χερσὶ θεούσης νηὸς ἔχοντα.

43. 9 539–40 κὰδ δ' ἔβαλε μετόπισθε νεὸς κυανοπρῴροιο

    τυτθόν, ἐδεύησεν δ' οἰήϊον ἄκρον ἱκέσθαι.

In the earlier lines *ib.* 482–3 the second has been wrongly added from 9 540, as
Merry observes.

44. 1 434, 480; XXIII 852, 878. = loom VI 491, 5 62.

45. 2 424 = 15 289 ἱστὸν εἰλάτινον.

46. 5 254 ἐν δ' ἱστὸν ποίει καὶ ἐπίκριον ἄρμενον αὐτῷ.

    and 318 τηλοῦ δὲ σπεῖρον καὶ ἐπίκριον ἔμπεσε πόντῳ.

47. XV 387–9 οἱ δ' ἀπὸ νηῶν ὕψι μελαινάων ἐπιβάντες

    μακροῖσι ξυστοῖσι, τά ῥά σφ' ἐπὶ νηυσὶν ἔκειτο

    ναύμαχα κολλήεντα κατὰ στόμα εἱμένα χαλκῷ.

48. XV 677–8 νώμα δὲ ξυστὸν μέγα ναύμαχον ἐν παλάμῃσι

    κολλητὸν βλήτροισι, δυωκαιεικοσίπηχυ.

49. 1 480 ἀνά θ' ἱστία λευκὰ πέτασσαν.

    2 426 = 15 291 ἕλκον δ' ἱστία λευκά.

    1 433 ἱστία μὲν στείλαντο.

    3 10–11 τοὶ δ' ἱστία νηὸς ἐΐσης

    στεῖλαν ἀείραντες.

50. 1 481 ἐν δ' ἄνεμος πρῆσεν μέσον ἱστίον.

    2 427 ἔπρησεν δ' ἄνεμος μέσον ἱστίον.

    Hymns, VII 33 ἔμπνευσεν δ' ἄνεμος μέσον ἱστίον.

    26 ἅμα δ' ἱστίον ἕλκεο νηός...

    32 Ὣς εἰπὼν ἱστόν τε καὶ ἱστίον ἕλκετο νηός.

51. 5 258–9 τόφρα δὲ φάρε' ἔνεικε Καλυψώ, δῖα θεάων,

    ἱστία ποιήσασθαι.

52. See 49 above.

53. 5 256–7 φράξε δέ μιν ῥίπεσσι διαμπερὲς οἰσυΐνῃσι

    κύματος εἶλαρ ἔμεν.

54. E.g. 2 389–90 καὶ τότε νῆα θοὴν ἅλαδ' εἴρυσε, πάντα δ' ἐν αὐτῇ

    ὅπλ' ἐτίθει, τά τε νῆες ἐΰσσελμοι φορέουσι.

Cf. the *hoplotheke* at Athens in the fourth century below, p. 189.

55. 2 422–3 Τηλέμαχος δ' ἑτάροισιν ἐποτρύνας ἐκέλευσεν

    ὅπλων ἅπτεσθαι· τοὶ δ' ὀτρύνοντος ἄκουσαν...

    427–32 ἔπρησεν δ' ἄνεμος μέσον ἱστίον, ἀμφὶ δὲ κῦμα

    στείρῃ πορφύρεον μεγάλ' ἴαχε νηὸς ἰούσης,

    ἡ δ' ἔθεεν κατὰ κῦμα διαπρήσσουσα κέλευθον,

    δησάμενοι δ' ἄρα ὅπλα θοὴν ἀνὰ νῆα μέλαιναν

στήσαντο κρατῆρας ἐπιστεφέας οἴνοιο.

λεῖβον δ᾽ ἀθανάτοισι θεοῖς αἰειγενέτῃσιν.

56. I 434. See 34 above.

57. 12 409–10   ἱστοῦ δὲ προτόνους ἔρρηξ᾽ ἀνέμοιο θύελλα

ἀμφοτέρους, ἱστὸς δ᾽ ὀπίσω πέσεν . . .

422–3   ἐκ δέ οἱ ἱστὸν ἄραξε ποτὶ τρόπιν· αὐτὰρ ἐπ᾽ αὐτῷ

ἐπίτονος βέβλητο, βοὸς ῥινοῖο τετευχώς.

58. 2 426 = 15 291   ἕλκον δ᾽ ἱστία λευκὰ ἐϋστρέπτοισι βοεῦσιν.

     Hymns, III 406–8 οὐδ᾽ ἔλυον λαῖφος νηὸς κυανοπρώροιο.

ἀλλ᾽ ὡς τὰ πρώτιστα κατεστήσαντο βοεῦσιν

ὣς ἔπλεον.

487   ἱστία μὲν πρῶτον κάθετον λύσαντε βοείας.

59. See 46, also 6 268–9

ἔνθα δὲ νηῶν ὅπλα μελαινάων ἀλέγουσι,

πείσματα καὶ σπεῖρα.

60. 5 260   ἐν δ᾽ ὑπέρας τε κάλους τε πόδας τ᾽ ἐνέδησεν ἐν αὐτῇ.

61. 10 32–3   αἰεὶ γὰρ πόδα νηὸς ἐνώμων, οὐδέ τῳ ἄλλῳ

δῶχ᾽ ἑτάρων.

62. *Hymns*, VII 33–4   ἀμφὶ δ᾽ ἄρ᾽ ὅπλα

κατ τάνυσαν.

63. I 436   ἐκ δ᾽ εὐνὰς ἔβαλον, κατὰ δὲ πρυμνήσι᾽ ἔδησαν.

64. XIV 410   χερμαδίῳ, τά ῥα πολλά, θοάων ἔχματα νηῶν . . .

65. XIV 75–7   νῆες ὅσαι πρῶται εἰρύαται ἄγχι θαλάσσης

ἕλκωμεν, πάσας δὲ ἐρύσσομεν εἰς ἅλα δῖαν,

ὕψι δ᾽ ἐπ᾽ εὐνάων ὁρμίσσομεν.

4 785   ὑψοῦ δ᾽ ἐν νοτίῳ τήν γ᾽ ὥρμισαν, ἐκ δ᾽ ἔβαν αὐτοί.

66. 12 32   οἱ μὲν κοιμήσαντο παρὰ πρυμνήσια νηός.

πρυμνήσια λῦσαι, e.g. 2 418, 15 286 and 552.

67. 9 136–9   ἐν δὲ λιμὴν εὔορμος, ἵν᾽ οὐ χρεὼ πείσματός ἐστιν

οὔτ᾽ εὐνὰς βαλέειν οὔτε πρυμνήσι᾽ ἀνάψαι,

ἀλλ᾽ ἐπικέλσαντας μεῖναι χρόνον εἰς ὅ κε ναυτέων

θυμὸς ἐποτρύνῃ καὶ ἐπιπνεύσωσιν ἀῆται.

68. 10 96   πέτρης ἐκ πείσματα δήσας.

ib. 126–7   τόφρα δ᾽ ἐγὼ ξίφος ὀξὺ ἐρυσσάμενος παρὰ μηροῦ

τῷ ἀπὸ πείσματ᾽ ἔκοψα νεὸς κυανοπρώροιο.

69. 13 77   πεῖσμα δ᾽ ἔλυσαν ἀπὸ τρητοῖο λίθοιο.

70. 22 465   πεῖσμα νεὸς κυανοπρώροιο.

71. 10 167–8   πεῖσμα δ᾽, ὅσον τ᾽ ὄργυιαν, ἐϋστρεφὲς ἀμφοτέρωθεν

πλεξάμενος συνέδησα πόδας δεινοῖο πελώρου.

72. 21 390–1   κεῖτο δ᾽ ὑπ᾽ αἰθούσῃ ὅπλον νεὸς ἀμφιελίσσης

βύβλινον . . .

HANDLING

The formulae describing the various operations of seafaring have been used extensively in the attempt to give an account of the structure and gear of the Homeric ship. In this section, at the risk of some repetition, the operations themselves will be reviewed.

The first action of a voyage is to haul the ship down from the beach to the sea[1]. If the ship has been ashore for a long period, the channel made for the keel must be cleared out, and the piles of stones acting as shores on each side of the ship removed[2]. When Odysseus returned to the Greek camp from the mission to Chryse, his ship was hauled up again high on the beach and the long piles of stones rebuilt[3].

The next action is to put the gear on board, the mast and the sail[4]; and for the crew to go on board themselves, untie the shore lines, and sit to the thole-pins[5]. The helmsman, the captain (*archos*), and any passenger there may be, sit on the stern *ikria*[6]. The oarsmen then row out to sea until a breeze springs up: 'first is the rowing, thereafter a breeze that is fair'[7]. At a command from the captain or the helmsman the crew apply themselves to the ropes, set up the mast, make it fast with forestays, hoist the sail (and sailyard), and shake out sail. 'The wind blows full in the middle of the sail, and the surging wave sings about the keel as the ship goes. The ship runs, accomplishing her course with a wave that follows. So then the crew make the tackle fast throughout the swift, black ship, and when they have finished they set up mixing bowls of wine, well-crowned, and pour libations to the immortal gods, created for ever[8].'

The poet does not give the whole formula, or all the formulae, on every occasion; nor are they always appropriate. Sometimes, presumably when the wind is right, a crew may make sail directly from the moorings[9]. Sometimes, again, the embarkation is in two stages: the crew haul down the ship into the water, place the gear in it, put out the oars and strap them to the tholepins, even shake out sail, but then moor the ship in deep water and go ashore for a meal before departure.

An arrival is described in the *Iliad* as follows. The ship makes harbour under canvas. Then the sail is furled and stowed, the mast is lowered onto the crutch, and the ship is rowed to the beach. As she grounds stern first, or rather a few seconds before grounding, the anchor stones are dropped out of the bows and lines run ashore and made fast. Then the crew go ashore[10]. In the

Odyssey Amphinomus catches sight of Antinous' ship a moment after she had reached the harbour at Ithaca. Some of the crew are furling the sails, while others still have the oars in their hands[11]. The word used for furling on another occasion suggests that the sail was brailed up (see below, p. 64, note 15). Sometimes in the context of a disembarkation the crew is said to 'let go the sails'[12]. This phrase seems to be a condensed expression for the operation of lowering sailyard and sail (after furling) by letting go the leathers by which both had been hoisted to the top of the mast. In the *Hymn to Apollo* the operation is described more explicitly: 'they lowered the sail, letting go the leathers'[13]. On an abnormal occasion when the ship runs aground in a fog the crew take down the sail ashore[14]. When Telemachus arrives at Pylos intending only a short stay, his crew 'raise the sail of the balanced ship and furl it, then moor the ship and go ashore'[15].

We can summarize the procedure of arrival as follows. A ship sails into a harbour where she can be beached or moored. The sail is first brailed up to the sailyard, then the halliards are let go, and the sailyard and sail are lowered into the ship. The mast is struck and laid on the crutch. The ship, with sail and sailyard stowed and mast lowered, is then rowed to the beach stern first. The word used in the *Iliad* and *Odyssey* for this operation, *proeressein* (rowing forward), may mean rowing astern since in this kind of rowing the oarsman rows in the direction he is facing. The ship is then moored from anchor-stones in the bow and lines taken ashore in the stern[16].

At the beginning of a voyage the crew sit to their oars, but they only row if, and as long as, there is no wind for sailing. Sometimes rowing is prolonged. There is the simile: 'as god gives a breeze to sailors who long for it, when they labour driving the sea with well-planed oars, and their limbs are paralysed with weariness'[17]. The excitment of relief is caught in the *Hymn to Dionysus*. The captain calls to the helmsman: 'Mark the breeze: hoist the sail and lay hold on every rope.' On three occasions in the *Odyssey* the voyage is pressed day and night[18]. A voyage from Crete to Egypt, in which there can have been no ports of call, is said to have taken four days with a following north wind[19]. Average speed for the four hundred miles would have been four knots. When the wind drops, the crew take down the sail before starting to row. In the sultry atmosphere which surrounds the Sirens 'at once the wind dropped and there was a windless calm, a god laid the waves to sleep. My companions stood and drew up the sail and stowed it in the hollow ship, while they sat to the oars and made the water white with planed blades'[20].

In a strong wind waves would run high and break over the ship's side, hence the wicker side screens on Odysseus' improvised ship[21]. In a northerly gale ships have their sails blown to tatters, lose steerage way and broach to. In this dangerous position they properly regain steerage way by furling sail and rowing[22].

TEXTS

1. E.g. 1 141   νῦν δ' ἄγε νῆα μέλαιναν ἐρύσσομεν εἰς ἅλα δῖαν.

      2 389   καὶ τότε νῆα θοὴν ἅλαδ' εἴρυσε. Cf. Ap. Rh. 1 371–90.

2. ΙΙ 153   οὐρούς τ' ἐξεκάθαιρον. . .ὑπὸ δ' ἤρεον ἕρματα νηῶν.

3. 1 485–6   νῆα μὲν οἵ γε μέλαιναν ἐπ' ἠπείροιο ἔρυσσαν
ὑψοῦ ἐπὶ ψαμάθοις, ὑπὸ δ' ἕρματα μακρὰ τάνυσσαν.

4. 2 389–90 (continuation of 1 above)   πάντα δ' ἐν αὐτῇ
ὅπλ' ἐτίθει, τά τε νῆες ἐΰσσελμοι φορέουσι.

     ΙΙ 2–3   νῆα μὲν ἄρ πάμπρωτον ἐρύσσαμεν εἰς ἅλα δῖαν,
ἐν δ' ἱστὸν τιθέμεσθα καὶ ἱστία νηῒ μελαίνῃ.

5. E.g. 9 177–80   ἐκέλευσα δ' ἑταίρους
αὐτούς τ' ἀμβαίνειν ἀνά τε πρυμνήσια λῦσαι.
οἱ δ' αἶψ' εἴσβαινον καὶ ἐπὶ κληῖσι καθῖζον,
ἑξῆς δ' ἑζόμενοι πολιὴν ἅλα τύπτον ἐρετμοῖς.

6. See above, p. 58, note 10.

7. ΙΙ 640   πρῶτα μὲν εἰρεσίῃ, μετέπειτα δὲ κάλλιμος οὖρος.

8. See above, p. 60, note 55.

9. E.g. 1 479–81, ΙΙ 4–8.

10. 1 432–7   οἱ δ' ὅτε δὴ λιμένος πολυβενθέος ἐντὸς ἵκοντο
ἱστία μὲν στείλαντο, θέσαν δ' ἐν νηῒ μελαίνῃ,
ἱστὸν δ' ἱστοδόκῃ πέλασαν προτόνοισιν ὑφέντες
καρπαλίμως, τὴν δ' εἰς ὅρμον προέρεσσαν ἐρετμοῖς.
ἐκ δ' εὐνὰς ἔβαλον, κατὰ δὲ πρυμνήσι' ἔδησαν·
ἐκ δὲ καὶ αὐτοὶ βαῖνον ἐπὶ ῥηγμῖνι θαλάσσης.

11. 16 353   ἱστία δὲ στέλλοντας ἐρετμά τε χερσὶν ἔχοντας.

12. 15 495–6   οἱ δ' ἐπὶ χέρσου
Τηλεμάχου ἕταροι λύον ἱστία.

13. *Hymns*, ΙΙΙ 487   ἱστία μὲν πρῶτον κάθετον λύσαντε βοείας.

14. 9 149   κελσάσῃσι δὲ νηυσὶ καθείλομεν ἱστία πάντα.

15. 3 10–11   οἱ δ' ἰθὺς κάταγον, τοὶ δ' ἱστία νηὸς ἐΐσης
στεῖλαν ἀείραντες, τὴν δ' ὅρμισαν, ἐκ δ' ἔβαν αὐτοί.

16. 15 496–8 (continuation of note 12)   κὰδ δ' ἕλον ἱστὸν
καρπαλίμως, τὴν δ' εἰς ὅρμον προέρεσσαν ἐρετμοῖς.
ἐκ δ' εὐνὰς ἔβαλον, κατὰ δὲ πρυμνήσι' ἔδησαν.

13 279   σπουδῇ δ᾽ ἐς λιμένα προερέσσαμεν.

17. VII 4–6   ὡς δὲ θεὸς ναύτῃσιν ἐελδομένοισιν ἔδωκεν
              οὖρον, ἐπεί κε κάμωσιν ἐϋξέστῃς ἐλάτῃσι
              πόντον ἐλαύνοντες, καμάτῳ δ᾽ ὑπὸ γυῖα λέλυνται...

18. 2 434; 10 28; 15 476 (Phoenicians)

19. 14 257–8   πεμπταῖοι δ᾽ Αἴγυπτον ἐϋρρείτην ἱκόμεσθα
              στῆσα δ᾽ ἐν Αἰγύπτῳ ποταμῷ νέας ἀμφιελίσσας.

20. 12 168–72 αὐτίκ᾽ ἔπειτ᾽ ἄνεμος μὲν ἐπαύσατο ἠδὲ γαλήνη
              ἔπλετο νηνεμίη, κοίμησε δὲ κύματα δαίμων.
              ἀνστάντες δ᾽ ἕταροι νεὸς ἱστία μηρύσαντο
              καὶ τὰ μὲν ἐν νηῒ γλαφυρῇ βάλον, οἱ δ᾽ ἐπ᾽ ἐρετμὰ
              ἑζόμενοι λεύκαινον ὕδωρ ξεστῇς ἐλάτῃσιν.

21. 5 256–7   See above, p. 60, note 53.

22. 9 67–73   νηυσὶ δ᾽ ἐπῶρσ᾽ ἄνεμον Βορέην νεφεληγερέτα Ζεὺς
              λαίλαπι θεσπεσίῃ, σὺν δὲ νεφέεσσι κάλυψε
              γαῖαν ὁμοῦ καὶ πόντον· ὀρώρει δ᾽ οὐρανόθεν νύξ.
              αἱ μὲν ἔπειτ᾽ ἐφέροντ᾽ ἐπικάρσιαι, ἱστία δέ σφιν
              τριχθά τε καὶ τετραχθὰ διέσχισεν ἲς ἀνέμοιο.
              καὶ τὰ μὲν ἐς νῆας κάθεμεν, δείσαντες ὄλεθρον,
              αὐτὰς δ᾽ ἐσσυμένως προερέσσαμεν ἤπειρόνδε.

DOCKYARDS, ETC.

Nothing resembling the ship-sheds and dockyards of fifth- and fourth-century Athens is of course to be found in the Homeric poems. In the *Iliad* the Greek ships are away from their home ports. They are hauled high up on the shore, along channels cut to receive their keels. That these channels were shallow, probably no more than grooves, is shown by the fact that 'long *hermata*' were built up on each side of the ship to act as shores, possibly also to protect the hulls from the weather. We saw that when Odysseus sets out on his voyage to Chryse, in a ship which had been laid up on the beach for several years, he 'first clears out the channels and removes the *hermata* from under it'[1]. On his return the crew haul up the ship and 'stretch out the long *hermata*'[2]. The meaning of *hermata* is 'heaps of stones'. Hesiod confirms that this is just what they were. He advises the farmer, when the Pleiades set, to haul up his ship and 'pack it with stones all round to withstand the power of the winds that blow damply'[3].

Two harbours are mentioned as particularly excellent[4]. There the anchor-stones and shore lines which are necessary on an unsheltered beach may be dispensed with, and the ship can ride to a single cable. The seaport of a seafaring people is described by Nausicaa in her proud account of her own city. 'There is a good harbour on each side with a narrow approach. To the road are drawn up ships horned fore and aft. They [i.e. the ships' captains] have sheds for their sails[5], each and all. And there they have a meeting place, about a fair temple of Poseidon...There they attend to the tackle of the black ships, mooring ropes and braces, and they plane the oars. For the Phaeacians take no interest in the bow and the quiver, only in masts and ships' oars and balanced ships, in which they take delight as they cross the grey sea[6].' We shall see that the dockyard at Athens in the fifth century resounded with the noise of the planing of oars[7], and was the scene of meetings of the Council when an expedition was being prepared[8].

When the ship which is to take Odysseus home leaves the Phaeacian harbour all the crew have to do is to cast off from a bollard[9]. That, we have seen, is the mark of a good harbour.

TEXTS

1. See above, p. 64, note 2.

2. See above, p. 64, note 3.

3. Hesiod, *Works and Days*, 624–5

> νῆα δ' ἐπ' ἠπείρου ἐρύσαι, πυκάσαι δὲ λίθοισι
> πάντοθεν, ὄφρ' ἴσχωσ' ἀνέμων μένος ὑγρὸν ἀέντων.

4. See above, p. 61, notes 67 and 68.

5. The word ἐπίστιον is translated by Liddell–Scott–Jones as 'slip or shed for a ship', and Rieu translates 'slip'. But there is nowhere else any suggestion of a slipway or ship-shed. The word should mean a place for masts and/or sails, as *epineion* later (see pp. 132, 186) means a place for ships. We have seen that at the end of a voyage the mast and sail were normally removed from a ship, and that the gear was replaced at the beginning of a new voyage. A well planned dockyard would undoubtedly have had a gear store, possibly each captain had his own.

6. 6 263–72.

> καλὸς δὲ λιμὴν ἑκάτερθε πόληος,
> λεπτὴ δ' εἰσίθμη· νῆες δ' ὁδὸν ἀμφιέλισσαι
> εἰρύαται· πᾶσιν γὰρ ἐπίστιόν ἐστιν ἑκάστῳ.
> ἔνθα δέ τέ σφ' ἀγορή, καλὸν Ποσιδήϊον ἀμφίς...
> ἔνθα δὲ νηῶν ὅπλα μελαινάων ἀλέγουσι,
> πείσματα καὶ σπεῖρα, καὶ ἀποξύνουσιν ἐρετμά.
> οὐ γὰρ Φαιήκεσσι μέλει βιὸς οὐδὲ φαρέτρη,

ἀλλ' ἱστοὶ καὶ ἐρετμὰ νεῶν καὶ νῆες ἐΐσαι
ᾗσιν ἀγαλλόμενοι πολιὴν περόωσι θάλασσαν.

For alternative interpretation of ἀμφιέλισσαι, see p. 37.

7. Aristophanes, *Acharnians*, 552

τὸ νεώριον δ' αὖ κωπέων πλατουμένων... (sc. πλέων).

8. See below, p. 192, note 44.

9. See above, p. 61, note 69.

FIFTH-CENTURY ACCOUNTS OF THE SHIPS OF
900–700 B.C.

Pindar appears to have said that the Achaean ships at Troy were pente-kontors[1]. Herodotus begins his history with an account of a Phoenician raid on Argos, which must have taken place after the beginning of the ninth century, since the Phoenicians do not seem to have penetrated the eastern Mediterranean till then. He says that they 'applied themselves to long voyages immediately after their arrival from the Red Sea and their occupation of the place which they now occupy'[2]. He tells the story of the Greek voyage to Aia in Colchis 'in a long ship', i.e. the *Argo*, as a reprisal for the raid on Argos, and of the carrying off of Medea[3]. When Herodotus speaks of the voyages of the distant past he usually specifies the ships as pentekontors or triakontors. The Pelasgians raid Attica in pentekontors[4], and Theras goes to Thera with some of the Minyans in three triakontors[5]. But the Aeginetans raid Attica in 'long ships'[6]. In one passage Herodotus speaks of ships being painted with red ochre in ancient times[7].

Thucydides emphasizes sea power in his account of the early history of Greece. He says that Minos of Crete was the earliest known possessor of a fleet and the first suppressor of piracy[8], and that Agamemnon's supremacy among the Greeks was due to his naval power[9]. Yet the expedition to Troy was, he says, comparatively speaking, small. 'For in a fleet of twelve hundred vessels Homer has represented the ships of the Boeotians as having a hundred and twenty men each, and those of Philoctetes as having fifty, indicating, it seems to me, the largest and the smallest ships; at any rate, no mention of the size of any others is made in the Catalogue of the Ships. But that all on board were at once rowers and fighting men he has shown in the case of the ships of Philoctetes; for he represents all the oarsmen as archers. And it is not likely that many supernumeraries sailed with the expedition, apart from the kings and those highest in office, especially as they were to cross the open sea with all the equipment of war, and, furthermore, had boats which were not provided with decks, but were built after the early style, more like pirate-boats. In any event if one takes the mean between the largest ships and the smallest, it is clear that not a large number of men went on the expedition, considering that they were sent out from all Hellas in common[10].'

With regard to the text of Homer Thucydides is in no better position than we are. He has no sources of information other than Homer's own words. He does, however, come to a different conclusion to the one we came to when we considered the texts[11]. Homer says that a hundred and twenty men 'went' in the Boeotian ships, and that Philoctetes' ships had fifty oarsmen. Thucydides' argument is that since the fifty oarsmen in Philoctetes' ships were also archers it follows that the fighting men in all the other ships were also oarsmen. Accordingly the hundred and twenty men in each of the Boeotian ships were all oarsmen, and the ships were unusually large types. We have mentioned the Attic bowl in the British Museum (Geom. 19, Pl. 4e) which shows thirty-nine oarsmen at two levels (see above, pp. 28 and 38 ff.) as well as a helmsman and a captain. If this is a real two-level ship of seventy-eight oarsmen, it still seems rather unlikely that the Boeotians in Homer had ships of as many as a hundred and twenty oarsmen. It is more likely that the Boeotian ships in Homer are parallel to the later troop-carrying *triereis* (see below, pp. 247–8) or to the pentekontors in Xerxes' fleet which carried thirty men in addition to the oarsmen[12]. Thucydides' argument is, in any case, not at all cogent. From a passage in Herodotus it is clear that there were pentekontors which could carry a great deal beside the oarsmen. The Phocaeans evacuated all their women and children, and movable property, from Asia Minor to the western Mediterranean in a fleet of these ships[13]. In Euripides' *Helen* we are told of a pentekontor which put to sea with a complete spare crew (see below, p. 200).

TEXTS

1. Pindar, fr. 274 Bowra καὶ Πίνδαρος πεντηκονταερέτμους φησὶ τὰς ναῦς τῶν Ἀχαιῶν εἶναι. Blass, in the Teubner edition of Bacchylides, introduces at XVI 87–8 the epithet ἑκατόντορον for Theseus' ship. Pollux I 82 is the only other instance of this word. Apart from the improbability of such an epithet for Theseus' ship, the emendation is unlikely.

2. Herodotus, 1 1[1] τούτους γὰρ ἀπὸ τῆς Ἐρυθρῆς καλεομένης θαλάσσης ἀπικομένους ἐπὶ τήνδε τὴν θάλασσαν καὶ οἰκήσαντας τοῦτον τὸν χῶρον τὸν καὶ νῦν οἰκέουσι, αὐτίκα ναυτιλίῃσι μακρῇσι ἐπιθέσθαι...

3. Herodotus, 1 2–4.

4. Herodotus, 6 138[1] οἱ δὲ Πελασγοὶ οὗτοι Λῆμνον τότε νεμόμενοι καὶ βουλόμενοι τοὺς Ἀθηναίους τιμωρήσασθαι, εὖ τε ἐξεπιστάμενοι τὰς Ἀθηναίων ὁρτάς, πεντηκοντέρους κτησάμενοι ἐλόχησαν Ἀρτέμιδι ἐν Βραυρῶνι ἀγούσας ὁρτὴν τὰς τῶν Ἀθηναίων γυναῖκας.

5. Herodotus, 4 148[3] συγχωρησάντων δὲ τῇ γνώμῃ τῶν Λακεδαιμονίων, τρισὶ τριακοντέροισι ἐς τοὺς Μεμβλιάρεω ἀπογόνους ἔπλωσε, οὔτι πάντας ἄγων τοὺς Μινύας ἀλλ' ὀλίγους τινάς.

6. Herodotus, 5 81[3] ἐπικειμένων γὰρ αὐτῶν Βοιωτοῖσι ἐπιπλώσαντες μακρῇσι νηυσὶν ἐς τὴν Ἀττικὴν κατὰ μὲν ἔσυραν Φάληρον, κατὰ δὲ τῆς ἄλλης παραλίης πολλοὺς δήμους.

7. Herodotus, 3 58[2] τὸ δὲ παλαιὸν ἅπασαι αἱ νέες ἦσαν μιλτηλιφέες.

8. Thuc. 1 4 Μίνως γὰρ παλαίτατος ὧν ἀκοῇ ἴσμεν ναυτικὸν ἐκτήσατο καὶ τῆς νῦν Ἑλληνικῆς θαλάσσης ἐπὶ πλεῖστον ἐκράτησε καὶ τῶν Κυκλάδων νήσων ἦρξέ τε καὶ οἰκιστὴς πρῶτος τῶν πλείστων ἐγένετο, Κᾶρας ἐξελάσας καὶ τοὺς ἑαυτοῦ παῖδας ἡγεμόνας ἐγκαταστήσας· τό τε ληστικόν, ὡς εἰκός, καθῄρει ἐκ τῆς θαλάσσης ἐφ' ὅσον ἐδύνατο, τοῦ τὰς προσόδους μᾶλλον ἰέναι αὐτῷ.

9. Thuc. 1 9[3] ἅ μοι δοκεῖ Ἀγαμέμνων παραλαβὼν καὶ ναυτικῷ δὲ ἅμα ἐπὶ πλέον τῶν ἄλλων ἰσχύσας τὴν στρατείαν οὐ χάριτι τὸ πλέον ἢ φόβῳ ξυναγαγὼν ποιήσασθαι.

10. Thuc. 1 104–5 πεποίηκε γὰρ χιλίων καὶ διακοσίων νεῶν, τὰς μὲν Βοιωτῶν εἴκοσι καὶ ἑκατὸν ἀνδρῶν, τὰς δὲ Φιλοκτήτου πεντήκοντα, δηλῶν, ὡς ἐμοὶ δοκεῖ, τὰς μεγίστας καὶ ἐλαχίστας· ἄλλων γοῦν μεγέθους πέρι ἐν νεῶν καταλόγῳ οὐκ ἐμνήσθη. αὐτερέται δὲ ὅτι ἦσαν καὶ μάχιμοι πάντες, ἐν ταῖς Φιλοκτήτου ναυσὶ δεδήλωκεν· τοξότας γὰρ πάντας πεποίηκε τοὺς προσκώπους. περίνεως δὲ οὐκ εἰκὸς πολλοὺς ξυμπλεῖν ἔξω τῶν βασιλέων καὶ τῶν μάλιστα ἐν τέλει, ἄλλως τε καὶ μέλλοντας πέλαγος περαιώσεσθαι μετὰ σκευῶν πολεμικῶν, οὐδ' αὖ τὰ πλοῖα κατάφαρκτα ἔχοντας, ἀλλὰ τῷ παλαιῷ τρόπῳ ληστικώτερον παρεσκευασμένα. πρὸς τὰς μεγίστας δ' οὖν καὶ ἐλαχίστας ναῦς τὸ μέσον σκοποῦντι οὐ πολλοὶ φαίνονται ἐλθόντες, ὡς ἀπὸ πάσης τῆς Ἑλλάδος κοινῇ πεμπόμενοι.

11. See above, p. 46.

12. Herodotus, vii 184[3] προσθήσω δ' ἔτι τούτῳ καὶ τῷ προτέρῳ ἀριθμῷ τοὺς ἐκ τῶν πεντηκοντέρων, ποιήσας, ὅ τι πλέον ἦν αὐτῶν ἢ ἔλασσον, ἀν' ὀγδώκοντα ἄνδρας ἐνεῖναι.

13. Herodotus, 1 164[3] οἱ Φωκαιέες... κατασπάσαντες τὰς πεντηκοντέρους, ἐσθέμενοι τέκνα καὶ γυναῖκας καὶ ἔπιπλα πάντα, πρὸς δὲ καὶ τὰ ἀγάλματα τὰ ἐκ τῶν ἱρῶν καὶ τὰ ἄλλα ἀναθήματα, χωρὶς ὅ τι χαλκὸς ἢ λίθος ἢ γραφὴ ἦν, τὰ δὲ ἄλλα πάντα ἐσθέντες καὶ αὐτοὶ ἐσβάντες ἔπλεον ἐπὶ Χίου.

THE ARCHAIC PERIOD: 700–480 B.C.

Sappho Fragment 16 (Page):

> οἱ μὲν ἰππήων στρότον οἱ δὲ πέσδων
> οἱ δὲ νάων φαῖσ' ἐπὶ γᾶν μέλαιναν
> ἔμμεναι κάλλιστον.

'Some say a host of horsemen, some a host of foot soldiers, others a host of ships is the most beautiful thing on the face of the dark earth.'

4

CATALOGUE OF
SHIP REPRESENTATIONS

c. 700–*c.* 650 B.C.

The representations are subdivided into three sections, Vases, Fibulae, and
Miscellaneous. The classification of all the fibulae in this period may be considered to be arbitrary in that a few of them may be a little later than 650,
and the gold fibula, Arch. 19, has been considered to be earlier, but they
have a distinctly homogeneous style and a common tradition.

VASES

Arch. 1. Plate 8*a* (photo: The National Museum, Athens). Early Protoattic fragment from Phaleron.
Athens NM. Kourouniotes, *Eph. Arch.* 1911, 251, fig. 19 (top left); Williams, *JHS* 1959, 160, fig. 1.

Section of hull amidships of a two-level ship. A part of the upper level of rowers can be
seen at the top of the fragment with their oars crossing the hull between the oars of the
lower-level oarsmen: these latter row through square ports; only their chests and arms
are showing. This ship resembles closely the Late Geometric two-level ships (Geom.
43–4), except that here the Protoattic artist is not averse to the overlapping of forms
involved in painting the oars of the upper level right across the hull.

Arch. 2. Plate 8*b* (photo: German Archaeological Institute, Athens). Early Protoattic fragment of
plaque from Sunium by the Analatos Painter. Athens NM. J. M. Cook, *BSA* 1934, pl. 40*b*; Zervos,
L'Art en Grèce, 48; Matz, pl. 192*b*; Kirk, fig. 7; Boardman, *Greek Art*, fig. 39.

After half of ship to left. Above the black hull is a reserved strip bounded at the top by
a pair of parallel lines and intersected by short verticals. It is difficult to judge whether
this reserved strip in fact represents void or corresponds to the reserved area just below
the gunwale on the seventh-century 'Rhodian' ships (Arch. 27–8) or to the painted
area in many sixth- and fifth-century Attic ships. The tholepins—the short parallel
oblique lines (above the topmost horizontal) to which the oar looms are attached—
would suggest that the horizontal is the gunwale and the reserved area below is part
of the hull. Above the horizontals sit five hoplites with shields. The stern compartment has its own rail with supports; the section corresponding to the reserved area
forward is here hatched. The helmsman holds a large steering oar (or is it two?). The
stern post seems to end in some sort of figure carving.

73

Kirk's statement that there are five warriors *standing* on a *deck* with *large* round shields is quite arbitrary. Small shields were the fashion at the time covering the upper part of the body. What appears just below their shields need not be their legs, but their waists and the upper part of their thighs as they sit. Kirk's deck is by no means as incontrovertible as he claims.

Arch. 3. Plaque fragment. Athens NM. Boardman, *BSA* 1954, pl. 16, 2.

Part of bow of ship. Boardman says that the fragment is a close contemporary of the Sunium plaque.

Arch. 3 *bis*. Early Protoattic fragment of a krater. Athens, Agora P. 3776. Brann, *Athenian Agora VIII*, pl. 22, 383.

Five marines seated on the line of the gunwale as in Arch. 2.

Arch. 3 *ter*. Early Protoattic fragment of a krater. Athens, Agora P. 21232. Brann, *Athenian Agora VIII*, pls. 22 and 43, 382.

Section of the hull of a ship moving to left, close to that of Arch. 2, but here there are two oarsmen rowing and marines are absent.

Arch. 4. Middle Protoattic fragment of a krater. Athens NM, from the Acropolis. Graef, no. 412; J. M. Cook, *BSA* 1934, pl. 55*c*; Kirk, p. 120*b*.

Stern of ship to left. The rail and supports of the stern compartment are clear: below is a hatched area, perhaps corresponding to the similar decoration in the same place of the Sunium ship; again there seems to be the black of the hull below this. On the right of the fragment, the black triangular area above the rail seems to be a support (cf. the François vase ship, Arch. 33, Pl. 11*a*) for the stern post, while the space between is closed to give some protection to the helmsman. The stern post curves forward and has one horizontal projection. The helmsman sits behind the rail. In front of him are two thick verticals such as occur for example on the François ship and on the Athens plate fragment, Arch. 58. Attached to the left-hand vertical are the stumps of two horizontals; the upper one may be an extension of the poop rail, the lower one perhaps the line of the gunwale, on which stands a human figure.

Arch. 5. Plate 9*a, b* (photos: Palazzo dei Conservatori, Rome) and *c*; krater of uncertain fabric, but probably West Greek, made by Aristonothos. Rome, Palazzo dei Conservatori, from Cervetri. Arias and Hirmer, *History of Greek Vase Painting*, 14–15 (where see bibliography; add Moll, B, VI*a*, 2; Lefebvre des Noëttes, *De la marine*, fig. 31; and Kirk, p. 120*c*).

Two ships bows on. The left-hand ship (Pl. 9*a*) is of the Greek type with ram. The exact shape of the ram is in doubt because of fractures; the stem post, too, has disappeared. A large 'eye' is set well back beneath the bow compartment. Beneath the gunwale, a row of six semicircular ports with five oars below. Above the heads of the five rowers is a horizontal line, on which three warriors stand (for a discussion of the interpretation of this line see the Summary, p. 80). The stern is high and the helmsman, protected by a shield, has a single steering oar; spears are resting against the stern.

The bow of the right-hand ship (Pl. 9*b*) is raised out of the water and has a down-pointing ram. Three planks project from the stem. A thick vertical stem post appears at the top of the bow. Above the gunwale and supported on struts is a horizontal line of difficult interpretation, on which three warriors stand. The ship has mast, shrouds, and halliards. At the top of the mast in a crow's nest is a warrior with shield and spear (cf. the Boeotian fibula, Arch. 8). The stern post, which is curved and heavy, ends in two divisions and is supported by a strut; the stern compartment has a rail extending beyond the stern, and two steering oars.

To the arguments put forward by Kirk (loc. cit.) supporting a western origin for the krater could be added the Etruscan pyxis, D. 150, in the Louvre, on which the left-hand ship is a fantastic version of the Aristonothos right-hand ship, including the man in the crow's nest, and the right-hand ship a version of the Aristonothos left-hand ship, including the rowers, warriors on 'deck' and their shield devices.

Arch. 6. Protocorinthian fragment of a skyphos. Eleusis. Skias, *Eph. Arch.* 1898, pl. 5, 3; Matz, pl. 7.

Rough sketch of a ship to left with five oarsmen. One steering oar is shown.

Arch. 7. Clazomenian fragment. Athens NM (on exhibition).

Only part of the hull, which is hatched, remains together with the ram and two oars.

FIBULAE

(1) *Group of Berlin 31013*

Hampe considered that Berlin 31013*a* and *b*, Arch. 8–9, were by the same hand, and that Arch. 10 and 13 came from the same workshop. The style of ship on Arch. 11–12 is so close to the rest as to warrant inclusion in the same group.

Arch. 8. Plate 8*c* (after Hampe). Fibula of bronze. Berlin 31013*a*, from Thisbe. Hampe, *Sagenbilder*, no. 62*a*, pl. 4; Moll, B, I, 43.

Ship to right. The ram is short and pointed. The bow has a curving stem post and four projections from the stem. The bow compartment has a side screen which is difficult to see on this fibula, but clearer on Berlin 31013*b*, which is probably by the same artist. There is a row of shields above the gunwale. Above the shields is a line on which warriors stand: I suspect that this is a rail (and not a deck; see Summary, p. 80) in line with the rail of the stern compartment set up to take the shields, which would afford protection for the rowers. The stern post is straight and has a sheer with a slight offset at the end. There are apparently short projections from the bottom of the hull aft of the steering oar. The mast has a single forestay and a square crow's nest from which emerges a head on a long neck.

75

Arch. 9. Fibula of bronze. Berlin 31013 *b*, from Thisbe. Hampe, *Sagenbilder*, no. 62 *b*, pl. 5; Moll, B, I, 44.

Ship to right on either side of the fibula.

(*a*) Horse in ship. Ram, bow screens, projection at stem, are as on the previous fibula. The stem post curves forward, then upwards and aft with two divisions at the end, the lower of which widens at the end. Stern compartment has a rail; the steering oar is set just forward of it; the stern post is in two divisions, which have a sheer.

(*b*) Warriors in ship. The bow has disappeared. A single shield remains above the gunwale; there may have been a row of them, as in 31013 *a*, and perhaps also a ground-line for the warriors with their long spears. There is a poop rail in the stern compartment with steering oar just forward. The stern post has a box-like addition at the top.

Arch. 10. Fibula of bronze. London 3204. Hampe, *Sagenbilder*, no. 100.

Ship to right. The ram is longer than on the previous two fibulae. The hull and fore-part of bow compartment are 'chased'. The after section of the bow compartment is divided roughly into squares and is probably meant to indicate a less solid part of the side screen. There are four triangular projections at the stem. The stem post curves forward, then upward; I think I can make out a thickening at its end. The stern compartment has poop rails and a steering oar forward; there are projections from the stern; the stern post is straight, has a sheer, and grows thicker towards the end. The high mast, with V top, has on the after side a crow's nest; on the forward side, a forestay.

Arch. 11. Fibula of bronze. Oxford 1893. 266. Hampe, *Sagenbilder*, no. 110.

Ship to right. The ram is close to those on the Berlin fibulae. Stem post curves slightly forward, then aft, and slightly upwards with the characteristic box-like protrusion at the end. The bow compartment has rails; the after edge of the solid section of the bow inclines down to the gunwale. A mast-rest remains, but nothing of the mast. The stern has poop rails, and a steering oar with central rib. The stern post has a pronounced sheer and has the characteristic protrusion at the top. There are projections from the stern. Some of the lines of the design are carefully doubled.

Arch. 12. Fibula of bronze. Thebes, from Chaeronea. Hampe, *Sagenbilder*, no. 140, pl. 6.

Ship to right. The pointed ram resembles that on the Berlin fibulae. There are rails in the bow compartment aft of the solid section. The stem post has the characteristic protrusion at the top. There are projections at the stem. A large mast-rest is set just forward of midship; mast and forestay are visible. The stern compartment has poop rails. The steering oar with the central rib is set farther forward than usual. The stern post has a pronounced sheer with the characteristic offset at the top, but it is also extended in line aft. There are projections from the stern.

Arch. 13. Fibula of bronze. Berlin 8396, from Thisbe. Hampe, *Sagenbilder*, no. 60, fig. 1; Moll, B, I, 42.

Ship with horse to left. The ram is beak-shaped; there are three large projections from the stem. The stem post has the offset characteristic of the group. The bow compartment has secondary rails aft. The hull is intersected by vertical lines. The stern compartment has rail and steering oar with central rib and right-angle projection at the top of the loom; the stern post has the characteristic offset at the top. Some of the lines of the design are carefully doubled.

This ship undoubtedly has characteristics of the Berlin 31013*a–b* ships—e.g. stern and stem posts, and bow and stern compartments, but the shape of the ram and the verticals down the hull are rather characteristic of the Ship Master (cf. the next group). However, Hampe attributes it to the same workshop as the Berlin 31013*a–b* fibulae.

(2) *Group of the Ship Master*

Hampe attributed the following two fibulae (Arch. 14–15) to his Ship Master; grave evidence definitely places him in the seventh century. Arch. 16–18 seem to show his influence, but lack his precision.

Arch. 14. Fibula of bronze. Athens NM 8199, from Thebes. Hampe, *Sagenbilder*, no. 13, pl. 11.

Ship to left. The ram is beak-shaped, and there are three projections from the stem. The stem post resembles those in the previous group, except that the top is diamond-shaped rather than square. The bow compartment is small. The hull is deeper, lacks the upward taper towards the stern, and is intersected by verticals. The stern compartment has a rail and a steering oar; three projections cut the stern. The stern post has the diamond-shaped top. The mast shows bisected V top and forestay and backstay.

Arch. 15. Fibula of bronze. London 121, from Thebes. Hampe, *Sagenbilder*, no. 93, pl. 11.

Ship to right almost identical with Athens 8199. Here the hull is 'chased', as well as intersected by verticals, and there is no rail in the stern compartment.

Arch. 16. Plate 8*d* (photo: National Museum, Copenhagen). Fibula of bronze. Copenhagen 4803. Hampe, *Sagenbilder*, no. 83.

Ship to right. The ram is pointed; the bow compartment is smaller and the hull, intersected by verticals, deeper as on the Ship Master's fibulae. There is no rail in the stern compartment; the steering oar is fitted with a tiller. The stern and stem posts are similar to those of the Ship Master, but the tops are not so carefully worked into a diamond shape. The mast shows mast-rest, a bisected V top, and forestay and backstay.

Arch. 17. Fibula of bronze. Oxford 1808. 624. Hampe, *Sagenbilder*, no. 108.

Ship to right. The ram is indefinite. In the bow compartment the top of the side screen is slanting instead of horizontal and mounts a very high stem post with a fin-like projection at the top. Two large extensions project from the stem. The hull is comparatively shallow and decorated with a lozenge chain. The stern post is very much more solid than usual and has a fin-like projection at the top. The steering oar, out of proportion and out of place, reaches as high as the top of the stern. Mast has a mast-rest, a bisected V top, and forestay and backstay.

Arch. 18. Fibula of bronze. Oxford G. 376. Hampe, *Sagenbilder*, no. 120.

Ship to right. A long ram protrudes from a comparatively low bow compartment; the stem post curves aft and is smaller than in the preceding example, but has the usual projection at the top. In the stern compartment there appear to be no rails, and it is now difficult to distinguish the stern post from the lower part of the backstay. Mast shows bisected V top, and forestay and backstay.

Arch. 19. Fibula of gold. London, BM (from Elgin Collection). Hampe, *Sagenbilder*, no. 88, 3, pl. 7; Kirk, fig. 8; Matz, pl. 38*b*; *JHS, Archaeological Reports* 1962–3, 53, fig. 3.

A careful engraving of a ship to left on a smaller scale. The ram is long; stem post curves forward and upward, and widens at the end. Aft of the bows is a post to which is attached the forestay. Mast has V top and rest; the backstay is attached to the rails in the stern compartment. Three planks project from the stern. The stern post is extremely high and has a box-like protrusion at the top.

This fibula has been dated to the eighth century B.C., but the ship has the style of the main body of fibula ships. The stern post with the box-like top, the stem post with the widening top, and the mast-rest are features which do not occur in Geometric, but are common on the fibulae. Its classification here is, however, tentative.

(3) *The Swan Master*

Hampe attributes the following two fibulae to the Swan Master. The ship in Athens 11765 is not far removed from the work of his Ship Master. Berlin 8145, 5 is not available for study.

Arch. 20. Plate 8*e* (photo: German Archaeological Institute, Athens). Fibula of bronze. Athens NM 11765. Hampe, *Sagenbilder*, no. 28, pl. 14; Boardman, *Greek Art*, fig. 19.

Ship to right. The ram is narrow but beak-shaped; three planks project from the stem. The stem post begins from the after side of the bow screen; it is widened at the top. The 'chased' hull is deeper than in the preceding groups, and the gunwale is defined by a lozenge chain. The stern compartment has a rail or side screen and a steering oar with a tiller. There are projections from the stern. The stern post is straight and inclines forward with a box-like projection at the top.

Arch. 21. Fibula of bronze. Berlin 8145, 5. Hampe, *Sagenbilder*, no. 55.

Ship. Attributed by Hampe to the same hand as the preceding, but it is not available for study at the moment.

(4) *Unclassified Fibulae*

Arch. 22. Fibula of bronze. Heidelberg. Hampe, *Sagenbilder*, no. 73.

Ship to left. The design on this fibula is very poorly preserved and it is impossible to make out the stern and stem posts. The ram is long and thin. The stem, in addition to the usual concave curve, has a straight line set in front of it (cf. the Rhodian plate fragment, London A. 720, Arch. 27). The hull and bow compartment are 'chased'. There is a rail with supports above the gunwale. Rails, too, can be made out in the stern compartment at a higher level than that amidships.

Arch. 23. Fibula of bronze, Louvre. Hampe, *Sagenbilder*, no. 133; Perrot and Chipiez, *Histoire*, fig. 129.

Ship to left. The pointed ram is short. The bow compartment has a pronounced sheer. There are heads and shoulders of six men above the gunwale. The stern post has an unusual backward curve. The mast is fitted with a bisected V top and a forestay and backstay.

Arch. 24. Fibula of bronze. Athens NM 8003, from Eleutherae. Hampe, *Sagenbilder*, no. 12, pl. 12.

Hull of ship with legs of four men engraved 'through' the hull. No bow or stern remains.

N.B. Two other fibulae with ship representations, Athens 30. 1 and 30. 3, Hampe 4 and 6, are not now available for study.

MISCELLANEOUS

Arch. 25. Engraving on bone. Ithaca. M. Robertson, *BSA* 1948, pl. 46.

Two ships to right. They overlap so that the bow of the left-hand ship is covered; the bow of the other is lost in a break. Hulls are engraved with hatching, as is also the steering oar. The gunwale is marked by a plain band. 'Subject and technique recall certain Late and Subgeometric Boeotian fibulae.' (Martin Robertson.)

Arch. 26. Bronze. Heraklion (from Idaean cave). Maraghiannis, *Antiquités crétoises I*, xlii; Kunze, *Kretische Bronzreliefs*, 42; Casson, *Technique of Early Greek Sculpture*, fig. 18; Moll, B, I, 37; Kirk, p. 116, n. 29.

Ship with five oarsmen in action. A warrior and a woman stand in the stern. The stern post ends in a straight bar which projects forward and a little aft. The ram appears to be short and blunt, and the stem post to be broken. Kirk (loc. cit.) rightly compares the fibula in the Thebes Museum, Arch. 12, and argues for a date later than the eighth century; the advanced technique (see Casson, op. cit. p. 47) would appear to substantiate his theory. The classification with this group is tentative.

SUMMARY

The two-level ship, which had appeared in Late Geometric (Geom. 42 ff.), is represented in the first half of the seventh century (Arch. 1), but the more usual class is the simple single-level long ship, which shows no radical difference from the Geometric examples. However, in this period there are depicted several features which do not occur in Geometric or earlier: the mast-rest (Arch. 11, 12, 17, 18, 19), the forestay and the backstay (Arch. 5, 12, 14, 16, 17, 18, 23), and the crow's nest (Arch. 5, 8, 10); the box-like projections at the top of the stem post and stern post, common on the fibulae, show refinements on the Geometric versions.

The chief problem of this period concerns the horizontal line on which the fighting men stand, e.g. on the Berlin fibula 31013*a* (Arch. 8) and the Aristonothos krater (Arch. 5). The points at issue can be simplified as follows:

1. *either* the warriors stood on an actual platform in the ship.

2. *or* the artist has distorted an actual part of the ship to give them a ground line, i.e. in fact they stood amidships.

3. *or* the line represents no actual part of a ship, but is simply an artificial ground line for the warriors.

1. this would indicate a deck; and gives rise to three possibilities (cf. introduction to Geometric):

(*a*) complete deck; the statement of Thucydides ought to preclude this (cf. pp. 160 ff).

(*b*) side deck; although this would give protection to the rowers, it would provide an unstable platform for the fighting men in anything but a calm sea. Further, the necessary supports are not always represented— a fact which tells strongly against a deck interpretation.

(*c*) central deck; this would connect the bow compartment with the stern compartment and would be raised to their level. It would impede the raising and lowering of the mast, and for this too the supports are lacking.

2. There are three possible distortions which occur to me:

(*a*) rail; very little distortion involved except perhaps in placing the rail higher than it was in fact; the distortion of course would lie in the placing of the fighting men above it, but this was the usual practice in Geometric and not surprising in the very early Orientalizing style.

(*b*) raised gangway amidships; this would not impede the raising and lowering of the mast to the same extent as a central deck, for the gangway need not be higher in fact than the benches and could be supported by them. On this the warriors would stand, but in representations it might be placed higher, so that all the warriors might be seen more clearly.

(*c*) far-side gunwale; if the artist were representing the profile view only, this could not be seen. It is unlikely that the perverse perspective of Geometric prevailed in early Orientalizing; for chariot floors, for example, are now drawn in correct perspective.

3. That the line is simply and solely a ground line and represents no actual part of the ship at all would be completely invalidated if the line were found without warriors or the like above it, but this does not happen, so that this possibility cannot be ignored.

Of these possibilities it seems to me that the rail interpretation is the most likely for the fibula Berlin 31013*a*, Arch. 8; for the Aristonothos krater, Arch. 5, I am tempted to think that the painter had the central gangway in mind, but here too the rail solution, though not so likely as for the fibula, cannot be disregarded.

c. 650–c. 600 B.C.

Arch. 27.* Plate 10*a* (photo: The British Museum). 'Rhodian' plate fragment. London A. 720.

Forepart of a ship to right drawn in outline. A few diagonal lines decorate the forward part of the ram, which has a rectangular outline. The outline of the stem is concave: in front of the concave line is a thick straight line running from the junction of the stem post and the stem to the point where the first diagonal line crosses the snout of the ram; between this straight line and the curved stem are several intersections. The interpretation of this line is perplexing (cf. a similar arrangement on the Heidelberg fibula, Arch. 22). A large eye set obliquely decorates the bow.

Aft of the eye is a thick curved line: if one judges from a similar arrangement in the later sections, the painter is clearly representing the angle or arris where the timbers of the hull begin to converge to the stem. (For the sake of convenience this may be called the cathead position. See Summary, p. 84.)

Topping this thick curve is a horizontal line, representing a wale, running right along the hull. Eighteen oars protrude from this line before the break in the fragment occurs. Overlapping segments, probably representing shields, are set above the

* Arch. 27–9 belong late in this period.

gunwale. That the oars protrude from well below the top of the gunwale indicates that the painter has in mind a ship with ports.

There is a line in the bow compartment just below the human head there which may represent a bow screen. The stem post has a pronounced sheer. Four planks project from the stem.

The general shape of this bow with its inclined stem post resembles the Corinthian (cf. the following section).

Arch. 28. Plate 10 *b* (photo: The British Museum). 'Rhodian' plate. London A. 719. Moll, B, VI *b*, 54.

Ship to left. The outline of the stem is convex.* The hull is solid black except for a reserved strip just below the gunwale. Above the gunwale runs a series of overlapping segments of circles, probably representing shields. Eleven oars protrude from below the gunwale; here again the artist probably had in mind a ship with ports. The bow compartment has a rail or side screen. The stem post has a sheer. The stern compartment has a similar rail or side screen. The stern post curves strongly forward, and ends in at least two divisions. Below the stern appear two steering oars.

Arch. 29. 'Rhodian' stemmed dish. Delos, B. 6013. *Délos* X, no. 67, pl. XIII.

A mere symbol of a ship with two steering oars, seven disproportionately large oars, and a shield superimposed on the central one.

Arch. 30. Plate 10 *c* (photo: The Museum of Fine Arts, Boston). Rhyton of uncertain fabric and date. Boston 99. 515. Fairbanks, *Cat. of Greek and Etruscan Vases in the Mus. of Fine Arts, Boston*, I, pl. 24; Kirk, *AJA* 1951, 339, pl. 34; Chamoux, *La Civilisation grecque*, fig. 29.

Rhyton in the form of a warship. The ram is unusually deep and almost oblong. The eye (with pupil and cornea) is set at the after end of the ram. In the strip of guilloche pattern which defines the upper part of the hull, underneath the centre of the bow screen, can be seen the inward angle of the ship's side towards the stem. The stern compartment has rails and a seated helmsman. The top of the stern serves as a drinking spout. Amidships is the filler; a pot-belly holds the fluid, and three legs support the whole. Kirk rightly rejects the eighth-century date previously given to the rhyton; the guilloche pattern along the hull must preclude a date earlier than Sub-geometric; but his arguments based on the shape of the stern and on the naturalistic eye are questionable. As he himself admits, the shape of the stern may be determined by the 'functional exigencies of the drinking-spout', and a naturalistic eye, though not found in Geometric, did appear in Mycenaean (BA. 7). However, I should be disinclined to place the vase earlier than this group because of the attempt at the representation of the cathead position, which appears now for the first time in painting on the BM Rhodian plate, Arch. 27. Kirk's Boeotian attribution seems very probable, especially in view of the Boeotian predilection for ship representations (cf. the Toronto and BM Geometric bowls, Geom. 42 and 19, both found in Thebes, and the several fibulae with ship representations).

* Cf. that of the Sicyonian metope, Arch. 38, and the Zankle–Messana coin, Arch. 89.

Arch. 31. Plate 10*d* (after *BSA*). Ivory plaque from Temple of Artemis Orthia, Sparta. Athens NM. Dawkins and Droop, *BSA* 1906–7, pl. 4; *Artemis Orthia*, pls 119–20; Koester, pl. 20; Moll, B, I, 47; Matz, fig. 294.

Ship to right. The pointed ram curves slightly upwards and the stem has a concave profile. The gunwale is defined by two lines running from stem to stern. Above is a rail with struts and affixed shields, above three of which are the heads of (?) oarsmen (no oars). The bow compartment has its own rail, higher than the main one, and a screen farther forward. The stem post curves aft. The stern compartment also has a poop rail higher than the main rail. The stern ends in a thick post which curves forward; underneath is the helmsman with his two steering oars; his head is lower than the heads of the two members of the crew facing him (oarsmen are usually lower than the helmsman), and it may be suspected that in fact the shields would have concealed the heads and shoulders of the oarsmen, if that is what they are, and in order to show them the artist has to raise them above the shields and therefore above the helmsman. Two men at the halliards have the greater part of their bodies showing, but there is no reason for supposing, certainly no proof, that these two men are standing on a deck, or at least on anything more than a central platform. Another man has his hands on the forestay as if he had just hauled up the mast, or, if this conflicts with the action of the captain (see below), standing ready to lower the mast. The mast, supported by forestay and backstay, has a ring top from which halliards hang: the sail is brailed to the yard with ropes below; braces are attached to the ends of the sailyard. At the stern the captain seems to be greeting a woman on landing, if the criterion is the direction of his movement (*sic* Beazley); a seaman is fishing from the bow compartment, and on the ram another seaman appears to be relieving himself. On the bow is inscribed, left to right, the word Orthaia, the name of the goddess to whom the relief was dedicated and perhaps the name of the ship as well.

Arch. 32. Gem. New York. Richter, *Catalogue of Greek Gems, Metropolitan Museum*, pl. 3, no. 14; *Handbook of Greek Art*, pl. 125*d*; *AJA* 1942, 489, fig. 1.

Bow of ship to left. The long ram has a rectangular tip. In front of the large circular eye are cut two curved lines in relief; aft of the eye and in the cathead position are three lines in less prominent relief, probably representing the angle where the hull planking curves inwards to the bows. These are topped by two horizontals (wale lines) with probably short vertical struts in between. Above is the gunwale surmounted by a rail, the supports of which are set in pairs. Forward is a strong stem post.

Richter attributes this gem to the second half of the seventh century, but the clamp lines over the ram and the markings in the cathead position (and, if I am correct in seeing struts between the pair of wale lines, the possibility of the ship being rowed by oars through ports) would suggest the second half of the sixth, and she does herself draw a parallel with the Exekian vases. On the other hand, the above features occur for the first time also on Arch. 27, so that it would be rash to deny that this gem could belong to the seventh century; but the sixth seems more likely.

SUMMARY

The adoption of the outline technique in vase-painting, as against the pure silhouette, allows more detail to be inserted in ship representations. For the first time there is depicted the angle on the hull where the hull planking curves towards the stem. At this point too would be set the catheads (*epotides*), but it is not until the period *c.* 550–*c.* 530 B.C. (see below, p. 96) that the markings in this position are such that one can visualize the cathead stanchions as well. Kleitias (Arch. 33) first painted an actual ear in this position, and indeed the term *epotides* suggests that the ear came first and later the *epotides* were set 'upon or over the ears'. The ship on the Rhodian plate, Arch. 27, has a horizontal line topping the curve in this position, a marking which becomes constant after 550 B.C.; for its interpretation see the Summaries on p. 90 and p. 97. Dr G. Buchner has told us of some terracotta models of ships from Ischia with interesting details of stern fittings, found in association with Transitional but mainly Early Corinthian pottery (*c.* 630–620 B.C.). The closest parallel for these sterns is on the right-hand ship of the Aristonothos krater, Arch. 5.

c. 600–*c.* 550 B.C.

VASES AND SCULPTURE

Arch. 33. Plate 11 *a* and *b* (photos: the Sopraintendenza alle Antichità, Florence). Attic black-figure volute-krater, painted by Kleitias. Florence 4209 (the François vase). *FR* pl. 13; Kirk, fig. 10; Koester, pl. 33 (less bow fragment); Moll, B, VI *b*, 75; Beazley, *ABV* 76/1; Devambez, *Greek Painting*, 75; Cook, *Greek Painted Pottery*, pl. 19 *b*; Hirmer and Arias, *History of Greek Vase Painting*, pl. 43 (where see bibliography).

Bow and after half of Theseus' ship to left. This bow conforms more to the shape of a boar's head than those of the preceding section. A mouth line (for an interpretation of this line see the Summary, p. 95) with two vertical strap-like markings above decorates the end of the ram. The eye is defined by a brow. Aft of this, Reichold drew an ear (not to be seen in the photograph) with a line dropping down below set in the position of the angle where the hull planking begins to curve to the stem. Aft of the line a series of indefinite small markings probably represents the boar's ruff. Topping the ear are three incised horizontal lines which represent the wales. A low bow screen has a rail above, which extends forward of the high stem post.

Three incised lines, probably a continuation of those which topped the ear, represent the planks of the gunwale and perhaps of the main wale; there is red paint between the upper two. Two horizontal rails above the gunwale are supported by struts, which extend above the upper rail; the rails are set outside the struts and are lashed to them; the whole balustrade was painted red.

The stern compartment has two rails, the lower one which is just a continuation of the lower main rail and which extends beyond the stern, and an independent one which is a little higher than the upper main rail. The stern rails also have struts, but these do not extend above. The helmsman, in *petasos* and cloak, has the looms of the steering oars in his lap; the port steering oar is fastened by cords (not shown in *FR*) to the lower rail; the blades have a swelling halfway down on each side. The stern ends in swans' heads, which are supported by a timber with a strut.

The rowers who have remained seated are all placed in line with the uprights of the rail, and clearly the benches must have been aligned with these uprights. It is, therefore, unlikely that the uprights also act as tholepins (*sic* Kirk), although the oars, which have lost a good deal of their original white paint, appear to emerge over the hull near them; the oars are rather in a half-shipped position and, with the blades thrown aft, the looms give the appearance of being attached in some cases to these uprights.

The mast is shown lowered towards the stern.

Arch. 34. Plate 11*c* (after Graef). Attic black-figure fragment. Athens, Acropolis 605. Graef, pl. 38, 605; Moll, B, VI*b*, 71; Beazley, *ABV* 78/1.

Stern of a ship to left. The gunwale is defined by two lines, the upper one red, the lower black; they are separated by an incised line, and an incised line tops the red along the hull. Below, a wider band of white; separating this from the lower part of the hull, which is painted black, are two more lines, the black this time above the red, the red again bounded by incised lines; these must represent the main wale. A rail runs above the gunwale supported by uprights which extend above it; another rail above, clear of the supports, is attached to the stern and presumably to a support on the forward side of the stern compartment (cf. the Kleitias ship). On the extreme right of this rail and projecting at an angle above it is part of the supporting strut for the swan's-head stern.

The loom of the starboard steering oar can be seen and most of the port steering oar, which is lashed to the gunwale: at this point, in the white area below the gunwale, is a narrow black band which might indicate a slot or a projection to facilitate this lashing. A parallel for this is the projection at about the same point on the Erechtheum ship lamp (Clas. 20). At the bottom left of the fragment is part of the stroke oar.

Of the cloaked helmsman there remain knees, lap, and an arm, which is extended behind him: across his hand is the hand of another figure. In front of the helmsman was a member of the ship's company; his right hand can be seen in front of the loom of the steering oar, his left (probably part of his left arm in the top left-hand corner of the fragment) holds the kantharos, of which the foot, stem, and part of the bowl survive.

This ship is close to that on the François vase; points of contact are as follows:

1. Upper rail independent of the lower one in the stern compartment.
2. Blade of steering oar.

3. Warm cloak of helmsman.

4. Supporting strut for the swan's-head stern.

5. The lashing of the steering oar, here to the gunwale, on the François vase to the lower rail.

6. Kantharos; a kantharos is placed in front of Peleus in the main frieze of the François vase.

In two other Acropolis fragments, 596 (Graef, pl. 29) and 598 (Graef, pl. 24), depicting dance scenes resembling that on the Theseus frieze of the François vase, Sir John Beazley sees the hand of Kleitias. I think this may well be one of the ships belonging to the scene. This ship has, however, considerably more depth of hull, as is shown by the inclusion of the main wale.

Arch. 35. Plate 11 *d* (photo: Chuzeville). Attic black-figure hydria. Louvre E. 735. De La Coste-Messelière, *Au Musée de Delphes*, pl. 13; Lefebvre des Noëttes, *De la marine*, pl. 22; Beazley, *ABV* 85/2.

Ship to left on the shoulder. The ram is long with a realistic rendering of a boar's head on the bow (but no ear). Seven incised lines run along the hull, placed at regular intervals with their forward ends curved downwards: these give the impression of a clinker-built hull. A *prorates* stands in the bow holding a spear (?), but there are no bow screens or stem post. Amidships the *keleustes* is a link between the *prorates* and the helmsman. Six pairs of oarsmen row from behind five shields set along the gunwale. Nine oars emerge from the hull well below the gunwale; where the oar leaves the hull is a pair of horizontal arcs which seem to indicate watertight sleeves covering the ports: the stroke oar, however, is rowed over the gunwale. The stern ends in two divisions, one of which is shaped to a swan's head, the other forked, and covered by a shield. The helmsman, wearing a *petasos* and encouraging the crew with his right hand, holds in his left the steering oar, which seems to pass through a plank at the stern. Aft of the steering oar protrudes a ladder. The painter does not seem to have much knowledge of ship construction, but he may be trying to characterize a mythical, obsolete ship, such as the *Argo*: the *prorates* would then be Lynceus, the helmsman Tiphys.

Arch. 36. Attic black-figure lid of lekanis, by the 'C' painter. Naples. Beazley, *ABV* 58/119 (where see bibliography); *Development of Attic Black-figure*, pl. 10.

Bow of ship as shield device. Of little importance, but it resembles Corinthian bows—e.g. Boston aryballos (Arch. 39)—as one would expect from this Corinthianizing painter.

Arch. 37. East Greek fragment. London 103/19, from Naukratis (M. Robertson suggested that it was Clazomenian). Moll, B, VI, 151.

Section of hull of ship. Heads of five of the crew showing above gunwale.

Arch. 38. Plate 12 *a*. Metopes from the Sicyonian Monopteros, Delphi. De La Coste-Messelière, *Au Musée de Delphes*, pl. 2 (small fragment) and pl. 11; Koester, pl. 38; Moll, B, II, 81.

Bow of *Argo* to left. The ram has a convex outline. A solid timber rises from the keel and then flattens out towards the tip of the ram (this is probably to strengthen the ram). Six horizontal lines in relief run from the stem along the hull: the lowest, as it extends beyond the stem, must be the line of a timber wale; nos 2 and 3 are probably also wales; it is less likely that they represent cables (*hupozomata*) secured round the ship, for if they had been cables, the artist would surely have differentiated them from the sharp-edged wales of timber; the fourth is also a wale, as it extends beyond the stem; nos 5 and 6 define the gunwale. A seventh line in relief represents a low rail. Above this rail in the bow compartment is a low screen. Over the gunwale are set overlapping shields. Against the low stem post, which has a sheer, rest a number of spears, as on the plaque Arch. 40: a break in the spears occurs where the ring for holding them together and to the stem post might have been. This ship is certainly in the same style as the ships on the Corinthian plaques.

Arch. 39. Plate 12 *b*. (Drawing: Museum of Fine Arts, Boston.) Late Corinthian aryballos, Boston. Payne, *Necrocorinthia*, 1282, pl. 36, 5; Pfuhl 173; Koester, fig. 23; Moll, B, VI *a*, 33.

Ship of Odysseus to right with Sirens. The extremity of the ram is rectangular. The eye is placed higher on the bow than is usual. The ear is elongated into a curved stem post. The gunwale is defined by a single line. Five oars are marked across a plain hull, and each oar is associated with a tholepin above the gunwale. Above the helmeted heads of the five rowers there is a horizontal line, attached to the stem post and supported by two struts, one amidships, which also does duty for a tholepin, and the other in the stern. This represents a rail rather than a deck, as Odysseus, who is tied to the mast, is seen through it. There are no bow screens in the bow. In the stern, apart from the ladder, there is an unusual square object, which seems to be drapery thrown over the rail (as on another Siren vase, Arch. 89). There is a halliard abaft the mast.

CORINTHIAN PLAQUES

Arch. 40. Plate 12 *c* (after *AD*). Corinthian plaque from Penteskouphia. Berlin F. 654 and 781. *AD* II, pl. 29, 4; Moll, B, VI *b*, 62–3; Koester, pl. 32 (bow only).

Bow and stern of ship (perhaps the same) to right. The ram has a vertical forward edge. The outline of the stem is concave and its curve is continued by an incised line indicating that the base of the stem post is in a deeper plane. The stem post has a sheer and is made up of spears held together by rings: in view of the fact that spears were stacked in the bow (and stern) in Homer and in Geometric ships, perhaps these are spears leaning against the stem post and secured by rings, although *three* rings seems an unnecessarily large number simply to secure spears that were likely to be used: but perhaps reference should be made to the Homeric pikes built up of many pieces of wood, tipped with bronze and clamped together with metal hoops (see p. 54). Four lines (certainly representing two separate planks) run from the stem outside the base of the stem post and may represent the rails in the bow compartment: the line of the gunwale is probably defined by the two incised lines below. Behind the stem post are the left arm, shield, and spear of a warrior, who must have been facing the stern.

Outside the ship are the head and outstretched arm of another figure: the attitude of the arm suggests support and guidance; if this is a representation of the *Argo*, as is probable, the figure is unlikely to be Athena, its chief supporter, because the torso would have been submerged in the sea, but the Triton comes to mind who guided the Argonauts through the shallows near Cyrene (p. 149 n. 76). Some Corinthian captain reaching port after a difficult voyage may have dedicated this appropriate plaque. The incised circle behind this figure is not a shield (the painter's shields are outlined with a pair of circles) but a representation of the curvature of the hull at this point.

In the stern fragment four lines (i.e. two timbers) define the gunwale with another wale line below. The helmsman, wearing a *petasos*, holds in his extended left arm the loom of a steering oar (?), and in his right what seems to be a yardarm brace, but there is not sufficient height in the plaque for a mast on this scale. Behind him are the loom of the other steering oar and part of a shield. At the bottom right of the fragment below the keel is probably the blade of the stroke oar.

Arch. 41. Plate 12 *d* (photo: Staatliche Museen Antiken-Abteilung, Berlin). Corinthian plaque from Penteskouphia. Berlin F. 650, with new fragment, see Pernice, loc. cit. *AD* II, pl. 24, 16; Pernice, *JdI* 1897, 27, fig. 16; Moll, B, VI *b*, 66.

Bow of ship to right. The extremity of the ram is rectangular; the two arcs at its top right corner and a few whisker-like lines over the snout are probably decorative. A large eye, with solid elliptical pupil, dominates the bow. Apart from a slight outward flare at the top, the forward edge of the stem post is approximately vertical; the line which forms the after edge curves back and meets the gunwale; a continuation of this line runs down through the hull to indicate the angle made by the converging of the hull planking towards the bows. This arrangement resembles that on the preceding aryballos, where the ear is extended to form the stem post. The two edges of the stem post are intercepted by a cross-line midway between the gunwale and the top of the stem post; on the after side of this line is a small elliptical object in solid paint. The line may represent the ring which occurs in this position on the 654/781 pinax (Arch. 40); as for the protrusion, compare Arch. 42 for a pair of posts in this position.

Pernice's additional fragment without a number gives what at first sight seems to be part of the rail; but it would be too high for the size of the ship and it is more likely to be part of the hull intersected by verticals which extended above the gunwale (cf. plaque, Arch. 44).

Arch. 42. Corinthian plaque (from Penteskouphia). Berlin F. 833. *AD* II, pl. 29, 21; Moll, B, VI *b*, 65.

Bow of ship to right. Two short mouth lines are intersected by a pair of diagonal lines running over the snout. Below the circular eye is a line roughly horizontal, running from the snout to two lines, the forward one vertical, the after curved. The presence of these two lines in the cathead position might suggest an attempt at the representation of the supports for the catheads (*epotides*), but the drawing is too rough for a firm conclusion (cf. the following section). Abaft the stem post, which has a sheer, are two posts or struts, set together, sloping slightly aft; some lines, which run around them, may perhaps be life-lines (cf. a similar fixture on the preceding plaque).

Arch. 43. Corinthian plaque from Penteskouphia. Berlin F. 835. *AD* II, pl. 23, 8*b*.

Bow of ship to left. Two vertical lines over the tip of the ram probably represent a collar or binding. Between these and the eye are markings which faintly resemble the forepart of a boar and which are probably decorative rather than functional. Running up the ram towards the stem post is a warrior with a shield. Under the bow is a strange pair of legs facing right with no corresponding torso above.

Arch. 44. Corinthian plaque from Penteskouphia. Berlin F. 621. *AD* II, pl. 39, 20; Moll, B, VI*b*, 64.

Ship to left. The hull is intersected by seven verticals. In the stern, the end of which is broken off, are the steering oars. The stem post is low and has a sheer. Amidships is a mast-rest or the stump of a mast.

Arch. 45. Corinthian plaque from Penteskouphia. Louvre. Collignon, *Mon. Grec.* II, 29, fig. 7.

Stern of ship ending in two swans' heads with spears set against the stern.

Arch. 46. Corinthian plaque from Penteskouphia. Berlin, no number. *AD* II, pl. 40, 12.

Hull of ship. A pair of lines runs along the hull; another pair defines the gunwale. On the gunwale are set tholepins and what appear to be rail supports, but these incline to the left.

Arch. 47. Corinthian plaque from Penteskouphia. Berlin F. 647 and 656. *AD* II, pl. 29, 12; Moll, B, VI*b*, 61; Koester, pl. 31.

Stern of ship to left. One incised line defines the bottom of the hull, another, a wale line, runs just over halfway up the hull. A row of four circular ports is set just below the gunwale, from three of which a spade-shaped oar protrudes; the oarsmen seem to be backing water. In the stern, which ends in two divisions, is a helmsman with two steering oars, both on the same side. Against the stern are set spears. The hull is painted red except for an area in the stern.

Arch. 48. Plate 12*e* (photo: Staatliche Museen Antiken-Abteilung, Berlin). Corinthian plaque from Penteskouphia. Berlin F. 646.* Koester, pl. 29, whence Williams, *JHS* 1958, pl. XV*f*.

Section of hull of ship to left. A horizontal line runs just above the water-level. Halfway up the hull runs a pair of wale lines bounding a row of circles: just below the gunwale, another pair of wale lines bounding another series of circles. These circles probably do not represent actual oarports because there are too many of them, as Kirk pointed out, but they need not be altogether decorative; they show that the painter had ports at least in mind and the two rows suggest a two-level ship (cf. Arch. 49). On the gunwale rest struts supporting a superstructure; it seems too substantial for a rail. In one 'room' appears a head; in another, a rough head and shoulders.

Arch. 49. Corinthian plaque from Penteskouphia. Berlin F. 652.

The middle part of an oared ship. The oars emerge from ports.

* I owe this reference to D. von Bothmer.

TWO-LEVEL SHIP

Arch. 50. Plate 12*f* (after *CVA*). Late Corinthian aryballos. Athens 281. Payne, *Necrocorinthia*, 1271; Williams, *Greece and Rome*, vol. 18, no. 54, pl. 88, 4*a*; *CVA* pl. 2, 5, whence Williams, *JHS* 1958, pl. xv (*d*).

Ship to right. The extremity of the ram is not in the picture, but there seems to be a short mouth line. Just above the eye, a roughly drawn horizontal projects beyond the stem and extends aft as far as an oblique line in the position of the angle where the hull planking turns in to the bows. A row of ports runs along the hull with oars protruding; the port farthest forward is painted in outline; the rest may have been filled in when the oars were painted. Above the gunwale sit five rowers (one is obscured by the *keleustes*) with *their* oars over the gunwale. There appear to be bow screens and a very high stem post. In the stern sits the helmsman with his steering oars. The stern ends in what may be a swan's head. The painting is rough and yet it is clear that the painter must have had in mind a two-level ship, although the two sets of oars are not being rowed in time together.

SUMMARY

Attic

Kleitias' ship (Arch. 33) sets the style of the Attic long ships for the rest of the century. There is no earlier strictly black-figure ship with incision, and it is interesting to observe how Kleitias uses this technique to apply additional details; the most important of these are the incised lines running along the top of and just below the gunwale indicating the wales running outside the hull in these positions. However, on the fragmentary ship, Arch. 34, Kleitias is representing a vessel with a much deeper hull. In the silhouette technique this depth could be indicated only by a reserved strip. From now on the stem post is straight and vertical, and becomes strictly a stem post as distinct from the curved horns of the Geometric style and the fibulae. The stern post now frequently ends in two divisions of equal length carved with swans' heads. Kleitias was also the first to indicate on Attic representations the ear and the brow of the boar's-head ram and the only artist to represent a lowered mast.

The Louvre hydria, Arch. 35, is an enigma: the ram takes the form of a boar's head, but the hull bears no relation to any other Greek ship, so much so that one may suspect that the artist was purposely depicting something bizarre in an attempt to characterize, perhaps, the *Argo*. The horizontal lines drawn along the hull with hooks at the forward end suggest the clinker-built vessel, whereas the absence of these lines (to be distinguished from the wales) on all other Greek ships shows that they were carvel-built, an observation which is confirmed by such actual remains of Greco-Roman ships as have survived (cf. Casson, *TAPA* 1963, 30, 'Ancient Shipbuilding', 28–33: 'Greco-Roman shipwrights. . .edge-joined the planks').

Corinthian

The main body of the evidence for Corinthian ships comes from the Penteskouphia plaques in Berlin and Paris. They have been grouped together in the first half of this century with the other Corinthian representations, although the Berlin pinax, 654/781 (Arch. 40), may well belong to the end of the seventh century. On the whole, painting is rough (Berlin 654/781 is exceptional), but there are several definite features which appear to be characteristic of Corinthian representations and which are not found on Attic:

1. The stem post on Corinthian ships generally has a sheer or a forward curve, and on the two most careful representations, the Sicyonian *Argo* relief, Arch. 38, and the Berlin pinax, 654/781, Arch. 40, is made up of spears, held together by rings.

2. The shape of the ram is generally similar to that of contemporary Attic, but the ram is usually shorter, and has a rectangular rather than a pointed extremity, nor has Attic any example of the convex outline to the bow such as appears on the Sicyonian *Argo* relief and Berlin *pinax*, 833, Arch. 42.

3. There is evidence on these Corinthian works for two-level ships. The Athens aryballos, Arch. 50 (and perhaps the pinax, Arch. 48), is a certain example of this system. The Attic examples of two-level ships belong to the end of the century, but the hull of the Kleitias fragment, Arch. 34, is deep enough for a two-level ship.

c. 550–*c*. 530 B.C. (EXEKIAN)

The first four vases are connected with Exekias, the greatest Attic black-figure vase-painter. The Vienna dinos, Arch. 51, I had associated with 'E' Group, the group which, as Sir John Beazley says, 'is, if not more, the soil from which the art of Exekias springs'; Beazley has confirmed this (*ABV* 140/3) and attributes the vase to the painter of the Vatican Mourner, near 'E' Group. The Munich cup, Arch. 52, has Exekias' signature as potter, and it has long been recognized that he also painted it. Exekias was also the potter of Arch. 53, the fragmentary *dinos* in Rome, but it is only recently (*ABV* 146/20) that Beazley has decided that it was also painted by Exekias; in *ABS* he had deferred judgment. The Coghill ships, Arch. 54, now in the Ashmolean Museum, Oxford, are in the same style as, but less precise than, those on the Exekias dinos, Arch. 53; and Sir John Beazley has given me his opinion that the vase belongs to one of the groups near 'E' Group. The ships on Arch. 55 (Louvre F. 62) are by the same painter as those on Arch. 54. The ships on Arch. 56 are sufficiently close to warrant their classification in this Exekian group.

Arch. 51. Plate 14*a* and *b* (photos: Kunsthistorisches Museum, Vienna). Attic black-figure dinos, near Group 'E' (Painter of the Vatican Mourner). Vienna 3619 (Masner 235). Williams, *Greece and Rome* 1949, pl. 87, 3*a*; Beazley, *ABV* 140/3.

Ships moving to left on inside rim. The ram is pointed. A long mouth line, in the right-hand ship of *b*, runs as far as the forward of two pairs of curved lines (the pairs are concave to each other) which bound the eye. These two pairs of lines and the eye they enclose will be called hereafter, in this section, the eye section. In *a* the mouth line runs right through the section: in the left-hand ship of *b* the forward pair of curved lines is omitted and the mouth line runs as far as the eye. For an interpretation of these lines see the Summary of this section.

Aft of the eye section in the right-hand ship of *b* are two curved lines, convex to the bow, joined by a horizontal, which clearly from the shape of the curves represent the supports for the catheads (*epotides*); the catheads were cross-timbers set athwart the line of the ship and projecting on either side of the bows. For the sake of convenience this area has been called the cathead position (see Summary, p. 96). On the left-hand ship of *b* the left-hand curved line is shaped roughly into the form of an ear, and the horizontal is omitted: in *a* there is only a single curved line.

Abaft the cathead position the hull is painted red, either in a continuous band or in patches between the oars. Above the red area and topping the curves in the cathead position are two horizontal lines close together extending from stem to stern: above these another incised line defines the gunwale (in *a* an exceptional intermediate line appears between the oars). These two sets of horizontal lines represent wales of timber outside the hull (see Summary, p. 97).

Above the gunwale is a rail (double in *a*) with supports, behind which are seven or eight oarsmen, their oars over the gunwale at the end of their stroke.

The bow officer (*prorates* or *proreus*) stands in the bow compartment, which is protected by side screens and has a tall, straight stem post. In the stern, at a higher level than the oarsmen, sits the helmsman with one of the steering oars in front of him. The main rail seems to end just short of the steering oar, and another rail of the same height with supports defines the stern compartment (cf. the Kleitias ship). The stern ends in a swan's head. The height of the bow officer and the helmsman above the oarsmen makes it clear that there were platforms in the bow compartment and the stern compartment.

Mast, sail, and eight or nine brailing ropes are depicted. No halliards are shown, but a pair of braces runs diagonally to the forward end of the yard.*

Arch. 52. Plate 13 (photo: Antikensammlungen, Munich). Attic black-figure cup signed by Exekias. Munich 2044. Beazley, *ABV* 146/21, where see bibliography; add Robertson, *Greek Painting*, pl. 71; Arias and Hirmer, *A History of Greek Vase Painting*, pl. XVI; and Devambez, *Greek Painting*, 92.

Inside the cup, Dionysus in ship to left. On the ram, which is of the same shape as those on the preceding, Arch. 51, the mouth line runs right through the eye section (*under* the two pairs of curved lines) as far as the curve in the cathead position. Just below the bow screens a single horizontal wale line runs from the stem to the curve in the cathead position, but abaft the curve the line is doubled and runs right along the hull. The band above this and below the gunwale has received additional colour. Another pair of wale lines runs along the top of the gunwale. The single rail is fitted outside the supports, but the stern compartment has no rail at all. The steering oars are in position; a slot or projection just under the gunwale must facilitate the fastening of the steering oar into position (cf. the Kleitias fragment, Arch. 34, and the Erechtheum lamp, Clas. 20). The ladder is shipped. Two hull planks extend well beyond the stern. The stern ends in a swan's head. The bow compartment has low bow screens and a straight, pointed stem post. On the mast (up which Dionysus' vine climbs) pairs of horizontals are incised at intervals (cf. Arch. 57). The triangular fitting at its top probably represents a truck. From the truck to the sailyard run halliards; the sailyard has single diagonal lines incised along it suggesting cords for attaching the sail to the sailyard. The sail has two braces and seven brailing ropes, and the two braces running diagonally to the forward end of the yard repeat those on the Vienna dinos. At the forward edge of the sail on its leeward side can be seen horizontal buntlines. Two dolphins, painted white, decorate the hull.

Arch. 53. Plate 14*c* and *d* (photos: Sopraintendenza alle Antichità dell'Etruria Meridionale). Attic black-figure dinos by Exekias. Rome, Villa Giulia Museum 50599. Mingazzini 446; Beazley *ABV* 146/20, where see bibliography.

Ships moving to left on inner rim. The ram is more pointed than on the preceding two and slightly shorter. The mouth line runs as far as the after pair of lines of the eye section (previous publications omit the left-hand pair). In the cathead position two curved lines represent the cathead stanchions. Aft of this position the hull is painted red. Topping the stanchions and running from stem to stern is a main wale represented by two horizontal lines, above which is a row of ports (24 on one, 26 on another). Immediately above the ports is a wale line, while another line defines the

* Dr H. A. Cahn possesses a fragment of an Attic bf dinos, which shows part of the sail, the stem post, bow screen and part of the gunwale aft of a ship to left. The bow screen is decorated in squares, as is Arch. 51, and not with the very much more common lozenges. Its drawing is coarser than in this group, but insufficient remains for closer classification.

gunwale: between these two lines in the bow compartment is a zigzag line, but aft on one ship (Pl. 14c) in this position is a chevron or semicircle roughly beneath each rower's head. The heads of these rowers, twenty-one on one ship, nineteen on another, with their oars, twenty-four in number, protruding over the gunwale, are framed in the 'rooms' formed by rail and supports. The very high bow screens in the bow compartment are decorated with a honeycomb pattern: the stem post is straight. The stern compartment has in one case a separate rail, but in others the main rail is continued aft. The helmsman sits at a higher level than the rowers with a steering oar in front of him, on the loom of which are markings probably representing lashings to the rail. Horizontal plankings project at the stern. In no case has any stern-post decoration survived. Mast, brailing ropes, and two forebraces to the forward end of the yard repeat the pattern of Arch. 51. If one judges by the number of oarsmen and oars, the ship is of pentekontor size: the presence of ports below the level of the bank of oars proves that this is a two-level ship.

Arch. 54. Plate 14e (photo: The Ashmolean Museum, Oxford). Attic black-figure dinos. Oxford 1932. 45 (ex Coghill). Millingen, *Vases from the Collection of John Coghill*, pl. 52; Baumeister, *Denkmäler* III, fig. 1662: both these representations include incorrect restorations.

Ships to left on inner rim. The ram is short as on Arch. 53. There is no mouth line. The eye section has a pair of chevrons on either side of the eye. There are two curves in the cathead position identical in shape with those on Arch. 53. A pair of wale lines runs right along the hull, and a single line defines the gunwale. Only on one ship does an incised line represent a rail. Above the gunwale there are at least twenty-five heads of rowers with their oars rowed over the gunwale. The bow compartment has a high bow screen decorated as on Arch. 53 and 55. The stern compartment has no rail: the helmsman sits well above the level of the oarsmen, holding his steering oar. The stern ends in a birdlike head. A mast and sail are depicted with brailing ropes and two braces running diagonally forward.

On Millingen's drawing the flag, flying against the direction of movement, and *two* sails are the figments of someone's imagination.

Arch. 55. Plate 14f (photo: Giraudon). Attic black-figure dinos. Louvre F. 62. *CVA* pl. I, 1–2, pl. II, 1; Moll, B, VI, 154 (left); Giraudon 3774–5, whence Williams, *JHS* 1957, 315, fig. 1; Casson, *The Ancient Mariners*, pl. 5b; Chamoux, *La Civilisation grecque*, 74 (but not from a Villa Giulia cup by Exekias as there stated).

Ships moving to left inside the rim. The shape of the ram is close to those on Arch. 51–3. No mouth line is inserted. The eye section and the two curves in the cathead position are identical with those on Arch. 54. These stanchion curves are topped by a pair of wale lines running the length of the ship. The gunwale is defined by a single wale line. Rails are incised above the gunwale, but no supports are indicated. Under the rail appear the heads of about twenty-two oarsmen rowing over the gunwale. The bow compartment has high bow screens, decorated as in Arch. 53–4, and a straight stem post. The stern compartment has no rail: the helmsman is again set well above the rowers and his steering oar has short diagonal markings on the handle indicating its attachment to the gunwale. The stern ends in a swan's head. Mast, sail, eight brailing ropes, and two diagonal braces running towards the forward end of the yard repeat the system of the preceding ships.

Arch. 56. Plate 14*g* (photo: Kohlroser). Attic black-figure dinos. Munich 781 (Jahn). Gerhard, *AV* 254.

Ships to left on inner rim. The ships in particular and the figures on the horizontal rim show a distinct resemblance to those on Louvre F. 62 which warrants placing this vase in this group. Apart from a small curve behind the eye there is no indication of the 'eye section'. On one ship there are two curves in the cathead position. A double wale line runs along the hull, a single one along the gunwale: on another ship the numbers are reversed, two for the gunwale, one for the main wale. There is no rail, but the heads of the rowers can be seen above the gunwale: their oars are rowed over the gunwale: in one ship the blades are in the water, in another at the end of the stroke out of the water. The bow compartment has the usual bow screens and a thickset stem post. The stern compartment shows helmsman and steering oar; the stern ends in the form of a bird's head. There are mast, sail, and brailing ropes, and the usual two braces running diagonally forward.

SUMMARY

Interpretation of constant features

1. *Lines on the ram.* There are several lines on the ram which recur and seem to have some special significance.

(*a*) Eye section: two pairs of chevrons concave to each other on either side of the eye. Occasionally the forward pair is omitted.

(*b*) Long mouth line (as distinct from a short porcine grin) running from the tip of the ram and extending, in the Munich cup, Arch. 52, through the eye section to the cathead position, on the Exekian dinos, Arch. 53, and on at least one of the Vienna ships, Arch. 51, as far as the after pair of lines of the eye section. Outside this Exekian section this long mouth line has been observed only on the Kleitias ship.

The question is whether these lines are simply decorative or whether they in fact represent some definite feature of the ram. The ram appears to have had a metal sheath (see Aeschylus, *Persians*, 408–9 on p. 157 below), so that the markings one would expect would be, first, the line where the metal ended and the timber began, and secondly, the clamps of the metal sheath onto the wooden core.

(*a*) The after pair of lines in the eye section is constant in this group—with the possible exception of the Munich dinos, Arch. 56—and seems to be the likeliest feature to represent the edge of the metal and the beginning of the timber. Along this edge, too, one might expect rivetings—possibly an extra band of metal to clamp the rivets in more securely; hence the double rather than a single line.

The forward pair of chevrons or curves may represent another clamp, but the fact that it is not constant may suggest that it could be decorative to balance the after pair.

(*b*) The horizontal mouth line could be put down as decorative if it had been a small one, but in this group it is particularly long. It is very unlikely that the metal for the ram would be cast in one piece; an easy and secure method would be to make two separate halves, an upper and a lower; the mouth line would then be the division between the two (see p. 280).

2. *The markings in the cathead position.* The catheads (*epotides*) were cross-beams set athwart the line of the ship and projecting on either side of the bows. In the cathead position on the representations there are usually incised two curved lines set apart and topped by a pair of horizontal lines (represent-ing wales of timber) running from stem to stern. The curved lines probably represent the curved stanchions supporting the projecting beams of the cat-heads. The correct perspective in the rendering of these stanchions, not un-naturally in this archaic period, gave trouble to the vase-painter, as can be seen from the varied ways employed in rendering these curved supports:

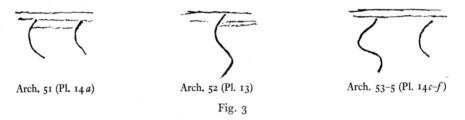

Arch. 51 (Pl. 14 *a*)   Arch. 52 (Pl. 13)   Arch. 53–5 (Pl. 14 *c–f*)

Fig. 3

Sometimes only a single curve is inserted, and then it is impossible to decide whether the artist is thinking of these supports or simply of the angle where the ship's timbers converge to the bow, but the chief advance made by the artists of the Exekias group in the representation of the ship's hull clearly lay in the area of this cathead position, nor did the painters of the following decades improve on the Exekian version.

An excellent illustration of catheads may be seen on the Apulian rhyton in Paris, Clas. 15, and just as on the ships of this group two horizontal lines run unbroken from the stem along the top of the cathead position, so on the rhyton, in the round, the two horizontal lines continue around the catheads.

3. *Lines along the hull.* It has already been suggested in Arch. 51 that the incised lines running along the gunwale and lower down the hull represent timber wales running outside the main planking; in some cases a pair of incised lines is found running along the top of the cathead position, but a single one along the gunwale; the implication is that in such a case the wale running along the hull is more substantial than the gunwale.

Characteristics of this section apart from the above markings

1. *Ram.* The ram is neat and pointed with a definite upward slope towards the stem.

2. *Rails.* The balustrade usually consists of a single horizontal rail with supports, but occasionally a double rail occurs. The stern compartment has no additional rail, or no rail at all, but the bow screens are high and solid.

3. *Rigging.* The mast is usually depicted with a sail, brailing ropes, and two braces running diagonally from a point between the mast and the stern to the forward end of the yard. Halliards do not appear. The markings along the sailyard on Arch. 52 make it clear that it consisted of two poles lashed together (cf. also Arch. 57).

4. *Oar-system.* It should be noted that Arch. 53 represents a two-level ship.

c. 530–*c.* 480 B.C.

GROUP CENTRED AROUND THE NIKOSTHENES CUP,
LOUVRE F. 123. *c.* 530–*c.* 510 B.C.

The cup thrown by the potter Nikosthenes, Louvre F. 123, Arch. 57, decorated with four finely painted ships and dated by Bloesch* to *c.* 530 B.C., is the chief vase of this group. The plate fragments from the Acropolis at Athens, Arch. 58, are close in style and probably from the same hand which painted Nikosthenes' cup. The eye cup, Arch. 59, is by a different hand and less precise, but seems to have been painted under the influence of the former. Arch. 60 and 61 are very much rougher works and resemble the Nikosthenes cup only in the pronounced boar-like quality of the ram and in the accent on the ear. Arch. 63 is closer to Arch. 57 in quality, but the

---

* *Formen attischer Schalen,* 10 ff.

development of the stern compartment suggests the next phase. Johansen in *CVA* Fasc. 8, Copenhagen, says that Arch. 64 is near the Swing painter, perhaps by the painter himself: however, it incorporates the characteristics of this group rather than those of the Exekian group above.

Arch. 57. Plate 15 *a* and *b* (photos: Chuzeville). Attic black-figure cup (type A) signed by the potter Nikosthenes. Louvre F. 123. *CVA* pls 95, 7–10, 12 and 96, 1 and 4; Beazley, *ABV* 231/8, where see bibliography: add Moll, B, VI *d*, 159; Koester, pl. 45; Arias and Hirmer, *A History of Greek Vase Painting*, 58; Chamoux, *La Civilisation grecque*, 73; and Casson, *The Ancient Mariners*, pl. 5 *c*.

Two ships on either side of the vase. The outline of the ram has a slight bulge to indicate the brow of the boar. The snout of the ram is squarer than in the Exekian group and painted red; just abaft the painted area is a pair of vertical incised lines (clamps): between these and a painted curved stripe reinforced by incision in front of the eye a short horizontal may represent the division between the upper and lower part of the bronze casing of the ram, while the curved stripe itself may represent a clamp on the edge of the metal. In the cathead position there is a pair of curves concave to the ram with an ear at the top of the lines, and another curve, a little further aft, convex to the ram; the intermediate area is painted red: such curves were noted in this position in the Exekian group and interpreted as the curved stanchions of the catheads. One ship has an incised ruff below the ear. A wale, represented by two incised lines, runs right along the hull above the cathead position, and two lines also define the gunwale; the area between the two wales is painted red, except for a row of semicircular ports, the straight sides of which adjoin the gunwale. The presence of ports, when they are part of the gunwale, does not imply a two-level ship. The main rail continues into the stern compartment, but here there are no supports. The stern ends in a swan's head of an ornate type with a turban-like addition, which has one streamer above and another in front. There are three protruding planks behind the stern. Behind the helmsman and his steering oars the ladder is shipped. In the bow compartment, on one side of the vase, the red bow screens have an eye painted on them; on the other side the screens have no eye, but here a bow officer (*proreus*) stands immediately behind the high stem post. The height of the bow officer above the screen again (cf. Arch. 51) makes it clear that there is a platform in the bow compartment. The ships are in full sail and show mast; yard (with vertical binding at intervals) and halliards; the single sail with horizontal buntlines on the leeward side and brailing ropes, which are double, on the windward side; sheets with circular attachments, painted white, at the lower corners of the sails; and a brace running from the bow to the after end of the yard.

Arch. 58. Attic black-figure plate fragments. Athens, Acropolis 2414 (Graef). Graef, pl. 98, 2414 *a–d*; Beazley, *ABV* 233.

2414 *a*. Stern of ship to left. The gunwale is defined by two lines right at the stern, but farther forward the lower line is doubled. In the body of the ship there are two rails with supports; the top rail continues into the stern compartment, but the lower stops short, nor are there any supports here. Behind the helmsman and his steering oars stands an *epibates* holding a 'streamer' from the stern (cf. Arch. 57 and 2414*d*). The rigging consists of sail, brailing ropes, and a sheet from the white circular attachment at the lower right-hand corner of the sail.

2414*b*. Sail of another ship to left. Part of the mast, yard, halliards and brailing ropes survive. Abaft the mast is the crest of an *epibates*' helmet; forward of the sail, the top of the stem post.

2414*c*. Two *epibatai* on board ship. Between their shields is the attachment for a sheet at the forward corner of the sail: brailing ropes hang behind the right-hand *epibates*.

2414*d*. The sterns of three ships, two moving to right, one to left. The ladders, the swan's-head sterns with the turbans and streamers, and the three extensions of the hull planking beyond the stern find close parallels on Arch. 57. The spear of an *epibates* cuts across the stern of the left-hand ship. At the bottom right-hand corner of the fragment is part of the steering oar of the ship to right, but what the griffin-like head between that and the ladder represents is not clear; perhaps part of a seabird.

Arch. 59. Plate 16*a*. Attic black-figure cup (type A). C. G. Bastis, New York.

Two bows back to back at either handle. There is a slight bulge in the outline of the ram to indicate the brow of the boar. Two pairs of lines are incised over the snout, probably representing clamps and the edge of the metal. Abaft the eye, in the cathead position, are a pair of longer lines and a ruff running up to the ear. A wale runs from the stem along the hull topping the ear. The area between this wale and the gunwale is painted red. The solid-looking balustrade consists of a single rail and supports. The bow compartment has the usual screens and stem post. The mast is shown and part of the yard and a halliard: the double brace running to the forward end of the yard and the horizontal buntlines and brailing ropes can be paralleled on the preceding cups.

Arch. 60. Plate 16*b* (photo: Nicholson Museum, University of Sydney). Attic black-figure cup (type A). Sydney 4703 (ex Cowdray). *Sydney Handbook*[2], 280, fig. 61; Beazley, *ABV* 207.

Foreparts of two ships adjoining back to back with common mast, but separate sails at either handle. A bulge in the outline of the ram indicates the brow. Three vertical lines are incised over the snout; two short lines above and behind the eye. A large ear is set high and two lines come down from it in the cathead position. The area between the main wale topping the ear and the gunwale is painted red. No rail is depicted but the heads of the rowers appear above the gunwale; their oars emerge from the line of the lower wale, so that the painter must have had in mind a ship with ports. The painting of the bow screens with solid red can be paralleled on the Nikosthenes cup (Arch. 57). Mast, halliards, and brailing ropes call for no comment. The sail is decorated with circles in outline.

7-2

Arch. 61. Plate 16*c* (photo: The Hermitage, Leningrad). Attic black-figure column-krater. Leningrad B. 1525.

Ships to left on inner rim. The bulge in the outline of the ram again indicates the brow of the boar. The markings over the snout, the curved line behind the eye, one or two arcs at the left-hand top edge of the large ear, seem rough renderings of the Nikosthenes version, Arch. 57. The gunwale is defined by a pair of lines. Heads of rowers fill the space between gunwale and rail, but there are no supports. Oars are only roughly indicated but they probably emerge over the gunwale. The stern compartment has no independent rail. The head of the helmsman is shown above the level of the oarsmen; one of the steering oars is shown behind him. Two planks project beyond the stern, which ends in a rough swan's head. The bow compartment has bow screens and a short stem post. Mast, sail and brailing ropes are roughly portrayed.

Arch. 62. Attic black-figure cup. New York* (Metropolitan Museum 56. 171. 36: ex Hearst, 9986). C. H. Smith, *Catalogue of the Forman Coll.* 322; *Sotheby Sale Catalogue*, July 1929, pl. 3, 14; von Bothmer, *MMA Bulletin*, March 1957, 172; Beazley, *ABV* 205/14.

Foreparts of two ships moving from the handle. The snout is carefully marked with a short mouth line and clamp-like curves; further larger curves represent the cheek and jaw line up to the ear. The brow above the eye is prominent, as in the other bows of this group. A line above the ear, in the usual position for the main wale, runs to the top of the rail (and not along the hull); a red band defines the area between the gunwale and the main wale. The rail has apparently no supports, but the heads of rowers appear above the gunwale with their oars over it. The bow compartment has stem post and high bow screens, the tops of which are decorated with red paint. There is a mast (but no halliards) and brailing ropes for the sail.

Arch. 63. Plate 16*d* (photo: Chuzeville). Attic black-figure band cup. Louvre F. 145. *CVA* pl. 88, 2, 5; Beazley, *JHS* 1932, 189.

The ram is long with little detail incised upon it apart from the eye. In the cathead position (abaft the eye) there is painted a patch of red with curved sides with an ear attached not to the forward edge, as usual, but to the after side. A single wale line tops the cathead curves, and double lines define the gunwale. The balustrade consists of two rails with uprights, and the heads of oarsmen appear just above the gunwale, over which their oars emerge. The stern ending in three divisions is very high out of the water, and the compartment has its own rail with supports, housing the helmsman and his steering oars. Two planks extend beyond the stern. A very high stem post curves back over the bow screens (cf. Arch. 57). Mast, yard and halliards, sail with horizontal buntlines on the leeward side and brailing ropes on the windward side (here grouped together, five appearing forward, five aft), sheets from circular attachments at the lower corners of the sail, and the single brace, all have points of comparison with the rigging on the ships of this section.

* Dr von Bothmer has kindly informed me that the Metropolitan Museum has also acquired on loan from Mr Mitchell the black-figure white ground cup, Hearst 9890 (*ABV* 236, 7), thrown by Pamphaios, a contemporary of Nikosthenes, which has a sketch of a ship.

Arch. 64. Attic black-figure krater fragment. Copenhagen VIII, 754. *CVA* pl. 322, 3*b*.

Bow of ship on inside rim (part of a file of ships). The tip of the ram is off the fragment: there is an eye and an ear (under the stem post) with ruff lines below. Above the ear is a single wale line; two lines define the gunwale, over which three oars appear belonging to the three oarsmen behind the double rails. The sail has horizontal buntlines and brailing ropes: two braces run to the forward end of the yard.

Summary

The ships of this group diverge particularly from the Exekian in the treatment of the ram. The long mouth line is not found, nor are the chevrons on either side of the eye forming the eye section, but the ram is made the most boar-like of all the groups in the period *c.* 530–*c.* 480 B.C.; a touch of realism is the bulge in the outline of the ram to indicate the brow of the boar and the reintroduction of the ear, which perhaps goes back to Kleitias. The snout becomes more bulbous, and as this has no connection with realism and as the same feature occurs in contemporary groups, it is possible that the shape of the tip of the ram was actually changed at this time. On Arch. 57 and 59 the markings on the ram still suggest a clamp near the snout and the reinforced edge of the metal forward of the eye. The representation of the cathead stanchions shows no advance on the Exekian. On the hull the main wale lacks the emphasis it receives in the Exekian and in the Antimenean examples, for on Arch. 57 and 59 it runs into the gunwale before it reaches the stern and on Arch. 61 it is omitted altogether, but on Arch. 63 (which incorporates other alien elements) it receives the normal attention. Again with the exception of Arch. 63, the stern compartments are given no rail of their own, but the main rail continues through to the stern: the lack of an additional rail in the stern compartment was also a feature of the Exekian ships. The extreme elaboration of the end of the stern on Arch. 57 and 58 cannot be paralleled. The representation of the rigging conforms to the Exekian pattern: noteworthy is, first, the insertion of the horizontal buntlines, a feature which had occurred in the Exekias group only on the large-scale Munich cup, Arch. 52 (another point which the latter has in common with Arch. 57 is the insertion of the lashings on the sailyard), and secondly the representation of the rings for the sheets at the bottom of the sail, a refinement which does not occur outside this group.*

* There may be a suspicion of such a ring on the after corner of the sail on the Munich cup, Arch. 52.

THE ANTIMENES AND LYSIPPIDES PAINTERS.
c. 530–c. 510 B.C.

Sir John Beazley has attributed the Madrid dinos, Arch. 65, to the Antimenes painter, who continued working in the old black-figure technique after the introduction of red-figure in c. 530 B.C.: Arch. 67 and 68 he assigned to his manner and to his circle respectively. Arch. 68, however, has no painting apart from the ships and might be associated with the San Francisco neck amphora, Arch. 78, which Beazley attributed more specifically to the Würzburg 199 Group in the circle of Antimenes, for the bow shield device on that amphora is closest to the Arch. 68 bows.* The Leningrad dinos, Arch. 66, cannot be separated from the Madrid dinos and should be attributed to the Antimenes painter himself. The painting on Arch. 69, Sir John Beazley informs me, is Antimenean, and the ships on it closely resemble those of Arch. 68. The ships of the Boston dinos, Arch. 73, resemble those on Arch. 69 and should belong to this group.

Although Sir John Beazley has attributed Arch. 74 *bis* to the Lysippides painter and has considered that Arch. 74 was 'not far from the Lysippides painter', the ships on both these vases seem to us sufficiently close to those from the Antimenes painter and his circle to warrant inclusion in the same group.

Arch. 65. Plate 17*a* (photo: Museo Arqueológico, Madrid). Attic black-figure dinos by the Antimenes painter. Madrid 10902. *CVA* pls 4–7; Williams, *Greece and Rome* 1949, pl. 87, 3*c*; Beazley, *ABV* 275/133.

Five ships sailing to right on inner rim. The tip of the ram is rounded and heavy, and marked by a short mouth line and two arcs over the snout; the eye is circular. Two pairs of arcs in the cathead position are topped by a wale line running from stem to stern. The gunwale is defined by a pair of lines, and attached to the lower one are semicircular ports, averaging fifteen, with oars protruding; the artist is clearly representing a triakontor. The area between the gunwale and the main wale is painted red on one ship at least. In each 'room' formed by the rail and supports is the head of a rower with the details of the face incised. The stern compartment has a rail of its own, higher and thicker than the main rail, supported by uprights and extending beyond the stern. The helmsman sits well above the level of the oarsmen and has the steering oars in front of him. The stern ends in a swan's head with a high crest. The bow com-

* See *JHS* 1957, 315 ff.

partment has the usual screens and stem post. The mast, halliards, and about eleven brailing ropes are cut short by the rim of the vase.

Arch. 66. Plate 17*b* (photo: The Hermitage, Leningrad). Attic black-figure dinos (with higher neck) by the Antimenes painter. Leningrad 86 (Stephani). Williams, *Greece and Rome* 1949, pl. 87, 3*b*; *JHS* 1957, 315, fig. 2.

These ships on the inner rim are almost identical with the Madrid ships. The differences are as follows:

1. These move to the left instead of to the right.
2. These have no ports, but the oars emerge from *below* the gunwale.
3. The heads of the oarsmen have no detail.

Arch. 67. Plate 17*c* (photo: Chuzeville). Attic black-figure dinos in the manner of the Antimenes painter. Louvre F. 61. *CVA* pl. 2, 2–4; Moll, B, VI, 154 (2) on right side of plate; Beazley, *ABV* 279/50.

These ships are very close to the preceding, but are not so carefully painted. The rams are the same. The forward pair of curved lines in the cathead position extends above the main wale line and cuts it off before it reaches the stem. At the top of these two curved stanchions is an ear, which reaches the gunwale lines. As on the Leningrad vase the oars emerge from below the gunwale. There are no supports for the rail, and the heads of the rowers are left without detail. Stern, bow, and mast are as on the preceding ships.

Arch. 68. Attic black-figure dinos (with deeper neck) in the manner of the Antimenes painter. Rome, Villa Giulia 959. *CVA* pls. 55, 3; 56, 1–3; Beazley, *ABV* 279/51.

Ships to left on inner rim. The shape and markings of the snout are the same as on the preceding. Behind and slightly above the circular eye is an ear. In the cathead position are two pairs of curved stanchions convex to each other. Topping these is a wale line. Two lines define the gunwale. The rail has supports and there is a head of a rower in each 'room' (*c.* 15 in all—another triakontor). Their oars emerge over the gunwale. Bow, stern, mast, halliards and brailing ropes as on the other ships of this group.

Arch. 69. Plate 17*d* (photo: Mrs Zancani). Attic black-figure dinos from the circle of the Antimenes painter. Paestum.* Stoop, *Atti e Mem. Soc. Magna Grecia*, NS VI–VII (1965–6), pls xxi *a–b* and xxiii *a*.

Ships to right on inner rim. The snout of the ram has not been given the prominence which it received on the other ships of this group. The ear is placed forward of the curved stanchions in the cathead position, as on Arch. 68, but the after curve in this position is much further aft than on Arch. 68. Above the cathead position is a main wale, and a pair of lines define the gunwale. The bow compartment, rail and sup-

* I am grateful to Sir John Beazley for drawing my attention to this vase.

ports, heads and oars of the rowers, and rigging, resemble those of Arch. 68, but the rail in the stern compartment and the helmsman do not receive the same prominence and precision, and only on one ship are the rail supports inserted.

Arch. 70. Attic black-figure dinos. Louvre C. 11244.* *CVA* pl. 154, 6.

Four ships to right on inner rim. The general shape of the ram is close to that in this section. There are two pairs of curves, convex to each other, in the cathead position: to the right of the forward pair is an ear set low, as in Arch. 69. A single wale line tops the cathead position and runs from stem to stern; a single line also defines the gunwale. Below the rail, which has no supports inserted, are the heads of the rowers; no blades are given to their oars. The bow compartment is typical of this section; the stern compartment is very close to that on Arch. 68, nor do the mast, halliards, brailing ropes, or sail differ.

Arch. 71. Attic black-figure fragments of a dinos. Louvre C. 11246. *CVA* pl. 155, 4–5.

Fragments of ships moving to right on inner rim. The bow of one ship, the oars and hull of another, have all the characteristics of this section.

Arch. 72. Attic black-figure dinos fragments. Louvre C. 11247. *CVA* pl. 155, 6–7.

File of ships moving to left. No ram, the most distinctive feature, remains, but what has survived, the hull painted red between the gunwale and main wale, neat rowers' heads, rail and stern compartment, warrants placing these fragments close to Arch. 66 of this section. There is, however, one detail here which does not occur elsewhere in this section, the horizontal buntlines on the far side of the sail.

Arch. 73. Attic black-figure dinos. Boston 90.154.

Ships to right on inner rim. The ram is obscured by waves. In the cathead position there is an ear and at least one pair of curves representing a stanchion, as on Arch. 69. There is a single main wale line and a pair of lines defining the gunwale. The thick rail, however, has no supports. Rowers' heads appear above the gunwale; their oars, emerging over it, amount to 25—a pentekontor. The stern compartment has no rail of its own; the stern, ending in a rough swan's head, is high. Bow compartment and mast and rigging reproduce those of this group.

Arch. 74. Plate 17*e* (photo: Staatliche Museen, Berlin). Attic black-figure band cup. Berlin 1800. Neugebauer, *Führer durch das Antiquarium Berlin*, II (Vasen), pl. 31; Beazley, *ABV* 265 (not far from the Lysippides painter); *JHS* 1932, 188–9.

Ships to left on inner rim. The ram has a curved line around the snout. The eye is set well forward. The cathead stanchions are represented by two pairs of curved lines (a single line may be substituted for the after curve) concave to the ram. A single wale line tops the cathead position. The hull below the wale is painted red. Two lines define the gunwale. The rail has supports with a rower's head in each 'room'. Fifteen oars

* Too little remains of the ships on Louvre C. 11245 for classification, but they seem to belong here.

emerge over the gunwale. Sometimes the stern compartment has an additional higher rail, sometimes the main rail runs right into the stern compartment, which has no rail of its own. The stern ends in a swan's head. The helmsman with his steering oar sits well above the level of the rowers. The bow compartment is close to those in this group. The mast, halliards, sail and brailing ropes reproduce those of this group, but the double brace running to the forward end of the sailyard is a feature of the Exekian section.

Arch. 74 *bis*. Attic black-figure cup, type A, by the Lysippides painter. Brussels, Musées Royaux. Beazley, *ARV*[2] 2, n. 1; Münzen und Medaillen A. G. List, November 1964, no. 68 and photo. D. Widmer 3192. We thank Dr Cahn for photographs of this and of Arch. 81 *bis* and 98 *bis*.

Around the inner rim five ships sailing to left. The markings on the ram, the ear and the stanchions in the *epotides* position, and the rigging are very close to those on Arch. 69, but the bow and stern compartments are here larger and the main rail is given supports on all the ships.

The Antimenes painter favoured a ship's bow or stern as a shield device, and the following come from his hand or from his circle.

Arch. 75. Attic black-figure hydria. London B. 316. *CVA* pl. 79, 4; Beazley, *JHS* 1927, 89, fig. 22; Moll, B, VI, 134; Koester, fig. 64; Beazley, *ABV* 268/24.

Ship's bow. Two short horizontal lines represent the mouth line. Two diagonal lines are incised over the snout. In the cathead position two pairs of curves, concave to the bow, represent stanchions. Along the top of these runs the main wale: a pair of incised lines defines the gunwale. The rail has supports which extend above it. The bow compartment has a high stem post.

Arch. 76. Attic black-figure hydria. Norwich Castle Museum. Chittenden and Seltman, *Greek Art*, pl. 14; Beazley, *ABV* 268/23.

Stern of ship. There is a rail above the gunwale and an additional rail in the stern compartment, which extends beyond the stern. The stern ends in a swan's head. Two steering oars.

Arch. 77. Attic black-figure hydria. Spencer-Churchill Collection, Northwick Park. Beazley, *JHS* 1927, 91, fig. 23; *ABV* 267/13.

Another stern close to that on the Norwich hydria.

Arch. 78. Attic black-figure neck amphora. San Francisco, Legion of Honor, 1814. *CVA* pl. 5, 1 *b*, pl. 7, 1 *d*; Beazley, *ABV* 287/3 (Group of Würzburg 199).

Ship's bow. A short horizontal mouth line is cut by two curved lines over the snout. In the cathead position there are two pairs of curves representing stanchions, the forward pair concave, the after convex to the ram as on Arch. 68. Above runs a single wale line, and the gunwale is defined by a pair of lines.

N.B. Two other bow shield devices, but with no markings whatsoever, are not connected with the Antimenes painter:

 (i) Attic black-figure hydria. London B. 343. *CVA* pl. 94, 3.

 (ii) Attic red-figure cup by Oltos. Boston 13.83. Beazley, *ARV* 57/40.

Summary

 The characteristics of the ships in this group are simple. All have a robust ram, usually with a pronounced snout: there is no example of the rendering of an eye section, the characteristic of the Exekian group, but the ear, which occurs on all the ships of the Nikosthenes group, is adopted by certain painters in the Antimenean circle or manner, but not by the Antimenes painter himself. In the cathead position two pairs of curves represent the stanchions. On the hull the main wale and the gunwale are clearly indicated. Arch. 65 has semicircular ports which are set just below the gunwale, and a similar structure must be imagined for Arch. 66 and 67, where the oars emerge from below the gunwale. The stern compartment has a solid rail of its own, higher than the main rail, which may be said to be one of the distinguishing features of this group. The painters do not attempt to show horizontal bunt-lines, nor do the diagonal braces appear.

SHIP REPRESENTATIONS FROM THE LEAGROS GROUP.
c. 510 B.C.

The paintings of this group are connected with the Leagros Group, a group of black-figure vases contemporary with the great trio of red-figure painters, Euphronios, Phintias and Euthymides. A complication arises from the fact that there were two hands working on one vase. The main designs on Arch. 79 and 80 are by one hand, that on Arch. 81 by another, but the ships on all three are by the same hand. I have tried to show in *JHS* 1957, 316 that this painter of the ships was the same one who painted the whole of Arch. 82, the London neck amphora B. 240, where the ship is not a subsidiary rim decoration but part of the main design. The small fragment Arch. 83 may also be classified here. The ships on the fine dinos with stand in Salerno, Arch. 84, are by another painter, but the rest of the painting seems to me to be Leagran.

 Another Leagran ship, but by a different hand, is classified with the two-level ships (Arch. 88).

Arch. 79. Plate 18*a* (photo: The British Museum). Attic red-figure cup (ships in black-figure). London, E. 2. Beazley, *ABV* 390/1 (Group of London E. 2); *ARV* 225/1; Walters, *History of Ancient Pottery* I, pl. 37, 1; Williams, *JHS* 1957, 315, fig. 4.

Ships on inner rim. The snout is slightly retroussé, and includes a short mouth line. Apart from the eye there is usually no further detail until the cathead position, where there are three irregularly curved arcs, which give little impression of stanchions. A single wale line tops these markings and runs from stem to stern. The gunwale is defined by two lines, by three in the stern compartment. The area between the gunwale and the main wale is painted red (in patches between the oars). There is a single rail; the painter does not insert both supports and the heads of the rowers; the dolichocephalic heads do duty for both. The stern compartment has a rail of its own, which is thick, and higher than the main rail, and dips slightly aft. The helmsman wears a hat (three of them wear the *petasos*, the fourth a tall pointed affair) and has a pair of ungainly steering oars in front of him. The stern ends in a rough rendering of a swan's head. The bow compartment has the usual stem post and bow screens; the top of the latter is defined by an incised line. Mast and halliards are depicted and a sail with horizontal buntlines on the leeward side of the sail and brailing ropes on the windward side.

Arch. 80. Attic red-figure cup fragment (ship in black-figure). Amsterdam 2182. Beazley, *ABV* 390/2 (Group of London E. 2); *ARV* 225/2; *CVA* pl. 6, 8–9.

Stern of ship identical with those of Arch. 79.

Arch. 81. Plate 18*b* (photo: Cabinet des Médailles, Paris). Attic black-figure cup. Paris, Cabinet des Médailles 322. Beazley, *ABV* 380/296 (The Antiope Group); *CVA* pls 52, 4–6; 53; Lefebvre des Noëttes, *De la marine*, fig. 35.

Ships sailing to left around the rim from the same hand as the *ships* on the last two vases. The shape of the ram is as on Arch. 79: the markings in the cathead position are also similar, but on one of these ships there are two groups of irregularly curved lines which give a more definite representation of cathead stanchions. This position is topped by the main wale line. The hull between the main wale and the gunwale, as in Arch. 79–80, is deeper than that in other groups. The gunwale is defined by two lines, except in the stern compartment, where there are three. Below the gunwale there are patches of red paint between the oars and a strip along the bow. Heads of rowers appear above the gunwale, over which their oars emerge, but there is no rail. The stern compartment is defined by a thick rail. The port steering oar has markings on the loom which probably represent securing ropes; just aft is the loom of the starboard steering oar. In two cases the helmsman wears a high pointed hat. The stern ends in a rough swan's head. The bow has high bow screens and stem post. Mast, halliards, sail and brailing ropes show nothing noteworthy.

Arch. 81 *bis*. Attic black-figure cup, type A. Haifa, Maritime Museum. Photo: D. Widmer 1839 (Münzen und Medaillen A. G., Basel).

Around the inner rim four pentekontors of similar style to those on Arch. 79–81, perhaps by the same hand and certainly from the same workshop.

Arch. 82. Plate 18*c* (photo: The British Museum). Attic black-figure amphora. London B. 240. *CVA* pl. 58, 4*a*; Moll, B, VI, 152; Williams, *JHS* 1957, 315, fig. 3.

The spirit of Achilles flying to the Islands of the Blessed past Cape Sigeum over the bow of a ship (Walters). The outline of the ram is not to be trusted, as there is a patch of restoration where the eye would have been. Two straight lines (mouth line) and a hooked curve near the snout have survived. Two sets of irregularly curved lines mark the cathead position, the nearest parallel for which can be seen on the previous cups. A single line defines the main wale and two the gunwale, with the area between the two painted red. There is a considerable depth of hull between the two wales. A single rail with thick uprights forms 'rooms' for the heads of the rowers; the heads are of the same shape as on Arch. 79. In the bow compartment there are high bow screens and stem post.

Arch. 83. Attic black-figure cup fragment. Tübingen 1206 (D. 43). Watzinger, *Griechische Vasen in Tübingen*, pl. 14, D. 43.

Section of hull of ship probably moving to left. To the left of the fragment on the lower part of the hull are two parallel incised lines set diagonally, which Watzinger suggests belong to the steering oar, but the steering oar is usually set under the stern and presents an acute angle to the ship, never an obtuse angle as here. These are in fact the markings in the cathead position similar to those of this group. Above them runs the wale, consisting of a single incised line. The gunwale is defined by two lines, and the area between them and the main wale is deep and painted red. Heads of rowers appear at the top of the fragment, and the break occurs before the level of a possible rail. There are definite points of contact with the ships of Arch. 79–82, which justify the inclusion of this fragment in the same group.

Arch. 84. Plate 18*d* (photo: Museo Provinciale, Salerno). Attic black-figure dinos. Salerno, Museo Provinciale. *Idea Fascista*, 31. 3. 1928, p. 2, fig. 5; Marzullo, *Annuario del R. Liceo T. Tasso*, 1935–6 (Salerno, 1937), 69.

Ships to right on inner rim. The shape of the ram varies from the flat Antimenean type to the more retroussé outline of this Leagros group; there are several rough incisions over the snout and larger ones in the cathead position. A single line represents the main wale and a pair of lines the gunwale: the distance between the two again varies from ship to ship. The single rail has no uprights inserted, but the rowers' heads appear above the gunwale; no oars are indicated. The stern compartment has a thick rail higher than, and independent of, the main rail. The helmsman's steering oars have both been placed on the port side. The stern ends in a plain swelling rather than in a swan's head. The bow compartment has the usual screens and stem post. Of the mast and rigging the horizontal buntlines occur on Arch. 79, but not in the Antimenean group.

Summary

From the point of view of ship construction this group provides nothing new. As in the Antimenean Group the stern compartment has a rail of its own higher than the main rail. As this feature does not occur in the group centred round the Nikosthenes cup or earlier, it is possible that the strengthening of the stern compartment was a development of ship construction in Athens at the end of the sixth century.

TWO-LEVEL SHIPS

Arch. 85. Plates 19 and 20*a* (photos: The British Museum). Attic black-figure cup. London B. 436. (Lefebvre des Noëttes, *De la marine*, fig. 33); Morrison, *Mariner's Mirror* 1941, vol. 27, no. 1, pl. 6*a*; Williams, *Greece and Rome* 1949, pl. 88, 4*c*; *JHS* 1958, pl. 14*e*; Casson, *JHS* 1958, pls 5–6; *The Ancient Mariners*, pl. 7.

Merchant vessel and two-level warship on either side of the vase.

A. (Warship with small ship at stern (Pl. 19).) The long ram has five corrugations incised across it as far as the eye. Abaft the ear a curved line with a row of dots on either side represents the ruff of the boar. Aft again there is a hooked marking in the cathead position. Topping the hook runs a pair of incised lines from stem to stern representing the main wale, below which the hull is painted red. Above this wale and below the two lines defining the gunwale is a row of ten ports with oars emerging from them; another bank of oars appears over the gunwale at positions intermediate between the ports. The heads and shoulders of oarsmen can be seen behind the balustrade of two rails and their supports. The stern is obscured by the towed ship and the handle of the vase, but a ladder can be seen to the right of the handle. The bow compartment has the stem post, but an unusual form of bow screen: it would seem to be a sort of tarpaulin (skin?) thrown over the rails in such a way that only a segment of rails at the side is obscured; the rails that are left uncovered have a black background. It is possible that the tarpaulin provided a temporary shelter. There is the usual mast, yard, halliards, sail and brailing ropes.

B. Similar (but without a towed ship, Pl. 20*a*) in points of construction, but at the lower level there are twelve ports with oars: only six oars are shown at the upper level, but some of the crew are busy with the sail. Casson argues that this is a *hemiolia*, which he defines as a two-level ship which has only the forward part of the upper level manned and the after part stripped for rapid adjustment of mast and rigging. The oarsmen here are set much lower than on A, for only their heads appear above the gunwale, but perhaps these are the lower-level oarsmen, who would be obscured in A by the upper level, so that only the lower level is here manned. The men who are busy with the sail seem to be standing on a gangway, which might have joined the bow and stern compartments, but it could be argued that they were standing on the thwarts of the upper level. Part of the stern here appears and includes the helmsman, steering oars and ladder; the planks of the gunwale and main wale are extended beyond the stern.

Arch. 86. Plate 20 *b* (photo: Anderson). Attic black-figure neck amphora. Tarquinia 678. *CVA* pl. 5, 1–3; *JdI* 1912, 76–7; Moll, B, VI *b*, 113–14; Anderson 41014, whence Williams, *Greece and Rome* 1949, pl. 88, 4 *b* and *JHS* 1958, pl. 15 *b*.

On either side Dionysus in a ship with satyrs and maenads.

A. Two-level ship to right. The outline of the ram shows a bulge to indicate the brow of the boar. Four curved lines are incised over its snout, and a few wrinkles above the bulge of the brow. The eye has a hooked line to the right, as on representations of horses. Below the ear is a feathered ruff. Four curved lines run from the top to the bottom of the hull in the cathead position with red paint between them. Running along the hull just above the water-line a pair of horizontal lines marks the line of the lowest wale; above, a row of circular patches of red paint. Immediately above this is another pair of horizontal wale lines with a row of circular ports between them: there were eight ports at this lower level (the one farthest forward has disappeared in a crack) with oars protruding. Above are three lines running along the gunwale; between the top two is set another row of eight circular ports, set not immediately above the lower ports, but in a staggered formation. Only in front of Dionysus is the rail depicted. The stern compartment has a low side screen; the steering oars are held by one of the satyrs; the stern ends in a swan's head. The bow compartment has high bow screens with a small eye near the stem. The stem post is high with a slight curve aft.

B. Single-level ship. The bow and stern are similar to A. Just above the water level a single wale line (or rope) runs along the hull; above, another single wale line. The gunwale is defined by a single line, between which and the wale below are circular patches of red paint. The balustrade consists of two rails with uprights (as in A), but the painter has carelessly painted ports along the lower rail instead of below the gunwale. Eighteen oars protrude from these ports. Three planks extend beyond the stern, and the stern again ends in a swan's head. From the stern there hangs a cloth, which presumably plays some part in the Dionysiac ritual, for it occurs in exactly the same position in the Dionysiac ship-carts (see Arch. 101 ff.).

Arch. 87. Plate 20 *c* (photo: The Ashmolean Museum, Oxford). Attic black-figure cup fragments. Oxford 1929.359. Williams, *JHS* 1958, pl. 15 *a*.

Two bows back to back. On the slender ram there appear two chevrons with their points aft and red paint between them: the eye has an equine hook on the after side. In the cathead position are two curved lines, the rear one of which incorporates the ear. Along the hull a wale line runs into the top of the ear: above this is a red strip, above which is a double wale line; between this and the gunwale lines is a row of ports. There are two rails, and their supports top the rail. The bow compartment has high side screens, only a segment of which is decorated, the remainder being black. The only parallel for this is the BM cup, Arch. 85. The stem post is short. The thick curved line in front of the bow is part of the cup's eye: the tapering curve above the bow is part of the ship's sail, but the white paint which originally covered it is almost completely lost; the vertical line aft is probably a brailing rope, although for this it is unusually thick. There are no oars shown but the structure of the ship is identical with that on Arch. 85, a two-level ship.

Arch. 88. Plate 20*d* (photo: The British Museum). Attic black-figure jug. London B. 508. *ABV* 426/10; Moll, B, VI, 136; Koester, pl. 46; Williams, *JHS* 1958, pl. 14*f*.

Forepart of ship to right. The ram is of the neat, pointed type common in the third quarter of the sixth century (see pp. 91 ff.). A small snout is marked off by a rectangle, smallest side uppermost, with a few horizontal lines inside. The eye has a small brow line above it. In the cathead position there is a single curved line. Topping this curve is a pair of wale lines, between which and the gunwale lines is a row of double arcs representing ports. Both the wales extend beyond the stem. In each 'room' formed by the rail and supports is a rower's head: above these, and larger than life, is a seated figure who may represent the upper level of oarsmen. The bow compartment has a thick stem post and side screens decorated with one large and five small eyes. The mast and rigging are unusually detailed: the yard is attached to the mast by a sling; the sail has brailing ropes which pass over the yard on special fittings; on the leeward side of the sail horizontal buntlines are shown. From the top of the mast run forestay and backstay. Although the identification of the large seated figure waving his hand with the upper level of oarsmen is only a possibility, the structure of the hull again suggests a two-level ship. In *JHS* 1958, 128 it was suggested that the scene may depict Arion being made to walk the plank (but his lyre is missing): it is less likely to represent a ship coming to land, as the mast and sail are still raised, and a ship usually beached stern first; the branches in the background are part of this workshop's stock-in-trade.

Arch. 89. Plate 20*e* (photo: The Ashmolean Museum, Oxford). Tetradrachm of Zankle–Messana. Oxford. Robinson, *NC* 1961, pl. 13, 1; Barron, *Silver Coins of Samos*, pls VII–VIII.

Bow of two-level ship to left. The ram has a blunt rectangular tip, and then the stem curves upward with a convex outline. From the tip of the ram a strengthening timber runs diagonally upwards as far as the lowest wale. There are three wales, each consisting of a pair of relief lines, all extending beyond the stem (this fact precludes their being cables (*hupozomata*)). Between the lowest wales and the centre pair, and between the centre ones and the top ones, there are horizontal struts forming squarish ports, which are set not directly one above the other but in a staggered formation. Curving upwards from the keel is a group of three narrow lines in relief which pass under the strengthening timber for the ram and curve upwards to the base of the stem post, and in fact seem to continue as the forward part of the stem post itself, which has a sheer as well as a curve. At the base of the stem post is a stout horizontal plank extending beyond the stem. The bow compartment has a screen. Behind this is the beginning of the deck—for the whole see Arch. 107. The two levels of ports make it clear that this Samian ship is at least a two-level ship. Robinson dates this coin to *c*. 489.

There is another contemporary representation of an undisputed two-level ship, but of Etruscan manufacture:

Plate 22*b* (photo: The British Museum). Etruscan black-figure hydria. London B. 60. Walters, *Catalogue of the Greek and Etruscan Vases in the British Museum*, vol. II, pl. 1; Koester, fig. 26; Casson, *The Ancient Mariners*, pl. 6*b*. Dohrn, *Die schwarzfigürigen etruskischen Vasen*, 96, dates this vase to *c*. 525– *c*. 485 B.C.

Two-level ship in action to left. The tip of the ram is concealed by the waves. Beneath the high stem post, curved slightly aft, is a large eye. At the level of the eye runs a broad line rendered in white over the black, from which the lower bank of oars protrudes: the upper bank is rowed from the gunwale amidships but from square ports forward, where there is a bow compartment more extended and elaborate than in Attic representations. Above the gunwale extend four uprights which are too large for tholepins and are not associated with the oars of the upper level; presumably they are part of a rail. In the stern compartment is a large steering oar held at the loom by the helmsman, who raises his other arm (not on the drawings) above the oar: this is better interpreted as the helmsman's arm than as the top of the stern post. Above the gunwale, and probably intended to be standing on a central gangway, are three *epibatai* amidships, and two archers in the bows and one in the stern, their position suggesting that there were decks at these points.

Summary

The first two vases of this group, Arch. 85 and 86, show two undisputed examples of two-level ships. The two banks of oars are clear and set in a staggered formation in relation to each other .·.·.·.. In Arch. 85 the lower level of oars is rowed through ports, set between the main wale and the gunwale; the upper level is rowed over the gunwale. In Arch. 86 both levels of oars are rowed through ports, and the hull is built up and strengthened with wales. Arch. 87 and 88 repeat the structure of Arch. 85 with ports, but no oars are represented, although Arch. 88 may have two levels of oarsmen. Arch. 89, the Zankle–Messana coin with a bow of Samian type, shows another definite two-level ship, although no oars are represented. Here too the square ports of each level are staggered in relation to each other. The shape of the ram on this Samian-type ship is quite different from the Attic and closely resembles that on the *Argo* of the Sicyonian monopteros, Arch. 38, and on Corinthian bows; this resemblance between the Samian and the Corinthian may be a result of the work done for the Samians by the Corinthian Ameinocles (see below, p. 159).

A MISCELLANEOUS GROUP. *c.* 520–*c.* 480 B.C.

Apart from Arch. 90 and 94 the ships of this group are of little interest and some of them are downright ugly. Arch. 94 has a carefully drawn mast and rigging and side screens, but the remainder of the ships provide no additional information for a study of the ships of the period. Arch. 101–4 represent Dionysus in a carnival ship-cart; this is of interest rather to the student of Dionysiac festivals.

Arch. 90. Plate 21*a* (photo: The Metropolitan Museum of Art). Attic black-figure column-krater. New York 07. 286. 76. Casson, *The Ancient Mariners*, pl. 5*a*.

Ships to right on inner rim. The ram is partly obscured by waves, but what is visible is undecorated apart from the eye: waves too obscure any possible markings in the cat-head position. Either one or two lines represent the main wale running along the hull; two lines define the gunwale: the area between the two wales is painted red in patches between the oars, which emerge over the gunwale. The single rail has supports with a head of a rower in each 'room'. The helmsman sits well above the level of the oars-men, with both his steering oars on the port side. The stern compartment is defined by a rail which declines about 45 degrees out of the horizontal, and there is as much rail extending outside the stern as there is inside. The stern ends in the shape of a swan's head with two horns. The bow screens are low, but the stem post is high. The mast is represented, but no halliards; a double brace runs diagonally forward from the stern (as in the Exekian group; see p. 91) across the brailing ropes.

Arch. 91. Plate 21*b* (photo: Martin von Wagner Museum, Würzburg). Attic black-figure neck and rim of a dinos now attached to a column-krater. Würzburg 527. Langlotz, *Griechische Vasen in Würzburg*, pl. 135, 527; Moll, B, VI*d*, 158.

Carelessly (?) drawn ships to left in so poor a state of preservation that it is difficult to classify them. The long ram has a bulbous snout and an eye; a pair of curved lines is set in the cathead position. In one ship there is a pair of lines representing the main wale topping the cathead position, on another ship a single line, which then swerves upward to the gunwale. One line defines the gunwale, over which the oars are rowed; patches of red are painted between the oars. The uprights which appear above the gunwale on one ship seem too large for tholepins (nor are tholepins found on Attic black-figure ship representations) and are probably supports for a rail which either was omitted or has perished. Heads of rowers are shown above the gunwale. One ship has a small section of balustrade just forward of the stern compartment. The helmsman raises his hand and seems to have no connection with the steering oars. The stern ends in a debased bird's head. The mast is shown, but no halliards; the sail has doubled horizontal buntlines on the leeward side and brailing ropes on the windward side.

Arch. 92. Plate 21 *c* (photo: Sopraintendenza alle Antichità della Campania, Naples). Attic black-figure column-krater. Naples (Heydemann, *Racc. Cum.* 246). *Mon. Ant.* XXII, pl. 60, 2.

Ships to left on inner rim. Each has a very long ram. The eye is set underneath the stem post with a curved line on either side concave to the ram; the after curve is slightly higher and approximately in the cathead position. The gunwale is defined by a wavy line. Rough diagonal lines cross the hull representing oars; heads of rowers appear above the gunwale, but no rail. The stern compartment seems to have a side screen, steering oars, and a shapeless helmsman, and the stern ends in four divisions, the forward one with bulges which may be means to represent a swan's head. The bow compartment has a long, low bow screen. The stem post is forked, with the after prong very much shorter than the forward. There are mast, yard, sail with brailing ropes and horizontal buntlines, but no halliards.

Arch. 93. Plate 21 *d* (photo: The British Museum). Attic black-figure cup. London B. 679.

Four thoroughly ugly ships to left. The bow has a short sawn-off type of ram. The details of jaw, eye, and ear are rendered both by incision and by heavy splashes of red paint. Two lines define the gunwale; only in one ship are there wale lines along the hull, and these have probably slipped from the gunwale. The rail has supports with a head of a rower in each 'room'; the oars are rowed over the gunwale. The stern compartment has a side screen. The painter has inserted steering oars but no helmsman. The stern ends in a debased swan's head. There are mast, halliards, sail, braces, brailing ropes, and two ropes fastened to the bow, which may be forestays.

Arch. 94. Plate 21 *e* (photo: The British Museum). Attic red-figure stamnos by the Siren painter. London E. 440. Beazley, *ARV* 289/1; *CVA* pl. 20, 1 *a–b*; Pfuhl 479; Lefebvre des Noëttes, *De la marine*, fig. 34.

Ship of Odysseus passing the Sirens; Odysseus is tied to the mast. The ram is short: the markings at the base of the stem suggest a shoe fitting over an inner core, i.e. the metal over the wood. A large eye decorates the bow. A painted line, probably representing the main wale, runs from stem to stern. The lines in the area of the gunwale are not precise, but the whole zone is painted red, except for seven circular ports. There are four oarsmen at the beginning of their stroke. The helmsman, seated high up, holds in his left hand the port steering oar; the starboard steering oar can be seen under the drapery thrown over the stern. The stern compartment has a rail which can be seen under the helmsman's left arm, but there is no rail amidships. The bow has a short stem post; the side screens, at least on the starboard side, extend beyond the mast, and it seems that these screens were adjustable and could be erected to form protection where and when required. The mast has at the top a fitting with rings on either side for the halliards; the sail is brailed up to the yard; the ends of the brailing ropes are bunched together at the stern; there are braces at the ends of the yard.

Arch. 95. Attic black-figure jug (white ground) by the Athena painter. Thebes 46, 83. Beazley, *ABV* 530/70; *Eph. Arch.* 1912, 102, fig. 1 and pl. 6.

Forepart of ship to right with flying Nike. The ram is partially covered by waves and there are only some indistinct incision lines, which may represent ear or eye. In the cathead position are two lines almost vertical, which reach the two lines defining the gunwale. A rail runs above the gunwale, its supports concealed by the looms of the oars. The after side of the bow screen is not straight, but, below the rail, it curves aft into the gunwale. A large eye decorates the side of the screen, above which rises a high stem post.

Arch. 96. Attic black-figure fragment of a jug. Tübingen D. 56. Watzinger, *Griechische Vasen in Tübingen*, pl. 15.

Section of a hull of a ship with a seated figure. A double wale line runs along the hull; a single line runs along the gunwale. Diagonal lines from the gunwale represent oars.

Arch. 97. Attic black-figure dinos fragments. Louvre C. 11248. *CVA* pl. 155, 9–10.

Remains of at least four ships on the inner rim moving to left. Their style bears little resemblance to that of any other section. The ram is long and marked by a vertical near the tip and diagonals further aft. Aft of the eye, at the base of the stem post, is an ear with ruff markings below; this is topped by a line representing the main wale; above are two bands, one painted white the other red, separated by an incised line; the red band defines the gunwale. The heads of nine rowers are depicted, their oars over the gunwale. The supports of the rail are abnormally high. In the bow compartment above the low bow screens appears the head of the bow officer, facing aft. The stern compartment has screens, an unusual feature, and above can be seen the head of the helmsman; his steering oars have an unusually long blade. Mast, halliards, sail and brailing ropes show no peculiarities.

Arch. 98. Attic black-figure column-krater. Louvre C. 11270. *CVA* pl. 173, 1.

Ships moving to left on inner rim in style not unlike those of Arch. 93.

Arch. 98 *bis*. Attic black-figure dinos fragment. Dr H. A. Cahn.

The stern of a ship to left. The helmsman is seated behind a shapeless steering oar. Two planks extend behind the stern, which ends in a roughly painted swan's head. The rail forward of the stern compartment is thicker than usual, and its uprights are pointed at the top. Heads of oarsmen are set in the 'rooms', from each of which an oar protrudes.

Arch. 99. Engraving on a tile from the vicinity of the Temple of Apollo Zoster, Vouliagmene, Attica. Athens. Stavropoulos, *Eph. Arch.* 1938, 22, fig. 25.

Ship to left with anchors down and secured to land by lines. The ram is not discernible: Stavropoulos distinguishes the eye on the bow. The stem post has a sheer. A single wale line runs along the hull, another along the gunwale. Above the gunwale is a rail.

The oars are in a shipped position. The end of the stern is vertical. Stavropoulos dates this to the second half of the sixth century. On Attic ships of this period stem posts are vertical; as Corinthian stem posts have a sheer it is likely that this is a Corinthian ship.

Arch. 100. Terracotta model, probably Corinthian. London. Higgins, *Catalogue of the Terracottas in the Department of Greek and Roman Antiquities*, vol. 1, 901, pl. 130.

Ship with ram, of coarse style, containing five warriors with their shields.

Arch. 100 *bis*. Relief sculpture. Basel, Antikenmuseum. Schefold, *Beschreibung*, 18 ff.

Ship to left in low relief in the style of the ships on the vases of the second half of the sixth century. To these it adds nothing of interest, except that the bow screens are extended farther amidships than is usual.

Arch. 101. Attic black-figure fragment of a skyphos by the Theseus painter. Athens, Acropolis 281. Haspels, *Attic Black-figure Lekythoi*, 250/29; Pickard-Cambridge, *Dithyramb, Tragedy and Comedy*, fig. 7; Graef, pl. 74; Moll, B, VI *b*, 117.

Ship-cart. The ram is lost, but the ear is just on the fragment. The 'hull' is decorated with vertical and horizontal lines, and the gunwale marked by two pairs of incised lines separated by a white zigzag line. An oblong object, covered with hatching, is attached to the stern: this object appears also on the next two ship-carts, and probably has some part in the ceremony depicted. A large eye is painted on the bow screen; the stem post is high.

Arch. 102. Attic black-figure skyphos by the Theseus painter. London B. 79. Haspels, *Attic Black-figure Lekythoi*, 250/30; Pickard-Cambridge, fig. 6.

A similar ship-cart.

Arch. 103. Attic black-figure skyphos. Bologna D.L. 109. *CVA* pl. 43, 2 and 4; Pickard-Cambridge, fig. 4; Moll, B, VI *b*, 116; Haspels, 253/15.

A similar ship-cart.

Arch. 104. Attic black-figure fragment of a skyphos. Tübingen, D. 53. Watzinger, *Griechische Vasen in Tübingen*, pl. 53.

Section of a ship-cart.

Arch. 105. Attic black-figure cup. Berlin 2961. Beazley, *ABV* 639/100; Moll, B, VI *b*, 111.

A very rough painting of Dionysus in a ship or ship-cart.

REPRESENTATIONS ON ARCHAIC COINS AND GEMS

Reference to the coin type of Zankle–Messana has already been made above (see p. 111), but sections of ships occurring on coins of the archaic period are usually on too small a scale to provide any evidence for ship construction in the period. Coins of Phaselis and the following gems may be regarded as exceptional.

Arch. 106. Phaselis Æ. Persic staters and subdivisions struck from the end of the sixth century until suppressed by the Athenians in the middle of the fifth century, then resumed in the fourth. Babelon, *Traité* II, pl. 23, 1–10; *BM Cat. Lycia*, pl. 16; von Aulock, *SNG* 4389–4436.

On the coins of Phaselis the bow of a ship is a constant obverse type. The bows are fairly uniform—in the shape of a boar with a foreleg and realistic eye. Shields are set along the gunwale. Along the hull three wale lines stand out in relief.

The stern on the reverses conforms to the characteristic type on later Phoenician coins and East Greek gems. Above the gunwale is a single rail with supports. On the rail and above each upright are small circles which Babelon thinks are heads, but seem just as likely to be shields.

Arch. 107. Gem (ex Evans Coll.). New York. Richter, *Catalogue of Greek Gems, Metropolitan Museum*, no. 43, pl. VII; Furtwängler, *Antike Gemmen*, pl. 6, 34.

Ship to left. The ram is in the form of a boar's head with tusks and an eye; another eye is depicted on the bow screen, from which rises a curving stem post. One wale line runs along the lower part of the hull; another pair, from which thirteen oars emerge, runs above. The gunwale is solid and above it are the heads and shoulders of five rowers in square ports formed by the struts of a deck on which appear the heads and shields of five hoplites. The helmsman sits with his feet on this deck, well above the level of the oarsmen, with his two large steering oars in front of him. The stern ends in three divisions, i.e. the planking of the deck, the gunwale, and the wales on either side of the oarports (but no oarports are visible).

This ship bears a close resemblance to the Zankle–Messana ships, Arch. 89, and may, in fact, represent a two-level ship.

Arch. 108. Gem. London. H. B. Walters, *Cat. of Engraved Gems and Cameos in the British Museum*, no. 449, pl. 8.

Ship to left. The bow terminates in a ram and has a large eye. In the stern is the *akrostolion* ornament. Twenty-six oars are shown and a helmsman with a large steering oar. Sixteen heads of rowers are indicated along the gunwale. Above, on a colossal scale compared with the oarsmen, are the upper parts of three warriors armed with helmet, shield and spear.

Arch. 109. Gem. London. H. B. Walters, *op. cit.* no. 491, pl. 8.

Ship to left with bow in form of a swan's head and neck, and ram in form of a boar's head projecting below. At the stern, *akrostolion* and two steering oars. Six oars are visible, but the heads of only four rowers. The helmsman is seated to left holding the tiller. On what appears to be an upper deck above the rowers are four armed men standing with their legs apart, each with a circular shield. On the ram stands a fifth holding a spear. The ship is of Corinthian style, bearing a resemblance to the Boston aryballos, Arch. 39.

5

LITERARY AND EPIGRAPHICAL TEXTS

The period between 700 and 480 B.C. is a time of considerable naval activity in the eastern Mediterranean. At its beginning, the Greek cities of the mainland and Asia were sending colonies to the north and north-east, and to the west. Close trading connections with Egypt were being developed. In the sixth century Samian sea power under Polycrates was being challenged by Sparta, Naxian sea power by Persia aided by other eastern Greek cities. Aegina and Athens were disputing the command of their home waters. The conquest of Phoenicia enabled Persia to use Phoenician sea power to subdue all the maritime Greek cities of Asia. At the end of the period came the Persian amphibious expeditions against the Greeks of the mainland, and their defeat. While, as we have seen, the period is rich in ship representations rendered with a new realism on bronze fibulae, and in the black- and later red-figure style of vase-painting, there were no contemporary writers to describe the voyages and expeditions and all the multifarious maritime activity of the age. Written evidence of the practice of seafaring in the period is provided by a few references in the poets and by a precious epigraphical record, the fourth-century text of the decree proposed by Themistocles and enacted by the Council and people of Athens just before the battles of Artemisium and Thermopylae. At the end of the period Pindar was writing odes in Sicily, and Aeschylus tragedies in Athens; but with one notable exception, the *Persians* of Aeschylus, these authors, when they mention ships, are speaking of ships of the heroic age. Furthermore, the passages of these authors to which we shall refer were written after the end of our period, and consequently, together with the later tragedies, form a category of evidence which it is convenient to take separately. If we believed that this category actually provided reliable evidence of seafaring in the heroic age, it would have been proper to include it in the literary evidence for the Homeric period. If however, as seems most likely, it relates rather to the practice of seafaring in the fifth century, it must be included, as we shall rather tentatively include it, among the literary evidence for seafaring in the classical period.

While the period is weak in contemporary records, it is strong in accounts of its seafaring activities written in the succeeding classical age. Herodotus provides a good deal of information about the naval activity before and during the Persian wars, and this information is supported and often confirmed by the briefer but more deliberately analytical treatment of Thucydides. These writers speak frequently of the *trieres*, and what they say must be given careful attention. To the accounts of the two historians must be joined the no less historical account of the battle of Salamis which Aeschylus gives in the *Persians*. A contemporary writer says that he was present at the battle[1]. All these three writers then speak with first-hand or near first-hand knowledge of the ships with which the Persian wars were fought.

1. LITERATURE

The poets of the period 700–480 B.C. were naturally much under the influence of Homer's language; and this influence is shown in the epithets they gave to ships. Archilochus and Solon speak of them as swift[2], Alcaeus as black[3]. Stesichorus speaks of a ship with good *selmata*[4], Alcaeus of a ship with good *zuga*[5]. Archilochus may have mentioned a pentekontor bringing Milesian ambassadors to Paros[6], an occasion demanding the best ship a city could muster. He speaks of a good helmsman[7]. Hipponax, who went into exile at Clazomenae about 542 B.C., provides the earliest literary reference to a *trieres*[8].

Archilochus speaks of the ship's *selmata* as the place where the wine was stored[9], i.e., probably, in the stern under the helmsman's eye. Alcaeus, in a description of a ship, probably the ship of state, in a storm, says 'the bilge water comes over the top of the mast-rest'[10]. It so happens that a box-like mast-rest is clearly visible in ships drawn on bronze fibulae of the period (see ch. 4, Arch. 16, Pl. 8*d*). The engraver of the fibulae seems to have exaggerated the height of the mast-rest. Alcaeus shows that it rose a foot or so above the keel and provided a means of measuring the height of the water in the bilge. Archilochus and Theognis speak, metaphorically, of the steering oar[11], Alcaeus of steering oars[12]. Archilochus uses the Homeric word *histion* for a sail[13], Alcaeus uses *laiphos*[14]. The latter talks of 'putting up side screens in haste' in a storm[15]. He also mentions *ankonnai*, which work loose in a storm[16]. These are possibly strops holding together the pieces of a composite sailyard (cf. Arch. 52, Pl. 13 and Arch. 57, Pl. 15). Later (see below, p. 300) we shall argue that they may be shrouds. Archilochus speaks of a ship's *hopla*, probably brailing ropes[17]. Theognis mentions the 'bonds' of a small ship, apparently the shore lines[18].

Hipponax urges a painter called Mimnes 'not to go on painting a snake on the many-benched side of a *trieres*, so that it seems to be running away from the ram towards the helmsman'[19] (possibly the ship's peculiar device or *semeion* (see pp. 131, 197–8)). The epithet 'many-benched' of a *trieres*' side seems to indicate a feature that was notable. The reference to the ram, as to the *trieres* itself, is the earliest in literature. Hipponax also mentions the waxing of the keel[20]. This operation is more likely to enable the ship to run smoothly on a runway than to make her watertight, as Liddell–Scott–Jones suggest. The poem may in fact have described the launching of a ship.

We find nothing new in these writers about the handling of ships. Archilochus, in what is probably a political allegory, cries to his companions to 'let down', i.e. shake out 'much of the sail, paying out the brailing ropes' and to make the most of a favourable wind[21]. Bailing in a storm is mentioned by Alcaeus[22]. Theognis, using the allegory of ship of state after Alcaeus, says: 'For now we are driven, taking down our white sails at the run, from the Melian sea through the black night. The crew will not bail, and the sea washes over both gunwales[23].' He speaks of beaching a ship which is down at the bow (or stern)[24], and of a ship being swallowed by the waves[25]. Hipponax probably speaks of people pouring libations from the stern of a ship into the sea[26], an act which seems to be depicted in a fragment of Attic black-figure vase-painting (see Arch. 34, Pl. 11*c*).

This age invented the image of the storm-tossed ship of state. If the invention has any significance it is to underline the hazards of the principal activities of contemporary Greece, politics and seafaring.

TEXTS

1. Ion of Chios, fr. 5a (von Blumenthal).
2. Archilochus, *Eleg.* fr. 5A 6–7 (Diehl[3]); cf. also note 13 below.

ἀλλ' ἄγε σὺν κώθωνι θοῆς διὰ σέλματα νηός
φοίτα καὶ κοίλων πώματ' ἄφελκε κάδων.

Solon, *Eleg.* fr. 7 3–4 (Diehl[3])

αὐτὰρ ἐμὲ ξὺν νηὶ θοῆ κλεινῆς ἀπὸ νήσου
ἀσκηθῆ πέμποι Κύπρις ἰοστέφανος.

3. Alcaeus, Z 2 4 (Lobel–Page, *Poetarum Lesbiorum Fragmenta*, 1955)

νᾶϊ φορήμμεθα σὺν μελαίνᾳ
χείμωνι μόχθεντες μεγάλῳ μάλα. (continued in note 10 below)

4. Stesichorus, 192 (Lobel–Page, *Poetae Melici Graeci*, 1962)

οὐδ' ἔβας ἐν νηυσὶν εὐσέλμοις.

5. Alcaeus, B 2 (*a*) 9 (Lobel–Page) εὐσδ[ύγ]ων θρῴσκοντ[ες] ἄκρα νάων. Cf. L 1 3 νᾶα φ[ερ]έσδυγον.

6. Archilochus, *Tetram.* fr. 51 p. 1 A 10 (Diehl[3]) See Diehl's note. πεντηκόντορον
εἰς Πάρον πρέσβεις ἄγουσαν ἀνέρας Μιλησίων
dixisse potest Archilochus.

7. Archilochus, *Iamb.* fr. 44 (Diehl[3]) κυβερνήτης σοφός.

8. Hipponax, *Iamb. Lib. Inc.* fr. 45 (Diehl[3])

Μιμνῆ κατωμόχανε μηκέτι γράψῃς
ὄφιν τριήρευς ἐν πολυζύγῳ τοίχῳ
ἀπ' ἐμβόλου φεύγοντα πρὸς κυβερνήτην·
αὕτη γάρ ἐστι συμφορή τε καὶ κληδών,
νικύρτα καὶ σάβαυνι, τῷ κυβερνήτῃ
ἢν αὐτὸν ὄφις τὠντικνήμιον δάκῃ.

9. See note 2 above.

10. Alcaeus, Z 2 6 (Page, *Sappho and Alcaeus*, 1965, 186–7: note *ad loc.*)

πὲρ μὲν γὰρ ἄντλος ἰστοπέδαν ἔχει,
λαῖφος δὲ πὰν ζάδηλον ἤδη,
καὶ λάκιδες μέγαλαι κὰτ αὖτο,
χόλαισι δ' ἄγκονναι, τὰ δ' ὀή[ϊα...

11. (i) Archilochus, *Tetram.* fr. 51 p. IV B 18 (Diehl[3])

σωφροσύνας οἴακα.

(ii) Theognis, *Eleg.* 1 457–60 (Diehl[3])

οὔτοι σύμφορόν ἐστι γυνὴ νέα ἀνδρὶ γέροντι·
  οὐ γὰρ πηδαλίῳ πείθεται ὡς ἄκατος,
οὐδ' ἄγκυραι ἔχουσιν· ἀπορρήξασα δὲ δεσμὰ
  πολλάκις ἐκ νυκτῶν ἄλλον ἔχει λιμένα.

12. See note 10 above.

13. Archilochus, 56 A (Diehl[3])

[– ∪ – βαθεῖ φέρο]νται νῆες ⟨ἐ⟩μ πόντῳ θοαί
[– ∪ – ⏓ – ∪ π]ολλὸν δ' ἱστίων ὑφώμεθα
[– ∪ – λύσαν]τες ὅπλα νηός, οὐρίην δ' ἔχε
[ἱκμένην σάου θ' ἑταί]ρους, ὄφρα σέο μεμνεώ⟨ι⟩μεθα.

14. See note 10 above.

15. Alcaeus, A 6 7 (Lobel–Page)

φαρξώμεθ' ὡς ὤκιστα [
ἐς δ' ἔχυρον λιμένα δρό[μωμεν·

16. See note 10 above.
17. See note 13 above.
18. See note 11 (ii) above.
19. See note 8 above.
20. Hipponax, *Iamb. Lib. Inc.* fr. 46 (Diehl[3])

    ἔπειτα μάλθῃ τὴν τρόπιν παραχρίσας.
21. See note 13 above.
22. Alcaeus, A 6 3 (Lobel–Page) ἄντλην; cf. v 1 12 ἀντλο[ῦ]ντες.
23. Theognis, *Eleg.* 1 671–4 (Diehl[3])

    οὕνεκα νῦν φερόμεσθα καθ᾽ ἱστία λευκὰ βαλόντες
    Μηλίου ἐκ πόντου νύκτα διὰ δνοφερήν·
    ἀντλεῖν δ᾽ οὐκ ἐθέλουσιν· ὑπερβάλλει δὲ θάλασσα
    ἀμφοτέρων τοίχων. . .
24. Theognis, *Eleg.* 1 855–6 (Diehl[3])

    πολλάκι δὴ πόλις ἥδε δι᾽ ἡγεμόνων κακότητα
    ὥσπερ κεκλιμένη ναῦς παρὰ γῆν ἔδραμεν.

Liddell–Scott–Jones translates κεκλιμένη 'wandering from her course'.
25. Theognis, *Eleg.* 1 680 (Diehl[3])

    δειμαίνω, μή πως ναῦν κατὰ κῦμα πίῃ.
26. Hipponax, *Iamb. Lib. Inc.* fr. 65 B (Diehl[3])

    πρύμνης ἀπ᾽ ἄκρας ἐς θάλασσαν σπένδοντες.

Maas σπένδοντες; MSS. Diehl σπεύδοντες.

2. THE DECREE OF THEMISTOCLES

Dr M. H. Jameson first published in 1960* an inscription on a stele of
Pentelic marble, found in Troizen and now in the Epigraphical Museum at
Athens, which purports to record an Athenian decree proposed by Themistocles setting out the preparations for meeting the Persian invasion of
480 B.C. The inscription is republished in the *Supplementum Epigraphicum
Graecum* of 1962 with some new readings[1] and a bibliography of published
discussions of the new discovery. Although its subject matter belongs to the
year 480, the forms of the letters clearly assign the inscription to a much later
date. Jameson thinks that it belongs to the years 330–322 B.C. Lewis and
Daux prefer 280 and 250 respectively. Jameson showed that a text of the
decree was certainly available not long before 346, since Demosthenes refers
to Aeschines' reading of it to the assembly in a speech of that date[2]. The
actual date of the cutting of the stone is therefore of no great importance.

* *Hesperia* XXIX, 198–223.

Lewis in a careful examination of the language of the decree* concludes: 'There are arguments which lead one to suspect an editor. I see no reason to suspect forgery. There are too many traces of official and archaic language.' What we appear to have in fact is a literary version of the original decree.† As such it provides some valuable information about the Athenian fleet, which can be listed as follows:

   (i)   the crews of the ships were to be made up of Athenians and resident aliens of military age;

   (ii)   the Athenian ships numbered two hundred;

   (iii)   the generals appointed the trierarchs;

   (iv)   the qualifications of trierarchs were the possession of land and a house at Athens, the possession of children born in wedlock, and age of less than fifty years;

   (v)   the generals also appointed ten *epibatai* to each ship, aged between twenty and thirty years, and four archers;

   (vi)   the generals also assigned the petty officers, *huperesia* (see below), to each ship;

   (vii)   the generals were to post the names of the crews on the notice-boards, Athenians from the registers of the demes, aliens from the lists in the possession of the polemarch;

   (viii)   the posting should be by companies and the names of the *trieres* and of the trierarch and of the petty officers should head the list of each company so that each company should know on which *trieres* to embark;

   (ix)   before the men went aboard, the Council and the generals should offer sacrifices to Zeus, Athena, Nike and Poseidon;

   (x)   half the fleet (i.e. one hundred ships) were to make a sortie to the temple of Artemis in Euboea, the other half were to patrol Salamis and Attica.

The matter of the decree fits the decisive moment, two or three days before the Persian fleet's arrival at Aphetae and the Persian army's arrival before Thermopylae, when the manning of the fleet was ordered.‡ As Herodotus records[3], 'They determined at a council, which was held after they had heard the oracle, to take the god's advice and meet the invader at sea with their

* *CQ* NS XI I (1961), 61–6.

† A. R. Burn (*Persia and the Greeks*, London, 1962, 364–77) believes that the literary version, possibly but not certainly based on an original preserved in the archives at Athens, was discovered by Aeschines when he was Secretary of the Council in 349–347, and edited by him to a greater or lesser degree.   ‡ See Map 1.

whole man-power (*pandemei*), and with any other Greeks who were willing to join them.' The story in Plutarch's *Life of Cimon*[4] of the young knights dedicating their bridles in the temple of Athena on the Acropolis and going on shipboard as marines symbolizes this total commitment to the sea. Its logical consequence was, as the decree shows, the evacuation of Attica, the women and children going to the safety of Troizen and the old men and slaves to Salamis, on which the fleet was to be based, where they would be useful as auxiliaries. The recall of the exiles to Salamis might also have been decided at the same council. Burn observes that the inscription seems to assemble together resolutions which must have been taken at different times. He regards, for example, the evacuation as the outcome of the defeat at Thermopylae. But the decision to commit her man-power to the ships must have been taken by Athens before Artemisium. A raid on Attica by a detachment of the Persian fleet was never an impossibility while the main Persian forces were still engaged north of Euboea. In fact a squadron of 200 ships appears to have been detached from the main fleet at Aphetae and might have carried out such a raid if it had not been destroyed by a storm. The original retention of half the Athenian fleet in Attic waters 'to guard the land', as the decree says, seems to have been intended as a counter to such a move. Certainly, after the destruction of the Persian task force the whole Athenian fleet was reunited at Artemisium. Herodotus says that the object of the task force was to seize the Euripus Strait behind the forward Greek fleet. It could have done both[5]. If the evacuation measures taken in the decree were in fact taken after the defeat at Thermopylae when the occupation of Attica was certain, it seems incredibly callous deliberately to sacrifice the treasurers and priestesses by instructing them to guard the property of the gods on the Acropolis. The order seems more understandable if the arrangements were made before the defeat.

Two further considerations which Burn* regards as 'the most stubborn obstacles to our believing that the inscription reproduces essentially the words of Themistocles' do not seem to present any great difficulty. The first is 'this last-minute deliberately fortuitous assembly of ships' companies which are to meet for the first time at the point of embarkation'. Examination of the text of the decree shows that it is only the allocation of ships which is done by lot. There is nothing to say that the trierarch, his petty officers and

* *Op. cit.* 368.

ship's company had not trained together. The posting on the notice-boards is done specifically so that 'men may know in which *ship* each company is to embark', not so that the trierarchs may know which petty officers or ship's company they have and *vice versa*. The second consideration which worries Burn is that the number of *epibatai* is only ten. He has not observed that the use of thirty or more *epibatai* by Ionian ships is probably to be linked with their development of the overall deck. The Athenian ships, not being decked from stem to stern, as Thucydides specifically tells us (see below, p. 160), could only employ a few *epibatai*. In fact, even when they had an overall deck, the Athenians did not increase the number above ten.

TEXTS

1. (*Supplementum Epigraphicum Graecum* 18 (1962), no. 153, pp. 56 and 245.) The new readings are incorporated.

Ἔδοξ[εν] τῆι βουλῆι καὶ τῶι δήμωι· | Θεμισ[τοκλ]ῆς Νεοκλέους Φρεάρριος εἶπεν· | τὴ[μ] μὲν πό[λιν παρακ]ατ[αθέ]σθαι τῆι Ἀθηνᾶι τῆι Ἀθηνῶ[μ [μεδεο]ύ[σηι] κ[αὶ τοῖς ἄλλ]οις θεοῖς ἅ[π]ασιν φυλαττει|5 ν κα[ὶ] ἀμ[ύνειν τὸμ βάρβ]αρ[ο]ν ὑπὲρ τῆς χώρας· Ἀθηναίου|[ς δὲ α]ὐτ[οὺ]ς καὶ τοὺς ξένο|υς τοὺς οἰκοῦντας Ἀθήνησι | [τὰ τέκ]ν[α καὶ τὰς γυναῖκ]ας ε[ἰς] Τροιζῆνα καταθέσθαι | [εἰς ὑποδοχὴν τοῦ Πιτθέως] τοῦ ἀρχηγέτου τῆς χώρας· τ|[οὺς δὲ πρεσβύτας καὶ τὰ] κτήματα εἰς Σαλαμῖνα καταθ| 10 ἐ[σ]θ[αι· τοὺς δὲ ταμίας καὶ τ]ὰς ἱερέας ἐν τῆι ἀκροπόλε|[ι μένειν φυλάττοντας τὰ τῶ]ν θεῶν· τοὺς δὲ ἄλλους Ἀθη|[ναίους ἅπαντας καὶ τοὺς ξέ]νους τοὺς ἡβῶντας εἰσβαί|νειν ε[ἰς τὰς ἑτοιμασθ]ε[ί]σ[α]ς διακοσίας ναῦς καὶ ἀμύ|νεσ[θαι] τ[ὸμ βάρβαρον ὑπὲρ τῆ]ς ἐλευθερίας τῆς τε ἑαυ| 15 τῶν [καὶ τῶν ἄλλων Ἑλλήνων] μετὰ Λακεδαιμονίων καὶ Κο|ριν[θίων καὶ Αἰγινητῶν] καὶ τῶν ἄλλων τῶμ βουλομένω|[ν] κοινω[νήσειν τοῦ κινδύνο]υ· καταστῆ|σαι δὲ καὶ τριη|[ρ]ά[ρχους διακοσίους, ἕνα ἐπὶ τὴν ναῦν ἑκάστην, τοὺς [σ]||τρατη[γ]-ού[ς ἀρχομένους τ]ῆι αὔριον ἡμέραι ἐκ τῶν κ[εκ]| 20 τημέν[ω]ν γ[ῆν] τ[ε κ]αὶ [οἰκί]αν Ἀθ[ή]νησι καὶ οἷς ἂμ παῖδ[ες] | ὦσι [γ]νή[σιοι μὴ πρεσβυτέρο]υς πεντήκοντα ἐτῶν κα[ὶ ἐ]|πικλ[ηρῶσαι αὐτ]οῖς [τ]ὰς ν[α]ῦς· vv καταλέξαι δὲ καὶ ἐπ[ι]|βάτας [δ]έκα [ἐφ' ἑκάστ]ην ναῦν ἐκ τῶν ὑπὲρ εἴκοσιν ἔτη [γ]|εγονότω[ν μέχρι τριάκ]οντα ἐτῶν καὶ τοξότας τέτταρ| 25 ας· διὰ[κληρῶσαι δὲ κ]αὶ [τ]ὰς [ὑ]πηρεσίας ἐπὶ τὰς ναῦς ὅτ|αμπερ κ[αὶ τοὺς τριηράρ]χους ἐπικληρῶσιν· ἀναγράψα|ι δὲ κα[ὶ τὰ πληρώματα τῶν] ν[εῶν] τοὺς στρατηγοὺς εἰς λ|ευκώ[ματα, τοὺς μὲν Ἀ]θηνα[ί]ο[υ]ς ἐκ τῶν ληξιαρχικῶν γρ|αμματεί[ων τοὺς] δὲ ξ[έν]ους ἐκ τῶν ἀπογεγραμμένων πα| 30 [ρ]ὰ τῶι [πολε]μ[άρχ]ω[ι]· ἀναγράφειν δὲ νέμοντας κατὰ τάξ|εις [ε]ἰ[ς] δι[α]κοσ[ί]α[ς] δώδεκα τὸν ἀριθμὸν καὶ ἐπιγράψα|ι [τ]ῆι [τάξε]ι ἑ[κά]στηι τῆς τρ[ι]ήρους τοὔνομα καὶ τοῦ τρι|ηράρχου καὶ τ[ῆς ὑ]πηρε[σί]ας ὅπως ἂν εἰδῶσιν εἰς ὁποί|αν τριήρη [ἐμ]βήσεται ἡ [τ]άξις ἑ[κ]άστη· ἐπειδὰν δὲ νεμη| 35 θῶσιν ἅπα[σ]αι αἱ τάξεις καὶ ἐπικληρωθῶσι ταῖς τριή|ρεσι, πληροῦν ἅ[π]άσας τὰς διακοσίας ναῦς τὴμ βουλὴν | καὶ τ[ο]ὺ̣ς̣τρατηγοὺ[ς θύ]σαντας ἀρεστήριον

τῶι Διὶ τῶι | Παγκρατεῖ κ[αὶ] τῆι Ἀθηνᾶι καὶ τῆι Νίκηι καὶ τῶι Ποσει|δῶνι τῶι Ἀσφα-
[λε]ίωι· *vv* ἐπειδὰν δὲ πεπληρωμέναι ὦσιν | 40 αἱ νῆες, τα[ῖ]ς μὲν ἑκατὸν αὐτῶν βοηθεῖν
ἐπὶ τὸ Ἀρτεμίσ|[ι]ον τὸ Εὐβοϊκὸν ταῖς δὲ ἑκατὸν αὐτῶν περὶ τὴν Σαλαμ|ῖνα καὶ τὴν
ἄλλην Ἀττικὴν ναυλοχεῖν καὶ φυλάττειν | τὴν χώραν· ὅπως δ' ἂν καὶ ὁμονοοῦντες
ἅπαντες Ἀθηναῖοι | ἀμύνωνται τὸμ βάρβαρον, τοὺς μὲν μεθεστηκότας τὰ [δ]| 45 [εκα]
ἔτη ἀπιέναι εἰς Σαλαμῖνα καὶ μένειν αὐτοὺς ἐ[κε]||[ῖ] ἕως ἄν τι τῶι δήμ]ωι δόξηι περὶ
αὐτῶν, τοὺς δὲ [ἀτίμου]||[ς ....]

The Council and the people decreed. Themistocles, son of Neocles, of
Phrearrhos, proposed: that the city be entrusted to the care of Athena
guardian of Athens and all the other gods, to protect it and to resist the
barbarian for the land's sake. As to the Athenians themselves and the aliens
who live in Athens, their children and wives shall be taken to Troizen to
the keeping of Pittheus founder of the country, while the old men and slaves
shall be taken to Salamis. The treasurers and priestesses shall remain on the
Acropolis protecting the property of the gods. All the other Athenians and
aliens who are of military age shall embark on the two hundred ships which
have been made ready and shall fight the barbarian for their own freedom
and the freedom of the rest of Greece, with the aid of the Spartans and
Corinthians and Aeginetans and the others who are willing to share the
peril. Beginning on the following day the generals shall also appoint two
hundred trierarchs, one for each ship, from those who not being more than
fifty years of age possess land and a house at Athens and who have
children born in wedlock, and shall assign the ships to them. They shall also
enrol ten *epibatai* for each ship from those that are above twenty and below
thirty years of age, and four archers; and they shall assign the petty
officers among the ships at the same time as they assign the trierarchs to
them. The generals shall also post up the ships' crews on the boards,*
Athenians from the deme-registers and aliens from the lists in the possession
of the polemarch. They shall post them up allocating (all of) them to
companies up to two hundred (and twelve)† in number and head the list of
each company with the names of the *trieres*, the trierarch and the petty officers,

* Cf. *IG* 1² 75 (*SEG* x 65 104), which is dated not long after the beginning of the Peloponnesian
war. A notice-board (*sanis*) for the posting of servicemen's names is mentioned three times (lines 5, 24
and 33).

† I can find no sense in the new reading δώδεκα in place of the πάντα read originally by Jameson.
I agree that πάντα cannot go with τὸν ἀριθμόν and that ἅπαντα is preferable. If ἅπαντα can be read
I should regard it as agreeing with πληρώματα. Otherwise, two hundred and twelve companies for two
hundred ships seems inexplicable. According to Burn (op. cit. p. 365, note 8a) Meritt believes that a
reading giving the meaning 'by hundreds' is indicated. This suggestion is no easier to understand.

so that each company may know on what *trieres* to embark. When all the companies are assigned and allocated to the *triereis*, the Council and the generals, after making sacrifice in propitiation to Zeus the Almighty, and Athena, and Nike, and Poseidon the Preserver, shall send the crews aboard all the two hundred ships. When the ships are manned, the generals shall make a sortie with a hundred of them to the temple of Artemis in Euboea, and with a hundred take up station on patrol round Salamis and Attica and guard the land. For the sake of concord of all Athenians in repelling the barbarian, those who have removed from the country for ten years shall go to Salamis and shall remain there until the people reach a decision about them, while those who have suffered loss of rights...

2. Demosthenes, 19 303 τὸ Μιλτιάδου καὶ ⟨τὸ⟩ Θεμιστοκλέους ψήφισμ' ἀναγιγνώσκων.

3. Herodotus, VII 144³ ἔδοξέ τέ σφι μετὰ τὸ χρηστήριον βουλευομένοισι ἐπιόντα ἐπὶ τὴν Ἑλλάδα τὸν βάρβαρον δέκεσθαι τῇσι νηυσὶ πανδημεί, τῷ θεῷ πειθομένους, ἅμα Ἑλλήνων τοῖσι βουλομένοισι.

4. Plutarch, *Life of Cimon* V 2 ὅτε γὰρ τὸν δῆμον ἐπιόντων Μήδων Θεμιστοκλῆς ἔπειθε προέμενον τὴν πόλιν καὶ τὴν χώραν ἐκλιπόντα πρὸ τῆς Σαλαμῖνος ἐν ταῖς ναυσὶ τὰ ὅπλα θέσθαι καὶ διαγωνίσασθαι κατὰ θάλατταν, ἐκπεπληγμένων τῶν πολλῶν τὸ τόλμημα πρῶτος Κίμων ὤφθη διὰ τοῦ Κεραμεικοῦ φαιδρὸς ἀνιὼν εἰς τὴν ἀκρόπολιν μετὰ τῶν ἑταίρων ἵππου τινὰ χαλινὸν ἀναθεῖναι τῇ θεῷ, διὰ χειρῶν κομίζων, ὡς οὐδὲν ἱππικῆς ἀλκῆς, ἀλλὰ ναυμάχων ἀνδρῶν ἐν τῷ παρόντι τῆς πόλεως δεομένης.

5. Herodotus, VIII 7¹ τῶν νεῶν πασέων ἀποκρίναντες διηκοσίας περιέπεμπον ἔξωθεν Σκιάθου, ὡς ἂν μὴ ὀφθείησαν ὑπὸ τῶν πολεμίων περιπλέουσαι Εὔβοιαν κτλ.

6

ACCOUNTS DERIVING FROM THE
LATER FIFTH CENTURY

HERODOTUS

In the account which Herodotus gives both of the successful resistance of
Miletus to the Lydians in the first half of the sixth century and of the rela-
tions of the Ionian islands with Croesus, he makes it clear that the Greeks of
the Asian seaboard were in control of the sea at the beginning of this period[1].
Later, when the Persians under Harpagus were able to employ the Phoenician navy, it is equally clear that the Greeks were brought into subjection.

USAGE OF TERMS AND TYPES

The most colourless word which Herodotus employs for a ship or boat is
ploion. He uses the word as a collective, or when he wants to say merely 'by
sea'[2]. The general term for oared warships seems to be 'long ships'. The
Argo is called a 'long ship', so are the Samian ships at the time of Croesus.
The Aeginetans attack Phalerum with 'long ships', and the Thasians use
their mining revenues to build walls and 'long ships'. The Naxians are said
to have eight thousand fighting men and many 'long ships'. Darius orders
the construction of 'long ships' and horse transports in preparation for the
first Persian expedition against Greece[3]. This expression certainly excludes
holkades, but seems likely to include all the other types of warship, triakontors,
pentekontors, and *triereis*, which Herodotus mentions.

Herodotus, as one would expect, frequently uses the word *naus*, ship,
without specifying the type. Most frequently the type is the *trieres*, and can
be seen to be so from the context. This leads to a usage by which the
equivalence *naus = trieres* is assumed. At VIII 1 2 the Ceians manned 'two
ships and two pentekontors', and *ib.* 46 4 the Cythnians provide 'one ship
and one pentekontor'[4]. It appears that Herodotus uses the more specific
term *trieres*, when the size[5], speed[6], or importance of the ship is to be stressed.
The catalogue of ships at Lade is given in 'ships' throughout but is summed

128

up as three hundred and fifty-three *triereis*[7]. When, however, the Athenians in 499 are said to have come to the help of the Ionians with 20 ships 'at the same time bringing five *triereis* of the Eretrians', there seems no other possible explanation for the change of term from 'ships' to '*triereis*' in the same sentence than that the Athenian ships were not all *triereis*. Admittedly Herodotus' contemporary, Charon of Lampsacus, appears to have said that the Athenians sailed with twenty *triereis*, but Herodotus seems, as Jacoby observed,* better informed than Charon on matters of detail and his testimony is therefore to be preferred[8].

Herodotus' first mention of the *trieres* is in connection with Necho's canal from the Mediterranean to the Red Sea, which he says was dug wide enough for two *triereis* to be rowed abeam. He says that some of Necho's *triereis* were built at the northern end and some in the Red Sea, and that slipways of the latter were visible in his own day[9]. Necho died in 593 B.C.; and if he built *triereis* they would antedate by fifty years the first mention of these ships in Greece. It is not very likely that the new type would have been invented in Egypt. Nevertheless, the mention by Hipponax at the beginning of the second half of the sixth century need not mark the date of their invention. Their invention in Greece before the end of the seventh century and introduction into Egypt by a dynasty noted for its philhellenism are by no means improbable.

Herodotus mentions *triereis* again in the last half of the sixth century in connection with Amasis, who sends one in chase of a fugitive[10]. A Mytilenian ship with a crew of two hundred in Cambyses' service[11] must also be a *trieres*, and Polycrates mans forty *triereis* with disaffected subjects and sends them to support Cambyses in his invasion of Egypt in 525[12]. This latter passage has been used to date the introduction of the *trieres*, since a decade or so earlier Polycrates is said to have founded his power on the acquisition of a hundred pentekontors and a thousand archers[13], and it is argued† that, had *triereis* been invented then, he would have acquired them, and not been content with pentekontors. The argument is not cogent, since Polycrates' navy of pentekontors (rather than *triereis*) may be regarded as the counterpart of his army of archers (rather than hoplites), and both as the armament proper to an aspiring pirate chief. Success made it possible for him later to

---

* *F. Gr. Hist.* IIIA, 262, F10: Commentary.

† By J. A. Davison, 'The First Greek Triremes', *CQ* 1947, 18 ff.

acquire *triereis*. It is surprising that he was able to acquire so many that he could afford to sacrifice forty. If the type had been invented a few years earlier, it is difficult to believe that he could have built and manned so many so quickly. The story of the defection of the forty may be true, but it may not be true that Polycrates deliberately manned them with his enemies. However, Polycrates, by Herodotus' account, was 'the first of the Greeks in our knowledge to have aimed at ruling the sea apart from Minos of Crete and any predecessor of his'[14]. He built ship-sheds[15], and Samian ships had a distinctive boar's-head bow[16]. It seems certain that by the time of Polycrates a fleet of *triereis* was the mark of a first-class naval power. Democedes and the Persian notables who are sent to reconnoitre Greece by Darius are able to charter two *triereis* in Phoenician Sidon[17]. In 494, at the time of the Ionian revolt, Chios could muster a fleet of a hundred *triereis*, and Miletus, Lesbos and Samos fleets of eighty, seventy and sixty *triereis* respectively. Athens' squadron consisted of only twenty ships, probably not all *triereis*. The relative naval strength of Athens and the Ionian states is strikingly illustrated.

The fleet which Darius sent under Datis to invade the Greek mainland in 490 numbered, according to Herodotus, six hundred *triereis* with horse transports in addition[18]. It sailed from the Aleian plain in Cilicia to Ionia and thence struck due west across the Aegean by way of Samos, Naxos, and Delos to Euboea[19]. There seems no substantial reason to believe that the number of six hundred was exaggerated, but it may have in fact included and not excluded, as Herodotus says, the horse transports. No sea-battle took place in this campaign. The Athenians were not tempted to commit themselves to the sea. After the defeat at Marathon the Persians withdrew eastwards. The Athenian fleet of seventy ships under Miltiades followed in their track as far as Paros, which had sided with the Persians, but failed to take it and returned home[20].

When in 481, under the threat of Xerxes' invasion, a delegation from the Greek congress came to Syracuse to ask Gelon's help, Herodotus tells how he promised two hundred *triereis* and a large military force provided he was given the command. Neither the Spartans nor the Athenians would allow this[21]. That he had two hundred *triereis* is confirmed by Ephorus, who says that with them he defeated the Carthaginians[22]. In 480 Corcyra's fleet of *triereis* numbered sixty[23].

The Chian *triereis* at Lade in 494 had fought with a complement of forty picked fighting men on deck[24]. In the second Persian invasion fleet we learn that there were on each ship, in addition to the normal complement of *epibatai*, a further detachment of thirty Persian, Median, or Sacan fighting men[25]. The normal complement of *epibatai* on Athenian ships at this time is probably given by the decree of Themistocles, i.e. ten hoplites, and there were four archers in addition. The disparity in number of *epibatai* between the east and west Greek fleets may have been the result of the lack of an over-all deck in the latter (see below, p. 161). The full complement of a *trieres* at this date appears to have been two hundred all told[26]. Its commander had the title of *trierarchos*, while *nauarchos* is used for the admiral of a fleet[27].

In spite of the pre-eminence of the *trieres*, pentekontors were still used on important occasions. Polycrates is twice described as going to sea in one[28]. In 540 B.C., when attacked by the Persians, the Phocaeans embark their families and possessions in pentekontors and retreat to the west[29]. It is probable that as J. A. Davison suggested* these are the ships with which, five years later, they fought the Carthaginians and Etruscans. On the latter occasion Herodotus calls the ships *ploia*[30]. After the fall of Sardis in 546 the Spartans send men to spy out Ionia in a pentekontor, and, during his Thracian expedition of 513, Darius as we learn from Ctesias makes a reconnaissance of the Black Sea coast with thirty pentekontors[31]. Gelon of Syracuse dispatches Cadmus to Delphi with three pentekontors to await the outcome of Xerxes' invasion[32]. There are pentekontors in Xerxes' fleet with crews of eighty, i.e. with the same number of non-rowers as a fourth-century *trieres*[33]. Pentekontors were also used, with *triereis*, in the construction of the bridge over the Hellespont[34]. There were also a few pentekontors in the Greek fleet which met the invaders[35].

Triakontors occur in the muster of the Persian fleet in 480, and their function can perhaps be seen when one is used at Artemisium to carry dispatches[36]. Horse transports are mentioned on four occasions by Herodotus. When Darius orders the construction of 'long ships' and horse transports[37] it may be inferred that the specifications of the two types were different.

DOCKYARDS, ETC.

Herodotus mentions slipways, which marked the site of Greek settlements in Egypt and the place on the Red Sea where Necho built his *triereis*. He attributes to Polycrates the building of ship-sheds, permanent buildings to house

* *Op. cit.*

ships and gear such as were possessed by the great naval powers of the succeeding age. He also informs us that at the time of the battle of Salamis
Phalerum was the Athenian naval station (*epineion*)[38].

HULL AND GEAR

The information which Herodotus provides about the hull and gear of the
ships in his narrative mostly relates to *triereis*. The ship in the story of Arion
however is an open, undecked, ship with a poop which is called *hedolia*, i.e.
'seating', presumably because the helmsman sat there[39].

The general structure of the *trieres* at this period is suggested by two passages. There is the story of Skylax[40], the captain of a Myndian ship taking
part in the Persian expedition of about 500 B.C. against Naxos under Megabates and Aristagoras. Megabates, making a night patrol, finds no one
keeping watch on Skylax' ship and orders him to be tied up inside the ship
with his head projecting through the oarport, a punishment no doubt
designed to encourage a good look-out. There can be little doubt that 'oarport' is the right translation for the word *thalamia*: 'but Megabates, taking a
serious view of the matter, told his guards to find the captain and tie him
through the *thalamia*, dividing him in such a way as to put his head outside
and his body inside.' The two-level ships which appear in the ship representations of this period had oarports for oarsmen of the lower level (see Arch.
85 ff., Pls 19 and 20). We have no clue at this stage to the position of the rest
of the oarsmen, but from another story in Herodotus[41] we can infer that all
the oarsmen were seated under the deck (*katastroma*). He tells how Xerxes on
his retreat from Salamis was said to have boarded a Phoenician ship at the
Hellespont for the passage to Asia. There was a storm and as there were
many deck-passengers accompanying Xerxes, the ship got into difficulties.
Asked if the ship could survive, the helmsman replied that she could not
unless they could get rid of the mass of deck-passengers; and on a word
from Xerxes they all jumped into the sea. Herodotus declares that the story
must be false because the king would undoubtedly have sent the Persians
below to row and made an equal number of Phoenician oarsmen leap
overboard. The *katastroma* is here contrasted with the ship's interior, *koile
naus*. It is not clear what sort of deck is meant. But the fact that the noun
katastroma is singular and that we know that on occasion as many as 40
fighting men were accommodated on it makes it likely that it was a single

overall deck and not a mere bow and stern platform like the Homeric *ikria* or later *selmata*.

Herodotus mentions the ram in his account of the defeat of the Phocaeans at Alalia in 535 B.C.[42]. It is probable that the Phocaean ships were pentekontors. Of their sixty ships they lost forty, and the twenty that survived the battle had their rams wrenched off. Like the later Athenian *triereis* they presumably had bronze rams which could be lost in battle. Ramming is the main offensive tactic in the sea-battles of the period, while the *epibatai* and archers perform a subsidiary role. The latter is well illustrated by an incident at the battle of Salamis[43]: 'a ship of Samothrace rammed an Athenian; the Athenian was going down when an Aeginetan vessel bore down on the Samothracian and sank her. Just before she was gone, the Samothracians, who were armed with javelins, drove the *epibatai* off the attacking vessel, leapt aboard, and captured her.'

The Persian ships at Marathon had the Homeric stern ornament, the *aphlasta*; and here too it was the object at which the enemy directed his attack. Herodotus tells how the Athenian Cynegeirus had his hand cut off as he was seizing the *aphlasta* of a Persian ship[44]. Speaking of the Samian exiles in Crete[45] he says that 'the Aeginetans with Cretan assistance defeated them and sold them into slavery, dedicating the *akroteria* of their ships with boar-headed bows in the temple of Athena in Aegina'. It has generally been assumed[46] that the *akroteria* were the actual boar-headed bows. There is an example of a boar-headed bow on a two-level pentekontor depicted on a black-figure vase of this period (see Arch. 85, Pls 19 and 20*a*), and it seems most unlikely that so large a part of a number of ships would have been transported back from Crete tò Aegina. Herodotus[47] records that among the spoils dedicated at Delphi after Salamis was a statue of a man holding in his hand the *akroterion* of a ship. This can hardly have been the whole bow section. There is finally a story in Polyaenus[48] about a certain Aristomachus who carried out a successful raid on a city by a piece of deception. He captured some enemy *triereis*, 'put his own oarsmen into them and decorated them with the *akroteria* of his own ships. Then he entered the enemy port with music playing, towing his own ships, and making his arrival late in the day. The enemy, thinking the squadron were their own ships returning victorious, came out to meet them and suffered casualties.' Here it is quite clear that the *akroterion* could not have been the forepart of the ship. It seems likely to have been the stern or bow ornament, which served, like a modern flag, to identify the ship's origin, and the loss of which was a mark of defeat and dishonour. The representations of ships of this period show a great variation of stern ornament (see Plates 11 ff.). At Salamis Artemisia's Halicarnassian ship had an *episemon* by which it could be recognized, and Themistocles' ship had an admiral's *semeion*. Diodorus speaks of the ships of the Athenian expedition to Sicily at the end of the fifth century B.C. having *episemata* in the bows. Polyaenus tells a story about Chabrias at the battle of Naxos. He told his captains to strike their own *semeia*, with the result that the Spartan helmsmen, failing to recognize the Athenian ships when they met them because they did not have the Attic *semeion*, sailed past without attacking[49]. There is some evidence from tragedy (see below, pp. 197–8) that ships had *semeia* painted on them. On the other hand the *semeia* in Polyaenus' story of Chabrias must have been flags or something which could have been struck, i.e. taken down, like the *akroteria*, which could clearly be removed. It seems likely then that ships had painted devices, like the snake which Mimnes painted on Hipponax' *trieres* (see above, p. 120), and other removable standards as well.

The general appearance of the Greek and Persian fleets at Artemisium seen from a distance seems to have been very similar. The silhouette from ahead or astern would not differ whether or not the overall deck was present, nor would this feature make much difference in the silhouette from abeam. Some of the Persian fleet mistake a Greek ambushing force for their own ships[50]. Yet there were differences in performance, which are ascribed sometimes to differences in the quality of the crews, sometimes to differences in the ships themselves. At the beginning of the Ionian revolt the Persian fleet in Cyprus was manned by Phoenicians and was defeated by a better-trained Ionian fleet in which the Samians were pre-eminent[51]; and later, after Salamis, the Samians, confident in their superiority over the Persian ships, bring the Greek fleet under Eurybiades to Mycale[52]. On the other hand at Artemisium the Persians are described as being aware that their own ships, besides being many times more numerous, were also 'better movers in the water'[53]. In the debate among the Greek captains before Salamis Themistocles argues against retreat to the Isthmus. If they fight there 'it will be in the open sea, which is least advantageous to us since our ships are heavier and fewer in number'[54]. Among the Greek ships those of the Athenians 'moved best in the water'[55]. We can only guess at the reason for a ship being light or heavy, moving well or badly. It seems unlikely that the reason lay in faulty shipbuilding, in different design, or in lack of skill in rowing. The main reason certainly lies in a condition of the ships, which could be, and was, accepted without shame or apology by Themistocles. It seems likely that the clue is contained in Herodotus' account of the approach of the Persian invasion fleet[56]: 'the naval commanders, on orders from Xerxes, moved all the ships from Doriscus to the adjoining beach. . .Here the ships were all hauled ashore and dried out.' The 'drying-out' operation no doubt included caulking. With the initiative of the attacker the Persians were able to arrive in Greek waters with dry bilges, while the Greeks, never knowing when the Persians might appear, could not risk taking their ships out of commission for a similar drying-out operation. In the crucial battles, then, the Greek ships were heavy compared with their adversaries.

Herodotus' word for sail is the Homeric *histia*[57]. He uses a collective word *tarsos* for a bank of oars, and *kope* for individual oars[58]. He also has a word for the timbers from which oars were made (*kopees*)[59]. He speaks of pikes for use in sea-fights[60], and ladders at Mycale where a landing on a hostile coast was expected[61]. The pictures show that ladders were part of the normal equipment of oared ships (for example: Arch. 52, Pl. 13; Arch. 57, Pl. 15). There are references to steering oars (*pedalia*) in the plural, but not in contexts which make it quite plain that more than one was used on each ship, although this conclusion is probably to be inferred from the phrase 'to use *pedalia*', meaning 'to navigate'[62]. From one account[63] it appears that the routine method of immobilizing a ship was to remove the steering equipment. There are references to anchors made of iron, and to anchoring off shore as a disagreeable alternative to beaching[64].

HANDLING

Herodotus does not give much information about the normal practice of navigation. He speaks of hauling ships up on the shore and down to the sea[65], and, as we have seen, of the process of hauling ships up on a beach to dry out the bilges[66]. He speaks of the use of the sounding lead and line[67]. The beaching of a ship which the crew is abandoning calls for a special word[68].

There is a good deal about the tactics of sea fighting. When the Ionian fleet gathered at Lade to relieve Miletus from the Persian attack in 494 B.C., a Phocaean named Dionysius was chosen commander. Herodotus describes his training methods[69], which proved a little too strenuous for the Ionians. He was clearly a tactician of genius. 'He took the fleet to sea regularly in line ahead to train the oarsmen by making the ships carry out a *diekplous* through each other's line, and get the *epibatai* under arms. For the rest of the day he kept the ships at anchor and gave the Ionians no break at all.' In the battle that followed it was only the Chians who, with the support of a few of their allies, 'fought using the *diekplous*'[70], and the Ionian fleet was defeated.

At Artemisium the fleet of the Greek allies was on the defensive. Herodotus gives its number as two hundred and seventy-one *triereis* and nine pentekontors at the outset, and says that it was joined later by a further fifty-three Athenian ships after the destruction of the Persian task force by storm off Euboea[71]. The original decision to split the Athenian fleet into equal halves and send only a hundred north to Artemisium had clearly been modified, and only fifty-three kept back 'to guard the land', while these too were sent north when the threat of the raiding force was lifted. The allied ships appear to have been slower than their opponents, for reasons which have just been discussed. The Persian fleet on the other hand, in spite of the losses it had suffered (at least four hundred ships, Herodotus says) when caught by a storm while for the most part at anchor off the inadequate beach between Kasthanaia and Cape Sepias[72], and in spite of the detachment of the task force to the south, must still have been more numerous than the fleet of the Greek allies. There is no substantial reason for following Hignett* in regarding the two fleets at Artemisium as about equal in numbers. Aeschylus' testimony that the Persian fleet at Salamis numbered one thousand ships, including the fast squadron, is hard to gainsay. Herodotus' numbers for the Persian fleet at Salamis can be harmonized with Aeschylus' if we suppose that Herodotus added the fast squadron to the total of a thousand. He says that between Artemisium and Salamis the Persians made up their losses in the storms, i.e. the four hundred ships lost off Magnesia, and the two hundred off Euboea. If we suppose that Herodotus, like ourselves, worked back from Salamis in his calculations, his mistake over the fast squadron would have affected his total of the Persian fleet at Doriscus, making it twelve hundred and seven (see p. 160) instead of a thousand, and at Artemisium we may suppose the Persian fleet to have numbered at least four hundred ships,† more likely five

* C. Hignett, *Xerxes' Invasion of Greece*, Oxford, 1963.
† I.e. one thousand less four hundred lost and two hundred detached. But Herodotus is likely to have exaggerated the losses.

hundred, as against the two hundred and eighty, later increased to three hundred and thirty-three, of the Greek allies. The advantage was considerable, but not overwhelming[73], and so it proved.

In the preliminary skirmishes the fleet of the allies is described[74] as taking the initiative against the more numerous and faster Persian fleet 'wishing to make trial of them in fighting and in the *diekplous*' or alternatively* 'wishing to make trial of their fighting tactics and their use of the *diekplous*'. If we recollect that the *diekplous* was a tactic which the Ionians, or some of them, had tried to employ at Lade, we may prefer the latter translation and suppose that the Greek allies would have expected the Persian fleet, in which the Ionians were serving, to employ it. Certainly the Greek allies do not seem to have themselves used the *diekplous* at Artemisium, since they were on the defensive being the slower in the water. Herodotus describes how the Persian ships sailed round them, and how they at the first signal turned their bows to the enemy and their sterns inwards to each other and at the second signal rowed against the enemy bow to bow and captured thirty ships. This manœuvre is clearly a planned defensive tactic against a *diekplous* which developed into a *periplous*. By abandoning their line and bunching together they frustrated the former, and by making a *kuklos* or 'hedgehog' from which they attacked radially they defeated the latter. The battle which the Peloponnesian squadron fought with Phormio in 429 is an example of the successful use of the *periplous* against a less well-drilled fleet which had attempted to employ, like the Greeks at Artemisium, a defensive *kuklos* (see below, p. 315).

The word *diekplous* appears to mean 'a passing through and out', and the nature of the manœuvre seems to be shown by the non-tactical use of the word on two occasions in Herodotus. In connection with the bridge of ships over the Hellespont the word is used to denote the gaps left in the line of ships, drawn up side by side just like a line of battle, to permit light traffic through the straits[75], and it is used on another occasion to mean a passage through shoals[76]. In battle tactics the word would then seem to mean the passage of a squadron of ships in line ahead, possibly the passage of ships one by one, through a gap or in the latter case through gaps in an enemy fleet drawn up opposite in line abreast. Since at the outset of the battle fleets normally faced each other in line abreast, it would have been the more manœuvrable and faster-moving fleet that could adopt the line ahead

* See Hignett, *op. cit.* p. 184.

formation as a preliminary to carrying out the *diekplous*. The breakthrough was presumably made at a prearranged place. This explanation well fits the description of Dionysius' practice runs before Lade. Once behind the enemy line, the fleet that had successfully made a *diekplous* would be in a position to ram the enemy ships as they tried to turn.

In a papyrus fragment of a work on the campaigns of Hannibal by Sosylus of Sparta[77] there is an interesting account of a tactical defence against the *diekplous*, here said to have been invented by Heracleides of Mylasa, presumably the same Heracleides of Mylasa whose ambush of a Persian army in the Ionian revolt is related by Herodotus[78]. Sosylus says: 'The Phoenicians when they meet an enemy face to face' (i.e. with both fleets line abreast) 'have the practice of bearing down as though to ram head on, but then do not ram immediately but row on through the enemy line and turn and ram the opposing ships on the now exposed quarter.' It may be that Sosylus in this condensed account has omitted the preliminary manœuvre of turning into line ahead, or he may have intended to describe the *diekplous* of a line of ships abreast, one by one. This latter tactic would only have been possible if the enemy line was widely spaced, but it may nevertheless have been a version of the *diekplous* practised by the Phoenicians. 'Now the Massaliotes' (i.e. the Greeks of Marseilles), Sosylus continues, 'had read in history about the battle of Artemisium fought by Heracleides of Mylasa, one of the most resourceful captains of his time, and accordingly they gave orders for a first line abreast to be followed by a second at appropriate intervals, the ships of which, as soon as the enemy passed through the line in front, should attack them while still passing. This was what Heracleides had done long before, and been the architect of victory.'

In Herodotus' account of the sea-battle off Artemisium in Euboea in 480 B.C. there is nothing which corresponds to the defensive tactics against the *diekplous* attributed by Sosylus to Heracleides, although there is the tradition in Herodotus that the Greek allies in that battle adopted defensive tactics, though of a different kind, against the *diekplous*. There are two possibilities, either that Heracleides fighting on the side of the Greek allies employed the double-line tactic, in circumstances which certainly called for it, in one of the engagements at Artemisium, but was not recorded by Herodotus as having done so, or that Heracleides employed this tactic on another occasion and his exploit was attributed to Artemisium because it was known that defensive tactics against the *diekplous* were used on that occasion. A third possibility is suggested by Munro: that the battle referred to by Sosylus belongs to the early struggles of the Phocaeans, engaged in colonizing Massilia, against the Phoenicians, and that the Artemisium is a temple built by the Phocaeans in honour of Ephesian Artemis near Massilia. Hignett discounts this last suggestion,* and since there is nothing else to connect Heracleides either with the Greek fleet at Artemisium or with Massilia the second possibility seems preferable.

The *diekplous*, at any rate, seems to have been a battle manœuvre which Dionysius knew and taught in one form before Lade and which in another, possibly Phoenician, form Dionysius' contemporary Heracleides countered with a double line. Herodotus describes another counter tactic as employed by the Greek allies at Artemisium, the *kuklos*, against which the attacker developed, there unsuccessfully, the *periplous*. Hignett certainly seems quite off the mark in concluding that the *diekplous* was an Athenian invention of the Peloponnesian war period.†

The remaining engagements off Artemisium, as described by Herodotus, afford little insight into tactical dispositions. For the final battle, which was hard-fought and indecisive, the Persians adopted a moon-shaped formation[79] suitable to a more numerous force seeking to envelop a smaller one. In such a formation the great Spanish Armada moved up the Channel in July 1588. Not the engagements at Artemisium but a defeat on land caused the withdrawal of the fleet of the Greek allies to Salamis.

The tactics of the battle of Salamis have been much discussed, most recently by Hammond,‡ Broadhead,§ Burn,‖ and Hignett.¶ Hammond has succeeded in making one certain identification, the site of the Greek fleet station on the island of Salamis before the battle. He places it on the southward- and eastward-facing shore of the modern Paloukia Bay.** His further identification of the island, mentioned in Aeschylus' and Herodotus' accounts of the battle under the name of Psyttaleia, with the modern island of St George, which lies less than half a mile south and east of the Greek station in the narrows between Salamis and Heracleum on the opposing shore of Attica, is much more doubtful. Burn†† puts up a stronger case for the alterna-

---

* *Op. cit.* Appendix VII.   † *Op. cit.* 184 f.   ‡ *JHS* LXXVI (1956), 32 ff.
§ In an appendix to his edition of Aeschylus, *Persians* (1960).
‖ *Op. cit.*   ¶ *Op. cit.*   ** See the map of Salamis and the adjacent waters, p. 330.
†† *Op. cit.* 453 f. See W. K. Pritchelt, *AJA* 1959, 251 ff.

tive identification of Psyttaleia with the modern Lipsokoutali, a larger island in the middle of the channel and between the rocky promontory of Salamis (which is probably the Cynosura of Herodotus) and Munichia. Fortunately this latter identification has no bearing on the main narrative.

Herodotus' account of the preliminaries to the battle compresses into two or three days operations which seem to need a longer period for their completion; but otherwise his narrative deserves close attention. The Persian fleet, he says, passed through Euripus, and in another three days arrived off Phalerum. The Persians were now in his opinion as strong in men and ships as they had been before the storms and the battles of Artemisium and Thermopylae, since they had received reinforcements. When he specifies the sources of these reinforcements, Malians, Dorians, Locrians, Boeotians, Carystians, Andrians, Tenians and the rest of the islanders, it seems quite impossible that these could have provided more than a fraction of the six hundred ships needed to replace those that had, he says, been lost. Herodotus' exaggeration of the Persian numbers at Sepias, and hence of the subsequent losses, here begins to show. Nevertheless we may safely believe that at least the same sort of disparity in numbers which existed between the Persian and Greek fleets at Artemisium prevailed also at Salamis. Diodorus says that Themistocles argued for a battle off Salamis because he believed that the narrow waters would favour the side 'fighting with few ships against superiority of numbers'[80]. (See Map 3, p. 330.)

A Persian council of war was followed by an embarkation 'against Salamis', where the Greek naval forces now lay. But an attack was postponed until the following day. Then follows the story of Themistocles' famous trick, told also by Aeschylus, whereby he made the Persian commanders believe that the Greek leaders were disunited and in panic and were planning to slip away. The Persian reaction is described in precise detail[81]: they put a large body of soldiers across to the island of Psyttaleia, and ordered the fleet to sea. Both operations were carried out in silence so that the enemy should not know what the Persians were doing. The dispositions of the fleet are equally precise: 'they put to sea, making an encircling move on the western wing. There put to sea too those who were given the station about Ceos and Cynosura, and they held the whole strait as far as Munichia with their ships.' Herodotus seems clearly to be reviewing the dispositions from west to east, beginning with the encircling move of the western wing of the fleet (the Egyptian squadron, according to Diodorus), round the southern coast of Salamis to the Megarian channel, which is attested by Aeschylus, passing next to the central section between Salamis and the island of Lipsokoutali (i.e. round Ceos and Cynosura) and finally to the eastern section between Lipsokoutali and Munichia. Yet Hammond with a curious perversity, while admitting that one squadron of the Persian fleet did occupy the Megarian strait, holds that this move took place earlier and that Herodotus' words 'they put to sea making an encircling move on the western wing' referred to a move by the right or *eastern* wing of the Persian fleet through the straits, 'the right wing swinging into position west of north and towards Salamis' so that it can at last become west of the rest of the fleet. Quite apart from the difficulty of supposing that the squadron to occupy the Megarian strait set out before the operation of Themistocles' trick, by getting Persian ships into the narrows so early Hammond falls into difficulties in his treatment of the battle the next morning.

The object of the manœuvres of the three squadrons of the Persian fleet is then given: 'so that the Greeks might not be able to slip away'. The object is achieved by closing the three approaches to the Bay of Eleusis, the Megarian channel in the west and the straits on either side of the island of Lipsokoutali in the east. It could not be achieved by less, or better achieved by more. The reason for the secret occupation of Psyttaleia, either, as Hammond thinks, right inside the straits but no more than three-quarters of a mile from the coast of Persian-occupied Attica, or in the approaches to the strait, was, Herodotus says, to save Persians and kill Greeks in the sea-battle which the Persians expected to take place in its vicinity. Herodotus remarks that the Persians spent a sleepless night in these preparations, a point which is the key to the tactical situation and is also emphasized by Aeschylus.

Herodotus then recounts the story of the arrival from Aegina of Themistocles' banished enemy Aristides. He had come presumably in response to the call, which we can now read in Themistocles' decree, for all Athenian exiles to come to Salamis. He made the dangerous passage by night, and was able to tell the Greeks that even if the Corinthians and Eurybiades wanted to sail away, he had now seen with his own eyes that it was impossible: 'for we are surrounded by the enemy'[82]. What he had seen with his own eyes through the darkness of the late summer night, possibly illumined by a rising moon, was the Egyptian squadron proceeding to take up its station in the Megarian strait and other ships patrolling the coast of Salamis. The fact of the total enclosure of the Greek allied fleet was confirmed by a Tenian ship which came in from the Persians, and the Greeks, no longer in any doubt as to what they had to do, prepared to fight.

Herodotus' account of the beginning of the battle is again clear and un-ambiguous[83]: at daybreak 'the Greeks put to sea with all their ships, and as they put to sea the barbarians attacked them'. Hammond invents a long intermediate move by the Greek fleet after they had put to sea and before the Persian attack. He thinks they first moved out of Paloukia Bay northwards, then went round behind Mt Aegaleos on the opposite Attic coast where they formed their order of battle, and finally emerged in line ahead turning left to face the Persian line, which he believes was by now stretching from the Attic shore north of the isle of St George to the tip of the projecting promontory of Salamis, Cynosura, and thus facing *south* of west. There is no support what-ever for this northward manœuvre of the Greek fleet. Both Herodotus and Aeschylus say that the battle was joined *immediately* the Greeks had put to sea. Aeschylus, as we shall see, says that the Greeks were at first not fully in view of the Persians as they came up the straits. If, as Hammond believes, the Persians were already north of the isle of St George and facing slightly south of west, he has to invent the northward manœuvre behind Mt Aegaleos to fit Aeschylus' clear testimony. But if the phrase describing the first of the Persian naval dispositions of the night, 'they put to sea making an encircling move on the western wing', means what it appears to say, there is no reason to bring the Persians into the strait so early. If they move up the strait as dawn breaks, the Greek fleet, putting out to sea on the northern and eastern side of Paloukia Bay, would first be screened from their view by the island of St George, and would come face to face with them in the channel between the island and the Attic coast. It would not have taken the Greek fleet more than about half an hour to clear the island and enter the main channel.

It seems then fairly clear what happened between midnight and the first contact between the fleets. The two Persian squadrons, which had spent the early hours of the morning blocking the passages each side of the island of Lipsokoutali, moved, as dawn began to break, round Cynosura and up the straits in line abreast facing north. The account in Diodorus mentions how the Persians as they moved up the narrowing channel had to shorten their line, and how this caused confusion. By the time they drew level with the isle of St George the channel was reduced to about 1300 yards. The line cannot have contained more than a hundred or a hundred and twenty ships. The rest presumably fell in behind. They had all spent at least six hours at the oar. As they drew level with the island, the Greek fleet appeared from behind it, having only just put to sea. Herodotus says that the Greeks at first backed water, then an Athenian ship led off by attacking a Phoenician, and became entangled, and the rest came to her aid and attacked.

Herodotus gives the information that the Phoenicians were stationed opposite the Athenians, who held the west wing towards Eleusis, and the Ionians were stationed opposite the Spartans, who held the east wing towards Piraeus[84]. The reference to Eleusis, which lies on about the same longitude as, and about five miles north of, the island of St George, is undoubtedly one of the reasons which has caused scholars to think that the lines of ships ran north and south, and not, as every other consideration suggests, east and west. Others, like Loeschke, have emended 'Eleusis' to 'Salamis'. But provided the lines are regarded as running east and west across the channel east of the island of St George, Eleusis is quite a reasonable point of reference for the western end, and Piraeus for the eastern end, of both lines. If Themistocles wanted to force a breakthrough, according to the tactic of the *diekplous*, it was reasonable for him to do so with an Athenian ship on the right wing off the friendly shore of Salamis. In fact, Aeschylus says that at the outset of the battle the right wing led and the rest followed.

The only other comment Herodotus makes on the battle is to remark on the Greeks' good order, and on the Persians' confusion and lack of good sense, and to speak about those who were stationed behind pressing on to perform some notable deed and falling foul of their own ships which were breaking off the action[85]. The ships behind were certainly those which had fallen in behind as the line was shortened. There is no indication that the fleet was drawn up at the outset in several ranks.

TEXTS

1. Ionian naval supremacy in the sixth century: 1 17³ τῆς γὰρ θαλάσσης οἱ Μιλήσιοι ἐπεκράτεον. Bias' (or Pittacus') *epilogos* to Croesus: 1 27⁴ ὦ βασιλεῦ, προθύμως μοι φαίνεαι εὔξασθαι νησιώτας ἱππευομένους λαβεῖν ἐν ἠπείρῳ, οἰκότα ἐλπίζων· νησιώτας δὲ τί δοκέεις εὔχεσθαι ἄλλο ἤ, ἐπείτε τάχιστα ἐπύθοντό σε μέλλοντα ἐπὶ σφίσι ναυπηγέεσθαι νέας, λαβεῖν ἀρώμενοι Λυδοὺς ἐν θαλάσσῃ, ἵνα ὑπὲρ τῶν ἐν τῇ ἠπείρῳ οἰκημένων Ἑλλήνων τείσωνταί σε, τοὺς σὺ δουλώσας ἔχεις;

Usage of terms and types

2. πλοίῳ = by sea, or by boat: III 4² ἐκδιδρήσκει πλοίῳ ἐξ Αἰγύπτου. VIII 8³ περὶ μέντοι τούτου γνώμη μοι ἀποδεδέχθω πλοίῳ μιν ἀπικέσθαι ἐπὶ τὸ Ἀρτεμίσιον. 75² ὅς τότε πλοίῳ ἀπικόμενος... (Sicinnus).

3. Long Ships: the *Argo*: I 2² καταπλώσαντας γὰρ μακρῇ νηΐ ἐς Αἶάν τε τὴν Κολχίδα καὶ ἐπὶ Φᾶσιν ποταμόν...

Samian ships at the time of Croesus: I 70² πυθόμενοι Σάμιοι ἀπελοίατο αὐτὸν (the bowl that the Spartans sent to Croesus) νηυσὶ μακρῇσι ἐπιπλώσαντες.

Thasian ships: VI 46² οἱ γὰρ δὴ Θάσιοι...νέας τε ναυπηγεύμενοι μακρὰς καὶ τεῖχος ἰσχυρότερον περιβαλλόμενοι...

Naxian ships: V 30⁴ πυνθάνομαι γὰρ ὀκτακισχιλίην ἀσπίδα Ναξίοισι εἶναι καὶ πλοῖα μακρὰ πολλά.

Darius' naval plans: VI 48² ...κήρυκας διέπεμπε ἐς τὰς ἑωυτοῦ δασμοφόρους πόλιας τὰς παραθαλασσίους, κελεύων νέας τε μακρὰς καὶ ἱππαγωγὰ πλοῖα ποιέεσθαι.

4. ναῦς = τριήρης, cf. VII 168² ἐπεὶ δὲ ἔδει βοηθέειν, ἄλλα νοέοντες ἐπλήρωσαν νέας ἑξήκοντα. These ships in 168⁴ are called *triereis*.

5. Word τριήρης used to stress size: II 158¹ εὖρος δὲ ὠρύχθη ὥστε τριήρεας δύο πλέειν ὁμοῦ ἐλαστρευμένας.

6. Word τριήρης used to stress speed: III 4² μεταδιώκει τῶν εὐνούχων τὸν πιστότατον ἀποστείλας τριήρεϊ κατ' αὐτόν. Cf. III 136; V 38²; VI 39¹.

7. VI 8¹⁻², see below, p. 164, note 2.

8. V 99¹ ἐπειδὴ οἵ τε Ἀθηναῖοι ἀπίκοντο εἴκοσι νηυσί, ἅμα ἀγόμενοι Ἐρετριέων πέντε τριήρεας... *F. Gr. Hist.* III A 262, F. 10: Ἀθηναῖοι δ' εἴκοσι τριήρεσι ἔπλευσαν ἐπικουρήσοντες τοῖς Ἴωσι...

9. II 158¹, see note 5 above; 159¹, see note 38 below.

10. III 4², see note 6 above.

11. III 13¹⁻² and 14⁴⁻⁵: 2000 punished, ten for each of the men from the Mytilenian ship who had been murdered.

12. III 44² ὁ δὲ ἐπιλέξας τῶν ἀστῶν τοὺς ὑπώπτευε μάλιστα ἐς ἐπανάστασιν ἀπέπεμπε τεσσεράκοντα τριήρεσι, ἐντειλάμενος Καμβύσῃ ὀπίσω τούτους μὴ ἀποπέμπειν.

13. III 39³ ἐν χρόνῳ δὲ ὀλίγῳ αὐτίκα τοῦ Πολυκράτεος τὰ πρήγματα ηὔξετο... ἔκτητο δὲ πεντηκοντέρους τε ἑκατὸν καὶ χιλίους τοξότας. ἔφερε δὲ καὶ ἦγε πάντας διακρίνων οὐδένα.

14. III 122² Πολυκράτης γὰρ ἐστι πρῶτος τῶν ἡμεῖς ἴδμεν Ἑλλήνων ὃς θαλασσοκρατέειν ἐπενοήθη, πάρεξ Μίνω τε τοῦ Κνωσσίου καὶ εἰ δή τις ἄλλος πρότερος τούτου ἦρξε τῆς θαλάσσης· τῆς δὲ ἀνθρωπηίης λεγομένης γενεῆς Πολυκράτης πρῶτος, ἐλπίδας πολλὰς ἔχων Ἰωνίης τε καὶ νήσων ἄρξειν.

15. III 45⁴ νεωσοίκους.

16. III 59³, see below, note 45.

17. III 136¹ καταβάντες δὲ οὗτοι ἐς Φοινίκην καὶ Φοινίκης ἐς Σιδῶνα πόλιν αὐτίκα μὲν τριήρεας δύο ἐπλήρωσαν, ἅμα δὲ αὐτῇσι καὶ γαῦλον μέγαν παντοίων ἀγαθῶν.

18. VI 95[1-2] ἐπῆλθε μὲν ὁ ναυτικὸς πᾶς στρατὸς ὁ ἐπιταχθεὶς ἑκάστοισι, παρεγένοντο δὲ καὶ αἱ ἱππαγωγοὶ νέες. . .ἔπλεον ἑξακοσίῃσι τριήρεσι ἐς τὴν Ἰωνίην.

19. VI 95[2] ff.

20. VI 132–135[1].

21. VII 157 ff.

22. *F. Gr. Hist.* IIᴀ 70, F. 186.

23. VII 168[1-4]. Cf. Diodorus XI 15 1.

24. VI 15[1] Χῖοι. . .οἳ παρείχοντο μέν, ὥσπερ καὶ πρότερον εἰρέθη, νέας ἑκατὸν καὶ ἐπ’ ἑκάστης αὐτέων ἄνδρας τεσσεράκοντα τῶν ἀστῶν λογάδας ἐπιβατεύοντας.

25. VII 184[2] ἐπεβάτευον δὲ ἐπὶ τουτέων τῶν νεῶν, χωρὶς ἑκάστων τῶν ἐπιχωρίων ἐπιβατέων, Περσέων τε καὶ Μήδων καὶ Σακέων τριήκοντα ἄνδρες.

26. E.g. VII 184[1], where the number of men given for the 1207 Persian ships is 241,400, i.e. 1207 × 200, and see note 11 above.

27. Trierarchos, VII 181, 182; VIII 85[2], 93[2].

Nauarchos, VII 59[2], 100[3], 161[2]; VIII 42[1], 131[2].

28. III 41[2] πεντηκόντερον πληρώσας ἀνδρῶν ἐσέβη ἐς αὐτήν.

124[2] ἰόντος αὐτοῦ ἐπὶ τὴν πεντηκόντερον ἐπεφημίζετο.

29. I 164[3] ἐν ᾧ ὦν ὁ Ἅρπαγος ἀπὸ τοῦ τείχεος ἀπήγαγε τὴν στρατιήν, οἱ Φωκαιέες ἐν τούτῳ κατασπάσαντες τὰς πεντηκοντέρους, ἐσθέμενοι τέκνα καὶ γυναῖκας καὶ ἔπιπλα πάντα. . .αὐτοὶ ἐσβάντες ἔπλεον ἐπὶ Χίου.

30. I 166[1-2] καὶ ἦγον γὰρ δὴ καὶ ἔφερον τοὺς περιοίκους ἅπαντας, στρατεύονται ὦν ἐπ’ αὐτοὺς κοινῷ λόγῳ χρησάμενοι Τυρσηνοὶ καὶ Καρχηδόνιοι νηυσὶ ἑκάτεροι ἑξήκοντα. οἱ δὲ Φωκαιέες πληρώσαντες καὶ αὐτοὶ τὰ πλοῖα, ἐόντα ἀριθμὸν ἑξήκοντα, ἀντίαζον ἐς τὸ Σαρδόνιον καλεόμενον πέλαγος. συμμισγόντων δὲ τῇ ναυμαχίῃ Καδμείη τις νίκη τοῖσι Φωκαιεῦσι ἐγένετο. αἱ μὲν γὰρ τεσσεράκοντά σφι νέες διεφθάρησαν, αἱ δὲ εἴκοσι αἱ περιεοῦσαι ἦσαν ἄχρηστοι· ἀπεστράφατο γὰρ τοὺς ἐμβόλους.

31. I 152[2] Λακεδαιμόνιοι δὲ ἀπωσάμενοι τῶν Ἰώνων τοὺς ἀγγέλους ὅμως ἀπέστειλαν πεντηκοντέρῳ ἄνδρας, ὡς μὲν ἐμοὶ δοκέει, κατασκόπους τῶν τε Κύρου πρηγμάτων καὶ Ἰωνίης. Ctesias: *F. Gr. Hist.* IIIᴄ 688, F. 13 (19).

32. VII 163[2] πέμπει πεντηκοντέροισι τρισὶ Κάδμον. . .ἐς Δελφούς, ἔχοντα χρήματα πολλὰ καὶ φιλίους λόγους, καραδοκήσαντα τὴν μάχην τῇ πεσέεται.

33. VII 97 τριηκόντεροι δὲ καὶ πεντηκόντεροι καὶ κέρκουροι καὶ ἱππαγωγὰ πλοῖα σμικρὰ συνελθόντα ἐς τὸν ἀριθμὸν ἐφάνη τρισχίλια.

184[3] See above, p. 69, note 12.

34. VII 36[1] ἐζεύγνυσαν δὲ ὧδε· πεντηκοντέρους καὶ τριήρεας συνθέντες. . .

35. VIII 1[2] Κήιοι δύο τε νέας καὶ πεντηκοντέρους δύο. Λοκροὶ δέ σφι οἱ Ὀπούντιοι ἐπεβοήθεον πεντηκοντέρους ἔχοντες ἑπτά.

36. VII 97, see note 33 above.

VIII 21[1] ὡς δ’ αὔτως ἦν Ἀβρώνιχος ὁ Λυσικλέος Ἀθηναῖος καὶ παρὰ Λεωνίδῃ ἕτοιμος τοῖσι ἐπ’ Ἀρτεμισίῳ ἐοῦσι ἀγγέλλειν τριηκοντέρῳ ἤν τι καταλαμβάνῃ νεώτερον τὸν πεζόν.

37. VI 48[2], see note 3 above.

Slipways, etc.

38. (i) II 154⁵ ἐξ ὧν δὲ ἐξανέστησαν χώρων ἐν τούτοισι δὴ οἵ τε ὁλκοὶ τῶν νεῶν καὶ τὰ ἐρείπια τῶν οἰκημάτων τὸ μέχρι ἐμεῦ ἦσαν.

(ii) II 159¹ καὶ τριήρεες αἱ μὲν ἐπὶ τῇ βορηίῃ θαλάσσῃ ἐποιήθησαν, αἱ δ᾽ ἐν τῷ Ἀραβίῳ κόλπῳ ἐπὶ τῇ Ἐρυθρῇ θαλάσσῃ, τῶν ἔτι οἱ ὁλκοί εἰσι δῆλοι.

(iii) III 45⁴ τῶν δὲ ὑπ᾽ ἑωυτῷ ἐόντων πολιητέων τὰ τέκνα καὶ τὰς γυναῖκας ὁ Πολυκράτης ἐς τοὺς νεωσοίκους συνειλήσας εἶχε ἑτοίμους, ἢν ἄρα προδιδῶσι οὗτοι πρὸς τοὺς κατιόντας, ὑποπρῆσαι αὐτοῖσι τοῖσι νεωσοίκοισι.

(iv) VI 116 Φαλήρου (τοῦτο γὰρ ἦν ἐπίνειον τότε τῶν Ἀθηναίων).

Hull and Gear

39. I 24⁴ ἀπειληθέντα δὲ τὸν Ἀρίονα ἐς ἀπορίην παραιτήσασθαι, ἐπειδή σφι οὕτω δοκέοι, περιιδεῖν αὐτὸν ἐν τῇ σκευῇ πάσῃ στάντα ἐν τοῖσι ἑδωλίοισι ἀεῖσαι· ἀείσας δὲ ὑπεδέκετο ἑωυτὸν κατεργάσεσθαι. καὶ τοῖσι ἐσελθεῖν γὰρ ἡδονὴν εἰ μέλλοιεν ἀκούσεσθαι τοῦ ἀρίστου ἀνθρώπων ἀοιδοῦ, ἀναχωρῆσαι ἐκ τῆς πρύμνης ἐς μέσην νέα.

40. V 33² περιιόντος Μεγαβάτεω τὰς ἐπὶ τῶν νεῶν φυλακὰς ἐπὶ νεὸς Μυνδίης ἔτυχε οὐδεὶς φυλάσσων· ὁ δὲ δεινόν τι ποιησάμενος ἐκέλευσε τοὺς δορυφόρους ἐξευρόντας τὸν ἄρχοντα ταύτης τῆς νεός, τῷ οὔνομα ἦν Σκύλαξ, τοῦτον δῆσαι διὰ θαλαμίης διελόντας τῆς νεὸς κατὰ τοῦτο, ἔξω μὲν κεφαλὴν ποιεῦντας, ἔσω δὲ τὸ σῶμα.

41. VIII 118²–119 πλέοντα δέ μιν ἄνεμον Στρυμονίην ὑπολαβεῖν μέγαν καὶ κυματίην. καὶ δὴ μᾶλλον γάρ τι χειμαίνεσθαι, γεμούσης τῆς νεὸς ὥστε ἐπὶ τοῦ καταστρώματος ἐπεόντων συχνῶν Περσέων τῶν σὺν Ξέρξῃ κομιζομένων, ἐνθαῦτα ἐς δεῖμα πεσόντα τὸν βασιλέα εἰρέσθαι βώσαντα τὸν κυβερνήτην εἴ τις ἔστι σφι σωτηρίη. καὶ τὸν εἶπαι· Δέσποτα, οὐκ ἔστι οὐδεμία, εἰ μὴ τούτων ἀπαλλαγή τις γένηται τῶν πολλῶν ἐπιβατέων. καὶ Ξέρξην λέγεται ἀκούσαντα ταῦτα εἰπεῖν· Ἄνδρες Πέρσαι, νῦν τις διαδεξάτω ὑμέων βασιλέος κηδόμενος· ἐν ὑμῖν γὰρ οἶκε εἶναι ἐμοὶ ἡ σωτηρίη. τὸν μὲν ταῦτα λέγειν, τοὺς δὲ προσκυνέοντας ἐκπηδᾶν ἐς τὴν θάλασσαν, καὶ τὴν νέα ἐπικουφισθεῖσαν οὕτω δὴ ἀποσωθῆναι ἐς τὴν Ἀσίην...

οὗτος δὲ ἄλλος λέγεται λόγος περὶ τοῦ Ξέρξεω νόστου, οὐδαμῶς ἔμοιγε πιστός, οὔτε ἄλλως οὔτε τὸ Περσέων τοῦτο πάθος. εἰ γὰρ δὴ ταῦτα οὕτως εἰρέθη ἐκ τοῦ κυβερνήτεω πρὸς Ξέρξην, ἐν μυρίῃσι γνώμῃσι μίαν οὐκ ἔχω ἀντίξοον μὴ οὐκ ἂν ποιῆσαι βασιλέα τοιόνδε, τοὺς μὲν ἐκ τοῦ καταστρώματος καταβιβάσαι ἐς κοίλην νέα, ἐόντας Πέρσας καὶ Περσέων τοὺς πρώτους, τῶν δ᾽ ἐρετέων ἐόντων Φοινίκων ὅκως οὐκ ἂν ἴσον πλῆθος τοῖσι Πέρσῃσι ἐξέβαλε ἐς τὴν θάλασσαν.

42. See note 30 above.

43. VIII 90² ἐνέβαλε νηὶ Ἀττικῇ Σαμοθρηικίη νηῦς. ἥ τε δὴ Ἀττικὴ κατεδύετο καὶ ἐπιφερομένη Αἰγιναίη νηῦς κατέδυσε τῶν Σαμοθρηίκων τὴν νέα. ἅτε δὲ ἐόντες ἀκοντισταὶ οἱ Σαμοθρήικες τοὺς ἐπιβάτας ἀπὸ τῆς καταδυσάσης νεὸς βάλλοντες ἀπήραξαν καὶ ἐπέβησάν τε καὶ ἔσχον αὐτήν.

44. VI 114 τοῦτο δὲ Κυνέγειρος ὁ Εὐφορίωνος ἐνθαῦτα ἐπιλαμβανόμενος τῶν ἀφλάστων νεός, τὴν χεῖρα ἀποκοπεὶς πελέκεϊ πίπτει...

45. III 59³ ἕκτῳ δὲ ἔτεϊ Αἰγινῆται αὐτοὺς ναυμαχίῃ νικήσαντες ἠνδραποδίσαντο μετὰ Κρητῶν καὶ τῶν νεῶν καπρίους ἐχουσέων τὰς πρῴρας ἠκρωτηρίασαν καὶ ἀνέθεσαν ἐς τὸ ἱρὸν τῆς Ἀθηναίης τῆς ἐν Αἰγίνῃ.

46. Liddell–Scott–Jones (*s.v.* ἀκρωτηριάζω) take πρῴρας as the object of ἠκρωτηρίασαν and translate 'cut the beaks off the prows', but *s.v.* κάπριος they properly take πρῴρας as the object of ἐχουσέων. It seems clear that a cognate object, i.e. ἀκρωτήρια, has to be supplied with ἠκρωτηρίασαν and that the genitive phrase τῶν νεῶν καπρίους ἐχουσέων τὰς πρῴρας depends on that cognate accusative as a genitive of possession. J. E. Powell's translation 'and they cut off the fore-parts of the ships, which were in the shape of boars' seems mistaken.

47. VIII 121² τὰ ἀκροθίνια ἀπέπεμψαν ἐς Δελφούς, ἐκ τῶν ἐγένετο ἀνδριὰς ἔχων ἐν τῇ χειρὶ ἀκρωτήριον νεός, ἐὼν μέγαθος δυώδεκα πήχεων.

48. Polyaenus V 41 Ἀριστόμαχος, Καρδιανῶν τριήρεις λαβών, μετεμβιβάσας τοὺς ἐρέτας καὶ κοσμήσας τοῖς ἀκρωτηρίοις τῶν αὑτοῦ νεῶν, αὐλούμενος κατέπλει, τὰς ἰδίας ναῦς ἐφέλκων, τὴν καταγωγὴν ὀψὲ ποιούμενος. Καρδιανοὶ μὲν πρὸς ⟨τὰς⟩ ναῦς ὥρμησαν ἐκ τῆς πόλεως ὡς οἰκείας καὶ νικώσας, οἱ δὲ Ἀριστομάχειοι τῶν νεῶν ἐκβάντες πολλοὺς Καρδιανῶν ἀπέκτειναν.

49. VIII 88², Artemisia's ἐπίσημον. 92², Themistocles' σημήιον. Cf. Diodorus XIII 3 2, the *triereis* of the Sicilian expedition κεκοσμημέναι τοῖς ἐπὶ ταῖς πρῴραις ἐπισήμασι (ἐπιστήμασι MSS.), and Polyaenus III 11 11 τὸ Ἀττικὸν σημεῖον.

50. VII 194¹ ἔδοξάν τε δὴ τὰς σφετέρας εἶναι οἱ βάρβαροι καὶ πλέοντες ἐσέπεσον ἐς τοὺς πολεμίους.

51. V 108², Phoenicians.

V 112¹ νηυσὶ μέν νυν Ἴωνες ἄκροι γενόμενοι ταύτην τὴν ἡμέρην ὑπερεβάλοντο τοὺς Φοίνικας, καὶ τούτων Σάμιοι ἠρίστευσαν.

52. IX 90³ τάς τε γὰρ νέας αὐτῶν κακῶς πλέειν καὶ οὐκ ἀξιομάχους κείνοισι εἶναι.

53. VIII 10¹ τὰς μέν γε τῶν Ἑλλήνων ὁρῶντες ὀλίγας νέας, τὰς δὲ ἑωυτῶν πλήθεΐ τε πολλαπλησίας καὶ ἄμεινον πλεούσας.

54. VIII 60a πρὸς μὲν τῷ Ἰσθμῷ συμβάλλων ἐν πελάγεϊ ἀναπεπταμένῳ ναυμαχήσεις, [ἐς] τὸ ἥκιστα ἡμῖν σύμφορόν ἐστι νέας ἔχουσι βαρυτέρας καὶ ἀριθμὸν ἐλάσσονας.

55. VIII 42² νέας δὲ πολλῷ πλείστας τε καὶ ἄριστα πλεούσας παρείχοντο Ἀθηναῖοι.

56. VII 59²⁻³ τὰς μὲν δὴ νέας τὰς πάσας ἀπικομένας ἐς Δορίσκον οἱ ναύαρχοι κελεύσαντος Ξέρξεω ἐς τὸν αἰγιαλὸν τὸν προσεχέα Δορίσκῳ ἐκόμισαν...ἐς τοῦτον τὸν αἰγιαλὸν κατασχόντες τὰς νέας ἀνέψυχον ἀνελκύσαντες.

57. IV 110²; VI 14²; VIII 56²; 94¹ ἱστία.

58. VIII 12¹ ταρσὸς τῶν κωπέων.

59. V 23² κωπέες.

60. VII 89³ δόρατα ναύμαχα.

61. IX 98² ἀποβάθρας.

62. IV 110² πηδαλίοισι χρᾶσθαι.

63. III 136² τοῦτο μὲν τὰ πηδάλια παρέλυσε τῶν Μηδικέων νεῶν, τοῦτο δὲ αὐτοὺς τοὺς Πέρσας εἶρξε ὡς κατασκόπους δῆθεν ἐόντας.

64. VII 36²; IX 74¹ (of iron); VI 12¹ τὰς νέας ἔχεσκε ἐπ' ἀγκυρέων. Riding at anchor opposed to beaching: VII 188¹ αἱ μὲν δὴ πρῶται τῶν νεῶν ὅρμεον πρὸς γῆ, ἄλλαι δ' ἐπ' ἐκείνῃσι ἐπ' ἀγκυρέων.

Handling

65. Hauling up: VII 188³ ἀνασπᾶν; IX 96³ ἀνειρύειν; VII 59³, IX 98² ἀνέλκειν. Pulling down: I 164³, VII 193¹ κατασπᾶν; VIII 96¹ κατειρύειν (ναυήγια); VII 100² καθέλκειν.

66. VII 59³ ἀναψύχειν τὰς νέας.

67. II 5², 28² καταπειρητηρίη.

68. VI 16¹ ἐποκέλλειν; VII 182 ἐξοκέλλειν.

69. VI 11²–12¹. Dionysius addresses the Ionians, promising them toil and sweat, but ultimate victory if they can put up with hardship. ταῦτα ἀκούσαντες οἱ Ἴωνες ἐπιτρέπουσι σφέας αὐτοὺς τῷ Διονυσίῳ. ὁ δὲ ἀνάγων ἑκάστοτε ἐπὶ κέρας τὰς νέας, ὅκως τοῖσι ἐρέτῃσι χρήσαιτο διέκπλοον ποιεύμενος τῇσι νηυσὶ δι' ἀλληλέων καὶ τοὺς ἐπιβάτας ὁπλίσειε, τὸ λοιπὸν τῆς ἡμέρης τὰς νέας ἔχεσκε ἐπ' ἀγκυρέων, παρεῖχέ τε τοῖσι Ἴωσι πόνον δι' ἡμέρης.

70. VI 15² διεκπλέοντες ἐναυμάχεον.

71. VIII 14¹ οὗτοι μὲν νυν περὶ τὰ Κοῖλα τῆς Εὐβοίης διεφθείροντο...τοῖσι δ' Ἕλλησι ἐπεβοήθεον νέες τρεῖς καὶ πεντήκοντα Ἀττικαί.

72. VII 188¹ ὁ δὲ δὴ ναυτικὸς στρατὸς ἐπείτε...κατέσχε τῆς Μαγνησίης χώρης ἐς τὸν αἰγιαλὸν τὸν μεταξὺ Κασθαναίης τε πόλιος ἐόντα καὶ Σηπιάδος ἀκτῆς, αἱ μὲν δὴ πρῶται τῶν νεῶν ὅρμεον πρὸς γῆ, ἄλλαι δ' ἐπ' ἐκείνῃσι ἐπ' ἀγκυρέων· ἅτε γὰρ τοῦ αἰγιαλοῦ ἐόντος οὐ μεγάλου πρόκροσσαι ὅρμεον τὸ ἐς πόντον καὶ ἐπ' ὀκτὼ νέας.

190 ἐν τούτῳ τῷ πόνῳ νέας, οἳ ἐλαχίστας, λέγουσι διαφθαρῆναι τετρακοσιέων οὐκ ἐλάσσονας.

73. Diodorus gives the total number of *triereis* in the Persian fleet as more than 1200 (XI 2 1, 3 7) and puts the losses at 300+200 (12 3). When the task force is reported lost (VIII 13), Herodotus says: ἐποιέετό τε πᾶν ὑπὸ τοῦ θεοῦ ὅκως ἂν ἐξισωθείη τῷ Ἑλληνικῷ τὸ Περσικὸν μηδὲ πολλῷ πλέον εἴη.

And Diodorus echoes him (13 1): ὥστε δοκεῖν τὸ θεῖον ἀντιλαμβάνεσθαι τῶν Ἑλληνικῶν, ἵνα τοῦ πλήθους τῶν βαρβαρικῶν νεῶν ταπεινωθέντος ἀντίπαλος ἡ τῶν Ἑλλήνων δύναμις γένηται καὶ πρὸς τὰς ναυμαχίας ἀξιόχρεως.

Neither of these pious observations need make us believe that either author was of the opinion that the superiority of the Persian fleet was actually less than each had stated. We can believe that the superiority was in fact less, but still quite considerable. Although the numbers are exaggerated by him, the impression that the Persians got before the engagements at Artemisium seems to have been truly reported by Herodotus (VIII 10¹), that the Greek ships were few, and their own considerably more numerous (πλήθεϊ πολλαπλησίας) and better movers in the water.

74. VIII 9 μετὰ δὲ τοῦτο, ὡς οὐδείς σφι ἐπέπλεε, δείλην ὀψίην γινομένην τῆς ἡμέρης φυλάξαντες αὐτοὶ ἐπανέπλεον ἐπὶ τοὺς βαρβάρους, ἀπόπειραν αὐτῶν ποιήσασθαι βουλόμενοι τῆς τε μάχης καὶ τοῦ διεκπλόου.

75. VII 36² διέκπλοον δὲ ὑπόφαυσιν κατέλιπον τῶν πεντηκοντέρων καὶ τριηρέων διχοῦ* ἵνα καὶ ἐς τὸν Πόντον ἔχῃ ὁ βουλόμενος πλέειν πλοίοισι λεπτοῖσι καὶ ἐκ τοῦ Πόντου ἔξω.

76. IV 179³ πειθομένου δὲ τοῦ Ἰήσονος οὕτω δὴ τόν τε διέκπλοον τῶν βραχέων δεικνύναι τὸν Τρίτωνά σφι.

77. *F. Gr. Hist.* 176 F 1.

78. V 118–21.

79. VIII 16¹ οἱ δὲ βάρβαροι μηνοειδὲς ποιήσαντες τῶν νεῶν ἐκυκλεῦντο ὡς περιλάβοιεν αὐτούς.

80. VII 184¹ τῶν νεῶν τῶν ἐκ τῆς Ἀσίης ἐουσέων ἑπτὰ καὶ διηκοσιέων καὶ χιλιέων.

VII 185¹ νέας μέν νυν οἱ ἀπὸ Θρηίκης Ἕλληνες καὶ ἐκ τῶν νήσων τῶν ἐπικειμένων τῇ Θρηίκῃ παρείχοντο εἴκοσι καὶ ἑκατόν.

VIII 66¹ ὡς μὲν ἐμοὶ δοκέειν, οὐκ ἐλάσσονες ἐόντες ἀριθμὸν ἐσέβαλον ἐς τὰς Ἀθήνας κατά τε ἤπειρον καὶ τῇσι νηυσὶ ἢ ἐπί τε Σηπιάδα ἀπίκοντο καὶ ἐς Θερμοπύλας.

Cf. Diodorus XI 15 4 πολλὰ γὰρ πλεονεκτήσειν ἐν ταῖς στενοχωρίαις τοὺς ὀλίγοις σκάφεσι διαγωνιζομένους πρὸς πολλαπλασίας ναῦς.

81. VIII 70¹ ἐπειδὴ δὲ παρήγγελλε ἀναπλεῖν, ἀνῆγον τὰς νέας ἐπὶ τὴν Σαλαμῖνα, καὶ παρεκρίθησαν διαταχθέντες κατ' ἡσυχίην. τότε μέν νυν οὐκ ἐξέχρησέ σφι ἡ ἡμέρη ναυμαχίην ποιήσασθαι· νὺξ γὰρ ἐπεγένετο· οἱ δὲ παρεσκευάζοντο ἐς τὴν ὑστεραίην.

76¹⁻³ τοῖσι δὲ ὡς πιστὰ ἐγίνετο τὰ ἀγγελθέντα, τοῦτο μὲν ἐς τὴν νησῖδα τὴν [Ψυττάλειαν] μεταξὺ Σαλαμῖνός τε κειμένην καὶ τῆς ἠπείρου πολλοὺς τῶν Περσέων ἀπεβίβασαν· τοῦτο δέ, ἐπειδὴ ἐγίνοντο μέσαι νύκτες, ἀνῆγον μὲν τὸ ἀπ' ἑσπέρης κέρας κυκλούμενοι πρὸς τὴν Σαλαμῖνα, ἀνῆγον δὲ οἱ ἀμφὶ τὴν Κέον τε καὶ τὴν Κυνόσουραν τεταγμένοι, κατεῖχόν τε μέχρι Μουνιχίης πάντα τὸν πορθμὸν τῇσι νηυσί. τῶνδε δὲ εἵνεκα ἀνῆγον τὰς νέας, ἵνα δὴ τοῖσι Ἕλλησι μηδὲ φυγεῖν ἐξῇ, ἀλλ' ἀπολαμφθέντες ἐν τῇ Σαλαμῖνι δοῖεν τίσιν τῶν ἐπ' Ἀρτεμισίῳ ἀγωνισμάτων. ἐς δὲ τὴν νησῖδα τὴν Ψυττάλειαν καλεομένην ἀπεβίβαζον τῶν Περσέων τῶνδε εἵνεκα, ὡς ἐπεὰν γένηται ναυμαχίη, ἐνθαῦτα μάλιστα ἐξοισομένων τῶν τε ἀνδρῶν καὶ τῶν ναυηγίων (ἐν γὰρ δὴ πόρῳ [τῆς] ναυμαχίης τῆς μελλούσης ἔσεσθαι ἔκειτο ἡ νῆσος), ἵνα τοὺς μὲν περιποιῶσι, τοὺς δὲ διαφθείρωσι. ἐποίευν δὲ σιγῇ ταῦτα ὡς μὴ πυνθανοίατο οἱ ἐναντίοι. οἱ μὲν δὴ ταῦτα τῆς νυκτὸς οὐδὲν ἀποκοιμηθέντες παραρτέοντο.

Cf. Diodorus XI 17 2 εὐθὺς οὖν τὸ τῶν Αἰγυπτίων ναυτικὸν ἐξέπεμψε, προστάξας ἐμφράττειν τὸν μεταξὺ πόρον τῆς τε Σαλαμῖνος καὶ τῆς Μεγαρίδος χώρας. τὸ δὲ ἄλλο πλῆθος τῶν νεῶν ἐξέπεμψεν ἐπὶ τὴν Σαλαμῖνα.

82. VIII 79⁴ ἐγὼ γὰρ αὐτόπτης τοι λέγω γενόμενος ὅτι νῦν οὐδ' ἢν θέλωσι Κορίνθιοί τε καὶ αὐτὸς Εὐρυβιάδης οἷοί τε ἔσονται ἐκπλῶσαι· περιεχόμεθα γὰρ ὑπὸ τῶν πολεμίων κύκλῳ.

* τριηρέων διχοῦ is Hude's plausible conjecture for the MSS. τριχοῦ or τριχῇ.

83. VIII 83²–84¹ ἐνθαῦτα ἀνῆγον τὰς νέας ἁπάσας ⟨οἱ⟩ Ἕλληνες. ἀναγομένοισι δέ σφι αὐτίκα ἐπεκέατο οἱ βάρβαροι. οἱ μὲν δὴ ἄλλοι Ἕλληνες [ἐπὶ] πρύμνην ἀνεκρούοντο καὶ ὤκελλον τὰς νέας, Ἀμεινίης δὲ Παλληνεὺς ἀνὴρ Ἀθηναῖος ἐξαναχθεὶς νηΐ ἐμβάλλει. συμπλεκείσης δὲ τῆς νεὸς καὶ οὐ δυναμένων ἀπαλλαγῆναι οὕτω δὴ οἱ ἄλλοι Ἀμεινίῃ βοηθέοντες συνέμισγον.

Diodorus XI 18 4 οἱ δὲ Πέρσαι τὸ μὲν πρῶτον πλέοντες διετήρουν τὴν τάξιν, ἔχοντες πολλὴν εὐρυχωρίαν· ὡς δὲ εἰς τὸ στενὸν ἦλθον, ἠναγκάζοντο τῶν νεῶν τινας ἀπὸ τῆς τάξεως ἀποσπᾶν, καὶ πολὺν ἐποίουν θόρυβον.

84. VIII 85¹ κατὰ μὲν δὴ Ἀθηναίους ἐτετάχατο Φοίνικες (οὗτοι γὰρ εἶχον τὸ πρὸς Ἐλευσῖνός τε καὶ ἑσπέρης κέρας), κατὰ δὲ Λακεδαιμονίους Ἴωνες· οὗτοι δ' εἶχον τὸ πρὸς τὴν ἠῶ τε καὶ τὸν Πειραιέα.

The disposition of the contingents in the account of Diodorus is quite different and must be wrong. He places the Phoenicians on the right wing and the Greek contingent of the Persian fleet on the left wing of the Persian line, while in the line of the Greeks the left wing was held by the Athenians *and* the Spartans, and the right wing by the Aeginetans and the Megarians. (Diodorus XI 173–82.)

85. VIII 86 ἅτε γὰρ τῶν Ἑλλήνων σὺν κόσμῳ ναυμαχεόντων, τῶν δὲ βαρβάρων οὔτε τεταγμένων ἔτι οὔτε σὺν νόῳ ποιεόντων οὐδέν. . .

89² ἐπεὶ δὲ αἱ πρῶται ἐς φυγὴν ἐτράποντο, ἐνθαῦτα αἱ πλεῖσται διεφθείροντο. οἱ γὰρ ὄπισθε τεταγμένοι ἐς τὸ πρόσθε τῇσι νηυσὶ παριέναι πειρώμενοι ὡς ἀποδεξόμενοί τι καὶ αὐτοὶ ἔργον βασιλέϊ, τῇσι σφετέρῃσι νηυσὶ φευγούσῃσι περιέπιπτον.

AESCHYLUS, 'PERSIANS'

The importance of Aeschylus' account of the battle of Salamis, and of the ships engaged in it, was well assessed by Munro:* 'Of our literary sources Aeschylus, an eye-witness writing in the fresh memory of the battle, is obviously the best. We may not find a systematic account of the battle in the *Persians*, but the pictures given are assuredly trustworthy as far as they go.' This opinion is quoted with approval by Broadhead,† who adds specific qualifications. The poet may have presented the actions of the Greeks in too favourable a light. As a dramatist he was not bound to adhere slavishly to historical facts, and even if he did adhere to them a dramatized version in the limited space available could hardly do more than bring out the salient points, especially those that were good dramatic material. He adds: 'Since such salient points, however, would be precisely those best remembered by the audience, they would be least likely to suffer serious distortion.' Here we shall be concerned only with the salient facts about the ships and

* *JHS* XXII (1903), 326. † *Op. cit.* 322.

their employment in the battle. Most of the points at issue have already been treated.

The messenger who brings the Persian queen-mother, Atossa, news of the Persian defeat at Salamis first reports that her son is alive, then lists the principal casualties, among whom is 'Tharybis leader of five times fifty ships'[1]. Atossa asks how many the Greek ships were that dared to attack the Persian fleet with 'ships' rams'[2]. The messenger gives the number of the Greek ships as 'three hundred all told, but ten were set apart'. Their peculiarity becomes clear from the number given for the Persian fleet. The messenger confidently states that Xerxes had a thousand ships, 'and two hundred and seven were especially fast'[3]. Herodotus gives the number of the Greek fleet at Salamis as two hundred and forty, including the last-minute Tenian deserter. Herodotus says that the number of the Persian fleet at Phalerum, in spite of the losses it had incurred, was about the same as at Sepias, i.e. twelve hundred (see above, p. 136). Broadhead is certainly right in his opinion that Aeschylus intended his round numbers of one thousand for the Persian and three hundred for the Greek fleet at Salamis to be inclusive of the special fast *triereis*. It looks then as if the number of 1207, which Herodotus gives for the Persian fleet at Doriscus and which can be derived by misinterpretation from Aeschylus, is at the bottom of Herodotus' calculations, which are accordingly to be regarded as that much exaggerated. Aeschylus' figures are unlikely to be far wrong.

The messenger then proceeds to an account of the battle[4]. He begins with the story of the deserter's false tale: 'at nightfall the Greeks would leap upon the *selmata* of the ships and slip away to safety'. By *selmata* Aeschylus certainly means here, not thwarts, as the editors generally translate, but the poop. He is probably thinking of the action, not of the crews, though these of course would have access to the thwarts by the landing ladder and poop, but of the trierarchs, helmsmen, *epibatai* etc., whose place was on the poop (cf. p. 121, note 5). As an 'officer' himself, the messenger is thinking in terms of the action of officers. We must remember that the Athenian *triereis* at any rate did not have an overall deck.

The messenger then recounts[5] Xerxes' order to the *nauarchoi* to post the main body of the fleet in three squadrons for the task of guarding 'the exits and narrow sea-races', and the rest of the ships 'round about the island of Ajax', i.e. Salamis. The words *stiphos*, pack, which is here translated 'main body', and *stoichoi*, files, which are translated 'squadrons', have led to some difficulty. They have been thought to imply formation in several ranks, and to look forward to the final battle lines on the following morning. Even if the battle line was to be composed of several ranks, which seems to be very doubtful, there is no reason for a line of three ranks for the tasks assigned to the fleet during the hours of darkness. Such an arrangement would have been inviting confusion. With Hammond we take the word *stoichos* here to mean a squadron of ships, which would normally move in line, ahead or abreast; and *stiphos* to mean the main body, possibly opposed to the 'others' which patrolled round the south of Salamis. These may possibly have been the fast *triereis*. There were then in practice four squadrons, each of which is likely to have had a separate task. We saw, when we were considering Herodotus' account, that he speaks of three tasks for the fleet in the early hours, guarding the Megarian strait, and blocking the channels on each side of the island of Lipsokoutali. When Aeschylus speaks of the three squadrons 'guarding the exits and the narrow sea-races', we can recognize this as a description of Herodotus' three tasks; and Aeschylus mentions a fourth task and a fourth squadron, patrolling round the south of the island of Salamis. We recall that in the casualty list Tharybis was described as leader of five times fifty ships. It seems likely then that the squadrons numbered about two hundred and fifty ships. Three squadrons of two hundred and fifty, and a fast squadron of two hundred and seven ships, bring the total to nearly a thousand.

The messenger then describes[6] the orderly preparations as the Persian crews take a meal, and fit their oars to the tholepins. At sunset they go aboard, 'every oarsman and every man of *hopla*'. Our previous experience of *hopla* in connection with ships would suggest that the word should mean the standing and running tackle of the mast and sail, but there are two reasons why this meaning must be rejected here. The first is that sail is never used in action. If sail is raised in action, it is to break off the engagement[7]. Secondly there undoubtedly was a large number of hoplites, as well as archers, on the decks of the Persian ships. It must be these who are meant by the expression 'every man of *hopla*'.

As the ships move off, 'company calls to company of the long ship'. The decree of Themistocles speaks of posting up lists of the *trieres*-companies or *taxeis*; and it seems, though the readings of the inscription at this point are far from certain, that the whole crew is regarded as a single *taxis*. Aeschylus' phrase suggests different *taxeis* within a single ship. He may then be thinking of the various categories of oarsmen, which we shall come to recognize (see pp. 268–71). The maintenance of strict time, particularly when picking up the stroke, would have been of great importance. One way of keeping time would have been by a sort of simple sea-shanty, company calling to company. The captains kept the whole Persian fleet on patrol throughout the night. In the morning[8] they could hear the Greeks singing. Instead of the panic and disunity they had been led to expect, the Greeks were in good spirits. The two squadrons which had the task of blocking the two eastern channels had presumably joined and were swinging round Cynosura northwards into the single narrow channel. The Greek fleet, just moving off the beaches of Paloukia half a mile the other side of the island of St George, could be heard but not yet seen. 'Straightway, at a signal, the oars fell as one and smote the deep water, and in a moment all were clearly seen.' The Greek fleet moved into view from behind the island of St George. 'First,' the messenger continued, 'the right wing was leading in orderly station, then the whole fleet followed.' Broadhead and Hammond speak of the attack of the Persians, hoping to take the Greeks by surprise. What Aeschylus suggests is something rather different. The two Persian squadrons after a night at the oar make at first light a reconnaissance in force of the Greek station, expecting to find panic and disunity. The surprise attack is made by the Greeks, whose tactical plan is to destroy the two squadrons who were weary with patrolling, before the rest of the fleet could come up. Five hundred ships, only able to present a narrow front because of the constricted water in which they found themselves, and rowed by tired crews, would be at most on equal terms with a force of three hundred ships with fresh crews. Herodotus' description of the Greeks backing water as the Persian squadrons approached may be an Ionian captain's misinterpretation of the manœuvre of changing from line abreast into line ahead. The first contact, the messenger says, was between a Greek ship and a Phoenician. Broadhead and Hammond follow Diodorus and suppose that the Greek ship was on the Greek *left* wing (see above, p. 143), and that in spite of the fact that the right wing was leading, first contact with the enemy was made at the other end of the line. According to the interpretation of the passages in Herodotus which is put forward above, the Phoenicians would have been on the Persian left facing the Athenians on the

Greek right. The Greek fleet, in line ahead with its former right wing leading, attempted a breakthrough, according to the principles of the *diekplous*, on the side where they would enjoy the not inconsiderable advantage of a friendly shore. While the ships of the Greek allies were passing through the gap they had created by ramming several ships on the Persian left wing, the rest of the Persian fleet carried on a little way from their initial momentum, but then, when they tried to turn, fell into confusion, ramming one another and shearing off one another's oars. The Greek allies were then able to row round them and complete their destruction.

The main difference between Aeschylus' and Herodotus' accounts is that Aeschylus makes the Persian squadrons begin their patrolling after sunset, while Herodotus makes them start at midnight. Aeschylus is more likely to be right, and we can perhaps see a reason for Herodotus' difference in the elaborate sequence of events with which he builds up the dramatic tale of the night's happenings. Otherwise the two accounts supplement and confirm each other remarkably. There is difference of emphasis on certain points, e.g., Herodotus, whose sources are likely to have been Ionian Greek, emphasizes that the Persians attacked the Greeks, whereas in Aeschylus, whose sources were Athenian, the attack described is that of the Greek allies. In both cases the action narrated is consistent with the same set of circumstances, an attempt at a *diekplous* by the Greek allies attacking in line ahead at a point at the western end of the Persian line of ships, which was advancing in line abreast up the narrowing channel against them. The salient points both in the nocturnal Persian preparations and in the battle itself seem equally clear in both authors. The Greek fleet had succeeded in overcoming the disadvantage of slower movement by attacking the enemy when he was tired after many hours at the oar, and it had overcome the disadvantage of considerably smaller numbers by attacking a part of the enemy fleet advancing on an artificially restricted front.

The information which Aeschylus gives about the ships at Salamis is not much. It confirms the practice of ramming, and the use of a bronze ram, the carrying of hoplites on deck, the Greek tactic of the *diekplous*, the use of the word *selmata* for the poop, and the recognition of different *taxeis* of oarsmen. In the lyric passages the ships are described as 'equal-winged', 'dark-eyed', and 'with three tholepins'[9]. The first epithet probably refers to the balanced oar-banks, the second to the eyes which appear in the representations on each side of the bow. The third is important since, as a partial variant of *trieres*, it suggests the meaning of the latter. *Trieres* means by derivation 'three-rowing', the latter part of the word being formed from the root *erē* which occurs in *eretes* and many other words connected with rowing, including the names of all oared-ship types (in -*oros*, -*eros*, and -*eres*). The word *triskalmos* tells us that the *trieres* was regarded as having three tholepins, clearly not three tholepins in all, but three tholepins in a unit division which in other types had a different number of them. The development of a ship of two levels of oarsmen emerges clearly from the ship representations of the period 700–480 B.C. (pp. 112–20, Pls 19–20). The fact that there is extreme scarcity of literary evidence giving details of the oared ships of the period makes the total lack of literary evidence for the two-level oared ship not really surprising. For the fifth-century writers who give accounts of the earlier period the development of the *trieres* is the new feature which steals the limelight, and it must be assumed that the term pentekontor, for them as for earlier writers, covered the two-level type. In the ship with oars rowed at two levels it is plain that there were two tholepins in the unit of length which is basic to the oared ship, i.e. the yard or so which is the fore-and-aft measurement of the space required by an oarsman to work his oar. The name for this oar-space is *metron* in Greek, *interscalmium* in Latin. In English it is sometimes called 'the room'. An increase in the number of tholepins and hence of oars to this unit of length meant an increase in power not offset by a corresponding increase in overall length. The epithet *triskalmos* indicates that the *trieres* was regarded as a ship which had three tholepins to the basic unit of length. The epithet *triskalmos* tells us nothing about the position of the new third oarsman, but it does tell us the reason for the new series of names for ship types which begins with *trieres*, and that is very valuable indeed.

TEXTS

Persians (Oxford text of Gilbert Murray)

1. 323   Θάρυβίς τε πεντήκοντα πεντάκις νεῶν
           ταγός.

2. 334   *Atossa* ναῶν πόσον δὴ πλῆθος ἦν Ἑλληνίδων,
           ὥστ' ἀξιῶσαι Περσικῷ στρατεύματι
           μάχην συνάψαι ναΐοισιν ἐμβολαῖς;
           Messenger πλήθους μὲν ἂν σάφ' ἴσθ' ἕκατι βάρβαρον
           ναυσὶν κρατῆσαι. καὶ γὰρ Ἕλλησιν μὲν ἦν

ὁ πᾶς ἀριθμὸς ἐς τριακάδας δέκα

ναῶν, δεκὰς δ᾽ ἦν τῶνδε χωρὶς ἔκκριτος·

Ξέρξη δέ, καὶ γὰρ οἶδα, χιλιὰς μὲν ἦν

3. 34²   ὧν ἦγε πλῆθος, αἱ δ᾽ ὑπέρκοποι τάχει

ἑκατὸν δὶς ἦσαν ἑπτά θ᾽· ὧδ᾽ ἔχει λόγος.

Cf. Herodotus VII 184¹ Μέχρι μέν νυν τούτου τοῦ χώρου (i.e. the restricted beach between Kasthanaia and Cape Sepias) καὶ Θερμοπυλέων ἀπαθής τε κακῶν ἦν ὁ στρατὸς καὶ πλῆθος ἦν τηνικαῦτα ἔτι, ὡς ἐγὼ συμβαλλόμενος εὑρίσκω, τὸν μὲν ἐκ τῶν νεῶν τῶν ἐκ τῆς Ἀσίης, ἐουσέων ἑπτὰ καὶ διηκοσιέων καὶ χιλιέων, τὸν μὲν ἀρχαῖον ἑκάστων τῶν ἐθνέων ἐόντα ὅμιλον...

4. 355   ἀνὴρ γὰρ Ἕλλην ἐξ Ἀθηναίων στρατοῦ

ἐλθὼν ἔλεξε παιδὶ σῷ Ξέρξη τάδε,

ὡς εἰ μελαίνης νυκτὸς ἵξεται κνέφας,

Ἕλληνες οὐ μενοῖεν, ἀλλὰ σέλμασιν

ναῶν ἐπενθορόντες ἄλλος ἄλλοσε

δρασμῷ κρυφαίῳ βίοτον ἐκσωσοίατο.

5. 366   τάξαι νεῶν μὲν στῖφος ἐν στοίχοις τρισίν,

ἔκπλους φυλάσσειν καὶ πόρους ἁλιρρόθους,

ἄλλας δὲ κύκλῳ νῆσον Αἴαντος πέριξ.

6. 374   οἱ δ᾽ οὐκ ἀκόσμως, ἀλλὰ πειθάρχῳ φρενὶ

δεῖπνόν ⟨τ᾽⟩ ἐπορσύνοντο, ναυβάτης τ᾽ ἀνὴρ

τροποῦτο κώπην σκαλμὸν ἀμφ᾽ εὐήρετμον.

ἐπεὶ δὲ φέγγος ἡλίου κατέφθιτο

καὶ νὺξ ἐπήει, πᾶς ἀνὴρ κώπης ἄναξ

ἐς ναῦν ἐχώρει πᾶς θ᾽ ὅπλων ἐπιστάτης·

380   τάξις δὲ τάξιν παρεκάλει νεὼς μακρᾶς·

πλέουσι δ᾽ ὡς ἕκαστος ἦν τεταγμένος,

καὶ πάννυχοι δὴ διάπλοον καθίστασαν

ναῶν ἄνακτες πάντα ναυτικὸν λεών.

καὶ νὺξ ἐχώρει, κοὐ μάλ᾽ Ἑλλήνων στρατὸς

385   κρυφαῖον ἔκπλουν οὐδαμῇ καθίστατο·

7. E.g. the Samians at Lade (Herodotus VI 14² ἀειράμενοι τὰ ἱστία ἀποπλῶσαι ἐκ τῆς τάξιος ἐς τὴν Σάμον) and the Athenian story of the Corinthian commander Adeimantus at Salamis (id. VIII 94¹ τὰ ἱστία ἀειράμενον οἴχεσθαι φεύγοντα).

8. 386   ἐπεί γε μέντοι λευκόπωλος ἡμέρα

πᾶσαν κατέσχε γαῖαν εὐφεγγὴς ἰδεῖν,

πρῶτον μὲν ἠχῇ κέλαδος Ἑλλήνων πάρα

μολπηδὸν ηὐφήμησεν, ὄρθιον δ᾽ ἅμα

390   ἀντηλάλαξε νησιώτιδος πέτρας

ἠχώ· φόβος δὲ πᾶσι βαρβάροις παρῆν

γνώμης ἀποσφαλεῖσιν· οὐ γὰρ ὡς φυγῇ

παιᾶν' ἐφύμνουν σεμνὸν Ἕλληνες τότε,
ἀλλ' ἐς μάχην ὁρμῶντες εὐψύχῳ θράσει·
σάλπιγξ δ' ἀυτῇ πάντ' ἐκεῖν' ἐπέφλεγεν.
εὐθὺς δὲ κώπης ῥοθιάδος ξυνεμβολῇ
ἔπαισαν ἅλμην βρύχιον ἐκ κελεύματος,
θοῶς δὲ πάντες ἦσαν ἐκφανεῖς ἰδεῖν.
τὸ δεξιὸν μὲν πρῶτον εὐτάκτως κέρας
ἡγεῖτο κόσμῳ, δεύτερον δ' ὁ πᾶς στόλος
ἐπεξεχώρει, καὶ παρῆν ὁμοῦ κλύειν
πολλὴν βοήν, 'ὦ παῖδες Ἑλλήνων ἴτε,
ἐλευθεροῦτε πατρίδ', ἐλευθεροῦτε δὲ
παῖδας, γυναῖκας, θεῶν τε πατρῴων ἕδη,
θήκας τε προγόνων· νῦν ὑπὲρ πάντων ἀγών.'
καὶ μὴν παρ' ἡμῶν Περσίδος γλώσσης ῥόθος
ὑπηντίαζε, κοὐκέτ' ἦν μέλλειν ἀκμή.
εὐθὺς δὲ ναῦς ἐν νηὶ χαλκήρη στόλον
ἔπαισεν· ἦρξε δ' ἐμβολῆς Ἑλληνικὴ
ναῦς, κἀποθραύει πάντα Φοινίσσης νεὼς
κόρυμβ', ἐπ' ἄλλην δ' ἄλλος ηὔθυνεν δόρυ.
τὰ πρῶτα μέν νυν ῥεῦμα Περσικοῦ στρατοῦ
ἀντεῖχεν· ὡς δὲ πλῆθος ἐν στενῷ νεῶν
ἤθροιστ', ἀρωγὴ δ' οὔτις ἀλλήλοις παρῆν,
αὐτοὶ δ' ὑπ' αὐτῶν ἐμβόλοις χαλκοστόμοις
παίοντ' ἔθραυον πάντα κωπήρη στόλον,
Ἑλληνικαί τε νῆες οὐκ ἀφρασμόνως
κύκλῳ πέριξ ἔθεινον...
ὁμόπτεροι κυανώπιδες.
πᾶσαι γᾷ τᾷδ'
ἐξέφθινται τρίσκαλμοι
νᾶες ἄναες ἄναες.

395

400

405

410

415

9. 559
677

Cf. 1074.

THUCYDIDES

That part of Thucydides' survey of ancient history which covers the period
700–480 B.C.[1] lays great emphasis on maritime affairs. It is extremely condensed, and at important points inexplicit, but some of the information is
important and precise. Furthermore, it throws light on aspects of Greek
maritime history on which Herodotus is silent.

'As Hellas became more powerful and was accumulating wealth even more
than before, tyrannies were commonly established in the cities as public

revenues became greater (earlier there had been hereditary kingships based on fixed perquisites); and Hellas began to fit out navies and to rely more on the sea. The Corinthians are said to have been the first to take up naval affairs in a manner closely resembling the modern fashion; and *triereis* are said to have been built first in Corinth, while Ameinocles a Corinthian shipwright appears actually to have built four ships for the Samians. It is about three hundred years between the end of this war and the time that Ameinocles went to Samos. The earliest sea-fight too, that we know of, was between the Corinthians and the Corcyraeans, and this was two hundred and sixty years before the same date. For the Corinthians had their city on the isthmus, and so from the very earliest times maintained an *entrepôt* because the Hellenes within and without the Peloponnese communicated with each other in early times by land rather than by sea and hence through Corinthian territory. They became rich and powerful, as has been shown by the early poets, who called the place "wealthy". Further, when the Hellenes came to use the sea more, the Corinthians acquired warships and put down piracy, and offering an *entrepôt* for both seaborne and landborne merchandise made their city powerful through its revenues of money.'

The period of greatest Corinthian naval and commercial growth is connected by Thucydides with the rise of tyranny; but the Cypselid dynasty with its associations with Egypt and Lydia inherited an already dominant Corinthian sea power which had early planted colonies in Corcyra and Syracuse. It is in such a milieu that we might expect the invention of the *trieres*. The sea-battle between Corinth and Corcyra, to which Thucydides refers, took place either in 664 or in 680 according to the interpretation of the phrase 'the end of this war'. Conditions of acute naval rivalry between Corinth and her colony, brought into subjection by Periander in 610 B.C., could have provided the stimulus to invention. From Corinth knowledge of the new type would quickly have been passed to Egypt, where the philhellene Necho might well have exploited it in his preparations for the invasion of Syria. It is not necessary to go as far back as the eighth century for the invention. Ameinocles is not said by Thucydides to have built four *triereis* for the Samians in 704 B.C. (or 720), as is often assumed. Samian naval reputation, resting mainly on the achievements of Polycrates, was high in the fifth century, as Herodotus testifies. Seeking to support his assertion that Corinth was the first power to adopt modern naval methods, Thucydides makes two separate points: first that she invented the *trieres*, and second that as early as 704 Ameinocles built four ships for no less a people than the Samians. As Cary has suggested,* comparing the entries in the Chronicle of Athena Lindia, he is likely to have derived the latter information from a Samian temple inscription. It would seem most unreasonable not to accept what Thucydides says about the *trieres*, since it complements Herodotus' testimony, as substantially correct: i.e. that the *trieres* was invented in Corinth probably before the middle of the seventh century, at any rate before the end of the century, when Corinthian sea power seems to have declined. Had the invention of the *trieres* occurred in the reigns of Cypselus (655–625 B.C.) or Periander (625–585 B.C.), it is likely to have been associated with their names. The fact that it is not suggests that the invention took place in the period of Corinthian naval and commercial power, and rivalry with Corcyra, before the institution of the tyranny.

Thucydides proceeds: 'The Ionians too afterwards acquired naval power in the time of Cyrus, who was first king of the Persians, and of his son Cambyses. While at war with Cyrus they managed to control their home waters for some time. Polycrates also, who was tyrant of Samos in Cambyses' time, was strong at sea, and reduced several islands including Rheneia, which he captured and dedicated to Delian Apollo. The Phocaeans, when engaged in colonizing Massilia, defeated the Carthaginians in a sea-fight.'

Thucydides, as Gomme observes,† is here not quite in agreement with Herodotus, who places Ionian sea power in the first half of the sixth century, and their subjection by Harpagus in the time of Cyrus. He confirms Herodotus' account of Polycrates' supremacy at sea. A defeat of the Carthaginians by the Phocaeans, engaged in the colonization of Massilia, which was founded about 600 B.C., yet at a date by inference later than Polycrates, sounds improbable, and is not elsewhere attested.‡

To continue with Thucydides: 'These, then, were the most powerful of the fleets: but it appears that even these, though they were established many

---

* M. Cary, *CR* LX (1946), 28. R. T. Williams (*JHS* 1958, 121 ff.) has suggested that the ships which Ameinocles made for the Samians are two-level ships and that the Greek word for four in the MSS. of Thucydides is a corruption of the word for two-level ships. The earliest representation of a Samian ship (*c.* 489 B.C., Arch. 89) shows a ship of two levels, so that Thucydides might well have regarded Ameinocles' action as bringing coals to Newcastle (*even* for the Samians). It was certainly about this time (700 B.C.) that Greek two-level ships are first represented (Geom. 40–2, Arch. 1) and that Phoenician ships of two levels appear in Assyrian art (Pl. 22 *a*).

† A. W. Gomme, *Commentary on Thucydides*, I, 123.

‡ Unless Sosylus (see above, p. 138) refers to this battle.

generations after the Trojan expedition, employed only a few *triereis* and were still, like it, equipped with pentekontors and long vessels (*ploia makra*). A short time before the Persian invasions and the death of Darius, who succeeded Cambyses as king of the Persians, the tyrants on the Sicilian coasts and the Corcyraeans acquired *triereis* in large numbers, so that these were the last naval powers of note to be established in Hellas before Xerxes' expedition. The Aeginetans and Athenians, and other such peoples, possessed small fleets, and most of these ships were pentekontors. It was only quite recently that Themistocles persuaded the Athenians when they were at war with the Aeginetans, and when too the Persians were expected, to construct the ships with which they actually fought [at Salamis]. And these ships did not yet have decks throughout their length.'

There are three points in this passage which need discussion: the small number of *triereis* in fleets before the Persian wars, Athenian naval construction between Marathon and Salamis, and the absence of a continuous deck in the *triereis* of Themistocles' fleet.

Thucydides is constantly concerned to minimize the importance of earlier conflicts in comparison with the war which he is setting out to describe. Herodotus' testimony, on the other hand, confirmed less specifically by Thucydides, must require us to attribute a large fleet of *triereis* to Polycrates, probably as many as a hundred. Nor is there any reason to disbelieve his statement that at Lade in 494 there were three hundred and fifty-three *triereis*, including contingents of a hundred Chian, eighty Milesian, seventy Lesbian and sixty Samian ships of that rating[2]. In a later chapter[3] Thucydides explains the reasons which inhibited the growth of the Greek states: 'For example, after the Ionians had achieved a great advance in prosperity, Cyrus and the Persian empire after subduing Croesus...made war on them and enslaved the cities on the mainland; and later Darius, fortified by the possession of the Phoenician fleet, enslaved the islands also.' Herodotus does not tell us the size of the Ionian and Aeolian contingents in the six hundred *triereis* of Datis' force, but Xerxes' force of one thousand two hundred and seven *triereis* included Greek contingents of three hundred and seven, as well as the hundred and fifty *triereis* from Cyprus. The Phoenician fleet numbered three hundred and the Egyptian two hundred ships of *trieres* rating[4]. It appears then that Thucydides does not take sufficient account of the East Greek fleets of *triereis* in the period before Salamis. On the other hand he may be quite correct in his attribution of large fleets of *triereis* to the cities of West Greece just before the war. Gelon, according to Herodotus, offered two hundred *triereis* to the Greeks in 490, but only on the condition, which was refused, of taking command of the whole Greek navy himself; and the Corcyraeans sent sixty *triereis* which never arrived[5].

His statement that Athens only constructed her *triereis* just before Xerxes' invasion seems likely to have been in the main correct[6]. Her help to the Ionian revolt consisted of twenty ships which were probably not all *triereis*. Just before Marathon Herodotus speaks of an Athenian expedition against Aegina consisting of fifty ships of her own and twenty borrowed from Corinth[7]. After Marathon Miltiades takes an Athenian fleet of seventy ships to Paros[8]. But at Artemisium ten years later she possessed, to face the Persian invaders, at first a hundred and forty-seven *triereis*, some with Plataean and twenty with Chalcidian crews, and later a further fifty-three, to make up the total of two hundred of which she was able to dispose at Salamis[9]. Such a marked increase must have been the result of a deliberate building programme.

The third point which Thucydides makes, and which must be examined, lies in the assertion that Themistocles' *triereis* were 'still without decks throughout their length'. The question of the deck-space of *triereis* is tied up with the question of how many *epibatai* they carried. Herodotus' testimony is that the Chians used forty *epibatai*, and that in Xerxes' fleet, in addition to the normal number, there were a further thirty Persian, Median, or Sacan *epibatai*. Of these it is likely that the Sacae at any rate were archers[10]. The decree of Themistocles appears to record ten *epibatai* and four archers on each of the Athenian ships. Plutarch[11] says that there were fourteen hoplites and four archers on the ships at Salamis. It seems clear that Xerxes', and the Chian, *triereis* found room for a considerably larger number of soldiers on their decks than did the *triereis* of the Athenians at Salamis.

There is some ground for the belief that ships of one and two oar-levels very early developed some kind of continuous deck linking the fo'c'sle and poop, for the accommodation, not of course of oarsmen, but of hoplites and archers. Pliny[12] attributed the invention of the continuous deck to the Thasians, a colony of Paros which became wealthy in the last half of the sixth century, and built a fleet. But before the middle of the seventh century a single-level ship on the Aristonothos vase (see Arch. 5, Pl. 9) suggests the existence of at least a gangway connecting fo'c'sle and poop for the use of soldiers, and the Sennacherib relief of about 700 (see Pl. 22 a) shows a Phoenician ship of two oar-levels which has a continuous deck with high side screens carrying a number of people. An Etruscan black-figure hydria of 525–485 B.C., again (see Pl. 22 b), shows a ship of two oar-levels with an enlarged fo'c'sle and poop, both manned by archers. In between on what is possibly a deck, possibly a connecting gangway, there stand one hoplite and two other armed men.

The conclusion would seem to be that the employment of large numbers of soldiers on deck by the Chians and by Xerxes necessitated a continuous deck, and that there is enough evidence to justify that assumption. On the other hand, Thucydides may have been quite right in saying that the Athenian *triereis* at Salamis had no continuous deck, since in these ships the number of soldiers on deck was small. Plutarch's account of Themistocles' tactics is also interesting in this connection. He took care, he says[13], not to send his *triereis* bow on against the enemy until the time arrived when a fresh breeze from the sea and a swell through the straits usually arose. 'This breeze had no effect on the Greek ships, which were of shallow draught and lay low in the water, but was fatal to the Persian ships, which had high sterns and decks and great momentum when under way. It caught them and offered them broadside to the enemy.' Plutarch's evidence has been thought to clash with Herodotus' statements about the condition of the two fleets (see p. 134). We saw that Herodotus is probably talking about the state of their hulls as affecting their speed under oar in open water, since the Persians had had the advantage of drying out before they entered Greek waters, while Plutarch is talking about the manoeuvrability of the Persian ships as a result of their build, and their ability to keep station in a stiff breeze. We saw (see above, p. 132) from the story of the obedient Persian notables how numbers of men on the deck could affect a ship's seaworthiness in rough weather. The presence of the overall deck with thirty or forty extra men on it would be likely to have just the effect Plutarch describes.

Confirmation of this conclusion is to be found in Plutarch's account of Cimon's naval operations in Ionia in 467 B.C. He says[14] that Cimon took over a fleet of two hundred *triereis* which 'had been from the beginning well constructed by Themistocles for speed and manoeuvrability', i.e. the Salamis fleet. 'He made them broader and put a bridge between their decks so that they might be able to attack the enemy in a more formidable fashion with many hoplites.' We may note that the Chians, who appear to have favoured this theory of naval warfare, were sailing with him on this occasion. Cimon's political tendencies may have inclined him to a theory which relied more on the hoplite and less on the oarsman, but for whatever reason he seems clearly to be giving up the Themistoclean theory which saw the ship primarily as an oar-powered machine for ramming and sinking the enemy, and adopting the opposing theory by which the ship was merely a platform for the accommodation of as large a force of hoplites and archers as possible. The phrase 'making the ships broader' must be taken to refer to the *katastroma*, which overhung the gunwale. In the realm of naval theory, as of politics, Cimon represents a backward eddy in a stream which was, for more than a century, to flow the other way.

TEXTS

1. I 13–14[3] Δυνατωτέρας δὲ γιγνομένης τῆς Ἑλλάδος καὶ τῶν χρημάτων τὴν κτῆσιν ἔτι μᾶλλον ἢ πρότερον ποιουμένης τὰ πολλὰ τυραννίδες ἐν ταῖς πόλεσι καθίσταντο, τῶν προσόδων μειζόνων γιγνομένων (πρότερον δὲ ἦσαν ἐπὶ ῥητοῖς γέρασι πατρικαὶ βασιλεῖαι), ναυτικά τε ἐξηρτύετο ἡ Ἑλλάς, καὶ τῆς θαλάσσης μᾶλλον ἀντείχοντο. πρῶτοι δὲ Κορίνθιοι λέγονται ἐγγύτατα τοῦ νῦν τρόπου μεταχειρίσαι τὰ περὶ τὰς ναῦς, καὶ τριήρεις ἐν Κορίνθῳ πρῶτον τῆς Ἑλλάδος ναυπηγηθῆναι. φαίνεται δὲ καὶ Σαμίοις Ἀμεινοκλῆς Κορίνθιος ναυπηγὸς ναῦς ποιήσας τέσσαρας· ἔτη δ' ἐστὶ* μάλιστα τριακόσια ἐς τὴν τελευτὴν τοῦδε τοῦ πολέμου ὅτε Ἀμεινοκλῆς Σαμίοις ἦλθεν. ναυμαχία τε παλαιτάτη ὧν ἴσμεν γίγνεται Κορινθίων πρὸς Κερκυραίους· ἔτη δὲ μάλιστα καὶ ταύτῃ ἑξήκοντα καὶ διακόσιά ἐστι μέχρι τοῦ αὐτοῦ χρόνου. οἰκοῦντες γὰρ τὴν πόλιν οἱ Κορίνθιοι ἐπὶ τοῦ Ἰσθμοῦ αἰεὶ δή ποτε ἐμπόριον εἶχον, τῶν Ἑλλήνων τὸ πάλαι κατὰ γῆν τὰ πλείω ἢ κατὰ θάλασσαν, τῶν τε ἐντὸς Πελοποννήσου καὶ τῶν ἔξω, διὰ τῆς ἐκείνων παρ' ἀλλήλους ἐπιμισγόντων, χρήμασί τε δυνατοὶ ἦσαν, ὡς καὶ τοῖς παλαιοῖς ποιηταῖς δεδήλωται· ἀφνειὸν γὰρ ἐπωνόμασαν τὸ χωρίον. ἐπειδή τε οἱ Ἕλληνες μᾶλλον ἔπλωζον, τὰς ναῦς κτησάμενοι τὸ λῃστικὸν καθῄρουν, καὶ ἐμπόριον παρέχοντες ἀμφότερα δυνατὴν ἔσχον χρημάτων προσόδῳ τὴν πόλιν. καὶ Ἴωσιν ὕστερον πολὺ γίγνεται ναυτικὸν ἐπὶ Κύρου Περσῶν πρώτου βασιλεύοντος καὶ Καμβύσου τοῦ υἱέος αὐτοῦ, τῆς τε καθ' ἑαυτοὺς θαλάσσης Κύρῳ πολεμοῦντες ἐκράτησάν τινα χρόνον. καὶ Πολυκράτης Σάμου τυραννῶν ἐπὶ Καμβύσου ναυτικῷ ἰσχύων ἄλλας τε τῶν νήσων ὑπηκόους ἐποιήσατο καὶ Ῥήνειαν ἑλὼν ἀνέθηκε τῷ Ἀπόλλωνι τῷ Δηλίῳ. Φωκαῆς τε Μασσαλίαν οἰκίζοντες Καρχηδονίους ἐνίκων ναυμαχοῦντες· δυνατώτατα γὰρ ταῦτα τῶν ναυτικῶν ἦν. φαίνεται δὲ καὶ ταῦτα πολλαῖς γενεαῖς ὕστερα γενόμενα τῶν Τρωικῶν τριήρεσι μὲν ὀλίγαις χρώμενα, πεντηκοντόροις δ' ἔτι καὶ πλοίοις μακροῖς ἐξηρτυμένα ὥσπερ ἐκεῖνα.

* τέσσαρας codd.: δικρότους R. T. Williams, *JHS* 1958, 121 ff. ἔτη δ': καὶ ταῦτα ἔ[τη] v.l. Π[19].

ὀλίγον τε πρὸ τῶν Μηδικῶν καὶ τοῦ Δαρείου θανάτου, ὃς μετὰ Καμβύσην Περσῶν
ἐβασίλευσε, τριήρεις περί τε Σικελίαν τοῖς τυράννοις ἐς πλῆθος ἐγένοντο καὶ Κερκυραίοις·
ταῦτα γὰρ τελευταῖα πρὸ τῆς Ξέρξου στρατείας ναυτικὰ ἀξιόλογα ἐν τῇ Ἑλλάδι
κατέστη. Αἰγινῆται γὰρ καὶ Ἀθηναῖοι, καὶ εἴ τινες ἄλλοι, βραχέα ἐκέκτηντο, καὶ τούτων
τὰ πολλὰ πεντηκοντόρους· ὀψέ τε ἀφ' οὗ Ἀθηναίους Θεμιστοκλῆς ἔπεισεν Αἰγινήταις
πολεμοῦντας, καὶ ἅμα τοῦ βαρβάρου προσδοκίμου ὄντος, τὰς ναῦς ποιήσασθαι αἷσπερ
καὶ ἐναυμάχησαν· καὶ αὗται οὔπω εἶχον διὰ πάσης καταστρώματα.

2. Herodotus VI 8[1-2] ἐτάσσοντο δὲ ὧδε· τὸ μὲν πρὸς τὴν ἠῶ εἶχον κέρας αὐτοὶ
Μιλήσιοι, νέας παρεχόμενοι ὀγδώκοντα· εἴχοντο δὲ τούτων Πριηνέες δυώδεκα νηυσὶ καὶ
Μυήσιοι τρισὶ νηυσί, Μυησίων δὲ Τήιοι εἴχοντο ἑπτακαίδεκα νηυσί, Τηίων δὲ εἴχοντο
Χῖοι ἑκατὸν νηυσί· πρὸς δὲ τούτοισι Ἐρυθραῖοί τε ἐτάσσοντο καὶ Φωκαιέες, Ἐρυθραῖοι μὲν
ὀκτὼ νέας παρεχόμενοι, Φωκαιέες δὲ τρεῖς· Φωκαιέων δὲ εἴχοντο Λέσβιοι νηυσὶ ἑβδομή-
κοντα· τελευταῖοι δὲ ἐτάσσοντο ἔχοντες τὸ πρὸς ἑσπέρην κέρας Σάμιοι ἑξήκοντα νηυσί.
πασέων δὲ τουτέων ὁ σύναπας ἀριθμὸς ἐγένετο τρεῖς καὶ πεντήκοντα καὶ τριηκόσιαι
τριήρεες.

3. I 16 ἐπεγένετο δὲ ἄλλοις τε ἄλλοθι κωλύματα μὴ αὐξηθῆναι, καὶ Ἴωσι προχω-
ρησάντων ἐπὶ μέγα τῶν πραγμάτων Κῦρος καὶ ἡ Περσικὴ βασιλεία Κροῖσον καθελοῦσα
καὶ ὅσα ἐντὸς Ἅλυος ποταμοῦ πρὸς θάλασσαν ἐπεστράτευσε καὶ τὰς ἐν τῇ ἠπείρῳ
πόλεις ἐδούλωσε, Δαρεῖός τε ὕστερον τῷ Φοινίκων ναυτικῷ κρατῶν καὶ τὰς νήσους.

4. (i) The first Persian expedition:

Herodotus VI 95[2] ἔπλεον ἑξακοσίῃσι τριήρεσι ἐς τὴν Ἰωνίην.

(ii) The second Persian expedition:

Herodotus VII 89[1] τῶν δὲ τριηρέων ἀριθμὸς μὲν ἐγένετο ἑπτὰ καὶ διηκόσιαι καὶ
χίλιαι, παρείχοντο δ' αὐτὰς οἵδε, Φοίνικες μὲν σὺν Συρίοισι τοῖσι ἐν τῇ Παλαιστίνῃ
τριηκοσίας...

89[2] Αἰγύπτιοι δὲ νέας παρείχοντο διηκοσίας...

90 Κύπριοι δὲ παρείχοντο νέας πεντήκοντα καὶ ἑκατόν...Κίλικες δὲ
ἑκατὸν παρείχοντο νέας.

91 Πάμφυλοι δὲ τριήκοντα παρείχοντο νέας.

92 Λύκιοι δὲ παρείχοντο νέας πεντήκοντα.

93 Δωριέες δὲ οἱ ἐκ τῆς Ἀσίης τριήκοντα παρείχοντο νέας...

94 Ἴωνες δὲ ἑκατὸν νέας παρείχοντο.

95[1] νησιῶται δὲ ἑπτακαίδεκα παρείχοντο νέας.

Αἰολέες δὲ ἑξήκοντα νέας παρείχοντο.

95[2] Ἑλλησπόντιοι δὲ πλὴν Ἀβυδηνῶν...οἱ δὲ λοιποὶ ⟨οἱ⟩ ἐκ τοῦ Πόντου στρατευόμενοι παρείχοντο μὲν ἑκατὸν νέας...οὗτοι δὲ Ἰώνων καὶ Δωριέων ἄποικοι.

5. Herodotus VII 158[4] ἕτοιμός εἰμι βοηθεῖν παρεχόμενος διηκοσίας τε τριήρεας...
ἐπὶ δὲ λόγῳ τοιῷδε τάδε ὑπίσχομαι, ἐπ' ᾧ τε στρατηγός τε καὶ ἡγεμὼν τῶν Ἑλλήνων
ἔσομαι πρὸς τὸν βάρβαρον.

168[2], see above, p. 144, note 4.

6. VII 21[3] ξυνανέπειθε δὲ καὶ ὁ Ἑρμοκράτης οὐχ ἥκιστα, τοῦ ταῖς ναυσὶ μὴ ἀθυμεῖν
ἐπιχειρῆσαι πρὸς τοὺς Ἀθηναίους, λέγων οὐδ' ἐκείνους πάτριον τὴν ἐμπειρίαν οὐδ'

ἀίδιον τῆς θαλάσσης ἔχειν, ἀλλ' ἠπειρώτας μᾶλλον τῶν Συρακοσίων ὄντας καὶ ἀναγκασθέντας ὑπὸ Μήδων ναυτικοὺς γενέσθαι.

7. Herodotus VI 89 οἱ δὲ Κορίνθιοι, ἦσαν γάρ σφι τοῦτον τὸν χρόνον φίλοι ἐς τὰ μάλιστα, Ἀθηναίοισι διδοῦσι δεομένοισι εἴκοσι νέας... ταύτας τε δὴ λαβόντες οἱ Ἀθηναῖοι καὶ τὰς σφετέρας, πληρώσαντες ἑβδομήκοντα νέας τὰς ἁπάσας, ἔπλεον ἐπὶ τὴν Αἴγιναν.

8. Herodotus VI 132 αἰτήσας νέας ἑβδομήκοντα.

9. Herodotus VIII 1¹ Ἀθηναῖοι μὲν νέας παρεχόμενοι ἑκατὸν καὶ εἴκοσι καὶ ἑπτά.

    1² καὶ Χαλκιδέες ἐπλήρουν εἴκοσι, Ἀθηναίων σφι παρεχόντων τὰς νέας.

    14¹ τοῖσι δὲ Ἕλλησι ἐπεβοήθεον νέες τρεῖς καὶ πεντήκοντα Ἀττικαί.

10. Herodotus VI 15¹, the Chians. See above, p. 145, note 24.

   id. VII 96¹, the Persian ships: ἐπεβάτευον δὲ ἐπὶ πασέων τῶν νεῶν Πέρσαι καὶ Μῆδοι καὶ Σάκαι; and 184², see above, p. 145, note 25. The Sacai were Scythians (VII 64) and so probably archers.

11. Plutarch, *Life of Themistocles* XIV 1 τῶν δὲ Ἀττικῶν ἑκατὸν ὀγδοήκοντα τὸ πλῆθος οὐσῶν (i.e. he is not counting the twenty that were manned by the Chalcidians) ἑκάστη τοὺς ἀπὸ τοῦ καταστρώματος μαχομένους ὀκτωκαίδεκα εἶχεν, ὧν τοξόται τέσσαρες ἦσαν, οἱ λοιποὶ δ' ὁπλῖται.

12. Pliny VII 56 209 tectas longas Thasii (invenerunt). antea ex prora tantum et puppi pugnabatur.

13. Plutarch, *ibid.* 2 Δοκεῖ δ' οὐχ ἧττον εὖ τὸν καιρὸν ὁ Θεμιστοκλῆς ἢ τὸν τόπον συνιδὼν καὶ φυλάξας μὴ πρότερον ἀντιπρώρους καταστῆσαι ταῖς βαρβαρικαῖς τὰς τριήρεις, ἢ τὴν εἰωθυῖαν ὥραν παραγενέσθαι, τὸ πνεῦμα λαμπρὸν ἐκ πελάγους ἀεὶ καὶ κῦμα διὰ τῶν στενῶν κατάγουσαν· ὃ τὰς μὲν Ἑλληνικὰς οὐκ ἔβλαπτε ναῦς ἁλιτενεῖς οὔσας καὶ ταπεινοτέρας, τὰς δὲ βαρβαρικὰς ταῖς τε πρύμναις ἀνεστώσας καὶ τοῖς καταστρώμασιν ὑψορόφους καὶ βαρείας ἐπιφερομένας ἔσφαλλε προσπῖπτον καὶ παρεδίδου πλαγίας τοῖς Ἕλλησιν ὀξέως προσφερομένοις καὶ τῷ Θεμιστοκλεῖ προσέχουσιν, ὡς ὁρῶντι μάλιστα τὸ συμφέρον.

14. Plutarch, *Life of Cimon* XII 2 ὥρμησεν ἄρας ἀπὸ Κνίδου καὶ Τριοπίου διακοσίαις τριήρεσι, πρὸς μὲν τάχος ἀπ' ἀρχῆς καὶ περιαγωγὴν ὑπὸ Θεμιστοκλέους ἄριστα κατεσκευασμέναις, ἐκεῖνος δὲ τότε καὶ πλατυτέρας ἐποίησεν αὐτὰς καὶ διάβασιν τοῖς καταστρώμασιν ἔδωκεν, ὡς ἂν ὑπὸ πολλῶν ὁπλιτῶν μαχιμώτεραι προσφέροιντο τοῖς πολεμίοις.

THE CLASSICAL PERIOD: 480–322 B.C.

μέγα γὰρ τὸ τῆς θαλάσσης κράτος.

Thucydides I 143[5]

'Sea power is indeed a great thing.'

7

CATALOGUE OF
SHIP REPRESENTATIONS

c. 480–*c*. 400 B.C.

The earliest literary reference to a *trieres* belongs to the second half of the sixth century (see above, p. 120), but it is not until the second half of the fifth century that we can confidently point to a representation of a ship of this rating. The earliest example in this section has been dated* about the middle of the fifth century after a gap of about twenty-five years in the succession of remaining Greek ship representations. It seems likely that the ship had become so complicated a subject to depict, with its three banks of oars and the problems of perspective which these, as well as the outrigger supports and deck-stanchions, presented, that artists in general had been avoiding the task.

There are nevertheless three clear representations of the *trieres* in this section.† The earliest (Clas. 3), the Vienna University fragment, is very small and has some puzzling features, but the side view it gives of a small part of the port side of an oared ship agrees with the views of the starboard side near the bow and of the stern provided by the Lenormant relief (Clas. 1) and the Talos vase (Clas. 2) respectively. Both these are dated at the end of the fifth century. There would be a strong presumption that a representation of an oared ship of complicated design coming from that period would depict a *trieres*. The written evidence for this type suggests that it was rowed by oarsmen at three levels. The thranite oarsmen worked their oars through an outrigger, the *zugioi* worked theirs either over a gunwale or through oarports, and the *thalamioi*, sitting at the lowest level below and behind the *zugioi*, rowed theirs through an oarport which, being no more than eighteen inches or so above the water-line, was fitted on the outside with a leather sleeve to prevent the water from coming in. All these inferences are confirmed by the

---

* H. Kenner, *CVA, Vienna University*, 32.

  † Casson has suggested to us a fourth, published by E. Schmidt, *The Treasury of Tersepolis*, Chicago, 1939, fig. 24, and dated between 520 and 331 B.C.

three representations. The Lenormant relief and the Talos vase also show supports for the outrigger, to take the vertical and longitudinal strain; and all three show stanchions canted outwards to take the weight of the deck. In the Vienna fragment the deck has a low rail.

A further category of representations of this period (Clas. 15–16, see pp. 177–8) show the bows of ships which are probably but not certainly *triereis*.

TRIEREIS

Clas. 1. Plates 23*a* and 24 (photos: The British Museum). Athens NM, the so-called Lenormant relief from the Erechtheum (another fragment in Magazin 12 of the NM). Cast in BM. *JHS* 25, 111, fig. 3; *Jh.* 18, Beiblatt; Moll, B, II, 82; Lefebvre des Noëttes, *De la marine*, 38; Morrison, 'The Greek Trireme', *Mariner's Mirror* 1941, 14 ff.; Chamoux, *La Civilisation grecque*, 75.

Forward section of hull of *trieres* to right. Passing from top to bottom we can observe the following features:

(1) *Deck-stanchions.* The shelter protecting the visible row of oarsmen is a solid deck, since there are figures reclining on it forward (at the right-hand end of the photograph). Its edge is cut in high relief, and is likely therefore to have extended outboard of the oarsmen. The stanchions of the deck are represented as curving left, i.e. aft. It is reasonable to suppose that the curve is the result of conventional perspective and shows the outward cant of the stanchions. Their foot must have rested on a solid base, probably the thwarts. Conventional perspective of this kind can be paralleled, e.g. on the red-figure calyx-krater (New York 07.286.86, Buschor *G.V.* 214), where the hind legs of the frontal horse are splayed outwards in an attempt to render frontally the bend of the hind leg. A similar convention is used by the artist of the Talos vase and of the Vienna fragment to depict the same feature. The deck must, of course, have been supported by other stanchions inboard of the oarsmen. Part of the oarsman visible on the extreme right appears to be concealed by the terminal housing of the deck, which is clearly shown on the Cian coins (Clas. 16). He is therefore the bow oarsman.

(2) *Outrigger* (see below, pp. 281–3). The two uppermost longitudinal courses of planking beneath the visible oarsmen are in higher relief than the lower courses. Since also the oars of those oarsmen in no case appear to cross the higher of the two uppermost courses but in some cases are cut crossing the lower course, the two uppermost courses seem to constitute the outrigger suggested by the written evidence, i.e. the *parexeiresia*, through which the visible oarsmen, i.e. the *thranitai*, worked their oars.

Between the two courses of the outrigger there are a number of uprights, four to each unitary repeated section. One is the tholepin of the thranite oar. Another appears from its position to be a support for the thranite oarsman's seat. The remaining two are set close together, the one further forward being in higher relief than the other, which occurs immediately beneath each of the deck-stanchions. The latter is then readily explained as the lower continuation of the deck-stanchion as it extends downwards to its footing on the *zugon*. The former may be associated with the upper end of one of the outrigger struts (see (4) below).

(3) *Oars*. Between the outrigger and the waterline run two further courses of planking, which can be called wales since they must lie directly on the ship's side. The oar of the visible thranite oarsman appears in high relief in the gaps on either side of and between the wales and on most occasions in low relief as it crosses the wales.

Forward of the oar belonging to the visible oarsman is shown what appears to be another oar slanting from beneath the outrigger to the waterline. It appears only in the gaps between and on either side of the wales, although in the forward-most unit shown the stone may show traces of low relief as it crosses the wales. This seems to be the zygian oar. An oarport for this oar could have been picked out in colour.

Forward of the second oar at the waterline is what appears to be a third oar entering the water. It starts in a cap-shaped hump immediately above the lower wale; and in no case is it shown crossing it in relief. This appears to be the thalamian oar and the cap-shaped hump appears to be the *askoma* (see below, pp. 283–4).

The reason why these oars are not in most cases cut in relief as they cross the wales is probably that they were originally also picked out in colour. Gardner writes:* 'In relief work colour was more freely used than in sculpture in the round. . . ; the background was usually painted red or blue: details and accessories were very frequently added in colour only: indeed in some cases the artist trusted quite as much to colour as to the relief for the effect he wished to produce.'

(4) *Struts*. There remain to be noticed the features immediately forward of the second oar in the gaps between the outrigger and the upper wale and between the upper and lower wales. They are to be seen to the best advantage in the unit farthest forward; but units 1 and 5 should also be examined. In the upper gap there appear to be two members, although in some of the examples the two seem almost fused together. The forward of the two is shaped like the middle third of an S; the other is straight, slanting parallel to the oars, and is continued in the lower gap unlike the other. There is no indication of the latter crossing the upper wale in relief; but this deficiency can be explained, as in the case of the oars, by the original use of colour.

The function of these two members in this position, apparently resting one on each of the wales, seems to be to support the outrigger. This structure would need support both from beneath and also against the longitudinal thrust from bow to stern when the oars were pulled. It looks as if the two struts were designed to take the vertical and longitudinal strains respectively.

Figure 4 shows the conclusions reached above from examination of the details of the relief. It is an idealized picture of a single unit.

* *Handbook of Greek Sculpture*, 141.

The deck-stanchion is likely to have had its footing on the thwart; and in fact if we reckon the distance between the tholepin of the zygian oarsman and his seat on the basis of the visible distance between the tholepin of the thranite oarsman and his seat, it can be seen that the thwart (on which the zygian oarsman sat) must have come roughly at the same point longitudinally as the foot of the deck-stanchion. The longer strut, if, as we have inferred, it was designed to take the vertical thrust, should be vertical

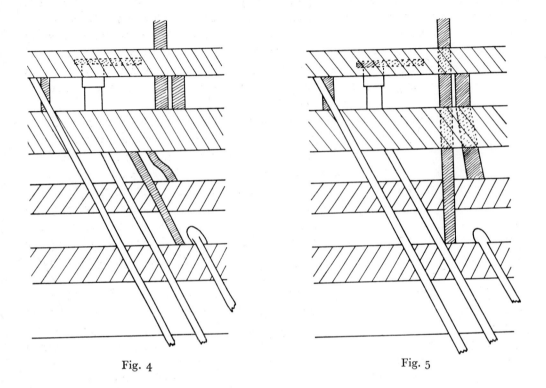

Fig. 4   Fig. 5

and not, as it appears, oblique. This difficulty is cleared up if we suppose that the struts are shown oblique in an attempt by conventional perspective to show their outward cant. We have already noticed conventional perspective of this kind in the case of the deck-stanchions. We can then correct the longer strut to a vertical position, while the S shape of the shorter strut gives it an obliquity which survives the correction.

The assumption of conventional perspective, while solving the difficulty noticed, also explains the only feature of the relief still unaccounted for. The vertical member seen through the courses of the outrigger beside and forward of the lower part of the deck-stanchion will appear to be a bracket connecting with the upper end of the shorter strut. By means of this bracket the shorter strut would then take the longitudinal thrust directly off both courses of the outrigger, to which it is imparted equally by the tholepin. Figure 5 shows the idealized unit as we may now suppose it to have been in reality. Pl. 25 shows a projection of the relief and Pl. 23 *c* and *d* photographs of a model made* on the basis of the projection.

Note: On Pl. 23 *b* we show a fragment of a Roman relief from Aquila (Museo Civico, *RM*, vol. 27, 306; A. Rumpf, Römische Fragmente 95, Winckelmannsprogramm). It seems to be part of a Roman copy of a relief of the same type as the Lenormant relief, and shows the section of a *trieres* near the stern. Steering oars are perhaps visible at the far left-hand side. In the unit nearest the stern only the thranite oar is shown. In view of the fact that there appear to have been more thranite oarsmen than those of the other two classes such a feature is to be expected. The details and measurements (cf. Rumpf, *loc. cit.*) are the same as on the Lenormant relief, i.e. deck, curved stanchions, position of the visible oarsmen and their oars, the out-rigger, and oarsmen's seats. There are also two wales below the outrigger. There are however as in the Vienna fragment no struts, and the third oar appears to emerge from the side, like the second oar, below the outrigger. The copyist seems to have confused the third (thalamian) oar and the struts.

Clas. 2. Plate 26 *a* (after *FR*). Attic red-figure. Volute-krater by the Talos painter. Ruvo, Jatta, 1501. Beazley, *ARV* 1338/1 (where see bibliography; add Morrison, 'The Greek Trireme', *Mariner's Mirror* 1941, 14 ff.).

Before considering in detail the picture of the ship on this vase we must make three points. In the first place the human figures are greatly out of proportion to the ship, which is a stage property in a scene depicting the kidnapping of Talos by the Argo-nauts. The second point is that the ship, if it is, as we shall argue, a *trieres*, is a case of anachronism. The third point to be noticed is that the port side of the ship is shown on the vase, and the starboard side on the relief which we have just been considering. In order to facilitate comparison of detail, fig. 6 shows a tracing of the ship on the vase in mirror image. For the sake of clarity the different features are distinguished by various kinds of hatching.

A first glance shows that, with the exception of the oars, all the features of the ship on the relief are present in the ship of the painting. There is a deck supported by curved stanchions, an outrigger of two courses of planking braced by two struts, one

---

* A model made by Mr Sinclair Morrison in 1939 and now in the Nautical Museum at Greenwich. The model was made on the basis of the projection which appears in the *Mariner's Mirror* 1941, 14 ff. Certain improvements of a minor kind have been made in the projection which appears in Pl. 25. The thwarts on which the *zugioi* sit are lower, and do not project to form part of the outrigger. The deck-stanchions do not rest on these thwarts outboard of the gunwale, and the deck overhangs the gunwale but not the outrigger. The model does not therefore correspond completely with the projection as published here.

straight and one S-shaped, and two wales lying on and along the ship's side. In between the courses of the outrigger there appear, besides the continuation of the deck-stanchion, only two uprights instead of the three of the relief. On the other hand, there is a flat object appearing just over the rim of the lower course of the outrigger and behind one of the uprights. This object would seem to be the seat of the thranite oarsman, which in the relief was kept out of sight by the upper course of the outrigger and whose support we concluded one of the uprights there to be. In the painting, where we are looking up through the courses of the outrigger, we see the seat instead of its support.

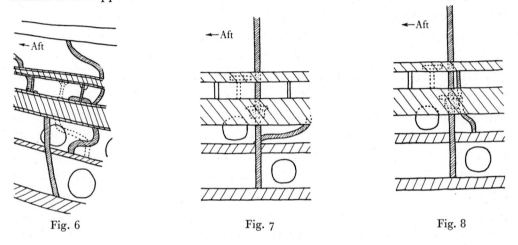

Fig. 6   Fig. 7   Fig. 8

Although no oars appear in the painting (they would be shipped when the vessel was beached), there is visible accommodation for a system of oars at three levels *en échelon*. The seat and tholepin of the thranite oarsman are visible. Between the lower course of the outrigger and the upper wale there is a porthole for the zygian oar, and another for the thalamian oar between the upper and lower wales. The upper porthole appears lower than we should expect, but this appearance is accounted for by the fact that we are looking up under the outrigger. The lower porthole is fitted with some sort of loose sleeve, presumably the *askoma* (see Pl. 26 a: not in fig. 6).

The question of perspective is more complicated in the painting than in the relief. The latter represents a ship for its own sake, and the point of view is accordingly the simplest possible, i.e. directly abeam. Further, the artist does not take up a single standpoint, but regards each part of the ship directly from the side, using conventions to represent members that project towards him. There is no true, as opposed to conventional, perspective, either vertical or horizontal. In the painting, however, the ship forms part of a larger composition, in which it has position and orientation. We may expect therefore in the painting true perspective, both vertical and horizontal, as well as conventional 'perspective', i.e. falsification of the actual appearance of the ship for purposes of explanation.

Examination of the painting reveals several indications, of which the position of the ladder is perhaps the most conclusive, that the ship is pointing away from the eye at an angle of about 45°. Determination of the horizon of perspective, i.e. the position of the eye in the vertical plane, is confused by the upward slant of the deck, outrigger and wales. This slant does not indicate that the horizon of perspective is above the deck. It is an actual slant, since the ship is drawn up on a sloping beach. A clue to the height of the horizon is provided by a point already noticed. In the painting the position of the outrigger in relation to the seat of the uppermost oarsman and the tholepin of the middle oarsman is higher than in the relief, where the ship is viewed directly from the side. Since the outrigger projects from the side of the ship, the fact that in relation to points farther inboard it is higher in the painting than in the relief shows that in the former either the point of view must be below the level of the outrigger or the ship must be tilted on one side. It is true that in both cases, whether the ship is lying on her side or is being regarded from beneath, the underside of the deck should be visible, and it is not. The artist may have neglected to draw the underside of the deck by oversight or because he deliberately only concerned himself with the external features of the ship. The upper portholes are blacked out like the space under the deck, although the inside of the ship would be visible through them.

The conclusion is that on the Talos vase we are looking at a ship which points away from us and which enables us to look up under her outrigger. In order to produce a diagrammatic picture of the external features of one port-side unit (i.e. something which is directly comparable with our idealized picture of one unit of the Lenormant relief, fig. 5) we must eliminate both horizontal and vertical perspective from the mirror image (fig. 6), and we must also restore the ship to an even keel.

The considerable curve of the deck-stanchion seems to indicate that its foot rests on the thwart some distance inboard of the deck's edge. By the elimination of horizontal perspective the deck-stanchion becomes straight and forms a single vertical line which is continued below the outrigger by the longer strut. The part of the deck-stanchion visible between the courses of the outrigger moves with the seat and its support between the two uprights of the outrigger. The inner end of the S-shaped strut, where it springs from the top of the lower wale, now falls behind the longer strut. By elimination of vertical perspective the whole outrigger descends so that its lower course partly covers the zygian porthole and the upper course hides the seat but not the support of the seat of the thranite oarsman. The result of these adjustments appears in fig. 7.

If fig. 7 is now compared with fig. 5, there will be seen to be complete correspondence between the relief and the painting with the exception of two points. There is a difference in respect of the shorter strut and of the upright which lies forward of the lower part of the deck-stanchion. When discussing the relief we inferred that this upright was in fact the upper end of the shorter strut, so that the difference between the two representations seems to concern the shorter strut only. It is however not necessary to leave the matter there, although the detail involved is of small significance. The shorter strut was seen in the relief to perform a definite and essential structural function, to bear the longitudinal thrust exerted on the outrigger by the action of rowing. In the painting the strut is drawn in a way which would make it impossible for it to perform this function. It can be seen in fact to have been drawn the wrong way round. It is perhaps not unreasonable to conclude that the artist has drawn it wrong by mistake, and altered the position of the upright to suit. The correct method of drawing the strut so as to give it a proper mechanical function is shown in fig. 6 in dotted lines. When this final correction has been made, we get fig. 8, which now corresponds in all particulars with fig. 6.

Clas. 3. Plate 26*b* (photo: Vienna University). Attic red-figure cup fragment. Vienna University 503.48. *CVA* pl. 21, 8.

A small section of a *trieres*. The deck has a rail and is supported by stanchions which curve right. We see therefore part of the port side. Below the stanchion run three pairs of planking courses. The uppermost is presumably the outrigger, the middle has a semicircular porthole, presumably the porthole for the zygian oar, above the lower wale, and the lowest again a semicircular porthole, the thalamian, above the lower wale. Behind the rail on the deck is the drapery of a standing figure. Below the ship the sea is shown. On this ship then, as on the Talos vase, both zygian and thalamian oarsmen rowed their oars through ports. The upright lines visible between the deck and the outrigger are puzzling: they may be intended to portray the internal supports of the deck, but seem unnecessarily numerous.

NONDESCRIPT

Clas. 4. Attic red-figure calyx-krater by the Kadmos painter. Syracuse 17427. Beazley, *ARV* 1184/4; *CVA* pl. 10, 4.

Stern of ship to right. The deck, on which a figure reclines, is supported by curved struts—i.e. the deck is offset. The wales along the hull are rendered simply by lines, one along the gunwale, another along the keel, and a pair in between (cf. the lines running along the hull of the Talos ship below the lower ports). The stern ends in four divisions and is crowned by a wreath. Another figure mounts the ladder set against the stern. The steering oars above his head are in the shipped position.

Clas. 5. Attic red-figure calyx-krater by the Kadmos painter. Bologna 303. Beazley, *ARV* 1184/6; *CVA* pl. 94, 9.

Stern of a ship close to that on Clas. 4, but here there is no ladder and the steering oars are in the ready position.

Clas. 6. Attic red-figure fragment. Bonn 1216, 179. *CVA* pl. 32, 14.

Stern of ship to left. The deck, the vertical edge of which is decorated with dots, is supported on struts, which, although they are not as curved as on the Talos vase, are yet not straight, and again indicate the offset of the deck. The gunwale is defined by chevrons, while a single line defines the keel. The two steering oars are in position.

Clas. 7. Attic red-figure hydria by the painter of the Louvre Centauromachy. Munich 2429. Beazley, *ARV* 1094/102; *CVA* pls 229 ff.

Ship's stern in a landing of Danaos providing no detail of interest.

Clas. 8. Attic red-figure kalpis. Howe, *AJA* 1957, pl. 101, 2.

Stern of the Argo showing deck, stanchions and steering oar.

Clas. 9. Campanian red-figure hydria by the Caivano painter. Karlsruhe 350; Beazley, *JHS* 1943, 81; Moll, B, VI, 165.

Stern of ship to left ending in five divisions, from which four fillets fly. It is supported by a pole and a strut. Near the top of the pole is a cross-piece with the inscription Z[E]ΥΣ ΣΩΤHP. In front of the low side screen is a bottle-shaped object, which may be the handle of the starboard steering oar; the port steering oar projects above the ladder.

Clas. 10. South Italian red-figure volute-krater by the Amykos painter. Ruvo, Jatta, 1095. *FR*, vol. 1, 304; Moon, *BSR*, vol. xi, 38.

Stern of ship to left. Between the gunwale, decorated with dotted semicircles between lines, and the deck there is a stanchion.

Clas. 11. Parthenon metope in position on north side. Praschniker, *Parthenonstudien*, pl. II; Picard, *La Sculpture classique*, 433, fig. 179.

Fragmentary stern of ship showing ladder and steering oar.

Clas. 12. Heroon of Gjölbaschi. Vienna, Kunsthistorisches Museum. Moll, B, II, 88, 89; Körte, *JdI* 31, 257.

Sterns of ships of little interest from the point of view of ship construction.

Clas. 13. Stele of Demokleides. Athens NM. Conze, *Die Attischen Grabreliefs*, 122.

Ship's bow to left in relief. Only details of the profile contour are rendered. There are two steps from the level of the ram to the foot of the bow screen, which inclines aft: the stem post inclines forward.

Clas. 14.* Electrum stater of Cyzicus. Greenwell, *Electrum Coinage of Cyzicus*, pl. 6, 35.

On the obverse, a bow of a ship to left. The ram is in the form of an animal's head, with wings on the bow. The stem post is straight, but curves aft at its base as a wale for the bow compartment: above this is a rail.

c. 400–*c.* 322 B.C.

Of the fourth-century representations Clas. 15–19 form a distinct group: Clas. 15–16, at least, seem to have room for three banks of oars and should represent *triereis*. In this connection it is interesting to note the close resemblance between Clas. 15–16 on the one hand and the bow on the Zankle–

* For Phaselis issues of this period with ship representations, see Arch. 106.

Messana coin, Arch. 89, on the other, which we described as being 'at least a two-level ship', but in the latter case the engraver had not represented the *epotides*. Clas. 20, the Erechtheum ship-lamp, reverts to the single-level long ship, but provides an elucidation of the way in which the steering oar was attached to the ship's hull. In some cases it was lashed to the rail in the stern compartment, but in Arch. 34 and 52 there is a marking on the outside of the gunwale, which might have been a slot or a projection: Clas. 20 shows a projection at this point.

Clas. 15. Plate 26*c* (photo: Musée du Petit Palais). Apulian rhyton. Paris, Petit Palais 411. *CVA* pl. 47, 1.

Rhyton in the form of a ship's bow. In profile the ram has an outline approximating to a three-pronged fork with its planks running along the hull just above the keel-line, as on Clas. 16, Pl. 27*a*. The stem has two 'steps', i.e. projecting planks: beneath the lower 'step' there is a line in paint which runs right along the hull (cf. the wale above the 'eye' on the stem of Clas. 16): the line above merges into the *epotides* (again cf. Clas. 16). The dolphin, which is all eye, resembles the very large 'eye' at the base of the stem post on Clas. 16. The *epotides*, surmounted by the handles of the rhyton, project at right-angles to the line of the ship: on the forward side of these between two lines is a pair of circles; that they are in relief suggests that they may be subsidiary rams (see p. 280). Above the stem, between the handles, there is a superstructure corresponding to that on Clas. 16. The spout of the rhyton has, of course, no connection with a ship.

Clas. 16. Plate 27*a*. Coins (N and R) of Cius in Bithynia; they may have been first struck near the limit of our period. Babelon, *Traité*, pl. CLXXX, 1–26; Koester, fig. 28.

On the reverse a bow of a ship. A deep plank in high relief runs along the hull above the keel-line, then drops slightly and continues to the extremity of the ram, where it ends in three divisions. Above, two wales run along the hull and just project beyond the stem. At the base of the curved stem post is a broken elliptical pattern, which on other dies is clearly a large 'eye'. Aft of this and parallel to the wales is a deep rectangular projection the forward end of which is marked by a triangle: the triangle represents the *epotides* and the rectangle aft is the projection of the *parexeiresia*. The deck ends in a solid superstructure in the bow compartment.

The following two miniature paintings of a bow closely resemble Clas. 15–16. They incorporate the following details: (i) the ram ending in three divisions; (ii) the representation of the wales above the ram, which in Clas. 15–16 project beyond the stem; (iii) the 'eyes' above.

Clas. 17. Attic Panathenaic amphora. London B. 610. *CVA* pl. 4, 3*a*; Beazley, *ABV* 417 (where see bibliography).

Nike standing on a ship's bow on the top of the pillar.

Clas. 18. Attic Panathenaic amphora. Sèvres 7230. *CVA* pl. 17, 19–22; Beazley, *ABV* 415/6 (where see bibliography).

Nike on a bow.

Clas. 19. Diobols of Samos. Barron, *Silver Coins of Samos*, pl. XXII.

On the reverse, bow resembling those of Clas. 16.

Clas. 20. Plate 27*b* (photo: Athens NM). Bronze lamp in the form of a ship, from the Erechtheum. Athens. Ridder, *Bronzes de l'Acropole*, 425, fig. 95.

The tip of the ram is rectangular in profile and pointed in plan view. There is a lip and aperture in front of the stem post to hold the wick. Along the hull run four incised lines from stem to stern, which probably represent wales. Above these and below the gunwale has been engraved a row of compass-drawn circles to represent ports. The top of the gunwale is defined by a rope, which runs between the bow and the stern compartments and may inadequately represent a *hupozoma* (see pp. 294–8). The stern compartment has a rail supported by a strut, and is decked with planks just below the level of the gunwale, with one strong thwart, in the position of the *threnus*, forward. The stern ends in two divisions, where it is decorated with an engraved 'eye'. On the outside of the hull is a rectangular projection, to which the steering oar would be attached (see above, p. 49). The bow compartment is also decked and has bow screens. Amidships there appears to be the mast-rest (*histopede*; see Arch. 16 and p. 119).

Judging from the form of the letters of the inscription on the hull—IEPON ΤΗΣ ΑΘΗΝΑΣ—R. P. Austin* would date this ship to the fourth century B.C.: also from the account of the finding of the ship (Paton, *Erechtheum*, 572) it appears that it was an original Erechtheum offering, not a chance find on the site; accordingly one would date it later than the completion of the Erechtheum in 406 B.C., unless of course it had been in the possession of the dedicator for some time before it was inscribed and dedicated to Athena.

Clas. 21. Terracotta model. Corpus Christi College, Cambridge. Koester, fig. 19. Kirk 116, n. 29.

Rough model of a warship. The ram has survived, but the stem and stern posts have broken off. Above the gunwale are set thick uprights supporting an overall deck. A solid protrusion on either side of the hull forward probably represents the *epotides*.

The date of this terracotta is uncertain, but possibly Hellenistic.

RELEVANT REPRESENTATIONS AFTER *c.* 322 B.C.

The three following representations have been chosen either to confirm theories already advanced (Hel. 1 and 3) or to illustrate a feature not yet represented (Hel. 2).

* Communication to J. S. M.

Hel. 1. Plate 27*c* (photo: the National Museum, Copenhagen). Terracotta model. Copenhagen. Breitenstein, *Catalogue of Terracottas in the Danish National Museum*, pl. 63, fig. 520.

This model of a *trieres* has been included to confirm the theory, if further proof be needed, that the *trieres* was propelled by three banks of oars, for nobody can dispute that there is one level below the gunwale, another bank of oars rowed over the gunwale, and a third through what must be the *parexeiresia*.

Breitenstein included this terracotta under Hellenistic, but we are not sure on what grounds.

Hel. 2. Plate 27*d*.* Relief carving, the so-called ship of Hagesandros. Lindus, Rhodes.

Ship's stern illustrating the *koruphaion* (see p. 297), a plaited rope running vertically down and under the hull to secure a *hupozoma*; it can be seen running down under the forward part of the steering oar.

Hel. 3. Plate 28 (photo: Giraudon 1935). The Nike from Samothrace. Louvre 2369.

A comparison with Clas. 16, Pl. 27*a*, shows that the square plinth of the goddess rests on the deck superstructure in the bow compartment. The projecting *epotides* below are clear and can be paralleled on Clas. 15, Pl. 26*c*. The stem post and the ram are broken off and lost.

* The surface has deteriorated since this photograph was taken.

8

THE SHIP-SHEDS

The most famous ship-sheds* in Greece, and the best-known from preserved remains, were those of Piraeus. The remains are of the fourth-century ship-sheds, but we may presume that in many cases the Athenians reused the foundations of the fifth-century buildings, which had been demolished after Athens' defeat in 404 B.C., since rock-cut foundations are difficult to demolish, and that Athens possessed under Pericles nearly as many ship-sheds as she employed later. The number of ship-sheds was probably always some-what less than the number of ships in the fleet; the balance will often have been at sea, but we do hear of ships standing 'in the open air'.† The ship-sheds were finally destroyed by Sulla in 86 B.C., together with the famous naval storehouse of Philo.‡

Our knowledge of these ship-sheds derives mainly from the excavations of Dragatzes and Dörpfeld on the east side of Zea harbour in 1885.§ The actual ship-sheds were partly cut in the bedrock, partly built up with blocks of the local stone, and run down into the sea with a gentle gradient of 1 in 10. No remains of keel-slots have been found at Zea, but there is slight evidence that they existed in Munichia. The possibility of wooden runners cannot be dis-missed. The stone slips are roughly three metres (9 ft 10 in.) wide, and have

---

* *Neosoikoi*. Other terms are found: *neolkion* (a late word) and *neon* (an Ionic word according to Photius *s.v. neonas*, cf. Hesychius *s.v.*). The Attic word *neosoikos* seems to have become standard.

The usage of the word *neorion* is confusing. In the singular it can mean 'the dockyard'; in the plural it can mean roughly the same, as we say 'the docks' meaning the whole complex of harbour installa-tions. But sometimes it is used, especially in the plural, as a synonym for *neosoikos*.

† *hupaithrioi* in *IG* 2² 1611 6, the catalogue of 357/6 when not all the ship-sheds had been rebuilt; but the number of ship-sheds never quite caught up with the number of ships. See Wachsmuth, *Die Stadt Athen im Alterthum*, II 1 (1890), pp. 63–4.

‡ Appian, *Mith.* 41; Plutarch, *Sulla*, 14; Strabo C 396.

§ *Praktika tēs Archaiologikēs Hetaireias* (1885), pp. 63–8 and pls 2–3, whence Pl. 29*a* and *b*. Supple-mentary excavations in 1899–1900 were inadequately published by Dragatzes and Angelopoulos in *Praktika* (1899), pp. 37–41, and (1900), pp. 35–7. Observations had earlier been made by Graser, who measured 38 ship-sheds in Zea and nine in Munichia and saw a few more, *Philologus* XXXI (1872), pp. 1–65; also by von Alten and Milchhöfer, *Karten von Attika, Erläuternder Text*, I (1881), pp. 14–15, 57–9. Doubts have, however, been raised on whether the remains in Munichia described by von Alten are ship-sheds at all (cf. Belger, *Berliner Philologische Wochenschrift* 1887, p. 724), and our conclusions must be based on the properly studied remains in Zea.

an average dry length of thirty-seven metres (121 ft 5 in.). They naturally are continued into the water, but their lower ends have nowhere been established.*

The ship-sheds were roofed in pairs, with a pitched roof whose ridge sloped seawards (Pl. 29a and b). Unfluted columns of local stone in rows alternately closely and more widely spaced supported the ridge and eaves, and formed the partitions between the individual ship-sheds. The clear (intercolumnar) width is just under six metres (19 ft 6 in.) in the Zea ship-sheds and somewhat less in those in Munichia.† The 1885 excavations in Zea revealed one partition which was a solid wall, and it is reasonable to suppose that the ship-sheds were divided into groups which were closed off by solid walls for extra security and fire protection; much valuable wooden gear was stored by the ships.‡ The more open column partitions within the group allowed easy movement and better ventilation—always an important point. Evidence of similar grouping was apparently found in Munichia.§ At the back of the ship-sheds a continuous wall of local stone ran right round the military harbours, and outside this perhaps a road. There must have been some doors through this wall; none have been found, but the wall was only preserved to a height of two or three courses and the doors may have been

* This is an important gap in our knowledge, not only as regards Piraeus. According to Curtius the harbour bottom falls away sharply at a depth of six feet all round the basin of Zea (cf. Graser, *loc. cit.* p. 21), but this has never been confirmed. Also the possibility of a change in the relative sea level since antiquity has not always been taken into account in discussions of the ship-sheds, though if it were established it would affect all the length measurements of the ship-sheds and any conclusions drawn therefrom on the dimensions of the *trieres*, and also the general picture one tries to form of what ancient military harbours looked like. It is also very relevant to one of the main unsolved problems concerning the Piraeus ship-sheds: how 196 ship-sheds were fitted into the harbour of Zea, which has a present shoreline of *c.* 1120 metres, when the known ship-sheds have an interaxial width of 6·50 m. (For the details of this controversy *vide* Judeich, *Topographie von Athen²*, pp. 437–9; Lehmann-Hartleben, *Die antiken Hafenanlagen des Mittelmeeres*, pp. 113–14, cf. pp. 138 ff.; Miltner, P.W. *RE* XVI 2, p. 2473 *s.v. neorion*; Marstrand, *Arsenalet i Piraeus*, p. 41. I hope to discuss the problem in detail later.)

In his restored section of the ship-sheds (Pl. 29a) Dörpfeld curiously made the slip end at sea level, though on his plan (Pl. 29b) he showed the lines running on into the water. Some of these slips can still be seen in the water at certain times, and a small section of the upper end of these same slipways (between points *B-a-z-k* on Pl. 29b) has been preserved in the basement of a block of flats, across the road from a public lavatory which was in fact built on the slips as a foundation.

† The total (interaxial) width in Zea averages 6·50 m. and the lower diameter of the columns 0·58 m.; the total width in Munichia is 6·25 m. and the lower diameter of the columns is not given.

‡ Cf. *IG* 2² 1611 *passim*. The Athenians were naturally very concerned about the danger from fire, cf. Arist. *Achar.* 920 ff. It must be noted, however, that the original excavators regarded the solid wall as a later addition.

§ Angelopoulos, *Praktika* (1899), p. 40; but the account gives few details and the promised full publication never appeared.

fairly high up and approached by wooden steps of which no trace has survived. The doors may have been few in number and access to the ships fairly restricted, though probably not with the severity of Hellenistic Rhodes, where unlawful entry into the dockyard was a capital offence.* The general appearance of the ship-sheds must have been of a continuous line of narrow hangars sloping down to and into the water.

The *triereis* may have been simply manhandled up the slips, but it seems more likely that winches or pulleys were used. Rollers may have been used as well, but only on those slips which were flat in cross-section, as at Piraeus. Some stones were found at the head of slips in Munichia which may have served as bollards for securing the ships.† Where the slips were flat in cross-section wooden shores may have helped to keep the *triereis* upright.‡ One must assume that there was water to a depth of at least one metre at the lower end of the slips. Anything much less would not have allowed the ships to enter the slip, and a much greater depth would have been a waste of labour.§ The wooden gear of the ships was stored by them in the ship-sheds, while the rigging and other tackle was kept in the store-rooms in the dockyard, in the later fourth century mainly in Philo's arsenal. The wooden gear will have been put on board before launching, but the ships were manned and received the last of their equipment and provisions later, in the main harbour of Kantharos at or near a jetty called Choma.‖

In the second half of the fourth century *tetrereis* and *pentereis* were introduced into the Athenian fleet (see below, p. 249). They must have been housed like the *triereis*, but there is no evidence yet on whether or not special ship-sheds were needed for them, either at Piraeus or elsewhere.¶ The closest parallel to the Piraeus ship-sheds is a group of ten ship-sheds found recently at Apollonia, the harbour of Cyrene (Pl. 30).**The slips are formed by quarrying in the rock, as are also the bases of the partition walls cut in steps for a

---

* Strabo C 653; Eustathius, *G.G.M.* II 312. † von Alten, *op. cit.* 14–15 and figs 7, 9.

‡ Perhaps the *parastatai* of the Naval Catalogues were such props (see below, p. 293).

§ The tide is an unimportant factor in Piraeus; the modern tide range varies from 10 to a maximum of 28 cm.

‖ (Dem.) 50 6; cf. 51 4, *IG* 2² 1629, 184 ff. The ships of the Sicilian expedition also clearly all left together from Kantharos, Thuc. VI 30–2.

¶ Graser (*loc. cit.* p. 24) thought he could distinguish groups of ship-sheds of varying sizes, for pentekontors, *triereis*, *tetrereis* and *pentereis* (cf. his chart opposite p. 62). But we have only his verbal descriptions, and the evidence is not conclusive. Cf. Wachsmuth, *op. cit.* pp. 72–3.

** Flemming in *Marine Archaeology* (ed. du Plat Taylor, 1965), pp. 170–8 and figs 69–70, whence Plate 30 *a* and *b*. These are the only slips whose lower end has been found.

superstructure of stone blocks, possibly with columns also, for four columns were found lying on the slips. Six of the slips have a narrow central runner, one of which has a keel-slot cut in it. The runner is wider and the slot shallower at the foot of the slip for easy entry. The slips are just under forty metres (157 ft 5 in.) long and have a clear width of six metres (19 ft 8 in.); the gradient is 1 in 14, so slight that ships could probably have been man-handled up them. The slips are now completely flooded, with a depth of 2·80 m. at their foot, but there has been a relative rise in sea level at Apollonia of about 2 m. since antiquity. With 0·80 m. of water at their foot the slips would have had a dry length of twenty-eight metres (110 ft 3 in.). Flemming dates them to the Greek period,* and they must be fairly early since they were built over in antiquity.

A third group of similar ship-sheds were found at Oeniadae in Acarnania.† Five ship-sheds were built in a chamber cut into the bedrock, now silted up and overgrown. They are divided by rows of columns, each with the same distance between columns, so that the excavators suggested that here each slip was separately roofed. Unlike those in Piraeus and Apollonia the slips here are hollowed out in the rock to a depth of up to 75 cm., with bevelled sides, and swing up at the upper end to fit the ship's stern when in position. The roof, which was about 7 m. high, probably swung up correspondingly at the upper end. The slips are estimated to be 47 m. long, and the excavated slip is 3·25 m. wide with a total clear width between the columns of just over 6 m.‡ The gradient, except at the top, is slightly less than 1 in 6. Gear was stored in small rock-chambers at the head of the slips, and in an empty space at one side of the group of ship-sheds. No indication is given on the published plan and section of present ground water level or of the estimated ancient sea level.§ The excavators dated the ship-sheds to the third century B.C. at the latest, and probably earlier.

The only other well preserved ship-sheds in Greece are two at Sunium, intended to house two guardships, much smaller than *triereis*, at this strategic

---

* But they are not Greek just because 'the Romans did not use slipways', since there is no evidence for this statement.

† Partly excavated by the American School in 1900–1: *AJA* VIII (1904), 227–37 and pls IX–XI, cf. Lehmann-Hartleben, *op. cit.* 115–18.

‡ The interaxial width is given as 6·78 m., and the columns have a lower diameter of 0·72 m.

§ Assuming that the total length of the slips is 47 m. and that the gradient remains even, 1 m. depth of water at the foot would give a dry length of just over 38 m.; this would mean a relative rise of some 2 m. since antiquity.

point.* They had short slips, over 21 m. long and 2·60 m. wide, narrowing to 1·15 m., with a shallow ledge on either side which may have held wooden runners. Here as at Oeniadae the slips are cut deep (1·25 m.) into the rock. The gradient is much steeper than elsewhere (1 in 3·5). The purpose of this may have been partly to prevent waves from washing up the slips, which face the prevailing north-west wind, but also partly to minimize the amount of rock cutting needed in a place where the bedrock slopes up steeply from the shore. For the ship-sheds may well have been built in a hurry, in a crisis in 413–412 B.C.†

Certainly with this gradient it would have been difficult to manhandle ships up the slips. A bronze ratchet-wheel found on the site may perhaps have belonged to a winch, and a stone found by one slip probably served as a bollard. The roof seems to have been a gable roof in two parts, both with a horizontal ridge.

These are the only remains of ship-sheds which have been properly studied. From them we may reasonably deduce that most Greek ship-sheds had a fairly uniform clear width, though clearly some narrower ones were built for smaller craft. Of the other famous harbours, the military harbour at Carthage contained 220 ship-sheds, which were among the most impressive of antiquity, and occupied the entire shore of the harbour and its central island. A description survives in Appian,‡ who compares the total effect to that of a colonnade surrounding the harbour. It has plausibly been suggested that the layout of the harbour was the work of a Greek architect. These ship-sheds each had an upper storey where the ship's tackle was stored, an arrangement which was a considerable advance. They were demolished after 146 B.C., and the Romans built quays over the foundations. Some remains of the ship-sheds have been found, but little reliable information has ever been published. The same is true of the remains found in the

---

* Well published by Kenny in *BSA* XLII (1947), 194–200 and pls 31–4. Again it is not clear how far the slips ran on into the water, since they are covered by fallen rock; the dry length is now *c.* 18 m.

† This seems to me a more plausible date for their construction than the mid-third-century date suggested by Kenny.

‡ *Lib.* 96 (a description of the capture of Carthage by the Romans in 146 B.C., based on the eye-witness account of Polybius); Strabo C 832. Some remains here indicate a clear width of 5·40–5·60 m.; for a survey of the evidence *vide* Lehmann-Hartleben, *op. cit.* 142–4; G. Picard, *Carthage* (1964), 195. Lehmann-Hartleben suggested that the ship-sheds on the island were only 2·70 m. wide and intended for the smaller units of the fleet. There is no concrete evidence for this, but it is difficult to see how 220 ship-sheds all with an interaxial width of 5·90 m. could have been fitted into the shore space available in the harbour.

Little Harbour at Syracuse.* Here the number of ship-sheds was even larger, reaching a total of 310 in the two harbours after the building work of Dionysius I at the end of the fifth century. According to Diodorus most of the 160 new ship-sheds built by Dionysius took two ships.†

A number of other structures have been interpreted as ancient ship-sheds, in almost every case wrongly.‡ But despite the paucity of actual remains we must assume that all Greek cities which had warships must have had ship-sheds in their harbours.§

DOCKYARDS, ETC.

There are very few references to permanent naval installations before the Persian wars. There was a sail store in the well planned port of Homeric Phaeacia, which the later Corcyraeans claimed as the forerunner of their city[1]. Polycrates built ship-sheds[2], but elsewhere we hear only of ordinary slipways for hauling ships up out of the water[3]. In the fifth and fourth centuries we have a good deal of information about the naval installations of Piraeus. There is some information too about dockyards elsewhere in Greek lands.

In 455 the Athenian general Tolmides sailed into the Gulf of Laconia and burnt the Spartan dockyard[4]. Later Xenophon tells us that this was at Gytheum[5]. The naval station which was constantly used by Peloponnesian fleets was Cyllene in Elis, since it was convenient as a base for operations against Athenian fleets at Naupactus and Corcyra. It was burnt by the Corcyraeans in 434 B.C.[6]. Thucydides calls Cyllene an *epineion* rather than a

* Cavallari spoke of foundations of ship-sheds along the shore, their width varying from 2·50 m. to 6 m. (Cavallari & Holm, *Topografia archeologica di Siracusa* (1883), 30). One must assume that the majority had a width of 6 m. or a little less. It has been suggested that Cavallari took central runners for partition walls, and that therefore his measurement of 2·50 m. is less than half the full width of the ship-sheds in question. Certainly there will have been only a small proportion of narrow ship-sheds. No length measurements have been obtained at Syracuse, or at Carthage. It is to be doubted whether the remains now visible at Syracuse are of ship-sheds at all.

† D.S. XIV 42 45; cf. Lehmann-Hartleben, *op. cit.* 84–5, 106–7, but his arguments are not always convincing. For example, it is not certain that these ship-sheds took the two ships side by side, as he asserts, rather than one behind the other (cf. Aelius Aristides, xxv, 4 on Rhodes). Diodorus simply says 'ship-sheds...the majority taking two ships'. Admittedly Plato's words (*Critias* 116B) 'double ship-sheds' (*neosoikous diplous*) imply a side-by-side arrangement, but one cannot be sure that he had Syracuse in mind throughout his description of Atlantis.

‡ E.g. at Pyrrha, Thoricus, Calauria, Halae; Aegina is an exception. I hope later to discuss these remains in detail.

§ There are a number of literary references to ship-sheds in other Greek cities: *vide* Lehmann-Hartleben, *op. cit.* 240–87 ('Katalog') and especially P.W. *RE* XIII 1, p. 564, *s.v. limen*.

neorion. There must have been dockyards at Corinth, but we hear of them only once. Argive *neoria* are mentioned by Xenophon in the fourth century[7]. There was a Megarian *neorion* at Nisaea[8]; and we hear that Sparta when she established the colony of Heracleia on the Malian Gulf built dockyards there[9]. The Syracusan *neorion* in 415 was in the small harbour on the north side of the city[10]. Old ship-sheds were, however, still in existence on the northern shore of the large harbour[11]. A temporary naval station is called a *naustathmon*, i.e. a place for beaching ships[12]. Aristotle speaks in the *Politics* of many countries and cities possessing *epineia* and harbours conveniently situated with regard to the city, so as not to form part of the city itself, yet not too far away, connected to it by walls and other defence works[13].

We shall see (pp. 225 f.) that the growth and fortification of Athens' *neorion* at Piraeus and its connection with Athens by the Long Walls was the direct result of the naval policies which are associated with the names of Themistocles and Pericles. In Aristophanes' *Birds* Sovereignty, the consort of Zeus, is said to look after his thunderbolt and all his other valuables—good counsel, good laws, good sense, and the dockyards[14]. Athens was very proud of them. An anonymous comic writer of the fifth or fourth century puts the dockyards as first among the glories of Athens[15]. In 425 fear of their being destroyed by fire was an anxiety to be played on by informers[16]; and we hear that from the time of Aristides there were five hundred special guards for them[17], and that in the time of Demosthenes a certain Antiphon had promised Philip that he would burn them down[18]. Thucydides says that at the beginning of the Peloponnesian war the whole enclosed area of Piraeus, including Munichia, was sixty stades in circumference[19]. At the end of our period, when Antipater sent a force to occupy the Athenian naval installations, Pausanias says that the force seized first Munichia, and then Piraeus and the Long Walls[20]. It looks as if at this time Munichia was not within the perimeter. In the naval lists of 330/29, 326/5, and 325/4 the number of ship-sheds in use is given as 372, divided between Munichia (82), Zea (196), and Kantharos (94)[21]. In an earlier list the number of *triereis* taken over by the dockyard overseers in 357/6 is given as 283, divided into those in the ship-sheds, those in the open air, and those in commission[22]. It looks as if the number of ship-sheds was considerably smaller at this date than twenty-five years later. We shall see that the rebuilding probably began about 347 B.C.

As we have seen, these ship-sheds were built in pairs with a space of less than six metres (19 ft 6 in.) between the lines of columns and with a dry length of thirty-seven metres (121 ft 5 in.). The actual stone slipways were roughly three metres (9 ft 10 in.) wide. A fragment of Cratinus suggests that reed mats were laid on the slipways for the bilges to rest on (see note 24 below).

Only the harbour of Kantharos is mentioned in fifth-century literature[23]. But it seems likely that the other two harbours were in use then. There certainly were ship-sheds in the fifth-century dockyard, since Cratinus mentions them and one is mentioned in the *Acharnians* of Aristophanes[24]. Andocides, in a speech which contains much historical inaccuracy, says that the Athenians built ship-sheds in the period of peace before the Peloponnesian war[25]. This statement in any case seems likely to be true. Isocrates speaks of a thousand talents having been spent on the naval installations of Piraeus, which were sold by the Thirty (during the Spartan occupation) for three talents[26]. Lysias confirms the destruction of the dockyards by the Thirty. The destruction cannot, however, have been complete since in a speech delivered in 399 he remarks that the ship-sheds were then falling to pieces. The historian of the Oxyrhyncus papyrus also mentions them as being in existence at about this time[27].

Between 399 and 377/6, when the first of the fourth-century naval lists are available, the condition of the dockyards is unknown. The first big list makes no reference to ship-sheds or gear stores, but the anchors and other gear said to be 'in the dockyard' must have been somewhere under cover[28], perhaps they were in the building referred to later as the 'old storehouse'[29]. The first mention of a gear store comes in 370, when 'hanging gear' is said to be housed in 'the *oikema*'[30]. In 357/6 there is a list of gear taken over by the dockyard overseers in the *neoria* and in the *skeuotheke*[31]. Our literary sources suggest that preparations for the rebuilding of the Athenian naval installations began in earnest under the influence of Eubulus, who was in control of financial policy from 354 to 350 B.C. The *Poroi* of Xenophon (355) is a treatise on economics which urges the Athenians to adopt financial reforms which will enable them, among other things, to repair the walls and dockyards. Dinarchus implies that the ship-sheds were built under Eubulus' direction[32]: and Aeschines says that public confidence in Eubulus resulted in the building of dockyards and a gear store (*skeuotheke*)[33]. But an inscription of 302/1 is preserved honouring two foreigners for contributing from 347 to 322 to the annual property tax levied at Athens to raise ten talents for the building of the ship-sheds and gear store[34]. It looks then as if the works were not actually begun until after Eubulus. In 339/8, Philochorus says, the works concerning the ship-sheds and the gear store were interrupted because of the war with Philip[35]. We are told however by [Plutarch] that Lycurgus, who took over the control of financial policy at Athens in the following year, completed the half-built ship-sheds and gear store[36]. This latter building must be the famous stone '*hoplotheke*' or 'hanging gear store' of which Philo was architect and which is mentioned by Strabo: 'now in early times Munichia was walled...including within the circuit of its walls both Piraeus and the harbours which were full of naval installations, among which was the hanging gear store built by Philo'[37]. An inscription gives full architectural details of this building, for which Philo is said to have accounted to the Athenians in the Assembly[38].

There was more than one *skeuotheke*. A list of 330/29 speaks of wooden *skeuothekai* for the gear of 277 *triereis*[39]. We also hear of gear for a hundred *triereis* stored, as a reserve, on the Acropolis[40]. The same list and another for 325/4 record miscellaneous gear kept 'in the big *oikema* at the gates'[41].

The dockyard authority was the board of overseers, who perhaps in the fifth century may have been called *neoroi*[42], but in the fourth century were *epimeletai*, ten annual officers elected one from each tribe[43]. They were responsible for the gear, its issue to the trierarchs and its recovery from them at the end of their period of office. Gear not repaid had to be paid for at a valuation. The naval lists, fragmentary in the fifth century but full and informative for a number of years in the middle of the fourth century, are largely statements of the accounts of these officers, of ships, gear and buildings received and handed over in turn together with lists of outstanding debts.

One picture may perhaps stay in our memory as we leave the dockyards of Athens. When the dispatch of an expedition was urgent, the presiding committee of the Assembly would meet 'on the jetty', and stay there in continuous session until the ships left[44].

TEXTS

1. Thuc. I 25[4] ναυτικῷ δὲ καὶ πολὺ προύχειν ἔστιν ὅτε ἐπαιρόμενοι καὶ κατὰ τὴν Φαιάκων προενοίκησιν τῆς Κερκύρας κλέος ἐχόντων τὰ περὶ τὰς ναῦς.

2. See p. 130 above.

3. See p. 129 above.

4. Thuc. i 108⁵ καὶ τὸ νεώριον τῶν Λακεδαιμονίων ἐνέπρησαν.

5. Xen. *HG* vi 5 32 Γυθείῳ δέ, ἔνθα τὰ νεώρια τοῖς Λακεδαιμονίοις ἦν, καὶ προσέβαλλον τρεῖς ἡμέρας.

6. Thuc. i 30² καὶ Κυλλήνην τὸ Ἠλείων ἐπίνειον ἐνέπρησαν.

       ii 84⁵ παρέπλευσαν δὲ καὶ οἱ Πελοποννήσιοι εὐθύς. . .ἐς Κυλλήνην τὸ Ἠλείων ἐπίνειον.

  Cf. iii 69¹, 76¹; vi 88⁹.

7. Xen. *HG* iv 4 12 and 19.

8. Thuc. ii 93² καθελκύσαντας ἐκ Νισαίας τοῦ νεωρίου αὐτῶν τεσσαράκοντα ναῦς.

9. Thuc. iii 92⁶ καταστάντες δὲ ἐτείχισαν τὴν πόλιν ἐκ καινῆς, ἣ νῦν Ἡράκλεια καλεῖται. . .νεώριά τε παρεσκευάζοντο.

10. Thuc. vii 22¹ καὶ ἀπὸ ξυνθήματος πέντε μὲν καὶ τριάκοντα ἐκ τοῦ μεγάλου λιμένος ἐπέπλεον, αἱ δὲ πέντε καὶ τεσσαράκοντα ἐκ τοῦ ἐλάσσονος, οὗ ἦν καὶ τὸ νεώριον αὐτοῖς.

11. Thuc. vii 25⁵ πρὸ τῶν παλαιῶν νεωσοίκων.

12. Thuc. iii 6²; vi 49⁴.

13. Aristotle, *Politics*, vii 5 5 1327a 32 ἐπεὶ δὲ καὶ νῦν ὁρῶμεν πολλαῖς ὑπάρχοντα καὶ χώραις καὶ πόλεσιν ἐπίνεια καὶ λιμένας εὐφυῶς κείμενα πρὸς τὴν πόλιν, ὥστε μήτε τὸ αὐτὸ νέμειν ἄστυ μήτε πόρρω λίαν, ἀλλὰ κρατεῖσθαι τείχεσι καὶ τοιούτοις ἄλλοις ἐρύμασι. . .

14. Aristophanes, *Birds*, 1537–40

    Pisthetaerus τίς ἐστιν ἡ βασίλεια;

    Prometheus   καλλίστη κόρη,

        ἥπερ ταμιεύει τὸν κεραυνὸν τοῦ Διὸς

        καὶ τἄλλ᾽ ἀπαξάπαντα, τὴν εὐβουλίαν

        τὴν εὐνομίαν τὴν σωφροσύνην τὰ νεώρια.

15. Com. Adespot. 340 Edmonds

        δέσποιν᾽ ἁπασῶν πότνι᾽ Ἀθηναίων πόλι,

        ὥς μοι καλόν σου φαίνεται τὸ νεώριον,

        ὡς καλὸς ὁ Παρθενών, καλὸς δ᾽ ὁ Πειραεύς.

16. Aristophanes, *Acharnians*, 916 ff.

17. Aristotle, *Ath. Pol.* 24 3 καὶ φρουροὶ νεωρίων πεντακόσιοι.

18. Demosthenes 18 132 τίς γὰρ ὑμῶν οὐκ οἶδεν τὸν ἀποψηφισθέντ᾽ Ἀντιφῶντα, ὃς ἐπαγγειλάμενος Φιλίππῳ τὰ νεώρια ἐμπρήσειν εἰς τὴν πόλιν ἦλθεν;

19. Thuc. ii 13⁷ καὶ τοῦ Πειραιῶς ξὺν Μουνιχίᾳ ἑξήκοντα μὲν σταδίων ὁ ἅπας περίβολος.

20. Pausanias i 25 5 φρουρά τε Μακεδόνων ἐσῆλθεν Ἀθηναίοις, οἳ Μουνιχίαν, ὕστερον δὲ καὶ Πειραιᾶ καὶ τείχη μακρὰ ἔσχον.

21. *IG* 2² 1627 397 νεώσοικοι οἰκοδομημένοι καὶ ἐπεσκευασμένοι ΗΗΗ⅏ΔΔΙΙ· τούτων Μουνιχίασιν ⅏ΔΔΔΙΙ ἐν Ζέᾳ Η⅏ΔΔΔΔΓΙ ἐν Κανθάρου λιμένι ⅏ΔΔΔΔΙΙΙΙ.

  Cf. 1628 552, 1629 1030.

22. *IG* 2² 1611 3 ἀ]ριθμὸς τριήρων ὧν [ἐ]ν νεωσοίκοις ἀν[ειλ]κυσμένων κατελά-
βομεν καὶ τῶν ὑπαιθρί[ω]ν καὶ τῶν ἐκπεπλευ[κ]ότων παραδοθεισῶν ΗΗ𐅄ΔΔΔΙΙΙ.

23. Aristophanes, *Peace*, 145
ἐν Πειραιεῖ δήπου 'στι Κανθάρου λιμήν.

24. Cratinus, fr. 197 Kock (speaking of *triereis*)
οὐ δύνανται πάντα ποιοῦσαι νεωσοίκων λαχεῖν
οὐδὲ κάννης.

Aristophanes, *Acharnians*, 95, see below, p. 288, note 25.

25. Andocides 3 7 νεωσοίκους τε ᾠκοδομησάμεθα.

26. Isocrates 7 66 τοὺς δὲ νεωσοίκους ἐπὶ καθαιρέσει τριῶν ταλάντων ἀποδο-
μένους.

27. Lysias 30 22 τοὺς δὲ νεωσοίκους ⟨καὶ⟩ τὰ τείχη περικαταρρέοντα.

Hell. Ox. 1 1 καθελκύσας ναῦν ἐκ τῶν νεωσοίκων ἀναγόμενος ἔπλει πρὸς
Κόνωνα.

28. *IG* 2² 1604 72 ταύτης τὰ] πηδάλια ἐν τῷ νεωρίῳ ἐστίν.

29. *IG* 2² 1627 352 ἐν τῇ ἀρχαίᾳ σκ[ευ]οθήκῃ.

30. *IG* 2² 1610 6 [κ]ρεμαστὰ σκε[ύη] ἐν τῷ οἰκήμα[τι] παρέδομεν.

31. *IG* 2² 1611 10 ἀριθμὸς σκευῶν ξυλί[νω]ν καὶ κρεμαστῶν [ὧ]ν ἐν τοῖς νεωρίοις
[καὶ] ἐν τῇ σκευοθήκῃ [κατ]ελάβομεν.

32. Xen. *Poroi*, 6 1; Dinarchus *Against Demosthenes* 96 ποῖαι γὰρ τριήρεις εἰσὶ
κατεσκευασμέναι διὰ τοῦτον, ὥσπερ ἐπ' Εὐβούλου, τῇ πόλει; ἢ ποῖοι νεώσοικοι
τούτου πολιτευομένου γεγόνασι;

33. Aeschines 3 25 διὰ δὲ τὴν πρὸς Εὔβουλον γενομένην πίστιν ὑμῖν οἱ ἐπὶ τὸ
θεωρικὸν κεχειροτονημένοι. . .καὶ νεώριον καὶ σκευοθήκην ᾠκοδόμουν.

34. *IG* 2² 505 12 εἴς τε τὴν οἰκοδομίαν τῶν νεωσοίκων καὶ τῆς σκευοθήκης εἰσ-
φέροντες τὰς εἰσφορὰς καθ' ἕκαστον τὸν ἐνιαυτὸν τὰς εἰς τὰ δέκα τάλαντα καλῶς καὶ
προθύμως ἀπὸ Θεμιστοκλέους ἄρχοντος μέχρι Κηφισοδώρου.

35. Philochorus, fr. 135 Λυσιμαχίδης Ἀχαρνεύς· ἐπὶ τούτου (339/8) τὰ μὲν ἔργα
τὰ περὶ τοὺς νεωσοίκους καὶ τὴν σκευοθήκην ἀνεβάλοντο διὰ τὸν πόλεμον πρὸς
Φίλιππον.

36. [Plutarch], *Vit. X or.* VII 851 D (Lycurgus) πρὸς δὲ τούτοις ἡμίεργα παραλαβὼν
τούς τε νεωσοίκους καὶ τὴν σκευοθήκην. . .ἐξεργάσατο.

Cf. Hyperides, fr. 118.

37. Strabo 9 1 15 τὸ μὲν οὖν παλαιὸν ἐτετείχιστο καὶ συνῴκιστο ἡ Μουνιχία
παραπλησίως, ὥσπερ ἡ τῶν Ῥοδίων πόλις, προσειληφυῖα τῷ περιβόλῳ τόν τε Πειραιᾶ
καὶ τοὺς λιμένας πλήρεις νεωρίων, ἐν οἷς καὶ ἡ ὁπλοθήκη Φίλωνος ἔργον.

38. *IG* 2² 1668 (347/6 B.C.) 1–7 [σ]υγγραφαὶ τῆς σκευοθήκης τῆς λιθίνης τοῖς
κρεμαστοῖς σκεύεσιν Εὐθυδόμου Δημητρίου Μελιτέως, Φίλωνος Ἐξηκεστίδου Ἐλευ-
σινίου. σκευοθήκην οἰκοδομῆσαι τοῖς κρεμαστοῖς σκεύεσιν ἐν Ζείᾳ ἀρξάμενον ἀπὸ τοῦ
προπυλαίου τοῦ ἐξ ἀγορᾶς προσιόντι ἐκ τοῦ ὄπισθεν τῶν νεωσοίκων τῶν ὁμοτεγῶν
μῆκος τεττάρων πλέθρων πλάτος πεντήκοντα ποδῶν καὶ πέντε σὺν τοῖς τοίχοις.

Cic. *de or.* 1 62 Philonem illum architectum, qui Atheniensibus armamentum fecit, constat perdiserte populo rationem operis reddidisse.

Val. Max. 8 12 2 Philonem rationem institutionis suae in theatro reddidisse constat.

39. *IG* 2² 1627 396 σκευοθῆκαι ξύλιναι σκεύεσιν τριήρων ΗΗℲΔΔΓΙΙ.

40. *IG* 2² 1627 56 ff. e.g. καὶ ἐν ἀκροπόλει ὑποζώματα ἐπὶ ναῦς Η.

41. *IG* 2² 1627 279 καὶ τάδε παρελάβομεν ἐν τῷ οἰκήματ[ι] τῷ [με]γάλῳ τῷ πρὸς τ[αῖ]ς [πύ]λαις.

42. *IG* 1² 74 (before 430 B.C.), II 11 *h*]οι νεωροί [

      IG 1² 126 (405 B.C.) = 2² 1 30 ἅπαντα ἐξαλειψά]ντων οἱ νεωροὶ ἀπανταχό-θεν. . .

43. See *IG* 2² 1607 (373/2 B.C.) *ad init.*

44. *IG* 2² 1629 247 τοὺς δὲ πρυτάνεις ποεῖν βουλῆς ἕδραν ἐπὶ χώματι περὶ τοῦ ἀποστόλου συνεχῶς, ἕως ἂν ὁ ἀπόστολος γένηται.

9

WRITTEN EVIDENCE

GENERAL NOTE

The written evidence falls into a number of well-defined categories. In the first category are the tragic and lyric poets, who may be speaking of ships either in the context of their plot or tale or as an image drawn from their own experience of seafaring. In the former case, with the unique exception of Aeschylus' *Persians* discussed above (pp. 150–5), the ships they purport to describe are the ships of the heroic age, about which they have learnt from Homer, or at which they may have guessed from observation of the smaller ships of their own age. Anachronism, attributing to the heroic age the ships and practice of seafaring which belong to their own age, is to be expected. The vase-painter, fortunately for us, appears to be guilty of it on occasion. The degree and frequency of anachronism among the writers can only be a matter of conjecture; but it seems very likely that in image-making they will naturally reflect their own experience.

The second category of evidence consists of the accounts of naval warfare given by the historians of the period. These writers assume that the reader is well aware of the structure and method of working of the ships mentioned. In our case the assumption is false, and we are left to deduce what we can from chance references.

The third category includes all those writers, Herodotus, the comic poets, the orators and the philosophers, who are not speaking specifically about the seafaring of the period, but from whose writings information may be gleaned either in an incidental statement or in a tale or in an image.

The fourth category consists of the many inscriptions concerning naval matters. Nothing as important historically as the decree of Themistocles is available for this period. But there are inventories of gear and ships handed over from one board of dockyard superintendents to another, records of offerings of naval gear in temples, and other miscellaneous records from which information can be gathered. With a few valuable exceptions all these inscriptions derive from the middle half of the fourth century.

The first of these categories of evidence, because of its ambiguous nature, will have to be treated separately, though the information derived from it may be used with caution in the task of building up a picture of the seafaring and naval activity of the period. The remaining three can be taken together and will provide the basic elements of the picture.

THE TRAGIC AND LYRIC POETS

THE EPITHETS

The epithets[1] which Pindar, Bacchylides and the tragic poets use to describe ships are mostly the Homeric ones, 'swift', 'many-oared', 'crossing the sea', 'with good *selmata*', 'with good bows', 'with good stern', 'with good oars'. Aeschylus and Bacchylides speak of 'dark-faced ships', Bacchylides of ships 'with dark prows', Euripides of ships 'with dark rams'. Bacchylides' epithets draw attention to the lightness of the stern, and to the way its wet surface flashes in the sun, and to the fine workmanship of its structure. Euripides has some graphic epithets: 'most manoeuvrable', 'with bronze ram', 'made of pinewood', 'with a good emblem'. It is difficult to believe that these pictures were not evoked by, and meant to evoke in the reader's mind, the contemporary reality.

TYPES

Pentekontors are the normal type, if one is specified. Pindar compares a snake to a pentekontor, taking it presumably as the largest type of ship[2]. He apparently said that the Achaean ships at Troy were pentekontors[3]. In the *Helen* of Euripides Menelaus and Helen escape from Egypt in a brand-new Phoenician pentekontor, which is described as having fifty units (*metra*) of benches and oars[4]. In Euripides' *Iphigeneia in Tauris*, Orestes' ship is described as a pentekontor, and it is said that fifty oarsmen sat at her tholepins. At the outset of the play Orestes and his company are spoken of as 'moving through the water with the double surge of their pinewood oars'[5]. The word translated 'double' (*dikrotos*) is used in Xenophon (see below, p. 310) of a *trieres* when only two of its banks of oars are being worked, and later of ships with two banks of oars[6]. Platnauer* thinks the phrase 'double surge' means the waves cast up by the oars on 'each side of the ship'. But it seems more likely in view of the later use of the word, and since two-level pentekontors

* In his edition of the *Iphigeneia*, Oxford, 1938.

were undoubtedly in use in the sixth century (pp. 109–12), probably in the seventh century (pp. 38–40), that Euripides is attributing this type of ship to Orestes.

The 'hundred-oared ship' which appears in the text of Bacchylides[7] is the invention of a modern editor.

SHIP'S COMPANY

Aeschylus calls Agamemnon *nauarchos*, as commander of the Greek fleet. In the *Persians* he gives captains of squadrons the same title[8]. A ship's captain is called *archos* in Pindar. In Aeschylus he is called *naukleros*, and the verb *nauklerein* is used metaphorically in the sense of ruling a city[9]. *Prumnetes*, 'officer of the poop', appears twice metaphorically in Aeschylus for the ruler of the city, and the phrase 'in the stern' as meaning 'in command'[10]. *Prumnetes* has usually been translated 'helmsman', but in view of the captain's place in the stern it may just as well be rendered 'captain'. The *prorates*, 'bow officer', occurs in a fragment of Sophocles' *Assembly of the Greeks*. Telephus is addressed: 'Sitting at the steering oar you will tell the bow officer to keep a look-out for the path to Troy of the sons of Atreus.' Telephus is a real seaman, and 'guide of oars by sea'[11]. *Prorates* is used again metaphorically in another Sophoclean fragment with the apparent meaning of 'commander of the army'[12]. This usage, nautically incorrect, appears to be derived from the metaphorical use of *prora*, the bow, to mean 'first', as, e.g., in a fragment of Sophocles where Hestia is addressed quaintly (as Pearson observes *ad loc.**) as '*prora* of a drink offering', and in the epithet *bouproros* attached to sacrifices in several inscriptions to indicate that the first animal to be sacrificed was a bull[13].

The helmsman appears in these writers almost always as the metaphorical figure of the ruler. Pindar, Aeschylus, and Euripides call him *oiakostrophos*, i.e. 'he who turns the tiller'; and an order to a real helmsman in Euripides is 'Turn the tiller'. Pindar speaks of 'turning the twin steering oars'. These instances suggest that the steering oar was not moved laterally in the water but revolved about its long axis[14]. In one fragment of Sophocles the helmsman is called the guardian of the ship, in another and in Aeschylus her shepherd[15].

Rowing frequently occurs in metaphor. The word *eressein* is used of any

* *The Fragments of Sophocles*, Cambridge University Press, 1917, II, p. 329.

lively motion, e.g. moving feet, handling a bow, redoubling threats, revolving thoughts. The most startling metaphor of all is the use of *eiresia* for Astyanax feeding at his mother's breast[16]. In Sophocles a real oarsman is said to 'sit on the swift thwart of rowing'[17]. In the *Troades* Euripides gives a list of the seamen's duties in a storm. One is at the tiller, another at the sails, while a third bails out the ship[18].

In Euripides the *keleustes* appears as an officer who shouts commands to the crew[19]. Orpheus is called *auletes* or bo'sun to the Argonauts in Euripides' *Hypsipyle*. He stands by the mast amidships, his lyre 'playing the oarsmen a measure for the long sweep of their oar, now a swift stroke now a pause for the blade of pine'. As Orpheus he plays on the lyre, not the pipe (*aulos*), but his function is that of the *auletes*, although it is to be noted that his measure is described as *keleusmata*[20]. Later writers give us the word *trieraules* for this officer in the *trieres*[21]. In Euripides' *Electra*, again, the dolphin is said to be fond of the pipe (*philaulos*) as he 'leaps beside the dark-rammed prows', presumably because, by the pathetic fallacy, he is thought to enjoy the bo'sun's call. In the *Iphigeneia in Tauris* Euripides speaks of the bo'sun's call as accompanying the oars[22]. In the same play we hear of archers on the poop[23].

HULL AND GEAR

In Bacchylides Theseus leaps into the sea at Minos' challenge from the 'well-built *ikria*'[24] (see above, pp. 47–8). So in Euripides the helmsman sits in the highest part of the stern[25], and a passenger is carried there[26]. In Aeschylus' *Agamemnon* it is part of Clytemnestra's complaint that Cassandra has been brought back from Troy sharing the *selmata* with her husband, i.e. as a first-class passenger[27]. Sophocles describes the helmsman who in a squall will not pay out the mainsheet, ending the voyage with the *selmata* upside down[28]. In Euripides Odysseus is asked if he has brought the wine with him to the Cyclops' cave or left it in the ship's *selmata*[29], and we remember that Archilochus speaks of the wine stored there (see above, p. 119). If the *selmata* are commonly the poop on which the helmsman and all the important people travel, Aeschylus' image in the *Agamemnon*, whereby the gods are described as occupying the 'proud *selma*', becomes a vivid one[30]. The poop is also sometimes called *hedolia*, seating, in these writers. In Sophocles' *Ajax* Teucer speaks of the topmost *hedolia* of the ships having been set on fire. And in the *Helen* of Euripides, Helen, an honoured passenger in Menelaus' ship, sits 'in the middle of the *hedolia*'[31]. As in Homeric ships we saw that there were *ikria* in the bow as well as the stern (see above, p. 48), so these writers mention *selmata* in the bow as well. In the *Helen* a bull for sacrifice is put aboard on the *selmata* of the bow[32]. So we find in Herodotus the Persians sacrificing in the bow of a ship one of the first prisoners they took at sea in the second invasion[33]. Finally, in Sophocles' *Philoctetes* we learn the three places where a passenger could be carried in an oared ship. Philoctetes asking to be taken aboard says he would be content to go anywhere, in the hold, on the bow or on the stern, i.e. as a third-, second- or first-class passenger[34].

We have noticed the bold image in the *Agamemnon*, of the gods sitting on the proud *selma*, and have had no difficulty in recognizing this position as the ship's poop. There are two other similar images, one in the *Agamemnon* and the other in Euripides' *Phoenician Women*, which are a little more confusing. Aegisthus reminds his rebellious subjects: 'You say this sitting at the oar below, while those who are on the *zugon* rule the ship[35].' In the *Phoenician Women* there is the phrase 'you sit upon the *zuga* of command', with which may be compared the phrase in the *Ion* 'the first *zugon* of the city'[36]. *Zugon* normally means the oarsman's thwart[37], but in the passage in the *Agamemnon* seems actually to be contrasted with the oarsman's position. The possibility that the upper thwarts of a two-level ship are being contrasted with the lower thwarts is ruled out by the consideration that the upper thwarts would not be in control of the ship any more than the lower. There can be only one explanation. *Zugon* in the singular can mean one particular important thwart, possibly the lineal descendant of the seven-foot *threnus* of the Homeric ship (see above, pp. 48–9), which marked the forward limit of the poop. In these phrases, then, 'on the *zugon*' means 'on the poop'.

A choric ode in Euripides' *Iphigeneia at Aulis* tells of the assembly of the Achaean fleet for the Trojan expedition. The emblems (*semata, semeia*) of the various squadrons are described. Achilles' squadron of fifty ships had an emblem of a golden Nereid at the high point of the stern. The emblem of the Attic ships was Athena in a winged chariot. The Boeotian ships had *semeia* consisting of Cadmus with a golden snake 'about the *korumba* of the ships'. The stern emblem of Nestor's ships was the river-god Alpheus, footed like a bull[38].

Aeschylus in the *Myrmidons*[39] apparently spoke of the device of a 'tawny horsecock' as painted on one of the Greek ships set on fire by the Trojans and 'dripping off' as the ships burned. We thus have the important information that the devices were painted on the hull. We have mentioned the stern ornaments of earlier oared ships (see above, p. 120). Here we have some actual examples of such emblems, and may perhaps infer that they were generally used as identification marks for national fleets.

We have seen that the forepart of the ship had a platform for the accommodation of the *prorates* (see above, p. 197), and for passengers, and that sacrifices were made there. From the *Suppliants* of Aeschylus it appears that the bow has eyes to see the way ahead[40]. This feature is very common in the representations of the sixth and fifth centuries (see Index *s.v.* eye). Pollux attributes to Sophocles in the *Nauplius* the use of the word *holkia* and says that it there meant *pedalia*, i.e. steering oars[41]. He quotes in support the 'planed *epholkaion*' of *Odyssey* 14 350. It was argued above (p. 49) that this was in fact neither a steering oar nor a lading plank, as Munro suggests, but a towing bar, a cross-beam corresponding to the seven-foot *threnus* in the stern, projecting on each side of the bows and thus offering a foothold for anyone going over the side there (as Odysseus said he did), as well as a point of attachment for towing ropes. In Apollonius Rhodius, the third-century Alexandrian imitator of Homer, the Triton towing the *Argo* to the sea 'holds on to the *holkeion*'[42] (see perhaps Arch. 40, Pl. 12 *c*). Pindar describes the *Argo*'s anchors as being 'slung above the ram'[43]. Euripides shows in the *Iphigeneia in Tauris* how this is done. The crew of a departing ship sling the anchor 'from the *epotides*'. When the representations (see Pls 11 *b–d*, 12 *b–d* ff.) exhibit the Greek habit of making the forepart of the ship into the appearance of an animal mask with eyes and ears, it would have been an easy guess that these ear-like timbers were projections on each side of the bows, if we had not in fact been told by Thucydides, in connection with *triereis*, that they were exactly that (see below, p. 282). The conclusion then is that *epotis* is the fifth-century word for a feature which in Homer is called *epholkaion* and in Sophocles, possibly, *holkion*, both these latter words deriving from the part it played in towing. The identification of the *epholkaion* with the *epotis* is confirmed by Euripides in the *Helen*. There the Phoenician messenger escapes from the ship which Menelaus has seized by an act of barratry in exactly the same way that Odysseus says that he did from the Phoenician ship, but whereas in Odysseus' case the ship had its anchors out and he went over the side by the 'planed *epholkaion*', the Phoenician messenger says he 'let himself down beside the anchor', which, since the ship was at sea, was slung, as in the

Iphigeneia in Tauris, from the *epotis*[44]. Finally, two fixed parts of the hull are mentioned in connection with the oarsmen, the thwarts[45] and the tholepins[46]. In Aeschylus' *Suppliants* a ship is said to be 'sewn with linen', and elsewhere in the same play a ship is described as 'pegged with ship's cords' and 'bound together with pegs'. The pegs presumably caulked the holes for the cords which held together the planks of a primitive kind of carvel-built hull (see p. 50). A shipwright's tool for drilling such holes is mentioned by Euripides in the *Cyclops*[47]. Bilge water is also mentioned and provides a vivid natural metaphor[48].

Turning to the 'wooden gear', we can observe that in these writers the steering oar is sometimes singular, sometimes plural. Once they are described as twin, and once as attached with cords[49]. There is a curious epithet for steering oars in the *Iphigeneia in Tauris*[50]. The chorus speaks of the 'sleeping' (*eunaion*) steering oars hissing as the ship moves forward before a wind which fills the sails. The oars would make a hissing sound as they cut the fast-moving wake. 'Sleeping' is more difficult to explain. Platnauer* suggests that the word means that the steering oars were never shipped, unlike the ordinary rowing oar. But the steering oars were, we know (see above, p. 135, and below, p. 292), removed when a ship was out of commission or immobilized; and in any case the point would be a curious one for the poet to make. It is better to suppose that the steering oars were housed, i.e. secured with the blades feathered in the water. Thus they could be said to sleep, since they do no work.

Oars and mast are often mentioned[51]. At the top of the mast is a sort of truck through which the halliards were worked. This fitting is quite clearly shown in a number of representations of the archaic period. In a cup of Exekias (Arch. 52, Pl. 13) it takes the form of an isosceles triangle base upwards with the mast passing through the downwards-pointing apex and bisecting, and continuing through, the base. A similar truck is visible in the Spartan ivory relief (Arch. 31, Pl. 10*d*), but the shape here is circular in profile. The clearest picture of the truck is on Arch. 94 (Pl. 21*e*). Here it appears to be a metal sleeve fitted over the top of the mast with ring-like ears through which the ropes passed. The word *karchesion* used by Pindar and Euripides is certainly this truck. Hippocrates speaks of a mast, with a *karchesion*, planted in the ground as an alternative to the use of lowering tackle from a wheel or pulley[52].

* *Euripides: Iphigeneia in Tauris,* ed. M. Platnauer, Oxford, 1938.

These authors mention sailyards[53], poles[54] and landing ladders. In the *Helen* of Euripides the sacrificial bull refuses to go aboard 'by the plank'. The plank must have been a special gangway for use on such occasions[55].

'Hanging' gear mentioned are sails[56], anchors[57], side screens[58], and various kinds of ropes. The anchor as a symbol of security appears often in metaphor. In a fragment of Sophocles children are said to be 'anchors of life for a mother', and in Aeschylus travellers say that it is time for them 'to cast anchor in a house of hospitality'. Stern cables (*prumnesia*) occur in Aeschylus and Euripides[59]. Mooring ropes (*peismata*)[60] and shrouds (*protonoi*)[61] appear in the same two authors. Sophocles and Euripides mention the sheet[62]. The passage in the *Troades* of Euripides where the wooden horse is said to have been introduced into Troy 'like the black hull of a ship with girdles of woven flax' is an almost certain reference to the rope girdles or swifters (*hupozomata*) with which *triereis* and probably other types of ship too were fitted when they were in commission (see below, p. 295), and suggests that their fitting was connected with the constant hauling up and down beaches to which the oared ship was subject[63].

HANDLING

Two passages, one in the *Helen* and the other in the *Iphigeneia in Tauris* of Euripides, give extended accounts of the departure of an oared ship. In the *Helen* a messenger relates the escape from Egypt of Helen and the disguised Menelaus. Helen succeeds in procuring a pentekontor for the pretended purpose of sacrificing a bull at sea in honour of Menelaus supposedly drowned. There is a description of the fitting out of a new ship of fifty oars. One line of the Greek text is unfortunately corrupt, but in what remains we hear of the provision of mast and oars, and the fitting of steering oars by means of cords. Then the bull is put aboard on the *selmata* of the bow, and Helen mounts the ladder and takes her seat in the middle of the *hedolia* with the disguised Menelaus beside her, as captain. Then Menelaus' crew go aboard with swords concealed in their clothing and sit on each side of the ship beside the Phoenician oarsmen. There was clearly room for fifty extra men in a pentekontor. At an order from the *keleustes* rowing started. When the ship gets out to sea, the helmsman asks Menelaus, as captain, if they have gone far enough. He agrees, and begins the sacrifice of the bull on the bow platform. At this point the oarsmen begin to feel uneasy and want to return.

They call to the *keleustes* and helmsman to take action. Unfortunately the command of the *keleustes* is not preserved correctly in the MSS. It probably was 'Give way starboard oars', a manœuvre which would bring the ship about. They tell the helmsman to put his helm over. At this Menelaus gives the word to the Greeks to attack the Phoenicians and drive them overboard, while the *keleustes* replies with a similar order to the Phoenicians, to fight with anything they can lay hands on, thwarts and oars, and Helen encourages the Greeks from the stern. The Greeks capture the ship and take over the oars. Menelaus compels the helmsman to steer a course for Greece. The messenger makes his escape over the bows 'beside the anchor', and lives to tell the tale[64].

This account is clearly a valuable one. A number of its details have already been used in the section on the hull and gear of ships mentioned by these authors. Since the intention is only a short voyage offshore, there is naturally nothing about making sail until the ship has been seized. What is particularly interesting is the information it gives about the relative functions of captain, helmsman, and *keleustes*. The captain gives commands to the helmsman direct, and to the oarsmen through the *keleustes*.

There is a similarly detailed account of a departure by sea in the *Iphigeneia in Tauris*, in places unfortunately obscured by difficulties with the Greek text. A messenger, again, describes how Orestes and Pylades, with Iphigeneia's help, make their escape from Tauri, and take her with them, in spite of rough weather and a lee shore.

The messenger and his companions, escorting Iphigeneia and the two prisoners to a sacrifice, let the three Greeks go on ahead, and as they come up catch sight of Orestes' ship, with oars run out and her fifty oarsmen holding them at the tholepins. Orestes and Pylades stand in the stern. They had been freed by Iphigeneia, and had made contact with their hidden ship. Platnauer finds great difficulty in the two men being in the ship at this point, when the messenger catches sight of her, and subsequently coming ashore to carry off Iphigeneia. But there is no difficulty. Orestes and Pylades are getting the ship ready for departure. She has been run down into the sea, and is waterborne: the anchors are being weighed. They are naturally aboard to supervise operations. 'Some of the seamen kept the bow steady with poles', since with the anchors up there was a danger of the bow swinging round and the ship broaching to. 'Others slung the anchors from the *epotides*.' Others were hauling in the stern cables, running out the ladders and lowering them into the water for Orestes and Pylades to go ashore to fetch Iphigeneia. The messenger and his companions react by holding on to Iphigeneia and the stern cables, and try to immobilize the ship by removing the steering oars. There follows a battle of fists, neither side being armed with swords, in which Orestes and Pylades succeed in coming ashore and carrying off Iphigeneia under the covering fire of archers on the pentekontor's poop. 'Then, for a big wave drove the ship up the beach, and the girl was afraid to get her feet wet, Orestes took her over his left shoulder, strode into the sea, leapt on the ladder, and set her inside the ship. . .' But their troubles were not yet over. 'With a joyful shout they smote the sea' (i.e. began to row), but getting a big ship off a lee shore is not so easy. The scene hitherto described has suggested high wind and sea, the use of poles to keep the ship from broaching to, the big wave that prompts Orestes to carry his sister aboard. So, as the ship gets away, she meets a heavy swell and is in difficulties. 'A great squall came and suddenly thrust the stern backwards.' The word translated 'stern' here is *prumnesia*, normally used, as we have seen, for stern cables. If the word is not to be emended, we have to suppose that it means here the high stern ornament, which would certainly catch the wind. The Oxford text of Gilbert Murray reads Mekler's emendation, which introduces a sail. One thing is certain. No one in his senses would have hoisted sail under these conditions. In spite of the set-back, the oarsmen redouble their efforts, and their enemies try to drag the ship in. Athena eventually intervenes and the Greeks row away[65]. Of particular interest in this story is the use of the archers on the poop to cover a withdrawal from a hostile shore. It confirms too for this age the procedure of a ship's departure with which Homer has made us familiar.

The procedure of weighing anchor and slinging it above the ram is described twice in Pindar[66], and in Sophocles the same word is used for weighing anchor as is used in Homer for brailing up sail[67]. Pindar describes the setting forth of the *Argo* in the Fourth Pythian Ode[68]: first Jason numbers the Argonauts, then Mopsus assigns the places by lot. (It is noticeable how in the parallel description in Apollonius Rhodius the two heaviest, Herakles and Ankaeus, are given the places in the middle of the boat and exempted from the draw[69].) Then, after the anchors have been slung, the captain pours a libation, presumably in the stern, and prays for a swift voyage and safe return. Mopsus, as *keleustes*, then gives the order to row 'and, before they were sated, their swift hands gave up rowing, and sent on their way by the south wind' (i.e. under sail) 'they came to the mouth of the Inhospitable Sea'. The various traditional stages in the departure are somewhat obscured by Pindar's elliptical style, but they are mostly there. The lyric style of a chorus in the *Iphigeneia in Tauris*, describing the homeward journey of the Argive pentekontor, similarly does its best to conceal the well-known pattern. 'You will go with threshing oars, and then in the air the forestays' (by dint of hauling up the mast) 'will spread out in the bow above the ram the foot of the swift ship' (i.e. her sail). The language is deliberately elliptical, but in its highly poetic way it gives a good impression of swift movement, first under oar, then under sail, with a fair breeze filling the canvas[70].

There is a passage in Euripides' *Helen* where, in a calm, oar and sail seem to be employed simultaneously, but the text is certainly corrupt. It seems likely that in an ode addressed first to 'Swift Phoenician Oar, dear mother of Sidonian rowing' sailors are adjured in a calm to cease trying to sail and to take up their pinewood oars[71]. Pindar speaks of changing sail (i.e. the amount of sail) as the wind drops[72]. In a squall the helmsman avoids capsizing by paying out the sheet[73]. Jason fleeing his wife's bitter tongue in the *Medea* likens himself to a wise helmsman who flees from a storm with shortened sail[74]. In one passage of an unknown tragic poet the helmsman 'escapes from the black sea furling his mainsail'[75]. We shall see that Xenophon is the first historical writer to speak of two sails (see below, pp. 298–9). In these three passages it is to be noted that the helmsman is in charge of the sail. In extremely bad weather the sail and sailyard are lowered entirely, as in Aeschylus, who in a metaphor advises the lowering of sail 'when the creaking sailyard labours'[76]. The same metaphor occurs in Sophocles[77]. When the wind blows fair, the helmsman shakes out sail by paying out the sheet and the brailing ropes. Euripides has the metaphorical phrase 'let go every rope' meaning 'go as fast as possible'[78]. With a fair wind the sail bellies out and presses against the forestays[79]. Sailing by night is mentioned in a fragment of Sophocles[80].

The surge and beat of rowing is expressed often in the lyric and dramatic writers by the words *rothios*[81] and *pitulos*[82]. In Sophocles we find expressions of Athens' pride in her expert oarsmanship[83]. The excellence of Phoenician, and in particular Sidonian, oarsmanship is also mentioned by Euripides[84].

Finally, there is the procedure of coming to land. In Aeschylus the leading ship of the Egyptian squadron approaching Attica comes near to the land, then brails up sail and rows with all oars to the beach. The beach of fine pebbles is ideal for landing, as an anonymous *skolion* of the fifth or fourth century says: 'Cease going forward, loosen the sheet, and let go the wings of canvas, make with all speed for the finely pebbled beaches.' If there is no beach, a ship must anchor off shore. Pindar, as he comes to the end of an ode, exclaims metaphorically: 'Easy oar, swiftly let the anchor grapple the shore from the bow, a protection from the rocky reef[85].' The image is of a ship coming ashore as always[86] stern first, suddenly seeing a reef and letting go her anchor from the bow to keep her off it. Aeschylus tells how worrying it is for a good helmsman to anchor off an unsheltered shore at night[87]. We hear, in a metaphor, that two anchors were better than one[88].

DOCKS, ETC.

The lyric and tragic poets naturally tell us little about permanent naval establishments. The *Rhesus* mentions *holkoi*, slipways, and in the *Helen* Euripides speaks of the Egyptians' dockyard surrounded by a wall[89].

TEXTS

Epithets

1. Pindar, θοός, *Nem.* VII 28; *Pyth.* IV 25; V 87; *Ol.* VI 101; XII 3; fr. 208 Bowra
     κοῖλος, *Ol.* VI 10
     ὑπόπτερος, *Ol.* IX 24
     ὠκύπορος, *Pyth.* I 74
   Bacchylides (ed. Blass), αἰολόπρυμνος, I 114
                   εὔπρυμνος, XII 150
                   κυανῶπις, XII 160
                   κυανοπρῷρα, XVI I
                   εὐδαίδαλος, XVI 88, fr. 15, 3
                   λεπτόπρυμνος, XVI 119
   Aeschylus, ὠκύπτερος, *Suppl.* 734
          εὔπρυμνής, *Suppl.* 989; ἐκ πρυμνῆς Sidgwick
          κυανῶπις, *Suppl.* 743, *Pers.* 559
          ὁμόπτερος, *Suppl.* 559
   Sophocles, ὠκύαλος θοός, *Ajax* 710
          πολύκωπος, *Trach.* 656
          ποντόπορος, *Ph.* 721; *Ajax* 250

Euripides, θοός, fr. 304, 2

    ὠκύπομπος, *I.T.* 1136

    πολύκωπος, *I.T.* 981

    ποντόπορος, *Tr.* 811

    εὐήρετμος, *Ion* 1160

    ἰσήρετμος, *I.A.* 242

    εὔσελμος, *Rhesus* 97

    εὔπρυμνος, *I.T.* 1000 and 1337

    καλλίπρῳρος, *Medea* 1335

    εὔσημος, *I.T.* 1383

    εὐστροφώτατος, *I.A.* 293

    χαλκεμβολάς, *I.A.* 1319

    θούριος, *I.A.* 238

    πευκᾶεν σκάφος, *Andr.* 865

    κυανέμβολοι πρῷραι, *El.* 436

    κελαινόν σκάφος, *Tr.* 537

    ἀμφῆρες δόρυ, *Cyclops* 15.

Types

 2. Pindar, *Pyth.* IV 244–5 δράκοντος...ὃς πάχει μάκει τε πεντηκόντορον ναῦν κρατεῖ.

 3. Fr. 274 Bowra καὶ Πίνδαρος πεντηκονταερέτμους φησὶ τὰς ναῦς Ἀχαιῶν εἶναι.

 4. Euripides, *Helen* 1412–13

    ναῦν τοῖσδε πεντηκόντορον

    Σιδωνίαν δὸς κἀρετμῶν ἐπιστάτας.

    1531–3. See note 64 below.

 5. Euripides, *I.T.* 1123. See note 70 below.

    1347. See note 65 below.

    407–9

    ἢ ῥοθίοις εἰλατίνας

    δικρότοισι κώπας ἔπλευ-

    σαν ἐπὶ πόντια κύματα.

 6. Arrian, *Anabasis* 6 5 2 ὅσαι τε δίκροτοι αὐτῶν τὰς κάτω κώπας οὐκ ἐπὶ πολὺ ἔξω ἔχουσαι τοῦ ὕδατος.

 Cf. Aeschylus, *Suppl.* 723 παγκρότως ἐρέσσεται.

 7. Bacchylides XVI 87

    κατουρον pap.: ἑκατόντορον Blass.

Ship's Company

 8. Aeschylus, *Choephoroe* 722–4

    ὦ πότνια χθὼν καὶ πότνι' ἀκτὴ

    χώματος, ἢ νῦν ἐπὶ ναυάρχῳ

    σώματι κεῖσαι τῷ βασιλείῳ...

    Persians 363
    πᾶσιν προφωνεῖ τόνδε ναυάρχοις λόγον.

9. Pindar, *Pyth.* IV 194
    ἀρχὸς ἐν πρύμνᾳ. . .

  Aeschylus, *Suppl.* 176–7
      ξὺν φρονοῦντι δ’ ἥκετε
    πιστῷ γέροντι τῷδε ναυκλήρῳ πατρί.

    Seven 652
    σὺ δ’ αὐτὸς γνῶθι ναυκληρεῖν πόλιν.

10. Aeschylus, *Eumenides* 16
    Δελφός τε χώρας τῆσδε πρυμνήτης ἄναξ.
     765–6
    μήτοι τιν’ ἄνδρα δεῦρο πρυμνήτην χθονὸς
    ἐλθόντ’ ἐποίσειν εὖ κεκασμένον δόρυ.

    Septem 2–3
    ὅστις φυλάσσει πρᾶγος ἐν πρύμνῃ πόλεως
    οἴακα νωμῶν, βλέφαρα μὴ κοιμῶν ὕπνῳ.

11. Sophocles, *Achaion Sullogos* 142 col. ii 3 Pearson, 1–10
    σύ τε π[ηδ]αλίῳ παρεδρεύ[ων]
    φράσε[ις τῷ] κατὰ πρῶ⟨ι⟩ρα[ν]
    εὐθὺς Ἰ[λίο]υ πόρον
    Ἀτρει[δᾶν ἰ]δέσθαι.
    σὲ γὰρ Τε[γ]εᾶτις ἡμῖν,
    Ἑλλάς, οὐ[χ]ὶ Μυσία, τίκτει
    ναύταν σύν τινι δὴ θεῶν
    καὶ πεμπτῆρ’ ἁλίων ἐρετμῶν.

12. Sophocles, *Polyxena*, fr. 524 Pearson, 1–2
    οὐ γάρ τις ἂν δύναιτο πρῳράτης στρατοῦ
    τοῖς πᾶσιν εἶξαι καὶ προσαρκέσαι χάριν.

13. Sophocles, *Chryses*, fr. 726 Pearson
    ὦ πρῷρα λοιβῆς Ἑστία, κλύεις τάδε;
Inscriptions: e.g. *SIG* 604 8 (Delphi, 2nd century B.C.) βούπρωρος ἑκατόμβη.

14. E.g. Euripides, *Suppl.* 879–80
      ἐπεί τοι κοὐδὲν αἰτία πόλις
    κακῶς κλύουσα διὰ κυβερνήτην κακόν.

  Sophocles, *O.T.* 922–3 (referring to the king)
    ὡς νῦν ὀκνοῦμεν πάντες ἐκπεπληγμένον
    κεῖνον βλέποντες ὡς κυβερνήτην νεώς.

  Pindar, *Isthm.* IV 78–9 (referring to the trainer)
    κυβερνατῆρος οἰακοστρόφου
    γνώμᾳ πεπιθὼν πολυβούλῳ.

Aeschylus, *Persians* 767
    φρένες γὰρ αὐτοῦ θυμὸν ᾠακοστρόφουν.
Euripides, *Medea* 522–5 (Jason speaks to Medea)
    δεῖ μ', ὡς ἔοικε, μὴ κακὸν φῦναι λέγειν,
    ἀλλ' ὥστε ναὸς κεδνὸν οἰακοστρόφον
    ἄκροισι λαίφους κρασπέδοις ὑπεκδραμεῖν
    τὴν σὴν στόμαργον, ὦ γύναι, γλωσσαλγίαν.
    Helen 1591. See note 64 below.
Pindar, fr. 20 Bowra, 1–2
    δίδυμον | στρέφοισα πηδάλιον.

15. Sophocles, *Achaion Sullogos*, fr. 143 Pearson
    ὡς ναοφύλακες νυκτέρου ναυκληρίας
    πλήκτροις ἀπευθύνουσιν οὐρίαν τρόπιν.
  Nauplius, fr. 432 Pearson, 10
    νεῶν τε ποιμαντῆρσιν ἐνθαλασσίοις.
Aeschylus, *Suppl.* 766–7. See note 87.

16. Euripides, *I.A.* 138–9
    ἀλλ' ἴθ' ἐρέσσων σὸν πόδα, γήρᾳ
    μηδὲν ὑπείκων.
Sophocles, *Philoctetes* 1134–5 (Philoctetes to his bow)
    ἄλλου δ' ἐν μεταλλαγᾷ
    πολυμηχάνου ἀνδρὸς ἐρέσσῃ.
  Ajax 251–3
     τοίας ἐρέσσουσιν ἀπει-
    λὰς δικρατεῖς Ἀτρεῖδαι
    καθ' ἡμῶν.
  Antigone 158
     Κρέων . . .
    χωρεῖ τίνα δὴ μῆτιν ἐρέσσων;
Euripides, *Tr.* 570–1
    παρὰ δ' εἰρεσίᾳ μαστῶν ἕπεται
    φίλος Ἀστυάναξ, Ἕκτορος ἶνις.

17. Sophocles, *Ajax* 249
    θοὸν εἰρεσίας ζυγὸν ἑζόμενον.

18. Euripides, *Tr.* 688–91
    ναύταις γὰρ ἦν μὲν μέτριος ᾖ χειμὼν φέρειν
    προθυμίαν ἔχουσι σωθῆναι πόνων,
    ὁ μὲν παρ' οἴαχ', ὁ δ' ἐπὶ λαίφεσιν βεβώς,
    ὁ δ' ἄντλον εἴργων ναός.

19. Euripides, *Helen* 1595–6. See note 64 below.

20. Euripides, *Hypsipyle* 61–7 (Page, *Gk. Lit. Pap.* 1 1942, p. 86)

μέσῳ δὲ παρ' ἱστῷ
'Ασιάδ' ἔλεγον ἰήιον
Θρῆσσ' ἐβόα κίθαρις 'Ορφέως
μακροπόλων πιτύλων ἐρέτῃσι κε-
λεύσματα μελπομένα, τότε μὲν ταχύ-
πλουν τότε δ' εἰλατίνας ἀνάπαυμα πλάτας.

21. Demosthenes 18 129 ὁ τριηραύλης Φορμίων, ὁ Δίωνος τοῦ Φρεαρρίου δοῦλος...

Cf. Philodemus, *Mus.* p. 72 K, Pollux 1 96, 4 71.

22. Euripides, *Electra* 432–7

κλειναὶ νᾶες, αἵ ποτ' ἔβατε Τροίαν
τοῖς ἀμετρήτοις ἐρετμοῖς
πέμπουσαι χοροὺς μετὰ Νηρήδων
ἵν' ὁ φίλαυλος ἔπαλλε δελ-
φὶς πρῴραις κυανεμβόλοι-
σιν εἱλισσόμενος.

I.T. 1125. See note 70 below.

23. Euripides, *I.T.* 1377. See note 65 below.

Hull and Gear

24. Bacchylides XVI 82–4

ἀλλ' εὐ-
πάκτων ἀπ' ἰκρίων
σταθεὶς ὄρουσε.

25. Euripides, *Cyclops* 14–15

ἐν πρύμνῃ δ' ἄκρᾳ
αὐτὸς λαβὼν ηὔθυνον ἀμφῆρες δόρυ.

26. Euripides, *Ion* 1238–43

τίνα φυγὰν πτερόεσσαν ἢ
χθονὸς ὑπὸ σκοτίων μυχῶν πορευθῶ,
θανάτου λεύσιμον ἄταν
ἀποφεύγουσα τεθρίππων
ὠκιστᾶν χαλᾶν ἐπιβᾶσ'
ἢ πρύμνας ἐπὶ ναῶν;

27. Aeschylus, *Agamemnon* 1440–3

ἥ τ' αἰχμάλωτος ἥδε καὶ τερασκόπος
καὶ κοινόλεκτρος τοῦδε, θεσφατηλόγος
πιστὴ ξύνευνος, ναυτίλων δὲ σελμάτων
ἰσοτριβής. ἄτιμα δ' οὐκ ἐπραξάτην.

28. Sophocles, *Antigone* 715–17

    αὔτως δὲ ναὸς ὅστις ἐγκρατῆ πόδα
    τείνας ὑπείκει μηδὲν ὑπτίοις κάτω
    στρέψας τὸ λοιπὸν σέλμασιν ναυτίλλεται.

29. Euripides, *Cyclops* 144

    ἐν σέλμασιν νεώς ἐστιν, ἢ φέρεις σύ νιν;

30. Aeschylus, *Agamemnon* 182–3

    δαιμόνων δέ που χάρις βιαίως
    σέλμα σεμνὸν ἡμένων.

31. Sophocles, *Ajax* 1276–8

            ἀμφὶ μὲν νεῶν
    ἄκροισιν ἤδη ναυτικοῖς ἐδωλίοις
    πυρὸς φλέγοντος...

    Euripides, *Helen* 1571. See note 64 below.

32. Euripides, *Helen* 1565–6. See note 64 below.

33. Herodotus VII 180 τὴν μὲν δὴ Τροιζηνίην τῆς ἦρχε Πρηξῖνος, αὐτίκα αἱρέουσι ἐπισπόμενοι οἱ βάρβαροι· καὶ ἔπειτα τῶν ἐπιβατέων αὐτῆς τὸν καλλιστεύοντα ἀγαγόντες ἐπὶ τὴν πρώρην τῆς νεὸς ἔσφαξαν.

34. Sophocles, *Philoctetes* 481–2

         ἐμβαλοῦ μ' ὅποι θέλεις ἄγων
    ἐς ἀντλίαν, ἐς πρῷραν, ἐς πρύμνην...

35. Aeschylus, *Agamemnon* 1617–18

    σὺ ταῦτα φωνεῖς νερτέρᾳ προσήμενος
    κώπῃ, κρατούντων τῶν ἐπὶ ζυγῷ δορός;

36. Euripides, *Phoenician Women* 74–5

          ἐπεὶ δ' ἐπὶ ζυγοῖς
    καθέζετ' ἀρχῆς.

    Ion 595

    ἐς τὸ πρῶτον πόλεος ὁρμηθεὶς ζυγόν.

37. See e.g. note 17 above and Euripides, *Helen* 1532–3 in note 64 below.

38. Euripides, *I.A.* 235–76

       καὶ κέρας μὲν ἦν
    δεξιὸν πλάτας ἔχων
    Φθιώτας ὁ Μυρμιδὼν Ἄρης
    πεντήκοντα ναυσὶ θουρίαις.
    χρυσέαις δ' εἰκόσιν κατ' ἄκρα Νη-
240   ρῇδες ἔστασαν θεαί,
    πρύμναις σῆμ' Ἀχιλλείου στρατοῦ.
    Ἀργείων δὲ ταῖσδ' ἰσήρετμοι
    νᾶες ἔστασαν πέλας·
    ὧν ὁ Μηκιστέως στρατηλάτας

245   παῖς ἦν, Ταλαὸς ὃν τρέφει πατήρ,
         Καπανέως τε παῖς
         Σθένελος· Ἀτθίδας δ' ἄγων
         ἐξήκοντα ναῦς ὁ Θησέως
         παῖς ἑξῆς ἐναυλόχει, θεὰν
250   Παλλάδ' ἐν μωνύχοις ἔχων πτερω-
         τοῖσιν ἄρμασιν θετόν,
         εὔσημόν γε φάσμα ναυβάταις.

         Βοιωτῶν δ' ὅπλισμα πόντιον
         πεντήκοντα νῆας εἰδόμαν
255   σημείοισιν ἐστολισμένας·
         τοῖς δὲ Κάδμος ἦν
         χρύσεον δράκοντ' ἔχων
         ἀμφὶ ναῶν κόρυμβα·
         Λήιτος δ' ὁ γηγενὴς
260   ἄρχε ναΐου στρατοῦ·
         Φωκίδος δ' ἀπὸ χθονὸς
         Λοκρᾶς τε τοῖσδ' ἴσας ἄγων
         ναῦς ⟨ἦλθ'⟩ Οἰλέως τόκος κλυτὰν
         Θρονιάδ' ἐκλιπὼν πόλιν.

265   Μυκήνας δὲ τᾶς Κυκλωπίας
         παῖς Ἀτρέως ἔπεμπε ναυβάτας
         ναῶν ἑκατὸν ἠθροϊσμένους·
         σὺν δ' Ἄδραστος ἦν
         ταγός, ὡς φίλος φίλῳ,
270   τᾶς φυγούσας μέλαθρα
         βαρβάρων χάριν γάμων
         πρᾶξιν Ἑλλὰς ὡς λάβοι.
         ἐκ Πύλου δὲ Νέστορος
         Γερηνίου κατειδόμαν
275   πρύμνας σῆμα ταυρόπουν ὁρᾶν,
         τὸν πάροικον Ἀλφεόν.

39. Aeschylus, *Myrmidons*, fr. 134 Nauck²
         ἐπ' αἰετὸς δὲ ξανθὸς ἱππαλεκτρυὼν
         στάζει...θέντων φαρμάκων πολὺς πόνος.

40. Aeschylus, *Suppl.* 716
         καὶ πρῷρα πρόσθεν ὄμμασιν βλέπουσ' ὁδόν.

41. Sophocles, *Nauplius*, fr. 438 Pearson. Pollux 10 134 καὶ ὁλκία δὲ τὰ πηδάλια ἐν Ναυπλίῳ ὠνόμασε (sc. Sophocles) παρὰ τοῦ Ὁμήρου (ξ 350) ʽξεστὸν ἐφόλκαιον'.

42. Apollonius Rhodius 4 1609–10

ὣς ὅ γ' ἐπισχόμενος γλαφυρῆς ὁλκήιον Ἀργοῦς
ἦγ' ἅλαδε προτέρωσε.

43. Pindar, *Pyth.* IV 191–2

ἐπεὶ δ' ἐμβόλου
κρέμασαν ἀγκύρας ὕπερθεν...

44. Euripides, *I.T.* 1350–1. See note 65 below.
Helen 1613. See note 64 below.

45. See Sophocles, *Ajax* 249 (note 17 above), Euripides, *Helen* 1531–3 and 1598 (note 64 below).

46. Euripides, *Helen* 1598. See note 64 below.
I.T. 1347. See note 65 below.

47. Aeschylus, *Suppl.* 134–7

πλάτα μὲν οὖν λινορραφής τε
δόμος ἅλα στέγων δορὸς
ἀχείματόν μ' ἔπεμπε σὺν
πνοαῖς.

440–1   καὶ γεγόμφωται σκάφος
στρέβλαισι ναυτικαῖσιν ὡς προσηγμένον.

στρέβλαι seem more likely to be cords, i.e. tensions, than screws, as L-S-J.

846
γομφοδέτῳ τε δόρει διώλου.

Euripides, *Cyclops* 460–1

ναυπηγίαν δ' ὡσεί τις ἁρμόζων ἀνὴρ
διπλοῖν χαλινοῖν τρύπανον κωπηλατεῖ.

48. E.g. Pindar, *Pyth.* VIII 8–12

τὺ δ' ὁπόταν τις ἀμείλιχον
καρδίᾳ κότον ἐνελάσῃ
τραχεῖα δυσμενέων
ὑπαντιάξαισα κράτει τιθεῖς
ὕβριν ἐν ἄντλῳ.

See notes 18 and 34 above.

49. Pindar, *Pyth.* I 86–7

νώμα δικαίῳ πηδαλίῳ στρατόν.

Fr. 20 Bowra. See note 14 above.

Aeschylus, *Agamemnon* 663

θεός τις, οὐκ ἄνθρωπος, οἴακος θιγών.

802
οὐδ' εὖ πραπίδων οἴακα νέμων.

Aeschylus, *Suppl.* 716–18

καὶ πρῷρα. . .
οἴακος εὐθυντῆρος ὑστάτου νεὼς
ἄγαν καλῶς κλύουσα. . .

Seven 2–3

ὅστις φυλάσσει πρᾶγος ἐν πρύμνῃ πόλεως
οἴακα νωμῶν. . .

Sophocles, fr. 143. See note 15 above.

Euripides, *Alcestis* 440

πηδαλίῳ τε γέρων νεκροπομπὸς ἵζει (a small boat).

Andromache 480

κατὰ πηδαλίων.

Helen 1536. See note 64 below.
1578. See note 64 below.
but 1591. See note 64 below.

I.T. 1357. See note 65 below.

50. Euripides, *I.T.* 430–2

πλησιστίοισι πνοαῖς
συριζόντων κατὰ πρύμναν
εὐναίων πηδαλίων.

51. Oars: κώπη, Pindar and tragedians
πλάτη, tragedians
ἐρετμόν, Pindar and tragedians
Mast: ἱστός, Euripides.

52. Mast-head or truck: καρχήσιον. Pindar, *Nem.* v 51[b] ζυγὸν καρχασίου the
sailyard.
Euripides, *Hecuba* 1261 πεσοῦσαν ἐκ
καρχησίων.

Cf. Hippocrates, *Art.* 43.

53. Aeschylus, *Eumenides* 553–7

τὸν ἀντίτολμον δέ φαμι. . .
. .βιαίως σὺν χρόνῳ καθήσειν
λαῖφος, ὅταν λάβῃ πόνος
θραυομένας κεραίας.

54. Euripides, *Helen* 1601. See note 64 below.

Alcestis 254

ἔχων χέρ' ἐπὶ κοντῷ Χάρων.

I.T. 1350. See note 65 below.

55. Sophocles, fr. 415 Pearson

ἀποβάθρα.

Euripides, *I.T.* 1351. See note 65 below.
1382. See note 65 below.

Helen 1556. See note 64 below.

56. Sails: Pindar, *Nem.* iv 70 ἔντεα ναός.

        λαῖφος, λαίφεα, tragedians

        σινδών, Euripides, fr. 773 42 (lyr.)

        ἱστίον, ἱστία, Pindar, Bacchylides, Euripides.

57. Anchors: ἄγκυρα, Pindar, *Pyth.* x 51. See note 85 below.

        νεῶν ἰσχάς, Sophocles, fr. 761 Pearson

        ἐν ἀγκυρουχίαις, Aeschylus, *Suppl.* 766

    Two anchors: Pindar, *Ol.* vi 101. See note 88 below.

        Euripides, *Phaethon* 134 (fr. 774 1). See note 88 below.

    Metaphor: e.g. Sophocles, fr. 685 Pearson

        ἀλλ᾽ εἰσὶ μητρὶ παῖδες ἄγκυραι βίου.

        Aeschylus, *Choephoroe* 661–2

        ὥρα δ᾽ ἐμπόρους μεθιέναι

        ἄγκυραν ἐν δόμοισι πανδόκοις ξένων.

Cf. note 85 below.

58. Aeschylus, *Suppl.* 714–15

        εὔσημον γάρ· οὔ με λανθάνει

        στολμοί τε λαίφους καὶ παραρρύσεις νεώς.

59. Stern hawsers: Aeschylus, *Agamemnon* 984

        πρυμνησίων ξυνεμβολαῖς.

        Euripides, *Hypsipyle* 56–8 (Page, *Gk. Lit. Pap.* i, p. 86)

        ὀρούσ-

        ας ἐπ᾽ οἶδμα γαλανεί-

        ας πρυμνήσι᾽ ἀνάψαι.

        I.T. 1352. See note 65 below.

        1355–6. See note 65 below.

    Metaphor: Euripides, *Hercules* 478–9

        ὡς ἀνημμένοι κάλως

        πρυμνησίοισι βίον ἔχοιτ᾽ εὐδαίμονα.

Cf. *Tr.* 811   ναύδετ᾽ ἀνήψατο πρυμνᾶν.

  Medea 770   πρυμνήτην κάλων.

60. Mooring ropes: Aeschylus, *Suppl.* 765. See note 87 below.

        Agamemnon 192–5

        πνοαὶ δ᾽ ἀπὸ Στρυμόνος μολοῦσαι…

        ναῶν τε καὶ πεισμάτων ἀφειδεῖς…

        Euripides, *Hippolytus* 760–2

        Μουνίχου δ᾽ ἀκταῖσιν ἐκ-

        δήσαντο πλεκτὰς πεισμάτων

        ἀρχάς.

        Hecuba 1081–2

        ναῦς ὅπως ποντίοις πείσμασιν, λινόκροκον

        φᾶρος στέλλων.

Cf. Euripides, *I.T.* 1043

οὗ ναῦς χαλινοῖς λινοδέτοις ὁρμεῖ σέθεν.

Hecuba 539–40 χαλινωτήρια

νεῶν.

61. Shrouds: Aeschylus, *Agamemnon* 897

σωτῆρα ναός πρότονον.

Euripides, *I.T.* 1134. See note 70 below.

Phaethon 90 (fr. 773 42)

σινδών δὲ πρότονον ἐπὶ μέσον πελάσει.

Hecuba 111–12

τὰς ποντοπόρους δ᾽ ἔσχε σχεδίας

λαίφη προτόνοις ἐπερειδομένας.

62. Sheet: Sophocles, *Antigone* 715. See note 28 above.

Euripides, *Orestes* 706–7

καὶ ναῦς γὰρ ἐνταθεῖσα πρὸς βίαν ποδί

ἔβαψεν, ἔστη δ᾽ αὖθις, ἢν χαλᾷ πόδα.

Cf. *Skolion*, perhaps Attic, of fifth–fourth century B.C. in Page, *Gk. Lit. Pap.* I, p. 390

παῦε] παραπροιών, ὑφίει πόδα,

λῦ᾽ ἐανοῦ πτέρυγας, τάχος ἵεσο

λεπτολίθων [ἐπ᾽ ἀγῶ]ν.

Note: In Pindar, *Nem.* VI 57, and Euripides, *I.T.* 1134, ποῦς is used in a non-technical sense and, in spite of the nautical content, does not mean 'sheet'.

63. Swifter (*hupozoma*): Euripides, *Tr.* 537–8

κλωστοῦ δ᾽ ἀμφιβόλοις λίνοιο ναὸς ὡσεὶ

σκάφος κελαινόν.

Cf. Apollonius Rhodius I 367–70

νῆα δ᾽ ἐπικρατέως Ἄργου ὑποθημοσύνῃσιν

ἔζωσαν πάμπρωτον εὐστρεφεῖ ἔνδοθεν ὅπλῳ

τεινάμενοι ἑκάτερθεν, ἵν᾽ εὖ ἀραροίατο γόμφοις

δούρατα καὶ ῥοθίοιο βίην ἔχοι ἀντιόωσαν.

Handling

64. Euripides, *Helen* 1530–1614

ὡς δ᾽ ἤλθομεν σῶν περίβολον νεωρίων,

Σιδωνίαν ναῦν πρωτόπλουν καθείλκομεν

3υγῶν τε πεντήκοντα κἀρετμῶν μέτρα

ἔχουσαν. ἔργου δ᾽ ἔργον ἐξημείβετο·

ὃ μὲν γὰρ ἱστόν, ὃ δὲ†* πλάτην καθίσατο

1535 ταρσόν τε χειρί,† λευκά θ᾽ ἱστί᾽† εἰς ἓν ἦν,†
πηδάλιά τε ζεύγλαισι παρακαθίετο.

κἂν τῷδε μόχθῳ, τοῦτ᾽ ἄρα σκοπούμενοι,
Ἕλληνες ἄνδρες Μενέλεῳ ξυνέμποροι
προσῆλθον ἀκταῖς ναυφθόροις ἠσθημένοι

1540 πέπλοισιν, εὐειδεῖς μέν, αὐχμηροὶ δ᾽ ὁρᾶν.
ἰδὼν δέ νιν παρόντας Ἀτρέως γόνος
προσεῖπε δόλιον οἶκτον ἐς μέσον φέρων·
ὦ τλήμονες, πῶς ἐκ τίνος νεώς ποτε
Ἀχαιίδος θραύσαντες ἥκετε σκάφος;

1545 ἆρ᾽ Ἀτρέως παῖδ᾽ ὀλόμενον συνθάπτετε,
ὃν Τυνδαρὶς παῖς ἥδ᾽ ἀπόντα κενοταφεῖ;
οἳ δ᾽ ἐκβαλόντες δάκρυα ποιητῷ τρόπῳ,
ἐς ναῦν ἐχώρουν Μενέλεῳ ποντίσματα
φέροντες. ἡμῖν δ᾽ ἦν μὲν ἥδ᾽ ὑποψία

1550 λόγος τ᾽ ἐν ἀλλήλοισι, τῶν ἐπεσβατῶν
ὡς πλῆθος εἴη· διεσιωπῶμεν δ᾽ ὅμως
τοὺς σοὺς λόγους σῴζοντες· ἄρχειν γὰρ νεὼς
ξένον κελεύσας πάντα συνέχεας τάδε.

καὶ τἄλλα μὲν δὴ ῥᾳδίως ἔσω νεὼς

1555 ἐθέμεθα κουφίζοντα· ταύρειος δὲ ποὺς
οὐκ ἤθελ᾽ ὀρθὸς σανίδα προσβῆναι κάτα,
ἀλλ᾽ ἐξεβρυχᾶτ᾽ ὄμμ᾽ ἀναστρέφων κύκλῳ,
κυρτῶν τε νῶτα κἀς κέρας παρεμβλέπων
μὴ θιγγάνειν ἀπεῖργεν. ὁ δ᾽ Ἑλένης πόσις

1560 ἐκάλεσεν· ὦ πέρσαντες Ἰλίου πόλιν,
οὐκ εἶ᾽ ἀναρπάσαντες Ἑλλήνων νόμῳ
νεανίαις ὤμοισι ταύρειον δέμας
ἐς πρῷραν ἐμβαλεῖτε, φάσγανόν θ᾽ ἅμα
πρόχειρον ὤσει σφάγια τῷ τεθνηκότι;

1565 οἳ δ᾽ ἐς κέλευσμ᾽ ἐλθόντες ἐξανήρπασαν
ταῦρον φέροντές τ᾽ εἰσέθεντο σέλματα,
μονάμπυκον δὲ Μενέλεως ψήχων δέρην
μέτωπά τ᾽ ἐξέπεισεν ἐσβῆναι δόρυ.

τέλος δ᾽, ἐπειδὴ ναῦς τὰ πάντ᾽ ἐδέξατο,

1570 πλήσασα κλιμακτῆρας εὐσφύρου ποδὸς
Ἑλένη καθέζετ᾽ ἐν μέσοις ἐδωλίοις,
ὅ τ᾽ οὐκέτ᾽ ὢν λόγοισι Μενέλεως πέλας·

---

* The sense of the obelized passages in 1534 and 1535 is clear, but no satisfactory emendations have been proposed. The best I can suggest is: ὁ δὲ πλατῶν καθίσατο | ταρσόν κατήρη λευκά θ᾽ ἱστί᾽ ἐνετίθει.

215

ἄλλοι δὲ τοίχους δεξιοὺς λαιούς τ' ἴσοι
ἀνὴρ παρ' ἄνδρ' ἔζονθ', ὑφ' εἵμασι ξίφη
λαθραῖ' ἔχοντες, ῥόθιά τ' ἐξεπίμπλατο
βοῆς κελευστοῦ φθέγμαθ' ὡς ἠκούσαμεν.
  ἐπεὶ δὲ γαίας ἦμεν οὔτ' ἄγαν πρόσω
οὔτ' ἐγγύς, οὕτως ἦρετ' οἰάκων φύλαξ·
Ἔτ', ὦ ξέν', ἐς τὸ πρόσθεν—ἢ καλῶς ἔχει—
πλεύσωμεν; ἀρχαὶ γὰρ νεὼς μέλουσι σοί.
ὃ δ' εἶφ'· Ἅλις μοι. δεξιᾷ δ' ἑλὼν ξίφος
ἐς πρῷραν εἷρπε κἀπὶ ταυρείῳ σφαγῇ
σταθεὶς νεκρῶν μὲν οὐδενὸς μνήμην ἔχων,
τέμνων δὲ λαιμὸν ηὔχετ'· Ὦ ναίων ἅλα
πόντιε Πόσειδον Νηρέως θ' ἁγναὶ κόραι,
σώσατέ μ' ἐπ' ἀκτὰς Ναυπλίας δάμαρτά τε
ἄσυλον ἐκ γῆς. αἵματος δ' ἀπορροαὶ
ἐς οἶδμ' ἐσηκόντιζον οὔριοι ξένῳ.
καί τις τόδ' εἶπε· Δόλιος ἡ ναυκληρία.
πάλιν πλέωμεν· δεξιὰν κέλευε σύ,
σὺ δὲ στρέφ' οἴακ'. ἐκ δὲ ταυρείου φόνου
Ἀτρέως σταθεὶς παῖς ἀνεβόησε συμμάχους·
Τί μέλλετ', ὦ γῆς Ἑλλάδος λωτίσματα,
σφάζειν φονεύειν βαρβάρους νεώς τ' ἄπο
ῥίπτειν ἐς οἶδμα; ναυβάταις δὲ τοῖσι σοῖς
βοᾷ κελευστὴς τὴν ἐναντίαν ὄπα·
Οὐκ εἶ' ὃ μέν τις λοῖσθον ἀρεῖται δόρυ,
ὃ δὲ ζυγ' ἄξας, ὃ δ' ἀφελὼν σκαλμοῦ πλάτην
καθαιματώσει κρᾶτα πολεμίων ξένων;
  ὀρθοὶ δ' ἀνῇξαν πάντες, οἳ μὲν ἐν χεροῖν
κορμοὺς ἔχοντες ναυτικούς, οἳ δὲ ξίφη·
φόνῳ δὲ ναῦς ἐρρεῖτο. παρακέλευσμα δ' ἦν
πρύμνηθεν Ἑλένης· Ποῦ τὸ Τρωικὸν κλέος;
δείξατε πρὸς ἄνδρας βαρβάρους· σπουδῆς δ' ὕπο
ἔπιπτον, οἳ δ' ὠρθοῦντο, τοὺς δὲ κειμένους
νεκροὺς ἂν εἶδες. Μενέλεως δ' ἔχων ὅπλα,
ὅποι νοσοῖεν ξύμμαχοι κατασκοπῶν,
ταύτῃ προσῆγ' ἐχθροῖσι δεξιῶς ξίφος,
ὥστ' ἐκκολυμβᾶν ναός· ἠρήμωσε δὲ
σῶν ναυβατῶν ἐρετμά. ἐπ' οἰάκων δὲ βὰς
ἄνακτ' ἐς Ἑλλάδ' εἶπεν εὐθύνειν δόρυ.
οἳ δ' ἱστὸν ἦρον, οὔριαι δ' ἦκον πνοαί.
  βεβᾶσι δ' ἐκ γῆς. διαφυγὼν δ' ἐγὼ φόνον
καθῆκ' ἐμαυτὸν εἰς ἅλ' ἄγκυραν πάρα.

1575

1580

1585

1590

1595

1600

1605

1610

65. Euripides, *I.T.* 1327–35, 1342–57, 1377–1410

ἐπεὶ πρὸς ἀκτὰς ἤλθομεν θαλασσίας,
οὗ ναῦς Ὀρέστου κρύφιος ἦν ὡρμισμένη,
ἡμᾶς μέν, οὓς σὺ δεσμὰ συμπέμπεις ξένων

1330 ἔχοντας, ἐξένευσ' ἀποστῆναι πρόσω
Ἀγαμέμνονος παῖς, ὡς ἀπόρρητον φλόγα
θύουσα καὶ καθαρμὸν ὃν μετῴχετο,
αὐτὴ δ' ὄπισθε δέσμ' ἔχουσα τοῖν ξένοιν
ἔστειχε χερσί. καὶ τάδ' ἦν ὕποπτα μέν,

1335 ἤρεσκε μέντοι σοῖσι προσπόλοις, ἄναξ...

φόβῳ δ' ἃ μὴ χρῆν εἰσορᾶν καθήμεθα
σιγῇ· τέλος δὲ πᾶσιν ἦν αὐτὸς λόγος
στείχειν ἵν' ἦσαν, καίπερ οὐκ ἐωμένοις.

1345 κἀνταῦθ' ὁρῶμεν Ἑλλάδος νεὼς σκάφος
ταρσῷ κατήρει πίτυλον ἐπτερωμένον,
ναύτας τε πεντήκοντ' ἐπὶ σκαλμῶν πλάτας
ἔχοντας, ἐκ δεσμῶν δὲ τοὺς νεανίας
ἐλευθέρους πρύμνηθεν ἐστῶτας νεώς.

1350 κοντοῖς δὲ πρῷραν εἶχον, οἳ δ' ἐπωτίδων
ἄγκυραν ἐξανῆπτον· οἳ δέ, κλίμακας
σπεύδοντες, ἦγον διὰ χερῶν πρυμνήσια,
πόντῳ δὲ δόντες τοῖν ξένοιν καθίεσαν.
ἡμεῖς δ' ἀφειδήσαντες, ὡς ἐσείδομεν

1355 δόλια τεχνήματ', εἰχόμεσθα τῆς ξένης
πρυμνησίων τε, καὶ δι' εὐθυντηρίας*
οἴακας ἐξηροῦμεν εὐπρύμνου νεώς...

...ἀλλ' εἶργον ἡμᾶς τοξόται πρύμνης ἔπι
σταθέντες ἰοῖς, ὥστ' ἀναστεῖλαι πρόσω.
κἂν τῷδε—δεινὸς γὰρ κλύδων ὤκειλε ναῦν

1380 πρὸς γῆν, φόβος δ' ἦν ⟨παρθένῳ⟩ τέγξαι πόδα—
λαβὼν Ὀρέστης ὦμον εἰς ἀριστερόν,
βὰς ἐς θάλασσαν κἀπὶ κλίμακος θορών,
ἔθηκ' ἀδελφὴν ἐντὸς εὐσήμου νεώς,
τό τ' οὐρανοῦ πέσημα, τῆς Διὸς κόρης

1385 ἄγαλμα. ναὸς ⟨δ'⟩ ἐκ μέσης ἐφθέγξατο

---

* δι' εὐθυντηρίας is explained by Platnauer thus: 'The εὐθυντηρίαι were two holes in the stern bulwarks, one on either side, through which the steering oars (οἴακες) passed.' I am not aware that any of the ship representations we have show such holes. The steering oars seem rather to be secured to the outside of the hull and to have a handle or tiller, at right-angles to the steering blade, coming inboard over the gunwale (see above, p. 85 and Index *s.v.* tiller). διευθυντηρίους would be a word not otherwise met with, but quite a plausible one.

βοή τις· ˀΩ γῆς Ἑλλάδος ναῦται, νεὼς
λάβεσθε κώπαις ῥόθιά τ᾽ ἐκλευκαίνετε·
ἔχομεν γὰρ ὧνπερ οὕνεκ᾽ ἄξενον πόρον
Συμπληγάδων ἔσωθεν εἰσεπλεύσαμεν.

1390
οἳ δὲ στεναγμὸν ἡδὺν ἐκβρυχώμενοι
ἔπαισαν ἅλμην. ναῦς δ᾽, ἕως μὲν ἐντὸς ἦν
λιμένος, ἐχώρει,* διαπερῶσα δὲ στόμα
λάβρῳ κλύδωνι συμπεσοῦσ᾽ ἠπείγετο·
δεινὸς γὰρ ἐλθὼν ἄνεμος ἐξαίφνης νεὼς

1395
ὠθεῖ παλίμπρυμν᾽ ἱστί᾽· οἳ δ᾽ ἐκαρτέρουν
πρὸς κῦμα λακτίζοντες· ἐς δὲ γῆν πάλιν
κλύδων παλίρρους ἦγε ναῦν. σταθεῖσα δὲ
᾽Αγαμέμνονος παῖς ηὔξατ᾽· ˀΩ Λητοῦς κόρη
σῶσόν με τὴν σὴν ἱερέαν πρὸς Ἑλλάδα

1400
ἐκ βαρβάρου γῆς καὶ κλοπαῖς σύγγνωθ᾽ ἐμαῖς.
φιλεῖς δὲ καὶ σὺ σὸν κασίγνητον, θεά·
φιλεῖν δὲ κἀμὲ τοὺς ὁμαίμονας δόκει.
ναῦται δ᾽ ἐπευφήμησαν εὐχαῖσιν κόρης
παιᾶνα, γυμνὰς ἐκ ⟨πέπλων⟩ ἐπωμίδας

1405
κώπῃ προσαρμόσαντες ἐκ κελεύσματος.
μᾶλλον δὲ μᾶλλον πρὸς πέτρας ᾔει σκάφος·
χὠ μέν τις ἐς θάλασσαν ὡρμήθη ποσίν,
ἄλλος δὲ πλεκτὰς ἐξανῆπτεν ἀγκύλας.
κἀγὼ μὲν εὐθὺς πρὸς σὲ δεῦρ᾽ ἀπεστάλην,

1410
σοὶ τὰς ἐκεῖθεν σημανῶν, ἄναξ, τύχας.

66. Pindar, *Pyth.* IV 24–5
ἁνίκ᾽ ἄγκυραν ποτὶ χαλκόγενυν
ναῒ κρημνάντων ἐπέτοσσε, θοᾶς ᾽Αργοῦς χαλινόν.
191 (see note 68 below).

67. Sophocles, fr. 761 Pearson
ναῦται δ᾽ ἐμηρύσαντο νηὸς ἰσχάδα.
Cf. *Od.* 12 170 and Apollonius Rhodius 4 889.

68. Pindar, *Pyth.* IV 189–204
καὶ ῥά οἱ
μάντις ὀρνίχεσσι καὶ κλάροισι θεοπροπέων ἱεροῖς
Μόψος ἄμβασε στρατὸν πρόφρων. ἐπεὶ δ᾽ ἐμβόλου
κρέμασαν ἀγκύρας ὕπερθεν,

---

* The MSS. reading ἐχώρει στόμια διαπερῶσα δὲ has no obvious sense. I once suggested (*CR* LXIV I (1950), p. 4) that ἐχώρει στομία might mean 'accepted the bit', i.e. 'progressed steadily and under control', which is the sense required. But ἐχώρει by itself really gives the necessary sense of 'progressed' and Murray's suggestion διαπερῶσα δὲ στόμα removes the difficulty of the delayed δέ and the unusual use of στόμια = στόμα which Platnauer's punctuation after ἐχώρει introduces.

χρυσέαν χείρεσσι λαβὼν φιάλαν
ἀρχὸς ἐν πρύμνᾳ πατέρ' Οὐρανιδᾶν ἐγχεικέραυνον Ζῆνα καὶ
    ὠκυπόρους
κυμάτων ῥιπὰς ἀνέμων τ' ἐκάλει...
      κάρυξε δ' αὐτοῖς
ἐμβαλεῖν κώπαισι τεράσκοπος ἀδείας ἐνίπτων ἐλπίδας·
εἰρεσία δ' ὑπεχώρησεν ταχειᾶν ἐκ παλαμῶν ἄκορος,
σὺν Νότου δ' αὔραις ἐπ' Ἀξείνου στόμα πεμπόμενοι
ἤλυθον...

69. Apollonius Rhodius 1 395–400

κληῖδας μὲν πρῶτα πάλῳ διεμοιρήσαντο
ἄνδρ' ἐντυναμένω δοιὼ μίαν· ἐκ δ' ἄρα μέσσην
ἧρεον Ἡρακλῆι καὶ ἡρώων ἄτερ ἄλλων
Ἀγκαίῳ...
τοῖς μέσσην οἴοισιν ἀπὸ κληῖδα λίποντο
αὔτως, οὔτε πάλῳ.

70. Euripides, *I.T.* 1123–36

  καὶ σὲ μέν, πότνι', Ἀργεία
πεντηκόντορος οἶκον ἄξει·
  συρίζων θ' ὁ κηροδέτας
  κάλαμος οὐρείου Πανὸς
    κώπαις ἐπιθωΰξει,
  ὁ Φοῖβός θ' ὁ μάντις ἔχων
  κέλαδον ἑπτατόνου λύρας
  ἀείδων ἄξει λιπαρὰν
  εὖ σ' Ἀθηναίων ἐπὶ γᾶν.
    ἐμὲ δ' αὐτοῦ λιποῦσα
    βήσῃ ῥοθίοισι πλάταις·
ἀέρι δὲ [ἱστία] πρότονοι κατὰ πρῷραν ὑ-
πὲρ στόλον ἐκπετάσουσι πόδα*
    ναὸς ὠκυπόμπου.

71. Euripides, *Helen* 1451–64

  Φοίνισσα Σιδωνιὰς ὦ
ταχεῖα κώπα ῥοθίοισι, μᾶτηρ
  εἰρεσίας φίλα,
  χοραγὲ τῶν καλλιχόρων
    δελφίνων, ὅταν αὔραις
    πέλαγος ἀνήνεμον ᾖ,
  γλαυκὰ δὲ Πόντου θυγάτηρ
    Γαλάνεια τάδ' εἴπῃ·

---

* In the last sentence the non-technical use of πόδα for sail has caused the gloss ἱστία to be inserted in the text after ἀέρι δ'. Bothe and Murray regard the word as intrusive.

Κατὰ μὲν ἰστία* πετάσατ' αὔραις λιπόντες εἰναλίαις,*
λάβετε δ' εἰλατίνας πλάτας,
ὦ ναῦται ναῦται
πέμποντες εὐλιμένους
Περσείων οἴκων Ἑλέναν ἐπ' ἀκτάς.

72. Pindar, *Pyth.* iv 291–3

ἐν δὲ χρόνῳ
μεταβολαὶ λήξαντος οὔρου
ἰστίων.

73. Sophocles, *Antigone* 715. See note 28 above.
   Euripides, *Orestes* 706. See note 62 above.
   Trag. Adespot. 341

μικρὸν δὲ δεῖ ποδὸς
χαλάσαι μεγάλη κύματος ἀλκῇ.

74. Euripides, *Medea* 523. See note 14 above.
75. Trag. Adespot. 377 Nauck[2]

φεύγει μέγα λαῖφος ὑποστολίσας
ἐρεβώδεος ἐκ θαλάσσης.

76. Aeschylus, *Eumenides* 556. See note 53 above.
77. Sophocles, *Electra* 335

νῦν δ' ἐν κακοῖς μοι πλεῖν ὑφειμένη δοκεῖ.

78. Pindar, *Pyth.* i 91–2

ἐξίει δ' ὥσπερ κυβερνάτας ἀνὴρ
ἰστίον ἀνεμόεν.

   Euripides, *Medea* 278

πάντα δὴ κάλων ἐξιᾶσι.

Cf. *Hercules* 837

φόνιον ἐξίει κάλων.

79. See note 61 above.
80. Sophocles, *Achaion Sullogos*, fr. 143 Pearson. See note 15 above.
81. ῥόθιος adj., see e.g. Euripides, *I.T.* 407, note 5 above; *id. ib.* 1133, note 70
above; *Helen* 1452, note 71 above; also *Cyclops* 16–17

παῖδες δ' ἐρετμοῖς ἥμενοι γλαυκὴν ἅλα
ῥοθίοισι λευκαίνοντες ἐζήτουν σ', ἄναξ.

Helen 1117

ὅτ' ἔδραμε ῥόθια πεδία βαρβάρῳ πλάτᾳ.

ῥόθια subst., Euripides, *I.T.* 1387. See note 65 above.

* The words κατὰ μὲν ἰστία suggest that taking down the sails is to be complementary to taking
to the oar, and this is exactly what the context requires. The words which follow must then be
corrupt. If they are to be emended, I suggest the following: κατὰ μὲν ἰστία παύετ' αὐ-|ρῶν λειφθέντες
εἰναλίων.

Helen 1269
ὥστ' ἐξορᾶσθαι ῥόθια χερσόθεν μόλις.

1501–2
γλαυκὸν ἔπιτ' οἶδμα κυανόχροά τε κυμάτων
ῥόθια πολιὰ θαλάσσας.

82. πίτυλος: see Euripides, *Hypsipyle* 64, note 20 above.

I.T. 1050
καὶ μὴν νεώς γε πίτυλος εὐήρης πάρα.

Tr. 1123–5
Ἑκάβη, νεὼς μὲν πίτυλος εἷς λελειμμένος
λάφυρα τἀπίλοιπ' Ἀχιλλείου τόκου
μέλλει πρὸς ἀκτὰς ναυστολεῖν Φθιώτιδας.

83. Sophocles, *Oedipus at Colonus* 707–19
ἄλλον δ' αἶνον ἔχω ματροπόλει τᾷδε κράτιστον,
δῶρον τοῦ μεγάλου δαίμονος, εἰπεῖν, χθονὸς αὔχημα μέγιστον,
εὔιππον, εὔπωλον, εὐθάλασσον.
ὦ παῖ Κρόνου, σὺ γάρ νιν εἰς
τόδ' εἷσας αὔχημ', ἄναξ Ποσειδάν,
ἵπποισιν τὸν ἀκεστῆρα χαλινὸν
πρώταισι ταῖσδε κτίσας ἀγυιαῖς.
ἁ δ' εὐήρετμος ἔκπαγλ' ἁλία χερσὶ παραπτομένα πλάτα
θρῴσκει, τῶν ἑκατομπόδων
Νηρήδων ἀκόλουθος.

84. Euripides, *Helen* 1272
Φοίνισσα κώπη ταχύπορος γενήσεται.

1451. See note 71 above.

85. Aeschylus, *Suppl.* 722–3
αὐτὴ δ' ἡγεμὼν ὑπὸ χθόνα
στείλασα λαῖφος παγκρότως ἐρέσσεται.

For *skolion* see note 62 above.

Pindar, *Pyth.* x 51–2
κώπαν σχάσον, ταχὺ δ' ἄγκυραν ἔρεισον χθονὶ
πρῴραθε χοιράδος ἄλκαρ πέτρας.

86. E.g. Euripides, *I.A.* 1319–22
μὴ...πρύμνας Αὐλὶς δέξασθαι τούσδ'
ἐς ὅρμους ὤφελεν.

Electra 1022
πρυμνοῦχον Αὖλιν.

87. Aeschylus, *Suppl.* 764–70
οὔτοι ταχεῖα ναυτικοῦ στρατοῦ στολή
οὐδ' ὅρμος, οὐδὲ πεισμάτων σωτηρία
ἐς γῆν ἐνεγκεῖν, οὐδ' ἐν ἀγκυρουχίαις

221

θαρσοῦσι ναῶν ποιμένες παραυτίκα,
ἄλλως τε καὶ μολόντες ἀλίμενον χθόνα
ἐς νύκτ' ἀποστείχοντος ἡλίου. φιλεῖ
ὠδῖνα τίκτειν νὺξ κυβερνήτῃ σοφῷ.

Cf. *Agamemnon* 664–5

τύχη δὲ σωτὴρ ναῦν θέλουσ' ἐφέζετο
ὡς μήτ' ἐν ὅρμῳ κύματος ζάλην ἔχειν.

88. Euripides, *Phaethon* 134, fr. 774 1

ναῦν τοι μί' ἄγκυρ' οὐδαμῶς σῴζειν φιλεῖ.

Pindar, *Ol.* VI 100–1

ἀγαθαὶ δὲ πέλοντ' ἐν χειμερίᾳ
νυκτὶ θοᾶς ἐκ ναὸς ἀπεσκίμφθαι δύ' ἄγκυραι.

Docks, etc.

89. Euripides, *Rhesus* 136, 244, 448, 591, 602

ναύσταθμα.

145–6

ὁλκοὶ νεῶν.

Helen 1530. See note 64 above.

10

SEA POWER IN THE AEGEAN:
480–322 B.C.

The composition of the Greek fleet at Salamis indicates the relative naval strength of the cities of central Greece. Athens, with two hundred ships, one hundred and eighty of them manned by Athenians, is stronger than all the rest put together. Corinth with forty ships gives some hint of her earlier predominance. Aegina and Megara with thirty and twenty ships respectively are the next strongest. The Spartan contingent numbers sixteen[1].

On the Persian side the main contingents were Phoenician, Egyptian, and Asian Greek[2]. In the year after Salamis when the Greek fleet under the Spartan Leotychidas met and defeated the remains of the Persian fleet at Mycale in Asia Minor, the Ionian Greeks had already defected to their fellow countrymen of the Greek mainland. In the confederacy of Delos, led by Athens, the lesser Ionian cities paid tribute instead of ships to the Greek cause, but the larger islands, Samos, Chios and Lesbos, maintained large fleets of their own[3]. Samos nearly wrested the control of the sea from Athens in 440[4], Lesbos had a large navy at the beginning of the Peloponnesian war, and Chios in 413 could man a fleet of sixty ships[5]. We hear nothing of Egyptian fleets after Salamis, until in the eighties of the next century Egypt revolts from Persia and sends a contingent of fifty ships to support Evagoras of Cyprus[6]. A Phoenician fleet remained in being after Mycale. It was defeated by Cimon leading a confederate Greek fleet at the Eurymedon river probably in 466, and again off Cyprus in 451[7]. No Phoenician war fleets entered Greek waters again for forty years, until in 411 the Persian satrap Tissaphernes brought a Phoenician fleet as far north as Aspendus, but it saw no action[8]. After the fall of Athens the Persian policy was to play off Sparta and Athens against each other. Phoenician fleets were put first at Conon's disposal against Sparta, and then at Sparta's disposal against Athens.

In western Greece Gelon had developed the harbour of Syracuse as a strong naval base, and had promised two hundred *triereis* against the

Persian invaders[9]. The fact that, though the *triereis* were not sent, he did not challenge at sea the Carthaginian invading force in 480, but defeated it on land when it was besieging Himera[10], suggests that this navy was not as strong as his promise might suggest. Later, Syracusan naval power increased under the stimulus of the Athenian attack of 415. Thereafter, she sent a contingent to strengthen the Peloponnesian fleet operating against Athens in the Aegean[11], and Dionysius who ruled Syracuse from 405 to 367 was a firm ally of Sparta until her defeat at the battle of Leuctra in 371. Athens had made approaches to Dionysius as early as 393, but without success until her alliance with Sparta brought with it also friendship and ultimately alliance with him[12]. Although the west Greek part in naval activity was not distinguished, it must be remembered that Sparta at the outset of the Peloponnesian war hoped to raise a naval force of five hundred *triereis* mostly to be built in Italy and Sicily, and that Thucydides observes that Sicily 'contains many *triereis* and many crews'[13].

Corcyra, on the trade route from mainland Greece to the west at the point where it stood out across the Adriatic, and like Syracuse a colony of Corinth, was the other western city to promise aid against Persia. She sent sixty ships which got no further than Cape Malea, a fleet larger than any except that of Athens[14]. At the beginning of the Peloponnesian war Thucydides could make the Corcyraean envoys at Athens say: 'The Greeks have only three fleets worthy of mention, yours, ours and the fleet of the Corinthians'[15].

Against this picture of present and future naval power the development of the Athenian navy after Salamis may be set. Thucydides describes vividly the attitude of her allies to Athens at this moment: 'fearing the size of her navy which was not previously in existence, and the aggressive spirit she had shown in the face of the Persian attack'[16]. Elsewhere he remarks how she had begun to practise the art of seamanship immediately after the Persian wars[17]. He is in no doubt that Themistocles was the mainspring both of her aggressive spirit and of her naval ambitions. Speaking of the rebuilding of the Athenian walls after the retreat of the Persians he says: 'Themistocles persuaded them also to finish the building of Piraeus (a beginning had been made of it previously during the tenure of the office which he had held annually at Athens). He considered that the place with its three natural harbours was ideal, and that if the Athenians became seamen they would take great strides towards the acquisition of power. It was Themistocles indeed who had the courage to say that they must cleave to the sea...And on his proposal they built the wall to the thickness which is now visible round Piraeus...But the wall was completed only to half the height he had intended. His idea was that enemy attacks would be held off by its size and thickness and that a guard of a few of the least able-bodied men would be sufficient, while the rest manned the ships. Themistocles laid most store by the ships in my opinion because he had observed that the Persian expeditionary force had found it easier to move to the attack by sea than by land. He believed that Piraeus was more useful than the upper city and often advised the Athenians if they were hard pressed by land to go down to Piraeus and resist all their opponents with their ships[18].' Diodorus, who is probably using the fourth-century historian Ephorus, says that Themistocles persuaded the Athenians each year to construct and add twenty *triereis* to the fleet they already possessed[19]. In 431 and in the fourth century we find that the Council has the responsibility for building a certain number of ships each year—probably ten[20]. The provision almost certainly goes back to Themistocles.

It appears that Aristides, who with Themistocles was a leader of the popular party, shared the latter's naval policy. He is said to have 'urged the people to lay hold of the leadership of the confederacy of Delos, and to quit the country districts and live in the city'[21]. It was however Cimon, not Themistocles or Aristides, who led the confederate fleet in driving the Persians from the Aegean and its coasts, who reduced a recalcitrant member of the confederation, and defeated a Phoenician fleet at the Eurymedon.

Thucydides' discussion of Themistocles' naval policy suggests that the latter envisaged a situation in which Athens would be at war with neighbouring Greek land powers. He could hardly have expected another Persian invasion. Cimon, his rival, pursued a policy of active war with Persia and peace with Sparta; but this policy was reversed and Cimon ostracized on Athens' rebuff by Sparta in 462 B.C. Pericles emerges at this juncture as the heir to Themistocles' policies, and he was so regarded by his later countrymen. In Plato Gorgias says: 'You know I suppose that these dockyards and walls of Athens and the equipment of the harbours came into existence on Themistocles' proposal, and some on Pericles' proposal.' Socrates replies: 'That is the story, Gorgias, about Themistocles and I myself heard Pericles when he was advising us about the middle wall[22].' Aristotle too says that

Pericles 'turned the policy of the state in the direction of sea power'[23]. Between 461 and 456 Athens began the construction of the Long Walls which connected Athens with her old port of Phalerum and her new one of Piraeus. The policy of Themistocles and Aristides was thus implemented, Attica was treated as expendable, and the power of Athens concentrated in a fortified triangle subtended by the sea. Before the walls were completed Thucydides tells that there was a party in Athens who were prepared to introduce a Spartan army into Attica if they would thereby put an end to the democracy and the building of the Long Walls[24]. Democracy and naval policy were inextricably connected. We can read in Plato's *Laws* the scornful aristocratic attitude to seafaring[25]. Conversely the character Demus in Aristophanes' *Knights*, who represents the Athenian people, speaks of *his* seamen[26]. The middle wall which Socrates mentioned was probably built in 444/3 and ran parallel to the Athens–Piraeus wall on its inner side. It may well have been the result of the Spartan invasion of 445, and also of the abandonment of the old harbour of Phalerum.

Between the emergence of Pericles and the outbreak of the Peloponnesian war, which was the logical outcome of his policies, there is thirty years of mixed fortunes for Athens as a naval power. From 460 to 454 she poured ships and men into Egypt, but was forced in the end to withdraw with a loss in ships which has been reckoned as at least 250[27]. The enterprise was no less rash, and a good deal more costly, than the better documented Sicilian expedition. On the other hand her near neighbour and naval rival, Aegina, was forced to submission in 458, and in 431 ceased to be an independent state[28]. In 454 the supposed presence of a Phoenician fleet on the Aegean coast was the pretext for moving the treasury of the Delian confederation to Athens.

Athens' ill-judged attempts to gain a land-empire in the years which followed Cimon's expedition to Cyprus and death there were concluded by the thirty years' peace of 445. The navy had not been neglected in this period, since in 440 Pericles was able to take a fleet of two hundred *triereis* to quell the revolt of Samos which ceased thereafter to hold her privileged place in the confederation[29]. In 434 an inscription records the decision to use the surplus of the revenues in that year 'for the dockyard and the walls'[30].

The theory of sea power seems to have been worked out with characteristic realism in Athens during the years immediately preceding the war. The author of the *Constitution of Athens*, attributed to Xenophon, who seems to be writing in 432 just before the outbreak of the war, sets it out clearly. His points are these. A sea power does not need a first-class hoplite force, only one sufficient to keep its allies in order. A land power may be resisted by a united force of small cities, but islanders cannot unite to resist a sea power. Of the mainland cities ruled by Athens, the large ones are held by fear, the small ones by need. No commerce can take place without the permission of the sea power. A sea power can invade the territory of a stronger power, can make a landing where there are none or few to resist them, and sail away when a force approaches. Distance means nothing to a sea power. A land power can only pass through friendly territory, or fight their way. If crops fail, a sea power can easily import food from abroad. They can import luxuries, and ideas, from the whole world, and alone can have a high standard of living. By occupying an island or a headland they can inflict damage on their enemies. The one weakness of a sea power is if it is not an island. Since the Athenians have not been granted the initial advantage of living on an island, they manage as follows: they place their property on the islands trusting in their command of the sea, but they put up with the ravaging of Attic soil by the enemy, realizing that if they are moved by sentiment for it they will lose other greater benefits[31].

In 431 Pericles' discussion of the relative power of Athens and Sparta, in a speech before the Athenian assembly, makes many of the same points. He begins by claiming that the Spartans have no accumulated surplus of revenue such as is necessary for carrying on a protracted war. They can build a fort on Athenian territory only with great difficulty, but the Athenians can easily use their sea power, which is greatly superior to the Spartan, to establish forts on their coast and to carry out reprisals by naval raids. 'Sea power is indeed a great thing. Just consider: if we were islanders, who would be more unassailable? As things are we must regard ourselves as such as near as may be, and abandon our land and our farmsteads, but stand guard over the sea and over the city[32].' A year later, when Athens had suffered two invasions of her cultivated land, Thucydides makes Pericles state the theory even more bluntly: 'You think that it is only over your allies that your empire extends, but I declare that of the two divisions of the world that man can use, the land and the sea, you are absolute masters of the whole of the latter, both to the extent to which you now employ it and to any further extent you may wish; and there is no one, either the King of Persia or any other nation on earth, who can prevent you from sailing with the naval armament you now possess. This power is not to be compared with the use of your fields and farmsteads, those great losses which you think you have suffered[33].'

The particular instructions given by Pericles to the Athenians at the beginning of the war exactly reflect the theory thus evolved. They were to bring in their property from the fields and come into the city, acting on the defensive by land, while equipping their fleet for offensive operations and using it to ensure the regular payment of tribute by the allies[34]. Pericles lays great stress on the financial aspect of their preparedness, the 6000 talents on the Acropolis, and on the three hundred *triereis* ready for sea. As in Themistocles' plan the able-bodied men were to man the fleet while the walls were guarded by men above and below military age. After the Spartan invading army had withdrawn from its first incursion into Attica, the popular assembly decided 'to set apart a thousand talents of the money stored on the Acropolis as a special reserve fund, and not to spend it, but to use the rest to carry on the war... And along with this sum of money they set apart for special service each year one hundred of the very best *triereis*, appointing trierarchs to command them, and no one of these ships was to be used in any other way than in connection with this particular fund in dealing with the same danger should the emergency arise[35].' The *Constitution of Athens* of 432 speaks of the people appointing four hundred trierarchs each year: i.e. three hundred for the active fleet and one hundred for the reserve[36]. It is not until the crisis of 412 that the reserve was employed[37]. In the fourth century we hear of gear for a hundred ships being stored on the Acropolis, presumably a similar reserve when gear was in short supply.

A papyrus fragment which seems likely to be part of a commentary on Demosthenes' speech *Against Androtion* gives a more detailed account of the decree instituting the reserve fund. The commentator has access to the text of the *psephisma* to which Thucydides refers. He dates the decree by the archon of 431, names Pericles as proposer, and adds a further clause about the annual naval building programme of ten ships which Thucydides omits. It is further clear from this author that the Council at this time had responsibility for the navy[38]. Both these latter points are confirmed by the Aristotelian *Constitution of Athens* (see above, p. 225, note 20).

If Wilcken's supplements are to be accepted, the passage also tells us that the Council is required to hand over each year a hundred of the old *triereis* as a reserve.

One further point must be made about the responsibility of Athenian sea power in a war planned according to the theories of Themistocles and Pericles, although it is not mentioned by Thucydides. The *Constitution of Athens* of 432 makes a sort of indirect reference to it[39]. Athens, cut off from her farmlands, had to be fed. Even with the resources of Attica her urban population could not have been fed without imports of grain. The grain route was from the Hellespont and the north-east Aegean to Piraeus, and its safeguarding was a constant preoccupation. This factor is a key to the naval operations in the late fifth and fourth centuries when the Sicilian disaster had struck at the root of Athenian naval supremacy.

The naval power of Athens at the beginning of the war with Sparta was then considerable. Her fleet of three hundred *triereis* must be set against the hundred and twenty which Corcyra could man at the outset although she claimed that she, Athens, and Corinth, were the foremost naval powers of Greece. The Corinthians sent a fleet of seventy-five ships against Corcyra in 434 which was defeated by a Corcyraean fleet of eighty ships, and in the following year mustered a fleet of a hundred and fifty ships including ninety of their own. The ten Athenian ships present when this Corinthian fleet met a hundred and ten Corcyraean ships succeeded in preventing a Corcyraean defeat. Thucydides says that the Peloponnesian league aimed at building a fleet of 500 *triereis* mostly in Italy and Sicily, but nothing like this aim was ever achieved. Corinth hardly makes her mark at all as a sea power during the war. The Athenian squadron at Naupactus at the entry to the Corinthian Gulf was certainly a contributory factor to her impotence. But her inventive genius made a decisive intervention. She developed the modification to the bow of the *trieres* which led to the Athenian naval defeats in the bay of Syracuse.

Thucydides makes an interesting comment on the Athenian naval operations in the year 428. He had been speaking of the fleet of a hundred ships with which the Athenians raided the Peloponnese while they were at the same time dealing with the revolt of Lesbos. The passage seems to have suffered the intrusion of glosses, but there is no reason for rejecting it entirely. He says that, at the time when these ships were at sea, about the largest number of ships were on active service that the Athenians ever had. 'For one hundred ships were guarding Attica, Euboea and Salamis, and another hundred were cruising off the Peloponnese, besides those at Potidaea and other places, so that the total number in service at the same time in a single summer was all told two hundred and fifty. It was this effort, together with Potidaea, which chiefly exhausted their resources of money.' He adds that the hoplite was paid two drachmas a day, one for himself and one for his auxiliary, and that the sailors were paid at the same rate, i.e. at one drachma a day[40]. We must remember that in addition to the two hundred and fifty ships at sea in 428 there were also a hundred in reserve. The largest single expedition which the Athenians mounted was the expedition to Sicily, one hundred and thirty-four *triereis* and two pentekontors. The reinforcing fleet was seventy-three *triereis*. Against them the Syracusans mustered seventy-six *triereis* in the first battle.

The destruction of the Athenian fleet at Syracuse threatened the whole basis of Athenian power. Her losses in ships were serious, still more damaging was the loss of skilled officers. She immediately set about collecting tribute and timber for ship-building from whatever source she could[41]. Meanwhile the Spartans began seriously to build a navy; and, taking a leaf out of Athens' book, made demands on their allies for this purpose. Thucydides reports that the Spartans 'made requisitions upon the states for the building of one hundred ships, fixing the levy for themselves and the Boeotians at twenty-five each, for the Corinthians at fifteen, for the Arcadians, Pellenians and Sicyonians at ten and for the Megarians, Troezenians, Epidaurians and Hermionians at ten'[42]. The comparatively humble position of the Corinthians in this list is interesting.

The effect of the naval effort by the Spartan league was an immediate threat to the Athenian corn-route from the Hellespont. The Spartan fleet at Miletus was soon on equal terms with the Athenian fleet at Samos[43]. The former was paid by the Persian satraps Tissaphernes and Pharnabazus, content to play one fleet off against the other until a Phoenician fleet could be brought up from the south[44]. The revolt of Chios in 412 was considered sufficiently serious to justify the Athenians drawing on their war reserve[45]. Under Astyochus in 411 the Spartans mustered a hundred and twelve ships off Samos, where the Athenians had a fleet of eighty-two ships which were reinforced by a further twenty-six from the Hellespont under Strombichides. But the Spartans would not risk an engagement which might have been decisive[46]; and although Tissaphernes brought a Phoenician fleet of a hundred and forty-seven ships as far as Aspendus he did not commit them to battle[47]. Then the tide turned in Athens' favour when at Cynossema in the Hellespont seventy-six Athenian ships defeated a Spartan fleet of eighty-six. Later in the year at Abydos, and early in 410 at Cyzicus, Athenian ships won decisive victories which re-established their supremacy on the sea, and safe-guarded the corn-route[48]. In the Peloponnesian fleet which she defeated was a squadron from Syracuse.

In 407 Sparta reinforced her fleet in Asia Minor under a new commander, Lysander, who obtained strong financial support from the Persian prince, Cyrus, now placed in control of the whole of the Aegean provinces of the Persian empire. Lysander advised Cyrus to make four obols (two-thirds of a drachma) the pay for the seamen in his fleet. Cyrus accepted his advice, agreeing to be paymaster of the Spartan fleet and to give a month's pay in advance[49]. These economic measures appear to have weakened the Athenian fleet, and strengthened the Spartan, which now had another new commander, Callicratidas. The Athenian fleet, defeated at Notium and now at Samos under Conon, was blockaded in the harbour of Mytilene, but a vessel succeeded in breaking through to Athens. In thirty days the Athenians manned a hundred and ten ships with crews of all classes, slaves and foreigners; and in the following year defeated Callicratidas at Arginusae. The Athenian ships were slow in the water, and adopted a formation of two lines to frustrate a *diekplous* by the faster Spartan ships[50].

In September of the next year (405) Lysander, who had returned to Asia Minor at Cyrus' request and had mustered a large naval force, sailed to the Hellespont, challenging Athens at her vital spot and thereby attracting thither the whole Athenian fleet of 180 ships. At Aegospotami the Athenians' over-confidence allowed Lysander to catch them off their guard with most of their ships on the beach or half-manned. Only Conon's squadron escaped[51]. After this disaster, given the facts of a strategy to which Athens' safety was wholly committed, her capitulation was only a matter of time. In April 404 Lysander sailed into Piraeus, and the walls (i.e. presumably the Long Walls and the fortifications of the naval base) were demolished. By the terms of her surrender she gave up all her *triereis* except twelve[52].

The government of the Thirty set up in Athens under Spartan influence after her defeat did its best to destroy the remaining instruments of sea power, connected now as always with democratic imperialism. The fortifications and Long Walls had been destroyed by Lysander. They dismantled the dock-yards, and sold the ship-sheds for demolition[53]. It does not appear that the demolition was in fact carried out, since later Demosthenes could speak of the ship-sheds, with the Parthenon, as one of the glories of Athens[54]. But they were certainly not kept in repair, and Lysias in 399 could describe the ship-sheds and walls as being in a ruinous condition[55]. Aegina, with its old inhabitants restored, now became a Spartan naval station, posing a constant threat to the Athenian installations at Piraeus. Spartan disagreements led to the restoration of the democracy at Athens in 403, but Sparta with a large fleet remained in control of the Aegean until Athenian sea power was re-established by Conon.

After Aegospotami Conon sailed with his squadron to Cyprus, where he had a friend in Evagoras. From there Pharnabazus, who had obtained permission and money from the Persian king to raise a fleet of 100 *triereis*, recruited him as commander[56]. The Athenian popular party seems to have sent arms and petty officers to this fleet[57]. Its first exploit was a raid on Cilicia with 40 ships, but Conon was caught and blockaded in Caunus by a Spartan fleet of 100 ships under Pharax and had to be extricated by reinforcements from Cyprus. Pharax withdrew to Rhodes but was expelled from there by a revolt of the citizens who received Conon and the eighty ships he had now been able to muster[58]. In August 394 at the head of a fleet of over 90 *triereis* he met the Spartan Aegean squadron of 85 ships under Peisander at Cnidus, and inflicted a decisive defeat[59].

Having broken the Spartan naval domination of the south-western Aegean Conon was now free with Pharnabazus to establish a base on Melos, raid the Spartan coast, and set up an Athenian governor on the island of Cythera. Finally, he sailed into Piraeus, and with Persian money, and the labour of the men from his eighty *triereis*, completed the rebuilding of the Long Walls and the refortification of Piraeus. Some part of the walls had already been reconstructed by the Athenians with the help of the Boeotians and other allies[60]. It appears that Conon also tried to bring about the alliance of Dionysius with Evagoras and hence with Athens, and that he had some temporary success[61]. During 392 Athenian settlers reoccupied their farms on Lemnos, Imbros and Skyros, from which they had been driven by Lysander in 404. Thrasybulus was dispatched to the northern Aegean with

forty ships in 390. He secured control of the Bosphorus, financing his operations by a tax on shipping through the straits. Moving south he re-established
Athenian influence on the seaboard of Asia Minor. Sparta maintained a
small fleet in this area, but sought no engagement. At this juncture the
Athenian orator Lysias states the strategical position with a brutal realism.
At the Olympic games of 388, pleading with the mainland Greeks to give up
their warfare with each other, he says, 'You are aware that empire is for those
who command the sea, that the king of Persia has control of the money, that
the Greeks are the creatures of those who have the financial power, that the
king has many ships, and so has the tyrant of Sicily[62].'

Athens' recent successes had been due to Persian assistance. Now her support of Evagoras of Cyprus, who was in revolt against Persia with a fleet of
200 ships, led to her loss of that assistance. She sent ten ships, which were
intercepted and captured by a Spartan fleet under Teleutias on its way to
support the pro-Spartan party in Rhodes. Later Chabrias took another ten
and others followed. A Spartan fleet under Antalcidas, which included a
squadron sent by Dionysius, now regained control of the straits[63]. By the
peace of Antalcidas in 386 Persia's title to the Ionian Greek cities was recognized, as was Athens' title to Imbros, Lemnos and Skyros[64]. But the two
major naval powers, Persia and Syracuse, were now both on Sparta's side,
and a Spartan fleet dominated Greek waters. Evagoras continued his war
against Persia and seized Tyre, but after a Persian invasion of Cyprus he was
defeated at Citium in 382, besieged in Salamis, and finally accepted terms[65].

At this unpropitious moment, with her friend Evagoras defeated, and
Sparta allied to Persia and Syracuse, which Isocrates calls in a speech of this
period 'the greatest of Hellenic states'[66], and threatening her from Aegina on
her very doorstep, Athens took the first steps to form her second confederation. Thebes, Chios, and Byzantium became equal allies, Athens executive
authority of a common council. Between 377 and 374 the alliance grew
fast[67]. Steps were taken to placate Persia. The charter specifically excluded
any of the Persian king's subjects. Chabrias, who was in Egypt helping the
Egyptian king Acoris against the Persians, was recalled, and Iphicrates was
sent to Asia Minor to act in alliance with the Persians who were preparing
an invasion of Egypt with 300 *triereis*. He sailed with the invasion fleet but
when it made no progress returned to Athens in disgust[68]. In 376 the Aegina-
based Peloponnesian squadron of 65 *triereis* under Pollis began to blockade

the approaches to the Saronic Gulf, and was defeated off Naxos by a large Athenian fleet of 83 ships under Chabrias[69]. A year later Chabrias was operating with a squadron off the Thracian coast, and in western waters Timotheus, Conon's son, with a fleet of sixty ships defeated fifty-five Spartan ships off Acarnania[70]. Peace negotiations were set on foot between Athens and Sparta, but these did not prevent Sparta from sending a fleet to take Corcyra in conjunction with ten ships sent by Dionysius. Iphicrates returning from service with Persia in 373, and hurriedly dispatched with an untrained squadron from Athens, intercepted Dionysius' ships and raised the siege[71].

By the King's Peace of 371 the Persians recognized both the Athenian and the Spartan confederations of autonomous cities, and the Spartan claim to lead on land as the Athenians commanded the sea[72]. Sparta's attempt however to impose the peace on a reluctant Boeotia resulted in her defeat at Leuctra and her eclipse as a land power. Athens, allied to Sparta since before Leuctra, now became also an ally of Dionysius of Syracuse[73]. But Dionysius died shortly after launching in 368/7 an unsuccessful attack with 300 *triereis* against the Carthaginian cities in Sicily[74]. At a meeting of envoys of the Greek states at Susa in 367 the Persians, now giving their support to Boeotia, proposed terms which included the withdrawal of the Athenian fleet from active service[75]. On Athens' refusal to comply there ensued a period of hostilities between her and Boeotia. Already, after Leuctra, Athens had sent thirty ships to the aid of Alexander of Pherae when he was attacked by Thebes[76]. Boeotia built a fleet of 100 *triereis* which proceeded to the Bosphorus in the summer of 363 and interfered with Athenian shipping there, besides stimulating the secession of Byzantium and other cities in an area previously adhering to the Athenian confederation. The Athenian commander in the area was overawed but Timotheus later was more successful[77]. Demosthenes is evidence for the acute shortage of skilled oarsmen at this time, and of their readiness to desert to the other side[78].

In 357 Chios, Rhodes and Cos seceded from the Athenians, and were supported by Byzantium and the Persian ruler of Caria. Chabrias was killed and his fleet defeated at Chios, but the Athenian commander Chares held on in the Chersonese with sixty ships, while the rebels with a hundred ships raided Lemnos and Imbros[79]. In the autumn of the next year Chares was joined by reinforcements of sixty ships from Athens under the command of Timotheus and Iphicrates. The combined fleet, sailing south through the channel between Chios and the mainland to attack Samos, appears to have met the rebel fleet off Embatum, the naval station of Erythrae, but to have failed to engage it in bad weather. Timotheus and Iphicrates were accused of cowardice by Chares, fined and removed from their command[80]. Chares tried to strengthen his position by joining Artabazus who was in revolt from the Persian king; but the Athenians, afraid to bring the Persian fleet of 300 ships against them, disowned Chares and made peace with the rebels[81]. A speech attributed to Demosthenes is evidence of an extreme shortage of naval gear at Athens at this juncture[82].

In the five years from 355 to 351 Athenian trade and finances improved under the direction of Eubulus. The surplus of the revenues was used to repair the docks and fortifications of Piraeus, and to build *triereis*[83]. In 353 Chares sailed to the Hellespont and seized Sestos. But now a new threat to Athenian shipping in the north-eastern Aegean was posed by Philip of Macedon, who captured Methone. When Philip succeeded in defeating Onomarchus of Phocis after capturing Pagasae, Chares, Diodorus says, 'happened to be sailing by'[84]. The peace treaty of Athens with Philip in 346 was of short duration. By 343 three hundred Athenian *triereis* were equipped for service, and Diopithes was operating off the Chersonese with an Athenian fleet[85]. In 340 Philip moved against Athenian corn ships in the straits, but withdrew when Athens sent a large fleet to the relief of Byzantium, now again on her side[86]. This crisis caused a temporary suspension of work on the new ship-sheds and naval storehouse at Athens[87]. Athenian attacks on Macedonian shipping in the north Aegean proved ineffective. Philip's strength was on land, and it was in a land battle that he defeated Athens and Thebes, united in the face of the common danger, at Chaeronea in 338. In the peace settlement that followed Athens was compelled to disband her confederation. Nevertheless, under the direction of Lycurgus, who controlled Athenian finances from 338 to 326, the new ship-sheds and naval storehouse were completed[88]. While Philip was engaging Athens, the Persian king Artaxerxes Ochus was dealing with a revolt of Cyprus and Phoenicia, in addition to the continuing revolt of Egypt. Sidon was able to launch more than 100 *triereis* and *pentereis* against the 300 *triereis* of Persia[89].

The league of Corinth, which was formed in 337 under Philip's leadership, declared war on Persia, and a joint army advanced into Asia Minor.

On Philip's death, Alexander pressed on with the invasion of Asia which was to take him finally to the Punjab. The naval side of these vast land conquests was naturally very minor. The fleet supplied by the Greek league at the outset consisted of a hundred and sixty *triereis*, including a contingent of twenty from Athens[90]. The Persians mustered a larger naval force, but Alexander did not need to risk an engagement. When he had taken Miletus in 334 he disbanded the navy, relying on his control of the land. For a brief period in 332 when Memnon manned 300 ships for Darius, captured Chios and Lesbos, and was rumoured to be contemplating a descent upon Euboea, this neglect of sea power seemed rash; but the threat passed on Memnon's death and with it the hope of a Persian counter-offensive by sea[91]. When Alexander was besieging Tyre in 332 he collected a second fleet, chiefly of Phoenician ships which had deserted from the Persians, to meet the Tyrian fleet of eighty *triereis*[92]. When in 326 he wished to return from India by sea, he built a thousand light river craft and sailed in them down the Indus and through the Indian Ocean to the Persian Gulf. Alexander completed the journey overland, giving the ships to Nearchus to bring back to Mesopotamia, and reached Susa in the spring of 324[93]. During the following winter he assembled a fleet at Thapsacus on the upper Euphrates. Some of the ships had been brought up river from the Persian Gulf, others overland in pieces from Phoenicia. The fleet was then sent down river to Babylon where a basin and shipyards had been prepared[94]. The expedition was frustrated by Alexander's death in 323.

On Alexander's death Athens made one last attempt to reassert her power at sea. She organized a revolt against Macedon, manned 170 ships and sent them to the Hellespont. But a Macedonian fleet succeeded in holding the straits. Joined by another under Antipater it defeated the Athenians at Amorgos[95]. Athens was forced to unconditional surrender; and in September 322 a Macedonian garrison occupied Munichia, dominating the naval installations of Piraeus[96].

The theory of sea power wielded by a city state 'cleaving to the sea', exacting revenue from subject allies, and importing food and skill, while treating its metropolitan territory as expendable, had served Athens well for over a hundred years. Her resilience and pertinacity were amazing, perhaps most amazing of all was the thoroughness with which she pursued and carried out a daring strategical idea. She failed in the fifth century because her ambitions in Egypt and in Sicily outstripped her ability and her resources. In the fourth century, when she had learnt caution, she tried again and again, but failed because the world in which her strategical ideas had been conceived was changing. She had captains of skill and initiative in Conon, Chabrias, Iphicrates and Timotheus, and statesmen like Eubulus and Lycurgus who could build and supply the ships, but the power of Macedon under a Philip or an Alexander was something with which an Athens, even successful in all her undertakings, would still have found it hard to deal. Antipater's occupation of Munichia marked the end of the chapter.

TEXTS

1. See above, p. 161, note 9.

2. See above, p. 160, note 4.

3. Thuc. I 19, the Athenians maintained their hegemony: ναῦς τε τῶν πόλεων τῷ χρόνῳ παραλαβόντες, πλὴν Χίων καὶ Λεσβίων, καὶ χρήματα τοῖς πᾶσι τάξαντες φέρειν.

   id. III 13[7], speech of the Lesbian envoys to Sparta: βοηθησάντων δὲ ὑμῶν προθύμως πόλιν τε προσλήψεσθε ναυτικὸν ἔχουσαν μέγα. . .

   Aristotle, Ath. Pol. 24 2 λαβόντες τὴν ἀρχὴν τοῖς συμμάχοις δεσποτικωτέρως ἐχρῶντο πλὴν Χίων καὶ Λεσβίων καὶ Σαμίων.

4. Thuc. I 117[1] καὶ τῆς θαλάσσης τῆς καθ' ἑαυτοὺς ἐκράτησαν ἡμέρας περὶ τέσσαρας καὶ δέκα καὶ ἐσεκομίσαντο καὶ ἐξεκομίσαντο ἃ ἐβούλοντο.

5. Thuc. VIII 6[4] ὡς ἐκεῖ (i.e. at Chios) οὐκ ἔλασσον ἢ ἑξήκοντα ἀφ' ὧν οἱ Χῖοι ἔλεγον ὑπαρχουσῶν.

6. Diodorus XV 2, 3; 3, 4.

7. Thuc. I 100[1] ἐγένετο δὲ μετὰ ταῦτα καὶ ἡ ἐπ' Εὐρυμέδοντι ποταμῷ ἐν Παμφυλίᾳ πεζομαχία καὶ ναυμαχία Ἀθηναίων καὶ τῶν ξυμμάχων πρὸς Μήδους καὶ ἐνίκων τῇ αὐτῇ ἡμέρᾳ ἀμφότερα Ἀθηναῖοι Κίμωνος τοῦ Μιλτιάδου στρατηγοῦντος, καὶ εἷλον τριήρεις Φοινίκων καὶ διέφθειραν τὰς πάσας ἐς διακοσίας.

   Cf. Diodorus XI 60, Plut. Cimon XII.

8. Thuc. VIII 81[3], Alcibiades boasts that Tissaphernes had promised τὰς. . .ἐν Ἀσπένδῳ ἤδη οὔσας Φοινίκων ναῦς κομιεῖν Ἀθηναίοις καὶ οὐ Πελοποννησίοις.

9. See above, p. 161, note 5.

10. Herodotus VII 166; Diodorus XI 20 ff.

11. Thuc. VIII 26[1] τῶν τε γὰρ Σικελιωτῶν, Ἑρμοκράτους τοῦ Συρακοσίου μάλιστα ἐνάγοντος ξυνεπιλαβέσθαι καὶ τῆς ὑπολοίπου Ἀθηναίων καταλύσεως, εἴκοσι νῆες Συρακοσίων ἦλθον καὶ Σελινούντιαι δύο.

12. Xen. HG VI 2 33 δέκα τριήρεις παρὰ Διονυσίου, βοηθήσουσαι τοῖς Λακεδαιμονίοις. VI 3 Rapprochement of Athens and Sparta before Leuctra. Treaty of Dionysius with Athens in 367 B.C. IG 2[2] 105. GHI 136. Cf. earlier Athenian rapprochements with Dionysius in 393 B.C. (GHI 108) and 368 B.C. (GHI 133).

13. Thuc. II 7² καὶ Λακεδαιμονίοις μὲν πρὸς ταῖς αὐτοῦ ὑπαρχούσαις ἐξ Ἰταλίας καὶ Σικελίας τοῖς τἀκείνων ἑλομένοις ναῦς ἐπετάχθησαν ποιεῖσθαι κατὰ μέγεθος τῶν πόλεων, ὡς ἐς τὸν πάντα ἀριθμὸν πεντακοσίων νεῶν ἐσομένων. VI 20⁴ πολλαὶ δὲ τριήρεις καὶ ὄχλος ὁ πληρώσων αὐτάς.

14. Herodotus VII 168⁴ ἔφασαν πληρῶσαι μὲν ἑξήκοντα τριήρεας, ὑπὸ δὲ ἐτησίεων ἀνέμων ὑπερβαλεῖν Μαλέην οὐκ οἷοί τε γενέσθαι.

15. Thuc. I 36³ τρία μὲν ὄντα λόγου ἄξια τοῖς Ἕλλησι ναυτικά, τὸ παρ᾽ ὑμῖν καὶ τὸ ἡμέτερον καὶ τὸ Κορινθίων.

16. Thuc. I 90¹ τῶν ξυμμάχων . . . φοβουμένων τοῦ τε ναυτικοῦ αὐτῶν τὸ πλῆθος, ὃ πρὶν οὐχ ὑπῆρχε, καὶ τὴν ἐς τὸν Μηδικὸν πόλεμον τόλμαν γενομένην.

17. Thuc. I 142⁷ οὐδὲ γὰρ ὑμεῖς μελετῶντες αὐτό (i.e. τὸ τῆς θαλάσσης ἐπιστήμονας γενέσθαι) ἀπὸ τῶν Μηδικῶν ἐξείργασθέ πω.

Cf. VII 21³ ξυνανέπειθε δὲ καὶ ὁ Ἑρμοκράτης οὐχ ἥκιστα ταῖς ναυσὶ μὴ ἀθυμεῖν ἐπιχειρῆσαι πρὸς τοὺς Ἀθηναίους, λέγων οὐδὲ ἐκείνους πάτριον τὴν ἐμπειρίαν οὐδὲ ἀΐδιον τῆς θαλάσσης ἔχειν, ἀλλ᾽ ἠπειρώτας μᾶλλον τῶν Συρακοσίων ὄντας καὶ ἀναγκασθέντας ὑπὸ Μήδων ναυτικοὺς γενέσθαι.

18. Thuc. I 93³ ἔπεισε δὲ καὶ τοῦ Πειραιῶς τὰ λοιπὰ ὁ Θεμιστοκλῆς οἰκοδομεῖν (ὑπῆρκτο δ᾽ αὐτοῦ πρότερον ἐπὶ τῆς ἐκείνου ἀρχῆς ἧς κατ᾽ ἐνιαυτὸν Ἀθηναίοις ἦρξε) νομίζων τό τε χωρίον καλὸν εἶναι, λιμένας ἔχον τρεῖς αὐτοφυεῖς, καὶ αὐτοὺς ναυτικοὺς γεγενημένους μέγα προφέρειν ἐς τὸ κτήσασθαι δύναμιν (τῆς γὰρ δὴ θαλάσσης πρῶτος ἐτόλμησεν εἰπεῖν ὡς ἀνθεκτέα ἐστί), καὶ τὴν ἀρχὴν εὐθὺς ξυγκατεσκεύαζεν. καὶ ᾠκοδόμησαν τῇ ἐκείνου γνώμῃ τὸ πάχος τοῦ τείχους ὅπερ νῦν ἔτι δῆλόν ἐστι περὶ τὸν Πειραιᾶ· δύο γὰρ ἅμαξαι ἐναντίαι ἀλλήλαις τοὺς λίθους ἐπῆγον. ἐντὸς δὲ οὔτε χάλιξ οὔτε πηλὸς ἦν, ἀλλὰ ξυνῳκοδομημένοι μεγάλοι λίθοι καὶ ἐντομῇ ἐγγώνιοι, σιδήρῳ πρὸς ἀλλήλους τὰ ἔξωθεν καὶ μολύβδῳ δεδεμένοι. τὸ δὲ ὕψος ἥμισυ μάλιστα ἐτελέσθη οὗ διενοεῖτο. ἐβούλετο γὰρ τῷ μεγέθει καὶ τῷ πάχει ἀφιστάναι τὰς τῶν πολεμίων ἐπιβουλάς, ἀνθρώπων τε ἐνόμιζεν ὀλίγων καὶ τῶν ἀχρειοτάτων ἀρκέσειν τὴν φυλακήν, τοὺς δ᾽ ἄλλους ἐς τὰς ναῦς ἐσβήσεσθαι. ταῖς γὰρ ναυσὶ μάλιστα προσέκειτο, ἰδών, ὡς ἐμοὶ δοκεῖ, τῆς βασιλέως στρατιᾶς τὴν κατὰ θάλασσαν ἔφοδον εὐπορωτέραν τῆς κατὰ γῆν οὖσαν· τόν τε Πειραιᾶ ὠφελιμώτερον ἐνόμιζε τῆς ἄνω πόλεως, καὶ πολλάκις τοῖς Ἀθηναίοις παρῄνει, ἢν ἄρα ποτὲ κατὰ γῆν βιασθῶσι, καταβάντας ἐς αὐτὸν ταῖς ναυσὶ πρὸς ἅπαντας ἀνθίστασθαι.

19. Diodorus XI 43³ (Themistocles) ἔπεισε δὲ τὸν δῆμον καθ᾽ ἕκαστον ἐνιαυτὸν πρὸς ταῖς ὑπαρχούσαις ναυσὶν εἴκοσι τριήρεις προσκατασκευάζειν.

20. Aristotle, *Ath. Pol.* 46 1 ἐπιμελεῖται δὲ (sc. ἡ βουλή) καὶ τῶν πεποιημένων τριήρων καὶ τῶν σκευῶν καὶ τῶν νεωσοίκων, καὶ ποιεῖται καινὰς δέκα* τριήρεις ἢ τετρήρεις, ὁποτέρας ἂν ὁ δῆμος χειροτονήσῃ, καὶ σκεύη ταύταις καὶ νεωσοίκους.

21. Aristotle, *Ath. Pol.* 24 1 μετὰ δὲ ταῦτα θαρρούσης ἤδη τῆς πόλεως καὶ χρημάτων ἠθροισμένων πολλῶν, συνεβούλευεν ἀντιλαμβάνεσθαι τῆς ἡγεμονίας καὶ καταβάντας ἐκ τῶν ἀγρῶν οἰκεῖν ἐν τῷ ἄστει.

* MSS. δέ.

22. Plato, *Gorgias* 455 *d–e* οἶσθα γὰρ δήπου ὅτι τὰ νεώρια ταῦτα καὶ τὰ τείχη τὰ Ἀθηναίων καὶ ἡ τῶν λιμένων κατασκευὴ ἐκ τῆς Θεμιστοκλέους συμβουλῆς γέγονεν, τὰ δ᾽ ἐκ τῆς Περικλέους, ἀλλ᾽ οὐκ ἐκ τῶν δημιουργῶν. Λέγεται ταῦτα, ὦ Γοργία, περὶ Θεμιστοκλέους· Περικλέους δὲ καὶ αὐτὸς ἤκουεν ὅτε συνεβούλευεν ἡμῖν περὶ τοῦ διὰ μέσου τείχους.

23. Aristotle, *Ath. Pol.* 27 1 (Pericles) καὶ μάλιστα προὔτρεψεν τὴν πόλιν ἐπὶ τὴν ναυτικὴν δύναμιν.

24. Thuc. I 107[1–4]: ἤρξαντο δὲ κατὰ τοὺς χρόνους τούτους καὶ τὰ μακρὰ τείχη Ἀθηναῖοι ἐς θάλασσαν οἰκοδομεῖν, τό τε Φαληρόνδε καὶ τὸ ἐς Πειραιᾶ...ἔδοξε δὲ αὐτοῖς (a Lacedaimonian army of 25,000 hoplites) ἐν Βοιωτοῖς περιμείνασι σκέψασθαι ὅτῳ τρόπῳ ἀσφαλέστατα διαπορεύσονται. τὸ δέ τι καὶ ἄνδρες ἐπῆγον αὐτοὺς τῶν Ἀθηναίων κρύφα, ἐλπίσαντες δῆμόν τε καταπαύσειν καὶ τὰ μακρὰ τείχη οἰκοδομούμενα.

25. Plato, *Laws* 706 *b*, the Athenians were unable to withstand the sea power of Minos, ἔτι γὰρ ἂν πλεονάκις ἑπτὰ ἀπολέσαι παῖδας αὐτοὺς συνήνεγκε, πρὶν ἀντὶ πεζῶν ὁπλιτῶν μονίμων ναυτικοὺς γενομένους ἐθισθῆναι πυκνὰ ἀποπηδῶντας δρομικῶς ἐπὶ τὰς ναῦς ταχὺ πάλιν ἀποχωρεῖν κ.τ.λ.

26. Aristophanes, *Knights* 1065–6
τοῖς ναύταισί μου / ὅπως ὁ μισθὸς πρῶτον ἀποδοθήσεται.

27. Thuc. I 109–110.

28. Thuc. I 108[4] ὡμολόγησαν δὲ καὶ οἱ Αἰγινῆται μετὰ ταῦτα τοῖς Ἀθηναίοις, τείχη τε περιελόντες καὶ ναῦς παραδόντες φόρον τε ταξάμενοι ἐς τὸν ἔπειτα χρόνον.

29. Thuc. I 117[3] καὶ ναυμαχίαν μέν τινα βραχεῖαν ἐποιήσαντο οἱ Σάμιοι, ἀδύνατοι δὲ ὄντες ἀντισχεῖν ἐξεπολιορκήθησαν ἐνάτῳ μηνὶ καὶ προσεχώρησαν ὁμολογίᾳ, τεῖχός τε καθελόντες καὶ ὁμήρους δόντες καὶ ναῦς παραδόντες καὶ χρήματα τὰ ἀναλωθέντα ταξάμενοι κατὰ χρόνους ἀποδοῦναι.

30. *IG* I[2] 91, 31 ἐς τὸ νεόριον καὶ τὰ τείχε τοῖς περιõσι χρέσθαι χρέμασ[ιν.

31. [Xen.] *Ath. Pol.* II 1–16. For date see Frisch, *The Constitution of the Athenians*. Copenhagen, 1942, pp. 47–62.

32. Thuc. I 141[2]–143 in particular 143[5] μέγα γὰρ τὸ τῆς θαλάσσης κράτος. σκέψασθε δέ· εἰ γὰρ ἦμεν νησιῶται, τίνες ἂν ἀληπτότεροι ἦσαν; καὶ νῦν χρὴ ὅτι ἐγγύτατα τούτου διανοηθέντας τὴν μὲν γῆν καὶ οἰκίας ἀφεῖναι, τῆς δὲ θαλάσσης καὶ πόλεως φυλακὴν ἔχειν, καὶ Πελοποννησίοις ὑπὲρ αὐτῶν ὀργισθέντας πολλῷ πλέοσι μὴ διαμάχεσθαι (κρατήσαντές τε γὰρ αὖθις οὐκ ἐλάσσοσι μαχούμεθα καὶ ἢν σφαλῶμεν, τὰ τῶν ξυμμάχων, ὅθεν ἰσχύομεν, προσαπόλλυται· οὐ γὰρ ἡσυχάσουσι μὴ ἱκανῶν ἡμῶν ὄντων ἐπ᾽ αὐτοὺς στρατεύειν), τήν τε ὀλόφυρσιν μὴ οἰκιῶν καὶ γῆς ποιεῖσθαι, ἀλλὰ τῶν σωμάτων· οὐ γὰρ τάδε τοὺς ἄνδρας, ἀλλ᾽ οἱ ἄνδρες ταῦτα κτῶνται. καὶ εἰ ᾤμην πείσειν ὑμᾶς, αὐτοὺς ἂν ἐξελθόντας ἐκέλευον αὐτὰ δῃῶσαι καὶ δεῖξαι Πελοποννησίοις ὅτι τούτων γε ἕνεκα οὐχ ὑπακούσεσθε.

33. Thuc. II 62[2–3] οἴεσθε μὲν γὰρ τῶν ξυμμάχων μόνων ἄρχειν, ἐγὼ δὲ ἀποφαίνω δύο μερῶν τῶν ἐς χρῆσιν φανερῶν, γῆς καὶ θαλάσσης, τοῦ ἑτέρου ὑμᾶς παντὸς κυριωτάτους ὄντας, ἐφ᾽ ὅσον τε νῦν νέμεσθε καὶ ἢν ἐπὶ πλέον βουληθῆτε· καὶ οὐκ ἔστιν ὅστις τῇ

ὑπαρχούσῃ παρασκευῇ τοῦ ναυτικοῦ πλέοντας ὑμᾶς οὔτε βασιλεὺς οὔτε ἄλλο οὐδὲν ἔθνος τῶν ἐν τῷ παρόντι κωλύσει. ὥστε οὐ κατὰ τὴν τῶν οἰκιῶν καὶ τῆς γῆς χρείαν, ὧν μεγάλων νομίζετε ἐστερῆσθαι, αὕτη ἡ δύναμις φαίνεται.

34. Thuc. II 13² παρῄνει δὲ καὶ περὶ τῶν παρόντων ἅπερ καὶ πρότερον, παρασκευά-ζεσθαί τε ἐς τὸν πόλεμον καὶ τὰ ἐκ τῶν ἀγρῶν ἐσκομίζεσθαι, ἔς τε μάχην μὴ ἐπεξιέναι, ἀλλὰ τὴν πόλιν ἐσελθόντας φυλάσσειν, καὶ τὸ ναυτικόν, ᾗπερ ἰσχύουσιν, ἐξαρτύεσθαι, τά τε τῶν ξυμμάχων διὰ χειρὸς ἔχειν, λέγων τὴν ἰσχὺν αὐτοῖς ἀπὸ τούτων εἶναι τῶν χρημάτων τῆς προσόδου, τὰ δὲ πολλὰ τοῦ πολέμου γνώμῃ καὶ χρημάτων περιουσίᾳ κρατεῖσθαι.

35. Thuc. II 24¹⁻² ἀναχωρησάντων δὲ αὐτῶν οἱ Ἀθηναῖοι φυλακὰς κατε-στήσαντο κατὰ γῆν καὶ κατὰ θάλασσαν, ὥσπερ δὴ ἔμελλον διὰ παντὸς τοῦ πολέμου φυλάξειν· καὶ χίλια τάλαντα ἀπὸ τῶν ἐν τῇ ἀκροπόλει χρημάτων ἔδοξεν αὐτοῖς ἐξαίρετα ποιησαμένοις χωρὶς θέσθαι καὶ μὴ ἀναλοῦν, ἀλλ᾽ ἀπὸ τῶν ἄλλων πολεμεῖν· ἢν δέ τις εἴπῃ ἢ ἐπιψηφίσῃ κινεῖν τὰ χρήματα ταῦτα ἐς ἄλλο τι, ἢν μὴ οἱ πολέμιοι νηίτῃ στρατῷ ἐπιπλέωσι τῇ πόλει καὶ δέῃ ἀμύνασθαι, θάνατον ζημίαν ἐπέθεντο. τριήρεις τε μετ᾽ αὐτῶν ἐξαιρέτους ἑκατὸν ἐποιήσαντο κατὰ τὸν ἐνιαυτὸν ἕκαστον τὰς βελτίστας, καὶ τριηράρ-χους αὐταῖς, ὧν μὴ χρῆσθαι μηδεμιᾷ ἐς ἄλλο τι ἢ μετὰ τῶν χρημάτων περὶ τοῦ αὐτοῦ κινδύνου, ἢν δέῃ.

36. [Xen.] Ath. Pol. III 4 καὶ τριήραρχοι καθίστανται τετρακόσιοι ἑκάστου ἐνιαυτοῦ. Thuc. II 13⁸ καὶ τριήρεις τὰς πλωίμους τριακοσίας.

Cf. 24².

Aristophanes, Acharnians 544-5
       καὶ κάρτα μεντἂν εὐθέως καθείλκετε
       τριακοσίας ναῦς. . .

37. Thuc. VIII 15¹ ἐς δὲ τὰς Ἀθήνας ταχὺ ἀγγελία τῆς Χίου ἀφικνεῖται· καὶ νομίσαντες μέγαν ἤδη καὶ σαφῆ τὸν κίνδυνον σφᾶς περιεστάναι. . .τά τε χίλια τάλαντα ὧν διὰ παντὸς τοῦ πολέμου ἐγλίχοντο μὴ ἅψασθαι. . .ἐψηφίσαντο κινεῖν καὶ ναῦς πληροῦν μὴ ὀλίγας.

38. U. Wilcken, 'Der Anonymus Argentinensis', Hermes 42, 1907, pp. 414-15. His text is as follows: ἑκάστῳ ἔ]τει τὴν βουλὴν τῶν παλαιῶν τριή[ρων ἑκατὸν ἐξαιρέτους παραδ]ιδόναι, καινὰς δ᾽ ἐπιναυπηγεῖν ἑκάσ[τοτε   δ]έκα.

39. [Xen.] Ath. Pol. II 12 καὶ ἐγὼ μὲν οὐδὲν ποιῶν ἐκ τῆς γῆς πάντα ταῦτα ἔχω διὰ τὴν θάλατταν.

40. Thuc. II 17¹⁻⁴ καὶ κατὰ τὸν χρόνον τοῦτον ὃν αἱ νῆες ἔπλεον ἐν τοῖς πλεῖσται δὴ νῆες ἅμ᾽ αὐτοῖς ἐνεργοὶ κάλλει ἐγένοντο, παραπλήσιαι δὲ καὶ ἔτι πλείους ἀρχομένου τοῦ πολέμου. τήν τε γὰρ Ἀττικὴν καὶ Εὔβοιαν καὶ Σαλαμῖνα ἑκατὸν ἐφύλασσον, καὶ περὶ Πελοπόννησον ἕτεραι ἑκατὸν ἦσαν, χωρὶς δὲ αἱ περὶ Ποτείδαιαν καὶ ἐν τοῖς ἄλλοις χωρίοις, ὥστε αἱ πᾶσαι ἅμα ἐγίγνοντο ἐν ἑνὶ θέρει διακόσιαι καὶ πεντήκοντα. καὶ τὰ χρήματα τοῦτο μάλιστα ὑπανήλωσε μετὰ Ποτειδαίας. τήν τε γὰρ Ποτείδαιαν δίδραχμοι ὁπλῖται ἐφρούρουν (αὑτῷ γὰρ καὶ ὑπηρέτῃ δραχμὴν ἐλάμβανε τῆς ἡμέρας), τρισχίλιοι μὲν οἱ πρῶτοι, ὧν οὐκ ἐλάσσους διεπολιόρκησαν, ἑξακόσιοι δὲ καὶ χίλιοι μετὰ Φορμίωνος,

οἳ προαπῆλθον· νῆές τε αἱ πᾶσαι τὸν αὐτὸν μισθὸν ἔφερον. τὰ μὲν οὖν χρήματα οὕτως ὑπανηλώθη τὸ πρῶτον, καὶ νῆες τοσαῦται δὴ πλεῖσται ἐπληρώθησαν.

41. Thuc. VIII 1³ ὅμως δὲ ὡς ἐκ τῶν ὑπαρχόντων ἐδόκει χρῆναι μὴ ἐνδιδόναι, ἀλλὰ παρασκευάζεσθαι καὶ ναυτικόν, ὅθεν ἂν δύνωνται ξύλα ξυμπορισαμένους, καὶ χρήματα, καὶ τὰ τῶν ξυμμάχων ἐς ἀσφάλειαν ποιεῖσθαι, καὶ μάλιστα τὴν Εὔβοιαν, τῶν τε κατὰ τὴν πόλιν τι ἐς εὐτέλειαν σωφρονίσαι, καὶ ἀρχήν τινα πρεσβυτέρων ἀνδρῶν ἑλέσθαι, οἵτινες περὶ τῶν παρόντων ὡς ἂν καιρὸς ᾖ προβουλεύσουσιν. πάντα τε πρὸς τὸ παραχρῆμα περιδεές, ὅπερ φιλεῖ δῆμος ποιεῖν, ἕτοιμοι ἦσαν εὐτακτεῖν.

42. Thuc. VIII 3² Λακεδαιμόνιοι δὲ τὴν πρόσταξιν ταῖς πόλεσιν ἑκατὸν νεῶν τῆς ναυπηγίας ἐποιοῦντο, καὶ ἑαυτοῖς μὲν καὶ Βοιωτοῖς πέντε καὶ εἴκοσι ἑκατέροις, ἔταξαν, Φωκεῦσι δὲ καὶ Λοκροῖς πέντε καὶ δέκα, καὶ Κορινθίοις πέντε καὶ δέκα, Ἀρκάσι δὲ καὶ Πελληνεῦσι καὶ Σικυωνίοις δέκα, Μεγαρεῦσι δὲ καὶ Τροιζηνίοις καὶ Ἐπιδαυρίοις καὶ Ἑρμιονεῦσι δέκα.

43. Thuc. VIII 53² ἀντιλεγόντων δὲ πολλῶν καὶ ἄλλων περὶ τῆς δημοκρατίας καὶ τῶν Ἀλκιβιάδου ἅμα ἐχθρῶν διαβοώντων ὡς δεινὸν εἴη εἰ τοὺς νόμους βιασάμενος κάτεισι, καὶ Εὐμολπιδῶν καὶ Κηρύκων περὶ τῶν μυστικῶν δι' ἅπερ ἔφυγε μαρτυρομένων καὶ ἐπιθειαζόντων μὴ κατάγειν, ὁ Πείσανδρος παρελθὼν πρὸς πολλὴν ἀντιλογίαν καὶ σχετλιασμὸν ἠρώτα ἕνα ἕκαστον παράγων τῶν ἀντιλεγόντων, εἴ τινα ἐλπίδα ἔχει σωτηρίας τῇ πόλει, Πελοποννησίων ναῦς τε οὐκ ἐλάσσους σφῶν ἐν τῇ θαλάσσῃ ἀντιπρῴρους ἐχόντων καὶ πόλεις ξυμμαχίδας πλείους, βασιλέως τε αὐτοῖς καὶ Τισσαφέρνους χρήματα παρεχόντων, σφίσι τε οὐκέτι ὄντων, εἰ μή τις πείσει βασιλέα μεταστῆναι παρὰ σφᾶς. Cf. *id. ib.* 78¹, 87⁴.

44. Thuc. VIII 46¹ παρῄνει δὲ (sc. Alcibiades) καὶ τῷ Τισσαφέρνει μὴ ἄγαν ἐπείγεσθαι τὸν πόλεμον διαλῦσαι, μηδὲ βουληθῆναι ἢ κομίσαντα ναῦς Φοινίσσας ὥσπερ παρεσκευάζετο ἢ Ἕλλησι πλείοσι μισθὸν πορίζοντα τοῖς αὐτοῖς τῆς τε γῆς καὶ τῆς θαλάσσης τὸ κράτος δοῦναι.

45. Thuc. VIII 15¹. See note 37 above.

46. Thuc. VIII 79¹⁻⁶.

47. Thuc. VIII 81³. See note 8 above.

48. Cynossema, Thuc. VIII 104 ff.; Abydos, Xen. *HG* I 1 5; Cyzicus, Xen. *HG* I 1 14 ff.

49. Xen. *HG* I 5 4–5 οἱ δὲ (sc. Λακεδαιμόνιοι) ταῦτ' ἐπῄνουν καὶ ἐκέλευον αὐτὸν τάξαι τῷ ναύτῃ δραχμὴν Ἀττικήν, διδάσκοντες ὅτι, ἂν οὗτος ὁ μισθὸς γένηται, οἱ τῶν Ἀθηναίων ναῦται ἀπολείψουσι τὰς ναῦς, καὶ μείω χρήματα ἀναλώσει. ὁ δὲ καλῶς μὲν ἔφη αὐτοὺς λέγειν, οὐ δυνατὸν δ' εἶναι παρ' ἃ βασιλεὺς ἐπέστειλεν αὐτῷ ἄλλα ποιεῖν. εἶναι δὲ καὶ τὰς συνθήκας οὕτως ἐχούσας, τριάκοντα μνᾶς ἑκάστῃ νηὶ τοῦ μηνὸς διδόναι, ὁπόσας ἂν βούλωνται τρέφειν Λακεδαιμόνιοι. ὁ δὲ Λύσανδρος τότε μὲν ἐσιώπησε· μετὰ δὲ τὸ δεῖπνον, ἐπεὶ αὐτῷ προπιὼν ὁ Κῦρος ἤρετο τί ἂν μάλιστα χαρίζοιτο ποιῶν, εἶπεν ὅτι Εἰ πρὸς τὸν μισθὸν ἑκάστῳ ναύτῃ ὀβολὸν προσθείης. ἐκ δὲ τούτου τέτταρες ὀβολοὶ ($\frac{2}{3}$ dr.) ἦν ὁ μισθός, πρότερον δὲ τριώβολον.

50. Xen. *HG* I vi 18–34 in particular 31 οὕτω δὲ ἐτάχθησαν, ἵνα μὴ διέκπλουν διδοῖεν· χεῖρον γὰρ ἔπλεον.

51. Xen. *HG* II 1 27–9; Diodorus XIII 106 1–7.

52. Xen. *HG* II 2 20–3; Lysias 13 5, 14, 15, 34, 46; Plutarch, *Lysander* xv 1–4; Diodorus XIII 107 4.

53. Lysias 12 99; Isocrates 7 66.

54. Demosthenes 13 28; 22 76; 23 207; 24 184.
Cf. Dinarchus 3 13.

55. Lysias 30 22 τοὺς δὲ νεωσοίκους ⟨καὶ⟩ τὰ τείχη περικαταρρέοντα.

56. Xen. *HG* II 1 29; Diodorus XIII 106 6, XIV 39 1–4; Isocrates, 4 142; Cratippus of Athens, *F. Gr. Hist.* II A 64 *T* 2: Κόνωνα πάλιν ἐμβιβάζοντα τὰς ᾿Αθήνας εἰς τὴν θάλασσαν.

An alternative version in Diodorus XIV 81 4 says that he chose Pharnabazus.

57. *Hell. Ox.* II 1 ἀπέπεμπον μὲν γὰρ (sc. οἱ πολλοὶ καὶ δημοτικοί) ὅπλα τε καὶ ὑπηρεσίας ἐπὶ τὰς ναῦς τὰς μετὰ τοῦ Κ[όνωνος.

Isocrates 4 142 ἐν δὲ τῷ πολέμῳ τῷ περὶ ῾Ρόδον ἔχων μὲν τοὺς Λακεδαιμονίων συμμάχους...χρώμενος δὲ ταῖς ὑπηρεσίαις ταῖς παρ᾿ ἡμῶν, στρατηγοῦντος δ᾿ αὐτῷ (i.e. the Persian king) Κόνωνος.

58. Diodorus XIV 39 4, 79 4–8; *Hell. Ox.* x.

59. Xen. *HG* IV 3 11 ff.; Diodorus XIV 83 4–7.

60. Xen. *HG* IV 8 7–10; Diodorus XIV 84 3–5, 85.

61. Lysias 19 19–20. *GHI* 108 records an honour for Dionysius at Athens in 393 B.C.

62. Xen. *HG* IV 8 25; Lysias 33 5 ἐπίστασθε δὲ ὅτι ἡ μὲν ἀρχὴ τῶν κρατούντων τῆς θαλάττης, τῶν δὲ χρημάτων βασιλεὺς ταμίας, τὰ δὲ τῶν ῾Ελλήνων σώματα τῶν δαπανᾶσθαι δυναμένων, ναῦς δὲ πολλὰς αὐτὸς κέκτηται πολλὰς δ᾿ ὁ τύραννος τῆς Σικελίας.

63. Lysias 19 21; Xen. *HG* IV 8 24, v 1 10 and 28; Demosthenes 20 76.

64. Xen. *HG* v 1 31.

65. Diodorus XIV 2–4, 8, 9 1–2; Isocrates 4 141.

66. Isocrates 3 23.

67. *GHI* 121, 122, 123; Diodorus xv 28–30. The charter of the confederacy dates from February or March 377 B.C.

68. Diodorus xv 29 2–4, 43.

69. Xen. *HG* v 4 61; Diodorus xv 34 3; Polyaenus III 11 2 and 11.

70. Diodorus xv 36 4 (Chabrias); Xen. *HG* v 4 65, Isocrates 15 109 (Timotheus).

71. Xen. *HG* VI 2 3–39.

72. Xen. *HG* VI 3 12, 5 1; Diodorus xv 50 4.
Cf. 38 4.

73. Xen. *HG* VI 3 (before Leuctra), *GHI* 133 and 136.

74. Diodorus xv 73.

75. Xen. *HG* VII 1 36 ᾿Αθηναίους ἀνέλκειν τὰς ναῦς.

76. Diodorus xv 71 3.

77. Diodorus xv 78, 79, 81.

78. Demosthenes 50 7 and 14.

79. Diodorus XVI 7 and 21; Nepos XII 4.

80. Diodorus XVI 21. Embatum, see Thuc. III 29 Ἔμβατον τῆς Ἐρυθραίας, and Steph. Byz. *s.v.* See also Nepos XIII 3 and Polyaenus 3 9 29.

81. Diodorus XVI 22.

82. Demosthenes 47 *passim*.

83. Dinarchus I 96.

84. Diodorus XVI 35 5 τυχικῶς παραπλέοντος τοῦ Ἀθηναίου Χάρητος μετὰ πολλῶν τριηρῶν.

85. Demosthenes 8.

86. Diodorus XVI 77 1–2.

87. Philochorus, fr. 135.

88. Diodorus XVI 87–8; Plutarch, *Vit. X or.* VII 853.

89. Diodorus XVI 40 3 ff.; *pentereis*, *ib.* 44 6.

90. *GHI* 177; Diodorus XVI 89 5.

91. Diodorus XVII 7 2, 22 5, 29 2–4.

92. Diodorus XVII 41 1, 42 3; Arrian 2 20 7.

93. Diodorus XVII 86 3 (triakontors on the Indus), 95 3–4 (*aphraktoi* and *huperetikoi*). 104 3 Nearchus takes over the fleet.
   Cf. Arrian, *Anab.* VI 1 1.

94. Arrian, *Anab.* VII 19 3 ff.

95. Diodorus XVIII 11–17; Plutarch, *Demetrius* XI 3.

96. Pausanias I 25 5.

II

WRITTEN EVIDENCE

USAGE OF TERMS AND SHIP TYPES

The usage of terms noticed in Herodotus is in general followed by other fifth- and fourth-century writers. The general term for a ship is *naus* or *ploion*, and these terms can be used of all types of ship: e.g. *ploion strongulon* (round, i.e. merchant ship)[1], *naus pentekontoros*[2], *holkadikon ploion*[3]. Both terms are used without qualification in a special sense. *Naus* by itself commonly means a *trieres*[4], and *ploion* by itself often means one of the lighter types of oared ship in contrast to the *trieres*, once or twice in contrast to the *pentekontoros*[5]. The epithets 'long' and 'round' are used to distinguish the slim galleys from the ships of burden. These latter are of two types, either oared *ploia*[6] or *holkades* (which appear never to have been rowed). An example of the oared *ploion* is the *eikosoros*, a twenty-oared cargo ship[7] (see p. 46).

These conclusions about the use of terms are largely confirmed by a passage in the *Constitution of Athens* attributed to Xenophon and probably written before 432. The subject is the training of oarsmen and helmsmen. The writer says that experience at the helm is gained first on *ploia* and on *holkades*. From these ships helmsmen are appointed to *triereis*. The great majority are able to row from the moment they go aboard a *naus* since they have had experience man and boy all their life[8]. In this passage then we have *ploia* and *holkades* distinguished from each other and both from *triereis*. Finally *naus* is used to mean the ships of the Athenian navy, i.e. at that time exclusively *triereis*. One distinction is not made; round *ploia* are not distinguished from long *ploia*.

The *holkas* appears not to have been an oared ship. Aristotle says[9] that certain insects fly clumsily and weakly, as if a *holkas* were to attempt to move by means of oars. She was broad and deep, and probably did not beach like a long ship but was moored in deep water[10]. A black-figure kylix dated in the last half of the sixth century (Arch. 85, Pl. 20*a*) shows just such a ship. She sailed on the high seas, but we are left to guess how she entered and left the often land-locked harbours of the eastern Mediterranean. The normal navigational use of the oar in an oared ship was for this purpose. A ship without oars would have to be towed. Towing is exactly what the name *holkas* suggests, since it certainly is cognate with the verb *helkein* 'to tow'. There are one or two passages to confirm this conclusion. Thucydides says that there sailed, carrying necessary supplies for the main Sicilian expedition, 'thirty corn-carrying *holkades*... and a hundred *ploia* which necessarily accompanied the *holkades*'[11]. He also tells us that the Cyrenaeans sent two *triereis* to accompany Spartan troop-carrying *holkades*[12]. In both these cases the escort probably had also a protective purpose. In the fighting at Syracuse, when the Syracusans took the forts on Plemmyrium, Thucydides says that some of the garrison got away with difficulty in *ploia* and a *holkas* when pursued by a fast *trieres*[13]. The *holkas* would never have got away under sail; it must have been towed. Demosthenes speaks of Athenian *triereis* towing grain-ships, called *ploia* but certainly *holkades*, from Thasos to Stryme, a distance of about fifty miles[14]. Finally Aristophanes mentions people 'who lay thick ropes for *holkades*'[15]. Thick ropes were used in warships for anchor cables and *hupozomata* (swifters: see p. 294). 'Thick ropes for *holkades*' must have been specially thick ropes, thicker than those used for warships. The purpose of such ropes must have been for use in towing.

The only oared cargo ship we hear of is the *eikosoros*. It is referred to in a fragment of middle comedy, and in Demosthenes is described as carrying three thousand jars of wine[17]. It was clearly a very useful hybrid.

The smallest type of oared boat is the *akatos* or *akation*. The small mast, sail and sailyard on a fourth-century *trieres* appear to have been of a size suitable to an *akatos* (see below, p. 293). A herald is sent in one by the Corcyraeans to forbid the Corinthian fleet to advance. Elsewhere in Thucydides it has an epithet which suggests that it was rowed by pairs of sculls. In the list of vessels used to form the boom closing the Great Harbour at Syracuse *akatoi* come last. Public *akatoi* are mentioned in the naval lists[16]. *Keles* or *keletion* is mentioned by Thucydides several times as a small boat used by pirates. The fourth-century comic poet Ephippus gives *keles* the epithet *penteskalmos*, i.e. with five tholepins[17]. In a small vessel of this kind it may be assumed that there were five oarsmen a side, ten in all. Aeschines and Aristotle speak of an *epaktrokeles*, and Xenophon of an *epaktris*[18]. We can only guess at their nature. The usage of the word *epagein* to which *epaktris* is cognate suggests that these may have been boats hoisted aboard much larger vessels. The *hemiolia* appears in Theophrastus and in Arrian as a pirate craft[19]. The name 'one-and-a-half-er' suggests that it may have resembled a ship depicted on a black-figure vase (Arch. 85, Pl. 20 a) which is shown with one and a half banks of oars.

In the period before Salamis pentekontors appear to have been still in frequent use, and for many cities remained capital ships. Triakontors were employed as swift dispatch boats. In the fifth century pentekontors became rare. A pentekontor and a triakontor appear in an Athenian inscription of 450/49[20]. When Phormio met the Corinthian fleet in the summer of 429, they formed a circle of *triereis* putting the light *ploia* inside[21]. These light *ploia* are almost certainly triakontors. Two pentekontors were sent by Rhodes as her contribution to the Sicilian expedition, and three Tyrrhenian pentekontors joined it on arrival[22]. When the Ten Thousand reach the Black Sea they acquire a pentekontor and a triakontor[23]. But pentekontors do not appear at all in the naval lists of the middle half of the fourth century; and when Alexander musters a fleet at Thapsacus on the upper Euphrates, bringing the ships overland in pieces from the Mediterranean coast, there are *pentereis*, *tetrereis*, *triereis* and up to thirty triakontors, but no pentekontors[24]. It appears that the pentekontor, when it lost its position as a capital ship, dropped out of use altogether.

The triakontor remains in use throughout the period. Thucydides' only mention of a triakontor is when a Messenian privateer of that rating, accompanied by a *keles*, turns up at Pylos and supplies arms to the Athenian occupying force[25]. The ship which made the annual voyage to Delos from Athens was apparently a triakontor[26]. In the fourth century the type occurs frequently in the naval lists, twice in the neuter form *triakontorion* which is used by Aristotle[27]. Plato speaks of his friend Archytas of Tarentum sending a triakontor to Dionysius of Syracuse on his behalf[28].

Our information about *triereis* comes almost exclusively from Athens. When two Athenian travellers are asked in Aristophanes their country of origin, they reply 'where the fine *triereis* come from'[29]. *Triereis* seem to have been divided into three categories 'fast', 'troop transports' and 'horse transports'. The ships in the first Sicilian expedition are divided into sixty fast ships and forty troop transports and we are told that they moored their fast ships under the forts at Plemmyrium[30]. In the *Knights* Aristophanes speaks of 'fast, money-collecting ships'[31]. The category of fast ships occurs a number of times in Demosthenes. He asks for ten fast ships in addition to a fleet of *triereis* and horse transports: 'for since Philip has a navy we need fast *triereis* to ensure the safety of the expeditionary force'[32]. By inference the ships which are not fast are, as in the Sicilian expedition, troop transports, and only the ships which are fast are in a state to fight a naval action. The state *trieres*, *Paralos*, like its sister ship the *Salaminia*, was undoubtedly a fast *trieres*, since it was sent on special missions of state. At the time of the oligarchic revolution at Athens it was sent to Athens by the Athenian democrats in the fleet at Samos. On arrival two or three of the crew were put in prison, while the rest were transferred to a troop transport and sent to carry out guard duties off Euboea[33].

Transport *triereis* occur in an Athenian inscription of 450–449[34]. Thucydides mentions that twenty of a fleet of seventy Samian ships which had been carrying out an attack on Miletus in 440 were troop transports[35]. The proportion in the Sicilian expedition, 40 per cent, was, as we saw, much higher. When we are told that the *stratiotis* to which the crew of the *Paralos* was transferred was sent on guard duty, we may perhaps make the inference that *stratiotis* was a category of ship rather than one actually carrying troops, since it is unlikely that troops would be carried on a guard ship. Two other texts strengthen this conclusion. Thucydides relates that in 411 the Athenian general Strombichides went to restore the situation in Lampsacus and Abydos with twenty-four ships, some of which were *stratiotides* 'carrying troops'[36]. The words suggest that some of the ships might have been *stratiotides* without actually carrying troops. Again, Xenophon in the *Hellenica* speaks of a fleet of fifteen ships which were *stratiotides rather than fast*[37]. What qualified a ship for being a *stratiotis* appears to have been its slowness. The word *hoplitagogos*, 'hoplite-carrier', is an alternative to *stratiotis*. Nicias estimated that the force needed against Syracuse was a hundred *triereis* and as many Athenian *hoplitagogoi* as they decide, with others requisitioned from the allies. Later the city is said to have provided forty empty *hoplitagogoi* for the expedition. These are later described as *stratiotides*[38]. In 412 Phrynichus sailed to Samos with forty-eight ships some of which were *hoplitagogoi*, and in the following spring Strombichides sails against Chios with thirty ships and some of the Athenian hoplites who had been brought by Phrynichus 'whom they took on *hoplitagogoi*'[39]. In none of these cases is it possible to guess the number of hoplites which a *stratiotis* or *hoplitagogos* could carry. The fact that the *Paralos'* crew, except the two or three who were put in prison, were transferred to a *stratiotis* suggests that there was no real difference in the rowing force of the two types. There is an inscription which dates from shortly after the beginning of the Peloponnesian war and is concerned with the manning of an expedition of thirty ships. Forty hoplites are to sail on each, in addition to five 'volunteers', ten archers and peltasts of a number not preserved[40]. Since, as we shall see, fast *triereis* carried a force of ten *epibatai* and four archers, the additional troops on these ships were about fifty[41]. If we assume that there were no more than 14 soldiers on each of the 60 fast *triereis* which sailed from Corcyra on the Sicilian expedition, we shall see that the remaining seventy-seven transports could have taken seventy-two fighting men each.

In the naval lists from 377/6 to 370/69 *triereis* are listed as 'new' or 'old'[42]. There is unfortunately nothing to show when a *trieres* became old. A further division of *triereis* appears in Demosthenes and in the naval lists. Demosthenes, in putting forward his proposal for symmories (boards to finance trierarchies) in 354, speaks of three classes of *triereis*, first, second and third[43]. In the naval list for 357/6 there is a record of the number of ships in the port of Zea in that year, divided into four classes: 'first' sixteen ships, 'second' forty-six ships, 'third' eight ships, and 'select' entered according to their date of building (ten in the previous year)[44]. There is no indication of the qualification for any of these classes. It does however seem likely that the select class, being the newest, correspond to the earlier class of new ships, and that the remaining three are the older ships in various grades.

The final category of *triereis* in the Athenian navy were the horse transports (*hippagogoi*). Herodotus had mentioned horse-carrying *ploia* and *nees* in Darius' fleet, and later in Xerxes'. On one occasion they are called small[45]. Thucydides says that Pericles' expedition against the Peloponnese in 430 contained three hundred cavalry in horse transports, which then for the first time had been made out of old ships (i.e. *triereis*)[46], and it appears from the *Knights* of Aristophanes that cavalry were regularly transported by sea in the Peloponnesian war. The innovation in fact was not to transport horses in ships but to use ships of the rating of *triereis* to transport horses. We learn later that each *trieres* could carry thirty cavalry[47]. The naval lists tell us also that each such *trieres* was rowed by sixty oarsmen[48]. The cavalrymen and grooms were presumably carried too. That *triereis* continued to be used for this purpose is shown by a reference in Demosthenes to horse-transport *triereis*[49]. In the naval lists *hippagogos* is shortened to *hippegos*. There too they are *triereis*[50].

The *trieres* on which the fleet commander sails is called the *strategis*. We hardly need to be told by Lysias that commanders chose the fastest ships[51].

In the naval lists of 330/29 *tetrereis* appear for the first time. The lists are so fragmentary that it is not to be assumed that they were introduced into the Athenian navy in this year. In this list there are eighteen of them compared with 492 *triereis*. They appear in the lists after *triereis* but before triakontors[52]. It does not look as if they were regarded as a new type which would take the place of the *trieres* as a capital ship. In the fleet that Alexander assembled at Thapsacus in 324 the *pentereis* and *tetrereis* are placed above *triereis* in the list as drawn up by the fourth-century historian Aristobulus[53].

According to Pliny, Aristotle ascribed the invention of *tetrereis* to the Carthaginians[54]. Diodorus says that in 398 Dionysius of Syracuse began to build *tetrereis* and *pentereis*, being the first to have thought of the latter arrangement of oars[55]. Here and elsewhere it is clear that Diodorus is only ascribing the invention of *pentereis* to Dionysius. The latter was in constant contact with Carthaginian shipping, so that Aristotle's statement about the origin of the *tetreres* may well be true. Dionysius' alliance with Athens, after Leuctra in 371, would have resulted in naval contacts and may well be responsible for the somewhat cautious inclusion of these new types in the Athenian navy. In the list of 325/4 seven *pentereis* and forty-three *tetrereis* are recorded[56]. We shall consider in its place what the nature of the new types may have been.

TEXTS

1. Xen. *HG* v 1 21 καὶ καταδύειν μὲν οὐδὲν εἴα στρογγύλον πλοῖον οὐδὲ λυμαίνεσθαι ταῖς ἑαυτῶν ναυσίν· εἰ δέ που τριήρη ἴδοιεν ὁρμοῦσαν, ταύτην πειρᾶσθαι ἄπλουν ποιεῖν.

2. Thuc. vi 103[2] ἐκ δὲ τῆς Τυρσηνίας νῆες πεντηκόντεροι τρεῖς.

3. Aristotle IA 710a19; see note 9 below.

4. E.g. Aristophanes, *Knights* 1070–1

ἀλλὰ ναῦς ἑκάστοτε

αἰτεῖ ταχείας ἀργυρολόγους οὑτοσί.

In contrast to *ploia* = lesser oared ships Thuc. ii 83[5], vi 30[1], 44[1], vii 7[3].

5. The ship sent annually to Delos is called a *ploion* in Plato, *Phaedo* 58a7. We learn in Aristotle, *Ath. Pol.* 56 3, that the ship was a triakontor. For *ploia* in contrast to pentekontors see Thuc. I 14[1] τριήρεσι μὲν ὀλίγαις χρώμενα, πεντηκοντέροις δ' ἔτι καὶ πλοίοις μακροῖς ἐξηρτυμένα and VI 44[1], where the hundred *ploia* are contrasted with *triereis*, pentekontors and *holkades*.

In Xen. *HG* I 2 1 the phrase τὰ ψηφισθέντα πλοῖα refers to the *triereis* mentioned at I 1 34. However in *Anabasis* VI 6 5 we read δύο τριήρεις ἔχων, πλοῖον δ' οὐδέν.

6. Thuc. IV 118[5] μὴ μακρᾷ νηΐ, ἄλλῳ δὲ κωπήρει πλοίῳ.

7. Demosthenes 35 18–19 τὰ δὲ τρισχίλια κεράμια ἄγεσθαι ταῦτα εἰς τὸν Πόντον ἐν τῇ εἰκοσόρῳ ἣν Ὑβλήσιος ἐναυκλήρει... οὐδὲ πεντακόσια κεράμια εἰς τὸ πλοῖον ἐνέθεντο.

Cf. Nicostratus, 10 Edmonds.

8. [Xen.] *Ath. Pol.* I 19–20 πρὸς δὲ τούτοις διὰ τὴν κτῆσιν τὴν ἐν τοῖς ὑπερορίοις καὶ διὰ τὰς ἀρχὰς τὰς εἰς τὴν ὑπερορίαν λελήθασι μανθάνοντες ἐλαύνειν τῇ κώπῃ αὐτοί τε καὶ οἱ ἀκόλουθοι· ἀνάγκη γὰρ ἄνθρωπον πολλάκις πλέοντα κώπην λαβεῖν καὶ αὐτὸν καὶ τὸν οἰκέτην, καὶ ὀνόματα μαθεῖν τὰ ἐν τῇ ναυτικῇ. καὶ κυβερνῆται ἀγαθοὶ γίγνονται δι' ἐμπειρίαν τε τῶν πλόων καὶ διὰ μελέτην· ἐμελέτησαν δὲ οἱ μὲν πλοῖον κυβερνῶντες, οἱ δὲ ὁλκάδα, οἱ δὲ ἐντεῦθεν ἐπὶ τριήρεσι κατέστησαν· οἱ δὲ πολλοὶ ἐλαύνειν εὐθέως οἷοί τε εἰσβάντες εἰς ναῦς, ἅτε ἐν παντὶ τῷ βίῳ προμεμελετηκότες.

9. Aristotle, *IA* 710a15 βραδεῖα δ' ἡ πτῆσις τῶν ὀλοπτέρων ἐστὶ καὶ ἀσθενὴς διὰ τὸ μὴ κατὰ λόγον ἔχειν τὴν τῶν πτερῶν φύσιν πρὸς τὸ τοῦ σώματος βάρος, ἀλλὰ τὸ μὲν πολύ, τὰ δὲ μικρὰ καὶ ἀσθενῆ. ὥσπερ ἂν οὖν εἰ ὁλκαδικὸν πλοῖον ἐπιχειροίη κώπαις ποιεῖσθαι τὸν πλοῦν οὕτω ταῦτα τῇ πτήσει χρῆται.

10. Thuc. II 91[3] ἔτυχε δὲ ὁλκὰς ὁρμοῦσα μετέωρος.

Arrian, fr. 19 ap. Suidam *s.v.* ναῦς. (= Pa. 67 Roos) εἶχε δὲ ἡ ναῦς μῆκος μὲν κατὰ τριήρη μάλιστα, εὖρος δὲ καὶ βάθος καθ' ὁλκάδα.

11. Thuc. VI 44[1] τούτοις δὲ τὰ ἐπιτήδεια ἄγουσαι ὁλκάδες μὲν τριάκοντα σιταγωγοί... πλοῖα δ' ἑκατόν, ἃ ἐξ ἀνάγκης μετὰ τῶν ὁλκάδων ξυνέπλει.

12. Thuc. VII 50[1–2] ὁ δὲ Γύλιππος ἄλλην τε στρατιὰν πολλὴν ἔχων ἦλθεν ἀπὸ τῆς Σικελίας καὶ τοὺς ἐκ τῆς Πελοποννήσου τοῦ ἦρος ἐν ταῖς ὁλκάσιν ὁπλίτας ἀποσταλέντας, ἀφικομένους ἀπὸ τῆς Λιβύης ἐς Σελινοῦντα. ἀπενεχθέντες γὰρ ἐς Λιβύην καὶ δόντων Κυρηναίων τριήρεις δύο καὶ τοῦ πλοῦ ἡγεμόνας... ἀφίκοντο ἐς Σελινοῦντα.

13. Thuc. VII 23[2] καὶ ἐκ μὲν τοῦ πρώτου ἁλόντος χαλεπῶς οἱ ἄνθρωποι, ὅσοι καὶ ἐς τὰ πλοῖα καὶ ὁλκάδα τινὰ κατέφυγον, ἐξεκομίζοντο ἐς τὸ στρατόπεδον· τῶν γὰρ Συρακοσίων ταῖς ἐν τῷ μεγάλῳ λιμένι ναυσὶ κρατούντων τῇ ναυμαχίᾳ ὑπὸ τριήρους μιᾶς καὶ εὖ πλεούσης ἐπεδιώκοντο.

14. Demosthenes 50 22 καὶ πλοῖα ἑλκόντων ἐκ Θάσου ἐς Στρύμην, 32 ἑλκύσας τὰ πλοῖα εἰς Στρύμην.

15. Aristophanes, *Peace* 36–7

ὥσπερ οἱ τὰ σχοινία
τὰ παχέα συμβάλλοντες ἐς τὰς ὁλκάδας.

16. Thuc. I 29³ οἱ Κερκυραῖοι κήρυκά τε προύπεμψαν αὐτοῖς ἐν ἀκατίῳ ἀπεροῦντα μὴ πλεῖν ἐπὶ σφᾶς.

IV 67³ ἀκάτιον ἀμφηρικὸν ὡς λῃσταί. . .εἰώθεσαν ἐπὶ ἁμάξῃ. . .διὰ τῆς τάφρου κατακομίζειν τῆς νυκτὸς ἐπὶ τὴν θάλασσαν καὶ ἐκπλεῖν.

VII 25⁶ ἔκ τε τῶν ἀκάτων ὤνευον ἀναδούμενοι τοὺς σταυρούς.

59³ ἔκλῃον οὖν τόν τε λιμένα εὐθὺς τὸν μέγαν. . . τριήρεσι πλαγίαις καὶ πλοίοις καὶ ἀκάτοις ἐπ' ἀγκυρῶν ὁρμίζοντες.

IG 2² 1627 372 ἐπὶ τὰς ἀκάτους τὰ[ς δη]μοσίους πηδάλια.

Cf. 1628 531–2.

17. κέλης Thuc. IV 9¹ at Pylos Demosthenes gets arms for his oarsmen ἐκ λῃστρικῆς Μεσσηνίων τριακοντέρου καὶ κέλητος. . .οἳ ἔτυχον παραγενόμενοι.

120² ὁ Βρασίδας διέπλευσε νυκτὸς ἐς τὴν Σκιώνην, τριήρει μὲν φιλίᾳ προπλεούσῃ, αὐτὸς δὲ ἐν κελητίῳ ἄπωθεν ἐφεπόμενος, ὅπως εἰ μέν τινι τοῦ κέλητος μείζονι πλοίῳ περιτυγχάνοι, ἡ τριήρης ἀμύνοι αὐτῷ. . .

VIII 38¹ ἀποπλέων ἐν κέλητι ἀφανίζεται.

κελήτιον Thuc. IV 120² ἐν κελητίῳ.

Thuc. I 53¹ ἔδοξεν οὖν αὐτοῖς ἄνδρας ἐς κελήτιον ἐμβιβάσαντας ἄνευ κηρυκείου προσπέμψαι τοῖς Ἀθηναίοις.

Ephippus 18a, 19: 17–18 Edmonds (= 5K)

περιπλεῖν δ' ἐπὶ τοῖς ἄμβωσιν ἄνω
πέντε κέλητας πεντασκάλμους.

18. Aeschines I 191; Aristotle *Int.* 16a26 ἐπακτροκέλης.

Xen. *HG* I I 11 ἐνταῦθα δὲ καὶ Ἀλκιβιάδης ἧκεν ἐκ τῶν Κλαζομενῶν σὺν πέντε τριήρεσι καὶ ἐπακτρίδι.

19. Theophrastus, *Char.* XXV 2 ὁ δὲ δειλὸς ⟨τοιοῦτός⟩ τις οἷος πλέων τὰς ἄκρας φάσκειν ἡμιολίας εἶναι. Cf. Arrian, *Anab.* III 2 5.

20. *IG* I² 23

τῷ ἀγάγον]
τι τὴν τρια[κόντερον καὶ τεν]
πεντεκόντε[ρον καὶ τὰς τὸς στ]
ρατιότας ἀ[γόσας

21. Thuc. II 83⁵ καὶ οἱ μὲν Πελοποννήσιοι ἐτάξαντο κύκλον τῶν νεῶν ὡς μέγιστον οἷοί τ' ἦσαν μὴ διδόντες διέκπλουν, τὰς πρῴρας μὲν ἔξω, ἔσω δὲ τὰς πρύμνας, καὶ τά τε λεπτὰ πλοῖα ἃ ξυνέπλει ἐντὸς ποιοῦνται καὶ πέντε ναῦς τὰς ἄριστα πλεούσας, ὅπως ἐκπλέοιεν διὰ βραχέος παραγιγνόμεναι, εἴ πῃ προσπίπτοιεν οἱ ἐναντίοι.

22. Thuc. VI 43 καὶ δυοῖν Ῥοδίοιν πεντηκοντέροιν.

Thuc. VI 103². See note 2 above.

23. Xen. *Anab.* V I 15 and 16 ἔλαβον δὲ καὶ πεντηκόντερον παρὰ τῶν Τραπεζουντίων. . .ἔλαβον δὲ καὶ τριακόντερον.

24. Arrian, *Anabasis* VII 19 3 κατέλαβε δὲ ἐν Βαβυλῶνι, ὡς λέγει Ἀριστόβουλος, καὶ τὸ ναυτικόν, τὸ μὲν κατὰ τὸν Εὐφράτην ποταμὸν ἀναπεπλευκὸς ἀπὸ θαλάσσης τῆς Περσικῆς ὅτιπερ σὺν Νεάρχῳ ἦν· τὸ δὲ ἐκ Φοινίκης ἀνακεκομισμένον, πεντήρεις μὲν δύο

τῶν ἐκ Φοινίκων, τετρήρεις δὲ τρεῖς, τριήρεις δὲ δώδεκα, τριακοντόρους δὲ ἐς τριάκοντα· ταύτας ξυντμηθείσας κομισθῆναι ἐπὶ τὸν Εὐφράτην ποταμὸν ἐκ Φοινίκης ἐς Θάψακον πόλιν. ἐκεῖ δὲ ξυμπηχθείσας αὖθις καταπλεῦσαι ἐς Βαβυλῶνα.

25. Thuc. IV 9¹. See note 17 above.

26. Aristotle, *Ath. Pol.* 56 3 καθίστησι δὲ (sc. ὁ ἄρχων)...ἀρχ[ιθ]έω[ρον τ]ῷ τριακοντορίῳ τῷ τοὺς ἠθέους ἄγοντι.

27. *IG* 2² 1627 (330–29), 1628 (326–5), 1629 (325–4).

28. Plato, *Ep.* VII 350 B 1 οἱ δὲ πρόφασίν τινα πρεσβείας πορισάμενοι παρὰ τῆς πόλεως πέμπουσι τριακόντορόν τε καὶ Λαμίσκον αὐτῶν ἕνα ὃς ἐλθὼν ἐδεῖτο Διονυσίου περὶ ἐμοῦ.

29. Aristophanes, *Birds* 108

ποδαπὼ τὸ γένος; ὅθεν αἱ τριήρεις αἱ καλαί.

30. Thuc. VI 31³ τοῦ μὲν δημοσίου...ναῦς παρασχόντος κενὰς ἑξήκοντα μὲν ταχείας, τεσσαράκοντα δὲ ὁπλιταγώγους.

43¹ τούτων Ἀττικαὶ μὲν ἦσαν ἑκατόν, ὧν αἱ μὲν ἑξήκοντα ταχεῖαι, αἱ δὲ ἄλλαι στρατιώτιδες.

VII 4⁵ διακομίσας οὖν στρατιὰν καὶ τὰς ναῦς ἐξετείχισε τρία φρούρια. καὶ ἐν αὐτοῖς τά τε σκεύη τὰ πλεῖστα ἔκειτο καὶ τὰ πλοῖα ἤδη ἐκεῖ τὰ μεγάλα ὥρμει καὶ αἱ ταχεῖαι νῆες.

31. Aristophanes, *Knights* 1071. See note 4 above.

32. Demosthenes 4 22 εἶεν· τί πρὸς τούτοις ἔτι; ταχείας τριήρεις δέκα· δεῖ γάρ, ἔχοντος ἐκείνου ναυτικόν, καὶ ταχειῶν τριήρων ἡμῖν, ὅπως ἀσφαλῶς ἡ δύναμις πλέῃ.

Cf. 10 19.

33. Thucydides VIII 74¹⁻², the *Paralos* with Chaereas aboard is sent from Samos to Athens. καὶ καταπλευσάντων αὐτῶν εὐθέως τῶν μὲν Παράλων τινὰς οἱ τετρακόσιοι δύ᾿ ἢ τρεῖς ἔδησαν, τοὺς δὲ ἄλλους ἀφελόμενοι τὴν ναῦν καὶ μετεκβιβάσαντες ἐς ἄλλην στρατιῶτιν ναῦν ἔταξαν φρουρεῖν περὶ Εὔβοιαν. And see Aristophanes, *Birds* 1204.

34. *IG* 1² 22 τριη[ρὸν καὶ] τὸν στρατιωτίδ[ον

35. Thuc. I 116¹ τεσσαράκοντα δὲ ναυσὶ καὶ τέσσαρσι Περικλέους δεκάτου αὐτοῦ στρατηγοῦντος ἐναυμάχησαν πρὸς Τραγίᾳ τῇ νήσῳ Σαμίων ναυσὶν ἑβδομήκοντα, ὧν ἦσαν αἱ εἴκοσι στρατιώτιδες.

36. Thuc. VIII 62² Στρομβιχίδης δὲ ἐκ τῆς Χίου πυθόμενος κατὰ τάχος βοηθήσας ναυσὶν Ἀθηναίων τέσσαρσι καὶ εἴκοσι ὧν καὶ στρατιώτιδες ἦσαν ὁπλίτας ἄγουσαι.

37. Xen. *HG* I 1 36 δόξαντος δὲ τούτου, πληρωθεισῶν νεῶν ἔκ τε Μεγάρων καὶ παρὰ τῶν ἄλλων συμμάχων πεντεκαίδεκα στρατιωτίδων μᾶλλον ἢ ταχειῶν ᾤχετο.

38. Thuc. VI 25² τριήρεσι μὲν οὐκ ἔλασσον ἢ ἑκατὸν πλευστέα εἶναι (αὐτῶν δ᾿ Ἀθηναίων ἔσεσθαι ὁπλιταγωγοὺς ὅσαι ἂν δοκῶσι, καὶ ἄλλας ἐκ τῶν ξυμμάχων μεταπεμπτέας εἶναι). And see note 30 above.

39. Thuc. VIII 25¹ ἐκ δὲ τῶν Ἀθηνῶν τοῦ αὐτοῦ θέρους τελευτῶντος χίλιοι ὁπλῖται Ἀθηναίων καὶ πεντακόσιοι καὶ χίλιοι Ἀργείων...καὶ χίλιοι τῶν ξυμμάχων ναυσὶ δυοῖν δεούσαις πεντήκοντα, ὧν ἦσαν καὶ ὁπλιταγωγοί.

40. *IG* ɪ² 97 (*SEG* x 106, 119). See B. D. Meritt, *Studies presented to D. M. Robinson*, ɪɪ 298–303, 1953. Meritt gives good reasons for not identifying the expedition of the inscription with the Melian expedition of 416 B.C. as *GHI* 76. Instead he supposes that it is an expedition sent to collect tribute shortly after the beginning of the Peloponnesian war, *c.* 431 B.C. Meritt's restoration is as follows:

h[οἰ δὲ σ]τρ

[ατεγοὶ ἐθελοντὰς ἐπιβάτα]ς πεντέκοντα καὶ h[εκατ]ον κα

[τὰ τὸν νόμον καταλεχσάσ]θον κατὰ φυλὰς ἐχς Ἀθ[εν]αίον κα

[ὶ hος τάχιστα καθελκυσά]σθον τριάκοντα τρι[έ]ρες· στρατ

[ιὰν δὲ τὲν ὑπόλοιπον κατ]αστεσάσθον ἐκ τὸν ἐλεχότον τα

[ῖς τριέρεσιν· πλευσάντο]ν δὲ ἐν ταύταις ταῖ[ς] ναυσὶν Ἀθε

[ναίον ἄνδρες ἐν ἑκάστει] τῇ νεῒ πέντε μὲν [ἐ]χς ἐθελοντõ

[ν ἐπιβατõν, ἐπὶ τούτοις δ]ὲ ὁπλῖται τεττ[αρά]κοντα ἐν ἑκά

[στει τῇ νεῒ ἐχς ἴσο κατὰ] φυλάς, τοχ[σόται δὲ]κα πελταστ[α]

[ὶ δέκα ἔχς ἴσο ἔκαστοι Ἀθε]ναίον [καὶ τõν χσυ]μμάχον·

41. See below, pp. 263 ff.

42. *IG* 2² 1604, 1605, 1606, 1607, 1608.

43. Demosthenes 14 18 τὰς δὲ τριήρεις πῶς; τὸν ἄπαντ' ἀριθμὸν κελεύω τριακοσίας ἀποδείξαντας, κατὰ πεντεκαιδεκαναῖαν εἴκοσι ποιῆσαι μέρη, τῶν πρώτων ἑκατὸν πέντε, καὶ τῶν δευτέρων ἑκατὸν πέντε, καὶ τῶν τρίτων ἑκατὸν πένθ' ἑκάστῳ μέρει διδόντας...

44. *IG* 2² 1611 65–128

[τῶν πρώτων] εὐπρεπῆ Εὔχαριν Λαμπάδα κ.τ.λ.

  74   τῶν δευτέρων· Τροπαίαν Ἀποτομάδα Εὔνοιαν κ.τ.λ. (46)

  97   τῶν τρίτων· Κλεοστράτην Ἀξιονίκην κ.τ.λ. (6)

102   ἕτεραι δύο ὄ[ν]ο[μα οὐκ] ἔχ[ο]υ[σ]αι

106   τῶν ἐξ[αιρετῶν] τῶν ἐπὶ [Χ]αρ[ι]κλείδ[ου] ἄρχοντο[ς ποηθεισῶν]

          Ἑλλη[ν...] Ὑγίει[αν

          τῶν ἐ[πι ... κ.τ.λ.

121   τῶν ἐπὶ Κηφισοδότο[υ] Ψαμάθην Φῶς κ.τ.λ. (11)

          ἑτέρα τριήρης ᾗ ὄνομά ἐστιν Βοήθεια Ἀρχενίδου

          ἔργον· ταύτην ἡμίεργον παραλαβόντες ἐκ τῶν Τηλεγονείων

          [ναυπηγί]ων ἡμεῖς...

45. Herodotus vɪ 48² (Darius) ἱππαγωγὰ πλοῖα. The same at 95¹ ἱππαγωγοὶ νέες.

          vɪɪ 21² (Xerxes) ἱππαγωγὰ πλοῖα. 97 ἱππαγωγὰ πλοῖα σμικρά.

46. Thuc. ɪɪ 56² ἦγε δ' ἐπὶ τῶν νεῶν ὁπλίτας Ἀθηναίων τετρακισχιλίους καὶ ἱππέας τριακοσίους ἐν ναυσὶν ἱππαγωγοῖς πρῶτον τότε ἐκ τῶν παλαιῶν νεῶν ποιηθείσαις.

Cf. Aristophanes, *Knights* 595 ff. The chorus praise the horses.

ἀλλὰ τἀν τῇ γῇ μὲν αὐτῶν οὐκ ἄγαν θαυμάζομεν

ὡς ὅτ' ἐς τὰς ἱππαγωγοὺς εἰσεπήδων ἀνδρικῶς...

47. Thuc. vi 43 καὶ ἱππαγωγῷ μιᾷ τριάκοντα ἀγούσῃ ἱππέας.

48. *IG* 2² 1628 154 f. καὶ ἱππηγῶν τριῶν ταρρούς, κώπας ἑκάστης ⊦Δ (= 60).

49. Demosthenes 4 16: πρὸς δὲ τούτοις τοῖς ἡμίσεσι τῶν ἱππέων ἱππαγωγοὺς τριήρεις.

50. 1627 241 τριήρεις τάσδε ἱππηγοὺς εἰς πλοῦν δοθείσας.

51. Thuc. ii 84³ καὶ οἱ Ἀθηναῖοι προσπεσόντες πρῶτον μὲν καταδύουσι τῶν στρατηγίδων νεῶν μίαν.

Andocides 1 11 τριήρης ἡ στρατηγὶς ἡ Λαμάχου.

Lysias 21 6 τὸν δὲ χρόνον ὃν ἐτριηράρχουν, ἡ ναῦς ἄριστά μοι ἔπλει παντὸς τοῦ στρατοπέδου. τεκμήριον δὲ τούτου ὑμῖν μέγιστον ἐρῶ. πρῶτον μὲν γὰρ Ἀλκιβιάδης, ὃν ἐγὼ περὶ πολλοῦ ἂν ἐποιησάμην μὴ συμπλεῖν μοι, οὔτε φίλος ὢν οὔτε συγγενὴς οὔτε φυλέτης ἔπλει ἐπὶ τῆς ἐμῆς νεώς. καίτοι ὑμᾶς οἶμαι εἰδέναι ὅτι στρατηγὸς ὤν, ᾧ ἐξῆν ποιεῖν ὅ τι ἐβούλετο, οὐκ ἄν ποτε ἀνέβη ἐπ' ἄλλην ναῦν εἰ μὴ τὴν ἄριστα πλέουσαν, μέλλων αὐτὸς κινδυνεύσειν.

Cf. Demosthenes 47 78 and Herodotus viii 92².

52. *IG* 2² 1627. 22 τετρήρεις δ' ἐμ μὲν τοῖς νεωρίοις παρέδομεν ΓΙΙΙ· ἐμ πλῷ δὲ Δ.

53. See note 24 above.

54. Pliny, *N.H.* 7.207 = Rose 600. quadriremem Aristoteles auctor est fecisse Carthaginienses.

Clem. Alex. *Strom.* 1 p. 132 Sylb. Καρχηδόνιοι δὲ πρῶτοι τετρήρη κατεσκεύασαν ἐναυπήγησε δ' αὐτὴν Βόσπορος αὐτοσχέδιον.

55. Diodorus xiv 42 2 ἤρξατο δὲ (Διονύσιος) ναυπηγεῖσθαι τετρήρεις καὶ πεντηρικὰ σκάφη, πρῶτος ταύτην τὴν κατασκευὴν τῶν νεῶν ἐπινοήσας. (Cf. 41 3.) διενοεῖτο γὰρ κατασκευάσας ναῦς τετρήρεις καὶ πεντήρεις οὐδέπω κατ' ἐκείνους τοὺς χρόνους σκάφους πεντηρικοῦ νεναυπηγημένου. 44 7 ἀπέστειλεν πεντήρη, πρῶτον νεναυπηγημένην.

56. 1629.808 τετρήρεις δ' μὲν τοῖς νεωρίοις παρέδομεν ΔΔΔΔΙΙΙ καὶ πεντήρεις ΓΙΙ, τετρήρεις δ' ἐμ πλῷ ΓΙΙ.

SHIP'S COMPANY

We have seen that the Persian ships in Xerxes' fleet had, according to Herodotus, a complement of two hundred men with thirty extra *epibatai* on each ship[1]. The implication is that this total of two hundred normally included in addition to the oarsmen at least the *epibatai*, probably also all the rest of the crew. Another passage in Herodotus, relating that Cleinias joined the fleet at the Eurymedon with his own ship and two hundred men, suggests that this total of two hundred included the whole of the crew but did not include the trierarch[2]. In the decree of Themistocles there is assigned, to each ship, a trierarch, *huperesia*, ten *epibatai*, and four archers, as well as a company of seamen, i.e. oarsmen (see above, pp. 122–7). We should expect these to add up to two hundred. This remains the total complement throughout the Peloponnesian war. The Athenian ambassadors who went to Sicily in 416 brought back sixty talents (i.e. 60 × 6000 drachmae) as pay for sixty ships for a month[3]. This works out at a drachma a day if the crews are two hundred. A drachma a day was the pay for Athenian seamen at the beginning of the war[4]. When at the end of the war Thucydides speaks of Tissaphernes' payments to the Spartan fleet the same total of two hundred men is assumed for each ship. In Demosthenes too the crews are two hundred.[5]

That the *huperesia* was a special category of men distinct from the *epibatai*, archers and seamen is clear from Themistocles' decree. In the historian of the fourth century B.C. preserved in the Oxyrhyncus Papyrus *huperesiai* and *epibatai* are distinguished from seamen, and this is regularly the case in Demosthenes[6]. Lysias has the phrase 'the crew (*pleroma*) and the *huperesia* as well' which is repeated in a passage in Arrian derived from the fourth-century historian Aristobulus[7]. The Greek phrase 'the *huperesia* as well' could mean equally well 'the rest of the *huperesia*', but in that case the oarsmen would be included in the *huperesia* and this does not seem to have been the case. In the description of the preparations for the Sicilian expedition Thucydides notes that the trierarchs gave extra pay 'to the thranite class of seamen and to the *huperesiai*'[8]. There is a passage in Pericles' speech at the beginning of the Peloponnesian war in which, as reported by Thucydides, he assesses Athens' naval resources. He first refers to the seamen, then to the helmsmen, whom he claims are citizens, and lastly to the 'rest of the *huperesia*', whom he claims are more numerous and better than those of all the rest of Greece[9]. Here the same phrase which was translated in Lysias 'the *huperesia* as well' must be translated in the alternative way 'the rest of the *huperesia*' because the helmsman appears to be included in the *huperesia*. An almost exactly similar usage occurs in an inscription recording a decree about the Sicilian expedition[10]. Plato implies that it is incorrect to call a helmsman a seaman[11]. If he is not a seaman, there is no other category for him to belong to other than the *huperesia*. It is conceivable that like the trierarch he belongs to no category. The only support for such a solution is the passage in Aristotle where the bow officer is referred to as the *huperetes* of the helmsman. If all the *huperesia* were thought of as the *huperetai*, aides, of the helmsman, then the helmsman's position outside the categories is explained. But it is perhaps more likely that the helmsman and the rest were regarded as the aides of the trierarch.

The writer of the *Constitution of Athens* of 432 says: 'The people row the ships and give the city its power, the helmsmen too and *keleustai* and *pentekontarchoi* and bow officers and shipwrights—these are the people who make the city powerful, and not the hoplites. . .[12]' Plato says much the same thing in the *Laws* written about the middle of the fourth century: 'States which owe their power to a navy also bestow the reward for their security on an inferior element of their forces. As they owe their security to the arts of the helmsman, the *pentekontarchos* and the oarsmen, a mixed and not very reputable crowd, it would not be possible to give honours rightly to the various individuals[13].' In an inscription belonging to the beginning of the fourth century we have a number of lists, none perfectly preserved, of the crews of various *triereis*. They are headed by two trierarchs, since double trierarchies were now regular; then follow ten *epibatai*, a helmsman, a *keleustes*, a *pentekontarchos*, an *auletes*, a shipwright, a bow officer, and three (sometimes two) archers[14]. We can then list the following members of the *huperesia*: the six men, petty officers is perhaps the best term for them, who follow the *epibatai* in the inscription, and possibly the archers, who are two or three in the inscription but are four on other occasions. The archers are definitely distinguished from the *epibatai*, who are hoplites, and should then belong to the *huperesia*, since they are not listed separately on occasions when, as often in Demosthenes, the ship's company is referred to as *huperesia*, *epibatai* and *nautai*[15]. The *huperesia* seems then to have numbered about ten.

The number of oarsmen in a *trieres* is never given. The crew-lists in the inscriptions just mentioned are not complete enough for any deductions to be drawn. We do on the other hand have the number of oars in a *trieres* given several times in the inventories. It is clear that there were normally sixty-two thranite oars, and fifty-four oars each in the zygian and thalamian classes, besides thirty spare oars[16]. The significance of these classes will be discussed later. Here it is to be noted that the *tarros* or complement of oars in use in a *trieres* was a hundred and seventy. With ten *epibatai*, ten members of the *huperesia* and a hundred and seventy oarsmen we get a total ten short of the two hundred total. It will have been obvious that among the crew members we have mentioned there have been none who were what we should call deck hands, i.e. men to manage the sails and rigging when the ship was under sail. The oarsmen would of course have been free, but the management of sails calls for a specialist. There is one hint that the helmsman and bow officer had men at their bidding—Xenophon says in the *Anabasis*: 'Do you not notice how the bow officer is angry with those in the bow, and the helmsman is angry with those in the stern for a mere nod, when there is a storm and high sea? For in such a crisis even small mistakes are enough to cause complete disaster[17].' If there were ten deck hands, five forward and five aft, they would have fallen into the category of *nautai*, seamen, and would not therefore call for special mention. Alternatively the ten may have been spare oarsmen. It is interesting to remember that a pentekontor like a *trieres* carried thirty men in addition to the oarsmen. The Persian pentekontors in Xerxes' fleet carried crews of about eighty men (see above, p. 131).

In Themistocles' decree we saw that the Athenian *triereis* at Salamis were manned by citizens and resident aliens, and that the trierarchs had to have certain age and property qualifications. At the beginning of the Peloponnesian war Pericles claimed that the helmsmen in the Athenian fleet were all citizens (it went without saying that the trierarchs were), and that although there were foreign mercenary oarsmen serving, if they were lured away by higher pay, the Athenians could if need be man their fleet with citizens and resident aliens[18] (i.e. as they had done at Salamis) and as they were to do again in time of emergency[19]. As to the *huperesiai* the Greek text is rather ambiguous. He may be claiming that they were composed of citizens, or he may be merely saying that they were the best and most numerous in Greece. It seems likely that Athens attracted skilled seamen as resident aliens, since the author of the *Constitution of Athens* of 432 says that the city needs resident aliens 'because of the many crafts and because of the navy'[20]. Isocrates says that the earlier generation manned their *triereis* with the scum and riff-raff of Greece, and that the present generation support any Greek who will be prepared to row their ships[21]. The extent to which slaves were used in the Athenian fleet is not clear. Isocrates says in 355 B.C., possibly with more regard for his epigram than for historical truth, 'Then' (when we had an empire) 'if we manned *triereis* we sent foreigners and slaves aboard as seamen, but we sent our citizens out under arms (i.e. as *epibatai*). Now we use foreigners as hoplites, and compel our citizens to row[22].' Corcyraean *triereis* had slaves among their crews at the beginning of the war[23]. In Sicily Thucydides says that mercenaries in the Athenian fleet persuaded trierarchs to let them substitute slaves at their places at the oar[24]. At the end of the century slaves and freemen were employed side by side in Chian ships[25]. The first indication of regular practice of using slaves in the fleet at Athens is the entry of *therapontes* in the crew-lists at the beginning of the fourth century[26]. The word *therapontes* suggests body servants. We are reminded of the *huperetes* who accompanied each hoplite at Potidaea, and of the attendants (*akolouthoi*) of Athenian travellers who like them learned to row *en voyage* and thus made good oarsmen in the fleet, as the author of the *Constitution of Athens* of 432 tells us[27]. Perhaps Athenian citizens had their servants accompany them, or substitute for them at the oar. In 406, of course, when Conon's fleet was blockaded in Mytilene, the relieving fleet was manned by everyone available of military age, slave or free[28]. The circumstance was clearly unprecedented at this time, and the slaves were given their freedom after the fleet's victory at Arginusae. Some have thought that the crew-lists which mention *therapontes* were in fact casualty lists for that battle. The conclusion must be that although slaves were used at the oar outside Athens as early as the beginning of the Peloponnesian war, they were almost certainly not used in normal circumstances in Athenian ships in the fifth century.

We have seen that early in the war and in the Sicilian expedition the payment of a ship's company was at the rate of a drachma a day. For the Sicilian expedition the trierarchs gave additional payment to the thranite oarsmen and to the *huperesiai*[29]. Lysias says that for the whole period of his trierarchy, which was before 405, he employed the foremost Greek helmsman, Phantias, 'persuading him with money'[30]; and Demosthenes later says that he acquired the strongest *huperesia* he could get, offering much higher pay than anyone else[31]. The trierarchs clearly had to offer much more than the basic state pay to get good petty officers. They probably had to pay extra in the fourth century to get good oarsmen too. Apollodorus, in Demosthenes' speech *Against Polycles*, tells how he as a trierarch was provided with conscripted seamen, but they failed to turn up and he had to hire others on his own account[32].

The full pay was a drachma a day, but the whole of it does not seem always to have been paid at once. In the *Knights* of Aristophanes, Demos, the character representing the Athenian people, is asked how he will govern. First, he says, he intends to pay the disembarking seamen *in full*[33]. The implication is that seamen had a balance of pay due to them when they reached port, but did not always get it. Thucydides tells how Tissaphernes in 412/11 paid the Spartan fleet at the rate of a drachma a day for one month, but said that in future he could only give 3 obols (half a drachma) until the Persian king authorized the full drachma. He adds later that Alcibiades, by his advice to Tissaphernes, 'cut down the pay of the Spartan troops so that instead of an Attic drachma only three obols were given and that not regularly, and he urged Tissaphernes to tell them that the Athenians, who had had experience of naval matters for a longer time, gave only three obols to their men not so much through lack of money as with the intention of keeping their seamen from becoming well-off and insolent. Some were likely to injure their health by spending their money on things which made them ill, others would desert, because they had no balance of pay, as a kind of hostage, to wait for.' He explained that the men could have their pay in full later on[34]. This enlightening passage shows that the inference from the *Knights* was correct and that Athenian seamen only received three obols on service and were entitled to the balance of their pay when they reached their home port. A similar system, also designed to discourage desertion, was employed in the British Navy from the seventeenth to the nineteenth century. When Lysander was appointed to the command of the Spartan fleet in Asia Minor in 407, after asking Cyrus to pay the Spartan fleet at the rate of an Attic drachma a day he succeeded in persuading him to give four obols and a month's pay in advance[35]. These measures made it profitable for deserters to join the Spartan fleet. In Demosthenes there is a case where an Athenian trierarch, replacing deserters in Sestos, is obliged to hire local men 'at full pay'[36]. Naturally it would be no good to them to have half their pay waiting for them at Athens.

In addition to the *misthos* the ship's company also received rations. Hermocrates of Syracuse urged his countrymen to send out a fleet with two months' rations to intercept the Athenian expedition[37]. On service the generals issued ration money to the trierarchs at 10 dr. a month for each man[38].

We may perhaps conclude the general account of a ship's company by a paragraph of Xenophon: 'Why is a *trieres* packed with men terrible to an enemy but an inspiring sight to a friend, if not for its speed? Why do the men on board not get in each other's way? Is it not because they take seats in order, swing forward and backward in order, embark and disembark in order?[39]'

THE TRIERARCH

In Themistocles' decree before Salamis the Council of the Areopagus and the people instruct the generals to appoint two hundred trierarchs the following day and assign them to the ships that had been made ready. These arrangements suggest a quite different organization to that which was prevalent in the later fifth and fourth centuries. In the later period the trierarchs draw hull, gear (if they wish), and crew from the state, have full financial responsibility and are liable for loss or damage. It is their responsibility too to make the ships ready for sailing[40]. In the later fifth century the people appoint the trierarchs[41], but in the last half of the fourth century the appointment appears to have again been placed in the hands of the generals[42]. The fourth-century work *Oeconomica* includes the trierarchy with other liturgies which it attributes to the sixth century[43]. Such a trierarchy must have been held under conditions similar to those described in the decree of Themistocles, but since the word trierarchy implies *triereis* which are likely to have been very few in Athens in the sixth century the author of the *Oeconomica* is probably guilty of anachronism. Aristotle, in the *Constitution of Athens*, relates how a hundred of Themistocles' ships came to be built. In 483 'in the archonship of Nicodemus the mines of Maroneia were discovered and the state made a profit of a hundred talents from the working of them. Some people advised the city to make a distribution of the money among themselves, but this was prevented by Themistocles. He refused to say on what he proposed to spend the money, but he bade them lend it to the hundred richest men in the city, one talent to each, and then, if the manner in which it was employed pleased the people, the expenditure should be charged to the state, but otherwise the state should receive back the sum from those to whom it was lent. On these terms he received the money and with it he had a hundred *triereis* built, each of the individuals building one; and it was with these ships that they fought the battle of Salamis against the barbarians[44].' Thucydides says that the fortifications of Piraeus were begun 'during the office which Themistocles held year by year at Athens'[45]. Themistocles was a general at Salamis, and it is not improbable that the office which Thucydides mentions and which gave him the initiative in naval affairs in the years before Salamis was the office of general. In the fourth century we hear of two generals 'for Piraeus'[46]. As the generals appointed the trierarchs before Salamis, so also they had the responsibility for building the *triereis* and getting them ready for sea. When Herodotus says that at Artemisium an Athenian, Cleinias son of Alcibiades, distinguished himself 'campaigning with two hundred men and his own ship', this is clearly noteworthy as an exception.

The *Constitution of Athens* of 432 tells us that the popular Assembly appointed four hundred trierarchs each year[47]. A hundred of these were presumably for the hundred *triereis* held in reserve for use in an emergency, and the rest for the active fleet of three hundred with which Athens began the war[48]. The men appointed could appeal to the people to be relieved of the liturgy, and the people again adjudicated in cases where the trierarch had not returned his ship in good repair[49]. In the fragments of naval lists from about 430 we find opposite the name of each ship the words *dokima kai entele* which indicate that the ship's gear is recorded as complete and in good order[50]. Such a record implies the trierarch's responsibility to return the gear as well as the ship in such a state. These conclusions are confirmed by a passage in Aristophanes' *Knights*, produced in 424, in which Cleon threatens that he will make his rival a trierarch (presumably by proposing his name to the popular Assembly) and give him an old ship on which he will continually have to spend money on repairs. He will contrive too that he draws a rotten sail (which he would have to replace)[51]. The financial obligations of the trierarchs are indicated in Thucydides' description of the preparations for the Sicilian expedition. The fleet, he says, was equipped at great expense to the trierarchs and to the city, the city providing pay for the seamen, the empty ships, and the strongest possible contingents of petty officers for them, while the trierarchs gave additional pay to the thranite oarsmen and to the petty officers, and smartened up the ships regardless of expense[52].

Trierarchies at Athens began to be shared between two men at the end of the fifth century, probably in the period of financial stringency after the war. Lysias mentions such an arrangement in a speech which refers to a period before 400 and says that the cost to each man was four-fifths of a talent[53]. In the fourth century we hear of the two trierarchs making an agreement to divide their active duties, each going on board for six months[54]. Demosthenes' speech *Against Polycles*, which refers to the late sixties of the fourth century, shows how the burdens of the trierarchy were at this time becoming very heavy, chiefly owing to the scarcity of skilled oarsmen and their readiness to desert 'confident in their ability to row'. The speaker,

Apollodorus, describes the dispatch of an expedition to north-eastern Greece in 362: 'You Athenians voted that the trierarchs should launch their ships and bring them up to the jetty, that the Council and the demarchs should make out lists of the demesmen and of seamen, and that the expedition should be dispatched without delay.' The conscripted men, he says, turned out to be few and incompetent and he dismissed them. He borrowed money and was the first to man his ship, hiring the best seamen possible by giving each man 'large bonuses and advance payments'. He drew no gear from the public stores, and hired the strongest possible contingent of petty officers. When the expedition sailed he had to pay the petty officers and *epibatai* mostly out of his own pocket, since the generals only handed over three months' pay of the seventeen months' pay due, apart from the 'ration money' (p. 259). When the ship put back to Piraeus before the end of his period of office, he had to give the crew extra inducements to sail again. A number of his crew deserted and he had to hire replacements at 'full pay in Sestos'[55]. Shortly after this speech Periander introduced a measure to lighten the trierarchs' burdens. Demosthenes describes its effect in the speech *Against Meidias*: 'I was a trierarch in the old days as soon as I came of age, when we trierarchs were in pairs and all the expenses were from our private purses and we ourselves manned the ships. But this fellow had not yet performed a liturgy when he had reached the age I am now. He had his first experience of it when you appointed the twelve hundred "contributors", the city providing the gear and the crews[56].' We have seen in the case of Apollodorus that the city did previously in theory provide the gear and the crews, but in practice the trierarch provided both. Periander's law laid the responsibility of commissioning ships on twenty navy boards (*summoriai*) each composed of sixty of the twelve hundred 'contributors', the richest men in the city. It also apparently did its best to make a reality of the theory that the state provided the gear and crews, as well as the ship. A speech delivered shortly after this law speaks of the shortage of sailcloth, hemp, and ropes for the fitting out of *triereis*, and says that the trierarchs were compelled by the law of Periander to take over debtors of gear and make them repay the gear owing[57]. It seems that trierarchs who had drawn gear from the state for their ships found, under conditions of shortage, that it was worth more than the valuation, and therefore kept it after the end of their trierarchy. The law of Periander seems to have aimed at getting the gear back into use on the ships.

Periander's measure clearly did not effectively restore the naval position at Athens, since in 354, in face of a 'Persian threat', Demosthenes urged a reformed system of navy boards in his first speech to the Assembly. Its most important provisions were the arrangements for the distribution of gear and for the manning of the three hundred ships envisaged[58]. His speech was not successful, but in 340 a proposal of his was made law by which the number of those liable to trierarchic service was reduced to three hundred. Small groups of these men commissioned each ship, and one man would be involved in the commissioning of several. Only the chief trierarch was mentioned in the naval records. Later Demosthenes claimed that his law saved the Athenian navy, by placing the burden fairly on those who were able to bear it[59].

The history of the trierarchy in the fourth century is more the concern of the economic than the naval historian. The trierarch became the financial backer rather than the captain of his ship. Many trierarchs never set foot on their ships[60]. Yet where the trierarch was a keen sailor he could become a real commander, like Apollodorus or the speaker in Demosthenes' speech *On the trierarchic Crown*, who acquired a good crew, a strong contingent of petty officers and trained the ship until it ran like an efficient machine. The city rewarded the first three trierarchs to bring their ships to the jetty after the order 'launch ship', so that, to quote a fourth-century inscription, 'the trierarch's ambition to deserve well of the people may be recognized'[61]. In the fifth century the single trierarch must have become deeply involved in the fortunes of his ship: in the bustle of preparation for an expedition, which Aristophanes describes, the cry is 'Where's the trierarch[62]?' Aristotle in the *Ethics* speaks of 'those public benefactions which are favourite objects of ambition, for instance the duty of equipping a chorus splendidly, or being a trierarch or even of giving a banquet to the public[63]'. As a method of getting rich men to pay heavy taxes and to enjoy doing it, the trierarchic liturgy was successful. It could only have worked as a method of raising a fighting force in a city of gifted amateurs.

EPIBATAI AND ARCHERS

The *epibatai* on the ships at Salamis were ten in number, they ranked immediately after the trierarch, and were enrolled from the citizens who were between twenty and thirty years of age. It is these whom Themistocles assembled and addressed immediately before the battle[64]. In the crew-lists from the beginning of the fourth century the number and position immediately after the trierarchs are the same[65].

In 426 the Athenian general Demosthenes was operating in north-western Greece with a fleet of thirty ships. For an inland march against the Aetolians he made up a land force of three hundred hoplites and an unspecified number of archers. These are clearly the *epibatai* and archers from the thirty ships. The archers therefore are likely to have numbered between sixty and 120 depending on whether four archers were carried as at Salamis, or two or three as in the crew-lists. The expedition was a disaster. Thucydides puts the number of hoplite casualties at 120 and comments: 'So great a number of men and all of the same age perished here, the best men in truth whom the city of Athens lost in this war[66].' It looks as if here, as at Salamis, the *epibatai* were the youngest and best of her hoplites. The number of ten hoplites a ship is confirmed by Thucydides' account of the first big expedition of 100 ships sent round the Peloponnese by Athens at the beginning of the war, which carried a thousand hoplites, and by the Spartan expedition of a hundred ships against Zacynthus which also carried a thousand hoplites[67].

The ships discussed in the previous paragraph were all 'fast' *triereis*. The question of the *epibatai* of troop carriers is more difficult. In the first Sicilian expedition of a hundred ships, seven hundred of the lowest of the Athenian property classes, the *thetes*, are said to have served as *epibatai*. Sixty of these ships were 'fast' and forty troop carriers[68]. The seven hundred *thetes* would be too numerous for the ten *epibatai* each needed by the fast ships. There is a further piece of evidence bearing on the question. An inscription, which we have already noticed, recording an Athenian expedition in the early years of the Peloponnesian war, mentions thirty ships containing 'five of the volunteer [*epibatai*] in each' together with forty hoplites, ten archers and an unspecified number of peltasts[69]. Unfortunately the word *epibatai*, though highly probable, has to be supplied. Excluding the thirty cavalry which had its own horse transport, the total fighting force of the Sicilian expedition is given by Thucydides as six thousand four hundred men to be carried on a hundred and thirty-seven *triereis*, two Rhodian pentekontors and a horse transport. To the hundred and thirty-four *triereis* said to have sailed from Corcyra must be added the three which had gone on ahead. If we then suppose that the sixty fast Athenian *triereis* carried ten hoplite *epibatai* and four archers each, that the remaining seventy-seven *triereis* were all troop carriers, and that the two Rhodian pentekontors were also troop carriers, we may conjecture that the troop *triereis* carried seventy-one fighting men each, and the pentekontors forty-six or seven. This compares with the forty-four fighting men carried into battle by the Persian *triereis* at Salamis, and the thirty fighting men on the Persian pentekontors there; and with the seventy fighting men aboard the *triereis* in the early Peloponnesian war expedition, if we conjecture that the number of peltasts there was fifteen. We may perhaps conjecture that the seven hundred thetic *epibatai* were five to each of the hundred and seventy ships. There would then have been five hoplite *epibatai* from the Athenian 'list' and four archers on each of the sixty fast *triereis*. How the rest were carried is quite uncertain.

The dilution of hoplite *epibatai* with *thetes* in the Sicilian expedition is probably an indication of a deterioration in the high quality of these troops which we noticed at the beginning of the war. When therefore towards its end Thucydides mentions that the fleet of Leon and Diomedon carried *epibatai* compulsorily enrolled from the 'list', he may be indicating a return to *epibatai* of high quality[70]. Later we read in Xenophon that Thrasybulus made up a force of four hundred hoplites from the *epibatai* of his forty ships[71].

The hoplite rank of the *epibates* is responsible for his superior position in the ship, next in rank to the trierarch. Aristotle observes in the *Politics* that there is no need for common seamen to be citizens in a city. The *epibatai* are free citizens and belong to the foot-soldier class. They are masters and control the ship[72]. At the departure of the Sicilian expedition they join with the trierarchs in the pouring of libations[73]. Xenophon speaks of them as leading men, like the trierarchs and helmsmen[74].

In battle their position was on deck, and there was so little spare room inside a *trieres* that they seem to have ordinarily occupied that position when at sea. Dionysus, in Aristophanes' *Frogs*, recalls how he served as an *epibates* with Cleisthenes, and read the *Andromeda* of Euripides on deck[75]. Conon, blockaded in Mytilene in 406, prepared two ships for a break-out, to get the news of his predicament to Athens. Before the attempt he ordered the *epibatai* inside the ships, so that the enemy would not realize that they were ready for sea[76].

The term *epibates* is used in Thucydides and Xenophon in quite another sense than that which we have been discussing, viz. for a Spartan naval officer[77].

The archers are mentioned together with the *epibatai*, but are always distinct from them. In an inscription they are given the epithet *paredroi*, 'sitting beside'[78]. It seems possible that they were stationed in the stern beside the helmsman. We have seen how in Euripides they could cover a withdrawal from a hostile shore from that position. They may also have had the task of protecting the helmsman. On the other hand an Etruscan black-figure vase (Pl. 20b) shows two archers on the bow of a ship, and in the description of the pyre of Hephaestion which Diodorus derives from Ephippus archers are represented on the *epotides* of *pentereis* (see below, p. 285).

PETTY OFFICERS (HUPERESIA)

The inscription which gives lists of ships' companies puts the petty officers in the following order: helmsman, *keleustes*, *pentekontarchos*, *auletes*, shipwright, and bow officer[79]. It seems likely that the order reflects their position in the ship from aft forward. The *keleustes*, who receives the helmsman's orders, must be next to him. When Orpheus is represented in Euripides as the *auletes* of the Argonauts he stands amidships beside the mast[80]. The bow officer is of course right up forward.

Helmsman and bow officer apparently worked closely together. The latter is essentially the helmsman's assistant, as Xenophon, Aristotle and Plutarch all say[81]. Aristophanes in the *Knights* tells us that a bow officer was a promoted oarsman, and a helmsman a promoted bow officer[82]. We have already noticed the passage in Xenophon where, in heavy weather, the bow officer gets irritated with the deck hands in the bow, and the helmsman with the deck hands in the stern for the merest nod[83]. In Aristophanes the bow officer looks out for squalls. Their co-operation was particularly required when the ship was under sail. He can be seen in a number of ship representations of the archaic period (see Arch. 35, Pl. 11d; Arch. 51, Pl. 14a and b; and Arch. 57, Pl. 15).

The helmsman has complete responsibility, under the direction of the trierarch, for the navigation of the ship both under sail and under oar. On one occasion we hear of Alcibiades leaving his helmsman in command of a squadron[84]. When the Spartan ships are trying to effect an opposed landing at Pylos on a rocky beach, Thucydides says that Brasidas, the Spartan commander, saw that the trierarchs and the helmsmen were unwilling to risk their ships, but he compelled his helmsman to run his ship ashore[85]. The helmsman shares the poop with the trierarch[86]. He holds the tiller in his hands, and also manages the sails, often holding the sheet[87]. The steering oars and the sails are his particular care, and he is responsible for seeing that they are in good condition[88]. Plato calls the helmsman 'the commander of the seamen', again he says that the art of helmsmanship is to give orders to the *keleustai* who are concerned with the oarsmen[89].

When the ship was under oars, then, the helmsman worked closely with the *keleustes* who transmitted his orders to the oarsmen. The latter also no doubt acted as their foreman during the operations of preparing a ship for sea[90]. We have seen in Euripides' *Helen* how the *keleustes'* shout was the signal to give way[91]. So, when in Aristophanes' *Frogs* Dionysus sits to the oar in Charon's boat, he says to Charon *katakeleue de* 'be *keleustes* then' and Charon proceeds *O opop, O opop*, thus setting the stroke. When they arrive Charon's orders are 'Way enough, oars alongside'[92]. When Xenophon describes a stealthy night pursuit by a *trieres*, he mentions that the *keleustes'* voice was replaced by the chink of stones, and that the oarsmen used a sliding stroke to muffle the sound[93]. In the *Oeconomicus* he gives a vivid description of the difference between a good and bad *keleustes*. 'For example, on a *trieres* when the ship is at sea and the oarsmen have to make a day's voyage under oar, some *keleustai* can say and do the sort of thing to stimulate the men to toil with a good heart, but some are so tactless that it takes them more than twice the time to complete the same voyage. In the first case *keleustes* and seamen come ashore sweating and congratulating each other, in the other they arrive cold hating their foreman and hated by him[94].' The whole of the *keleustes'* task, which is the same as that of the Roman *pausarius*, is summed up neatly by Ovid in the *Metamorphoses*:

> qui requiemque modumque
> voce dabat remis animorum hortator Epopeus[95].

In battle, where change of course, stopping and backing were frequent, the *keleustes* had a big part to play: and often the noise was such that he could not be heard[96]. On one occasion Diodorus says that a *keleustes* chanted the prayer before battle[97]. He is to be seen on at least two archaic representations (Arch. 35, Pl. 11*d*; Arch. 50, Pl. 12*f*).

The *auletes* would seem to some extent to have assisted the *keleustes*. He is not included in the list of petty officers in the *Constitution of Athens* and does not appear in our historical sources, although the *trieraules* in Demosthenes, Philodemus and Pollux is no doubt the same officer[98]. We have noticed references to him in tragedy[99]. On a long spell of rowing the *auletes* would no doubt take over from the *keleustes* the task of keeping the stroke steady. His music may also have lightened the oarsmen's work.

The *pentekontarchos* was clearly an important officer. In Plato his post is mentioned with helmsmanship and rowing as one which 'saves the city'[100]. In Demosthenes' speech *Against Polycles* Apollodorus relates that when some of his crew deserted he sent his *pentekontarchos* to Lampsacus to enrol the best crew he could get. He fell ill and had to be sent home. Apollodorus appointed another *pentekontarchos* who succeeded in filling the vacancies[101]. The name gives no clue whatever to his duties. 'Captain of fifty' is completely obscure for a single officer on a *trieres*. The only guess which seems at all plausible is that the commander of a pentekontor had this name, and that it was continued in the *trieres* to denote the trierarch's assistant officer. The shipwright, *naupegos*, is the remaining petty officer. He was clearly a necessary person on a wooden ship rowed by a hundred and seventy oarsmen. The oarsmen's seats, tholepins, the *parexeiresia*, and the whole internal structure would have been under constant working strain. The *naupegos* is not mentioned in our literary sources as the shipwright of a particular ship, but since *naupegoi* appear both in the list of petty officers in the *Constitution of Athens* and in the crew-lists there is no doubt that they belonged to the normal contingent of petty officers.

OARSMEN (NAUTAI)

The vase-paintings of ships of one and two levels of oarsmen show with sufficient clarity that in those ships one man rowed one oar. The Lenormant relief (before 401 B.C.) which we argue is a representation of a *trieres* shows a succession of oarsmen each rowing his own oar (see pp. 170–3). The other representations which we claim are of *triereis* do not show men at the oar. A passage in Thucydides describes a raid on the Attic coast by a Peloponnesian fleet in the winter of 429. 'It was determined that each seaman, taking his oar and *huperesion* and *tropoter*, should go on foot from Corinth to the sea on the Athenian side of the isthmus, and go aboard forty ships which happened to be at Nisaea[102].' It seems certain then that in the *trieres*, as in the earlier types, one man rowed one oar.

Besides his oar, each seaman, in the passage of Thucydides quoted above, took his *huperesion* and his *tropoter*. Isocrates in 355 B.C. complains that 'we compel our citizens to row our ships with the result that when they land in hostile territory these men, who claim the right to rule over the Hellenes, disembark with their *huperesion*, while men who are of the character I have just described take the field with shield and spear[103]'. The clue to the nature of the *huperesion*, which we should expect from Isocrates' remark to be a rather undignified object, is provided by a fragment of fifth-century comedy. Hermippus speaks of an oarsman going aboard with his *kopeter* and his *proskephalaion*[104]. The latter is certainly a cushion, and although by derivation it means a pillow, i.e. a head cushion, it is also used for a cushion to sit on, as for example in Theophrastus for cushions to sit on in the theatre[105]. There seems then no doubt that the oarsman's *huperesion*, which by derivation means a support, was a pad to save him from the consequences of rowing suffered by Dionysus in the *Frogs*[106]. The *tropoter* is the equivalent of the Homeric *tropos*, a leather loop to hold the oar to the tholepin, and *kopeter* in Hermippus looks like an alternative name for the same thing.

The oarsmen were divided into classes, of which the most important appears to have been the *thranitai*. Aristophanes speaks of 'the thranite crowd which saves the city[107]'; and in the Sicilian expedition the trierarchs gave additional pay to the thranite oarsmen as well as to the petty officers. The other class mentioned in Thucydides is the *thalamioi*. When the Athenians made their final attack on the Spartan force on Sphacteria they employed as soldiers the crews of the seventy ships with the exception of the *thalamioi*[108]. The reason may be either that they needed to keep some oarpower in the ships or that the *thalamioi* either had no arms or were disqualified from having them because they were slaves. The first of these three possibilities seems most likely, the last very unlikely. Aristophanes refers to the thalamian oarsman under the comic diminutive form *thalamax* in the *Frogs*. Aeschylus in Hades says that when he was alive the oarsmen in the state *trieres*, *Paralos*, only knew how to call for rations and shout *ruppapai*. 'Yes,' says Dionysus, 'and make wind into the face of the *thalamax*[109].' We must draw the inference that the thalamian oarsmen sat below and behind members of one of the other two classes.

There are also three passages where *thalamia* appears to mean an oarport, presumably therefore an oarport for the oar of the thalamian oarsman. We have already noticed the passage in Herodotus where the Ionian trierarch Skylax is tied up through the *thalamia* with his head outside and his body inside the ship[110]. In Aristophanes' *Peace* Trygaeus sits on a breastplate, which presumably stands upright with the neck opening uppermost, and says that he will use it as a commode. 'But however will you wipe yourself?' the breastplate merchant asks. 'Putting my hand through the *thalamia* on this side and on that (i.e. through the arm-holes)' answers Trygaeus. The merchant is surprised: 'With both hands at once then?' 'Yes of course' says Trygaeus, still thinking of the oarports, 'so that I shan't be caught concealing the ship's hole[111].' The editors explain this last sentence as referring to the practice of fraudulent trierarchs who drew pay from the state for unmanned oars[112]. Trygaeus puts his hand through each *thalamia* to show that each oar is manned. In the description of the preparations for an expedition in the *Acharnians* one of the operations which cause the din is the cutting of *thalamiai*, i.e. oarports[113]. These passages seem to show pretty conclusively that there were oarports for the thalamian oarsmen, and that originally, at any rate, these were oarports for these oarsmen alone. It would appear then that they sat lowest in the ship. The fragment Clas. 3 (Pl. 26*b*) which is dated in the middle of the fifth century and the Talos vase which is dated at the end of the century show oarports at two levels. In the two-level ship the lower oarsmen rowed their oars through oarports, the upper over the gunwale. We shall argue that in the *trieres* a third class of oarsmen was added to the two-level ship, and that they rowed their oars through an outrigger sitting outside and slightly higher than the upper level of oarsmen of the original two-level ship. If this account is correct the oarsmen representing the upper level of the original two-level ship would continue at first to row their oars over the gunwale. At the same time it would have made a drier ship if the gunwale had been built up and these oarsmen, like the *thalamioi*, had rowed their oars through ports. In spite of this development, the oarport *par excellence* in Herodotus and Aristophanes was that of the thalamian oarsmen.

In the naval lists four categories of oars are repeatedly given and the correct number of oars in each category is clear: thranite 62, zygian 54, thalamian 54, and *perineo* 30[114]. If, as we shall argue below, the *perineo* are spare oars, we can infer that the thranite class of oarsmen numbered sixty-two, and the zygian and thalamian fifty-four each. Whether there were spare oarsmen or not is uncertain. The ten men needed to make the total of 170 oarsmen, 10 *epibatai*, four archers and six petty officers up to two hundred, even if as we have conjectured they were deck hands, could have taken an oar if necessary. It seems reasonable to infer from the thranites' honourable reputation that they occupied the uppermost and outermost position which must certainly have been the least disagreeable. The *zygioi* then will occupy the position corresponding to the upper level of oarsmen in the two-level ship. The *thalamioi* as we have said occupy the position corresponding to the lower level in the two-level ship.

TEXTS

General

1. Herodotus VII 184[1-2]. See above, p. 131.

2. Herodotus VIII 17.

3. Thuc. VI 8[1] οἱ τῶν Ἀθηναίων πρέσβεις ἧκον ἐκ τῆς Σικελίας καὶ οἱ Ἐγεσταῖοι μετ' αὐτῶν ἄγοντες ἑξήκοντα τάλαντα ἀσήμου ἀργυρίου ὡς ἐς ἑξήκοντα ναῦς μηνὸς μισθόν, ἃς ἔμελλον δεήσεσθαι πέμπειν.

Pay for a ship of 200 men at 1 drachma a day for a month (30 days) is 6000 drachmae = 1 talent. Pay for sixty ships would be sixty talents.

4. Thuc. III 17[4] τήν τε γὰρ Ποτίδαιαν δίδραχμοι ὁπλῖται ἐφρούρουν (αὐτῷ γὰρ καὶ ὑπηρέτῃ δραχμὴν ἐλάμβανε τῆς ἡμέρας)...νῆές τε αἱ πᾶσαι τὸν αὐτὸν μισθὸν ἔφερον. VI 31[3] τοῦ μὲν δημοσίου δραχμὴν τῆς ἡμέρας τῷ ναύτῃ ἑκάστῳ διδόντος.

5. Thuc. VIII 29[1] μηνὸς μὲν τροφήν, ὥσπερ ὑπέστη ἐν τῇ Λακεδαίμονι. ἐς δραχμὴν Ἀττικὴν ἑκάστῳ πάσαις ταῖς ναυσὶ διέδωκε, τοῦ δὲ λοιποῦ χρόνου ἐβούλετο τριώβολον διδόναι...ὅμως δὲ παρὰ πέντε ναῦς πλέον ἀνδρὶ ἑκάστῳ ἢ τρεῖς ὀβολοὶ ὡμολογήθησαν. ἐς γὰρ πέντε ναῦς καὶ πεντήκοντα τριάκοντα τάλαντα ἐδίδου τοῦ μηνός.

I.e. he gave the pay for sixty ships at ½ dr. for 200 men for thirty days = thirty talents (180,000 dr.). Cf. Dem. 4 28.

6. *Hell. Ox.* 15[1] ὡς αὐτοῖς μὲν οὐ μέλλουσιν ἀποδιδόναι τὸν μισθὸν τὸν ὀφειλό-μενον, παρασκευάζονται δὲ διαλύσεις μόνον ταῖς ὑπηρεσίαις καὶ τοῖς ἐπιβάταις.

Demosthenes 50 7, 10, 24, 32, 36 (*bis*).

7. Lysias 21.10 παρεσκευασάμην δὲ καὶ τὸ πλήρωμα πρὸς ἐκεῖνον καὶ τὴν ἄλλην ὑπηρεσίαν ἀκόλουθον.

Arrian, *Anabasis* 19 4 πληρώματα δ' ἐς τὰς ναῦς καὶ τὰς ἄλλας ὑπηρεσίας.

8. Thuc. VI 31[3] τῶν δὲ τριηράρχων ἐπιφοράς τε πρὸς τῷ ἐκ δημοσίου μισθῷ διδόντων τοῖς θρανίταις τῶν ναυτῶν καὶ ταῖς ὑπηρεσίαις καὶ τἆλλα σημείοις καὶ κατα-σκευαῖς πολυτελέσι χρησαμένων.

9. Thuc. I 143[1] εἴ τε καὶ κινήσαντες τῶν Ὀλυμπίασιν ἢ Δελφοῖς χρημάτων μισθῷ μείζονι πειρῶντο ἡμῶν ὑπολαβεῖν τοὺς ξένους τῶν ναυτῶν, μὴ ὄντων μὲν ἡμῶν ἀντιπάλων ἐσβάντων αὐτῶν τε καὶ τῶν μετοίκων, δεινὸν ἂν ἦν· νῦν δὲ τόδε τε καὶ ὑπάρχει καί, ὅπερ κράτιστον, κυβερνήτας ἔχομεν πολίτας καὶ τὴν ἄλλην ὑπηρεσίαν πλείους καὶ ἀμείνους ἢ ἅπασα ἡ ἄλλη Ἑλλάς.

271

10. *IG* i² 98–99 = *SEG* x 107: Decrees of 416–415 B.C. about the Sicilian expedition. *GHI* 77.

20 ff. τὲν ἐ]
κκλεσίαν ποιόντον hόταν κε[ναὶ ὄσι αἱ νε͂ες ναυτῶν καὶ κυβερνετ]ο͂ν καὶ τε͂ς ἄλλες hυπερεσίας.

11. Plato, *Republic* 341c Τί δὲ κυβερνήτης; ὁ ὀρθῶς κυβερνήτης ναυτῶν ἄρχων ἐστὶν ἢ ναύτης; Ναυτῶν ἄρχων.

12. [Xen.] *Ath. Pol.* 1 2 ὁ δῆμός ἐστιν ὁ ἐλαύνων τὰς ναῦς καὶ ὁ τὴν δύναμιν περιτιθεὶς τῇ πόλει, καὶ οἱ κυβερνῆται καὶ οἱ κελευσταὶ καὶ οἱ πεντηκόνταρχοι καὶ οἱ πρῳρᾶται καὶ οἱ ναυπηγοί, οὗτοί εἰσιν οἱ τὴν δύναμιν περιτιθέντες τῇ πόλει πολὺ μᾶλλον ἢ οἱ ὁπλῖται καὶ οἱ γενναῖοι καὶ οἱ χρηστοί.

13. Plato, *Laws* iv 707a–b αἱ διὰ τὰ ναυτικὰ πόλεων δυνάμεις ἅμα σωτηρίας τιμὰς οὐ τῷ καλλίστῳ τῶν πολεμικῶν ἀποδιδόασι. διὰ κυβερνητικῆς γὰρ καὶ πεντηκοντ-αρχίας καὶ ἐρετικῆς καὶ παντοδαπῶν καὶ οὐ πάνυ σπουδαίων ἀνθρώπων γιγνομένης τὰς τιμὰς ἑκάστοις οὐκ ἂν δύναιτο ὀρθῶς ἀποδιδόναι τις.

14. *IG* 2² 1951.

15. See note 6 above.

16. *IG*² 1615–1618. *Thranite*; in the nine cases where the total is given, eight give sixty-two, one sixty-four. *Zygian*; in the twelve cases where the total is given, eleven give fifty-four, one fifty-two. *Thalamian*; in the thirteen cases where the total is given, twelve give fifty-four, one fifty-three. *Perineo*; in the sixteen cases where the total is given, all give thirty. It seems plain that in two of the three cases of deviation from the norm fifty-two and sixty-four is a simple error for fifty-four and sixty-two.

17. Xen. *Anabasis* v 8 20 ὅταν δὲ χειμὼν ᾖ καὶ θάλαττα μεγάλη ἐπιφέρηται, οὐχ ὁρᾶτε ὅτι καὶ νεύματος μόνον ἕνεκα χαλεπαίνει μὲν πρῳρεὺς τοῖς ἐν πρῴρᾳ, χαλεπαίνει δὲ κυβερνήτης τοῖς ἐν πρύμνῃ; ἱκανὰ γὰρ ἐν τῷ τοιούτῳ καὶ μικρὰ ἁμαρτηθέντα πάντα συνεπιτρῖψαι.

18. See note 9 above. Cf. Aristophanes, *Wasps* 1094 ff. Athenian oarsmanship.

19. E.g. when Lesbos revolted in 428 B.C. the Athenians manned a hundred ships (Thuc. iii 16¹): ἐσβάντες αὐτοί τε πλὴν ἱππέων καὶ πεντηκοσιομεδίμνων καὶ οἱ μέτοικοι.

20. [Xen.] *Ath. Pol.* 1 12 δεῖται ἡ πόλις μετοίκων διά τε τὸ πλῆθος τῶν τεχνῶν καὶ διὰ τὸ ναυτικόν· διὰ τοῦτο οὖν καὶ τοῖς μετοίκοις εἰκότως τὴν ἰσηγορίαν ἐποιήσαμεν.

21. Isocrates 8 79 τίς γὰρ ἂν ὑπέμεινε τὴν ἀσέλγειαν τῶν πατέρων τῶν ἡμετέρων, οἳ συναγαγόντες ἐξ ἁπάσης τῆς Ἑλλάδος τοὺς ἀργοτάτους καὶ τοὺς ἁπασῶν τῶν πονη-ριῶν μετέχοντας πληροῦντες τούτων τὰς τριήρεις ἀπηχθάνοντο τοῖς Ἕλλησι;

22. Isocrates 8 48 καὶ τότε μὲν εἰ τριήρεις πληροῖεν τοὺς μὲν ξένους καὶ τοὺς δούλους ναύτας εἰσεβίβαζον, τοὺς δὲ πολίτας μεθ' ὅπλων ἐξέπεμπον· νῦν δὲ τοῖς μὲν ξένοις ὁπλίταις χρώμεθα, τοὺς δὲ πολίτας ἐλαύνειν ἀναγκάζομεν.

23. Thuc. i 55¹. After the sea battle between the Corinthians and Corcyraeans: καὶ τῶν Κερκυραίων ὀκτακοσίους μὲν οἳ ἦσαν δοῦλοι ἀπέδοντο.

24. Thuc. VII 13² εἰσὶ δ' οἳ καὶ...ἀνδράποδα Ὑκκαρικὰ ἀντεμβιβάσαι ὑπὲρ σφῶν πείσαντες τοὺς τριηράρχους τὴν ἀκρίβειαν τοῦ ναυτικοῦ ἀφῄρηνται.

25. Thuc. VIII 15² τάς τε τῶν Χίων ἑπτὰ ναῦς...ἀπαγάγοντες τοὺς μὲν δούλους ἐξ αὐτῶν ἠλευθέρωσαν, τοὺς δ' ἐλευθέρους κατέδησαν.

26. *IG* 2² 1951 117. See Thuc. VII 13² ὑπηρέτης; Thuc. III 17⁴.

27. [Xen.] *Ath. Pol.* II 19.

28. Xen. *HG* I 6 24 εἰσβιβάζοντες τοὺς ἐν τῇ ἡλικίᾳ ὄντας ἅπαντας καὶ δούλους καὶ ἐλευθέρους.

Aristophanes, *Frogs* 190: *Charon* δοῦλον οὐκ ἄγω/εἰ μὴ νεναυμάχηκε τὴν περὶ τῶν κρεῶν.

29. See note 8 above.

30. Lysias 21 10 εἶχον γὰρ χρήμασι πείσας κυβερνήτην Φαντίαν ἅπαντα τὸν χρόνον.

31. Demosthenes 51 6 ἔτι τοίνυν ὑπηρεσίαν τὴν κρατίστην ἔλαβον, πολλῷ πλεῖστον ἀργύριον δούς.

32. Demosthenes 50 7 ἐγὼ δ' ἐπειδή μοι οὐκ ἦλθον οἱ ναῦται οἱ καταλεγέντες ὑπὸ τῶν δημοτῶν, ἀλλ' ἢ ὀλίγοι καὶ οὗτοι ἀδύνατοι, τούτους μὲν ἀφῆκα ὑποθεὶς δὲ τὴν οὐσίαν τὴν ἐμαυτοῦ καὶ δανεισάμενος ἀργύριον πρῶτος ἐπληρωσάμην τὴν ναῦν, μισθωσάμενος ναύτας ὡς οἷόν τ' ἦν ἀρίστους.

33. Aristophanes, *Knights* 1366–7
πρῶτον μὲν ὁπόσοι ναῦς ἐλαύνουσιν μακράς,
καταγομένοις τὸν μισθὸν ἀποδώσω 'ντελῆ.

34. Thuc. VIII 29¹. See note 5 above.

id. ib. 45² καὶ διδάσκαλος πάντων γιγνόμενος τήν τε μισθοφορὰν ξυνέτεμεν, ἀντὶ δραχμῆς Ἀττικῆς ὥστε τριώβολον, καὶ τοῦτο μὴ ξυνεχῶς, δίδοσθαι, λέγειν κελεύων τὸν Τισσαφέρνην πρὸς αὐτοὺς ὡς Ἀθηναῖοι ἐκ πλείονος χρόνου ἐπιστήμονες ὄντες τοῦ ναυτικοῦ τριώβολον τοῖς ἑαυτῶν διδόασιν, οὐ τοσοῦτον πενίᾳ ὅσον ἵνα αὐτῶν μὴ οἱ ναῦται ἐκ περιουσίας ὑβρίζοντες, οἱ μὲν τὰ σώματα χείρω ἔχωσι δαπανῶντες ἐς τοιαῦτα ἀφ' ὧν ἡ ἀσθένεια ξυμβαίνει, οἱ δὲ τὰς ναῦς ἀπολείπωσιν οὐχ ὑπομένοντες* ἐς ὁμηρείαν τὸν προσοφειλόμενον μισθόν.

35. Xen. *HG* I 5 4–7. See above, p. 231.

36. Demosthenes 50 18.

37. Thuc. VI 34⁴ καθελκύσαντες ἅπαν τὸ ὑπάρχον ναυτικὸν μετὰ δυοῖν μηνοῖν τροφῆς ἀπαντῆσαι Ἀθηναίοις ἐς Τάραντα καὶ ἄκραν Ἰαπυγίαν.

38. Demosthenes 50 10 παρὰ τῶν στρατηγῶν σιτηρέσιον μόνον λαμβάνων. 4 28.

39. Xen. *Oecon.* 8 8 καὶ τριήρης δέ τοι ἡ σεσαγμένη ἀνθρώπων διὰ τί ἄλλο φοβερόν ἐστι πολεμίοις ἢ φίλοις ἀξιοθέατον ἢ ὅτι ταχὺ πλεῖ; διὰ τί δὲ ἄλλο ἄλυποι ἀλλήλοις εἰσὶν οἱ ἐμπλέοντες ἢ διότι ἐν τάξει μὲν κάθηνται, ἐν τάξει δὲ προνεύουσιν, ἐν τάξει δ' ἀναπίπτουσιν, ἐν τάξει δ' ἐμβαίνουσι καὶ ἐκβαίνουσιν;

---

* B reads ὑπολιπόντες, the rest of the MSS ἀπολιπόντες. Neither reading makes satisfactory sense. It seems reasonable to suppose that ὑπομένοντες was corrupted by the proximity of ἀπολείπωσιν.

The Trierarch

40. The state provided the empty hull (Thuc. vi 31³) and the trierarch was responsible for returning it in good condition ([Xen.] *Ath. Pol.* iii 4). The trierarch did not always draw gear (Dem. 51 5 τὰ σκεύη τοίνυν, ὅσα δεῖ παρέχειν τὴν πόλιν τοῖς τριηράρχοις, ἐγὼ μὲν ἐκ τῶν ἰδίων ἀνήλωσα καὶ τῶν δημοσίων ἔλαβον οὐδέν), but if he did he was responsible for returning it in good condition (Aristophanes, *Knights* 912–918: see note 51 below). Crew were allocated to ships 'from the register' but did not always turn up or, if they did, pass muster (Demosthenes 50 7).

41. [Xen.] *Ath. Pol.* iii 4 καὶ τριήραρχοι καθίστανται τετρακόσιοι ἑκάστου ἐνιαυτοῦ.

42. Aristotle, *Ath. Pol.* 61 1, the people appoint the ten generals by open vote and assign them to different duties: ἕνα δ' ἐπὶ τὰς συμ[μο]ρίας, ὃς τούς τε τριηράρχους καταλέγει.

Cf. Demosthenes 39 8 and 35 48 (οἱ στρατηγοὶ) τριηράρχους καθιστᾶσιν.

43. Aristotle, *Oeconomica* ii 2 4 1347a11, Hippias allowed people to commute for liturgies.

44. Aristotle, *Ath. Pol.* 22 7 ἔτει δὲ τρίτῳ μετὰ ταῦτα (484/3) Νικοδήμου ἄρχοντος, ὡς ἐφάνη τὰ μέταλλα τὰ ἐν Μαρωνείᾳ καὶ περιεγένετο τῇ πόλει τάλαντα ἑκατὸν ἐκ τῶν ἔργων, συμβουλευόντων τινῶν τῷ δήμῳ διανείμασθαι τὸ ἀργύριον, Θεμιστοκλῆς ἐκώλυσεν, οὐ λέγων ὅ τι χρήσεται τοῖς χρήμασιν ἀλλὰ δανεῖσαι κελεύων τοῖς πλουσιωτάτοις Ἀθηναίων ἑκατὸν ἑκάστῳ τάλαντον, εἶτ' ἐὰν μὲν ἀρέσκῃ τὸ ἀνάλωμα, τῆς πόλεως εἶναι τὴν δαπάνην, εἰ δὲ μή, κομίσασθαι τὰ χρήματα παρὰ τῶν δανεισαμένων. λαβὼν δ' ἐπὶ τούτοις ἐνα[υ]πηγήσατο τριήρεις ἑκατόν, ἑκάστου ναυπηγουμένου τῶν ἑκατὸν μίαν, αἷς ἐναυμάχησαν ἐν Σαλαμῖνι πρὸς τοὺς βαρβάρους.

45. Thuc. i 93³ ἔπεισε δὲ καὶ τοῦ Πειραιῶς τὰ λοιπὰ ὁ Θεμιστοκλῆς οἰκοδομεῖν (ὑπῆρκτο δ' αὐτοῦ πρότερον ἐπὶ τῆς ἐκείνου ἀρχῆς ἧς κατ' ἐνιαυτὸν Ἀθηναίοις ἦρξε).

46. Aristotle, *Ath. Pol.* 61 1 δυὸ δ' (στρατηγοὺς) ἐπὶ τὸν Πειραιέα, τὸν μὲν εἰς τὴν Μουνιχίαν, τὸν δὲ εἰς τὴν Ἀκτήν, οἳ τῆς φ[υ]λακῆς ἐπιμελοῦνται καὶ τῶν ἐν Πειραιεῖ. And see inscriptions quoted in Sandys' note *ad loc.*

47. See note 41 above.

48. See above, p. 228.

49. [Xen.] *Ath. Pol.* iii 4 δεῖ δὲ καὶ τάδε διαδικάζειν, εἴ τις τὴν ναῦν μὴ ἐπισκευάζει.

50. *SEG* 353–5. Catalogi Navales *ca.* 430 B.C. See D. M. Robinson *AJA* xli, 1937, 292 f.
'Three small fragments, then, are all that is known of the naval inventories of the first Athenian league, presenting a remarkable contrast to the twenty-eight inventory lists, dating from the period of the second league and occupying eighty-five pages of the Editio Minor of the Greek Corpus. If we may venture to infer from these three fragments that the fifth-century B.C. inventories were of a very general character, merely listing the names of the ships according to their various classes and noting the

general condition of the equipment (with lavish use of space and an unheeding repetition of formula), on this score too they contrast strongly with the fourth-century inventories, which enter into great detail, giving the number and condition of each item of equipment, facts regarding the seaworthiness of the vessels, the builder, trierarchs, etc.'

51. Aristophanes, *Knights* 912–918

> ἐγώ σε ποιήσω τριη-
> ραρχεῖν, ἀναλίσκοντα τῶν
> σεαυτοῦ, παλαιὰν ναῦν ἔχοντ'
> εἰς ἣν ἀναλῶν οὐκ ἐφέ-
> ξεις οὐδὲ ναυπηγούμενος·
> διαμηχανήσομαί θ' ὅπως
> ἂν ἱστίον σαπρὸν λάβῃς.

52. Thuc. VI 31³. See note 8 above.

53. Lysias 32 24 οὗτος γὰρ συντριηραρχῶν Ἀλέξιδι τῷ Ἀριστοδίκου φάσκων δυοῖν δεούσας πεντήκοντα μνᾶς ἐκείνῳ συμβαλέσθαι...

54. Demosthenes 50 68 καὶ πρότερον Εὐριπίδῃ συντριήραρχος ὢν καὶ συνθηκῶν οὐσῶν αὐτοῖς τοὺς ἓξ μῆνας ἑκάτερον πλεῖν...

55. Demosthenes 50 *passim*. Cf. Aristophanes *Plutus* 172.

56. Demosthenes 21 154–5 κἀγὼ μὲν κατ' ἐκείνους τοὺς χρόνους ἐτριηράρχουν, εὐθὺς ἐκ παίδων ἐξελθών, ὅτε σύνδυ' ἦμεν οἱ τριήραρχοι καὶ τἀναλώματα πάντ' ἐκ τῶν ἰδίων καὶ τὰς ναῦς ἐπληρούμεθ' αὐτοί· οὗτος δέ, ὅτε μὲν κατὰ ταύτην τὴν ἡλικίαν ἦν ἣν ἐγὼ νῦν, οὐδέπω λῃτουργεῖν ἤρχετο, τηνικαῦτα δὲ τοῦ πράγματος ἧπται, ὅτε πρῶτον μὲν διακοσίους καὶ χιλίους πεποιήκατε συντελεῖς ὑμεῖς, ...εἶτα πληρώμαθ' ἡ πόλις παρέχει καὶ σκεύη δίδωσιν.

57. Demosthenes 47 19–20 ψηφισμάτων δὲ ὑμετέρων δήμου καὶ Βουλῆς καὶ νόμου ἐπιτάξαντος (the law of Periander as appears in 21), εἰσέπραξα τοῦτον ὀφείλοντα τῇ πόλει σκεύη τριηρικά· δι' ὅτι δὲ ἐγὼ ὑμῖν διηγήσομαι· ἔτυχεν ἔκπλους ὢν τριήρων καὶ βοήθεια ἀποστελλομένη διὰ τάχους· σκεύη οὖν ἐν τῷ νεωρίῳ οὐχ ὑπῆρχεν ταῖς ναυσίν, ἀλλ' ἔχοντες οἱ ὀφείλοντες οὐκ ἀπεδίδοσαν· πρὸς δὲ τούτοις οὐδ' ἐν τῷ Πειραιεῖ ὄντα ἄφθονα ὀθόνια καὶ στυππεῖον καὶ σχοινία οἷς κατασκευάζεται τριήρης ὥστε πρίασθαι· γράφει οὖν Χαιρέδημος τὸ ψήφισμα τουτί, ἵνα εἰσπραχθῇ τὰ σκεύη ταῖς ναυσὶ καὶ σῷα γένηται τῇ πόλει.

58. Demosthenes 14 16 ff.

59. Demosthenes 18 102–8.

60. Demosthenes 51 11 θαυμάζω δ' ἔγωγε, τί δή ποτε τῶν μὲν ναυτῶν τοὺς ἀπολειπομένους, ὧν τριάκοντα δραχμὰς ἕκαστος ἔχει μόνας, δοῦσι καὶ κολάζουσιν οὗτοι· τῶν δὲ τριηράρχων τοὺς μὴ συμπλέοντας, ὧν τριάκοντα μνᾶς εἰς τὸν ἐπίπλουν εἴληφεν ἕκαστος, οὐ ταὐτὰ ποιεῖθ' ὑμεῖς.

61. *IG* I² 1629 201 f. ὅπω[ς ἂν ᾖ] φανερὰ ἡ φιλοτι[μία ἡ εἰ]ς τὸν δῆμον τοῖς [τριηρ]άρχοις.

62. Aristophanes, *Acharnians* 546 περὶ τριηράρχου βοῆς.

63. Aristotle, *E.N.* 4 5 1122b23 καὶ ὅσα πρὸς τὸ κοινὸν εὐφιλοτίμητά ἐστιν, οἷον εἴ που χορηγεῖν οἴονται δεῖν λαμπρῶς ἢ τριηραρχεῖν ἢ καὶ ἐστιᾶν τὴν πόλιν.

Epibatai *and Archers*

64. Herodotus 8 83[1] ἠώς τε διέφαινε καὶ οἳ σύλλογον τῶν ἐπιβατέων ποιησάμενοι, προηγόρευε εὖ ἔχοντα μὲν ἐκ πάντων Θεμιστοκλέης.

65. *IG* 2² 1951. Cf. lines 79–82.

66. Thuc. III 95² καὶ Ἀθηναίων τριακοσίοις τοῖς ἐπιβάταις τῶν σφετέρων νεῶν. (Cf. 94¹ οἱ ἀπὸ τῶν τριάκοντα νεῶν Ἀθηναῖοι.)

97³ καὶ ἦν ἐπὶ πολὺ τοιαύτη ἡ μάχη, διώξεις τε καὶ ὑπαγωγαί, ἐν οἷς ἀμφοτέροις ἥσσους ἦσαν οἱ Ἀθηναῖοι. μέχρι μὲν οὖν οἱ τοξόται εἶχόν τε τὰ βέλη αὐτοῖς καὶ οἷοί τε ἦσαν χρῆσθαι, οἱ δὲ ἀντεῖχον (τοξευόμενοι γὰρ οἱ Αἰτωλοὶ ἄνθρωποι ψιλοὶ ἀνεστέλλοντο)· ἐπειδὴ δὲ τοῦ τε τοξάρχου ἀποθανόντος οὗτοι διεσκεδάσθησαν καὶ αὐτοὶ ἐκεκμήκεσαν καὶ ἐπὶ πολὺ τῷ αὐτῷ πόνῳ ξυνεχόμενοι, οἵ τε Αἰτωλοὶ ἐνέκειντο καὶ ἐσηκόντιζον, οὕτω δὴ τραπόμενοι ἔφευγον, καὶ ἐσπίπτοντες ἔς τε χαράδρας ἀνεκβάτους καὶ χωρία ὧν οὐκ ἦσαν ἔμπειροι διεφθείροντο· καὶ γὰρ ὁ ἡγεμὼν αὐτοῖς τῶν ὁδῶν Χρόμων ὁ Μεσσήνιος ἐτύγχανε τεθνηκώς.

98⁴ ἀπέθανον δὲ τῶν τε ξυμμάχων πολλοὶ καὶ αὐτῶν Ἀθηναίων ὁπλῖται περὶ εἴκοσι μάλιστα καὶ ἑκατόν. τοσοῦτοι μὲν τὸ πλῆθος καὶ ἡλικία ἡ αὐτή οὗτοι βέλτιστοι δὴ ἄνδρες ἐν τῷ πολέμῳ τῷδε ἐκ τῆς Ἀθηναίων πόλεως διεφθάρησαν· ἀπέθανε δὲ καὶ ὁ ἕτερος στρατηγὸς Προκλῆς.

67. Thuc. II 23² οἱ Ἀθηναῖοι ἀπέστειλαν τὰς ἑκατὸν ναῦς περὶ Πελοπόννησον ὥσπερ παρεσκευάζοντο καὶ χιλίους ὁπλίτας ἐπ᾽ αὐτῶν καὶ τοξότας τετρακοσίους.

66¹⁻² οἱ δὲ Λακεδαιμόνιοι καὶ οἱ ξύμμαχοι τοῦ αὐτοῦ θέρους ἐστράτευσαν ναυσὶν ἑκατὸν ἐς Ζάκυνθον τὴν νῆσον, ἣ κεῖται ἀντιπέρας Ἤλιδος· εἰσὶ δὲ Ἀχαιῶν τῶν ἐκ Πελοποννήσου ἄποικοι καὶ Ἀθηναίοις ξυνεμάχουν. ἐπέπλεον δὲ Λακεδαιμονίων χίλιοι ὁπλῖται καὶ Κνῆμος Σπαρτιάτης ναύαρχος.

68. Thuc. VI 43 μετὰ δὲ ταῦτα τοσῆδε ἤδη τῇ παρασκευῇ Ἀθηναῖοι ἄραντες ἐκ τῆς Κερκύρας ἐς τὴν Σικελίαν ἐπεραιοῦντο, τριήρεσι μὲν ταῖς πάσαις τέσσαρσι καὶ τριάκοντα καὶ ἑκατόν, καὶ δυοῖν Ῥοδίοιν πεντηκοντόροιν (τούτων Ἀττικαὶ μὲν ἦσαν ἑκατόν, ὧν αἱ μὲν ἑξήκοντα ταχεῖαι, αἱ δ᾽ ἄλλαι στρατιώτιδες, τὸ δὲ ἄλλο ναυτικὸν Χίων καὶ τῶν ἄλλων ξυμμάχων), ὁπλίταις δὲ τοῖς ξύμπασιν ἑκατὸν καὶ πεντακισχιλίοις (καὶ τούτων Ἀθηναίων μὲν αὐτῶν ἦσαν πεντακόσιοι μὲν καὶ χίλιοι ἐκ καταλόγου, ἑπτακόσιοι δὲ θῆτες ἐπιβάται τῶν νεῶν, ξύμμαχοι δὲ οἱ ἄλλοι ξυνεστράτευον, οἱ μὲν τῶν ὑπηκόων, οἱ δ᾽ Ἀργείων πεντακόσιοι καὶ Μαντινέων καὶ μισθοφόρων πεντήκοντα καὶ διακόσιοι), τοξόταις δὲ τοῖς πᾶσιν ὀγδοήκοντα καὶ τετρακοσίοις (καὶ τούτων Κρῆτες οἱ ὀγδοήκοντα ἦσαν) καὶ σφενδονήταις Ῥοδίων ἑπτακοσίοις, καὶ Μεγαρεῦσι ψιλοῖς φυγάσιν εἴκοσι καὶ ἑκατόν, καὶ ἱππαγωγῷ μιᾷ τριάκοντα ἀγούσῃ ἱππέας.

42², three ships sent on ahead.

69. See p. 253, note 40 above.

70. Thuc. VIII 24² εἶχον δ' ἐπιβάτας τῶν ὁπλιτῶν ἐκ καταλόγου ἀναγκάστους.
Cf. the volunteer *epibatai* in the inscription of 431 B.C. (p. 253).

71. Xen. *HG* IV 8 28 συντάξας τούς τε ἀπὸ τῶν ἑαυτοῦ νεῶν τετρακοσίους ὁπλίτας καὶ τοὺς ἐκ τῶν πόλεων φυγάδας (25. Θρασύβουλον τὸν Στειριέα σὺν τετταράκοντα ναυσίν).

72. Aristotle, *Pol.* VII 5 7 1327b τὸ μὲν γὰρ ἐπιβατικὸν ἐλεύθερον καὶ τῶν πεζευόντων ἐστιν, ὃ κύριόν ἐστι καὶ κρατεῖ τῆς ναυτιλίας.

73. Thuc. VI 32¹ καὶ ἐκπώμασι χρυσοῖς τε καὶ ἀργυροῖς οἵ τε ἐπιβάται καὶ οἱ ἄρχοντες σπένδοντες.

74. Xen. *HG* I 1 28 (cf. 30) οἱ δ' ἀναβοήσαντες ἐκέλευον ἐκείνους ἄρχειν, καὶ μάλιστα οἱ τριήραρχοι καὶ οἱ ἐπιβάται καὶ οἱ κυβερνῆται.

75. Aristophanes, *Frogs* 48–53

Dionysus   ἐπεβάτευον Κλεισθένει—

Heracles κἀναυμαχήσας; *Dionysus* καὶ κατεδύσαμέν γε ναῦς....

Heracles σφώ; *Dionysus* νὴ τὸν Ἀπόλλω. *Xanthus* κᾆτ' ἔγωγ' ἐξηγρόμην.

Dionysus καὶ δῆτ' ἐπὶ τῆς νεὼς ἀναγιγνώσκοντί μοι

τὴν Ἀνδρομέδαν . . .

76. Xen. *HG* I 6 19 καὶ τοὺς ἐπιβάτας εἰς κοίλην ναῦν μεταβιβάσας.

77. Thuc. VIII 61²; *Hell. Ox.* XVII 4; Xen. *HG* I 3 17.

78. *IG* I² 950 137.

Petty Officers

79. *IG* 2² 1951 lines 94–105.

80. See above, p. 196.

81. Xen. *Oeconomicus* 8 14 τὸν δὲ τοῦ κυβερνήτου διάκονον, ὃς πρῳρεὺς τῆς νεὼς καλεῖται.

Aristotle, *Politics* I 2 4 1253b28 τῶν δ' ὀργάνων τὰ μὲν ἄψυχα τὰ δὲ ἔμψυχα (οἷον τῷ κυβερνήτῃ ὁ μὲν οἴαξ ἄψυχον ὁ δὲ πρῳρεὺς ἔμψυχον).

Plutarch, *Agis* I 2 καθάπερ γὰρ οἱ πρῳρεῖς τὰ ἔμπροσθεν προορώμενοι τῶν κυβερνητῶν ἀφορῶσι πρὸς ἐκείνους καὶ τὸ προστάσσομενον ὑπ' ἐκείνων ποιοῦσιν, οὕτως οἱ πολιτευόμενοι. . .

82. Aristophanes, *Knights* 541–4 καὶ πρὸς τούτοισιν ἔφασκεν / ἐρέτην χρῆναι πρῶτα γενέσθαι πρὶν πηδαλίοις ἐπιχειρεῖν, / κᾆτ' ἐντεῦθεν πρῳρατεῦσαι καὶ τοὺς ἀνέμους διαθρῆσαι / κᾆτα κυβερνᾶν αὐτὸν ἑαυτῷ.

83. Xen. *Anabasis* 5 8 20. See note 17 above.

84. Xen. *HG* I 5 11 καταλιπὼν ἐπὶ ταῖς ναυσὶν Ἀντίοχον τὸν αὐτοῦ κυβερνήτην.

85. Thuc. IV 12¹ τὸν ἑαυτοῦ κυβερνήτην ἀναγκάσας ὀκεῖλαι τὴν ναῦν.

86. Theophrastus, *Char.* 22 5 καὶ τριηραρ(χῶν τὰ μὲν το)ῦ κυβερνήτου στρώματα αὑτῷ ἐπὶ τοῦ καταστρώματος ὑποστόρνυσθαι τὰ δὲ αὑτοῦ ἀποτιθέναι.

87. Plato, *Statesman* 272e τότε δὴ τοῦ παντὸς ὁ μὲν κυβερνήτης οἷον πηδαλίων οἴακος ἀφέμενος.

88. Plato, *Hipparchus* 226b τί δέ; κυβερνήτην μηδενὸς ἄξια ἱστία καὶ πηδάλια τῇ νηῒ παρεσκευασμένον ἀγνοεῖν οἴει ὅτι ζημιωθήσεται καὶ κινδυνεύσει καὶ αὐτὸς ἀπολέσθαι καὶ τὴν ναῦν ἀπολέσαι καὶ ἃ ἂν ἄγῃ πάντα;

89. Plato, *Republic* I 341c τί δὲ κυβερνήτης; ὁ ὀρθῶς κυβερνήτης ναυτῶν ἄρχων ἐστὶν ἢ ναύτης; ναυτῶν ἄρχων.

   Alcibiades 125d ὥσπερ ἂν εἴ σε ἐροίμην πάλιν τὰ νυνδή, κοινωνούντων ναυτιλίας ἐπίστασθαι ἄρχειν τίς ποιεῖ τέχνη; κυβερνητική.

90. Aristophanes, *Acharnians* 554.

91. See above, p. 201.

92. Aristophanes, *Frogs* 207: Dionysus: κατακέλευε δή. Charon: ὢ ὀπόπ, ὢ ὀπόπ.
   and 269: Charon: ὢ παῦε, παῦε, παραβαλοῦ τὼ κωπίω.

93. Xen. *HG* v 1 8 λίθων τε ψόφῳ τῶν κελευστῶν ἀντὶ φωνῆς...

94. Xen. *Oeconomicus* 21 3 οἷον καὶ ἐν τριήρει, ἔφη, ὅταν πελαγίζωσι καὶ δέῃ περᾶν ἡμερινοὺς πλοῦς ἐλαύνοντας οἱ μὲν τῶν κελευστῶν δύνανται τοιαῦτα λέγειν καὶ ποιεῖν ὥστε ἀκονᾶν τὰς ψυχὰς τῶν ἀνθρώπων ἐπὶ τὸ ἐθελοντὰς πονεῖν, οἱ δὲ οὕτως ἀγνώμονές εἰσιν ὥστε πλέον ἢ ἐν διπλασίῳ χρόνῳ τὸν αὐτὸν ἀνύτουσι πλοῦν. καὶ οἱ μὲν ἱδροῦντες καὶ ἐπαινοῦντες ἀλλήλους, ὅ τε κελεύων καὶ οἱ πειθόμενοι, ἐκβαίνουσιν, οἱ δὲ ἀνιδρωτὶ ἥκουσι μισοῦντες τὸν ἐπιστάτην καὶ μισούμενοι.

95. Ovid, *Metam.* III 618–19.

96. Thuc. II 84³ βοῇ τε χρώμενοι καὶ πρὸς ἀλλήλους ἀντιφυλακῇ τε καὶ λοιδορίᾳ οὐδὲν κατήκουον οὔτε τῶν παραγγελλομένων οὔτε τῶν κελευστῶν.

   VII 70⁶ καὶ τὸν κτύπον μέγαν ἀπὸ πολλῶν νεῶν ξυμπιπτουσῶν ἔκπληξίν τε ἅμα καὶ ἀποστέρησιν τῆς ἀκοῆς ὧν οἱ κελευσταὶ φθέγγοιντο παρέχειν.

97. Diodorus XX 50 6.

98. Demosthenes 18 129; Philodemus, *Mus.* p. 72 K; Pollux 1 96, 4 71.

99. See above, p. 196.

100. Plato, *Laws* IV 707a and b: see note 13 above.

101. Demosthenes 50 18.

Oarsmen

102. Thuc. II 93² ἐδόκει δὲ λαβόντα τῶν ναυτῶν ἕκαστον τὴν κώπην καὶ τὸ ὑπηρέσιον καὶ τὸν τροπωτῆρα πεζῇ ἰέναι ἐκ Κορίνθου ἐπὶ τὴν πρὸς Ἀθήνας θάλασσαν.

103. Isocrates 8 48 τοῖς μὲν ξένοις ὁπλίταις χρώμεθα, τοὺς δὲ πολίτας ἐλαύνειν ἀναγκάζομεν, ὥσθ᾽ ὁπόταν ἀποβαίνωσιν εἰς τὴν τῶν πολεμίων, οἱ μὲν ἄρχειν τῶν Ἑλλήνων ἀξιοῦντες ὑπηρέσιον ἔχοντες ἐκβαίνουσιν, οἱ δὲ τοιοῦτοι τὰς φύσεις ὄντες οἵους ὀλίγῳ πρότερον διῆλθον, μεθ᾽ ὅπλων κινδυνεύουσιν.

104. Hermippus, fr. 54
 A. ὥρα τοίνυν μετ᾽ ἐμοῦ χωρεῖν τὸν κωπητῆρα λαβόντα καὶ προσκεφάλαιον, ἵν᾽ ἐς τὴν ναῦν ἐμπηδήσας ῥοθιάζῃς.
 Β. ἀλλ᾽ οὐ δέομ᾽ ⟨οὐ⟩ πανικτὸν ἔχων τὸν πρωκτὸν ⟨προσκεφαλαίου⟩.

105. Theophrastus, *Char.* II 11 καὶ τοῦ παιδὸς ἐν τῷ θεάτρῳ ἀφελόμενος τὰ προσκεφάλαια αὐτὸς ὑποστρῶσαι.

106. Aristophanes, *Frogs* 236

ἐγὼ δὲ φλυκταίνας γ᾽ ἔχω.

107. Aristophanes, *Acharnians* 162–3

ὑποστένοι μεντἂν ὁ θρανίτης λεώς
ὁ σωσίπολις.

108. Thucydides IV 32² ἐκ μὲν νεῶν ἑβδομήκοντα καὶ ὀλίγῳ πλειόνων παντὸς πλὴν θαλαμιῶν.

109. Aristophanes, *Frogs* 1071–74

Aeschylus καὶ τοὺς Παράλους ἀνέπεισεν (sc. Euripides) / ἀνταγορεύειν τοῖς ἄρχουσιν. καίτοι τότε γ᾽ ἡνίκ᾽ ἐγὼ ᾽ζων, / οὐκ ἠπίσταντ᾽ ἀλλ᾽ ἢ μᾶζαν καλέσαι καὶ ῥυππαπαῖ εἰπεῖν.

Dionysus: νὴ τὸν Ἀπόλλω, καὶ προσπαρδεῖν γ᾽ ἐς τὸ στόμα τῷ θαλάμακι.

110. See above, p. 196.

111. Aristophanes, *Peace* 1228 ff. Trygaeus makes fun of a merchant trying to sell an armoured waistcoat:

Trygaeus ἐναποπατεῖν γάρ ἐστ᾽ ἐπιτήδειος πάνυ—
Merchant παῦσαί μ᾽ ὑβρίζων τοῖς ἐμοῖσι χρήμασιν.
Trygaeus ὡδὶ παραθέντι τρεῖς λίθους. οὐ δεξιῶς;
Merchant ποίᾳ δ᾽ ἀποψήσει ποτ᾽ ὦμαθέστατε;
Trygaeus τηδὶ διεὶς τὴν χεῖρα διὰ τῆς θαλαμιᾶς.
            καὶ τῇδ᾽. *Merchant* ἅμ᾽ ἀμφοῖν δῆτ᾽; *Trygaeus* ἔγωγε νὴ Δία.
ἵνα μή γ᾽ ἁλῶ τρύπημα κλέπτων τῆς νεώς.

112. Aeschines, *In Ctesiphontem* 146 μισθοφορῶν...κεναῖς κώπαις.

Cf. Cicero, *In Verrem* II 5 21 175.

113. Aristophanes, *Acharnians* 553 θαλαμιῶν τρυπωμένων: see p 320, note 2.

114. See note 16 above.

THE HULL

In Aristophanes pitch and timber are spoken of as the main materials of which *trsignificantly—triereis* were made[1], and pitch is joined with leather fittings and sail-cloth in a list of contraband whose export was forbidden from Athens[2]. Theophrastus in the fourth century tells us that ships' keels were made of oak to withstand the wear of hauling up and down beaches. Ribs, he says, were sometimes made of pine for lightness[3]. Presumably they were otherwise made of oak like the keel. Plato in the *Laws* gives full information about the rest of the wood used. The Athenian stranger asks: 'How is our district off for timber for shipbuilding?' Clinias replies, 'There is no fir to speak of nor pine and not much cypress; nor could one find much larch or plane, which shipwrights are always obliged to use for the interior parts of ships[4].' The use of pitch is presumably for caulking seams and generally making the ship watertight. In a miscellaneous list of naval stores in an inscription of 330 we find *hupaloiphe*, outside paint, in two varieties, 'white' and 'black'[5]. The black is presumably pitch. It seems likely that a new coat of pitch was put on before each new sailing[6]. The 'white' *hupaloiphe* may be just clear varnish of some kind, possibly wax with which Hipponax (sixth century) appears to have said the keel of a ship was smeared[7], possibly tallow.

Although pitch was used generously on *triereis'* hulls, they seem to have leaked water into the bilges fairly quickly. We have discussed this question in relation to the respective speeds in the water of the Persian and Greek fleets before Salamis. The Athenian ships at Syracuse became heavy and their speed reduced eighteen months after commissioning[8]. The first thing that Lysander did on his appointment to command the Spartan fleet in Asia Minor in 406 B.C. was to beach the ships and dry them out[9]. The function of the ship-shed was presumably to keep the hull in good condition out of the sea and sheltered from rain and sun. We learn of some ships which had become leaky through having been out of the sea for too long[10].

The offensive weapon of the *trieres* was the ram, *embolos*, and the object of all tactics was to bring the ram to bear on the enemy's flank or quarter. We have already learned that these rams were of bronze. That they were removable is shown by the entry of a number of rams in naval lists of gear. When a ship was broken up abroad the trierarch owed the ram to the dockyard[11]. In lists of 374 and 370 B.C. we hear of ships lacking 'the upper bronze' (see p. 96 (*b*)). The word translated 'bronze', *chalkoma*, is used for a ship's ram in Diodorus and Plutarch[12]. In a list of 353 B.C. there is a reference to the fore-ram, *proembolion*[13]. All these entries suggest that the ram was not just one single beak as in the picture of the single- and two-level ships. There is a suggestion in Thucydides that subsidiary rams may have been attached to the forward face of the *epotis*, and such may be visible in the rhyton in the shape of a ship's bow (Clas. 15, Pl. 26c). These would then constitute the 'upper bronze'. An incomplete entry in the earliest list suggests that the ram may have been somehow lashed to the hull[14]. There is a representation of such ropes attached to a trident ram in a Roman bronze showing the bow of a ship.*

At Salamis the ships on the Persian side had been decked throughout, and had carried on these decks a substantial number of soldiers. By the time of the

* Illustrated in Koester, pl. 40.

battle of the Eurymedon the Athenian ships had adopted the continuous deck, but did not apparently increase the number of *epibatai* and archers on board their fast *triereis* beyond the number they had employed at Salamis, when their ships had no continuous deck but only raised platforms at bow and stern. The *trieres* throughout the Greek world now became standard. In the Peloponnesian war Athenian and Peloponnesian *triereis* were indistinguishable[15].

Two structurally connected parts of the *trieres*, for which we have evidence in this period, are the *parexeiresia* and the *epotis*. The scholiasts and lexicographers declare that the former was the 'part beyond the rowing at the bow and stern'[16]; but clearly it was nothing of the kind. Thucydides describes the Spartan landing against the Athenian position on Pylos, when Brasidas forcing his helmsman to drive his ship ashore ran out a landing ladder and climbed on to it. The ships must have been driven ashore bow first and the ladder run out over the side. As Brasidas climbed on to it he was hit by an Athenian missile and fainted. As he collapsed into the *parexeiresia* his shield fell away into the sea[17]. The story is clear if the *parexeiresia* is a structure projecting from the ship's side.

While reinforcements were on their way to join the Athenian expedition at Syracuse, an inconclusive but highly significant engagement was fought at the entrance to the Corinthian gulf between a Corinthian squadron and the Athenian squadron based on Naupactus. Thucydides describes the result. None of the Athenian ships was sunk completely, but seven were put out of action. They had been rammed bow-to-bow and their *parexeiresiai* smashed and forced back by the Corinthian ships which were 'equipped with stouter *epotides* designed for this very purpose'[18]. We have seen from our discussion of passages in tragedy (see above, p. 198) that *epotides* were the projecting ends of a beam laid across the bow of a ship. In a collision bow-to-bow the rams of the opposing ships would have driven on past each other and the port (or starboard) *epotis* of one ship would have come hard up against the port (or starboard) *epotis* of the other. The Corinthian *epotides* had been deliberately made stouter with this particular manœuvre in view. It was the Athenian *epotides* accordingly which gave way under the impact, and as a result the *parexeiresiai* were smashed and forced back. This result can only imply that the *parexeiresiai* were projections from the side of the ship immediately aft of, and usually covered by, the *epotides*. The breaking of the *epotides*, then, led to the *parexeiresiai* being forced back, i.e. towards the stern. The stern shown on the Lindus relief (Hel. 2, Pl. 27d) and the bow base of the Nike of Samothrace (Hel. 3, Pl. 28) both show such projecting structures. Both representations are later than the classical period, and neither shows a *trieres*; but the feature appearing in them seems likely to be a development of the *parexeiresia* of a *trieres* as described by Thucydides.

The battle off Naupactus was significant because it showed the way by which the Athenian *trieres*, lightly built in the bows for speed[19], could be mastered. The Syracusans adapted their ships in the same way that the Corinthians had, 'They shortened the bows of their ships and strengthened them: they laid stout *epotides* on their bows, and fixed stays from the *epotides* to the ships' sides both inside and out[20].' The word translated 'fixed' is the geometrical term which makes the English word 'hypotenuse'. The stays were the hypotenuses of right-angles formed by the beam of the *epotides* and the ship's side, both inside and out.

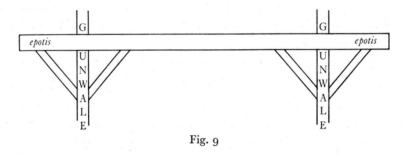

Fig. 9

Polyaenus mentions the *parexeiresia* twice in connection with the fourth-century Athenian commander Chabrias. Both passages confirm the conclusions we have reached. In the first passage he says that Chabrias fastened skins under the *parexeiresia* on each side of the ship to prevent the sea coming in. He also attached a vertical reed awning to the deck above and made it fast to the *parexeiresia*. These measures prevented the ship from running wet and stopped the seamen getting wet or taking fright at the sight of the waves[21]. To give any sense to this story the *parexeiresia* must be a projecting structure running the length of the part of the ship's side occupied by the oarsmen. Chabrias' methods of protecting the oarsmen foreshadow the completely enclosed superstructure which appears on the Samothrace bow and the Lindus stern just mentioned.

The second mention of the *parexeiresia* in Polyaenus concerns the double set of steering oars which Chabrias fitted in his ships. He used the ordinary set in fine weather, but when there was a high sea he ran out a second set through the *parexeiresia* beside the thranite oars[22]. This passage gives the clue we need to the purpose of the *parexeiresia*. It was an outrigger through which the thranite oars were worked. It also indicates that the first oars forward of the helmsman were thranite. This fact can be observed in the Aquila relief (see Pl. 23*b*) which appears to be a Roman copy of a monument which either is or closely resembles the Lenormant relief. Whereas the Lenormant relief shows the nine thranite oarsmen nearest the bow the Aquila relief shows the four thranite oarsmen nearest the stern. Of these four oarsmen the two nearest the stern certainly have no zygian or thalamian oars shown below them. We should in fact expect that four of the thranite oarsmen on each side would have no zygian and thalamian oarsmen beneath them since there were apparently (see p. 270) eight more thranite oars than zygian or thalamian.

In the earliest of the naval lists, that for 377/6, there appears to be a regular entry against each of the ships listed. Either they are said to be fitted with *askomata* or someone named is said to be in possession of the ship's *askomata*, or the dockyard authority is said to have the money for them (regularly 43 drachmae, 2 obols), or they are missing[23]. Literary references to *askomata* all come from Aristophanes. In the *Frogs* they are joined with sailcloth and pitch as articles of contraband, and the scholiast explains that they are leather fittings through which the oars are run out[24]. In the *Acharnians* the Persian king's ambassador, the King's Eye, is greeted as follows: 'Lord Heracles, by the gods, man, you look like a battleship. . .You seem to have an *askoma* about your eye below[25].' As van Leeuwen says,* the reference appears to be to the leather fitting about the oarports of a *trieres*. If this is the case, besides giving us an explanation of the *askoma*, the passage suggests an interpretation of three baffling entries in the naval lists. Twice it is said of a ship: 'Her eye is broken'; and again 'This ship has no gear and does not even have eyes'[26]. Eyes were painted on the forepart of a ship, as the representations often show. Such an eye could however hardly be said to be broken. The tholepin in an oarport might easily break, and it is possible that the oarports had not yet been made in an unfinished ship. The use of leather fittings in

* In his edition *ad loc.*

oarports has an obvious function. They could close the oarport when the oars were shipped. This would be necessary in rough weather. Such a fitting could also fasten tightly round the oar when in use and prevent the entry of water. Both the Lenormant relief and the Talos vase have features which may be interpreted as such a fitting for the thalamian oars only. If an oarport was called an eye, and only the lower oarports were fitted with *askomata* (because the upper oarports would not be liable to let the water in), the phrase addressed to someone who is said to look like a battleship 'an *askoma* about your eye below' is precise. Much later such fittings appear clearly on a Roman ship of A.D. 50 on a relief in the Vatican (see Koester, p. 150). If *askomata* are as we have described them we may perhaps recognize them under the word *askoi* next to *tropoteres* (tholepin leathers) in the description of the dispatch of a naval expedition in the *Acharnians*[27].

Finally, the 'gilding of Pallases' which was part of the naval preparations described in the *Acharnians* must suggest the emblems (*semeia*) which were provided by the trierarchs in the Sicilian expedition (p. 134). The emblems of the various national contingents of the Achaean fleet were described by Euripides in the *Iphigeneia in Aulis* (p. 197).

The picture of the *trieres'* hull which our written sources give us contains a certain amount of detail. This picture is confirmed and supplemented by the few representations of the *trieres* which we possess. We may safely attribute to it the general shape and appearance of the earlier simple long ships, with a number of important modifications. There is still the screened bow platform, forward of which is a low ram and on each side of which are the laterally projecting *epotides*, constituting a single beam resting on the gunwale. In the *trieres* the deck which covers the oarsmen, the *katastroma*, terminates at the bow, as the fourth-century coin of Cios (Clas. 16) shows, in a housing of some size. This housing is probably just visible in the Lenormant relief half concealing the bow thranite oarsman. On this terminal housing, though not of course in a *trieres*, the Victory of Samothrace stands (Pl. 28). In the stern the *katastroma* seems to continue in the poop on which the helmsman sits controlling the steering oars, one of which is probably just visible aft of the stroke oarsman in the Aquila fragment (Pl. 23 b). Under the deck and sitting very near to, but slightly above, the gunwale the thranite oarsmen work their oars through an outrigger, projecting possibly as much as two feet from the side of the ship, running from the *epotis* for thirty-two oarsmens' places aft to its termination just forward of the helmsman's seat at the point where the high up-curving stern begins to rise above the deck. In the main body of the ship the zygian and thalamian oarsmen worked their oars exactly as the two levels of oars were worked in the archaic two-level ships of which we have several pictures (Arch. 85–9, Pl. 20). It seems probable that the zygian oarsmen like the thalamian oarsmen often worked their oars through oarports (as shown on the Vienna fragment and the Talos vase), though no oarports appear for these oarsmen on the Lenormant relief.

The system of rowing the *triereis* which we can reconstruct undoubtedly required skilled oarsmen. The full system, with a hundred and seventy oarsmen rowing simultaneously, appears only to have been used in battle, and Vitruvius, in the first century B.C., lays down a principle which applied certainly to oared warships at all times: 'A sea-battle is only fought in calm water[28].' The difficulties of the unpractised Peloponnesian oarsmen when the sea became rough during an engagement at the outset of the Peloponnesian war underline these points[29].

The dimensions of the *trieres* may be inferred from the remains of the ship-sheds at Zea and Munichia (see above, p. 182). The dry length of these is an average of 37 metres (121 ft. 5 in.), and the breadth just under six metres (19 ft. 6 in.) at Zea and somewhat less at Munichia. Since we should not expect the ships to fit tightly into the slipways, an overall length of 35 metres (114 ft. 9 in.), and an overall breadth of 5 metres (16 ft. 5 in.), seems a reasonable inference. If the outrigger projected 61 cm. (2 ft.), the breadth of the hull from gunwale to gunwale at its widest point would be 3 m. 87 cm. We may note that the actual stone slips on which the ships were drawn up were roughly 3 metres wide (9 ft. 10 in.). This is probably the breadth of the ship's flat bottom.

Plate 31 embodies in a drawing of the starboard side of a complete *trieres* the conclusions of this section. It is based closely on the Talos vase ship, the Lenormant and Aquila reliefs, and the Cian coins.

There is only one piece of evidence relating to the hull of types other than the *trieres*. In Diodorus[30] the maximum breadth of a *penteres* between the extremities of the *epotides* on either side is probably deducible. The funeral pyre of Hephaestion is described as a square of which each side is a stade in length (i.e. 600 ft.). In the foundation course of it 'were set golden bows of *pentereis* close together two hundred and forty in all' (i.e. sixty a side). 'Upon the *epotides* each carried two kneeling archers four cubits in height and armed male figures five cubits high, while the intervening spaces were filled by red banners made out of felt.' It is of course impossible to tell what was the actual length of the foot Diodorus, or his source Ephippus, was using, but it looks as if he meant the bow of the *penteres* to measure not more than ten feet across the *epotides*. If the foot was the Attic one, that would be a little less than three metres. If the *pentereis* used the same ship-sheds as the *triereis*, as apparently they did at Athens, they can have been no broader amidships than the five metres we have allowed for the *triereis*. It appears then that *pentereis* tapered from a breadth of five metres amidships to about three metres across the *epotides*. It does not seem unreasonable to suppose that the same measurement applied also to *triereis*. If, in fact, the bows of *triereis* measured the same as those of *pentereis*, we may ask why the bows of *pentereis* were specified in Hephaestion's pyre. The answer probably lies in the greater solidity of the outrigger's build in the *penteres*, since larger multiple-handed oars had to be rowed through it. It is perhaps a reasonable guess that the bow on which the Nike of Samothrace is standing is the bow of a *penteres* or *tetreres* (see Pl. 28). In this ship oars are rowed at two levels through the outrigger.

TEXTS

1. Aristophanes, *Knights* 1310
   εἴπερ ἐκ πεύκης γε κἀγὼ καὶ ξύλων ἐπηγνύμην.

2. Aristophanes, *Frogs* 364
   ἀσκώματα καὶ λίνα καὶ πίτταν διαπέμπων εἰς Ἐπίδαυρον.

3. Theophrastus, *Hist. Plant.* v 7 2 τὴν δὲ τρόπιν τριήρει μὲν δρυΐνην (ποιοῦσι) ἵνα ἀντέχῃ πρὸς τὰς νεωλκίας, ταῖς δὲ ὁλκάσι πευκίνην, ὑποτιθέασι δὲ ἔτι καὶ δρυΐνην ἐπὰν νεωλκῶσι—ταῖς δὲ ἐλάττοσιν ὀξυΐνην.

   3 ἡ δὲ τορνεία τοῖς μὲν πλοίοις γίνεται συκα-μίνου μελίας πτελέας πλατάνου· γλισχρότητα γὰρ ἔχειν δεῖ καὶ ἰσχύν· χειρίστη δὲ ἡ τῆς πλατάνου· τάχυ γὰρ σήπεται· ταῖς δὲ τριήρεσι ἔνιοι καὶ πιτυΐνας ποιοῦσι διὰ τὸ ἐλαφρόν· τὸ δὲ στερέωμα πρὸς ᾧ τὸ χέλυσμα καὶ τὰς ἐπωτίδας μελίας καὶ συκαμίνου καὶ πτελέας· ἰσχυρὰ γὰρ δεῖ ταῦτ' εἶναι.

4. Plato, *Laws* 705c Τί δὲ δή; ναυπηγησίμης ὕλης ὁ τόπος ἡμῖν τῆς χώρας πῶς ἔχει; Οὐκ ἔστιν οὔτε τις ἐλάτη λόγου ἀξία οὔτ' αὖ πεύκη, κυπάριττός τε οὐ πολλή· πίτυν τ' αὖ καὶ πλάτανον ὀλίγην ἂν εὕροι τις, οἷς δὴ πρὸς τὰ τῶν ἐντὸς τῶν πλοίων μέρη ἀναγκαῖον τοῖς ναυπηγοῖς χρῆσθαι ἑκάστοτε.

   Cf. Euripides, *Andromache* 863: πευκᾶεν σκάφος.

5. *IG* 2² 1627 313 ὑπαλοιφὴ ἐμ φιδακνίῳ μέλαινα· ἑτέρα ἐν ἀμφορεῖ μέλαινα· ἑτέρα λευκὴ ἐμ φιδακνίῳ· ἐν ἀμφορεῦσι δυοῖν λευκή.

6. Aristophanes, *Acharnians* 189–90 (truces for five years)

οὐκ ἀρέσκουσίν μ’ ὅτι

ὄζουσι πίττης καὶ παρασκευῆς νεῶν. Cf. p. 305, note 31.

7. See p. 122, note 20 above.

8. Thuc. VII 12³ τὸ γὰρ ναυτικὸν ἡμῶν, ᾗ περ κἀκεῖνοι πυνθάνονται, τὸ μὲν πρῶτον ἤκμαζε καὶ τῶν νεῶν τῇ ξηρότητι καὶ τῶν πληρωμάτων τῇ σωτηρίᾳ· νῦν δὲ αἵ τε νῆες διάβροχοι, τοσοῦτον χρόνον ἤδη θαλασσεύουσαι, καὶ τὰ πληρώματα ἔφθαρται.

9. Xen. *HG* I 5 10 καὶ ὁ μὲν Λύσανδρος ἐπεὶ αὐτοῦ τὸ ναυτικὸν συνετέτακτο ἀνελκύσας τὰς ἐν τῇ Ἐφέσῳ οὔσας ναῦς ἐνενήκοντα ἡσυχίαν ἦγεν, ἐπισκευάζων καὶ ἀναψύχων αὐτάς.

10. Thuc. II 94³ ἔστι γὰρ ὅτι καὶ αἱ νῆες αὐτοὺς διὰ χρόνου καθελκυσθεῖσαι καὶ οὐδὲν στέγουσαι ἐφόβουν.

11. *IG* 2² 1623 6 ταύτην ὡμολόγησεν ἐπὶ τοῦ δικαστηρίου καινὴν ἀποδώσειν τῇ πόλει Εὐξένιππος Ἐθελοκράτους Λαμπτρ, τὴν δὲ παλαιὰν διαλύσειν καὶ τὸν ἔμβολον ἀποδώσειν ἐς τὰ νεώρια.

1628 49β ἐμβόλους παρελάβομεν παρὰ νεωρίων ἐπιμελητῶν || καὶ παρέδομεν ||.

Cf. 1629 813.

12. *IG* 2² 1606 32 and 89; 1609 24, 29; Diodorus xx 9; Plutarch, *Antony* 67 3.

13. *IG* 2² 1614 27 Εὐ[ετ]ηρία [Λυ]σεκράτους ἔργ[ον] [πρ]οεμβόλιον [οὐ]κ ἔχει.

14. *IG* 2² 1604 31 δεσμὰ τοῦ χαλκιω[.

15. Thuc. III 32³ ὁρῶντες γὰρ τὰς ναῦς οἱ ἄνθρωποι οὐκ ἔφευγον, ἀλλὰ προσεχώρουν μᾶλλον ὡς Ἀττικαῖς.

16. Schol. ad Thuc. IV 12 1 παρεξειρεσία ἐστὶν ὁ ἔξω τῆς νεὼς τόπος καθ’ ὃ μέρος οὐκέτι κώπαις κέχρηνται· ἔστι δὲ τοῦτο τὸ ἀκρότατον τῆς πρύμνης καὶ τῆς πρῴρας.

Schol. ad Thuc. VII 34 5 παρεξειρεσία ἐστὶ τὸ κατὰ τὴν πρῷραν πρὸ τῶν κωπῶν· ὡς ἂν εἴποι τις τὸ παρὲξ τῆς εἰρεσίας.

Hesych. παρεξειρεσίαν ⎫ παρὰ Θουκυδίδῃ τὸ κατὰ τὴν πρῷραν πρὸ τῶν
Suid. παρεξειρεσίας ⎭ κωπῶν· ὡς ἂν εἴποι τις τὸ παρὲξ τῆς εἰρεσίας.

Suid. ⎫
Photius ⎭ παρεξειρεσίαν· τὸ ἔξω τῶν ἐρεσσόντων ἐν δ' Θουκυδίδης.

17. Thuc. IV 12¹ ἐχώρει ἐπὶ τὴν ἀποβάθραν· καὶ πειρώμενος ἀποβαίνειν ἀνεκόπη ὑπὸ τῶν Ἀθηναίων, καὶ τραυματισθεὶς πολλὰ ἐλιποψύχησέ τε καὶ πεσόντος αὐτοῦ ἐς τὴν παρεξειρεσίαν ἡ ἀσπὶς περιερρύη ἐς τὴν θάλασσαν.

18. Thuc. VII 34⁵ καὶ τῶν μὲν Κορινθίων τρεῖς νῆες διαφθείρονται, τῶν δὲ Ἀθηναίων κατέδυ μὲν οὐδεμία ἁπλῶς, ἑπτὰ δέ τινες ἄπλοι ἐγένοντο ἀντίπρωροι ἐμβαλλόμεναι καὶ ἀναρραγεῖσαι τὰς παρεξειρεσίας ὑπὸ τῶν Κορινθίων νεῶν ἐπ’ αὐτὸ τοῦτο παχυτέρας τὰς ἐπωτίδας ἐχουσῶν.

19. Thuc. VII 36³ τὰς τῶν Ἀθηναίων ναῦς...λεπτὰ τὰ πρῴραθεν ἐχούσας.

20. Thuc. VII 36² τὰς πρῴρας τῶν νεῶν ξυντεμόντες ἐς ἔλασσον στεριφωτέρας ἐποίησαν, καὶ τὰς ἐπωτίδας ἐπέθεσαν ταῖς πρῴραις παχείας, καὶ ἀντηρίδας ἀπ' αὐτῶν ὑπέτειναν πρὸς τοὺς τοίχους ὡς ἐπὶ ἓξ πήχεις ἐντός τε καὶ ἔξωθεν ᾧπερ τρόπῳ καὶ οἱ Κορίνθιοι πρὸς τὰς ἐν τῇ Ναυπάκτῳ ναῦς ἐπεσκευασμένοι πρῴραθεν ἐναυμάχουν.

21. Polyaenus III 11 13 Χαβρίας πρὸς τὰς ἐπιβολὰς τῶν κυμάτων ὑπὸ τὴν παρεξειρεσίαν ἑκατέρου τοίχου δέρρεις κατελάμβανεν καὶ καλάμινον ἀρτήσας* τῷ καταστρώματι κατὰ τὸ ὕψος φράγμα κατελάμβανεν αὐτὸ πρὸς τὰς παρεξειρεσίας. τοῦτο δὲ ἐκώλυε τὴν ναῦν ὑποβρύχιον φέρεσθαι καὶ τοὺς ναύτας ὑπὸ τῶν κυμάτων βρέχεσθαι· καὶ τὰ ἐπιφερόμενα κύματα οὐχ ὁρῶντες διὰ τὴν τοῦ φράγματος προσθέσιν οὐκ ἐξανίσταντο διὰ τὸν φόβον οὐδὲ τὴν ναῦν ἔσφαλλον.

22. Polyaenus III 11 14 Χαβρίας πρὸς τοὺς πελαγίους πλοῦς καὶ τοὺς ἐν θαλάττῃ χειμῶνας κατεσκεύαζεν ἑκάστῃ τῶν νηῶν δισσὰ πηδάλια καὶ τοῖς μὲν ὑπάρχουσιν ἐν ταῖς εὐδίαις ἐχρῆτο, εἰ δὲ ἡ θάλασσα κοίλη γένοιτο, θάτερα διὰ τῆς παρεξειρεσίας κατὰ τὰς θρανίτιδας κώπας παρετίθει τοὺς αὐχένας ἔχοντα καὶ τοὺς οἴακας ὑπὲρ τοῦ καταστρώματος, ὥστε ἐξαιρομένης τῆς πρύμνης τούτοις τὴν ναῦν κατευθύνεσθαι.

23. *IG* 2² 1604.

24. Aristophanes, *Frogs* 364. See note 2 above.

Cf. E.M.: τὰ δέρματα τὰ ἐπιρραπτόμενα ταῖς κώπαις ἐν ταῖς τριήρεσι, διὰ τὸ μὴ εἰσφρεῖν τὸ θαλάσσιον ὕδωρ.

Suid. τὰ ἐν ταῖς κώπαις σκεπαστήρια ἐκ δέρματος, οἷς χρῶνται ἐν ταῖς τριήρεσι, καθ' ὃ τρῆμα ἡ κώπη βάλλεται.

Schol. Aristoph. *Ran.* 364 ἄσκωμα δερμάτινόν τι ᾧ ἐν ταῖς τριήρεσι χρῶνται, καθ' ὃ ἡ κώπη βάλλεται.

Pollux I 87 δι' ὧν δὲ διείρεται ἡ κώπη τρήματα· τὸ δὲ πρὸς αὐτῷ τῷ σκαλμῷ δέρμα ἄσκωμα.

25. Aristophanes, *Acharnians* 94–7
    Dionysus
                        ὦναξ Ἡράκλεις,
            πρὸς τῶν θεῶν ἄνθρωπε ναύφαρκτον βλέπεις;
            ἢ περὶ ἄκραν κάμπτων νεώσοικον σκοπεῖς;
            ἄσκωμ' ἔχεις που περὶ τὸν ὀφθαλμὸν κάτω.

26. *IG* 2² 1604 68 ὀφθαλμὸς κατέαγεν; 75 ὀφθαλμοὶ κατεα[.
        1607 24 α]ὕτη σκεῦος ἔχει οὐθέν, οὔθ' οἱ ὀφθαλμοὶ ἔνεισιν.

27. Aristophanes, *Acharnians* 549
            ἀσκῶν, τροπωτήρων...

28. Vitruvius IV 43 pugna navalis tranquillo committitur mari.

29. Thuc. II 84³ καὶ τὰς κώπας ἀδύνατοι ὄντες ἐν κλύδωνι ἀναφέρειν ἄνθρωποι ἄπειροι τοῖς κυβερνήταις ἀπειθεστέρας τὰς ναῦς παρεῖχον.

30. Diodorus XVII 115 1–2 ᾠκοδόμησε τετράπλευρον πυράν, σταδιαίας οὔσης ἑκάστης πλευρᾶς...μετὰ δὲ ταῦτα περιετίθει τῷ περιβόλῳ παντὶ κόσμον, οὗ τὴν μὲν κρηπῖδα

* κατὰ μόνας ἀρτίους MSS.: κατηλώσας ἀρτίως Woefflin. I suggest καλάθινον ἀρτήσας as nearer to the tradition.

288

χρυσαῖ πεντηρικαὶ πρῷραι συνεπλήρουν, οὖσαι τὸν ἀριθμὸν διακόσιαι τεσσαράκοντα, ἐπὶ δὲ τῶν ἐπωτίδων ἔχουσαι δύο μὲν τοξότας εἰς γόνυ κεκαθικότας τετραπήχεις, ἀνδριάντας δὲ πενταπήχεις καθωπλισμένους, τοὺς δὲ μεταξὺ τόπους φοινικίδες ἀνεπλήρουν πιληταί.

The description is possibly derived from Ephippus (*F. Gr. Hist.* IIB 126) who wrote on 'the Funeral of Alexander and Hephaestion'.

GEAR

Ships' gear is divided in the naval lists into two categories, 'wooden' and 'hanging'. In the former category are: oars, steering oars, ladders, poles, shores, main mast, boat mast, main sailyard, boat sailyard. In the latter are: swifters, main sail, boat sail, ropes, *hupoblema*, *katablema*, white side screens, hair side screens, cables, anchors.

'WOODEN' GEAR

Oars

The naval lists show, as we have seen, that a *trieres* in the fourth century B.C. normally carried two hundred oars in four classes. We have concluded that a hundred and seventy of the oars in the thranite, zygian, and thalamian classes were employed by the oarsmen of those names. There remains the class of *perineo*, which number thirty. The word *perineo* is used in Thucydides as a masculine noun meaning passengers on a ship as opposed to *proskopoi* the working oarsmen[1]. Used of oars, the word should mean oars which are not employed, i.e. do not belong to the working *tarros* or set of oars, the sixty-two thranite, fifty-four zygian and fifty-four thalamian oars. They are, in fact, spares. This conclusion is confirmed by an entry in the lists: '*tarros* complete, *perineo* lacking'[2]. It would not have been possible to make such an entry if, as has been suggested, the *perineo* were extra oars worked from the deck by the non-oarsmen, who were of course like the *perineo* thirty in number.

The length of the *perineo* is given. They are either of nine cubits (4·16 m. = 13 ft. 6 in.) or of nine and a half cubits (4·4 m. = 14 ft. 4 in.)[3]. We may compare the lengths of 12 ft. 6 in. for the oars of a racing eight, 12–14 ft. for the oars of a naval cutter-gig (or whaler), and 15–16 ft. for the oars of a naval cutter. In the case of the naval boats the oars in the bow and stern are shorter than those in the middle of the boat: and there seems to be no doubt that the difference of length of ten inches among the *perineo* was for the same reason. Aristotle says: the outermost finger is short for good reason and the middle finger long like the midships oar[4]. Galen explains the different lengths of the fingers in the same way: 'As, I believe, in *triereis* the ends of the oars extend to the same distance although they are not all of equal length. In the case of the *trieres* too they make the middle oars longest for the same reason[5].' The fourth-century *Mechanica* states that 'in the middle of the ship the largest proportion of the oar is inboard, for there the ship is broadest'[6]. This statement looks at the phenomenon from a different point of view, but is in harmony with Aristotle and with Galen. We are to imagine the oarsmen sitting directly behind one another in a straight line from stern to bow. The tholepins against which the oars are rowed are set in a curved line following the curve of the ship's gunwale or of the outrigger which follows it. The oars all extend to the same distance from the ship's side, so that the tips of the oars make a line which curves in correspondence with the curve of the side. The looms of the middle oars are longer than those towards bow and stern.

That the oars of the *trieres* should vary in length according to the oarsman's longitudinal position in the ship rather than according to his vertical distance from the waterline is surprising, but there seems to be no doubt that it was so. The two-level ship using oars all apparently of the same length is a matter of fact. The blades would enter the water at eighteen-inch intervals. If this is possible, and it appears to be so, the addition of the thranite oars presents no great problem. The spacing of the oars in the water is shown on the Lenormant relief (Pl. 23 *a*).

An inscription records that a new ship the *Trieteris* has lacking the seat of a zygian oar. The word seat (*hedra*) may indicate the piece of wood on which the oar rested. Alternatively 'the seat of the zygian oar' may indicate the seat of the zygian oarsman[7].

Hitherto we have been speaking of the oars of the *trieres*. When the higher denominations, the *tetreres* and *penteres*, appear in the naval lists their oars are only mentioned collectively under the word *tarros*. The only clue we have is the valuation of the *tarros* of a *tetreres* at 665 drachmae in 325/4[8]. Andocides relates that at the end of the fifth century he supplied oar timbers to the Athenian fleet at Samos at 5 drachmae apiece[9]. By the time they had been worked up into oars the value would have been greater. The value of a *trieres*' oars then at the end of the fifth century cannot have been less than a thousand drachmae. Comparisons with prices three-quarters of a century later are dangerous, but it seems unlikely that oars would have become cheaper over the period. We are then perhaps justified in drawing a very tentative conclusion that a *tetreres* had fewer oars than a *trieres*. The numeral in the names of types must certainly denote the number of men in each 'room' (see above, p. 155), rather than the number of banks of oars. The evidence that one man rowed one oar only concerns *triereis* and smaller ships, so that there is no evidence against the hypothesis that in *tetrereis* and higher denominations more than one man rowed at each oar. The *tetreres* could then have had four men to each 'room' (as the *trieres* had three) rowing two men to each of two oars. The oars of a *tetreres* would then have been larger, but only two-thirds as numerous as the oars of a *trieres*. The oar-system of a *penteres* is likely to have been similar, with three men to one oar and two to the other in each 'room'. The new oar-systems must have been designed to meet the shortage of skilled oarsmen, since for each oar there need have been only one skilled man.*

Steering Oars

We saw (p. 195) that the word 'turn' is used in poetry with *pedalion*, the steering oar, to suggest that the steering oar was turned about its axis. The evidence is against this conclusion for the larger ships of the fifth and fourth centuries. Two steering oars are standard equipment for *triereis* in the naval lists[10]. Plato speaks of 'the tiller of the steering oars'[11], suggesting that the inboard ends of the steering oars were joined together by a connecting bar. The same author in the *Alcibiades I* provides an enlightening passage. 'Suppose you were to sail in a ship. Would you be at a loss whether to move the tiller in or out and in your ignorance make a mistake, or would you sail in peace committing the tiller to the helmsman?'[12] 'Moving the tiller in or out' would mean moving the connecting bar in a lateral direction either towards yourself or away from yourself. The steering would then be effected by the lateral movement of the steering oar in the water, not by turning it on its axis. The fourth-century *Mechanica* confirms this inference. 'Why', the writer asks, 'is the steering oar, small as it is and operating at the extremity of the ship, powerful enough to move a heavy ship at the touch of one man sitting at the tiller?' He explains that the steering oar is a lever, and the

---

* For the assertion that the gear of a *tetreres* could be transferred to a *trieres*, see J. S. Morrison, *CQ* XLI (1947), pp. 121 ff.

fulcrum is the point at which the steering oar is attached to the ship[13]. This explanation implies the movement of the head of the steering oar to port for a turn to starboard and to starboard for a turn to port. The fulcrum is the point at which the oar is lashed to the ship's side. Such a lashing appears in the fragmentary representation of a pentekontor or triakontor in a black-figure sherd in the Acropolis museum (see above, Arch. 34; cf. 33, 35, Pl. 11).

It appears that the connecting bar was removable and that the position of the steering oar when not in use was a horizontal one. Such a position is frequently to be observed in representations of the stern of a beached ship, in particular, for a *trieres*, in the Talos vase ship (see Pl. 25a). There is a story in Polyaenus of the helmsman Calliades, who, being pursued by a faster ship, let go his steering oar repeatedly so that it cocked up on whichever side the ship tried to ram him. His object was that 'the pursuer coming up against the steering oar with his *epotides* would not be able to reach the hull with his ram which could only get as far as the first thranite oars'[14]. By letting go the head of the steering oar he let it take up the horizontal position under pressure from the water.

The fixture of the steering oar to the ship had then to allow movement round it in two dimensions. This fulcrum would also have to take the weight of the pressure of the water on the steering oar when it was in the steering position. On a bronze lamp made in the shape of a ship found in the Erechtheum and dated to the fourth century B.C. (p. 179, Pl. 27b), there is a projecting beam just at the point where we should expect the steering oar to be attached. In view of the nature of the attachment it seems reasonable to suppose that such a projecting beam was normal.

We saw in the *Helen*, where a ship is described as being fitted out, that 'steering oars were let down on each side of the ship with strops[15]'. That is to say, steering oars were fixed with strops on each side of the ship. When ships are immobilized, as we saw in Herodotus, their steering oars are unlashed[16]. Vegetius speaks of the ropes by which steering oars were tied and how in a sea-battle they were liable to be 'cut by skilful soldiers and seamen in small boats'[17].

There are two references in the naval lists to the 'wing' of the steering oar, as unserviceable. This part is likely to be the blade which would be liable to damage[18].

Ladders

Two ladders are standard equipment for a ship in the naval lists[19]. We noticed that ladders were run out in the stern in the kidnapping scene in the *Iphigeneia* (see p. 202). The many pictures of the sterns of beached ships occurring on red-figure vases show a single ladder in position. The word for the ladders we have been mentioning is *klimax* or *klimakis*. Another word *apobathra* is used of ladders used for a landing on a hostile shore[20]. These would probably be used over the side rather than over the stern and may be a different type.

Poles (*kontoi*)

Standard equipment for *triereis* seems to be two or three poles[21]. Sometimes a big pole is recorded in the naval lists, sometimes a small one[22]. Their use is demonstrated in a passage in Thucydides where a Peloponnesian fleet driven into a small compass by Phormio's encircling tactics uses poles to fend one ship off from another[23]. Another use of the pole was seen in the kidnapping scene in the *Iphigeneia* (see above, p. 202), to keep a ship, which was touching the shore with its stern, from broaching to in heavy weather.

Shores (*parastatai*)

Each ship has two[24]. They do not appear in literature and their function can only be guessed at. It seems a reasonable inference from their name that they were stakes placed on each side of a ship when she was drawn up on the beach to prevent her heeling over. In Homer and Hesiod we find *hermata*, piles of stones, performing just this function (see above, p. 65). Liddell–Scott–Jones suggest that they were props to stay the mast, but this does not seem at all likely.

Masts (*histoi*)

Two types of mast appear in the naval lists, corresponding to two types of sailyard and sail. In addition to the main mast (*histos megas*) there is the boat mast recorded on many ships[25]. The Greek name for the latter (*histos akateios*) means exactly 'boat mast'; it seems likely that it was a boat-size, i.e. small, mast used in addition to the main mast and almost certainly forward of it. Such small masts with small sailyard and sail are shown in representations of Roman ships.

Sailyards

It will be remembered that Aeschylus in the *Eumenides* says: 'In a storm the *keraiai* creak, then is the time to lower sail[26].' The word clearly means 'horns', and it is possibly for this reason that the plural form is often used in literature, always in the naval lists. In one or two of the representations of small ships under sail the sailyard appears to be composed of two spars lashed together, but generally the sailyard appears to be made of a single piece of wood. The plural form may either derive from a time when the sailyard was normally composite, or be the result of the idea that the sailyard was, as it were, the horns of the ship. Thucydides uses *keraia* twice in the singular to mean a ship's sailyard employed as a sort of crane by the Plataeans and hollowed out and used as a blow-pipe of giant proportions in the siege of Delium[27]. The third time he uses it of the sailyards of merchantmen protecting the entrances to the Athenian stockade in the bay of Syracuse with the destructive weights (*delphines*) attached to them[28]. Aristotle, demonstrating that jokes usually depend on some sort of ambiguity, gives as an example the ambiguity of the word which means both 'brail up (sail)' and 'hurry'. 'Where are you hurrying to?' might be taken to mean 'where are you brailing up the sail to?' The answer 'up to the sailyard' would seem funny to someone who meant to ask 'where are you hurrying to?'[29] Sails are then brailed up to the sailyard. The fourth-century *Mechanica* asks the question: 'When the *keraia* is higher, do ships sail faster with the same wind and sail?'[30] The sailyard could then be raised to the top of the mast, or in a storm lowered completely.

'HANGING' GEAR

Swifters

The first item in the lists of hanging gear are the *hupozomata*. They are likely therefore to be the most important, just as the oars, which come first in the lists of wooden gear, are the most important there. An inscription from the beginning of the Peloponnesian war appears to record a regulation prescribing the least number of men it was permissible to use when fitting a *hupozoma* to a *trieres*[31]. The operation would appear then to be quite a difficult one. In the *Knights* of 424 Cleon charges a man with exporting for

Peloponnesian *triereis—zomeumata*[32]. The word, which means soup, is presumably a comic substitution for *hupozomata*. They were as we should expect contraband of war, like *askomata*, sailcloth and pitch. In a list of 330/29 ships are said to have been fitted with *hupozomata* by a decree of the Council of 335/4[33]. Again, in a famous inscription of 325/4 recording its dispatch of an expedition to suppress piracy in the Adriatic, it is said that two extra *hupozomata* each were issued to the three *triereis* and one *tetreres* of the fleet. These *hupozomata* are described as coming from the number of those that had been removed from certain *triereis* by a resolution of the people proposed by Hagnonides[34]. The two *hippegoi* of the fleet were equipped with four of these *hupozomata* and the triakontors with two[35]. The fact that it was a political decision to fit or remove *hupozomata* suggests that ships on the active list were fitted with them, and that the decision concerned the number of ships to be retained on the active list. Two captured *triereis* in a list of 374/3 are noted as not fitted with *hupozomata*[36]. A passage from Polybius confirms this conclusion. He speaks of advice being given to the Rhodians to fit forty ships with *hupozomata* so that if there was an emergency call they would not be making their preparations after it had come, but would be in a state of preparation to do what was required[37]. It seems then that ships placed on the active list were fitted with *hupozomata*. When in 435 the Corcyraeans were threatened by a Corinthian fleet they 'yoked their old ships to make them seaworthy'. This practice is probably that of fitting *hupozomata* to ships which are not on the active list[38].

The normal number for each ship appears to have been four[39]. It seems unlikely that all would have been fitted at once. The extra two taken by the expedition to the Adriatic were presumably added because the fleet was going to be away from home for a long time. A list of dedications of the Delphic Amphiktyony contains an entry of *hupozomata* classing them with anchor ropes as opposed to small ropes such as *himantes* and *huperai*[40]. Ropes of the larger variety are divided in the naval lists into eight- and six-finger ropes[41]. *Hupozomata* were probably of the larger sort.

The method of fitting the *hupozoma* is nowhere described in detail. All we know is that it took a number of men to do it. The word *hupozoma* suggests an under-girdle. Such a girdle could be fitted either round under the keel or on the outside of the hull from stem to stern. Many considerations rule out the first alternative. In the first place a ship on the active list would await

295

launching with the girdle ready fitted. Thick ropes under the keel would make launching on a slipway impossible. In the second place we know the weight of four *hupozomata* which were the subject of a dedication: i.e. 17 talents 48 minas[42]. A single *hupozoma* works out at just under 257 lb. 250 lb. of modern lightly-tarred Italian hemp 5 in. rope would make a length of 280–340 ft.* Greek eight-finger (= 5 in.) rope would probably be somewhat heavier than this, but it is nevertheless quite clear that a *hupozoma* was long enough to pass round outside the hull of a 120 ft. *trieres* from end to end with something to spare. This conclusion can be confirmed from the information which we have about the monster *tessarakonteres* of Ptolemy Philopator of which we have Callixeinus' accurate description, including dimensions, preserved in Athenaeus and Plutarch[43]. It had two hulls and twelve *hupozomata*, six for each hull. Although the ship had two hulls it only had two, not four, *parexeiresiai*, so that the overall breadth of 38 cubits must be halved and reduced by the breadth of one *parexeiresia*, say three cubits, to produce a hull breadth of sixteen cubits. The ship's length was 280 cubits. Since the *hupozomata* were six hundred cubits long it is clear that they could pass from bow to stern outside the single hulls comfortably. A parallel to the use of *hupo* in *hupozoma* to mean not under the ship so much as on the outer surface of the hull is provided by the word *hupaloiphe* which means paint for the exterior of the hull (see above, p. 280).

The remainder of the evidence bears on the purpose and method of application of the *hupozoma*. Plato says: '*entonoi* and *hupozomata* in ships and taut sinews in the living creature have both the same nature. They are tensions whose preservation is essential to the safety of the ship and to the well-being of the body[44].' If tension is the essential quality of the rope girdle, some device must have been used to maintain the tension. Rope expands when dry and contracts when wet. The *hupozoma* must have been constantly getting wet and dry again in different parts of it. In the lists we find mention of *tonoi*, and on one occasion they are said to be *tonoi* of *hupozomata*[45]. These *tonoi* must be the same as the *entonoi* in the passage of Plato. The verb *enteino* from which the noun *entonos* is derived means, according to Liddell–Scott–Jones, to 'stretch or strain tight, especially any operation performed with straps or cords'. It seems that these *tonoi* or *entonoi* associated with *hupozomata* both in inscriptions and in Plato must have been just the tightening device which we have

* According to information kindly supplied by my friend Mr R. H. Tizard of Churchill College.

been looking for. In a list of hanging gear are included *kommata* and *koruphaia* of *hupozomata*[46]. The former are easily identified as pieces of *hupozomata*. *Koruphaia*, neuter plural, are more puzzling. *Koruphaiā*, feminine singular, is the headstall of a bridle, the strap which goes over the horse's head behind the ears[47]. There is on a number of reproductions of ships' sterns, of which the earliest is possibly the Lindus relief, a plaited rope passing round under the upward curving stern (see p. 180, Pl. 27 d). Since this is a plaited and not a laid rope it is unlikely to be part of the *hupozoma*, which like other naval ropes was almost certainly laid: but it might be the stern 'anchor' for the *hupozoma*. If so it might well be called a *koruphaion* by analogy with the horse's headstall. If the *koruphaion* had a bight at each end the *hupozoma* might be introduced inside the ship through these bights and be tightened up by a device at the helmsman's feet.

There are two further literary passages which are relevant. In Plato's *Republic* there is a story of the journey of the soul of Er the Armenian in the country of the dead. He journeys with others, and at one point 'they arrived at a place where they could see above stretched over the whole heaven and earth a straight light, like a pillar, but resembling the rainbow most of all, only brighter and purer. They arrived at this light after a day's journey, and saw there in the middle of the light, stretched from heaven, the ends of heaven's bonds. For this light is the constricting bond of heaven, like the *hupozomata* of *triereis*, thus keeping together the whole periphery; and from the ends the spindle of Necessity is attached[48].' Fortunately it is not necessary here to explain Plato's imagery in detail, for our purpose it is clear enough. A light surrounding and constricting the heaven is described at one point, seemingly in the far west, to have ends which, as it were, come inside the periphery and are attached to a spindle. The spindle, as it spun, would have tightened the 'bonds'. Finally this constricting light is compared to the *hupozomata* of *triereis*.

Apollonius Rhodius, describing the fitting out of the *Argo*, tells how before launching the ship 'they girded it with might and main, putting a tension on each side with a well-twisted rope from within, so that the planks should fit well with the dowels and withstand the opposing force of the sea'[49]. The 'well-twisted rope from within' sounds just like the *tonos* or *entonos*.

Our conclusions about the *hupozoma* are then as follows: the *hupozoma* was a rope long enough to pass round the hull from stem to stern on the outside. It was probably 'anchored' in the stern by means of a plaited strop round the curving stern where an ordinary rope would have had little purchase. The ends of the girdle were brought inside the ship in the stern and the whole girdle was tightened by means of a special device known as a *tonos* or *entonos*. The object of the girdle was to subject the outside skin to a constricting tension which would keep the structure from working loose under the stress of navigation under oar and sail, the shocks of battle, and the constant strains of hauling up and down beaches, and on occasion even across an isthmus[50]. A rope girdle constantly kept tight would undoubtedly have lengthened the ship's life. It was fitted to ships on the active list. In modern terminology it would probably be called a swifter.

Sails

The fifth-century *trieres* seems generally to have carried a single sail, but, in the fourth century, Xenophon speaks of main sails and boat sails; and the boat sail is mentioned in Aristophanes' *Lysistrata* of 411[51]. The latter, like the boat mast and the boat sailyard, seem to derive their name from the small craft (*akatoi*) for which they were suitable. We have no representations of *triereis* under sail, and can have no accurate idea of their rig. The main sail is however likely to have resembled the single sail of the earlier types of which we have representations. The boat sail is likely to have been a smaller sail of similar rectangular shape, rigged forward of the main sail, since we can observe such sails in later ships. A fragment of Aristotle speaks of *all* the sails of a ship, but we have no evidence for more than two[52].

The sails were made of linen, which is included with other naval materials as contraband of war in a list in Aristophanes[53]. This author also gives us the name for a sailmaker (*histiorraphos*)[54]. Another fifth-century writer of comedy, Hermippus, mentions sails and papyrus ropes coming from Egypt[55].

Ships going into action left their main sails behind, and main mast and tackle too very probably. The phrase 'raise the *akateion* (boat sail)' in Aristophanes with the meaning 'take to flight' indicates that the boat sail was taken into battle[56]. The Athenian fleet at Syracuse, which was constantly expecting action, left its sails in the forts on the promontory of Plemmyrium where they were captured when the forts fell[57]. Before the battle of Cyzicus Alcibiades fell in with two Athenian squadrons which had been collecting tribute and told them to put their main sails ashore and follow him[58].

Conon after Aegospotami captured the main sails which Lysander had put ashore before the battle[59]. And when Iphicrates set off on his voyage round the Peloponnese with raw crews he sailed 'as if he was expecting a sea-battle' and left his main sails behind but took his boat sails[60]. As a result he had plenty of opportunity of training his crews before he reached his destination.

Two kinds of sails are mentioned in the naval lists, light and heavy. Ships do not seem to have had two rigs. In a total of two hundred and eighty-eight sails in one list only seventy-four were light, and in another only sixty-three out of two hundred and eighty-one[61]. An entry in the list of 323/2 suggests that light sails were more valuable than heavy ones. A list of debts includes 'two light sails: in place of these the trierarchs handed back two heavy sails: for these they owe according to the schedule three hundred drachmae'[62]. It seems then that the light sails may have been employed on the ships of the highest rating. A light sail would certainly increase speed.

Ropes

(i) *Topeia.* This word seems to be used for the smaller rope tackle which is used in connection with the sails. In one of the naval lists there is an entry of complete sets of *topeia* for eighty-nine ships and in addition the following odd items: [1 *ankoina*], 2 *himantes*, 3 [*podes*], 3 *huperai*, 1 *chalinos*, and 8 *kalos*[63]. Again, there is a list of the hanging gear taken over by the overseers of the dockyards in 370. Apart from *hupozomata* and *tonoi*, with which we have already been concerned, the only other ropes mentioned are: *ankoinai, chalinoi, podes, huperai, kalos* and *himantes*[64]. There is also an entry in the same list: '*neia* untested 25'. That these were ropes seems clear from an entry in another list of hanging gear: 'In the old gear store new *neia* 2[5], among those which Eubulus bought. The majority are of five fathoms. Pieces of *neia* 4[65].' The word *neia* means merely 'belonging to a ship'. It seems likely then that these were lengths of rope which had not been made up into any specific piece of tackle. The six different types of rope mentioned on the two separate occasions probably then exhaust the kinds of *topeia*. Homeric usage showed that *podes* were the sheets attached to the bottom corners of the sail, and that *huperai* were probably braces attached to each end of the sailyard[66]. We are unable to attach any special meaning to *kaloi* in Homer. Herodotus speaking of the ships of his own time gives valuable information about them. He says that other nations 'attach the rings and *kaloi* to their sails on the outside', i.e. on the forward face, 'while the Egyptians attach them on the inside'[67]. In one black-figure vase-painting we can see very clearly brailing ropes passing over the sailyard through some kind of attached fitting, and apparently continuing out of sight down the forward side of the sail to its foot (see above, Arch. 88, Pl. 20*d*). We can readily believe that they passed through rings sewn to the sail at intervals to keep the brailing rope in position. Such rings are in fact shown on a representation of a Roman merchantship. *Kaloi, kalos* then are brailing ropes, and the phrase 'let out every kalos'[68] means to let the sail down to its fullest extent in a favourable wind. Seven or eight of these brailing ropes are often shown in ships on black-figure vases, and we can observe in these ships too that there are also horizontal ropes across the front of the sail, buntlines, which form with the brailing ropes a net-like structure against which the sail presses (see Arch. 88, Pl. 20*d*; Arch. 63, Pl. 16*d*).

There remain three members of the class of *topeia*, sail-tackle, *ankoinai*, *himantes*, and *chalinoi*. *Ankoinai* are likely to be the same as the *ankonnai* which in Alcaeus work loose or become slack in a storm as the sail develops holes[69]; but this does not help us very much. It has been suggested that since the sailyard was often made of two pieces of timber made to overlap and lashed together, *ankonnai* in Alcaeus were those lashings. In one of the naval lists there is an entry for a double *ankoina*[70]. The reason for using a double rope is to insure against breaking. There would be no point in doubling a rope for lashing. A stronger lashing would be achieved by using a longer rope. The fact that a double *ankoina* was sometimes used, and that this rope would work loose in a storm, suggests that it was a rope which normally took a strain. The word *himantes* means leather thongs. Since in the Homeric poems the sail and sailyard are regularly hauled up and let down 'with twisted ox-leathers' (see above, p. 55), it is reasonable to suppose that the use of leathers for this purpose continued and that *himantes* therefore are halliards. *Chalinoi* may have been buntlines, i.e. the horizontal ropes which with the vertical brailing ropes form a net on the forward face of the sail. The word is used in lyric poetry and tragedy for the anchor cable, and *chalinoteria* is used in the same sense[71], but anchor cables appear in the lists under the heading of *schoinia*, not *topeia*. The word *chalinos* means a bit or bridle. The buntlines which hold the sail in might well have such a name. We return then to *ankoinai* and ask if there are any strain-bearing ropes which appear not to have been mentioned in the list of sail tackle. In Homer shrouds (*protonoi*) and back-stay were prominent. The eight or so brailing ropes leading from the stern over the top of the yard-arm might have taken the place of a back stay. Furthermore the stability of the mast would be greatly increased in the *trieres* by the support of the deck through which it passed. On the other hand if the *trieres* sailed, as it appears to have done, with the wind abeam or on the quarter, shrouds would certainly have been necessary to give lateral support to the mast. *Ankoinai* may well be shrouds. The word means a bent arm, and thence metaphorically something which enfolds as in an embrace. It is perhaps a coincidence that the word shroud has a similar non-nautical meaning in English. The *ankoinai* may be regarded as embracing and supporting the mast.

(ii) The second category of ropes in the naval lists are *schoinia*. These are heavy ropes, distinguished as of eight fingers and of six fingers (i.e. ropes of 5·8 and 4·4 in. in circumference). Each ship was equipped with four of each size[72]. We are told that each ship had four anchor cables (one for each anchor and two spares), and two to four stern cables[73]. The anchor cable had the heavier work when a ship was riding in deep water and when her stern was beached. It was used also to haul the ship off the beach. We find anchor cables accordingly classed with *hupozomata*[74]. It seems reasonable to infer that the eight-finger cables were the anchor cables and the six-finger the stern cables. The latter are referred to in the naval lists as *epigua*[75]; and this word, which seems to have superseded *prumnesia* in common usage, appears in a fragment of Aristophanes: 'Bravo the *epibates* who dived overboard to carry the *epiguon* ashore[76].' The word *peismata* which is common in Homer and in tragedy for mooring cables appears in this sense in Plato[77].

Herodotus gives the material for the ropes used in the bridge over the Hellespont which was made for the Persian army as papyrus and hemp[78]. So when Hermippus in the fifth century speaks of 'hanging gear, sails and papyrus, coming from Egypt' we can infer that the papyrus was material for ropes[79]. In a description of a ship built by Hiero of Syracuse in the third century B.C. Moschion records that the material for the ropes was *leukaia* from Spain and hemp and pitch from the Rhône[80]. It seems likely that Athenian ropes in the fifth and fourth centuries were made of papyrus and hemp, and that they were prevented from rotting by some kind of pitch.

Katablema, hupoblema

The nature of these two items of the hanging gear is completely obscure. They occur in the singular, that is to say there was only one on each ship so that any piece of gear which would have had to be used on both sides of the ship is ruled out. Liddell–Scott–Jones describe *katablema* as a 'tarpaulin for keeping off missiles'. *One* tarpaulin capable of this function would necessarily have been much too large unless it merely covered the bow. We have one reference to the *katablema* as made of hair[81]. The interesting thing about the *hupoblema* is that it is always absent in lists of the hanging gear of *tetrereis*[82]. The new oar system somehow made it unnecessary. If the oar system of the *tetreres* dispensed, as we have suggested, with the thalamian oarsmen, the *hupoblema* may have been some kind of canvas equivalent of floor-boards, which was unnecessary in the absence of the thalamian oarsmen.

Parablemata, pararrumata

We have earlier met with side screens for the protection of the oarsmen. In the naval lists they occur as 'white', i.e. made of canvas, or as 'made of hair'[83]. On one occasion a *pararruma* of leather is mentioned in addition to the normal two kinds[84]. Canvas side screens are likely to have been used to protect the oarsmen from the weather, sun or spray, while the hair-cloth screens would have been effective against missiles, leather ones more effective still. In the *Hellenica* Xenophon describes an occasion where side screens were used so that the enemy would not know whether the ships were manned or not[85]. On another occasion he includes putting up the side screens among the preparations for battle[86]. One entry in the naval lists records that a ship needed its side screens nailing down[87]. It looks as if the covering was coming adrift from the framework. We have noticed Chabrias' devices for keeping his ships dry, as described by Polyaenus, consisting of screens from deck downwards and outwards to the outer end of the outrigger, and others on the underside of the outrigger (see above, p. 282).

Anchors

The final item in the list of hanging gear is the anchor. There were two in each ship, and they were made of iron[88]. Xenophon records an occasion when stones were used instead of anchors in the old Homeric fashion[89].

The normal use of the anchor was when approaching a beach stern foremost. An anchor was let go out of the bow. The ship was thus held from broaching to and when the time came for departure she could be hauled off. Ships also rode at anchor off shore. Two anchors were then sometimes used[90].

TEXTS

'Wooden' Gear

1. Thuc. 1 10⁴. The oarsmen in Homeric ships αὐτερέται δὲ ὅτι ἦσαν καὶ μάχιμοι πάντες, ἐν ταῖς Φιλοκτήτου ναυσὶ δεδήλωκεν· τοξότας γὰρ πάντας πεποίηκε τοὺς προσκώπους. περίνεως δὲ οὐκ εἰκὸς πολλοὺς ξυμπλεῖν ἔξω τῶν βασιλέων καὶ τῶν μάλιστα ἐν τέλει.

2. IG 2² 1614 30 ταύτῃ [παράκε]ιται ταρρὸς δόκιμος· ἐνδεῖ περίνεων.

3. IG 2² 1606 43 τούτ[ων ἐ]ννεαπήχεις III.

    1607   9 αὗται ἐν[νεαπήχεις
          14 ἐννεαπήχεις καὶ σπιθαμί
          22 αὗται ἐννεαπήχεις
          23 ἐννεαπήχεις
          51 ἐννέα πηχέων καὶ σπιθαμῆς
          55 τ]ούτων ἐννεαπήχεις Γ
          98 το]ύτων ἐννε[απ]ή[χ]εις.

4. Aristotle, *PA* 4 10 687b18 διὰ τί δὲ ἄνισοι πάντες ἐγένοντο (οἱ δάκτυλοι) καὶ μακρότατος ὁ μέσος; ἢ ὅτι τὰς κορυφὰς αὐτῶν ἐπὶ ἴσον ἐξικνεῖσθαι βέλτιον ἦν ἐν τῷ περιλαμβάνειν ὄγκους τινὰς μεγάλους ἐκ κύκλῳ...καθάπερ οἶμαι κἂν ταῖς τριήρεσι τὰ πέρατα τῶν κωπῶν εἰς ἴσον ἐξικνεῖται, καίτοι γ᾽ οὐκ ἴσων ἁπασῶν οὐσῶν· καὶ γὰρ οὖν κἀκεῖ τὰς μέσας μεγίστας ἀπεργάζονται διὰ τὴν αὐτὴν αἰτίαν.

5. Galen, *UP* 1 24 καὶ ὁ ἔσχατος (δάκτυλος) δὲ μικρὸς ὀρθῶς, καὶ ὁ μέσος μακρός, ὥσπερ κώπη μεσόνεως (Schneider: μέσον νεώς vulg.)· μάλιστα γὰρ τὸ λαμβανόμενον ἀνάγκη περιλαμβάνεσθαι κύκλῳ κατὰ τὸ μέσον πρὸς τὰς ἐργασίας.

Cf. Mich. Eph. Comm. in Arist. Graec. XXII 118 15 καὶ γὰρ καὶ αἱ μέσαι κῶπαι τῶν νεῶν μακρότεραι τυγχάνουσι τῶν ἄκρων.

6. Aristotle, *Mechanica* 4 850b10 ἐν μέσῃ δὲ τῇ νηῒ πλεῖστον τῆς κώπης ἐντός ἐστιν. καὶ γὰρ ἡ ναῦς ταύτῃ εὐρυτάτη ἐστὶν ὥστε πλεῖον ἐπ᾽ ἀμφότερα ἐνδέχεσθαι μέρος τῆς κώπης ἑκατέρου τοίχου ἐντὸς εἶναι τῆς νεώς.

7. IG 2² 1604 40 ἐνδεῖ — —]ίων τράφηκος ἕδρας κώπης ζυγίας. ταῦτα δεῖ Μενέξενον παραδοῦ[ναι.

8. IG 2² 1629 684 παρὰ Νεοπτολέμου Δεκελε ταρροῦ τετρηριτικοῦ ἀπελάβομεν Γ Η Γ Δ Γ.

9. Andocides 2 11 τούτους τε εἰσήγαγον τοὺς κωπέας καὶ παρόν μοι πέντε δραχμῶν τὴν τιμὴν αὐτῶν δέξασθαι οὐκ ἠθέλησα πράξασθαι πλέον ἢ ὅσου ἐμοὶ κατέστησαν.

10. *IG* 2² 1606 34 αὕτη ἔχει πηδάλια, τὸ ἕτερον ἀδό[κιμο]ν;

1608 74 αὕτη] ἔχει πη[δ]άλια ΙΙ· τοῦ ἑ[τέρου] ἡ πτέρυξ ἀδόκιμος [π]α[ράκει]ται.

1611 23, total of rudder oars is 469: enough for 234 ships with one over.

11. Plato, *Statesman* 272 e.

12. Plato, *Alcibiades* 117c–d τί δὲ εἰ ἐν νηΐ πλέοις, ἆρα δοξάζοις ἂν πότερον χρὴ τὸν οἴακα εἴσω ἄγειν ἢ ἔξω, καὶ ἅτε οὐκ εἰδὼς πλανῷο ἄν, ἢ τῷ κυβερνήτῃ ἐπιτρέψας ἂν ἡσυχίαν ἄγοις;

13. Aristotle, *Mechanica* 5 550 b 25 διὰ τί τὸ πηδάλιον μικρὸν ὂν καὶ ἐπ' ἐσχάτῳ τῷ πλοίῳ τοσαύτην δύναμιν ἔχοι ὥστε ὑπὸ μικροῦ οἴακος καὶ ἑνὸς ἀνθρώπου δυνάμεως, καὶ ταύτης ἠρεμαίας, μεγάλα κινεῖσθαι μεγέθη πλοίου; ἢ μὲν οὖν προσήρμοσται τῷ πλοίῳ, γίνεται ὑπομόχλιον, τὸ δὲ ὅλον πηδάλιον ὁ μοχλός, τὸ δὲ βάρος ἡ θάλασσα, ὁ δὲ κυβερνήτης ὁ κινῶν.

14. Polyaenus v. 43.

15. Euripides, *Helen* 1536. See p. 216.

16. Xen. *Anab.* 5 1 11 εἰ οὖν αἰτησάμενοι παρὰ Τραπεζουντίων μακρὰ πλοῖα κατάγοιμεν καὶ φυλάττοιμεν αὐτὰ τὰ πηδάλια παραλυόμενοι. . .

17. Vegetius iv 46. Per has (bipennes) in medio ardore pugnandi peritissimi nautae vel milites cum minoribus scaphulis secreto incidunt funes quibus adversariorum ligata sunt gubernacula.

18. See note 10 above.

19. E.g. *IG* 2² 1611 28, the total of ladders is 465: enough for 232 ships with one over.

20. See above, p. 135.

21. E.g. *IG* 2² 1609 90. The *Doris* has two poles. In *IG* 2² 1611 33 two poles are left over after an allocation of ? poles to 232 ships. The standard allocation must then be more than two.

22. Big pole: *IG* 2² 1607 21, 1606 51 and 94. Small pole: 1604 29 and probably 1606 94.

23. Thuc. ii 84³ καὶ ναῦς τε νηΐ προσέπιπτε καὶ τοῖς κοντοῖς διωθοῦντο.

24. *IG* 2² 1611 38 454 *parastatai* for 227 ships.

25. E.g. *IG* 2² 1604 48 ἐνδεῖ ἱστοῦ μεγάλου; 1604 64 ἐνδεῖ ἱστοῦ ἀκατείου.

26. See above, p. 212, note 53.

27. Thuc. ii 76⁴ καὶ δοκοὺς μεγάλας ἀρτήσαντες. . .ἀπὸ κεραιῶν δύο ἐπικεκλιμένων καὶ ὑπερτεινουσῶν ὑπὲρ τοῦ τείχους.

iv 100² καὶ κεραίαν μεγάλην δίχα πρίσαντες ἐκοίλαναν ἅπασαν.

28. Thuc. vii 42² ἔπειτα αὐτοὺς αἱ κεραῖαι ὑπὲρ τῶν ἔσπλων αἱ ἀπὸ τῶν ὁλκάδων δελφινοφόροι ἠρμέναι ἐκώλυον.

29. Aristotle, *Soph. Elench.* 33 182 b 17 καὶ γὰρ οἱ λόγοι σχεδὸν οἱ γελοῖοι πάντες εἰσὶ παρὰ τὴν λέξιν, οἷον ἀνὴρ ἐφέρετο κατὰ κλίμακος δίφρον, καὶ ποῖ στέλλεσθαι; πρὸς τὴν κεραίαν.

30. Aristotle, *Mechanica* 6 851 a 38 διὰ τί ὅσῳ ἂν ἡ κεραία ἀνωτέρα ᾖ, θᾶττον πλεῖ τὰ πλοῖα τῷ αὐτῷ ἱστίῳ καὶ τῷ αὐτῷ πνεύματι;

'Hanging' Gear

31. *IG* I² 73 ἐξέστω δὲ] μηδ' ἑνὶ ἀνέλκ[εν ἀνδράσιν ἐλάττοσι ἢ τετ]ταράκοντα καὶ [καθέλκεν ἐς τὴν θάλατταν] ἔλαττον ἢ εἴκο[σι ἀνδράσι μηδὲ πιττῶν μ]ηδὲ hυποζωνύνα[ι ἔλαττον ἢ πεντήκοντα ἀ]νδράσιν. . .

32. Aristophanes, *Knights* 278–9

τουτονὶ τὸν ἄνδρ' ἐγὼ 'νδείκνυμι, καὶ φήμ' ἐξάγειν
ταῖσι Πελοποννησίων τριήρεσι—ζωμεύματα.

33. *IG* 2² 1627 49 ὑποζώματα ἐπὶ ναῦς σὺν αἷς ἡ βουλὴ ὑπέζωσεν ἡ ἐπ' Εὐαινέτου ἄρχοντος Η Η ⱶ Γ Ι.

34. *IG* 2² 1629 11 ff. καὶ ἕτερα ὑποζώματα ἔλαβον τῶν ἐγλυθέντων δύο κατὰ ψήφισμα δήμου ὃ εἶπεν Ἁγνωνίδης Περγασῆθεν.

Cf. 31 ff., 53 ff.

35. *IG* 2² 1629 70 ὑποζώματα δὲ ΙΙΙΙ τριηριτικῶν.

83 ὑποζώματα δὲ ΙΙΙΙ τῶν ἐγλυθ. τριηρ.

36. *IG* 2² 1606 79 and 83 ἀνυπόζωστος.

37. Polybius 27 3 3 καὶ τετταράκοντα ναῦς συμβουλεύσας τοῖς Ῥοδίοις ὑποζων-νύειν, ἵνα ἐάν τις ἐκ τῶν καιρῶν γένηται χρεία, μὴ τότε παρασκευάζωνται πρὸς τὸ παρακαλούμενον, ἀλλ' ἑτοίμως διακείμενοι πράττωσι τὸ κριθὲν ἐξ αὐτῆς.

38. Thuc. 1 29³ ζεύξαντές τε τὰς παλαιὰς ὥστε πλωίμους εἶναι.

39. *IG* 2² 1631 671 ξύλινα ἐντελῆ· ὑ[ποζώματα] ΙΙΙΙ καὶ ἕτερα ΙΙ τῶν [ἐγλυθέν]των.

40. *IG* 2² 1649 11

ὑπ]οζώματα: Γ Ι: σχοινία ἀγκύρε[ια
Δ Δ Γ Ι Ι Ι: σὺν τοῖς μικροῖς· τού[των
στ]ύππινα Γ: ἵμαντες Ι Ι: ὑπέρ[αι
χαλι]νός

41. E.g. 1627 447 σχοινία ὀκτωδάκτυλα ΙΙΙΙ ἑξδάκτυλα ΙΙΙΙ.

42. *IG* 2² 1479B49 ὑποζώματα τέτταρα [σταθμὸν τά]λαντα ⋔[Ⱶ]ΤΤ μναῖ Δ Δ [Δ Δ] Γ [Ι Ι Ι.

Cf. 57 ὑποζώματα τέττ[αρα στ]αθμὸν [τ]άλαντα ⋔ⱵΤΤ μναῖ Δ[ΔΔΓΙΙΙ.

43. Athenaeus 5 37, Plutarch, *Demetrius* 43 4.

44. Plato, *Laws* 945c πολλοὶ καιροὶ πολιτείας λύσεώς εἰσι καθάπερ νεὼς ἢ ζῴου τινός, οὓς ἐντόνους τε καὶ ὑποζώματα καὶ νεύρων ἐπιτόνους μίαν οὖσαν φύσιν διεσπαρ-μένην πολλαχοῦ πολλοῖς ὀνόμασι προσαγορεύομεν.

45. *IG* 2² 1610 23; 1613 280 and 282; 1673 12 ὑποζωμάτων τέτταρας τόνους ἐλάβομεν ἐκ νεωρίων.

46. *IG* 2² 1610 26 and 21.

47. Xen. *Equ.* 3 2, 5 1, 6 7.

48. Plato, *Republic* 616b–c ἐπειδὴ δὲ τοῖς ἐν τῷ λειμῶνι ἑκάστοις ἑπτὰ ἡμέραι γένοιντο, ἀναστάντας ἐντεῦθεν δεῖν τῇ ὀγδόῃ πορεύεσθαι, καὶ ἀφικνεῖσθαι τεταρταίους ὅθεν καθορᾶν ἄνωθεν διὰ παντὸς τοῦ οὐρανοῦ καὶ γῆς τεταμένον φῶς εὐθύ, οἷον κίονα,

μάλιστα τῇ ἴριδι προσφερῆ, λαμπρότερον δὲ καὶ καθαρώτερον· εἰς ὃ ἀφικέσθαι προελθόντες ἡμερησίαν ὁδόν, καὶ ἰδεῖν αὐτόθι κατὰ μέσον τὸ φῶς ἐκ τοῦ οὐρανοῦ τὰ ἄκρα αὐτοῦ τῶν δεσμῶν τεταμένα—εἶναι γὰρ τοῦτο τὸ φῶς σύνδεσμον τοῦ οὐρανοῦ, οἷον τὰ ὑποζώματα τῶν τριήρων, οὕτω πᾶσαν συνέχον τὴν περιφοράν—ἐκ δὲ τῶν ἄκρων τεταμένον Ἀνάγκης ἄτρακτον.

49. Apollonius Rhodius 1 367–9

νῆα δ᾿ ἐπικρατέως Ἄργου ὑποθημοσύνησιν
ἔζωσαν πάμπρωτον εὐστρεφεῖ ἔνδοθεν ὅπλῳ
τεινάμενος ἑκάτερθεν.

50. E.g. Thuc. III 15¹. And cf. Aristophanes, *Thesmophoriazusae* 647–8.

51. Xen. *HG* VI 2 27 εὐθὺς μὲν γὰρ τὰ μεγάλα ἱστία αὐτοῦ κατέλιπεν ὡς ἐπὶ ναυμαχίαν πλέων· καὶ τοῖς ἀκατείοις δέ, καὶ εἰ φορὸν πνεῦμα εἴη, ὀλίγα ἐχρῆτο. (373 B.C.)

Aristophanes, *Lysistrata* 63–4 (van Leeuwen)

ἡ γοῦν Θεογένους
ὡς δεῦρ᾿ ἰοῦσα τἀκάτειον ἤρετο.

It is possible that when Thucydides in IV 100² speaks of a μεγάλη κεραία he means a main yardarm, not just a big one.

52. Aristotle, fr. 11 ναῦς πᾶσιν ἱστίοις εὐτρεπιζομένη.

53. Aristophanes, *Frogs* 364.

54. Aristophanes, *Thesmophoriazusae* 935.

55. Hermippus, fr. 63

ἐκ δ᾿ Αἰγύπτου τὰ κρεμαστά,
ἱστία καὶ βίβλους.

56. Aristophanes, *Lysistrata* 64 (see note 51 above).

57. Thuc. VII 24².

58. Xen. *HG* I 1 13 Ἀλκιβιάδης δὲ εἰπὼν καὶ τούτοις διώκειν αὐτὸν ἐξελομένοις τὰ μεγάλα ἱστία...

59. Xen. *HG* II 1 29 Κόνων δὲ ταῖς ἐννέα ναυσὶν φεύγων...κατασχὼν ἐπὶ τὴν Ἀβαρνίδα τὴν Λαμψάκου ἄκραν ἔλαβεν αὐτόθεν τὰ μεγάλα τῶν Λυσάνδρου νεῶν ἱστία.

60. See note 51 above.

61. *IG* 2² 1627 65; 1629 371.

62. *IG* 2² 1631 415 κρεμαστὰ τριηριτικὰ ἱστία λεπτὰ II ἀντὶ τούτων παρέδοσαν παχέα δύο ὑπὲρ τούτων προσοφείλουσι πρὸς τὸ διάγραμμα Η Η Η.

63. *IG* 2² 1611 54 τοπεῖα ἐπὶ ναῦς ἐντε]λῆ ΗᴿΔΔΔΓΙΙΙΙ [καὶ ἄγκοινα Ι ἱ]μάντες II [πόδες] III, ὑπέραι III, χαλιν]ός I, κ(ά)λως ΓΙΙΙ.

64. *IG* 2² 1610 9 ὑποζώ[μ]ατα III ἄγκοιν[α]ν I χαλινόν I πόδας II ὑπέρα I. 15 ἱμάντες II. 27 νεῖα οὐ δεδοκιμασμένα ΔΔΙΙΙΙΙ.

65. *IG* 2² 1627 353 ἐν τῇ ἀρχαίῳ σκ[ε]υοθήκῃ νεῖα καινὰ ΔΔ[Γ] ὧν Εὔβουλος ἐπρ[ία]το· τούτων τὰ πλεῖστα πεντώρυγα· νείων τόμοι ΙΙΙΙ.

66. See above, p. 56. Cf. Antiphon fr. 176 Th. ὁ ποδοχῶν = the helmsman.

67. Herodotus II 36⁴ τῶν ἱστίων τοὺς κρίκους καὶ τοὺς κάλους οἱ μὲν ἄλλοι ἔξωθεν προσδέουσι, Αἰγύπτιοι δὲ ἔσωθεν.

68. E.g. Aristophanes, *Knights* 756; Plato, *Protagoras* 338a and *Sisyphus* 389c.

69. See above, p. 119.

70. *IG* 2² 1627 151 ἄγκοιναν διπλῆν with ἱμάντες, πόδες, ὑπέραι and χαλινός.

71. Pindar, *Pyth.* 4 25; Euripides, *I.T.* 1043.

72. *IG* 2² 1624 117; 1627 447.

73. *IG* 2² 1611 393; 1611 254 (between two and four).

74. See note 40 above.

75. *IG* 2² 1611 255; 1622 292 σχοινίων ἐπιγύων III.

76. Aristophanes, fr. 80 (Babylonians)

εὖ γ᾽ ἐξεκολύμβησ᾽ οὑπιβάτης ὡς ἐξοίσων ἐπίγυον.

Cf. fr. 426 and *A.P.* 10 1 (Leonidas).

77. Plato, *Laws* 893b ἐχόμενοι δὲ ὥς τινος ἀσφαλοῦς πείσματος...

78. Herodotus 7 25¹ παρεσκευάζετο δὲ καὶ ὅπλα ἐς τὰς γεφύρας βύβλινά τε καὶ λευκολίνου.

Cf. 36³.

79. See note 55 above.

80. Athenaeus v 40 206 f. εἰς δὲ σχοινία λευκέαν μὲν ἐξ Ἰβηρίας κάνναβιν δὲ καὶ πίτταν ἐκ τοῦ Ῥοδανοῦ ποταμοῦ.

81. *IG* 2² 1631 418 καταβλήματα τρίχινα.

82. *IG* 2² 1627 466; 1628 333 and 605; 1629 1081.

83. E.g. 1611 244–249 παραρύματα λευκά, τρίχινα.

84. *IG* 2² 1627 348 παράρυμα κάτ[τυ]ος.

85. Xen. *HG* I 6 19 παραρύματα.

86. Xen. *HG* II 1 22 παραβλήματα.

87. *IG* 2² 1604 31 παραβλήματα κατηλῶσαι.

88. *IG* 2² 1609 114; 1611 259, two for each ship; 1627 449 ἀγκύρας σιδηρᾶς II.

89. Xen. *Anab.* 3 5 10 λίθους ἀρτήσας καὶ ἀφεὶς ὥσπερ ἀγκύρας εἰς τὸ ὕδωρ.

90. Demosthenes 56 44 ἐπὶ δυσὶν ἀγκυραῖν ὁρμεῖν.

12

HANDLING

ROUTINE NAVIGATION

At Athens, when the trierarchs were given the order to launch their ships, they were required to get them fitted out and to bring them round to the jetty as quickly as possible. Prizes were given to the first three trierarchs to bring their ships round.

The process of fitting out (*paraskeue*) is described vividly by Aristophanes in the *Acharnians*. 'When there is a *casus belli*', Dicaearchus tells the Athenians, 'you don't sit quiet; but in a moment[1] you would be launching three hundred ships and the city would be full of the hubbub of servicemen, of shouts for the trierarch, of wage-paying, Pallas-gilding, the echoing covered market, of doling out rations, of leathers, oar-loops and people buying casks, of garlic, olives, onions in nets, of trierarchic crowns, anchovies, flutegirls and black-eyes, while down at the dockyard the air would be full of the planing of oars, the hammering of dowel-pins, the fitting of oarports with leathers, of pipes, *keleustai*, trills and whistles[2].' Another passage in the *Acharnians* associates the fitting out of ships with the smell of pitch[3]. But this is perhaps an earlier stage than that described above.

When the ship has been manned the trierarch exercises it. Such exercises have already been noticed in the preparations for the battle of Lade (see above, pp. 135–6). Races as a means of practising a crew were undoubtedly used at Athens. Pindar refers to ship races[4]. There is a possibility that he is attributing such races to the Isthmian games. There is certainly a later tradition that the *Argo* won in a contest of ships at those games[5]. The young pleader in Lysias' speech claims that he won a victory with a *trieres* in the race at Sunium[6]: and the comic poet Plato, who was writing between 428 and 390 B.C., composed an epigram for Themistocles' tomb which suggests that ship races were a common sight in Piraeus[7]. Isocrates mentions that Evagoras, who set up as naval power in Cyprus at the beginning of the fourth century B.C., was, on his death, honoured by his son Nicocles with ship races[8]. Alexander, too, held ship races for his newly assembled fleet at Thapsacus[9].

The object of training and exercises was to get the crew of a hundred and seventy oarsmen moving together. A crew which is not well together is called *axunkrotetos* 'not with a unified beat' by Thucydides[10]. He was describing a raw Athenian fleet which had to put out against a Peloponnesian fleet at the end of the war. The same word is used positively by Xenophon. The Athenians propose to send sixty ships to Corcyra under Timotheus. He finds it impossible to man his ships at Athens and tries to recruit in the islands, 'thinking it a formidable matter to sail with a scratch crew against ships which had a unified beat'[11]. The Athenians had no patience with him and appointed Iphicrates in his place. Iphicrates solved the problem by taking untrained crews and training them in the course of the voyage west. He left his main sails behind and only used the boat sails sparingly, proceeding under oar most of the time. He organized races to the land, taking the fleet out line ahead, changing to line abreast and then giving the signal to start. He used to put out to sea immediately after dinner, and give the crews a rest running before the wind if it was favourable. Otherwise he gave the oarsmen rest in turn. Iphicrates' training voyage was an improvisation, but the exercising of trained crews when on active service seems to have been regular. Thucydides speaks of the exercises of the Syracusan fleet on a number of occasions[12], and Xenophon says that Alcibiades in conditions of bad visibility caught Mindarus' fleet exercising some way off shore before the battle of Cyzicus[13].

We have hitherto been considering the full oar power of a *trieres*, and the measures taken to achieve the difficult aim of a unified beat for a hundred and seventy oars. Full oar power was probably only developed in exercises and in battle, or on a short voyage of special urgency. The *trieres* which was sent from Athens to reprieve the Mytilenians made its maximum speed with the crew rowing and sleeping in turns[14]. Xenophon says that the voyage under oar from Byzantium to Heracleia about 140 miles east along the Black Sea coast of Asia Minor took 'a long day'[15]. If we assume that a long day means twelve hours, the speed is between eleven and twelve knots. If a long day means eighteen hours, the speed is reduced to less than eight knots. In normal voyaging under oar it seems likely that all the three banks of oars of a *trieres* were not commonly used together. Polyaenus relates a story of the Athenian commander Diotimus, a contemporary of Iphicrates, who disembarked by night a considerable number of men from each of his ships and laid an ambush with them. At daybreak he held his fleet off the place of ambush and gave orders for his soldiers on deck to prepare for action, and the oarsmen to pull in turn first the thalamian, then the zygian and then the thranite oars. The enemy observers presumably treated this as normal practice. When Diotimus' force attempted a landing the enemy attacked them and were taken in the rear by the ambushing troops[16]. The words used for ships employing less than the full complement of oarsmen are given in Xenophon's account of Conon's escape at Aegospotami. When Lysander attacked, Conon ordered the Athenian fleet to go into action; but, as the crews were scattered ashore, some of the ships put to sea *dikrotoi*, some *monokrotoi*, while some were quite empty[17]. The beat (*krotos*), which we saw was unified in a well-trained ship, had one component in a ship rowing only one bank of oars, and two when two banks were rowed. The word *trikrotos* is used of the *trieres* in later writers[18]. *Dikrotos* can also be used of a ship which has two banks of oars only. Arrian describes some of the triakontors in Alexander's fleet as *dikrotoi* and getting into difficulties because they did not have their lower oars far above the water[19].

The procedure of rowing, with a *keleustes* to call the time and an *auletes* to keep up the stroke, has already been described. As Nicias observed, peak performance of oarsmen lasts a short time, few of them both get the stroke going and also keep it up[20]. Rough water caused difficulties to unskilled men who found themselves unable to recover their oar after the stroke[21]. Way was checked by holding the oar in the water[22]; the next command was to ship or partially ship oars[23]. The oars of the two-level pentekontor on the kylix in the British Museum (Arch. 85, Pls. 19 and 20a) seem to be thus partially shipped, since the ship is under sail. A more complete method of stowing oars is described in the passage relating the launching of the *Argo* in Apollonius Rhodius: 'Turning up the oars high on either side they tied them about the tholepins with a cubit's length of the oar outboard[24].' Ovid describes the operation with his customary accuracy in the *Metamorphoses*: 'They left the port and the breeze shook the shrouds, thereat the oarsman turned the useless oars up at the ship's side[25].' Pictures of medieval galleys often show the oars in this raised position like the wings of a sea bird.

Oar power was used in this period, as always, to get a ship out of a land-locked harbour on to the open sea where a breeze might be expected. Xenophon tells how Critias charged Theramenes with being a turncoat:

'You must persevere like the seamen do (i.e. at the oar) until they get a favourable breeze[26].' Euripides, we saw (p. 202), gives a vivid picture of the dangers of a lee shore, even for an oared ship. An unfavourable wind could apparently prevent *triereis* setting out. An attack on Piraeus by a Peloponnesian fleet at the beginning of the war was abandoned for this reason[27]. Thucydides says it was lucky that no unfavourable wind hindered the *trieres* bringing the reprieve to Mytilene[28]. Demosthenes' fleet stayed at Pylos because of bad weather[29].

The operation of going astern under oar is often described. In only one passage in Thucydides does it denote the routine operation of beaching stern first[30]. It is Cicero who gives us the only accurate description of this manœuvre since Homer. He writes to Atticus: 'Now to return to that matter of the word *inhibere* you are interested in, I dislike it very much. It is a completely nautical word. I knew that, but I thought that rowing was stopped when the oarsmen received the command to *inhibere*. That this was not the case I learnt yesterday when a ship put in at my estate. They don't stop rowing, they row in a different way. *Inhibitio* of the oarsmen involves motion, and very violent motion too, as the oar power drives the ship sternwards instead of forwards[31].'

On service *triereis* were normally beached at night or when a prolonged stay was contemplated. *Hormein* and *kathormisasthai* in Thucydides, if unqualified, mean beaching[32]. Warships sometimes anchored off shore, but not if they could help it. One thing Apollodorus complained of in Demosthenes' speech *Against Polycles* was that he had had to spend the whole night at anchor in deep water off a hostile shore[33]. In Homer when a ship beached bow foremost a special word, *okellein*, was used: so in Thucydides *okellein* is used of the beaching of Brasidas' ships in the attempted landing on Pylos[34].

The noise of a large oared ship being rowed must have been considerable. Aristotle tells us that it was[35], and notices that the noise of the oars entering the water only reaches the land as they are being recovered at the end of the stroke[36]. The word for the noise is *rothion*. Aristophanes uses it metaphorically in the *Knights* for the applause in the theatre: the chorus urges the audience to 'raise a great surge for the poet, send him on his way with eleven oarstrokes': i.e. as we should say, 'give him eleven'[37].

Aristotle also noticed the rainbow which the oars make as they leave the water[38].

UNDER SAIL

Metaphorical passages in the *Knights* of Aristophanes throw light on sailing practice. When the wind blows a gale the helmsman brails up his sail and lets the ship drive. A phrase in the *Frogs* 'with sail brailed up using the sail's edge' indicates that in a high wind the canvas at the extremities of the sail-yard was used[39]. When a squall threatens he is warned by the bow officer and pays out the sheet. When the wind's force lessens he pays out the brailing ropes nearest the ends of the sailyard (*terthrioi*) and thus increases the canvas area there. Finally when the wind moderates he pays out every brailing rope, and the sail extends downward to its full length everywhere[40]. In these passages we are to suppose that the wind is astern or on the quarter. The measures taken concern its force, not its direction.

The fourth-century work *Mechanica*, attributed to Aristotle, gives us some information on sailing practice when the wind is not favourable. The question is asked: 'Why, when people want to sail a course with the wind's help, although the wind is not favourable, do they reef up the part of the sail near the helmsman, but let go the part near the bow, making a foot? It is because the steering oars cannot counteract the wind when it is powerful, but can do so when it is weak; and therefore they reduce (the area of canvas in the stern exposed to) it. The wind moves the ship forward, but the steering oar turns the wind into a favourable breeze resisting it and using the sea as a fulcrum. At the same time the seamen fight against the wind, for they lean their bodies against it[41].'

It is clear that the writer envisages a ship with the sailyard braced round so that it extends fore and aft. The seamen lean out to windward to trim the ship, like modern yachtsmen. The area of canvas abaft the mast is reduced so that the tendency of the ship to luff, i.e. come up into the wind, is lessened. As the writer says, the steering oars would not be able to counteract this tendency, being a comparatively weak form of rudder. There is no foot, i.e. point of attachment for a sheet, at the after corner of the sail since it is brailed up. The single foot is at the forward corner of the sail. The phrase 'make a foot' seems to indicate this special mode of sailing where the square sail has virtually been transformed into a triangular sail with the point downwards and forward. This foot cannot have been held, like the normal foot, by the helmsman, but must have been either made fast forward or held by the bow officer. There is a parallel case in Vergil where Aeneas 'gives orders for raising all the masts', i.e. the masts of all his ships, 'quickly and for the spreading of the sailyards with sail. With one accord they all make a foot (*fecere pedem*), in unison they all let out now the left-, now the right-hand folds of the sails. Together they brace the lofty sailyards this way and that. The fleet is borne along by a wind it makes its own[42].' The procedure is the same as that of the *Mechanica*, except that in Vergil both tacks are described, in the *Mechanica* only one. In the *Mechanica* the after part of the sail is brailed up and the forward part let down, 'they make a foot', the wind is not favourable. In Vergil 'they make a foot', they let down the sail on the port side (i.e. the forward part when the wind is from the port side). When they come about on the other tack and the wind comes from the starboard side, the starboard part of the sail is forward and it is let down in its turn. They 'make the wind their own', i.e. they make a wind which is unfavourable into one which helps them. For the procedure in two such very different writers in different languages to be so close, even in terminology, we must postulate a practice of tacking prevalent in the Mediterranean from at least the fourth century B.C.

Sailing into the wind is described unmistakeably by Nicander, who is probably to be dated in the second century B.C. He contrasts the straight course of the viper with the indirect approach of the *cerastes*: 'meandering on a crooked path with his scaly back, like to the dingy of a merchantman dipping her whole side in the brine when the wind is contrary, as she forces her way to windward when driven back by the south-westerly gale'[43]. The boat is the *akatos* of a merchantman. She is not in tow as a dingy normally is, but sailing on her own. Her course is 'crooked', as she goes about first on one tack and then on another.

BATTLE TACTICS

The accounts of battle tactics which we possess are all given by the historians Thucydides and Xenophon, and all belong to the fifth century B.C. As a result they all concern *triereis*. Athens' victory at Salamis, with light, manœuvrable ships carrying few soldiers on deck and themselves constituting the weapon of offence, laid down the tactics of fleets of *triereis* for nearly two centuries. The *diekplous* was the manœuvre of the faster fleet, and the slower had to evolve a disposition to defeat it. Although we have no details of naval engagements in the fourth century to compare with those given by Thucydides and Xenophon for the fifth, there is no indication that tactics changed. When the ships of larger denomination began to be included in Athenian fleets they seem not to have taken pride of place. The *trieres* remained the chief tactical weapon. These new ships did however begin a new, or possibly a reversion to an old, conception of naval warfare which came to its full development in the fleets of Alexander's successors. Huge ships, by the standard of the *trieres*, provided floating platforms on which the soldiers could fight it out. The conditions of the Great Harbour of Syracuse, which the Greek commanders there realized were the negation of all Athenian naval expertise, were now deliberately chosen.

We saw that the tactic of the *diekplous* had been developed among the Ionian Greeks before the Persian invasions (see above, p. 136). The fleet using it, confronted by an enemy fleet in line abreast, deployed line ahead and broke through at a chosen point. The formation line ahead is denoted in Thucydides either by the phrase *kata mian* (in column of one) or *epi keros* (to the flank)[44]. Line abreast[45] is regarded as the primary formation of a fleet, so that a 90° turn together to the flank is the simplest method of achieving line ahead. This manœuvre was employed with signal success by the fleet of Themistocles at Salamis. Although his ships were slower in the water than the Persians and greatly outnumbered, he brought his *diekplous* to bear on two squadrons of a fleet which had been at the oar most of the night, while his own men were fresh and newly embarked. Furthermore his own ships carried fourteen as against the Persian fleet's forty soldiers on deck. After the withdrawal of the Persians the Ionian Greeks who had been in the Persian fleet at Salamis now became part of the fleet of the confederacy of Delos under Athenian leadership. The Athenian ships now appear to have adopted the continuous deck of the Ionian ships, but not to have increased their deck force beyond the fourteen they had at Salamis—an indication of their confidence in the tactic of the ram. Thucydides describes the battle of Sybota fought between the Corinthians and the Corcyraeans in 433 B.C. 'Both fleets', he says, 'had many hoplites on deck and many archers and javelinmen, for they were still equipped rather inexpertly in the old-fashioned way. The sea battle was a fierce one, not so much because of the skill of both sides but because it was more like a land battle than a sea battle. For when the ships crashed into each other they did not easily get away because of the number and crush of ships and because they trusted for victory more to the hoplites on their decks. They fought a stand-up fight without the ships moving, and the battle was one of courage and brute strength rather than science. And there were no opportunities for the *diekplous*[46].'

In 429 B.C., after the outbreak of war between Athens and Sparta, the Athenian commander Phormio with twenty ships fell in with a Peloponnesian squadron of forty-seven ships at the approaches to the Corinthian Gulf. To avoid the Athenian *diekplous* the Peloponnesian ships formed a circle, with their fast ships in reserve and their light ships in the middle, and the bows of the rest facing outwards. The Athenians countered by forming line ahead and sailing round the enemy fleet until they had reduced it to confusion. Then they moved in to the attack[47].

A month later the same twenty ships of Phormio were faced with an even larger Peloponnesian fleet, seventy-seven ships, at the actual entrance to the Corinthian Gulf. Phormio, who was based on Naupactus, an Athenian station on the north shore of the Gulf, had not complete tactical freedom as he was obliged to defend his base against so large an armament. The two fleets beached opposite each other and prepared for an engagement. Thucydides represents the two commanders addressing their men in terms which are full of interest for us. The Spartan commander, Brasidas, admitted that the Athenians had greater technical skill, but claimed greater daring for the Spartans. Phormio emphasizes the Athenian experience, and makes the following remarks on the tactical situation: 'I shall not, if I can help it, bring the matter to issue in the Gulf, nor will I sail into it. For I am aware that a confined space is not an advantage to a few experienced and faster moving ships against a larger number of inexperienced ships. It is not possible to move in properly to ram if you cannot get a sight of your enemy from some way off, nor if you are in a tight corner can you retire when hard pressed. There are no opportunities for *diekplous* and *anastrophe* which are the proper manœuvres of faster moving ships; but the sea battle must necessarily degenerate into a land battle, and in those circumstances numbers tell[48].' *Anastrophe* is the sequel to the *diekplous*. After rowing through the enemy's line the column turns back to attack the enemy line from the rear. Alternatively it can row round them and throw them into confusion. Phormio's statement that the *diekplous* is the tactic of the faster fleet is not contradicted by Salamis for the reasons which have been given. It is confirmed very conclusively by the account Xenophon gives of the disposition of the fleets before Arginusae. Here the Athenians were in the unusual position of being the slower fleet, and were therefore on the defensive. They disposed their ships in four squadrons of fifteen ships each, and these squadrons were placed two deep on either wing (where the *diekplous* was most likely to take place). In the centre were three detachments of ships in line ahead. Xenophon says specifically that the Athenian fleet was drawn up in this way to avoid the *diekplous*, because they were the slower in the water. The Spartan ships, on the other hand, were all in formation of line ahead, prepared for the *diekplous* and *periplous*, because they were the faster. As it turned out, the Athenian defensive measures were successful[49].

We must now return to the fleets of Brasidas and Phormio facing each other at the entrance to the Corinthian Gulf. The engagement developed as follows. The Peloponnesians moved in column four deep eastwards along the southern shore of the Gulf with their twenty fast ships leading. The Athenian fleet, only a quarter as numerous, were forced to cover their move, which threatened Naupactus, and rowed in single file along the north coast. When the fleets were well inside the Gulf but had not yet reached the more open water off Naupactus, the Peloponnesian column suddenly made a 90° turn together into line abreast and bore down on the single line of twenty Athenian ships. Nine were trapped; but eleven got away, pursued by the twenty fast Peloponnesian ships, in the direction of Naupactus. Ten reached Naupactus and faced about to defend themselves. The eleventh swung round a merchant ship which was at anchor in deep water off the town, and rammed and sank the foremost of the twenty pursuers. The other nineteen Peloponnesian ships, thinking themselves victorious, were following in disorder. The leaders checked, waiting for the rest to come up, and were set upon and routed by the ten Athenian ships that had succeeded in facing about[50].

This famous feat of arms and the tactical manœuvres which led up to it illustrate very vividly the underlying principles of warfare with the *trieres*. Given tactical freedom Phormio's twenty fast ships were a match for the seventy-seven Peloponnesians of which only twenty were fast. On a later occasion twelve Athenian ships faced thirty-three Peloponnesian ships off Corcyra. They attacked and sank a ship on the enemy wing and then carried out a *periplous* which would have thrown the circle of enemy ships into confusion here as on the previous occasion, if a further twenty enemy ships had not come up and forced them to break off the engagement[51]. Brasidas however on this occasion was aware of the string which tied Phormio to Naupactus and used it to bring him to battle in the narrow waters of the entrance to the Gulf. If Phormio had been left to get through to the more open waters off Naupactus, as no doubt he hoped, he would have been less at a disadvantage. Nevertheless a tactical defeat was turned into a moral victory by the brilliant initiative of one nameless trierarch, and the readiness of ten others to support him at the end of an exhausting pursuit. It is clear that the Athenian naval superiority was not only technical.

Thucydides attracts our attention to another interesting tactical situation in connection with the transit of the Athenian expedition from Corcyra to Italy on its way to attack Syracuse in 415 B.C. He represents the Syracusan statesman Hermocrates as advising that the whole naval resources of his city and its allies should be dispatched to the heel of Italy. If, he argues, the whole fleet of the Athenians makes the crossing, it will straggle and be easy to attack. If, on the other hand, they make the crossing lightening their fast ships and concentrating them, we can attack these ships when the oarsmen are tired from the long voyage across. If we decide not to do so, we can retire to Tarentum. Their battle fleet will then find itself without resources on an inhospitable coast. The Syracusans were not ready to take Hermocrates' advice, so that the situation envisaged by him never in fact arose[52].

Ships in transit to a theatre of war were normally laden with extra gear and carried sails and extra men. They could not therefore be rated as fast. Hermocrates, we have just seen, argued that the fast ships in the Athenian Sicilian fleet would have to be lightened to make them ready for battle. So Brasidas, making excuses for the defeat of a Peloponnesian fleet, says: 'We were not at sea for a battle but rather for a military expedition[53].' The battle *trieres* was, as Cephisodotus is said to have described it, 'a complicated kind of mill[54]'—a piece of man-powered machinery in which weight was kept to the minimum.

All the principles of naval warfare with *triereis* which had been evolved by Greeks since their introduction were contravened in the naval warfare which developed in the Great Harbour of Syracuse between Athenians and Syracusans during the siege which began in 415 B.C. Nicias, writing to the Athenian Assembly in the autumn of 414 B.C., explained how it had come about that the Syracusans were preparing to challenge the Athenian fleet: 'As they know well, our fleet was originally in first-class condition, the ships dry and the crews unimpaired, but now the ships are leaky and the crews have deteriorated. It is not possible for us to beach our ships and dry them out, because the enemy fleet, our equal, indeed our superior, in numbers, keeps us constantly on the look-out for an attack. They are to be seen exercising and have the initiative, as well as a greater opportunity of drying out their ships, not being the blockading force[55].' The Athenians, he added, had to use their ships for convoy duties to ensure the arrival of supplies. He asked for a large reinforcement if the enterprise was not to be abandoned. The Athenians decided to send a further sixty ships.

Before the new fleet had arrived the Syracusans under their Spartan commander Gylippus succeeded in capturing the forts which commanded the entrance to the Great Harbour and which had served the Athenians as a gear store. The Athenian fleet was now confined to the Great Harbour and could only attack the stockades on the north side behind which were the old ship-sheds and some of the Syracusan fleet. While the Syracusans were undermining the position of the Athenians at Syracuse, a Corinthian squadron of twenty-five ships was sent to engage the attention of the eighteen Athenian ships at Naupactus and prevent them interfering with the reinforcements which were being sent from the Peloponnese to Gylippus. The Athenian squadron, reinforced by ten of the fastest ships from the new Sicilian expeditionary force and by others from Athens, was eventually engaged by the Corinthian squadron. In the battle there emerged a new tactical factor which was to be decisive in the subsequent fighting at Syracuse. The Corinthians had specially strengthened their ships' bows and, in consequence, were able to employ successfully the despised tactic of bow-to-bow encounter. In this battle the Corinthians in fact obtained no marked success; numbers were about equal and the Athenians were able to take avoiding action[56]. The importance of the battle, however, lies in the fact that the Syracusans adopted with enthusiasm the new tactic for their engagements with the Athenians in the narrow waters of the harbour. Thucydides gives the Syracusan thinking in two interesting paragraphs. 'In a contest with ships which had not been modified in the same way for defence against their own, but were light above the bows (because the Athenians did not employ bow-to-bow encounters but rowing round and ramming), they thought that they would not be at a disadvantage and that the fighting in the Great Harbour with many ships in a small space would be favourable to them. By employing the tactic of bow-to-bow encounters they would smash and force back their bow-structure striking with stout and thick rams against structures which were hollow and weak. The Athenians on the other hand would not be able to use either the *periplous* or the *diekplous* in the narrow space. . .[57]'

The effect of these measures is to be seen in the description of a later engagement. The Athenians attack; and 'the Syracusans received them and using bow-to-bow encounters, as they had planned to do, with their specially adapted rams smashed back the Athenian ships' outriggers to some distance. The soldiers on deck threw javelins and caused many casualties among the Athenians, but far greater damage was done by Syracusans who rowed around in small boats, got in among the oars of the enemy ships, ran alongside and threw javelins at the oarsmen[58].'

The 'stout and thick rams' of the former passage and the 'specially adapted rams' of the latter amount in fact, as Thucydides tells us and as we have seen earlier, to a strengthening of the projecting *epotides* on each side of the bow by means of struts inside and outside the hull (see above, p. 282). The Syracusans (and the Corinthians before them) did not strengthen the actual main ship's ram but made the subsidiary rams on the forward faces of the *epotides* more effective. The bow-to-bow attack naturally resulted in the main rams glancing off each other, and the starboard *epotis* of one ship coming hard up against the port *epotis* of the other. When the weaker *epotis* gave way the result would be the smashing back of the outrigger which terminated forward in, and was covered by, the *epotis*.

The special conditions of bow-to-bow fighting led to another variation of the usual tactical disposition. Javelin men belonged to the old-fashioned way of fighting sea battles condemned by Thucydides in his account of the engagement between the Corinthians and the Corcyraeans in 433 B.C. In his speech before the final battle in the harbour Nicias says: 'Many archers and javelin men will go on board, and a crowd which we would not employ if we were fighting in the open sea, because they would spoil the effects of our skill by making the ships heavy.' Against the bow-to-bow tactics of the Syracusans the Athenians devised grappling irons so that the ships once in contact could not separate. Nicias declared that he had been forced to fight a land battle on ship-board. In such a battle the object is to board the enemy ship with one's own hoplites and drive the enemy hoplites off the deck[59]. For this purpose the usual hoplite force of *epibatai* seems to have been much increased. Gylippus speaks of the 'many hoplites on the Athenian decks contrary to their accustomed usage', and of 'the many javelin men who will not know how to throw their javelins sitting down', as naval javelin men, presumably, had to learn to do[60].

In the battle which ensued two hundred and more ships fought in an area of little more than three square miles of water. None of the Athenian skill could be exercised, and their desperate attempts to adopt a new set of tactics directly contrary to those that they had learnt could not have inspired them with any confidence. The result was a foregone conclusion. The defeat was not, however, for the traditional Athenian tactics of sea warfare, but for the strategy which put them in a position where they had to be abandoned.

TEXTS

1. *IG* 2² 1629 178 ff. τοὺς μὲν τῶν νε[ωρί]ων ἐπιμελητὰς πα[ραδο]ῦναι τοῖς τριηράρ[χοις τ]ὰς ναῦς καὶ τὰ σκεύη [κατὰ τ]ὰ δεδογμένα τῷ δή[μῳ, το]ὺς δὲ τριηράρχους [τοὺς κα]θεστηκότας παρα[κομίζει]ν τὰς ναῦς ἐπὶ τὸ [χῶμα ἐ]ν τῷ Μουνιχιῶνι [μηνὶ π]ρὸ τῆς δεκάτης [ἱσταμέ]νου καὶ παρέχειν [παρεσ]κευασμένας εἰς [πλοῦν].

Cf. Demosthenes 51 4, 50 5.

2. Aristophanes, *Acharnians* 544–54

 καὶ κάρτα μέντἂν εὐθέως καθείλκετε
 τριακοσίας ναῦς, ἦν δ' ἂν ἡ πόλις πλέα
 θορύβου στρατιωτῶν, περὶ τριηράρχου βοῆς,
 μισθοῦ διδομένου, παλλαδίων χρυσουμένων,
 στοᾶς στεναχούσης, σιτίων μετρουμένων,
 ἀσκῶν, τροπωτήρων, κάδους ὠνουμένων,
 σκορόδων, ἐλαῶν, κρομμύων ἐν δικτύοις,
 στεφάνων, τριχίδων, αὐλητρίδων, ὑπωπίων·
 τὸ νεώριον δ' αὖ κωπέων πλατουμένων,
 τύλων ψοφούντων, θαλαμιῶν τροπουμένων,*
 αὐλῶν, κελευστῶν, νιγλάρων, συριγμάτων.

 *τρυπωμένων seems more likely cf. *Peace* 1234.

3. See above, p. 287, note 6.

4. Pindar, *Isthm.* 5 4–6

 καὶ γὰρ ἐριζόμεναι / νᾶες ἐν πόντῳ...

5. Dio Chrys. 37 15.

6. Lysias 21 5 νενίκηκα δὲ τριήρει μὲν ἁμιλλώμενος ἐπὶ Σουνίῳ ἀναλώσας πεντεκαίδεκα μνᾶς.

7. ap. Plutarch, *Them.* 32 5

> ὁ σὸς δὲ τύμβος ἐν καλῷ κεχωσμένος
> τοῖς ἐμπόροις πρόσρησις ἔσται πανταχοῦ
> τούς τ' ἐκπλέοντας εἰσπλέοντάς τ' ὄψεται
> χὠπόταν ἄμιλλ' ᾖ τῶν νεῶν θεάσεται.

8. Isocrates 9 1 ὁρῶν, ὦ Νικόκλεις, τιμῶντά σε τὸν τάφον τοῦ πατρὸς οὐ μόνον τῷ πλήθει καὶ τῷ κάλλει τῶν ἐπιφερομένων, ἀλλὰ καὶ χοροῖς καὶ μουσικῇ καὶ γυμνικοῖς ἀγῶσιν, ἔτι δὲ πρὸς τούτοις ἵππων τε καὶ τριήρων ἁμίλλαις. . .

9. Arrian 723 5 ἐν τούτῳ δὲ πολλάκις μὲν τοῦ ναυτικοῦ ἀπεπειρᾶτο πολλαὶ δὲ ἔριδες αὐτῷ τῶν τριήρων καὶ ὅσαι τετρήρεις κατὰ τὸν ποταμὸν ἐγίγνοντο, καὶ ἀγῶνες τῶν τε ἐρετῶν καὶ τῶν κυβερνητῶν καὶ στέφανοι τῶν νικώντων.

10. Thuc. viii 95 Ἀθηναῖοι δὲ κατὰ τάχος καὶ ἀξυγκροτήτοις πληρώμασιν ἀναγκασθέντες χρήσασθαι. . .

11. Xen. *HG* vi 2 12 οὐ φαῦλον ἡγούμενος εἶναι ἐπὶ συγκεκροτημένας ναῦς εἰκῇ περιπλεῦσαι.

12. Thuc. vii 21² καὶ ξυγκαλέσας τοὺς Συρακοσίους (ὁ Γύλιππος) ἔφη χρῆναι πληροῦν ναῦς ὡς δύνανται πλείστας καὶ ναυμαχίας ἀπόπειραν λαμβάνειν.

12⁵: Nicias' letter to the Athenian assembly: φανεραὶ δέ εἰσιν ἀναπειρώμεναι.

13. Xen. *HG* i 1 16 ἐπειδὴ δ' ἐγγὺς τῆς Κυζίκου ἦν, αἰθρίας γενομένης καὶ τοῦ ἡλίου ἐκλάμψαντος καθορᾷ τὰς τοῦ Μινδάρου ναῦς γυμναζομένας πόρρω ἀπὸ τοῦ λιμένος.

14. Thuc. iii 49³ καὶ οἱ μὲν ὕπνον ᾑροῦντο κατὰ μέρος, οἱ δ' ἤλαυνον.

15. Xen. *Anab.* 6 4 2 καὶ τριήρει μέν ἐστιν εἰς Ἡράκλειαν ἐκ Βυζαντίου κώπαις ἡμέρας μακρᾶς πλοῦς.

16. Polyaenus v 22 4 Διότιμος καταπλεύσας νυκτὸς ἐς χωρίον τῆς πολεμίας ἀφ' ἑκάστης νεὼς συχνοὺς ἄνδρας ἐκβιβάσας τοὺς μὲν εἰς ἐνέδραν ἀπέκρυψεν· ἀρχομένης δὲ ἡμέρας κατὰ τοὺς ἐνεδρεύοντας ταῖς ναυσὶν ἀνεκώχευε παραγγείλας τοῖς μὲν ἐπὶ τῶν καταστρωμάτων διασκευάζεσθαι πρὸς μάχην, τοῖς δ' ἐρέταις ἀνὰ μέρος ὁτὲ μὲν τὰς θαλαμιάς, ὁτὲ δὲ τὰς ζυγίας, ὁτὲ δὲ τὰς θρανίτιδας κώπας ἀναφέρειν, καί τινα τῶν σκαφῶν τῇ γῇ προσάγειν ἐπειρᾶτο. οἱ μὲν πολέμιοι προσδραμόντες ἐκώλυον τὴν ἀπόβασιν, τοῦ δὲ τὸ προσυγκείμενον σημεῖον ἄραντος οἱ μὲν ἐκ τῶν ἐνέδρων ἐπιφανέντες πολλοὺς τῶν πολεμίων ἐφόνευσαν, τοὺς λοιποὺς δ' ἐς φυγὴν ἐτρέψαντο. ὁ δὲ Διότιμος ἀσφαλῆ τὴν ἀπόβασιν ἐποιήσατο.

17. Xen. *HG* ii 1 28 διεσκεδασμένων δὲ τῶν ἀνθρώπων αἱ μὲν τῶν νεῶν δίκροτοι ἦσαν, αἱ δὲ μονόκροτοι, αἱ δὲ παντελῶς κεναί.

18. Aristides, *Or.* 25 (43) 4.

19. Arrian, *Anab.* 6 5 2 ὅσαι τε δίκροτοι αὐτῶν τὰς κάτω κώπας οὐκ ἐπὶ πολὺ ἔξω ἔχουσαι τοῦ ὕδατος.

20. Thuc. vii 14¹ βραχεῖα ἀκμὴ πληρώματος καὶ ὀλίγοι τῶν ναυτῶν οἱ ἐξορμῶντές τε τὴν ναῦν καὶ ξυνέχοντες τὴν εἰρεσίαν.

21. Thuc. II 84³ καὶ τὰς κώπας ἀδύνατοι ὄντες ἐν κλύδωνι ἀναφέρειν ἄνθρωποι ἄπειροι τοῖς κυβερνήταις ἀπειθεστέρας τὰς ναῦς παρεῖχον.

22. Thuc. II 91⁴ αἱ μέν τινες τῶν νεῶν καθεῖσαι τὰς κώπας ἐπέστησαν τοῦ πλοῦ.

23. Aristophanes, *Frogs* 180 and 269.

24. Apollonius Rhodius I 378–9

> ὕψι δ᾽ ἄρ᾽ ἔνθα καὶ ἔνθα μεταστρέψαντες ἐρετμὰ
> πήχυιον προύχοντα περὶ σκαλμοῖσιν ἔδησαν.

25. Ovid, *Metamorphoses* XI 474–7

> portibus exierant, et moverat aura rudentes:
> obvertit lateri pendentes navita remos
> cornuaque in summa locat arbore totaque malo
> carbasa deducit venientesque accipit auras.
> (*At line* 486 *when storms threaten*)
> sponte tamen properant alii subducere remos.

26. Xen. *HG* II 3 31 δεῖ δέ, ὦ Θηράμενες, ἄνδρα τὸν ἄξιον ζῆν οὐ προάγειν μὲν δεινὸν εἶναι εἰς πράγματα τοὺς συνόντας, ἂν δέ τι ἀντικόπτῃ εὐθὺς μεταβάλλεσθαι, ἀλλ᾽ ὥσπερ ἐν νηὶ διαπονεῖσθαι, ἕως ἂν εἰς οὖρον καταστῶσιν.

27. Thuc. II 93⁴ καί τις καὶ ἄνεμος αὐτοὺς λέγεται κωλῦσαι.

28. Thuc. III 49⁴ κατὰ τύχην δὲ πνεύματος οὐδενὸς ἐναντιωθέντος.

29. Thuc. IV 4¹ ἡσύχαζεν ὑπ᾽ ἀπλοίας.

30. Thuc. VII 40¹ καὶ οἱ Συρακόσιοι ἐξαίφνης πρύμναν κρουσάμενοι πάλιν πρὸς τὴν πόλιν ἔπλευσαν.

31. Cicero, *ad Atticum* XIII 21³, nunc ad rem ut redeam 'inhibere' illud tuum, quod valde mihi adriserat, vehementer displicet. est enim verbum totum nauticum. quamquam id quidem sciebam sed arbitrabar sustineri remos cum inhibere essent remiges iussi. id non esse eiusmodi didici heri cum ad villam nostram navis appelleretur. non enim sustinent sed alio modo remigant. id ab ἐποχῇ remotissimum est. . .inhibitio autem remigum motum habet et vehementissimum quidem remigationis navem convertentis ad puppim.

32. E.g. IV 26³ ὅρμος opposed to μετέωροι ὥρμουν: IV 45¹ καθορμίσασθαι.

33. Demosthenes 50 22 ἀναγκαῖον ἦν ἐπ᾽ ἀγκύρας ἀποσαλεύειν τὴν νύκτα μετεώρους.

34. Thuc. IV 11⁴, 12¹.

35. Aristotle, *HA* 4 8 533 b 6 (fish) ὅτι δὲ ἀκούουσι καὶ ὀσφραίνονται φανερόν· τούς τε γὰρ ψόφους φεύγοντα φαίνεται τοὺς μεγάλους, οἷον τὰς εἰρεσίας τῶν τριήρων.

36. Aristotle, *Meteor.* II 9 369 b 10 δηλοῖ δ᾽ ἐπὶ τῆς εἰρεσίας τῶν τριήρων· ἤδη γὰρ ἀναφερόντων πάλιν τὰς κώπας ὁ πρῶτος ἀφικνεῖται ψόφος τῆς κωπηλασίας.

37. Aristophanes, *Knights* 546

> αἴρεσθ᾽ αὐτῷ πολὺ τὸ ῥόθιον, παραπέμψατ᾽ ἐφ᾽ ἕνδεκα κώπαις.

38. Aristotle, *Meteor.* III 4 374 a 29 ἡ δὲ ἀπὸ τῶν κωπῶν τῶν ἀναφερομένων ἐκ τῆς θαλάττης ἶρις.

39. Aristophanes, *Frogs* 999–1000

    ἀλλὰ συστείλας ἄκροισι

    χρώμενος τοῖς ἱστίοις...

40. Aristophanes, *Knights* 430–41

Cleon   ἔξειμι γάρ σοι λαμπρὸς ἤδη καὶ μέγας καθιείς,

    ὁμοῦ ταράττων τήν τε γῆν καὶ τὴν θάλατταν εἰκῆ.

Sausage-seller   ἐγὼ δὲ συστείλας γε τοὺς ἀλλᾶντας εἶτ' ἀφήσω

    κατὰ κῦμ' ἐμαυτὸν οὔριον, κλάειν σε μακρὰ κελεύσας.

.   .   .   .

Demus   ἄθρει καὶ τοῦ ποδὸς παρίει·

.   .   .   .

Chorus   ἀνὴρ ἂν ἡδέως λάβοι· τοὺς τερθρίους παρίει·

    τὸ πνεῦμ' ἔλαττον γίγνεται.

41. Aristotle, *Mechanica* 7 851b6 διὰ τί, ὅταν ἐξ οὐρίας βούλωνται διαδραμεῖν μὴ οὐρίου τοῦ πνεύματος ὄντος, τὸ μὲν πρὸς τὸν κυβερνήτην τοῦ ἱστίου μέρος στέλλονται, τὸ δὲ πρὸς τὴν πρῷραν ποδιαῖον ποιησάμενοι ἐφιᾶσιν; ἢ διότι ἀντισπᾶν τὸ πηδάλιον πολλῷ μὲν ὄντι τῷ πνεύματι οὐ δύναται, ὀλίγῳ δέ, ὃ ὑποστέλλονται. προάγει μὲν οὖν τὸ πνεῦμα, εἰς οὔριον δὲ καθίστησι τὸ πηδάλιον, ἀντισπῶν, καὶ μοχλεῦον τὴν θάλατταν ἅμα δὲ καὶ οἱ ναῦται μάχονται τῷ πνεύματι· ἀνακλίνουσι ἐπὶ τὸ ἐναντίον ἑαυτούς.

42. Vergil, *Aeneid* v 828–32

    iubet ocius omnes

    attolli malos, intendi bracchia velis.

    una omnes fecere pedem, pariterque sinistros,

    nunc dextros solvere sinus; una ardua torquent

    cornua detorquentque; ferunt sua flamina classem.

43. Nicander, *Theriaca* 266–70. I have used Gow and Scholfield's translation and accepted their dating of Nicander.

44. Thuc. II 84[1] κατὰ μίαν ναῦν τεταγμένοι.

    II 90[4] κατὰ μίαν ἐπὶ κέρως.

45. Thuc. II 90[4]. The opposite of κατὰ μίαν ἐπὶ κέρως: μετωπηδὸν ἔπλεον.

Cf. Herodotus VII 100[3] and infantry movement in Xen. *Cyr.* 2 4 2 and 3.

46. Thuc. I 49[1] ξυμμείξαντες δέ, ἐπειδὴ τὰ σημεῖα ἑκατέροις ἤρθη, ἐναυμάχουν, πολλοὺς μὲν ὁπλίτας ἔχοντες ἀμφότεροι ἐπὶ τῶν καταστρωμάτων, πολλοὺς δὲ τοξότας τε καὶ ἀκοντιστάς, τῷ παλαιῷ τρόπῳ ἀπειρότερον ἔτι παρεσκευασμένοι. ἦν τε ἡ ναυμαχία καρτερά, τῇ μὲν τέχνῃ οὐχ ὁμοίως, πεζομαχίᾳ δὲ τὸ πλέον προσφερὴς οὖσα. ἐπειδὴ γὰρ προσβάλοιεν ἀλλήλοις, οὐ ῥᾳδίως ἀπελύοντο ὑπό τε τοῦ πλήθους καὶ ὄχλου τῶν νεῶν, καὶ μᾶλλόν τι πιστεύοντες τοῖς ἐπὶ τοῦ καταστρώματος ὁπλίταις ἐς τὴν νίκην, οἳ κατα-στάντες ἐμάχοντο ἡσυχαζουσῶν τῶν νεῶν· διέκπλοι δ' οὐκ ἦσαν, ἀλλὰ θυμῷ καὶ ῥώμῃ τὸ πλέον ἐναυμάχουν ἢ ἐπιστήμῃ.

47. Thuc. II 83[5] καὶ οἱ μὲν Πελοποννήσιοι ἐτάξαντο κύκλον τῶν νεῶν ὡς μέγιστον οἷοί τ' ἦσαν μὴ διδόντες διέκπλουν, τὰς πρῴρας μὲν ἔξω, ἔσω δὲ τὰς πρύμνας, καὶ τά τε λεπτὰ

πλοῖα ἃ ξυνέπλει ἐντὸς ποιοῦνται καὶ πέντε ναῦς τὰς ἄριστα πλεούσας, ὅπως ἐκπλέοιεν διὰ βραχέος παραγιγνόμενοι, εἴ πη προσπίπτοιεν οἱ ἐναντίοι. οἱ δ' Ἀθηναῖοι κατὰ μίαν ναῦν τεταγμένοι περιέπλεον αὐτοὺς κύκλῳ καὶ ξυνῆγον ἐς ὀλίγον, ἐν χρῷ αἰεὶ παραπλέοντες καὶ δόκησιν παρέχοντες αὐτίκα ἐμβαλεῖν.

48. Thuc. II 86⁵–89¹¹.

49. Xen. *HG* I 6 31 οὕτω δ' ἐτάχθησαν, ἵνα μὴ διέκπλουν διδοῖεν· χεῖρον γὰρ ἔπλεον. αἱ δὲ τῶν Λακεδαιμονίων ἀντιτεταγμέναι ἦσαν ἅπασαι ἐπὶ μιᾶς ὡς πρὸς διέκπλουν καὶ περίπλουν παρεσκευασμέναι, διὰ τὸ βέλτιον πλεῖν.

50. Thuc. II 90–2.

51. Thuc. III 77–8.

52. Thuc. VI 34⁵ εἰ δ' αὖ τῷ ταχυναυτοῦντι ἀθροωτέρῳ κουφίσαντες προσβάλοιεν, εἰ μὲν κώπαις χρήσαιντο, ἐπιθοίμεθ' ἂν κεκμηκόσιν, εἰ δὲ μὴ δοκοίη, ἔστι καὶ ὑποχωρῆσαι ἡμῖν ἐς Τάραντα· οἱ δὲ μετ' ὀλίγων ἐφοδίων ὡς ἐπὶ ναυμαχίᾳ περαιωθέντες ἀποροῖεν ἂν κατὰ χωρία ἐρῆμα.

53. Thuc. II 87² οὐχὶ ἐς ναυμαχίαν μᾶλλον ἢ ἐπὶ στρατείαν ἐπλέομεν.

54. Aristotle, *Rhet.* 1411 a 24 καὶ Κηφισόδοτος τὰς τριήρεις ἐκάλει μυλῶνας ποικίλους.

55. Thuc. VII 12³ τὸ γὰρ ναυτικὸν ἡμῶν, ὅπερ κἀκεῖνοι πυνθάνονται, τὸ μὲν πρῶτον ἤκμαζε καὶ τῶν νεῶν τῇ ξηρότητι καὶ τῶν πληρωμάτων τῇ σωτηρίᾳ· νῦν δὲ αἵ τε νῆες διάβροχοι τοσοῦτον χρόνον ἤδη θαλασσεύουσαι, καὶ τὰ πληρώματα ἔφθαρται. τὰς μὲν γὰρ ναῦς οὐκ ἔστιν ἀνελκύσαντας διαψύξαι διὰ τὸ ἀντιπάλους τῷ πλήθει καὶ ἔτι πλείους τὰς τῶν πολεμίων οὔσας αἰεὶ προσδοκίαν παρέχειν ὡς ἐπιπλεύσονται. φανεραὶ δ' εἰσὶν ἀναπειρώμεναι, καὶ αἱ ἐπιχειρήσεις ἐπ' ἐκείνοις καὶ ἀποξηρᾶναι τὰς σφετέρας μᾶλλον ἐξουσία· οὐ γὰρ ἐφορμοῦσιν ἄλλοις.

56. Thuc. VII 34⁵. See p. 287, note 18 above.

57. Thuc. VII 36³ ἐνόμισαν γὰρ οἱ Συρακόσιοι πρὸς τὰς τῶν Ἀθηναίων ναῦς οὐχ ὁμοίως ἀντινεναυπηγημένας, ἀλλὰ λεπτὰ τὰ πρῴραθεν ἐχούσας διὰ τὸ μὴ ἀντιπρῴροις μᾶλλον αὐτοὺς ἢ ἐκ περίπλου ταῖς ἐμβολαῖς χρῆσθαι, οὐκ ἔλασσον σχήσειν, καὶ τὴν ἐν τῷ μεγάλῳ λιμένι ναυμαχίαν, οὐκ ἐν πολλῷ πολλαῖς ναυσὶν οὖσαν, πρὸς ἑαυτῶν ἔσεσθαι· ἀντιπρῴροι[ς] γὰρ ταῖς ἐμβολαῖς χρώμενοι ἀναρρήξειν τὰ πρῴραθεν αὐτοῖς, στερίφοις καὶ παχέσι πρὸς κοῖλα καὶ ἀσθενῆ παίοντες τοῖς ἐμβόλοις. τοῖς δὲ Ἀθηναίοις οὐκ ἔσεσθαι σφῶν ἐν στενοχωρίᾳ οὔτε περίπλουν οὔτε διέκπλουν, ὧπερ τῆς τέχνης μάλιστα ἐπίστευον· αὐτοὶ γὰρ κατὰ τὸ δυνατὸν τὸ μὲν οὐ δώσειν διεκπλεῖν, τὸ δὲ τὴν στενοχωρίαν κωλύσειν ὥστε μὴ περιπλεῖν.

58. Thuc. VII 40⁵ οἱ δὲ Συρακόσιοι δεξάμενοι καὶ ταῖς [τε] ναυσὶν ἀντιπρῴροις χρώμενοι, ὥσπερ διενοήθησαν, τῶν ἐμβόλων τῇ παρασκευῇ ἀνερρήγνυσαν τὰς τῶν Ἀθηναίων ναῦς ἐπὶ πολὺ τῆς παρεξειρεσίας, καὶ οἱ ἀπὸ τῶν καταστρωμάτων αὐτοῖς ἀκοντίζοντες μεγάλα ἔβλαπτον τοὺς Ἀθηναίους, πολὺ δ' ἔτι μείζω οἱ ἐν τοῖς λεπτοῖς πλοίοις περιπλέοντες τῶν Συρακοσίων καὶ ἔς τε τοὺς ταρσοὺς ὑποπίπτοντες τῶν πολεμίων νεῶν καὶ ἐς τὰ πλάγια παραπλέοντες καὶ ἐξ αὐτῶν ἐς τοὺς ναύτας ἀκοντίζοντες.

59. Thuc. VII 62¹⁻⁴ ἃ δὲ ἀρωγὰ ἐνείδομεν ἐπὶ τῇ τοῦ λιμένος στενότητι πρὸς τὸν μέλλοντα ὄχλον τῶν νεῶν ἔσεσθαι καὶ πρὸς τὴν ἐκείνων ἐπὶ τῶν καταστρωμάτων

παρασκευήν, οἷς πρότερον ἐβλαπτόμεθα, πάντα καὶ ἡμῖν νῦν ἐκ τῶν παρόντων μετὰ τῶν κυβερνητῶν ἐσκεμμένα ἡτοίμασται. καὶ γὰρ τοξόται πολλοὶ καὶ ἀκοντισταὶ ἐπιβήσονται καὶ ὄχλος, ᾧ ναυμαχίαν μὲν ποιούμενοι ἐν πελάγει οὐκ ἂν ἐχρώμεθα διὰ τὸ βλάπτειν ἂν τὸ τῆς ἐπιστήμης τῇ βαρύτητι τῶν νεῶν, ἐν δὲ τῇ ἐνθάδε ἠναγκασμένῃ ἀπὸ τῶν νεῶν πεζομαχίᾳ πρόσφορα ἔσται. ηὕρηται δ᾽ ἡμῖν ὅσα χρὴ ἀντιναυπηγῆσαι, καὶ πρὸς τὰς τῶν ἐπωτίδων αὐτοῖς παχύτητας, ᾧπερ δὴ μάλιστα ἐβλαπτόμεθα, χειρῶν σιδηρῶν ἐπιβολαί, αἳ σχήσουσι τὴν πάλιν ἀνάκρουσιν τῆς προσπεσούσης νεώς, ἢν τὰ ἐπὶ τούτοις οἱ ἐπιβάται ὑπουργῶσιν. ἐς τοῦτο γὰρ δὴ ἠναγκάσμεθα ὥστε πεζομαχεῖν ἀπὸ τῶν νεῶν, καὶ τὸ μήτε αὐτοὺς ἀνακρούεσθαι μήτ᾽ ἐκείνους ἐᾶν ὠφέλιμον φαίνεται, ἄλλως τε καὶ τῆς γῆς, πλὴν ὅσον ἂν ὁ πεζὸς ἡμῶν ἐπέχῃ, πολεμίας οὔσης.

60. Thuc. VII 67² τά τε τῆς ἀντιμιμήσεως αὐτῶν τῆς παρασκευῆς ἡμῶν τῷ μὲν ἡμετέρῳ τρόπῳ ξυνήθη τέ ἐστι καὶ οὐκ ἀνάρμοστοι πρὸς ἕκαστον αὐτῶν ἐσόμεθα· οἱ δ᾽, ἐπειδὰν πολλοὶ μὲν ὁπλῖται ἐπὶ τῶν καταστρωμάτων παρὰ τὸ καθεστηκὸς ὦσι, πολλοὶ δὲ καὶ ἀκοντισταὶ χερσαῖοι ὡς εἰπεῖν Ἀκαρνᾶνές τε καὶ ἄλλοι ἐπὶ ναῦς ἀναβάντες, οἳ οὐδ᾽ ὅπως καθεζομένους χρὴ τὸ βέλος ἀφεῖναι εὑρήσουσι, πῶς οὐ σφαλοῦσί τε τὰς ναῦς καὶ ἐν σφίσιν αὐτοῖς πάντες οὐκ ἐν τῷ ἑαυτῶν τρόπῳ κινούμενοι ταράξονται;

GAZETTEER

Letters indicate position of place names on Maps 1, 2, and 3.

Abdera 2 Ca		Chalcis 2 Bb	
Abydos 2 Ca		Chios 2 Cb	
Acarnania 2 Ab		Cilicia 1 Cb	
Acheron, R. 2 Ab		Citium 1 Cb	
Acragas 1 Ab		Cius 2 Da	
Adriatic Sea 1 Aa		Clazomenae 2 Cb	
Aegaleos, M. 3		Cnidus 2 Cc	
Aegean Sea 1 Bb		Colchis 1 Ca	
Aegina 2 Bb		Corcyra 2 Aa	
Aegospotami 2 Ca		Corinth 2 Bb	
Aeolis 1 Bb		Corinthian G. 2 Bb	
Aetolia 2 Ab		Cos 2 Cc	
Aia 1 Ca		Crete 1 Bc	
Alalia 1 Aa		Cyllene 2 Ab	
Aleian Plain 1 Cb		Cyme 2 Cb	
Alpheus, R. 2 Bb		Cynossema 2 Ca	
Ambracia 2 Aa		Cyprus 1 Cb	
Amorgos 2 Cc		Cyrene 1 Bc	
Amphipolis 2 Ba		Cythera 2 Bc	
Anaphe 2 Cc		Cythnos 2 Bb	
Andros 2 Cb		Cyzicus 2 Ca	
Aphetae 2 Bb		Delium 2 Bb	
Apollonia 1 Bc		Delos 2 Cb	
Apulia 1 Ab		Delphi 2 Bb	
Arginusae 2 Cb		Doriscus 2 Ca	
Argos 2 Bb		Egypt 1 Cc	
Artemisium 2 Bb		Eleusis 3	
Asia Minor 1 Cb		Elis 2 Ab	
Asine 2 Bb		Embatum 2 Cb	
Aspendus 1 Cb		Ephesus 2 Cb	
Astypalaea 2 Cc		Epidamnus 2 Aa	
Athens 2 Bb		Erythrae 2 Cb	
Attica 2 Bb		Euboea 2 Bb	
Aulis 2 Bb		Euphrates 1 Cb	
Black Sea 1 Ca		Eurymedon, R. 1 Cb	
Boeotia 2 Bb		Gela 1 Ab	
Byzantium 2 Da		Gytheum 2 Bc	
Calauria 2 Bb		Halicarnassus 2 Cb	
Camarina 1 Ab		Hebrus, R. 2 Ca	
Caria 2 Db		Hellespont 2 Ca	
Carpathus 2 Cc		Heracleia 1 Ca	
Carthage 1 Ab		Himera 1 Ab	
Carystus 2 Bb		Icaria 2 Cb	
Caunus 2 Dc		Imbros 2 Ca	
Ceos 2 Bb		Iolcus 2 Ba	
Cephallenia 2 Ab		Ionian Sea 1 Ab	
Chaeronea 2 Bb		Ios 2 Cc	

326

Ithaca   2 Ab
Kasthanaia   2 Ba
Laconia, G. of   2 Bc
Lade   2 Cb
Lampsacus   2 Ca
Lemnos   2 Ca
Lesbos   2 Cb
Leucas   2 Ab
Libya   1 Bc
Lipsokoutali   3
Lydia   2 Db
Maeander, R.   2 Db
Magnesia   2 Ba
Marathon   2 Bb
Megara   3
Melos   2 Bc
Messenia   2 Ab
Metapontum   1 Ab
Methone   2 Ba
Miletus   2 Cb
Munichia   3
Mycale   2 Cb
Mycenae   2 Bb
Myconos   2 Cb
Mylasa   2 Db
Mysia   2 Ca
Mytilene   2 Cb
Naucratis   1 Cc
Naupactus   2 Bb
Naxos   2 Cb
Nile Delta   1 Cc
Oeniadae   2 Ab
Olynthus   2 Ba
Pagasae   2 Bc
Paros   2 Cb
Peloponnese   2 Bb
Peneus, R.   2 Ba
Phalerum B.   3
Phaselis   1 Cb
Pherae   2 Ba
Phocaea   2 Cb
Phocis   2 Bb
Phoenicia   1 Cc
Piraeus   3
Pithecussae   1 Ab
Pleuron   2 Ab
Potidaea   2 Ba
Pylos   2 Ab
Pyrrha   2 Cb

Rhegium   1 Ab
Rhodes   2 Dc
Rome   1 Aa
St George I.   3
Salamis   3
Salamis (Cyprus)   1 Cb
Samos   2 Cb
Samothrace   1 Ca
Sardis   2 Db
Saronic G.   2 Bb
Sciathos   2 Bb
Scione   2 Ba
Scyros   2 Bb
Sepias   2 Ba
Sestos   2 Ca
Sicily   1 Ab
Sicyon   2 Bb
Sidon   1 Cc
Sigeum   2 Ca
Sinope   1 Ca
Siphnos   2 Bb
Sparta   2 Bb
Sphacteria   2 Ab
Stryme   2 Ca
Strymon, R.   2 Bc
Sunium   2 Bb
Sybaris   1 Ab
Sybota   2 Aa
Syracuse   1 Ab
Syria   1 Cb
Tarentum   1 Ab
Tenos   2 Cb
Teos   2 Cb
Thapsacus   1 Cb
Thasos   2 Ba
Thebes   2 Bb
Thera   2 Cc
Therma   2 Ba
Thermopylae   2 Bb
Thesprotia   2 Aa
Thessaly   2 Aa
Thoricus   2 Bb
Thrace   2 Ba
Troizen   2 Bb
Troy   2 Ca
Tyre   1 Cc
Zacynthos   2 Ab
Zancle-Messana   1 Ab

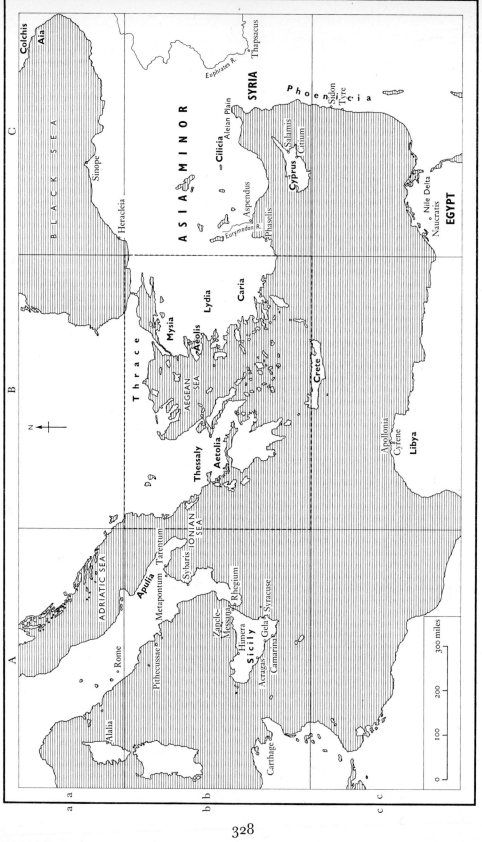

Map I

328

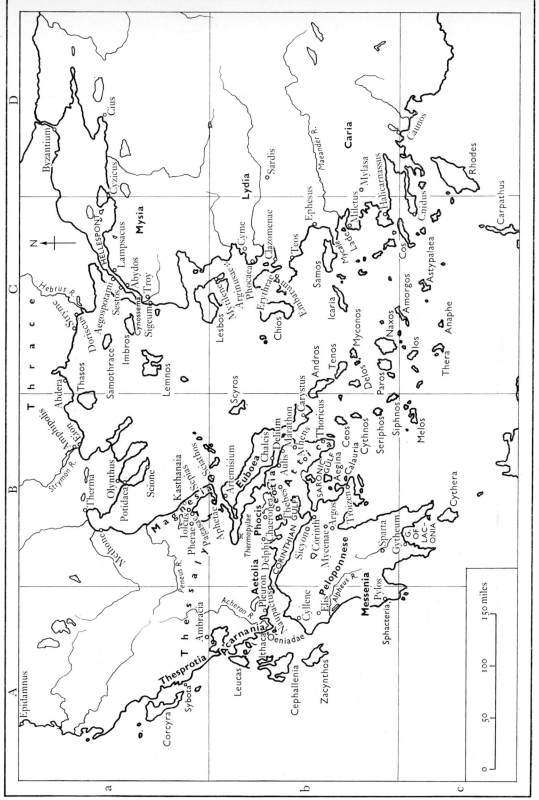

Map 2

329

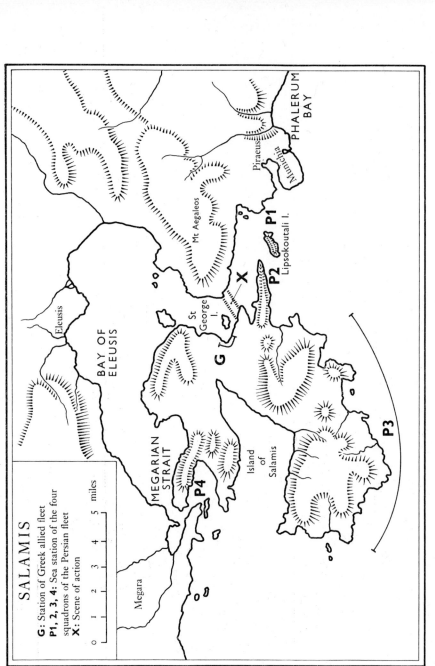

SALAMIS

G: Station of Greek allied fleet
P1, 2, 3, 4: Sea station of the four
squadrons of the Persian fleet
X: Scene of action

0 1 2 3 4 5 miles

PHALERUM BAY

Piraeus

Munichia

P1

Lipsokoutali I.

P2

X

Mt Aegaleos

St
George
I.

G

BAY OF
ELEUSIS

Eleusis

P3

Island
of
Salamis

MEGARIAN
STRAIT

P4

Megara

Map 3

330

BIBLIOGRAPHY AND
OPUS ABBREVIATIONS

Allen, T. W., *The Homeric Hymns*, 2nd ed. Oxford, 1936.

Alten, G. von and Milchhöfer, A. in E. Curtius and J. A. Kaupert: *Karten von Attika: Erläuternder Texte I* 1881, 14–15.

Angelopoulos, H. 'Peri tōn en Peiraiei anaskaphōn', *Praktika* 1899, 40.

Arias, P. E. and Hirmer, M. (rev. B. B. Shefton), *A History of Greek Vase Painting*. London, 1962.

Atkinson, T. D. *et al. Excavations at Phylakopi in Melos* (*JHS* Suppl. paper no. 4). London, 1904.

Babelon, E. *Traité des Monnaies Grecques et Romaines*. Paris, 1901.

Barron, J. P. *The Silver Coins of Samos*. London, 1966.

Baumeister, A. *Denkmäler des klassischen Altertums* III. Munich and Leipsig, 1885.

Beazley, Sir John. 'The Antimenes Painter', *JHS* 1927, 63 ff.; 'Little-Master Cups', *JHS* 1932, 167 ff.; 'Attic Black-figure: a sketch', *Proceedings of the British Academy* (= ABS), 1928; *Development of Attic Black-figure* (= Development), Berkeley, California, 1951; *Attic Black-figure Vase-painters* (= ABV), Oxford, 1956; *Attic Red-figure Vase-painters* (= ARV), Oxford, 1963.

Belger, C. Review of *Praktika* 1885, *BPhW* 1887, 724.

Blegen, C. 'Hyria.' *Hesperia*, Suppl. 8, 1949, 3 ff.

Bloesch, H. *Formen Attischer Schalen*. Berne, 1940.

Boardman, J. *Greek Art*. London, 1965; 'Painted votive plaques and an early inscription from Aegina', *BSA* 1954, 183 ff.

Boeckh, A. *Urkunden über die Seewesen des Attischen Staates*. Berlin, 1840.

Brann, E. T. H. 'A figured Geometric fragment from the Athenian Agora', *Antike Kunst* 1959, 35 ff. *Athenian Agora* VIII, Princeton, 1962.

Breitenstein, N. *Catalogue of Terracottas in the Danish National Museum*. Copenhagen, 1941.

Broadhead, H. D. *The Persae*. Cambridge, 1960.

Buchner, G. 'Figürlich bemalte spätgeometrische Vasen aus Pithekussai und Kyme', *RM* 1953–4, 37 ff. *Expedition* 1966, vol. 8, no. 4, p. 8.

Burn, A. R. *Persia and the Greeks*. London, 1962.

Buschor, E. *Griechische Vasen*. Munich, 1940.

Cary, M., *CR* lx, 1946, pp. 28 ff.

Casson, L. *The Ancient Mariners*. London, 1959; 'New Light on ancient Rigging and Boat-building', *American Neptune* xxiv 2. 1964, 81 ff.; 'Hemiolia and Triemiolia' *JHS* 1958, 14 ff.

Cavallari, I. S. e Holm, A. *Topografia archaeologica di Siracusa* 1883, 30.

Chamoux, F. 'L'école de la grande amphore du Dipylon', *RA* 1945, 55 ff. *La Civilisation Grecque*. Paris, 1963.

Chittenden, J. and Seltman, C. *Greek Art*. London, 1947.

Coldstream, J. N. *JHS* 1963, 212 (Review of J. M. Davison); *JHS* 1964, 217 (Review of Brann, *Athenian Agora* VIII).

Collignon, M. 'Penteskouphia Plaques', *Monuments Grecs* II, 23 ff.

Conze, A. *Die Attischen Grabreliefs*. Berlin, 1890.

Cook, J. M. 'Protoattic Pottery', *BSA* 1934–5, 206 ff.

Cook, R. M. *Greek Painted Pottery*. London, 1960.

Davison, J. A. 'The First Greek Triremes', *CQ* 1947, 18 ff.

Davison, J. M. *Attic Geometric Workshops*, Yale Classical Studies XVI (= Davison). 1961.

Dawkins, R. M. *The Sanctuary of Artemis Orthia at Sparta*. London, 1929.

Dawkins, R. M. and Droop, J. P. 'The sanctuary of Artemis Orthia', *BSA*, 1906–7.

Délos. X Explorations archéologiques de Délos. Paris, 1928.

Desborough, V. d'A. *Protogeometric Pottery*. Oxford, 1952.

Devambez, P. *Greek Painting*. London, 1962.

Dohrn, T. *Die Schwarzfigurigen Etruskischen Vasen*. Berlin, 1937.

Dragatzes, I. and Dorpfeld, W. *Praktika* 1885, 63–8.

Dunbabin, T. J. *The Greeks and their Eastern Neighbours*. London, 1957.

Fairbanks, A. *Museum of Fine Arts Boston. Catalogue of Greek and Etruscan Vases*. Boston, Mass., 1928.

Flemming, N. C. In *Marine Archaeology*, ed. du Plat Taylor, 170–8. 1965.

Froedin, O. and Persson, A. W. *Asine*. Stockholm, 1938.

Furtwängler, A. *Beschreibung der Vasensammlung im Antiquarium*, *I* (Penteskouphia plaques). Berlin, 1885; 'Pinakes von Penteskouphia', *AD* II, pls 23 ff.

Furtwängler, A. und Reichold, K. *Griechische Vasenmalerei* (= *FR*). Munich, 1904–32.

Furumark, A. *Mycenaean Pottery*. Stockholm, 1941; *The Chronology of Mycenaean Pottery*. Stockholm, 1941.

Gardner, E. *The History of Greek Sculpture*. London, 1896–7.

Gerhard, E. *Auserlesene Vasenbilder* (= *AV*). Berlin, 1840–58.

Gjerstadt, E. *The Swedish Cyprus Expedition*. Stockholm, 1934.

Gomme, A. W. *Commentary on Thucydides*. Oxford, 1945–56.

Gow, A. S. F. and Scholfield, A. E. *Nicander*. Cambridge, 1953.

Graef, B. und Langlotz, E. *Die Antiken Vasen von der Akropolis zu Athen* (= Graef). Berlin, 1925–33.

Graser, B. Athenische Kriegs-häfen. *Philologus*, 1872, 1–65.

Greenwell, W. *Electrum Coinage of Cyzicus* in *Numismatic Chronicle* 1887, 1 ff. and as separate reprint.

Hammond, N. G. L. 'The Battle of Salamis', *JHS* 1956, 32 ff.

Hampe, R. *Frühe Griechische Sagenbilder in Böotien* (= Sagenbilder). Athens, 1936; *Die Gleichnisse Homers und die Bildkunst seiner Zeit* (= Gleichnisse). Tübingen, 1952.

Haspels, C. H. E. *Attic Black-figured Lekythoi* (= *ABL*). Paris, 1936.

Higgins, R. A. *Catalogue of Terracottas in the Department of Greek and Roman Antiquities, British Museum*. London, 1954.

Hignett, C. *Xerxes' Invasion of Greece*. Oxford, 1963.

Hood, R. *Greek Vases in the University of Tasmania*. Hobart, 1964. 'A geometric oenochoe with ship-scene in Hobart', *AJA* 1967, 82.

Hornell, J. *Water Transport*. Cambridge University Press, 1946.

Howe, T. P. 'Sophocles, Mikon and the Argonauts', *AJA* 1957, 341 ff.

Jameson, M. H. 'A decree of Themistocles from Troizen', *Hesperia* XXIX, 1960, 293 ff.

JHS Archaeological Reports. London, 1962–3.

Johansen, K. F. *Les Vases Sicyoniens*. Paris–Copenhagen, 1923.

Judeich, W. *Topographie von Athen*². Munich, 1931.

Kahane, P. 'Die Entwicklungsphasen der attisch-geometrischen Keramik', *AJA* 1940, 464 ff.

Kenner, H. *CVA Vienna University*. Munich, 1942.

Kenny, E. *BSA* XLII 1947, 194–200.

Kirk, G. S. 'Ships on Geometric Vases', *BSA* 1949, 93 (= Kirk); *The Songs of Homer*. Cambridge, 1962; 'The ship rhyton in Boston', *AJA* 1951, 339.

Koester, A. *Das Antike Seewesen* (= Koester). Berlin, 1923.

Korte, G. 'Zu den Friesen von Gjölbaschi', *JdI* 1916, 257.

Kourouniotes, K. *Eleusis*. Athens, 1934; 'Ex Attikēs', *Eph. Arch.* 1911, 251; 'Pulou Messēniakēs tholōtos taphos', *Eph. Arch.* 1914, 108.

Kunze, E. 'Disiecta membra attischer Grabkratere', Oikonomos Festschrift, *Eph. Arch.* 1953, 162 ff. (= *O*); 'Bruchstücke attischer Grabkratere', *Neue Beiträge zur klassischen Altertumswissenschaft*. Schweitzer Festschrift, 48 ff. Stuttgart (= *S*), 1955; *Kretische Bronzereliefs*. Berlin, 1931.

La Coste Messelière, P. de. *Au Musée de Delphes*. Paris, 1936.

Langlotz, E. *Griechische Vasen in Würzburg*. Munich, 1932.

van Leeuwen, ed. *Ranae*. Leyden, 1896.

Lefebvre des Noëttes, R. J. E. C. *De la marine antique à la marine moderne*. Paris, 1935.

Lehmann-Hartleben, K. 'Die Antiken Hafenanlagen des Mittelmeeres', *Klio* XIV. 1923.

Lewis, D. M. 'Notes on the decree of Themistocles', *CQ* 1961, 61 ff.

Lorimer, H. L. *Homer and the Monuments*. London, 1950.

Lullies, R. *Antike Kleinkunst in Königsberg* II. Königsberg, 1935.

Maraghiannis, G. *Antiquités Crétoises* I, xlii. Vienna, 1906.

Marstrand, V. *Arsenalet i Piraeus*. Copenhagen, 1922.

Marwitz, H. 'Ein attisch-geometrischer Krater in New York', *Antike Kunst* 1961, 39 ff.

Matz, F. *Geschichte der griechischen Kunst, I. Die geometrische und die früharchaische Form* (= Matz). Frankfurt, 1950.

Mellaart, J. 'The Royal Treasure of Dorak', *Illustrated London News*, 28 Nov. 1959.

Meritt, B. D. 'An Athenian Decree', *Studies presented to D. M. Robinson II*, 298 ff. 1953.

Millingen, J. *Peintures antiques de vases grecs de la collection de Sir John Coghill Bart*. Rome, 1817.

Moll, F. *Das Schiff in der bildenden Kunst* (= Moll). Bonn, 1929.

Morrison, J. S. 'The Greek Trireme', *Mariner's Mirror* 1941, 14 ff.; 'Notes on certain Greek nautical terms, etc.', *CQ* 1947, 122 ff.

Munro, J. A. R. 'Some observations on the Persian Wars', *JHS* 1902, 294 ff.

Münzen und Medaillen A. G., Basel. List, Nov. 1964.

Murray, A. S. 'A new vase of the Dipylon class', *JHS* 1899, 198 ff.

Neugebauer, K. A. *Staatliche Museen zu Berlin. Führer durch das Antiquarium. II Vasen*. Berlin, 1932.

Nottbohm, G. 'Der Meister der grossen Dipylon-Amphora in Athen', *JdI* 1943, 1 ff.

Page, D. L. *The Homeric Odyssey*. Oxford, 1955.

Paton, J. M. (ed.). *The Erecthheum*. Cambridge, Mass., 1927.

Payne, H. *Necrocorinthia*. Oxford, 1931, *Photokorinthische Vasenmalerei*. Berlin, 1933.

Pernice, E. 'Über die Schiffsbilder auf den Dipylonvasen', *AM* 1892, 285 ff. (= Pernice); 'Die korinthischen Pinakes im Antiquarium der Königlichen Museen', *JdI* 1897, 27.

Perrot, G. and Chipiez, C. *Histoire de l'art dans l'antiquité*, vols. 9–10 by Perrot (= Histoire). Paris, 1911–14.

Pfuhl, E. *Malerei und Zeichnung der Griechen* (= Pfuhl). Munich, 1923.

Picard, C. *Manuel d'Archéologie Grecque. La Sculpture II*. Paris, 1939.

Pickard-Cambridge, A. W. *Dithyramb, Tragedy and Comedy*. Oxford, 1927.

Platnauer, M. *Iphigeneia in Tauris*. Oxford, 1938.

Praschniker, C. *Parthenonstudien*. Augsburg and Vienna, 1928.

Richter, G. M. A. *Catalogue of Greek Gems, Metropolitan Museum New York.* Rome, 1956; *Bulletin Metropolitan Museum VII* 29, 169 ff. 1934; *Handbook of Greek Art.* London, 1959.

Ridder, A. de. *Catalogue de Bronzes trouvés sur l'Acropole d'Athènes.* Paris, 1896.

Robertson, M. 'Excavations in Ithaca V. Objects other than the pottery', *BSA* 1948, 113 ff.; *Greek Painting.* Geneva, 1959.

Robinson, D. M. 'A new fragment of the 5th century Athenian naval catalogues', *AJA* 1937, 292 ff.

Robinson, D. M., Harcum, C. G. and Iliffe, J. F. *A Catalogue of the Greek Vases in the Royal Ontario Museum of Archaeology Toronto.* Toronto, 1930.

Rumpf, A. *Römische Fragmente*, 'Berliner Winckelmanns Programm 95'. Berlin, 1935.

Schaeffer, C. *Enkomi-Alasia*, 1952.

Schweitzer, B. 'Zum Krater des Aristonothos', *RM* 1955, 78 ff.

Skias, A. N. 'Panarchaia Eleusiniakē Nekropolis', *Eph. Arch.* 1898, 29 ff.

Smith, C. H. *Catalogue of the Forman Collection.* Sotheby, June 1899.

Snodgrass, A. M. *Early Greek Armour and Weapons.* Edinburgh, 1964.

Sotheby Sale Catalogue. London, July 1929.

Stauropoulos, D. S. 'Hieratikē oikia en Zōstēri tēs Attikēs', *Eph. Arch.* 1898, 29 ff.

Supplementum Epigraphicum Graecum 18 and 19 (= *SEG*). 1962 and 1963.

Tarn, W. W. 'The Greek Warship', *JHS* 1905, 137, 204.

Taylour, Lord William. *The Mycenaeans.* London, 1964.

Theochares, D. A. 'Iolkos, whence sailed the Argonauts', *Archaeology* 1958, 13 ff.

Thompson, H. *Buildings on the West Side of the Agora, Hesperia* VI, 1 ff. 1937.

Tod, M. N. *Greek Historical Inscriptions* (= *GHI*). Oxford: I, 1933; II, 1948.

Tölle, R. 'Figürlich bemalte Fragmente der geometrischen Zeit von Kerameikos', *Arch. Anz.* 1963, 642 ff.

Torr, C. *Ancient Ships* (= Torr). Cambridge, 1894; 'Les Ports de Carthage', *RA* 1894, 34.

Tsountas, C. 'Κυκλαδικά', *Eph. Arch.* 1899, 74 ff.

Ventris, M. G. F. and Chadwick, J. *Documents in Mycenaean Greek.* Cambridge, 1956.

Vermeule, E. *Greece in the Bronze Age.* Chicago, 1964.

Villard, F. *CVA Louvre* 11. Paris, 1954.

Wace, A. J. B. and Stubbings, F. H. *A Companion to Homer.* London, 1962.

Wachsmuth, C. *Die Stadt Athen in Altertum* II, 1. 1890.

Walters, H. B. *History of Ancient Pottery* I. London, 1905; *Catalogue of Engraved Gems and Cameos in the British Museum.* London, 1926.

Watzinger, C. *Griechische Vasen in Tübingen*. Reutlingen, 1924.

Webster, T. B. L. *From Mycenae to Homer*. London, 1964. 'Homer and Attic Geometric Vases', *BSA* 1955, 38 ff.

Weinberg, S. S. 'What is Protocorinthian Geometric Ware?', *AJA*, 1941, 30 ff.

Wilcken, U. 'Der Anonymus Argentinensis', *Hermes*. 1907.

Williams, R. T. 'Ships in Greek Vasepainting', *Greece and Rome* 1949, no. 54, 126 ff.; 'Notes on some Attic black-figure vases with ship representations', *JHS* 1957, 315 ff.; 'Early Greek ships of two-levels', *JHS* 1958, 121 ff.; 'Addenda to ships of two-levels', *JHS* 1959, 159.

Young, R. S. 'Late Geometric graves and a seventh-century well in the Agora', *Hesperia*, Suppl. 2. 1939.

Zervos, C. *L'Art en Grèce*. Paris, 1934.

Anon. 'Multum in Parvo', *AJA* 1942, 488.

PLATES

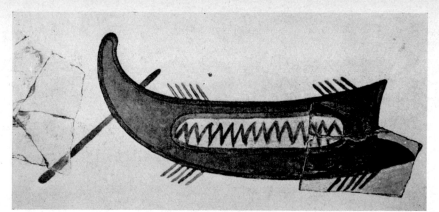

a BA. 1, p. 9

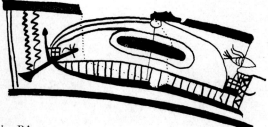

b BA. 2, p. 9

c BA. 3, p. 10

d Geom. 1, p. 12

e Geom. 2, p. 18

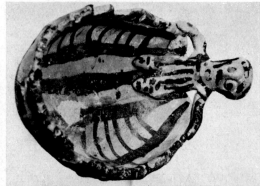

f Geometric boat in Heraklion
Museum (*photo*: Androulake), p. 17

PLATE I

a   Geom. 4, p. 19

b   Geom. 5, p. 19

c   Geom. 8 (1), p. 22

d   Geom. 8 (3), p. 22

PLATE 2

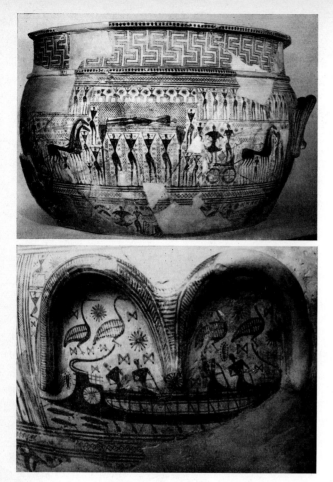

a Geom. 9, pp. 13, 22

b Geom. 9, p, 22

c Geom. 10, p. 23

d Geom. 10, p. 23

PLATE 3

a Geom. 11, p. 23

b Geom, 12, p. 24

c (i) Geom. 16, p. 24

c (ii) Geom. 16, p. 24

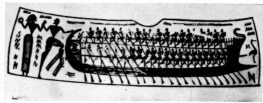

e Geom. 19, p. 28

d Geom. 17, p. 25

PLATE 4

Geom. 25, pp. 31-2

PLATE 5

a Geom. 25, pp. 31–2

b Geom. 25, pp. 31–2

c Geom. 26, p. 32

d Geom. 28, p. 32

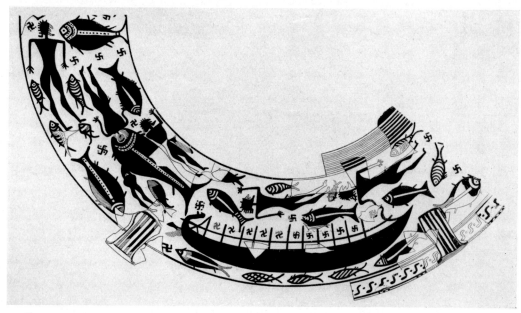

e Geom. 32, p. 34

PLATE 6

a Geom. 38, p. 35

b Geom. 39, p. 36

c Geom. 40, p. 36

d Geom. 42, p. 36

e Geom. 43, p. 37

f Geom. 44, p. 37

PLATE 7

a Arch. 1, p. 73

b Arch. 2, p. 73

c Arch. 8, p. 75   *d* Arch. 16, p. 77   *e* Arch. 20, p. 78

PLATE 8

a   Arch. 5, pp. 74–5

b   Arch. 5, pp. 74–5

c   Arch. 5, pp. 74–5

PLATE 9

a Arch. 27, p. 81

b Arch. 28, p. 82

c Arch. 30, p. 82

d Arch. 31, p. 83

PLATE 10

a Arch. 33, p. 84

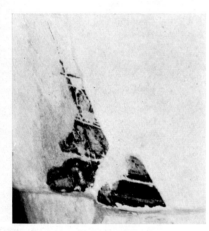

b Arch. 33 (bow), p. 84

c Arch. 34, pp. 85–6

d Arch. 35, p. 86

PLATE II

a　Arch. 38, p. 86

b　Arch. 39, p. 87

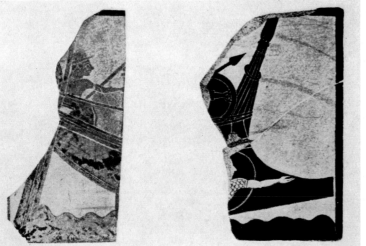

c　Arch. 40, p. 87

d　Arch. 41, p. 88

e　Arch. 48, p. 89

f　Arch. 50, p. 90

PLATE 12

Arch. 52, p. 93

PLATE 13

a   Arch. 51, pp. 92–3   *b*   Arch. 51, pp. 92–3

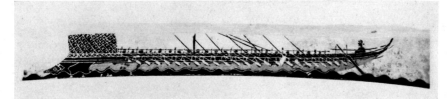

c   Arch. 53, pp. 93–4

d   Arch. 53, pp. 93–4

e   Arch. 54, p. 94   *f*   Arch. 55, pp. 94–5

g   Arch. 56, p. 95

PLATE 14

a   Arch. 57, p. 98

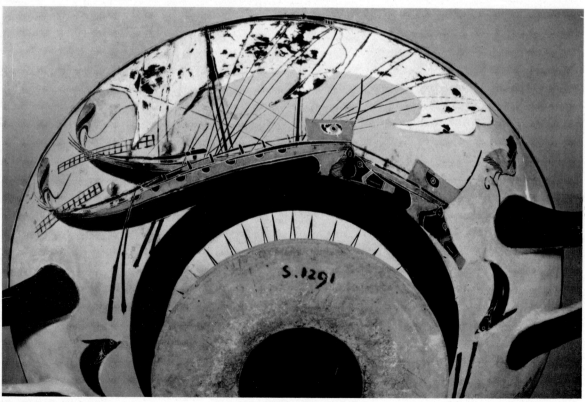

b   Arch. 57, p. 98

PLATE 15

b   Arch. 60, p. 99

a   Arch. 59, p. 99

c   Arch. 61, p. 100

d   Arch. 63, p. 100

PLATE 16

a Arch. 65, pp. 102–3

b Arch. 66, p. 103

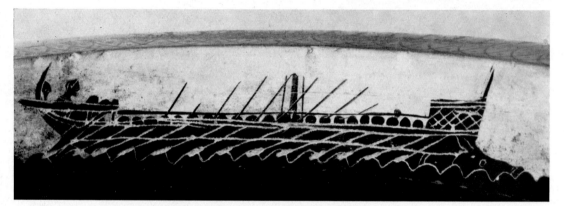

c Arch. 67, p. 103

d Arch. 69, pp. 103–4

e Arch. 74, pp. 104–5

PLATE 17

a   Arch. 79, p. 107

b   Arch. 81, p. 107

c   Arch. 82, p. 108

d   Arch. 84, p. 108

PLATE 18

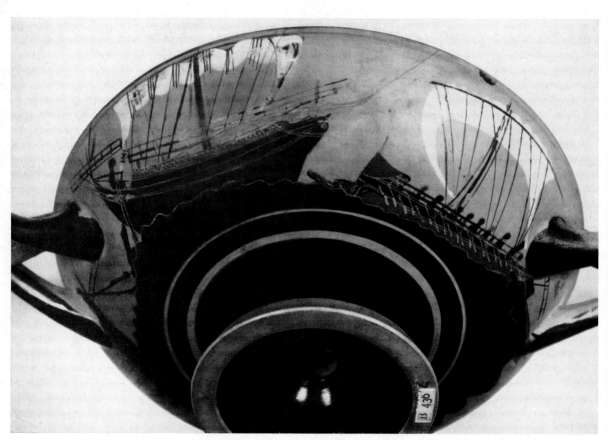

Arch. 85, p. 109

PLATE 19

a Arch. 85, p. 109

b Arch. 86, p. 110

d Arch. 88, p. 111

c Arch. 87, pp. 110–11

e Arch. 89, p. 111

PLATE 20

a Arch. 90, p. 113

b Arch. 91, p. 113

c Arch. 92, p. 114

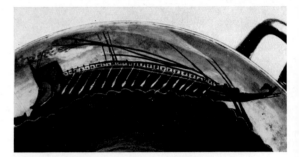

d Arch. 93, p. 114

e Arch. 94, p. 114

PLATE 21

a   Relief of a Phoenician ship from palace of Sennacherib, p. 162

b   Etruscan black-figure hydria, p. 112

(photos of *a* and *b* by courtesy of the Trustees of the British Museum)

PLATE 22

a   Clas. 1, pp. 170–3

b   Roman relief from Aquila, p. 173

c   Photograph of a model of a *trieres*, p. 173

d   Photograph of a model of a *trieres*, p. 173

PLATE 23

Section of Clas. 1, pp. 170–3

PLATE 24

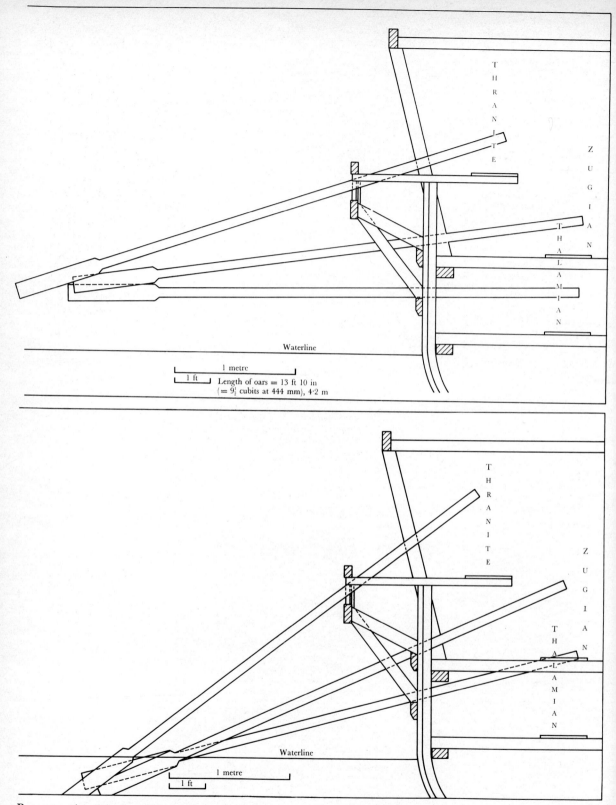

THRANITE

ZUGIAN

THALAMIAN

Waterline

1 metre

1 ft   Length of oars = 13 ft 10 in
(= 9½ cubits at 444 mm), 4·2 m

THRANITE

ZUGIAN

THALAMIAN

Waterline

1 metre

1 ft

Reconstructions based on Clas. 1 (detail), Plate 24, p. 173

PLATE 25

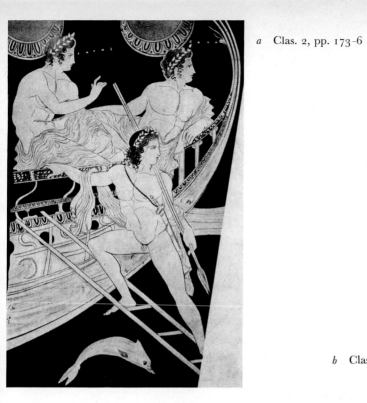

a Clas. 2, pp. 173-6

b Clas. 3, p. 176

c Clas. 15, p. 178

PLATE 26

a   Clas. 16, p. 178

b   Clas. 20, p. 179

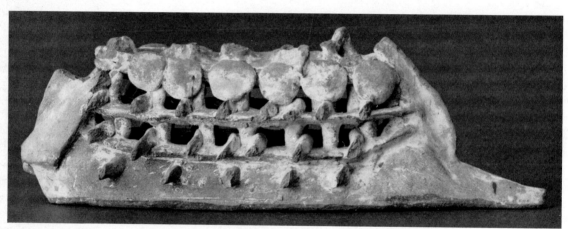

c   Hel. 1, p. 180

d   Hel. 2, p. 180

PLATE 27

Hel. 3, p. 180

PLATE 28

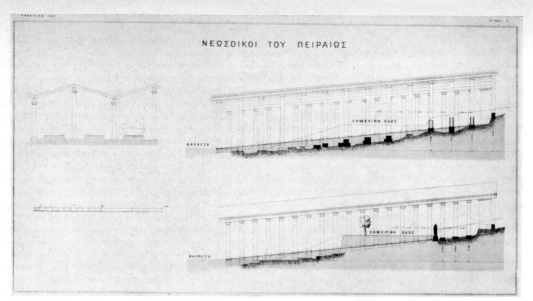

a Zea ship-sheds, pp. 181–2

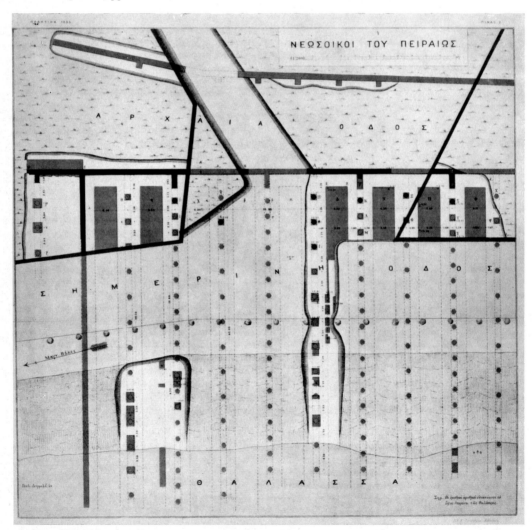

b Zea ship-sheds, pp. 181–2

PLATE 29

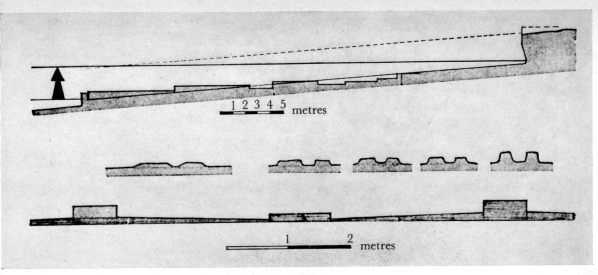

a   Sections across Apollonia slipways (N. C. Flemming), p. 183

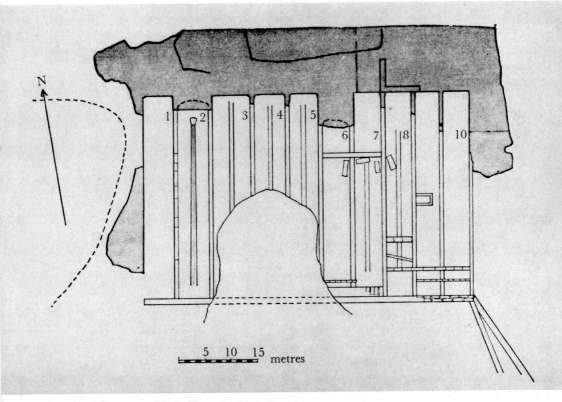

b   Plan of Apollonia slipways (N. C. Flemming), p. 183

PLATE 30

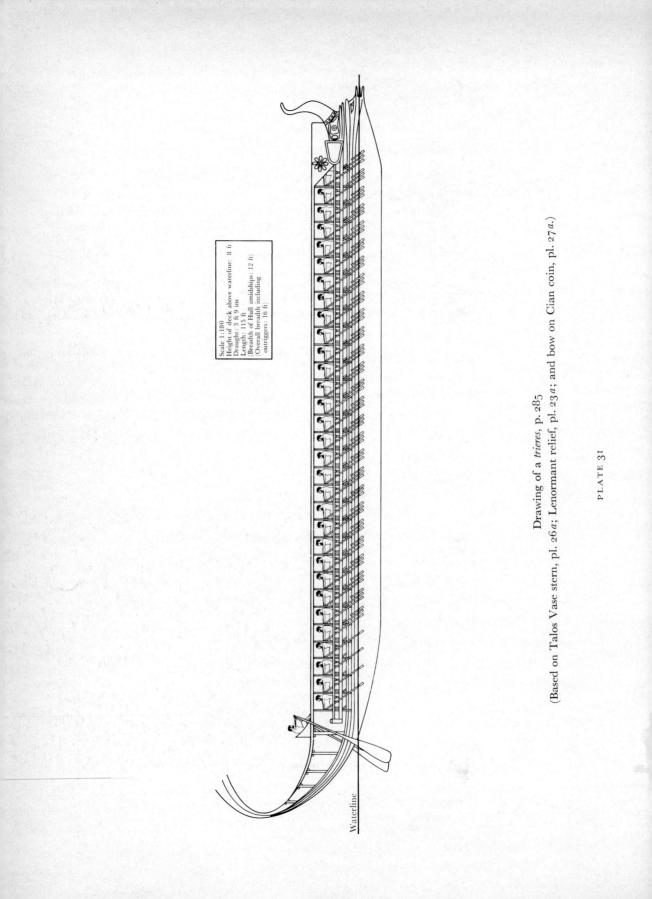

Scale 1:180
Height of deck above waterline: 8 ft
Draught: 3 ft 9 ins
Length: 115 ft
Breadth of Hull amidships: 12 ft
(Overall breadth including outriggers: 16 ft)

Waterline

Drawing of a *trieres*, p. 285

(Based on Talos Vase stern, pl. 26 *a*; Lenormant relief, pl. 23 *a*; and bow on Cian coin, pl. 27 *a*.)

PLATE 31

GLOSSARIES

ARCHAEOLOGICAL

AMPHORA. A two-handled vase with a relatively narrow neck for holding oil or wine.

ARYBALLOS. A small, usually round vase with a single handle and a narrow spout for holding oil.

BELL KRATER. A krater (*q.v.*) shaped like an inverted bell with simple handles set high.

BLACK-FIGURE. The name of a vase-painting technique in which the figures are painted in silhouette in black 'paint'; details are incised, and red and white sometimes used as washes. For the composition of this black 'paint' and the white and the red and the technique generally, see R. M. Cook, *Greek Painted Pottery*, 242 ff. or, more fully, Noble, *Techniques of Painted Attic Pottery*.

COLUMN KRATER. A krater (*q.v.*) with handles of columnar shape.

DINOS. A deep handleless bowl with rounded bottom and made to fit into a stand; used for mixing wine (sometimes, perhaps more correctly, called a lebes).

DIPYLON SHIELD. The large figure-of-eight shield characteristic of the Minoan period and occurring frequently on Geometric vases in a stylized form (*v.* p. 42).

FIBULA. A brooch in the form of a modern safety-pin on which the catch-plate is enlarged to receive an engraved design.

FRYING PAN. A flat terracotta vase of uncertain purpose.

HYDRIA. A vase having one vertical handle at the back and two horizontal handles at the sides with narrow neck for holding water.

HYDRISKOS. A small hydria (*q.v.*).

KANTHAROS. A large cup with two high vertical handles.

KRATER. A deep bowl with wide mouth and handles of varying shape for mixing wine and water.

LEKANIS. A shallow bowl with two handles and a lid.

MAEANDER. The Greek key pattern characteristic of Geometric art.

METOPE. In architecture, the approximately square slab in the Doric frieze often carved in high relief: in vase-painting, an approximately square area decorated with a prominent design and flanked by subsidiary vertical motifs.

NECK AMPHORA. An amphora (*q.v.*) on which the body meets the neck at a sharp angle.

PINAX. *Q.v.* PLAQUE.

PLAQUE. A square or rectangular terracotta plaque painted either for dedication with a wide range of subjects or for the exterior of a grave with a funerary subject.

PYXIS. A round handleless vase with a lid, used by women for cosmetics or articles of toilet.

RED-FIGURE. A vase-painting technique in which the design is left in the colour of the clay, which by virtue of its iron content fires red, and surrounded by black 'paint'; the interior details of the figures are applied with the same black 'paint' either in full strength or diluted to produce brown. For the technique, see R. M. Cook, or Noble, *op. cit.*

RESERVED AREA. An area left unpainted, i.e. reserved, in the colour of the clay and surrounded by paint.

RHYTON. A cup, usually in the shape of an animal's head, but in the case of Clas. 15 in the form of the bow of a *trieres*.

SKYPHOS. A deep cup with two horizontal handles.

STIRRUP VASE. A Mycenaean container for oil having on the shoulder a real spout and two handles joined by a false spout.

VOLUTE KRATER. A krater (*q.v.*) with handles in the form of spirals rising above the rim.

GREEK WORDS IN ENGLISH LETTERS OR FORM

ankonnai: ropes certainly connected with the rigging of mast and sail, but the precise function of which cannot be determined, = ankoinai.

aphlaston = akrostolion = akrōtērion: terminal ornament of bow or stern.

archos: homeric word for captain or admiral, later, *nauarchos.*

deme: parish of Attica, Greek *dēmos.*

diekplous: the battle tactic of deploying in line ahead and breaking through an enemy fleet drawn up with the ships in line abreast.

epēnkenides: horizontal planks forming a poop rail in Homer.

epholkaion: towing bar in Homer.

epibatēs: a heavy-armed soldier carried on the deck of a warship.

epikrion: sailyard in Homer.

episēmon: ship's ensign.

epitonos: stay of the mast.

epōtis: earlike plank projecting on each side of the ship in the bows and forming the forward termination of the *parexeiresia,* cathead.

eunē: anchor stone.

gomphoi: dowel-pins used to secure *harmoniai.*

harmonia: small piece of wood (modern tenon) used to make a joint between the planks of a carvel-built ship.

hedolia: poetic word for the helmsman's seat.

hekatomb: a sacrifice.

hermata: piles of stones used as shores in Homer.

histion, histia: sail.

histodokē: crutch to hold the mast when struck.

histopedē: footing for the mast, mast-rest.

histos: mast.

holkas: a bulk-carrying ship which did not employ oars.

hopla: ropes in Homer, arms in later writers.

hoplite: anglicized form of the Greek word *hoplītēs,* a heavy-armed soldier.

hupera: rope connected with the rigging of the sail, probably a brace for the sailyard.

hupēresia: a collective word for the petty officers on a *trieres.*

hupozōma, -ta: swifters, heavy cables passed round the outside of a ship's hull and made tight.

ikria: poop or fo'c'sle.

kalos, kalōs: rope connected with the rigging of the sail, a brailing rope in Herodotus.

katastroma, -ta: the continuous deck connecting poop and fo'c'sle in the developed *trieres.*

keleustēs: boatswain.

klēïdes: tholepins in Homer.

kōpē: oar.

kubernētēs: helmsman.

laiphos: sail (in poetry).

mesodmē: middle thwart with slot for the mast in Homer.

naus, nēes: general word for a ship (ships).

Nikē: statue of Victory.

oiēïon, oiax: tiller.

pararrumata, pararruseis: side screens.

parexeiresia: the outrigger through which the thranite oarsman worked his oar.

parodos: side-gangway.

pēdalion: steering oar.

peisma, -ta: mooring rope(s).

pentekontor: anglicized form of Greek *pentēkontoros,*

petasos: wide-brimmed hat.
a ship of fifty oars.

ploion: general word for a ship or boat.

polemarchos: the third archon at Athens (archons were the chief magistrates in Athens and were nine in number). Hence 'polemarch'.

pous, podes: the rope(s) forming the sheet.

prōreus, prōrātēs: bow officer, look-out.

protonoi: the stays of the mast, shrouds.

selma, -ta: structure of poop or fo'c'sle.

skalmos: tholepin.

skeuē kremasta: standing and running rigging, and anchors.

skeuē xulina: wooden gear.

sparta: ropes.

speira: rope connected with the sailyard in Homer.

steira: forefoot of ship.

stēlē: stone pillar on which records were inscribed.

tarros, tarsos: the oar system of a ship.

thalamios: oarsman who sat in the lowest part of a *trieres*, hence thalamian.

thrānīte: anglicized form of Greek *thrānītēs*, the oarsman who rowed his oar through the *parexeiresia*.

thrēnūs: probably a seven-foot thwart in the stern which provided a footrest for the helmsman.

triakontor: anglicized form of Greek *triakontoros*, a ship of thirty oars.

trierarch: anglicized form of Greek *triērarchos*, a *trieres* commander.

triērēs, -eis: = trireme, a ship in which there were three oarsmen to each unitary division or 'room', called in Latin 'interscalmium', the distance of about three feet between one thole-pin and the next at one level. *Tetrērēs, pentērēs* ships with four and five men to this division, probably rowing more than one man to each oar.

tropis: ship's keel in Homer.

zugios: the oarsman in the *trieres* who rowed his oar above and in between the thalamian oars, as the upper oarsman did in the two-level ship, hence zygian.

zugon: the thwart on which the oarsmen sat.

NAUTICAL

Belaying-pin: fixed wooden pin on which ropes are secured.

Bollard: post on quay to which mooring ropes are secured.

Bow oarsman: the oarsman furthest forward.

Bow screens: screens in the fo'c'sle to protect crew against spray.

Brace: rope attached to the end of the sail-yard.

Brailing ropes: ropes for controlling the area of sail.

Carvel-built ship: a ship whose hull planks are laid flush edge to edge.

Cathead: projecting timber from which the bow anchor can be slung.

Clinker-built ship: a ship whose hull planks overlap each other.

Crow's nest: a place at the top of the main mast where a look-out can be posted.

Crutch: a wooden prop on which the mast rests when struck.

Dowel-pins: wooden plugs used to secure tenons in carvel-built ships.

Gangplank: plank for disembarking.

Gunwale: the uppermost course of planks on a ship's side.

Halliards: ropes by which the sail and sailyard are hoisted.

Lay, laid: to lay a rope is to make it by twisting strands together.

Leeward: the side of the ship opposite to that from which the wind is blowing.

Loom: the inboard part of the oar.

Poop: the raised stern of a ship.

Port: the left-hand side of a ship looking forward.

Port, port-hole, oarport: in oared ships the opening in the side of the ship through which the oars of some of the oarsmen were rowed.

Ram: in Greek oared ships the keel terminated forward in a ram. In the *trieres* the ram was sheathed in bronze and was the chief weapon of offence.

Room: the space between one tholepin and the next on the same level, Latin *interscalmium*.

Sailyard: the spar from which the sail hangs.

Sheer: forward inclination (of the bow post).

Sheet: the rope attached to the lower corners of the sail.

Shores: posts used to support a beached ship on each side.

Stanchion: upright support.

Starboard: the right-hand side of a ship looking forward.

Stem post: the post stepped into the keel which forms the forward end of the fo'c'sle.

Stern balustrade = poop rails: the guard rails in the stern.

Stern post: the high curving post in which the stern of a Greek ship terminated.

Stroke oarsman: the oarsman nearest the stern.

Tenon: small, flat piece of wood used to join planks in a carvel-built ship.

Tholepin: pin against which the oar is worked.

Thwart: cross plank which serves as the seat of the oarsmen.

Tiller: lever fitted to the head of the steering oar.

Truck: fixed block at the top of the mast through which halliards work.

Wale: course of planking added on the outside of the ordinary hull planking.

Yard: sailyard.

INDEX TO COLLECTIONS

INDEX OF GREEK AND LATIN WORDS
IN ENGLISH LETTERS OR FORM

(Words are given in singular form except where indicated. Long vowels in
Greek words are so marked e.g. ankōn.)

GENERAL INDEX

(Gz. is placed after the names of places appearing in the Gazeteer.)

346

Jason, 29, 202, 203

Kadmos painter, 176
Kahane, 30
Kantharos, 183, 183 n., 187, 188
Kasthanaia, 136, 156, Gz.
Kastro tou Golou, 7
keel, 50, 120
keel-slot, 181, 184, cf. 65
Kerameikos, 35
King of Persia, 228
King's Peace, 234
Kirk, G. S., 15, 20, 23, 25, 29, 31, 33, 41, 74, 75, 82, 85, 89
Kleitias, 84, 85, 86, 90, 91, 92, 95; fragment, 93; ship, 95
Kourouniotes, 10
Kunze, 12 n., 18, 19, 21–28
Kunze painter, 12, 23, 26–28

ladder, 86, 87, 93, 98, 99, 109, 135, 175, 176, 177, 200, 202, 281, 282, 289, 293
Lade, 128, 130, 135, 137–9, 156, 160, 308, Gz.
Laestrygonian, 57
Lampsacus, 129, 247, 268, Gz.
Leagran ship, 106
Leagros, group, 106, 108
Leeuwen, van, 283
Lemnos, 29, 232, 233, 234, Gz.
Lenormant relief, 169, 172, 175, 268, 283, 284, 285, 290
Leon, 265
Leotychidas, 223
Lesbian ships, 160
Lesbos, 130, 223, 229, 239, Gz.
Leuctra, 224, 234, 249
Lewis, D. M., 122, 123
libations, 120, 265
Lindus relief, 282; stern, 282 (see Hagesandros)
Linear B, 2, 7; syllabary, 43
Linear Geometric, 39
Lipsokoutali, I., 140, 141, 142, 152, Gz.
Locrians, 140
Loeschke, 143
long ships, 67, 80, 90, 128, 131, 144
long vessels, 160
Long walls, 187, 226, 231, 232
Louvre centauromachy, painter, of 177
lowered mast, 85, 90
Lycophron, 47
Lycurgus, 235, 237
Lydia, 158, Gz.
Lydians, 128
Lynceus, 86

Lyrnessos, 42
Lysander, 231, 232, 259, 280, 298, 310
Lysias, 188, 232, 233, 249, 255, 258, 261, 308
Lysippides painter, 102, 105

Macedon, 236, 237
Macedonian garrison, 236; fleet, 236; troops, 3
Magnesia, 136, Gz.
Malea, C., 224
Malian Gulf, 187
Malians, 140
Marathon, 130, 133, Gz.
marines, 34, 74, 124, 133, (see epibatai)
Maroneia, 260, Gz.
Marseilles, 138
Marwitz, 30, 32
Massaliotes, 138
Massilia, 139, 159
mast, 53, 54, 293; boat, 245, 289, 293; main, 289, 293
mast-rest, 76, 77, 78, 80, 89, 119, 179
mast-top, 10 (cf. 34)
Mechanica, 290, 291, 294, 312, 313
Medea, 67
Median fighting men, 131; epibatai, 161
'Mediterranean moor,' 56 n.
Mediterranean sea, 2, 67, 68, 118, 129
Megabates, 132
Megara, 223, Gz.
Megarian channel, 141; neōrion, 187; strait, 141, 152
Mekler, 202
Melos, 232, Gz.
Melian sea, 120; expedition, 253
Memnon, 236
Menelaus, 32, 50, 194, 196, 198, 200, 201
merchantman, 8, 11
Meriones, 50
Meritt, B. D., 253
Mesopotamia, 236
Messenia, 7, 9, Gz.
Messenian privateer, 246
Methone, 235, Gz.
Michalowski, 24
Milesian ship, 160; ambassadors, 119
Miletus, 128, 130, 135, 230, 236, 247, Gz.
Miltiades, 130
Mimnes, 9 n., 120, 134
Mindarus, 309
Minos, 67, 130, 196
Minyans, 67
Mitchell, 100 n.
model, 8, 11, 84, 116, 173 n., 179, 180

351